About the author

Dr. Seenarine is a graduate of Columbia University and a former Assistant Professor at Hunter College, City University of New York. Seenarine is the author of "Recasting Indian Women in Colonial Guiana: Gender, labor and caste in the lives of indentured and free laborers," (1998) and *Voices from the Subaltern: Education and Empowerment Among Dalit (Untouchable) Women in India* (2004).

Seenarine's article on caste systems across the Globe was translated and published in Japan, and his work on women and caste in India has been cited by the FAO, UNESCO, Human Rights Watch, Anti-Slavery International, the Institute for the Study of Labor, World Council of Churches, and many others.

Praise for Cyborgs Vs the Earth Goddess

"Brilliant work showing the reality of what we have become since the domestication of animals... The evidence presented in this magnificent compilation of different fields of research can be used to greatly enhance our understanding of ourselves as a species." - Amina Rodriguez, Goddess feminist

"I have to say I was given a new prospective on feminism I didn't expect to find. And that's pretty remarkable." - Candyce Rusk, feminist writer & musician

"Seenarine proposes empowering women and animals as the solution to ecocide, but wonders if female governance will help to restore balance with nature and heal our relationship with animals... The inclusion of the Mother's Gift Economy in Seenarine's solution to restoring balance with nature is a radical and revolutionary truth that opposes the industrialized chaos we live in today." - Jennifer Renee Anthony, feminist activist

"This timely book takes a radically feminist approach to the environmental crisis. Until female agency and power are restored, Seenarine argues, and nature and nonhuman animals are honored and protected, there will be no reining in of catastrophic climate change. Heavily researched and passionately argued... It is truly heartening to see a man embrace radical feminist thought as passionately and as rigorously as Seenarine does. I especially appreciate the honoring of prehistory, the history of feminist resistance, and feminist lineage in general (now increasingly truncated if not erased)." - Lise Weil, founder and editor of the U.S. feminist review *Trivia: A Journal of Ideas* and of its online offshoot *Trivia: Voices of Feminism*

"After finishing the radfem summer festival circuit, I've finally had some down time to read pieces of your book... each time I went back I saw great detail and analysis that rang true for my knowledge." - Samantha Berg, anti-prostitution activist and keynote speaker

Cyborgs Versus the Earth Goddess

Men's Domestication
of Women & Animals
& Female Resistance

by

m seenarine

Xpyr Press | LA

dedicated to

Savitri ("relating to the sun")

Mangalbasi ("powerless comforter")

&

Lillian ("innocence; beauty")

I

For nonhuman Animals and human Females

who run free

and for those

still trapped

II

Male fantasies, male fantasies, is everything run by male fantasies?
Up on a pedestal or down on your knees,
It's all a male fantasy: that you're strong enough to take what they dish out,
or else too weak to do anything about it.
Even pretending you aren't catering to male fantasies is a male fantasy:
Pretending you're unseen, pretending you have a life of your own, that you can wash your feet and comb your hair unconscious of the ever-present watcher peering through the keyhole,
Peering through the keyhole in your own head, if nowhere else.
You are a woman with a man inside watching a woman.
You are your own voyeur.

- Margaret Atwood, *The Robber Bride*

III

"It is interesting that many women do not recognize themselves as discriminated against; no better proof could be found of the totality of their conditioning."

- Kate Millett, *Sexual Politics*

Table of Contents

Glossary

BP: Before Present (2017)

C: Celsius

Benevolent Sexism: less obvious than overt sexism; seems like a compliment, but it is rooted in men's feelings of superiority

Commodity Feminism: a variety of feminism that co-opts the movement's ideals for profit

Cyborg: 'angelic' males 'superior' to Earth, women and animals

Ecofeminism: combines ecological concerns with feminist ones, regarding both as resulting from male domination of society

Ecogynocentrism: or gynecology, is the merging of gynocentrism and ecology; it is grounded in respect for nature with a focus on long-term sustainability for women and the environment. The Earth, her forms and her laws for long-term, land management, are viewed as inter-related and worshiped as various Goddess figures

Essentialism: advocates maintain there are physical and other differences between females and males

F: Fahrenheit, a temperature scale in which freezing occurs below 32 degrees

Gender: the state of being female or male, typically used with reference to social and cultural differences, rather than biological ones

Gynocentrism: a dominant or exclusive focus on women in theory or practice; or to the advocacy of this. Anything can be considered gynocentric when it is concerned exclusively with a female (or specifically a feminist) point of view

Egg-producer: female, young-bearing, ovary being, pistillate

Empowerment Feminism: emphasis on feeling, self-expression, and how women can make changes to achieve success in the workplace

Equity Feminism (Conservative Feminism): focused on legal equality between women and men

Female: the sex that can bear offspring; egg-producer, ovary being, pistillate

Feminism: a movement to end sexism, sexist exploitation, and oppression

First Wave Feminism: from the 1848 Seneca Falls Convention to discuss the "social, civil, and religious condition of woman" to the 1920 passage of the 19th amendment giving women the right to vote

Hostile Sexism: openly insulting, objectifying and degrading women

Intersectional Feminism: how women's overlapping identities - including race, class, ethnicity, religion and sexual orientation - impact the way they experience oppression and discrimination

Internalized Sexism: when the belief in women's inferiority becomes part of one's own worldview and self-concept

Machismo: an overemphasis on masculinity and power, often associated with a disregard for consequences and responsibility

Male: the sex that produces sperm; phallic, staminate, cyborg

Male gaze: a way of looking at the world through a masculine lens that views women as sexual objects

Masculinity: is a set of attributes, behaviors and roles generally associated with boys and men, for example, virility, vigor, strength, muscularity, ruggedness, courage, independence and assertiveness

Matrifocal: a system based on the mother as the head of the family or household; fathers play a less important role in the home and in bringing up children

Matrilineal: a society in which lineage, birthright, and social classification are traced through the mother's ancestry rather than the father's, as is common in patriarchal societies

Matrilocal: a custom in marriage whereby the husband goes to live with the wife's community

Misandry: hatred of men; a misnomer like 'reverse-racism' that is used without reference to existing power relations

Misogynoir: misogyny directed toward black women

Misogyny: dislike of, contempt for, or ingrained prejudice against women

Neolithic: or New Stone Age, began about 12,000 BP (Before Present) in some parts of the Middle East, and 6,500 to 4,000 BP elsewhere

Objectification: the action of degrading a subject - a person or animal - to the status of a mere object

Paleolithic: a prehistoric time that covers roughly 95 percent of human technological prehistory; also referred to as the Stone Age, it extends from the earliest known use of stone tools, 2.6 million years ago, to around 10,000 BP

Patriarchy: a hierarchical-structured system in which the father or eldest male is head of the family and descent is traced through the male line; a society or government in which men hold power and women are mostly excluded from it

Pistillate: female; a pistillate flower is female, bearing only pistils; ovary being

Phallic: relating to, or resembling a penis; male-based; staminate, cyborg

Privilege: a special right, advantage, or immunity granted or available only to a particular person or group of people

Second Wave Feminism: began in the 1960s and bloomed in the 1970s with huge gains for women in legal and structural equality

Sexism: prejudice, stereotyping, or discrimination, typically against women, on the basis of sex; the idea that women are inferior to men

Sperm producer: male; staminate, cyborg

Staminate: male; a staminate flower is a male flower, bearing only stamens

Stone Age: an ancient time when people made tools from stone, wood, bones, and other materials that began 2.7 million years ago and lasted into the 20th century for some groups. End in the Neolithic or New Stone Age period.

Third Wave Feminism: began in 1990s, trying to make feminism more inclusive, intersectional and to allow women to define what being a feminist means to them personally

Title IX: protects Americans from discrimination based on sex in education programs or activities that receive federal financial assistance

Victim-blaming: when the victim of a crime or harmful act is held fully or partially responsible for it. No woman is guilty for violence committed by a man

Women of Color Feminism: a form of intersectional feminism that seeks to clarify and combat the unique struggles nonwhite women face

(Figure i: Gaia by m seenarine)

Acknowledgments

Any inquiry into suppressed female history undertaken by a born-male is suspect. All born-males have internalized misogyny, and the author is a member of the male oppressor group that is being rigorously condemned. So biology and cultural programming are underlying hypocrisies of the text, plus, in all likelihood, the researcher's 11-year old son, Jad, will in some ways reproduce the contemptible system of male supremacy and hegemony.

However, this critical look into female ancestors and the rise of patriarchy is not merely an exercise in man-hating, self-flagellation. Nor does this second published effort on women's studies serve to deflect the author's own need to change through the appropriation of women's suffering.

The motivation behind this project is to mend the relationship between humans and nature and restore females and animals to their rightful place in history. As a parent, it is a resolute attempt at family and planetary survival through writing and consciousness-raising.

Our study is foremost an acknowledgment of the hard work, struggles, and endless support of females past and present, whose combined efforts have made it possible to attempt this task. The work is dedicated to the author's mother, Savitri, and two grandmothers, Mangalbasi and Lillian, whose shattered lives serve as its primary inspiration.

The content grew out of several lifelong concerns and recent interests. In exploring the contributions of animal-based food to climate change in a previous book,[1] the author wanted to trace the historical development of men's exploitation of animals to understand men's underlying relationship to nature.

Further, there was an interest in examining how men's inconsideration of nature, and specifically of food-animals, affected their attitudes toward females and social development. Although distinct in scope and focus, the present inquiry was conceived as a prequel to our study on over-consumption and climate change, looking for fundamental causes.

In the past, did a women-based philosophy exist, or at least an alternative way of thinking about our life and relationship with others? The humanities field is almost exclusively based on the opinions of western men, and Indigenous beliefs are positioned as inferior in comparison. But it is this 'superior,' male-centered, school of thought that has brought us to the brink of ecosystem collapse in a few thousand years.

Ancient, women-based doctrines are the opposite of phallic beliefs on the purpose and meaning of life and death. Women's philosophy is communism and cyclical. It is centered on the needs of mothers and children, ecological sustainability, social balance, equity, and gift-giving. Understanding women's interpretations of existence honor female creativity and significance in the species and is vital to solving the crisis of capitalism and climate change.

Predictably, focusing on food-animals in an exploration of female prehistory and communism will be regarded by academic feminists and communists as essentialist mansplaining, divisive, and even anti-feminist. And, apart from animal studies, most experts in the humanities and sciences will dismiss this multidisciplinary analysis as lying outside of their specialization.

Anthropologists, evolutionary biologists, philosophers, historians, and sociologists alike will plainly ignore this unique inquiry as lacking in academic rigor, over-generalized, and interminably biased due to the male author's plant-based diet. Our effort will be characterized, if at all, as having limited social, practical, or theoretical implications for development agencies and social services.

This study has relevance beyond animal studies and ecofeminism. Food choice is intensely personal, but due to critical social and environmental effects, the exploitation of food and pet animals is also fundamentally political. Researchers, activists, and theorists who ignore domestication will miss a central aspect of patriarchy, and may fail to grasp its full implications for women, development, and the environment.

The open-minded reader who goes beyond defensive responses of personal choice in diet will explore how the histories and status of females and nonhuman animals are inter-related. They will gain a better grasp of the history and practice of carnivory, and insights into prehistoric diets, social, and environmental relations. Pet and animal lovers will appreciate discussions on the ancient symbolism of dogs, cats, bears, deer, horses, cows, snake, birds, and chickens, and expand their perception of human-animal inter-relationships.

Admittedly, the author started out being highly skeptical of the existence of female leadership during the Stone Age. Given the preponderance of phallic aggression in the present, it is tempting to accept the notion of 'man-the-hunter' and male rivalry for leadership during human's entire prehistory. Studies in anthropology do not include other social conditions, and students are warned to be wary of romanticizing a glorified past of peace-loving people.

Having an open mind, we eventually realized the danger of being trapped in confirmation bias. We started to explore Goddess culture, and thereby embarked upon a moving journey into suppressed, female prehistory. Since the patriarchal academy completely repudiates ecogynocentrism and Goddess cultures, the author had to carefully discover and re-interpret evidence, and get rid of learned biases.

After deconstructing phallic myths and prejudice across several disciplines, it became apparent that contrary to the male dominance theory, prehistoric women were the primary leaders of human cultures. And, it is obvious that the thousands of Goddess narratives and icons represents the dominant ideology during prehistory. Without glorifying the past, there is ample evidence that people flourished in peaceful, sustainable, plant-based communities for hundreds of thousands of years, by respecting the land, nature, and animals.

In developing a radical feminist analysis to explain the reduction in the status of non-human animals and human females that occurred with the ending of the Stone Age, the author was influenced by the work of numerous 1st and 2nd wave feminists. Women scholars such as Ida B. Wells (1862 to 1931), Charlotte Perkins Gilman (1860 to 1935), Katherine Burdekin (1896 to 1963), Mary Daly (1928 to 2010), Sally Miller Gearhart (1931-), Gerda Lerner (1920 to 2013), Sheila Jeffries (1948-), Michele Wallace (1952-), Ariel Salleh (1944-), and many others served as muses for the text. The study is influenced by the phenomenal writings and wisdom of these great women.

The Women's Liberation Movement resulted in a flowering of academic research on the origins of women's oppression. Our unique study contributes to this crucial body of work by including diet and nonhuman animals in a historical analysis of patriarchy. Importantly, it deconstructs how males' objectification of females is related to their colonization of other-than-human animals.

What's more, the inquiry documents the background of ecogynocentrism in three ways to provide a sense of the cultures and economies that existed before the patriarchal reversal. First, by examining Stone Age artifacts, such as Goddess figures, female cave art, and hand-prints. Second, the narrative includes stories of egg-producers living in pre-colonial societies, before their contact with patriarchal Europeans. And third, the text surveys female-centered cultures in the present.

Our interest in feminist studies began in the early 1990s under the academic guidance of Florence (Kiki) McCarthy, a socialist-feminist whose research work centered on women, development, and migration issues in Asia, Australia, and the US. Kiki was instrumental in my dissertation which looked at biological sex, caste, and class among Dalit (untouchable) women in India.[2]

In *Voices from the Subaltern* (2004), we argued that addressing social discrimination is critical for empowering minority women facing class-based oppression. At the same time, ending male abuse, domestic violence, and wider aspects of patriarchal oppression were also crucial to improving the status of Dalit and minority females.

The study followed the path of socialist-feminists, such as Maria Mies and Bina Agarwal, who examined the linkages between women, land, and modern development. As early as the 1980s, Mies argued that "Marx failed to appreciate that Man's freedom through labor and technology are made possible by the expropriation of a surplus from women and nonhuman nature."

Similar to the interdisciplinary work of socialist-feminists, our thesis on multiple oppressions faced by Dalit females preceded the 'discovery' of inter-sectionality by cultural feminists and identity activists. Even though 1st and 2nd wave feminists focused on intersectional issues, both are denied credit for holding multiple perspectives.[3] In its current framing, inter-sectionality is conflated with queer empowerment, while women's lack of access to land, cultural subjugation, and class oppression remain sidelined.[4]

Our interest in understanding the interconnections between women, culture, class, and development naturally led to the exploration of ecofeminism. The author was extremely fortunate to meet and interview the incredible Marti Kheel, whose book, *Nature Ethics* (2007) was a profound influence.

Mary Daly's *Gyn/Ecology* (1978) and later radical feminist texts were equally transformative. The author was likewise inspired by the feminist fiction of the brilliant Sally Miller Gearhart, especially *The Wanderground* (1978). Interviews with Kheel and Gearhart were combined in an unreleased documentary, *Nemesis: The Goddess of Divine Intervention* (2010), dedicated to Mary Daly. Marti, Mary, and Sally are the Triple-Goddesses of *Cyborgs Versus the Earth Goddess*.

While the study is written by a man, it is informed by feminist writings in several disciplines, including scientists such as Sarah Hrdy and Patricia Gowaty, and anthropologists like Marija Gimbutas and Heide Göttner-Abendroth. The theoretical insights of these feminist scholars are indispensable but unknown. Some faced a tremendous backlash in their opposition to the dominant male-centered narrative, for example, Gimbutas and Daly.[5] Our research makes a valuable contribution by disseminating their vital scholarship, and by countering their critics.

Our study is a collaborative effort, and the author is especially grateful for the tremendous support and insights offered by the brilliant and gracious, Charlotte Cressey. As we walk along the ecofeminist path, it is comforting to know that Charlotte is ahead. We especially benefited from online discussions held by hundreds of feminists on social media.

Critical insights were garnered from online friends including Africa Sankofa Johnson, Amira Davis, Angela MacDougall, Ava Park, Beata Murrell, Carla Clark, Caitlin Roper, Cheryl Seelhoff, Chris Cherry, Cynthia Stephen, Erin Anderson, Favianna Rodriguez, Helen Hye-Sook Hwang, Jennifer Bilek, Karen Pastore, Katha Pollitt, Kathleen Barry, Kirsten Savali, Lisa Blank, Lisa-Marie Taylor, MaryLou Singleton, Max Dashu, Meghan Murphy, Monique O'Reilly, Nohad Nassif, Olutosin Adebowale, Rachael Honeytone, Rasa Von Werder, Rinita Mazumdar, Rita Banerji, Sallie Ann Harrison, Samantha Berg, Sharmishta Ayyar, Sikivu Hutchinson, Swaneagle Fitzgerald, Trey Capnerhurst, Trista Hendren, Winnie Small, Zainab Amadahy, and other amazing feminists too numerous to name.

Our multidisciplinary inquiry of domestication addresses some burning questions in feminism. For instance, what caused members of the young-bearing sex to lose their higher status? What can account for females' 5,000 years of exclusion from the phallic-dominated historical process? And what could explain the long delay in women's coming to consciousness of their own subordinate position?

Systemic oppression, Global misogyny, and the ecological crisis are all highly intractable problems that are not easily solved. And just like self-defense in not a cure for violence against women, adopting the man's tools and weapons will not save females and animals. This work is not a panacea for solving the monstrous crimes of patriarchal capitalism, but it does offer clues. Likewise, the author is not an exception to machismo, although there are hints for deconstructing toxic masculinity.

This introductory study journeys from prehistory to the present, and due to its wide scope, there are significant omissions. Also, the project was limited by time, resources, space, purpose, theoretical focus and so on. In the interest of balancing breadth and depth, footnotes are used extensively to keep the text more succinct.

As with our other writings, the focus here in on presenting a subaltern perspective, one that is unrecognized and discredited in mainstream academia and culture. The ASIA's Journey narrative highlights themes, links chapters, and sketches a dystopian future that girls and women potentially face with the impending climate catastrophe.

The current environmental crisis is linked to men's oppression of other-than-human animals, girls and women. Climate change will not be solved until and unless females' agency and power are fully restored, and nonhuman animals and nature are honored and protected.

m seenarine, 9/6/17
long beach, ca

Preface by Kirsten Danielle

Thanks to Seenarine's painstaking investigation into ancient food practices among womyn, we are given a more complete picture of man's domestication of the female sex for his own gain. Seenarine's fictional narrative of a band of womyn trying to make female space in a patriarchal waste-land is juxtaposed against a historical narrative of past female-centered spiritualities, sensualities and connectedness to Earth and each other.

This juxtaposition reveals to the reader how patriarchy's practices of exploitation of earth, animals and human animals has lead to a planetary wide death spiral toward total destruction, ironically manifesting in fear of death through patriarchal sky-god religion. Seenarine's revelations expose how mankind has transformed humanity from interconnected consciousness with nature and reverence for the female life-giving divine to invasive-species hell-bent on preservation of alienation and resource extraction for the benefit of the few, at all costs to future generations, particularly to the female sex caste.

His investigation further cements that only a radical transformation of our treatment of the earth, animals, womyn and complete revolutionizing of our diets can possibly save Gaia and thus the species. This narrative traces the origins of Capitalism back its patriarchal roots and exposes the full-on academic backlash to the feminist analysis of Matriarchal society.

It's amazing how patriarchy has essentially erased all of women's technological contributions, which have been co-opted by men for male benefit. One of the main messages I take away from this book is that technology is not inherently bad or evil, but rather it depends on the hands into which it falls. There are technologies that humans have used in synchronicity with earth's processes and cycles for thousands of years that have benefited the planet. Under women-centered ideology we can see how technology would be used to help the earth rather than destroy it because humans are seen as part of the earth. When we separate ourselves from the earth, as is seen in men's mentality, that seems to be where the problem originates.

Despite the entirety of Anthropological evidence pointing to a female-centered evolutionary origin for humanity, the patriarchal lie has continued to promulgate the "man as natural rapist" lie, a contradiction patriarchy refuses to address in its claims to male superiority. Only a holistic view of humanity as part of nature will be our saving grace and prevent the horrid future Seenarine envisions for womyn and girl-children.

Foreword by Trista Hendren

(Trista Henren is a daughter, mother, and author of *The Girl God* series, *Hearts Aren't Made of Glass, Single Mothers Speak on Patriarchy,* and other books.)

Throughout my childhood, until my late teenage years, I quietly accepted the blatant lies of the world around me. When the truth began to unravel, I would often cry out - and sometimes scream in agony - "Why?"

Why, why, why, why - are things this way? This book provides many of those answers. For women who are hidden from their deep HERstories, the whys are critically important. We cannot heal the past if we don't even know what it entails.

> "Once we thoroughly understand how and why patriarchy acquired its power over us—the power of an entrenched mistake over the minds and lives of all people—once we understand and feel clearly that the fight of witch women is also the fight of earth's people everywhere against mechanical subjugation and exploitation - once we reestablish the magic link between the individual psyche and the earth's vital energy flow, between all-evolving matter and all-evolving spirit, and learn to encourage and teach others to do the same, in a loving return to what we always were - perhaps then, in the final time of crisis, the Serpent Goddess will shake herself loose from her deep exiled sleep in the earth's belly. Perhaps the serpent of life's flowing energy will begin to rise again, all luminous and of the earth, and the children of the Great Mother will rise up with it, and the universe will be our home again, as before. This flight is not an escape, but a return. The only way for human beings to survive the end is to return to the beginning."

- Monica Sjöö and Barbara Mor[6]

This understanding has brought some peace for me - and prodded a lot of doing and un-learning - and finally what Mary Daly describes as "Be-ing." However, even in my fourth decade, I know damned well that I am still not fully woke. I have come to realize it may take my entire lifetime, and a few more, to reach that point. The more I wake up, the more I realize how little I really "know" and must rely on memory and intuition as opposed to what was taught as "right."

It is excruciatingly painful to realize how many of our "loved ones" are in on this horrid indoctrination and how many benefit from it. However, once we finally accept this, it is easier to put the puzzle pieces back together. You catch on to why you never could "get ahead" as a single mom, despite having a good degree. You understand why you were blamed for your own rape instead of comforted and protected. And it's not just the big things, it's all the little things that we are taught from girlhood will make us "happy" - that thoroughly disappoint throughout our lives. Every single patriarchal religion has turned the universe ass-backwards. Most of us are so brainwashed, we can't even name what it is we are missing.

We are anesthetized from our deepest feelings - and hence, our power. In the pages herein, Seenarine fills in many of the blanks regarding our "civilization" and domestication - which Sonia Johnson wrote of decades ago:

> "Our eventual subjugation was accomplished, as all seasoning is accomplished, by a lethal combination of brainwashing and terrorism... It was the slow work of many, many centuries to tame us, to persuade us that this captivity, violence, and isolation was in our best interests, that it meant that we were loved and respected, that it was pleasant, that we liked it, that we wanted it, that we couldn't live without it, and - the ultimate doublespeak - that it was freedom."[7] - Sonia Johnson

As Seenarine notes, this does not happen accidentally or even haphazardly. Religion, violence, money and diet have all been used to tame females. After exploring religion and economics for many years, I have to wonder if diet is not the most insidious of all these.

The phrase, "You are what you eat," comes to mind here. If what we swallow is truly what we turn into, eating animal products becomes, at the very least, extremely troubling. What we eat affects our physical and mental health tremendously. Can we ingest abused and tortured animals and not absorb their suffering - or are we, in a sense, conspiring in our own abuse and the abuse of other women, children and animals?

The food we eat is deeply ingrained into our be-ing, which is why it's affects are so powerful. My best childhood memories are of cooking and eating with my grandmothers. We have recipes handed down from generations ago - such as my great, great grandmother's fried chicken - that I cherished throughout most of my life. As I child, I *lived* for that fried chicken. It was a rare treat in my often unkind world. That said, how do you reconcile that with how most chickens on our planet are treated today? If we know the pain of our own abuse, how can we take part in the abuse of another living being - let alone continue to enjoy it?

As someone who grew up as a fundamentalist Christian, I have had to re-wire my brain for more than 20 years. The hymns I once found so comforting, I now know to be toxic to my female core. The melodies are still branded into my brain, so in some cases, I have changed the words to make the songs (more) affirming. I've spent decades replacing the Bible verses I memorized as a child with woman-affirming texts. In order to find "new ways, we must replace the "old" ones with something else - or better yet, go back to the very beginning.

> "There was a time when you were not a slave... you walked alone, full of laughter, you bathed bare-bellied. You say you have lost all recollection of it, remember...You say there are no words to describe this time, you say it does not exist. But remember. Make an effort to remember. Or, failing that, invent." - Monique Wittig[8]

For those of us with amnesia, this book will serve as a vivid reminder of what was. Much like uncovering the rotten roots of patriarchy in our faith and families of origin, acknowledging the abuse involved in what and how we eat can be both challenging and painful. Females often become disassociated at a very young age. We are herded and prodded like animals to please the dominant patriarchal agenda. But if we are to get to the root of our suffering, we must confront it. Like our animal sisters and brothers, we have been stripped, not only of our own agency—but of our very divinity.

The past is worth re-membering. Mary Daly taught that the "Second Coming is not a return of Christ but a new arrival of female presence, once strong and powerful, but enchained since the dawn of patriarchy... The Second Coming, then, means that the prophetic dimension in the symbol of the great Goddess - later reduced to the "Mother of God" - is the key to salvation from servitude to structures that obstruct human becoming."[9]

Mother Earth is suffering tremendously under the selfish rule of the cyborgs. However, once we begin to know our HERstory, we can rediscover healthier ways of living. It is the duty of every person to do their best to live gently and humanely. None of us lives perfectly, but we owe it to ourselves, our communities and our Mother to continue to search our hearts and strive to be better.

Given the state our world is in, the "Second Coming" can't happen soon enough. This remarkable book, solidly grounded in the wisdom of so many of our beloved Foresisters, shatters capitalist patriarchy at its core. May the words within it set us free. While reading the text, I kept thinking of what Mary Daly wrote in her last book:

> "We grieve for our Foresisters and our contemporary Sisters who seem to be lost in the diaspora over time and space. We grieve for those burned alive...and for those whose books were burned before they even had a chance to write them. We grieve for our Sisters who have been raped, sexually abused and harassed, beaten, driven insane, mutilated, murdered.
>
> We grieve for our Sisters the Animals who have been tortured in laboratories, hunted down, destroyed by agribusiness. We grieve for our Sisters the Trees who have been slaughtered and for our Sisters the Seas, and Lakes, the Rivers that have been polluted. We grieve for our Sister the Air that has been filled with poisons and for our Sister the Sun that has been turned against us. We grieve for our Sister the Earth, who will survive the assaults of the patriarchs long after they have shriveled into oblivion.
>
> Our Grief is not passive. We do not consume our Time in depression. Our Grief combines with Rage. Our Wailing is our Railing.
>
> Knowing that Sound is a Potent Force, we Sound Out our Naming. We Name. We Blame. We do not settle for sitting in ashrams chanting an OM. Preferring to OM as we Roam, we Wander the Galaxies, especially the Firth, Re-Claiming our Home.
>
> Be-Speaking is Speaking into Be-ing. With Words we Concreate New Vortices of Force. By Naming what we know, we bring forth New Be-ing. We are more and more Here...But where is Here?"
>
> - Mary Daly, in *Quintessence...Realizing the Archaic Future: A Radical Elemental Feminist Manifesto*

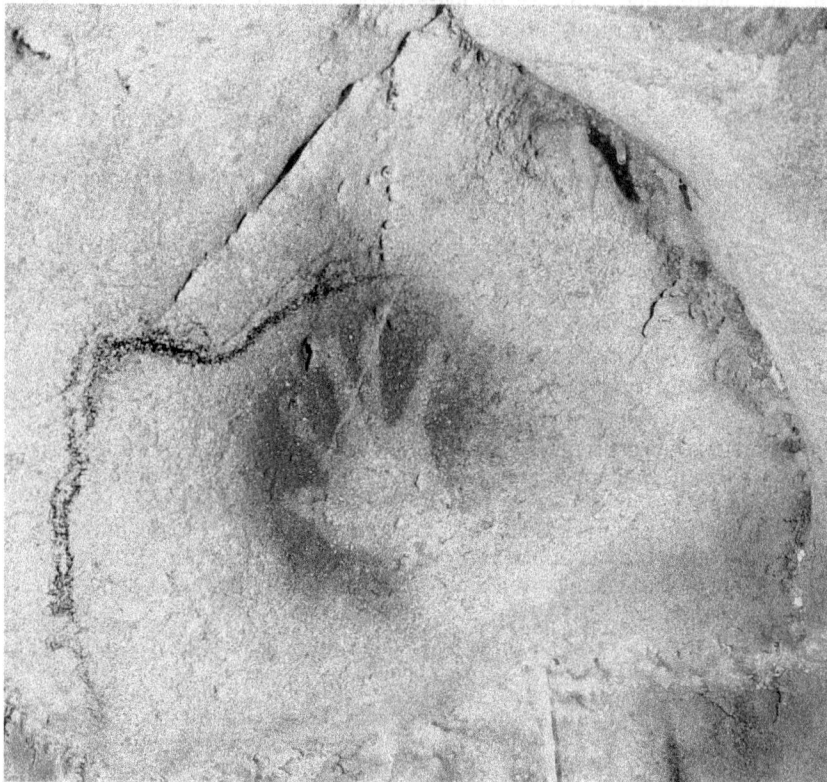

(Figure 1: Chauvet Cave Female Hand print c. 31,000 BP)

I: ECOGYNOCENTRISM

1: Reclaiming the Goddess

In making this metapatriarchal leap into our own Background, feminists are hearing/naming the immortal Metis, Goddess of wisdom, who presided over all knowledge. - Mary Daly

ASIA's Journey 2121.01

In the post-apocalyptic future, a group of 40 women and children are fleeing the physical and social effects of climate change. Parched and tired, the group is walking north to escape the triple-digit Spring heat and are running out of water.

Two adolescent females in the rear scurry the smaller children along and try to cover their tracks. It is 109 degrees Fahrenheit (43 degrees Celsius) with the sun directly overhead, and the humidity is at a dangerous 85 percent. A relative humidity of 60 percent or more hampers sweat evaporation, which hinders the body's ability to cool itself and can lead to heat exhaustion.

"Lower your voices, children." Nakeisha cautions from the middle of the group. The group wear similar full body, sand-colored clothing with head and face covering. The younger women use lose-fitting pants and long sleeve blouses, while the crones preferred wraps and shawls. With sand-colored backpacks, they were well camouflaged in the sparse desert.

The women were attacked twice already by pedophile hunters since leaving the Santa Barbara shelter two days ago. There was no other choice but to leave the over-crowded shelter filled with climate migrants. Gangs are daily kidnapping girls, and it is getting worse for females in the city overall. The women are determined to save the lives of 12 young girls who are being hunted by gangs for the sex-trade.

After the collapse of civilization, gold and girls became the main currency between militias. Pre-pubescent girls are the highest denomination and the most sought after commodity besides gold. Any female can be captured and sold, except crones who were of no value to men.

At the crest of a hill, a blast of hot, dry, desert air stings the women's exposed faces. The crones catch up and watch as the children roll down the hill playfully with the four dogs. It was getting close to sunset, and pedo-hunters were less likely to discover them in the dark.

In the depression between the hills, Zola, Hehewuti, Kuan-Yin, and other crones of ASIA started to make camp for the night. While they were at the shelter, Nakeisha helped to organize the group and came up with the name, All Sisters in Arms, or ASIA. The crones and grandmothers of ASIA decide where to camp, and Nakeisha and the other mothers follow with their children. The single women are responsible for setting up the security alarms and keeping watch over the group.

As they settled in for the evening, the fire-keeper was careful to keep the cooking fire low and covered to avoid detection in the dark night. The new Moon was completely in the Sun's shadow, lit only by Earthshine. After a simple dinner of lentil and rice, Zemora marked their daily passage on the

ASIA board for all to see. The women are emphatic and share a close bond. Their lives serve as mirrors for each other. Acting in concert, the females develop synchrony in their joint action.

It was Cronetime, and the children gathered around as Onaiwah, one of the elder mothers, read from the group's only book. "The Age of Sibyls," she began, "was the 'golden age' when female ancestors were rulers."

Naming the Problem - Men (♂)

As a woman, the most common form of violence you are likely to face is men's domestic aggression. Globally, an estimated 43,600 women are killed every year by an intimate phallic partner or family member.[1] This is equivalent to five females murdered every hour, or one every 12 minutes.

If nothing changes, by the year 2030, domestic violence committed by sperm-producers will take the lives of an additional half a million egg-producing humans. Despite the prevalence of this abominable problem, almost a quarter of countries in the World have no laws specifically protecting females from men's ferocity in their homes.[2]

Contrary to the general belief that phallic humans dominated our species from its inception, males' brutal rein is a relatively recent phenomena. Long before the dawn of our species, Homo sapiens, primate males were 'domesticated' by females. During vast intervals of human evolution, sperm-producers' ascendancy and hostility were generally curtailed by female-centered clans. In the millions of years of sexual relations, human egg-producers are just recovering equality, not inventing it.

Throughout the course of prehistory, human sperm-producers lived voluntarily in cooperative, gynocentric, or female-centered, communities. Childcare was the primary concern, and men shared responsibility for raising the young. However minimal the male-female variation may be, humans were aware of this divergence not only in sexual activities but in all social interactions.[3]

Respect for nature prevailed in our species from its origin, and most of the early human groups consumed a predominantly plant-based diet. Human clans co-existed in comparative harmony, sharing food, fire, tools, knowledge, and other resources. Stone Age humans practiced ecogynocentrism, and their philosophy was grounded in respect for nature with a focus on long-term sustainability for women and the environment. The Earth, her forms and her laws for long-term land management, were viewed as inter-related and worshiped as various Goddess figures.

This long-lasting era of female-led cooperation and sharing was shattered at the end of the Stone Age, 10,000 years ago. First, women began to intensify proto-agricultural practices around temporary settlements, and this evolved into farming. Interestingly, DNA evidence suggests that male migrants played a critical role in the spread of agriculture, rather than the adoption of new ideas by indigenous populations.

Millennia after the agrarian revolution, phallic humans began to enslave and transform herbivores into forms of transportation, labor, food, trade, and wealth. To put together this male-centered, animal-based economy, sperm-producers had to reject ancient gynecological principles for sustainable living, and this led to the unraveling of prehistoric, female-centered ideologies and organizations.

In turn, animal domestication was fundamental to the emergence and evolution of phallic identity, masculinity, male supremacy, male-centered ideologies, religions, and systems of social control. Men used competition against nonhuman animals to establish and maintain supremacist notions over nature and the Earth. And the colonization of animals also turned men away from consuming sustainable plant-based foods, to adopting an unethical and unsustainable, hyper-carnivorous diet.

As part of phallic-dominated, domesticating culture, masculine constructs and values have been internalized in the minds of females and males and embodied in social and cultural institutions. The social and psychological issues surrounding patriarchy and patriarchal thinking are the subjects of this book, as well as the female-centered philosophies that preceded them. The two chapters of this introductory section provide a brief overview of prehistoric ecogynocentrism. It also outlines the development of masculine identity and phallic humans' rule, which are the central themes of this study.

10,000 Years of ♂ Dis-order

From 10,000 years ago, unto the present, egg-producing humans have been constantly under attack by sperm-producers in the home and community, and by patriarchal structures in the wider society.[4] From birth to death, girls and women are viciously subordinated by male-dominated socialization and social organization.

In male-dominated systems, masculine ideologies are played out in power-based, social relations which govern the daily lives of individual females, and the entire society as well. It is this masculine undercurrent, not human-centeredness, that is behind the irrational behaviors displayed in current events, and the climate crisis itself.[5]

Feminist historian, Gerda Lerner, convincingly argues that male dominance over women is not "natural" or biological, but the product of domestication in the Near East and elsewhere.[6] This study makes the same argument, with a distinction between plant and animal domestication. And, like Lerner, it emphasizes that since patriarchy as a system of organizing society was established historically, it can be ended by a historical process as well.

The domesticating mindset that emerged at the beginning of so-called male 'civilization,' laid the foundation for rampant exploitation of females and nature on a global scale. The current crisis in social inequality and environmental disaster has precedence within male-centered development in the New Stone Age. Clearly, masculinity and masculine identity are critical issues that urgently need to be addressed. Yet, illustrative of the power of the patriarchy, the naming of males as 'the' problem is taboo in academia, the media, popular culture, and other male-controlled institutions.

Instead, males' private and public violence are glorified in art, politics, the economy, academy, and so on. And, correspondingly, female prehistory is suppressed and disparaged. But men were not always hyper-masculine, carnivorous warriors. In the Stone Age or Paleolithic, human males lived cooperatively as willing supporters of plant-based gynocentric social organizations.

During prehistory, masculinity was not defined in opposition to females, but as complementary to female roles. Sex roles were not binary since both sexes shared domestic chores and tasks, such as making tools and containers; foraging for food; searching for water and firewood; preparing a fireplace or hearth, and tending a fire; preparing and cooking food; serving and storing food; taking care of elders; child-care, and so on.

Female improvement of intensive plant cultivation around 15,000 BP followed sustainable gynecological principles, and the vast majority of female small-scale farmers in the present still do. The advancement of female-led agriculture was critical to the development of male-centered civilization and all of its subsequent technologies. And, if women had remained equal and powerful as societies formed unto the present-day, the planet may not be facing its sixth mass extinction event.

Men's Domesticating Mindset

A third of all women experience some form of violence in their lifetime, Men's violence against females is a global epidemic. It is a problem which threatens the lives of millions of women every day. And women living in poverty, and those facing other forms of discrimination, often face greater risk.

Despite the significant toll on the lives of women, basic questions of this male-caused epidemic remain taboo and ignored. For example, when did born-females become vulnerable to this pervasive violence? And what are the underlying causes for this long-lasting, female tragedy? To move beyond piece-meal responses and reforms, women's organizations and activists should engage in these critical issues.

Starting around 10,000 years ago, modern humans began to be radically transformed from female-centered settlements and harvesting communities into male-dominated pastoral communities that revolved around animal domestication. Men's taming of herbivores was, and is, unsustainable, and it created a fundamental shift in personal, social, ideological, and natural relations.

The enslavement of animals for transportation, labor, trade, and food signaled the "end" of the Stone Age, and of ecological, sexual, and social harmony. This momentous transformation marked the end of sexual equality among humans, and the emergence of male-centered rule, private accumulation, and hierarchies.

With the harvesting of domesticates' natural abilities, men gained super strength and powers they lacked before. Utilizing animal force, one man could accomplish the work of several, for example, in clearing land, tilling the soil, and carrying heavy loads. With their new-found capacity to tame, domesticating men began to regard themselves as superior to the Earth Mother and her animals. Assuming the role of the Earth Goddess herself, undeserving males became increasingly infantile and ecological heretics, fashioning themselves after the megalomaniac, sky-gods they invented.

By 8,000 BP, patriarchal cities and urban 'civilizations' were first established, their rapid growth driven by animal-based labor, trade, sacrifice, and male religion. The harnessing of nonhuman animal power eventually gave rise to industrial societies 250 years ago. And tragically, the carbon-based energy that was used to replace animal-based power in patriarchal economies has spawned the climate crisis we are currently facing.

With male enslavement of nonhuman animals, sex roles increasingly became binary. Male identity evolved to that of master/husband of animal, and became defined in opposition to that of servant/wife's domestic roles. With the bifurcation of masculinity, the roles of females were constrained and contained to the domestic sphere. Accompanying this reduction, the concept of femininity evolved to serve as mirrors that reflected and enlarged the image of men.

The new urban masculinity became defined as 'male-dominant behavior' expressed as superiority over females and nonhuman animals.

Correspondingly, urban femininity became defined as tamed, 'female-subordinate behavior' by conveying servility to men.

Sheila Jeffreys argues, "Masculinity cannot exist without femininity. On its own, masculinity has no meaning, because it is but one half of a set of power relations. Masculinity pertains to male dominance as femininity pertains to female subordination."[7]

The sexual binary, and merging of male and animal power at the end of the Stone Age contributed to the establishment of cyborg mind-set during the Bronze Age. A cybernetic organism or cyborg, is a theoretical or fictional being with enhanced abilities due to the integration of some artificial component or technology. Cyborg consciousness grew out of men's enslavement of nonhuman animals, and their myriad years of conquest was made possible by their appropriation of nonhuman labor.

The sexual binary and enslavement mind-set contributed to the development of toxic male identity and hyper-masculinity. Across the globe, the introduction of animal enslavement was soon followed by the overthrow of ancient female-centered power structures and the rise of patriarchy.

This introductory chapter commences with a discussion of men's false his-story. This is followed by a look at ecogynocentrism, and then men's rejection of ancient sustainable laws. Next, the chapter briefly covers men's taming of females, and then it concludes with a brief look at the remarkable pace of patriarchal mal-development.

♂ False His-story

Pre-agricultural humans are typically portrayed as victims of nature whose food availability and security were always subjected to the harsh whims of the environment. In the man-the-hunter tale, roaming bands of humans are imagined as constantly chasing fast-moving prey. As a result, they only had time to create simple stone tools, primitive weapons, and the occasional cave drawing.

For example, in the 18th century, Malthus theorized that prior to the novel occurrence of farming at the end of the Stone Age, human population was limited by their food supply. He contended that food uncertainty deprived pre-agriculturalists from having control over their lives and blocked their road to "civilization."[8]

Human prehistory is viewed as a progression from a plant-based diet to one that primarily consists of animal flesh. Following Malthus, the field of anthropology has promoted the theory that early humans primarily hunted nonhuman animals to acquire food and energy, especially protein. A significant part of history is viewed as a tale of men's ever-increasing skill and sophistication at hunting larger prey.[9]

A few scholars have critiqued this simplistic narrative, and one researcher suggested that rather than nutritional aims, big-game hunting was more related to the social, reproductive, and political goals of men.[10] Nevertheless, the animal-protein theory gained acceptance in other fields, especially in medicine where there was a similar misconception on the root cause of malnutrition.

In the 1930s, kwashiorkor, an extreme form of protein malnutrition, was discovered. The rare health issue was generalized, and by the 1950s and 1960s, most health professionals viewed protein as the root cause of malnutrition and hunger worldwide. But beginning in the 1970s, nutritionists took a broader look and concluded that the real problem of deficiency disease was inadequate overall calorie intake and shortages of various micronutrients.

Dietary studies have demonstrated that the absence of protein is not significant, but the hunter and animal-protein myths endure. So too the assumption that animal flesh and bones played a central role in human evolution.

Nonetheless, there is a limit to the amount of protein one can safely consume on a daily basis, as shown by the global obesity and chronic health crisis. Early humans would have had to expend a lot of time and energy to chase and capture giant animals. Hunters had to compete with other super predators, and guard the kill from scavengers. It was probably a lot easier, faster, and more reliable to fulfill daily protein and fat needs from plant-based foods.

The man-the-hunter tale is not only misguided, but it erases millions of years of female accomplishments and the entire background of 'herstory.' In addition, it perpetuates several spurious health, social, and historical myths. One is that hunting was the primary source of food throughout prehistory.

Another false assumption is that agriculture was only 'discovered' around 15,000 BP. A third notion is that nothing of major significance occurred among humans before the so-called 'agrarian revolution.' A related misconception is that the short time-span after intensive plant cultivation represents the best in human social development, organization, and behavior.

A fifth fallacy is that human leaders and innovators were always male - from aggressive Stone Age hunters to more 'civilized', Bronze Age herders, artists, and traders. And perhaps the most dangerous error is the assertion that human males were always engaged in clan warfare, and that competition, conflict, and violence are natural characteristics of the species.

These male-centric 'truths' are a-historical, anecdotal, and severely lacking in evidence, nuance, and complexity. The reality is that early villages and 'civilization' did not simply and suddenly emerge from the desert, fully formed by belligerent hunters around 15,000 BP. On the contrary, the formation of settlements, and cultivation of flora were gradual processes that occurred over tens of thousands of years, as described in this study.

Moreover, agrarian technology required meticulous timing, patience, and care, which were more likely formed under gynocentric cultures. The sudden emergence of farming skills in the New Stone Age is not congruent with the unchallenged narrative of aggressive, hyper-masculine hunters.

Man Versus 'Beast'

Jared Diamond and other leading scholars have argued that the domestication of nonhuman animals for food, clothing, labor, transportation and tools of war has helped in the advancement of human society.[11] The level of industrial exploitation of nonhuman animals is, therefore, an important measure of modernism, civilization, and human progress.

However, this so-called 'advancement' in male dominance has come at a horrible cost for females, nonhuman animals, and nature. From around 10,000 BP (before present), rule by man and his tamed-animal/machine subverted peaceful gynocentric systems which existed since the dawn of the species. And since then, men have blocked human females' path to power and knowledge, so it is not a fair comparison. If gynecological systems had prevailed, women may have achieved far greater accomplishments and progress than men, and with much less environmental costs.

Male-based 'civilization' would not have been possible without the subjugation of a wide range of nonhuman species.[12] Enslaved domesticates played a central role in the rise of patriarchy and male-dominated societies, from transport and trade, to rivalry and warfare. In addition, enslaved food animals were fundamental to the development of patriarchal economies, religions, and cultures, and to the domination of nature.

In the present, nonhuman animals are victimized in countless ways by male-centered maldevelopment. Animals are used for food, clothing, luggage, transportation, product testing, experiments, sport, entertainment, security, war, and more. Falsely entitled males' terrorism against nonhuman animals is unrelenting, and there are seemingly no limits to male commercial exploitation of nature and animals.

Each year, tens of thousands of lab animals, millions of pets, and billions of food and fiber animals are tortured, euthanized, and slaughtered by animal-based industries. It is important to note that many animals, including farm animals, do feel pain and emotions, and do grieve, as anthropologist Barbara Kings points out.[13]

The domesticating mindset is not only confined to elite males. This mentality has infected all of humanity, the vast majority of whom have normalized enslaving and abusing animals as part of human privilege. Across the globe, men of all races, classes, and religions advance themselves individually, and as a collective, by treating animals as machines and capital. And in cities and towns throughout the World, male-based states continue to use attack dogs and horses to curb protests and charge their enemies.

While lower class men bet on cock fights and fighting dogs for income, they may envy upper-class men who race horses for status, and the myriad male-led corporations that exploit tamed animals for profit in circuses and zoos, or in fiber and livestock plants. Men of all educational levels participate in the victimization of nonhuman animals. While educated cyborg males many use animals as trapped objects in scientific experiments, non-literate men use them for labor and transportation.

Significantly, the exploitation of nonhuman animals is gendered and closely related to the emergence of male-based hierarchies. Masculinity is linked to increased consumption of animal products. Accordingly, across race, class, religion, and location, males consume more animal carcass and dairy products than females.

Men's utilitarian view of nonhuman animals has led to the reduction and lowered status of human animals as well. Oppressed groups, like females and the Indigenous, are portrayed as being closer to nature and more animal-like, and so readily available exploitation. Thus, the colonization of herbivores, of objectifying nonhuman animals for male use, was extended to females and animalized 'others' such as the poor, minorities, and other marginalized groups.

The sex-species hierarchy developed by ecofeminists describes sex, race, class, and species oppression. At the top are 'humanized humans,' upper-class white men, considered the most rational, moral, and successful. Females are 'animalized humans,' viewed as inferior to men, irrational, and instinctual. People of color, minorities and the poor are 'animalized humans,' seen as uncivilized and immoral.

Regardless of their place in the sex-species hierarchy, men of all colors have proudly defeated the 'beasts' of the Earth, and neutralized threats from all giant animals, ranging from mammoths, rhinoceros, and tigers, to blue whales, giant squids, and groupers. Men's colonization of nonhuman animals developed rapidly, and it now at a tipping point for the next mass extinction. Countless species are now threatened with habitat loss and annihilation as land is cleared so male-led corporations can grow feed crops for the billions of domesticated food animals they market and sell daily.

Reclaiming Her-story (♀)

There are thousands of Goddess narratives and oral histories across the Globe. In addition, there are vast numbers of early, middle and late Stone Age Woman/Goddess figures, female hand-prints, sacred vulvas, birthing images, female-centered jewelry, and gynocentric rituals in Africa, Asia, Australia and elsewhere. Collectively, this evidence suggests that prehistoric cultures were female-centered, and women and girls enjoyed higher status compared to modern times.

There is nothing natural or preordained about male domination, which is a relatively recent phenomena within human communities. Before the catastrophic rule by men got started, females and nonhuman animals roamed the Earth, free from the multifarious aspects of male violence fatally impacting the Globe in the present. For millions of years, a relatively peaceful co-existence existed between humans and nonhuman animals, and human clans remained sustainable by following gynecological laws.

In her study of the New Stone Age in Eurasia, Marija Gimbutas found thousands of female figurines, female-honoring ritual artifacts, and temple models, with a ratio of 98 percent Woman figurines to male ones.[14] Gimbutas suggests these were figures of ancient Goddesses, and she traced them to remnants of a gynocentric tradition in later European cultures through works of art, language, literature, folklore, and so on.[15]

Gynocentrism is simply female-centered. It can be part of a matriarchy, which is defined as a family, group, or state governed by a woman. It can also be a viewed as a system of social organization in which descent and inheritance are traced through the female line.

Gynocentrism is an egalitarian system based on shared responsibilities of the sexes. It is not a system where women reign over men, but in fact, men do live better where women are in charge. This system increased human resiliency during numerous climatic changes and harsh terrains, while the man-the-hunter thesis of constant warfare increases survival risks, and may have resulted in humans going extinct during the Stone Age.

In matriarchies, mothers are at the center of culture without ruling over other members of society. The aim in these societies is not to have power over others and over nature, but to follow maternal values. That is, to nurture natural, social, and cultural life based on mutual respect among all sexes.

A male observer of the gynocentric Mosuo notes, "When women rule, it's part of their work. They like it when everything functions and the family is doing well. Amassing wealth or earning lots of money doesn't cross their minds. Capital accumulation seems to be a male thing. It's not for nothing that popular wisdom says that the difference between a man and a boy is the price of his toys."[16]

For millions of years, early humans collected and ate fruits, tubers, nuts, seeds, and other plant-foods as part of gynecological groupings. And tens of thousands of years prior to the intensive cultivation of plants, gynocentric groups used temporary settlements to exploit seasonal flora and vegetation that provided nutrients and resources. In the primeval Stone Age, human female animals were gathering seeds and cereals and making seed cakes.

Around 15,000 BP, the development of intensive cultivation was not an accidental occurrence in one location. Rather, farming among humans was a natural progression from earlier gynocentric agricultural technology and practice. Notably, around this time, at least 11 separate regions of the World were involved as independent centers of intensive cultivation, from China to South America. These 11 agri-cultures were all gynocentric at the end of the Stone Age and remained so during the early interval of animal colonization.

Remarkably, gynocentric groups, like the Mosuo and others, have resisted the rise of cyborgs and their endless terror campaign against women and nature. Geocentric groups in the present-day provide evidence of what was once the norm in human social, political, and economic organization. They are a testament to countless other female-centered communities that temporarily survived ten millennia of the male onslaught, by retreating further into the desert, forests, hills, and mountains, until there was nowhere left to hide.

Eons before the so-called 'agrarian revolution' and male 'civilization' got started, women were the primary leaders of human clans and collectives. Females were mid-wives, herbalists, teachers, counselors, guides, artists, tailors, traders, and so on, with full control over their bodies and sexuality. Even today, in modern gynocentric groups, a female can take as many sexual partners as she pleases and various types of romantic relationships are embraced. And since children live with their mothers, marriage is typically non-binding.

Among the Khasi, for example, children live with the mother's clan, and there is little to no stigma and hardship when women divorce. Moreover, even if a man abandons a woman he has impregnated, the children are never 'illegitimate.'[17] Notably, domestic violence is close to absent in gynocentric societies.[18]

Seven Domestications

This study argues that domestication is a long and varied process with at least seven separate phases. Each taming transformed the lives of our human ancestors and enabled the next step. Each skill built upon the prior one, and earlier domestications made later subjugations possible.

(i) The first taming occurred long before the Stone Age or Paleolithic began. Sometime in the remote past, female primates domesticated primate males, and greatly subdued male violence. Importantly, the great apes predominantly consume plant-foods. This plant-based, gynocentric system endured until the rise of patriarchy with the sixth domestication, roughly around 10,000 BP.

(ii) The second containment happened over a million years ago in the early Stone Age. This momentous innovation was the control and management of fire. The first taming was critical to this second step since human ancestors had to cooperate closely to capture, maintain, share, and transport fire over vast distances and climates.

Other forms of social relations may have precluded the use of fire. Among roving gangs of hyper-masculine hunters engaged in perpetual conflict, the upkeep of fire would have been arduous and risky. For instance, fire and smoke may reveal to enemies far away, your group's position, and that you have food.

In the early Stone Age, the gynocentric use of fire led to further improvements in female technology, like cooking, building hearth-fires, and constructing home-bases. Fire and cooking greatly expanded the range of edible plants to include hard roots and nuts, toxic fruit and seeds, and pungent tubers.

(iii) The third adaptation was profound for mankind as well. It occurred when females began using fire as part of proto-agriculture and land management. This practice began over 100,000 years ago as a critical switch took place in humans - gynocentric clans went from exploiting the Earth as it is, to actively changing nature to suit their needs.

Humans used fire to modify local land, to make it more productive for plant-foods, which they relied on for survival. Fire-foraging and fire-farming helped modern humans to survive and thrive under a gynecological system of long-term, sustainable, land management.

(iv) The fourth taming occurred earlier than 30,000 BP, when female humans tamed wolves and trained them to serve as guards. Importantly, these first pet animals were not used for food or protein. Dogs were viewed as individuals, and they were often buried with other members of the family.

Female-centered clans had natural laws relating to pet management, and canines became a sustainable part of the community. Dogs provided security of home-bases, and for protection for women and children while foraging. In addition, bitches or female dogs served as honored guardians of the Goddess and her sacred spaces.[19]

(v) According to the simplistic, man-the-hunter narrative, the fifth subjugation referred to here is erroneously viewed as the first domestication - the so-called 'agrarian revolution' that occurred around 15,000 BP. This narrow framing discounts the previous four tamings, and the entire prehistoric .

Not surprisingly, this false patriarchal tale excludes the fact that females were instrumental in this 'revolution' in food security and social organization. While men take the credit for this plant cultivation, it was primarily accomplished by females who used their ancient knowledge of proto-agriculture to intensify crop yields.

The (vi) sixth colonization was unsustainable and incompatible with previous tamings and philosophies. By 10,000 BP, women's knowledge, resources, innovations in fire use, use of pets, and intensive farming, were learned and co-opted by men to experiment with the enslavement of animals.

Men's capture and use of domesticates for transportation, labor, trade, and food represented an emphatic transformation in human and nonhuman animal relations. Further, it dramatically increased male power and men's practice of violence.

The (vii) seventh domestication was an extension of animal husbandry and men's ruinous change in ecological relations. This last step involved male ascendancy and men's brutal subjugation of females. By 8,000 BP, a drastic reduction in the status of females was accomplished by men across vast parts of Asia, Europe, the Middle East, and elsewhere.

The sixth and seventh subjugations created and cemented the domesticating cyborg mindset. Cyborg enterprises and economies give rise to the first cities, and rise of so-called 'civilization.' This blighted progress has mainly benefited males to the disadvantage of females, animals, and nature.

Moreover, male supremacy has led to the destruction of countless female-centered communities, and various forms of gynecological philosophies across the Earth. Tragically, after a mere 8,000 years of male so-called 'civilization', the Planet in now caught in the throes of its 6th mass extinction.

Having tamed land and sea, the dominant male order is fast domesticating Earth's atmosphere and placing in jeopardy millions of years of human evolution.

Ecogynocentrism

Long before male 'civilization' began, humans lived in female-centered, sustainable clans for thousands of years. Self-sufficient, gynocentric communities honored the Earth in all of her forms - as nature, animals, plants, water, soil, and so on. Sustainability was ensured by humans adherence to holistic, gynecological laws for long-term, land management. The Earth, her forms, and her laws were all inter-related and worshiped as various Goddess figures.

Reclaiming the Goddess means putting the interest of women and girls first. Further, it connotes a reclaiming of love for the Goddess and all of her forms - flora, fauna, land, water, and ice. Affirming the Goddess implies a profound concern for long-term female survival and well-being of the seventh generation of females. Sustainable gynocentrism, or ecogynocentrism, was accomplished in the past, and it can be achieved again in the future.

For millennia, the so-called 'pre-agrarians' were deliberately organizing communities of plants to make them more abundant, convenient, and predictable. Across the world, female-centered communities altered the landscape and surrounding flora for their own benefit, for instance, through fire-farming and forest gardening.

The Stone Age practice of forest gardening focused on fostering the growth of low-input, but productive and sustainable units of highly diversified trees, palms, bushes, and vines.[20] Stone Age women were experts at extracting vegetative matter for food, and using different flora for medicine, tools, ritual, and art. Living in harmony with nature was part of women's inner orientation. Plant food and other flora were integral parts of the gynocentric gift economy as well.

With long-term, land management techniques, early humans created vast plains through controlled and periodic 'patch burning.' This practice was called 'bushfire' in Australia and Africa, 'wildland fire' in North America, and 'jungle fire' in India. The Bantu of Africa have a detailed vocabulary to describe different stages of grass growth in relation to fire. And the nomadic Bushmen of South Africa burn old grass at the end of the dry season, in order to promote the growth of roots and bulbs in the coming rainy season.[21]

Using fire, Aborigines increased the amount and diversity of food available in Australia. They managed clearings, shrubs, forests, undergrowth, tree corridors, and other forms of vegetation with periodic burnings.

Aborigines maintained habitats for valuable plant species, for example, grassland for tubers, wetlands for reeds and rushes, and so on. Tubers like yam daisy were an essential staple, and they require areas of open country,[22] so fire-farming was used widely to encourage their growth.

Sustainable land management was practiced for millennia in the Stone Age by women in different regions of the globe. Female clan leaders adhered to ecological laws and sanctions passed down by their gynocentric ancestors. These laws demanded the continuance of every form of life, and they helped prehistoric women and men to remain sustainable over long periods of time.

Females were at the forefront of experiments related to plant domestication and females' plant technology allowed New Stone Age communities to feed rapidly increasing populations. Most gatherers could not easily store food for long due to their migratory lifestyle, whereas those with a sedentary dwelling could store their surplus grain. Farming required more long-term planning, tools, and facilities and women invented and shared these technologies as part of their gift economy.[23]

Amazingly, aspects of gynocentric cultures exist in the present-day to some extent. Women have preserved bits and pieces of their gynocentric past, which can provide answers to our Global social and economic crises. Across the Earth, female-centered societies worshiping Earth goddesses, evolved peacefully, cooperatively, and in harmony with nature.

Females not only have the solutions to end male violence, they have practiced equality for a very long-time. Women-led hominid clans survived many extreme climate changes, and they were thriving at the end of the last ice-age. However, the vast scale of female creativity, invention, technology, and accomplishment during the Stone Age have been entirely erased.[24] Yet, it was ecogynocentrism that made the modern era possible and may prove essential for our future survival.

♂ Ending of Ecogynocentrism

The Goddess is Earth. Humans cannot remove divinity from Earth. To do so is treason punishable by extinction. Belief in a male savior in the sky prevents us from saving ourselves from men's greed on Earth. People of faith feel that humans were granted dominion over earth, and the wealthiest one percent have earned the right to dominate human and earthly affairs.

Almost universal belief in sky magic is opportunistic and self-centered, merely cover for people's lust for money, power and prestige under the guise of security. But the more we seek individual security is the more insecure humans become collectively.

Earth is the hive and Queen, and humans are worker bees that are here to serve and protect her. Instead, we act arrogantly and do the opposite - using Gaia and her Earthlings to construct seven billion barren hives without a Mother.

Men's enslavement of food animals commences around 10,000 BP and this process is so new that the power of transportation machines is still measured in 'horse'-power. Unlike intensive agriculture which had a long history, the taming, enslaving, and breeding of herbivores was a sudden, extremist idea. By focusing on a few species at the expense of all others, men fundamentally contradicted and ignored ancient gynecological laws for long-term land management.

Since Goddess-based sanctions pertaining to the taming of fauna were ignored, sustainability became an ongoing issue for early herders up to the present. Rejecting ecological guidance regarding tamed animals contributed to their exploitation and over-use of local plant resources for feed. This in turn led to perpetual male conflict over grazing lands, frequent ecological collapse, and the reoccurring demise of patriarchal 'civilizations.'

Men's enslavement and breeding of herbivores are inherently unsustainable. To cite just one example, in the early 1800s, European colonists found open grasslands among the rainforest in the highlands of northern Tasmania. The grasslands were ideal for sheep, so European families imported several herds and settled down to become farmers.

At the same time, the colonists removed local Aborigines from the area, which prevented their regular burning of the highlands. Soon, sour grass and scrub replaced the open grassland, and sheep farming became unprofitable with imported grain. These European agricultural 'experts' lasted less than two decades, while Aborigines, who supposedly lacked any form of agricultural technology, survived for thousands of years on the same land.[25]

One Australian ecologist concluded, "Aboriginal people had, and in some parts of Australia still have, a more successful style of managing bushfire, and associated ecosystems, than do present Australian governments and their authorities, both state and federal."[26] Modern methods of land clearing, like slash-and-burn and clear cutting, ignore ancient ecological laws and goals.

Prior to their enslavement, nonhuman animals were respected, and their environments were carefully managed. Each animal species had a totem, and human clans shared responsibly for all of the animals long-term well-being. Interestingly, natural laws for the taming of food animals did not exist in the Stone Age. Perhaps gynocentric, long-term land management strategies generated nutritional abundance, so there was no need to hunt or enslave animals for food.

Before animal enslavement began in earnest, men were riding horses and traveling at speeds unimaginable before. These horsemen were the first cyborgs who broke away from ecogynocentrism to invade and destroy female-centered groups with limited means to respond. Roving bands of male warriors destabilized female-led communities across vast regions. The chaos that ensued helped to establish the dawn of cyborg rule, competition, and violence, that continues into the present.

Animal husbandry created a male monster that quickly unraveled ancient gynecological cultures that lasted throughout the Stone Age. The massive reduction of women's power led to cyborgs becoming a new Prometheus - the Greek creator of mankind, with dominion over all of the Earth.

Cyborgs, the New Prometheus

The gaining of new-found power over nature's creative forces by inherently insecure males' produced a primal shift in men's cosmological perspective that quickly reverberated across the Globe. With the enslavement and use of animal power, the cyborg's quixotic desire for transcendence over all of nature was born.

Men's enslaving mentality represent the essence of the domestication 'revolution,' and is at the heart of patriarchal so-called 'civilization.' This book explores the history of nonhuman animal use, especially the early patriarchal capitalization of animals, and animalization of capital.

The central themes of the male dominator mode, as Riana Eisler argues, are "reality and myth polarization and strife, conflict and separation, winning and losing, dominating and subduing, dismembering and disembodying, conquering and controlling, in short, force, fear, and violent disconnection."[27]

One consequence of men's ascendancy over tamed animals was a severing of the connection to untamed animals and the natural world. Another loss was an understanding of humans' inner, unrestrained nature as animals. The taming of human females marked a further de-evolution in the men's thinking. The confluence of masculinist views of nature and sexism led to animals being feminized, and females being animalized.

In a few thousand years, cyborgs have placed the whole Planet in crisis. The industrial revolution, or the mechanical bride of cyborg consciousness, started less than 300 years ago. Since then, male-centered maldevelopment has increased the global average temperature by one degree, and is already causing abrupt climate change. Undeterred, male-centered technological 'progress' is accelerating and this will cause even more planetary warming.

Males' terrorism and exploitation of nature and nonhuman animals are unnatural, unearthly, unprecedented, and unsustainable. In the past three centuries alone patriarchal capitalism has caused a rapid decrease in natural and social diversity.

Vandana Shiva describes the cyborgs' disdain for equality and biodiversity as follows: "Maldevelopment militates against this equality in diversity, and superimposes the ideologically constructed category of western technological man as a uniform measure of the worth of classes, cultures, and genders."[28] She continues, "unity and harmony in diversity, become epistemologically unattainable in the context of maldevelopment, which then becomes synonymous with women's underdevelopment and nature's depletion."

The current rate of biodiversity loss is greater than anything the Earth has experienced since the vanishing of the dinosaurs 65 million years ago. Moreover, the losses are occurring all over the planet - from the South Pacific Islands, to the Arctic sea ice, and from the deserts of Africa, to the mountaintops and valleys of the Himalayas.[29]

Only 20 percent of the world's original forest cover remains in sizable tracts of relatively undisturbed or 'frontier forest'.[30] As much as 50 percent of known vertebrate species died off in the last 50 years as a result of male maldevelopment, sports hunting, disease, habitat loss, and so on. And, the remaining 50 percent could die off in the next 40 years.[31]

Nature's destruction has been accompanied by explosive population growth, with over 7 billion humans, 70 billion domesticated animals, and hundreds of billions of farmed fish. The sheer quantity of animals and sea food caught and raised for consumption poses a grave threat to Earth's ecosystems and biodiversity.[32]

Along with the rapid growth in animals raised for profit, cyborgs' speed at killing food animals has increased exponentially. Automatic machines slaughter 9,000 chickens an hour, and hundreds of fish a minute. Daily, the monumental violence against nonhuman animals and nature goes unchecked. Cyborgs with fallacious rights, unhinged from ancient equality and sustainability practices, are terrorizing and extinguishing countless species of our fellow Earthlings.

It is possible that humans males were always this annihilating. But there may have been variation in socialization, and attendant behaviors, over long periods of time in different regions. This book attempts to explore some of these prehistorical spaces and breaks in male violence. This may help in conceptualizing new modes of understanding and interactions between human and non-human animals, and between females and males who understand and reject the notion of a 'cyborg.'

Conclusion

This study argues that the present-day ecological and social crises are caused by cyborg consciousness that developed with men's enslavement of nonhuman animals. Phallic superiority preceded all other forms of oppression and led to the creation of racism, classism, tribalism, religious intolerance, and so on.

Continuing a tragically misguided, patriarchal tradition, modern economic and social development are male dominated, top-down, and broadly dismissive of women and nature. Economic growth is paramount to all other concerns, including sustainability, climate change, biodiversity, and it seems, even human survival itself.

Male-centered violence is more persistent and pervasive than all other social and ecological persecutions. Part of the problem of male violence is that it remains unnamed and hidden in general categories, like human violence. The term cyborg addresses the invisibility of male aggression, as well as the mythology of sperm-producers' superiority.

'Not all men' are terrible, but 'yes all women' and most animals have to fear the numerous bad ones. The phallic 'minority' that is guilty of violence is dangerous and they have had a tremendous influence on human history. Moreover, they are continuously fostered, maintained, and re-created by patriarchal systems based on cyborg consciousness. Another critical aspect of men's violence is the portrayal of victims as inferior objects, and the next chapter delves into this issue.

(Figure 2: Goddess of Willendorf - 4.4 in (11.1 cm) tall figurine c. 28,000 BP)

2: ♀ Subjects to ♂ Objects

In patriarchal myth she [Metis] was swallowed by Zeus when she was pregnant with Athena. Zeus claimed that Metis counseled him from inside his belly. In any case, the Greeks began ascribing wisdom to this prototype of male cannibalism. - Mary Daly

ASIA's Journey 2121.02

It is early Spring, and it feels like walking into an oven in the 123-degree Fahrenheit (50 degrees Celsius) heat and 40 percent humidity. But young and old, that is what the women and children of ASIA have to do. Generations after the collapse, there are no public facilities or cooling stations. The entire western area of the continent is in its second decade of drought, and tens of thousands died last Summer in Santa Barbara alone. Summer is going to be hotter this year.

The group of females is taking their fifth break for the day, sitting in the shade of an overhanging boulder. Desert and brush stretched on for miles in the distance, like spots of mold on an old, dirty mirror.

"How long more do we have to go?" 12-year old Cha'Kwaina asks with a sad face. She looks at Xóchitl, who shrugs and says nothing. Lian stands up and explains, "If we walk 10 miles today, we have 11 days before we get to the safe house."

The 26-year old Lian and 24-year old Xóchitl are the primary members of the security team. As the fittest individuals in the group, they carry the most gear. The four dogs also carry backpacks. "But if it gets any hotter, we will have to take more frequent breaks," Lian continues. "So it could take two weeks."

"That's too long." Cha'Kwaina whimpers. She pauses then asks, "Why are the pedo-hunters trying to capture girls?" Onaiwah, her mother, replies, "They are rewarded for doing so by other men in the city,"

11-year old Iniko is puzzled. "But we are nice... and smart just like the boys." Iniko glances at her brother, Zaid. Thirty-eight-year-old, Onaiwah points at the three males in the group - two teens, Alex and Roshi, and 11-year old, Zaid. "They are sometimes taken," Onaiwah warns. "We have to watch out for them too."

The older boys laugh as they bully Zaid, who usually cries a lot.

Lian shakes her head and says, "Not nearly as much as girls, though. There is not a huge demand for boys." She checks her timer. "Alright, ASIA. That's our half-hour break. Let's get moving for another half-hour."

"It's too hot." Cha'Kwaina mutters with a heavy sigh. "Be brave," Hehewuti encourages in a raspy voice. Hehewuti is the eldest, at 84. "Wet your scarf, and wrap it around your head," she suggests to Cha'Kwaina.

Xóchitl walks ahead to check for any signs of pedophile hunters. She sees nothing and motions the group forward. The group move out of the shade into the blazing sun. They walk slowly and close together, using umbrellas to provide young children and elderly in the middle of the group with shade.

Since leaving the shelter, the crones' senses have become keener. Their speech and movement are synchronized, almost like a ritual. They work with the rhythms of nature and view their natural environment as the ultimate source of power, who they refer to as 'Gaia', the great Earth Goddess.

Introduction

The Earth and her organisms are wholesome, active entities. Each unique creature has individual and collective interests and relationships. However, acting like aliens, Cyborgs have reduced and eliminated the subjectivity of Earthlings to establish themselves as the only 'real' subjects in both theory and practice.

The status of being a subject is central to having rights and safeguards under a patriarchal society. Framing unique, individual beings as similar objects is a key strategy of patriarchal reduction and oppression. This second introductory chapter sketches female subjectivity during prehistory and their extraordinary decline in status when men gained control over human organization.

This chapter starts with a look at how female-centered societies were associated with Goddess ideologies. After this, the fall of the Greek Goddess, Metis, is explained, followed by an examination of the great fall in female status in the post-Stone Age. A discussion on the loss of subjectivity and how vibrant girls changed into male objects comes next. Then, the chapter explores resistance by the so-called 'fairer' sex,[1] and finally, it provides an outline of the book.

♀ Roles & the Goddess

Female-centered primate cultures existed for millions of years, and females held a high status within the earliest human groups, around two million BP. Also, from the dawn of the species over 200,000 years ago, females have been active participants in shaping culture, behavior, and human destiny.

The notion of a Goddess was central to Stone Age oral traditions, imagery, ecogynocentrism, and female-centered thinking. Gynocentric practices revolved around reverence for various Goddesses, and evolved along with our human-like ancestors.

The Goddess perspective was maintained during humans' continuous migration out of Africa to populate the Earth, so it was a Global one. Gynecological sanctions were part of Goddess narratives, and adhering to these environmental laws ensured long periods of sustainability for our species.[2]

Stone Age humans viewed the Earth as a providential Goddess and a fertile Mother, and females' prominent positions were connected to the bountiful Deity. Under the Goddess worldview, nature and animals were perceived as female - sacred, mighty, and nurturing. Men were active participants in female-led communities, with valuable roles and strong ties to their maternal clans.

As fully realized subjects, females led child-centered groups under the protection of various Earth Goddesses. Then, as now, egg-producing humans were creative, intelligent, reasonable, courageous, and powerful. They were likewise generous, compassionate, moral, socially responsible, and hard-working.

Prehistoric women lived in matrilocal kin groups based on maternal residence and group motherhood. Clans were also matrilineal, with inheritance based on maternal lineage.[3] The Goddess-centered economy was proportionate and equal, with gift-giving playing a primal role in fostering cooperation and solidarity between female communities.

The tightly-knit, female-centered social organization kept the power of human male animals in balance during the Stone Age. Lack of art and other physical evidence imply there was an absence of conflict, and the numerous successful migrations across the globe suggest vast periods of human cooperation.

In many parts of the World, Goddess worship and females held dominant roles, but over the past centuries, grave robbers pillaged a lot of this evidence. The burial of a 4,500 years old Siberian noblewoman from the ancient Okunev Culture that was found undisturbed provides a glimpse of the history that was wiped out.

The early Bronze Age grave include an incense burner decorated with solar symbols - three sun-shaped facial images which match ancient rock art in Siberia. There were also two jars, cases with bone needles inside, a bronze knife, 1,500 beads that once adorned the woman's costume, and 100 pendants made from animal teeth.[4]

In the Americas, female authority persisted into the last millennia. For example, the priestesses of Moche were renowned for their monumental architecture and rich visual culture. Regarded as the first state-level civilization in the Americas, the Moche inhabited the north coast of Peru from 2,000 to 1,200 BP.

The Moche flourished before the Incas, but at the same time, the Mayas thrived in Mexico and Central America. The Moche developed the inland desert with a complicated system of irrigation used for agriculture. They built adobe pyramids, and, like other gynocentric cultures, used an Earth Goddess to unify their society.[5]

The Moche had no written language but left thousands of ceramic vessels with intricate drawings portraying their daily lives and beliefs about the human and supernatural worlds. Moche artists crafted ceramic and metal objects of striking realism and visual sophistication depicting the Goddess and female life cycles.

The eight royal tombs of Moche priestess discovered contained extensive artifacts, and the complexity of the burial reveal the power and influence the women wielded in life. Archaeologists know the eight women were priestesses because of their resemblance to figures depicted in rituals scenes found in Moche art.

The women were priestesses, but they could have likewise been rulers. The political and religious realms were blended in ancient cultures, and rulers were often the priests. For instance, the Señora de Cao, who reined around 1,700 BP, is considered the first female sovereign of pre-Hispanic Peru.[6]

Greek Titaness: Metis/Wisdom

In Greek, Metis means 'wisdom,' 'skill,' or craft.' In pre-patriarchal Greek religions, Metis was of the older Titan generation and an Oceanid. Metis was born of Oceanus and his sister Tethys. She is of an earlier age than Zeus, the chief male god, and his siblings. This era was the age of the Goddess when male deities were rare or insignificant.

Metis was the Titan Goddess of good advice, planning, and cunning. She was the mother of wisdom and sound thought. After the decline of ecogynocentrism, Metis was reduced to a counsel and spouse of Zeus, and besides, his cousin.

A prophecy revealed that she was destined to bear a son greater than his father. Zeus became jealous and tricked Metis into turning herself into a fly. Then, he promptly swallowed her. Trapped, Metis spent the rest of her life giving Zeus advice from inside him.

Inside Zeus' belly, Metis conceived a daughter. In time, she began making a helmet and robe for her fetus, and her hammering caused Zeus great pain. Eventually, her daughter, Athena, re-birthed from the god's head fully grown and armed with a war-cry. Graves explains that worship of Athena was retained as a cult because it was too strong to be suppressed, but she was recast as a child of Zeus in new myths. Athena was given the role of justifying horrific crimes against the old gynocentric religious customs.

In later Greek mythology, after the solidification of patriarchal versions of earlier religions, poets described Athena as a "motherless goddess" and did not mention Metis. Other versions of Athena noted that Zeus, her father, later attempted to rape her. Athena killed him without hesitation and took his name and skin. In many different versions of the story, Athena never has a birth mother. Plato identified Athena with Neith, a much more ancient Triple Goddess from Libya.

Zeus swallowed Metis and made her a part of himself. But that was not enough. By having Athena born only from Zeus, the narrative gave males authority and power over something that had previously only been a female realm, the cycles of reproduction. Moreover, this framing of male-birthing removed all female association with wisdom.

In remembering Metis, this study is reclaiming female prehistory and wisdom as female-centered. It is asserting that gynocentric cultures existed among early humans and lasted throughout the Stone Age. Honoring Metis reminds us that ancient gynecological principles were sustainable and a return to these practices can slow down planetary heating and help to restore harmony on Earth.

The Great Fall of ♀

Stone Age gynecological worldviews that honored females and nature through various Earth Goddesses survived well into the so-called 'agrarian' era. But by the Bronze Age, even though some Goddesses remained, sex roles and status were totally reversed. Maleness became prized, at the detriment of other subjects, and females, nature, and the Goddess were collectively debased to objects for male use.

Men's opportunity arose with females' continuous innovations in cultivating plants during the Neolithic, or New Stone Age (12,200 to 4,500 BP). Sperm-producing humans embraced, learned, then took over female cultivation technologies, but this was not the end. The stupendous decline in female status and culture, and the attendant rise of patriarchy, are related to animal enslavement that occurred later.

By 9,500 to 9,000 BP, agricultural economies that relied on a mix of domesticated crops and farmed animals were fully crystallized in the Middle East. Soon after, many aspects of daily life in the Fertile Crescent were diffused into the Mediterranean and elsewhere.[7] The agrarian transfer package included subsistence agriculture, animal husbandry, social networks, and cyborg belief systems.

By 8,000 BP, male-dominated farming economies led to the rise to powerful cyborg city-states in Eurasia. The sovereignty of female clans honoring Earth Goddesses was comprehensively diminished, and egg-producing humans were prevented from amply expressing themselves in increasingly male-dominated societies. Formerly honored girls were disempowered and objectified into tools by the falsely entitled cyborg herders.

The Bronze-Age started around 5,000 BP, and durable weapons increased male violence across the Globe as embattled men competed to rule over each other. Across Europe, patriarchal ideology continued to replace matrilineal and matrifocal systems, which severely affected females' personal, social, and economic status.

The human young bearers[8] calamity intensified around 1,500 BP when Christians and Muslims began to replace thousands of female-honoring Goddess cultures in Africa and Eurasia with a single patriarchal god. In a short time span, in cultures across the world, once sovereign beings were objectified into reproductive objects and restricted to the domestic sphere.

In Gyn/Ecology, Mary Daly notes, "this attraction/need of males for female energy, seen for what it is, is necrophilia - not in the sense of love for actual corpses, but of love for those victimized into a state of living death." The domestication of 'ladies' is ongoing and so too is its resistance. Sarah Ditum argues that women cannot remain neutral on the feminist issue because the battlefield is our bodies: "There's no way to avoid picking a side when you yourself are the disputed territory."

While there has been some progress toward sexual equality in modern times, gains have also been eroded and "the much needed positive developments are not happening fast enough." This conclusion was made at the 2017 UN Commission on the Status of Women, by Phumzile Mlambo-Ngcuka, executive director of UN Women, the United Nations agency charged with promoting women's rights.[9]

In addition to receiving one-third less wages than a man, over half of all women workers around the world, and up to 90 percent in some countries, are informally employed. The informal economy consists of low-cost, female farm workers, street food vendors, care workers, and so on. These girls and women work without legal or social protection, and in India alone, this sector accounts for 190 million women. "They are the under-the-radar and under-valued cogs in the bigger wheels of the formal economy," Mlambo-Ngcuka said.

The UNW director also warned that changing discriminatory laws in over 150 countries "could affect more than three billion women and girls in the world." On the other hand, empowering females can lead to many positive changes, including economics. Phumzile Mlambo-Ngcuka suggested that "advancing women's equality in total could bring a potential boost of 28 trillion U.S. dollars to global annual GDP by 2025."

From Free ♀ to ♂ Tools

As a consequence of male 'progress,' the diversity of female-centered societies has been destroyed and replaced by a rigid machismo script of male ascendancy. Masculinity became redefined as part the New Stone Age, and men began constructing themselves as the only 'real' subjects. Male-dominance intensified with the objectification of human and nonhuman females. Both were stripped of subjectivity and transformed into objects for fulfilling insecure males' desire for wealth, power, taste, and sex.

A subject or having subjectivity is related to consciousness, agency, and independence. A subject is an individual who possesses conscious experiences, such as perspectives, feelings, beliefs, and desires. In contrast, an object is an abstraction of a subject. Others define objects in terms of use value.

According to Martha Nussbaum, a person can be objectified if one or a selection of the properties are adhered to. One factor is instrumentality, or being used as a tool for someone else's purposes. Another is denial of autonomy, as if the individual is lacking in agency or self-determination.

A third aspect of objectification is inertness, as if the creature is without action. A fourth is fungibility, or considering the person as interchangeable with 'objects' of the same type, or with objects of other types. There is the notion of ownership, and denial of subjectivity, as if there is no need for concern for their feelings and experiences.[10]

From valuable subjects under Stone Age ecogynocentrism, females and other-than-human animals became viewed as inert instruments under cyborg rule, reduced to bodily appearance, and silenced.[11] Egg-producing humans and animals entirely forfeit their independence and consent to male owners who treat them as disposable and interchangeable. Although rarely discussed, objectification lies at the heart of the so-called 'Neolithic revolution,' male civilization, and cyborg consciousness.

Exceptionally, first and second wave feminists resisted the sexual objectification of women, arguing that it contributed to second-class status. With third wave feminism, though, the same sexualizing treatment has been repackaged as female empowerment or women 'owning' their sexuality. Not by coincidence, this type of pistillate performance tends to be indistinguishable from the porn-inspired fantasies of heterosexual men.

Under the framing of 'choice' feminism even infants are encouraged to objectify themselves in the name of 'sex-positive' feminism. Any form of nudity is characterized as a revolutionary act since it subverts the conservative status quo. But exposure keeps men's attention firmly on feminized bodies and how they look, rather than on what women say or do. Choice empowerment, therefore, translates to reducing girls to object status on their terms.

Sometimes, an egg-producing human may try to console herself with the idea that females were thwarted by anatomy before men's defeat. That is, trapped by the cycles of menstruation and reproduction, women have never been free and creative agents outside of their homes. This justification reflects the magnitude of the calamity ovary beings face, and the immense value of suppressed female prehistory.

Sex differences among human animals is a central aspect in the construction of femininity and objectification, and Parts II and III examines cognitive and physical variations a variety of perspectives in. This book draws from studies on sex differences in genetics, neuroscience, evolutionary biology, archaeology, anthropology, and sociology. And, there are discussions on biological determination, sexual differentiation, sex differences, sexual characteristics, sex selection, the maternal brain, the y-chromosome, and on female and male bodies.

According to Lerner, patriarchy is a hierarchical, militaristic organization in which individuals and groups are allocated resources, property, status and privileges culturally defined gender roles. It manifests itself through male control of land, wealth, social institutions, female sexuality, and reproduction.

Before the rise of patriarchy, women and girls were responsible for reproduction, and culture itself may have been a female invention for child care in the early Stone Age. Women's prehistory has been entirely erased, an the male-dominated academy disputes any remaining trace with their man-the-hunter dogma. Evidence of gynocentric cultures do exist, and they are pivotal to understanding female subjectivity, and their subsequent reduction in the great fall of women.

This book examines the evidence for female-centered prehistory, including woman-the-gatherer's invention of tools for production and reproduction, cooking methods, nutrient storage devices, food preservation techniques, herbal medicine, and fiber and textile for clothing and accessories. This study of female prehistory also investigates female-centered art, sculpture, pottery, language, ritual, storytelling, script, culture, governance, theology, philosophy, astronomy, time, and agriculture.

♀ Resistance

The war against the Earth Goddess by cyborgs' mechanical consciousness is causing massive destruction that can only intensify with business as usual. Many species are going extinct, and soon, maybe ours as well. In the end, the Earth Goddess will certainly defeat male-centered maldevelopment. And irrespective of how tough and ambitious their plans are, cyborgs will lose.

Male desire for accumulation, ascendancy, and transcendence over the entire Earth is the primary cause for the current deplorable conditions of human females, nonhuman animals, and feminized nature. The demise of egg-producing humans and the natural World are integrally related to climate change, but how can females resist the patriarchy and environmental destruction at the same time?

The empowerment feminism mantra is that greed is especially good for girls and women. Accumulation is paramount, so it is time for females to lean into capitalism, and grab on to the horns of the corporate bull. With the popularity of third wave liberal feminism, 'feminism' can now be whatever you want it to be.

Anybody can be a feminist, including men, and any act can be a 'feminist' statement, even if it upholds institutions and structures that oppress and harm women as a whole, as long as a woman 'chooses' it. This framing is since feminism is a social movement for "human decency, not molding young girls in the image of a banking industry" and turning every woman into a CEO.[12] Embracing patriarchal market economies may be empowering for a token few, but it will not reform the greed-based system or prevent ecocide.

Women have to take survival very seriously as a collective and cannot depend on men to lead. Enduring abrupt climate change will be challenging and result in further reductions in females' status. Preventing a female dystopia requires a radical turnaround in men's hierarchy, male superiority, and alien consciousness, to a more equal, Earth-centered view. What is more, women have to make this shift in ecological awareness very quickly, in less than a few generations.

It is not the case that all women are inherently more virtuous humans than men. Not all sperm-producers are violent and not all women are nurturing. There are different group intensities, situational, and cultural variations of violence and nurturing among females and males. There are also ample individual differences, and within-group variability.[13]

Females have their means of creating conflict, for example, in competing for male interest. Girls and women have internalized sexism, and are complicit in their oppression. Also, women who share class, race, and other privileges with men, can exert power over other females. Nonetheless, humans with ovaries are much more resistant to male dis-order and programming because they benefit less and see its inherent contradictions in their lives.

Women are not exclusively victims, yet, female actions occur within the confines of patriarchal households, communities, and societies. Boys and men police female behavior and action in both private and public spheres. In conforming to toxic masculinity, sperm-producers are somewhat victimized, but males also benefit from sexism and male supremacy in overt and hidden ways.

It is in males' interest to be willfully ignorant of misogyny since they are the chief beneficiaries. Machismo also enables males to deny social responsibility for a range of issues, from anti-female bias to ecosystem collapse. Men have designed and operated the wretched speciesist[14] and sexist system and they are uneager to dismantle it. If there is to be any change in the unequal status quo and ecocidal business-as-usual, it will have to come from girls and women.

Fortunately, there were extensive periods of humans living more in harmony with nature and nonhuman animals to inspire change. For eons of time, prehistoric, child-centered cultures existed, who honored female deities and Earth Goddesses that represented all of life. As fully realized subjects, egg-producing humans lacked any of the current forms of objectification and sexualization built into cyborg societies. Moreover, during prehistory, males were not reduced to mere sex objects but enjoyed equality.

Even millenniums after the dramatic fall of gynocentric clans, some aspects of female subjectivity remained, though greatly diminished. Matrilocal unions continued, and women held relatively high status and power in Africa, China, Japan, Egypt, Greece, Rome, Northern Europe, the Americas, Pacific Islands, Australia, and elsewhere.

Significantly, remnants of the gynecological gift economy remain. This ancient practice may be applied to a wide range of human behaviors such as charity, emergency aid, help to coalition partners, tipping, courtship gifts, production of public goods, and environmentalism.

Restoring the Earth Goddess and female power cannot possibly undo the massive, deleterious effects of more than ten millennia of patriarchy. All the same, ecogynocentrism and female-led social organization may prove essential for our species survival in a rapidly changing climate.

Is 'Cyborgs' ♂ Bashing?

A cyborg is a hypothetical or fictional being with a combination of biological, mechanical, and electronic parts. Men's disastrous separation from nonhuman animals, nature, and the Earth is the foundation of their machine-like consciousness. The complete subjugation of nonhuman animals allows over-anxious males to think of themselves as surpassing nature to become a cyborg, a phantasmal half-god, half-shepherd, lording over feminized Earth.

The concept of cyborg utilized in this study is an organic one, and it involves the merging of nonhuman animals' power with human resources. A cyborg is an alpha mammal grounded on the supremacy of human animals. This definition is separate from the idea of companionship with pets, or the cyborg blending of human and electronic and mechanical devices.[15]

Violence against females, animals, and nature is over-overwhelmingly male, and the term 'cyborg' is used here to raise awareness of this fact. Pointing out ten millenniums of male sexism, misogyny, and animal oppression by referring to men who continue to participate in this offensive system as 'cyborgs' is not bashing, essentialist, or stereotyping.

From the point-of-view of nonhuman animals, there is no question males are monstrous. Sperm-producers treat animals like objects, mere organic devices. Men also use real machines to effect total domination over other-than-human animals and to incorporate their flesh and skin into thousands of products.

Beyond animal abuse, the problems of industrial civilization, including global warming, are integrally related to cyborg machismo and hyper-carnivory. Each tree, forest, and ecosystem destroyed, and animal product consumed, is a concrete expression of males' victory over femaleness and the female Earth.

Moreover, the colonization of nonhuman animals has profoundly affected individuals and society. Animal-based diets cause pollution, deforestation, loss of biodiversity, disease, health problems, and so on. Livestock's long shadow also extends into gender oppression and inequality. And with the policing of female sexuality, male tribalism developed into enslavement, race, caste, religious, and class oppression.

The machine-mindset places economic and ideological interests over life, and ancient gynecological laws and sanctions. Instead, cyborgs refer to Bronze Age rituals, books, and ideology that are woefully lacking in morality and relevance. Programmed for living in the profound past, they compete daily for servitude to a male god far removed the Earth that no one has ever seen, or can ever see.

Men's alien-like consciousness is manifested as dominant behavior and practiced as misogyny, entitlement, privilege, and the assumed right to domesticate Earthlings. The results of sperm-producers' machine-like misconceptions are hierarchy, greed, conflict, and predatory capitalism masking as religion, democracy, and development. Also, cyborgs terrorize each other in an endless cycle of one-upmanship.

For example, cyborgs kill people who are not strictly following their version of Iron Age ideologies. They bomb and occupy the lands of others and claim their 'god' gave it to them. And cyborg societies routinely discriminate and incarcerate the poor and people with darker skin.

Particularly, the term is used to show that the framing of male superiority over nature and females may have far-reaching influence in phallic identities. Coupled with the normalization of guns, porn, and war in media and games, a combination of nature and nurture can lead to a step-up in male violence and toxic masculinity.

Stoltenberg argues that "'manhood' - the personal, behavioral identity that is committed to gender, committed to 'being the man there' - cannot possibly coexist with authentic and passionate and integrated selfhood." Males grow up learning to fear other men's judgment of their masculine performance. However, Stoltenberg suggests the manhood act has become "an impediment to human harmony - perhaps even hazardous to our species' health. The more seriously anyone takes the manhood act, the more dangerous it becomes. Yet we cling to it still."[16]

Like the fabled Minotaur, a creature with the head of a bull and the body of a man, cyborgs are caught in a labyrinth, but of their own design - toxic masculinity. Characteristically, from the start of animal colonization, cyborgs idolized and imitated the bull in its hyper-sexualized and aggressive form.[17] The Greek Minotaur was eventually killed, but it may take a generation of sheroes to slay its modern equivalent, neoliberal patriarchal capitalism, and save the global village.

Perhaps, having an alien mindset played some role in the recent 'success' of our species. Even so, hyper-masculinity is now a major obstacle to existence, and empowering females, and dis-empowering men, are necessary for human survival. To accomplish this, men have to relinquish cyborg consciousness and its false notion of superiority over women, girls and feminized nature.

Only then can non-cyborg men re-learn a connection to nature and accept their responsibility to protect all Earthlings. Through negation of mechanized thinking, unbiased servitors can re-discover respect for females and once again support ecogynocentrism. Once free from all forms of masculinity and patriarchal ideology, non-alienated men can come down to Earth, and slowly begin to re-honor the Planet as the figurative 'Goddess.'

Outline

Exploring the past is important, since it may explain how we got to the present, and provide a glimpse into the future. The text is loosely organized from primates and female prehistory, to the emergence of male-centered civilization, unto the present. It surveys seven taming events and three subjects - biology, feminism, and diet.

Divided into 28 chapters and five parts, the text eclectically interweaves feminist theory from a broad range of disciplines. Intersecting with this, are discussions on diet and the historical relationship between human and non-human animals.

The two introductory chapters' brief discussion of gynocentric prehistory is explored in detail in the next two sections. Part II delves into the early Stone Age to examine diet and the achievements of egg-producing humans. Part III details female-centered organizations and practices during the Middle and Late Stone Age.

After uncovering the preponderance of evidence for female-centered prehistory, the book turns to analyze the emergence of patriarchy in the New Stone Age. Part IV investigates the colonization of nonhuman animals, and how this contributed to the outgrowth of misogyny and cyborgs' rule. Part V continues the unpacking of patriarchy with an overview of the current status of women and girls. Finally, Part VI looks at ecofeminist theory and resistance to patriarchal thinking.

Ecogynocentrism is the focus of Part II and Part III, which are the operative sections of this study. Various aspects of female prehistory are detailed in 15 chapters, starting with nine chapters in Part II. The section opens with a discussion of primates and then analyzes pre-humans starting around 3 million BP.

Part II goes up to 12,000 BP and analyses female child-care, cooperation, culture, cooking, shelter, ritual, dance, medicine, art, sexual choice, pottery, textile, language, script, and proto-agriculture. It also investigates myths about the Paleo diet, man-the-hunter, and male violence in the Stone Age.

The next section continues the exploration into ancient gynocentric cultures in six chapters. Part III begins around 12,000 BP and ends with the decline of ecogynocentrism about 7,000 years ago. This third part covers female intensive agriculture, settlement, social relations, governance, and economy in the late Stone Age.

Part III also focuses on female-centered theology and philosophy and introduces many Goddesses, such as Lady of the Beasts, Animal Goddesses, Earth Goddesses, Moon Goddesses, Triple Goddesses, and the Deer Goddess. The last chapter of Part III unpacks the political and academic opposition to ecogynocentrism and female-centered theory.

The fourth section covers the dawn of male-centered society and the twilight of ecogynocentrism from 8,000 to 5,000 BP. Part IV consists of five chapters that investigate male domination over nature, the taming of ovary beings, and men's economic, political, and symbolic use of animals. Part IV details cyborg's domestication of the Goddess and the evolution of male-centered religions.

The five chapters of Part V continues the critical analyses of cyborg societies with a summary of the current status of females under patriarchy. It details selected aspects of men's exploitation of women, male violence, and the representation of women in media. This fifth section also looks at critical debates in feminist theory as they relate to this study.

The last section has one chapter. The focus of the final chapter is an ecofeminist critique of the destructive patriarchal/cyborg worldview, especially in regards to nature, nonhuman animals, and women.

Conclusion

Objectification is a fundamental aspect of male-dominated societies. Turning nature, animals, and females from independent subjects into patriarchal objects simultaneously justify their oppression and makes them more vulnerable and available for use. Objectification is the basis of cyborg oppression, Part IV and V details men's framing of nonhuman animals and humans with ovaries.

This second chapter wraps up the introduction to the book's main themes - diet, gynocentrism, and domestication. Given false claims by mainstream patriarchal 'science,' and the ubiquitous nature of male subjugation, it is essential to note that women and nonhuman animals once roamed free, unhindered by constraints of cyborg rule and violence. This is revealed in Part II and III, which comes next.

(Figure 3: Bonobo)

II: PALEO ECOGYNOCENTRISM (3M to 12,000 BP)

3: Hominid

> We must remember that Metis was originally the parthenogenetic mother of Athena. - Mary Daly

> Note: Parthenogenesis is a type of asexual reproduction in which the offspring develops from unfertilized eggs.[1]

ASIA's Journey 2121.03

At an afternoon rest stop, the women gather in a circle under the shade of a giant cactus. Still five days away from the safe house, the women of ASIA discuss how to ration out the remaining food and water.

The language of crones, mothers, and the other women is free-flowing as if they understand each others' consciousness, fears, and desires. The women's individual and community dreams are the same, and at each meeting they effortlessly reach consensus.

It is 121 degrees F (49 degrees C) in the shade with a humidity of 75 percent. The children are eating a snack under a smaller tree. They like to create games, art, and tools out with sticks and stones, and invent new ways to tie and strap their backpacks.

The girls are eating and playing a guessing game when suddenly, the two male teenagers, Alex and Roshi, starts to chase Cha'Kwaina for her bread. Four girls immediately rush to her aid and stop the bullies from taking her food. But Cha'Kwaina falls to the ground and lies motionless on the hot sand.

Onaiwah screams when she sees her daughter not moving. "Quick! She fainted from heat exhaustion. Get her in the shade." Three women gently lifted Cha'Kwaina and carried her to the shade of the giant cactus. The children circle to look at their friend.

"Don't crowd her," Xóchitl warned. "She's needs air. Go back over there." Xóchitl points to the smaller tree. The children whisper as they walk away. "Is she dead?" Iniko tearfully ask of her best friend.

Kuan-Yin fans the air close to Cha'Kwaina with a piece of cardboard. Ramla strips off Cha'Kwaina's clothes and Zemora covers the child with wet towels. Onaiwah applies a wet cloth to Cha'Kwaina's forehead and places a water bottle to her daughter's lips. "Drink, Cha-Cha, drink," Onaiwah pleads with tears streaming down her eyes.

Cha'Kwaina does not move. Unconscious, her breathing is shallow and rapid. Nakeisha checks her with a stethoscope and announces, "Her pulse is high and weak, and her pressure is low."

"Is she going to be alright?" Onaiwah asks weakly.

"Maybe." Nakeisha looks at the older women. "She has to avoid physical activity for the rest of the day." The crones motion consent but they knew that ASIA did not have enough rations for an extra day.

Zemora glances around. The waxing crescent moon was still high over the hills to the west but moonset would be a few hours after sunset, so it would be a dark night. "Let's find a deep spot to camp in," Zemora suggests to the crones, who gesture in accord.

Onaiwah looks at the two male teens angrily. "You two, come here." She screams inside to avoid slapping them. She had known their mothers before they died at the shelter, and Onaiwah promised both women that she would take care of their sons. Grinding her teeth, Onaiwah seethes, "Go gather Cha'Kwaina's bread over there. Eat it well, as it may be our last."

Introduction

The human story is a few million years old, and it begins with the primate order and our immediate ancestors, the family of great apes, or Hominidae. As our cousins and most human-like creatures, understanding primate diet and social systems is useful for comprehending ourselves. Knowing how biological sex and power influence primate inter-personal and inter-group relations could similarly prove beneficial.

The great apes provide clues on how ancient human-like creatures may have survived and lived. Part II's exploration of Paleolithic ecogynocentrism commences with a discussion on diet and social relations among the three existing great apes. Then, a look at food consumption by the first human-like creatures follows.

The third chapter of this section goes into the evolution of modern humans, and the fourth one investigates the vital but discounted work of female gatherers during the Stone Age. The fifth chapter analyses the second adjustment, the taming of the flame, followed by the use of combustion in the third subjugation, fire farming. It also explores ancient women's ritual and dance.

The sixth chapter of Part II investigates Stone Age art and the commonly found Woman or Goddess figures. This chapter discusses the role of egg-producing human artists and their relevance to gynocentric cultures. The seventh chapter analyzes Darwinism and female choice in sex selection, and it surveys aspects of the fourth taming, that of dogs.

The eight chapter of Part II focuses on the 'evidence' for Stone Age male-centered violence, and on biological differences between pistillate and staminate humans. The ninth and final chapter of this section explores egg-producing bodies and inventions by ovary beings. It covers aspects of female civilization in the Stone Age, such as language, script, pottery, and textiles.

This first chapter of Part II argues that the first domestication was female apes' taming of males. This contention is significant because if the great apes are gynocentric, this shows that early humans may have shared similar forms of female-centered social organization.

The chapter begins with a brief discussion of measuring time and then provides an overview of the great apes. Diet and social relations among orangutans come next, followed by gorillas. The chapter closes by investigating food and social interactions among the pan primates - chimpanzee and bonobo.

Measuring Time

Across the globe, ancient humans have had to adapt to climate change numerous times. Early humans altered their environment as did their interventions with animals, which in turn influenced the climate. As human-animal and human-environment relationships changed, this affected social relations and these interrelated processes are ongoing into the present.

In Earth science, the Pleistocene lasted from approximately 2.5 million years BP to 11,500 BP. This era was marked by repeated glaciations in the World, ending in the last glacial interval and the commencement of intensive plant cultivation. In archaeology, the Pleistocene corresponds roughly with the Paleolithic or Stone Age.

The Stone Age represents time measured in terms of human technological artifacts. The onset of this archaeological era is the first known use of stone tools, probably by hominids such as Australopithecus, over three million years ago. The Paleolithic is characterized by the use of chipped stone tools, while the Neolithic or New Stone Age is known for its polished stone tools.

The Paleolithic covers 95 percent of human technological prehistory in which stone was used to make implements with an edge, a point, or a flat surface. The entire Stone Age era terminates with the Copper Age (6,500 to 5,500 BP),[2] which was succeeded by the Bronze Age (5,000 to 3,200 BP), and then the Iron Age (3,200 to 2,600 BP).

The Stone Age is sub-divided into three segments - the Early, Middle and Late Stone Age, or the Lower, Middle, and Upper Paleolithic. The Middle Stone Age or Mesolithic starts from approximately 300,000 BP and concludes close to 50,000 BP. Modern humans emerged during this era and migrated to Asia then Europe. The Late Stone Age ends with the Neolithic, or New Stone Age, around 12,000 BP.

Interestingly, stone tools dated to 3.3 million BP occur before the first appearance of the oldest Homo fossils about 2.8 million years old. Other primates and animals also use tools, so the defining characteristic of Homo or even of early humans is not their technological ingenuity.[3] Furthermore, the framing the human story almost exclusively in terms technological use limits our understanding of other salient factors, like diet and sexual relations.

1st Domestication: Male Apes

The subduing of mammalian males by females is an extensive and ongoing process in numerous species across the Globe. The first domestication realized among the great apes family in the primate order was the taming of sperm-producers by egg-producers. Even though balance between the sexes fluctuates, females wield great power in sex-selection.

Female reproductive achievement is limited by resource availability and acquisition. In contrast, male reproductive success is limited by access to mates and the number of fertilizations, and may therefore be more variable. Phallic apes have to obtain young-bearers' approval, who may have a preference for younger mates. So power relations among social primates are situational and constantly changing.

Primates are characterized by refined development of the hands and feet, a shortened snout, an ample brain, as well as an increased reliance on stereoscopic vision at the expense of smell, the dominant sensory system in most mammals.[4] Many primates have specializations that enable them to exploit particular foods, such as fruit, leaves, gum or insects.[5]

The great apes or Hominidae are sizable, tailless primates, with the smallest living species being the bonobo at 60 to 90 pounds (30 to 40 kg) in weight, and the largest being the eastern gorillas, with males weighing 300 to 400 pounds (140 to 180 kg). Fruit is the preferred food among all but some human groups. Human teeth and jaws are markedly smaller for their size than those of other apes, which may be an adaptation to eating cooked food.[6]

Similar to the male bias held by mainstream anthropologists, primate researchers are male-centric, and their work has focused on the role of phallic individuals vying for leadership of groups. Often viewed as more passive, egg-producing apes' manipulation of sex selection and other aspects of power are frequently understated and misinterpreted in primate studies.

The great apes have varying degrees of female-centered involvement in their cultures, from solitary orangutan mothers who avoid contact with males to female-led bonobo clans of over 100 individuals. The notion of phallic-dominated gorillas with a lone silverback defending a group of egg-producers is false since this leads to sexual insecurity for most sperm-producers. There are several advantages for alpha males to follow the wishes of female gorillas, for example, food and reproductive security.

The evolution of the primates occurred about 70 million BP. Their emergence was facilitated by the 'angiosperm revolution' in which flowering and fruiting trees provided niches for tree-living frugivores or fruit-eating organisms, and folivores, animals that feed on leaves.[7] Around 35 million BP, ape-like and monkey-like primates appeared, and by 20 million BP, recognizable apes were dispersed residents of the forests.

The Hominidae, whose members are known as great apes or hominids, are part of the primate family. The group is defined by an upright gait, increased brain cavity compared with other primates, a flattened face, and reduction in the size of the teeth and jaw. The great apes are considered more 'advanced' than other apes and monkeys, but they are not.

Worldwide there are more than 450 species of primates, and many use tools. Some Japanese primates even wash their food and soak in natural hot springs. Almost all primates eat a plant-based diet. Some monkeys consume five servings of fruit per hour, and as many as 50 portions of fruit in a single day.[8]

The Hominidae family include seven species in four genera. One genus is Pongo consisting of the Bornean and Sumatran orangutan. Another is Gorilla, with the eastern and western gorilla. A third genus is Pan comprising of the common chimpanzee and the bonobo. And finally, there is Homo, with human and near-human ancestors and relatives, like the Neanderthals.

The most recent common ancestor of all Hominidae lived roughly 16 to 19 million BP, when Pongos separated from the other three genera. The Hominidae group separated from the Hylobatidae (gibbons) family earlier than 20 million BP.[9] And, chimpanzee and human ancestry converge approximately 7 million BP.

Pongo: Orangutan

The ancestors of the Pongo subfamily split from the main ape line in Africa and eventually spread into Asia. The genus contains the extinct Gigantopithecus blacki, the largest known primate. Native to Indonesia and Malaysia, orangutans are currently found in only the rainforests of Borneo and Sumatra.

Orangutans are among the most intelligent Hominidae, and there may even be distinctive cultures within populations. Pongos use a variety of sophisticated tools and construct elaborate sleeping nests each night from branches and foliage. They may add additional features, such as 'pillows,' 'blankets,' 'roofs,' and 'bunk-beds' to their nests.

Orangutans are the most solitary of the great apes. Social bonds occur primarily between mothers and their dependent offspring, who stay together for the first two years. As with other primates, the presence of Orang mothers improve the survival of their daughters' offspring.

Resident females live in defined home ranges that overlap with those of other adult egg-producers, who may be their immediate relatives. Females tend to settle in home ranges that overlap with their mothers,[10] so female pongos live mostly within a gynocentric grouping.

One to several resident female home ranges is encompassed within the orbit of a resident male, who is their primary mating partner. Resident phallic orangs may form unions with females that can last days, weeks or months after copulation. This voluntary partnership is an example of the first adaptation, the restraining of Orangutan sperm-producers by egg-producers.

Orangutans have a 22 to 30-day menstrual cycle, like humans. Gestation lasts for nine months, with egg-producers giving birth to their first offspring between 14 and 15 years old. There is an eight-year separation between births, the longest inter-birth interval among the great apes. Orangutans can live over 30 years in untamed nature and captivity.

Fruit is the principal component of an orangutan's diet, but they also eat vegetation, bark, honey, insects, and bird eggs. They consume over 300 kinds of fruit, and for minerals, they sometimes eat soil. Mothers teach their babies what food to eat, in which trees to find it, and in what season.

Gorilla

Gorillas are ground-dwelling, predominantly herbivorous apes that inhabit the forests of central Africa. The DNA of gorillas is highly similar to that of humans, around 95 percent. Gorillas are the next closest living relatives to humans, after Pan, or chimpanzees and bonobos.

Like the other great apes, gorillas can laugh, grieve, have "rich emotional lives," develop strong family bonds, make and use tools, and think about the past and future. Some researchers believe gorillas have spiritual feelings or religious sentiments. They have cultures in various areas revolving around different methods of food preparation and show individual color preferences.[11]

Gorillas live in groups called troops. Both staminate and pistillate Gorillas emigrate from their natal groups, perhaps to avoid problems related to in-breeding. Notably, maternally related egg-producers in a troop tend to associate closely. And, by restricting sexual access to a single alpha silverback, or dominant male, egg-producers restrained sperm-producers by forcing them to compete to reproduce.

In a group, when the silverback dies, females and their offspring disperse to find a new troop. Without a silverback to protect them, infants may become victims of infanticide, so joining a new group is probably a female tactic to prevent this tragedy.[12]

Similar to Homo, gorillas mate year round. Female mountain gorillas first give birth at ten years of age and have four-year inter-birth intervals. Gorilla infants are vulnerable and dependent, so mothers, their primary caregivers, are critical to their survival. Male gorillas are not active in caring for the young.

Like other leaf-eating primates, gorillas prefer protein-rich leaves.[13] Fruits and herbaceous leaves comprise the majority of the diet.[14] The Western lowland gorilla consumes parts of at least 97 plant species. About 67 percent of their diet is fruit, 17 percent is leaves, seeds and stems, and three percent is termites and caterpillars. Eastern lowland gorillas will also eat insects, preferably ants.[15]

Pan: Chimpanzee

The closest relatives of Hominins, the two existing Pan species,[16] diverged around one million years ago. The most obvious differences between Pans are that chimpanzees are somewhat bigger, more aggressive, and male dominated, while the bonobos are smaller, peaceful, and female dominated.[17]

Anatomical variations between the common chimpanzee and the bonobo are slight, but sexual and social behaviors are markedly different. The two species behave quite differently even if kept under identical conditions.[18] Both can live over 30 years in untamed nature and captivity.

Chimps and bonobos are some of the most social great apes, with social bonds occurring among individuals in the community. They convey intended meanings in a manner that is similar to that of human nonverbal communication, using vocalizations, hand gestures, and facial expressions.

Chimpanzees are phallic-dominated. Sperm-producers typically attain dominance by cultivating allies who will support them during future ambitions for power. Egg-producing chimpanzees have to show deference to the alpha male by presenting their hindquarters. Female chimpanzees have a hierarchy which is influenced by their position within a group and young females may inherit lofty status from a high-ranking mother.[19]

Community acceptance by egg-producers is necessary for alpha phallic status since females ensure that their group visits places that supply them with enough food. A group of dominant females will sometimes oust an alpha male who is not to their preference and back another male chimp. Thus the need to maintain the favor of egg-producers serves to restrain even male-centered chimpanzees.

Western chimpanzees have some unique behaviors. They make wooden spears to hunt other primates, use caves as homes, share plant foods with each other, travel and forage during the night, and submerge themselves in water and play in it. The common chimpanzee has an omnivorous diet, a troop hunting culture based on beta males led by an alpha phallic chimp, and highly complex social relationships.

Plants are the primary component of a chimpanzee's diet including fruits, seeds, nuts, leaves, and flowers. While they are mostly herbivorous, they do eat honey, soil, insects, birds and their eggs, and small to medium-sized mammals, including other chimps and monkeys. [20]

Pan: Bonobo

The most successful first-domestication among the great apes was that of bobono sperm-producers by egg-producers. This taming can probably be traced to the split between the two Pans, around one million BP. In contrast to chimpanzees, bonobos are relatively egalitarian and nonviolent. They are not phallic-dominated but instead display a mix of gynocentrism and sexually receptive behavior.

Sharing 98.5 percent of the same DNA as humans, it is not surprising that bonobos possess very human-like qualities. They embody a profound intelligence and emotional capacity. Bonobos have picked up on many facets of human culture through simple observation, and have learned how to communicate in human languages, use tools, and play music.[21]

Egg-producing bonobos frequently form coalitions even though they are generally with non-relatives. All-female coalitions of two or more individuals form spontaneously to attack males, usually after the sperm-producers behaved aggressively towards one or more female bonobo.

Bonding enables bonobo females to dominate most of the males. Although male bonobos are individually stronger, they cannot stand alone against a united group of egg-producers. One researcher concludes, "coalitions in female bonobos might have evolved as a counter strategy against male harassment."[22]

Interestingly, bonobos have highly individualized facial features, as humans do. So like us, one individual may look significantly different from another bonobo. This adaption facilitated visual facial recognition in social interaction.

Bonobos can live in close-knit social groups of a hundred individuals or more. During the day, the group break into smaller groups to forage in different areas, but the whole clan sleeps together at night. The ancestors of humans might have adopted the same foraging and sleeping behavior. And they may have occupied temporary retreats, or settlements, for extensive periods of time. So human settlements, or what is commonly considered as 'domestication,' is much older than 12,000 years.

Between bonobo groups, social mingling may occur, in which members of different communities have sex and groom each other. This behavior is unheard of among common chimpanzees. While social hierarchies do exist, rank plays a less prominent role than in other primate societies. Primatologist Frans de Waal thinks that bonobos are capable of altruism, compassion, empathy, kindness, patience, and sensitivity. He describes "bonobo society" as a "gynecocracy."[23]

Egg-producers have a higher social status in bonobo society than the other great apes. Aggressive encounters between staminate and pistillate bonobos are rare, and sperm-producers are tolerant of infants and juveniles. Bonobos carry and nurse their young for four years and give birth every 4.6 years. Akin to the other great apes, bonobo mothers assume the entirety of parental care.

A male bonobo derives status from the social position of his mother, similar to chimpanzees, and hanging out with mom can boost a sperm-producer's chances of getting intimate with a fertile female.[24] The mother-son bond often stays strong and continues throughout life.[25]

Compared to chimps, bonobos show more sexual behavior in a greater variety of relationships. Bonobos frequently have sex, sometimes to help prevent and resolve conflicts. Bonobos are the only non-human animal to have been observed engaging in tongue kissing, and oral sex. Bonobos and humans are the only primates that engage in face-to-face genital sex.[26]

Bonobos do not form permanent monogamous sexual relationships with individual partners. They also do not discriminate in their sexual behavior by sex or age either. When bonobos come upon a new food source or feeding ground, the increased excitement will usually lead to communal sexual activity, presumably decreasing tension and encouraging peaceful feeding.[27]

Female bonobos engage in mutual genital behavior, possibly to bond socially and form a female nucleus of bonobo society. Egg-producers rub their clitorises together rapidly for ten to twenty seconds, and this behavior, "which may be repeated in rapid succession, is usually accompanied by grinding, shrieking, and clitoral engorgement."[28] Adolescent females often leave their native community to join another community. Sexual bonding with other egg-producers establishes these new females as members of the group.

The bonobo's diet is for the most part vegetarian. Foraging in small groups, bonobos feast primarily on fruit, but they also eat leaves, flowers, bark, stems, roots, insect larvae, worms, crustaceans, honey, eggs, and soil. Occasionally, they hunt small mammals like flying squirrels or small antelopes.

Conclusion

This chapter surveyed the closest relatives to humans and chartered the physical, social, and dietary landscape from which modern humans emerged. This segment argued that the first taming occurred long before human prehistory commenced, with the subduing of sperm-producing primates by egg-producers. And, it showed that sustainable, plant-based foods are the primary diet of the great apes.

The female-centered nature of bonobo and other primate societies show that male domination among humans is an anomaly among primates, and that it can be changed. Within the Hominidae family, bonobo females hold relatively higher status compared to human girls and women. To illustrate this, Part V documents sexual caste and the multiple oppressions human egg-producers face, from street harassment and media objectification, to domestic violence and femicide. As a reflection of cyborg ecocidal 'progress,' the other members of Hominidae face rapid habitat loss and imminent extinction in nature. Can our related Homo genus avoid a similar fate?

The next chapter moves the clock forward to the start of human prehistory. The few fossils discovered from the first human-like creatures who separated from the other great apes offer fascinating hints on various aspects of their lives.   Interestingly, there were many human-like creatures in the Stone Age, but only one survived.

So much of this primordial era is unclear. Did sexual relations and diet have anything to do with the demise of the others? Did female-centered social organization help the ancestors of modern humans to survive? What can a few bones from the past tell us about these vital questions? These questions are explored next.

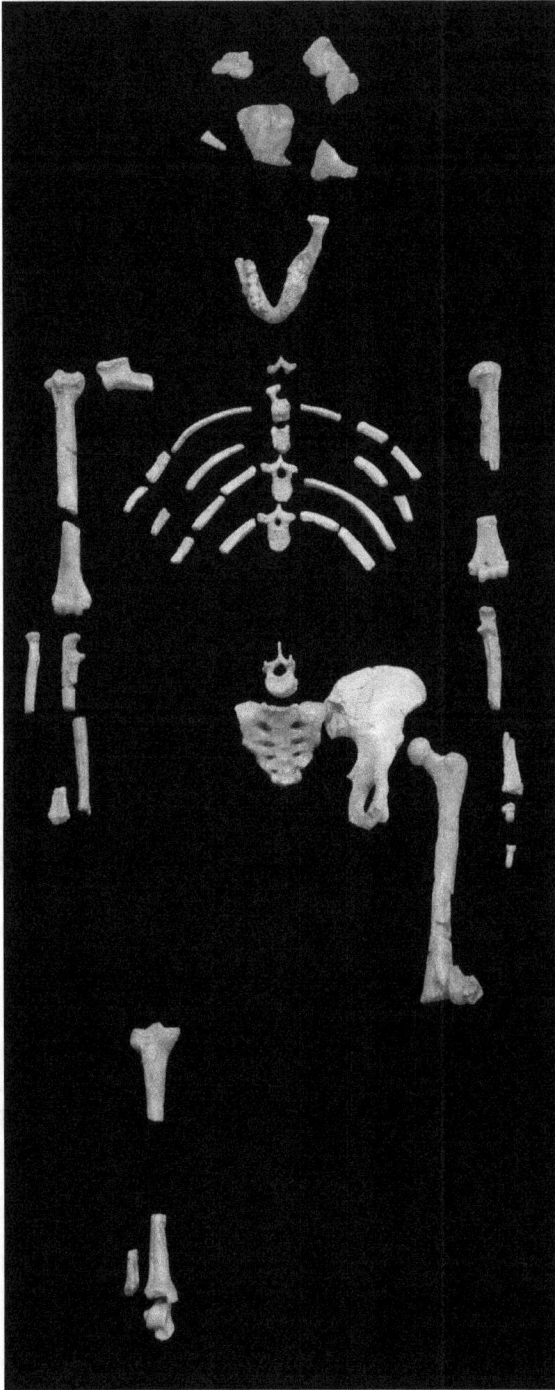

(Figure 4: Lucy, Australopithecus afarensis, c. 3.2 million BP)

4: Hominin

After Athena was "reborn" from the head of Zeus, her single "parent", she became Zeus's obedient mouthpiece. She became totally male-identified, employing priests, not priestesses, urging men on in battle, siding against women consistently. - Mary Daly

ASIA's Journey 2121.04

It's mid-day, windless, 127°F (52°C) in the sun with low humidity. The women know that the cells in their bodies start to die around 106°F (41°C) to 113°F (45°C). If hydrated, their bodies can survive higher temperatures, but not for long.

The group is slowly making their way north, across a scorching stretch of red dirt. The sky is clear with a faint dusty haze to the west. A pair of vultures circles high overhead, oblivious to the heat below. Two girls were suffering from muscle and abdominal cramps. Three women have nausea, vomiting, and diarrhea. There is little food and water left, and the safe-house is three days away. A lot could happen before then and the crones are worried.

While scouting ahead, Xóchitl unexpectedly discovers a small spring at the bottom of a natural depression. Upon hearing this news, the entire group races down the hill, elated. There is enough water to get a soak, and everyone takes advantage of this. The children splash each other excitedly while adults happily rinse off weeks-old dirt from their skin and clothes. After days of walking and sleeping in the heat, it is heaven to just sit in cool water.

An owl hoots and the group instantly freezes. It is their security alarm, and everyone becomes silent and alert. Lian at the top of the ridge signals them to move and hide. The pedo-hunters were probably close. Instinctively, Onaiwah goes after Cha'Kwaina. She gathers Iniko and the other girls around her and exits the water.

"Go and hide behind the bushes and shrubs," Onaiwah tells the girls and points the side of the hill. Ramla and the other mothers form into a semi-circle around the children. The women set up a defensive perimeter and the children help to dig a trench.

"Boys," Hehewuti calls Alex and Roshi over to her. "Go and help Lian and Xóchitl up there." She points to the hill top. "Listen to Xóchitl and do exactly what she tells you."

Hehewuti and the women sit and wait. At the top of the ridge, Xóchitl points to the left. The boys follow her and all three disappear from view on the other side.

"Xóchitl's plan is to lure the pedo-hunters away from here," Hehewuti said, looking pleased. "Let's hope her plan succeeds."

Introduction

This chapter extends the discussion of diet and social relations among the great apes by exploring the ape-like creatures that emerged during the last 4 to 6 million years, who may have been the ancestors of modern humans. However, unlike the great apes, there are no populations of these creatures that can be studied, and only a few scattered artifacts remain of their existence.

Bones, tools, and ornaments offer tantalizing clues about early humans, and how they might have lived and eaten. This section discusses artifacts found, especially what they may suggest about diet and female modes of production, such as gathering. This second chapter of Part II on Stone Age ecogynocentrism centers on the biological variations among early humans, and continues the inquiry into the first domestication and diet.

The chapter begins by defining primates, hominids, and human-like creatures, or hominins. Artifacts from four human-like species - Floresiensis, Naledi, Neanderthal, and Denisovan - are examined next. The chapter ends by critically analyzing the notion that progress in the Stone Age was related to an increase in carnivory or male modes of production.

Hominid to Hominin

Approximately 15 to 20 million BP, hominids, or the great apes, evolved from the primate order that is 70 million years old. Humans are just the latest in a long line of hominid species that have emerged in the past six to eight million years from apes.[1]

Hominin is a special group of hominids consisting of modern humans, extinct human-like species, and their immediate ancestors. In this group are members of the genera Ardipithecus, Australopithecus, and Homo. The evolution of these great apes were part of primates' response to ecological shifts as African forests transformed to woodlands and savannas. This flatter landscape favored the adaptation of bipedalism.[2]

Hominins modified their diet to suit their wooded environments by consuming new floral resources like seeds and roots. Humans emerged from the brush, as Growlett argues, "Rather than apes who came down from the trees, as traditionally seen, our ancestors were the bush country apes."[3]

Ardipithecus was an early transition species, neither human nor ape. It was bipedal with reduced jaws and teeth, and a longer thumb.[4] Next to evolve were the australopiths, with their sturdy builds, lengthy arms, short legs, and smaller brains. Curiously, bonobo body proportions closely resemble those of Australopithecus, so bonobos may be a living example of this distant human ancestor.

Experts consider Australopithecus as the original "killer ape" who went to the savanna to hunt. Accordingly, early humans' first technology is presumed to be weapons. But researchers found plant remains in the two-million-year-old dental plaque of A. sediba's teeth.[5] The animals were consuming bark, leaves, sedges, grasses, fruit, and palm, not flesh.[6]

One of the earliest hominin finds is Australopithecus afarensis or bones from the famous Lucy fossil. Her 3.2-million-year-old skeleton was discovered in Ethiopia in 1974.[7] Stone tools associated with afarensis date to 3.4 million BP,[8] so they were the first hominin known to use implements.

Close to three million years BP, australopiths were joined by the first members of the genus Homo, with their longer legs, stiffer walking feet, more dexterous fingers, and much larger brains. Rather than a clear, linear evolution from early hominins, a more complex picture of the first Homo sapiens has emerged. There were regional diversities and smaller brains than expected. Plus, Homo sapiens coexisted alongside australopiths for at least 1.5 million years.

The Homo[9] genus consist of several primeval types such as Homo habilis (2.8 to 1.5 million BP). H. habilis was short and had disproportionately lengthy arms compared to modern humans. And they had a cranial capacity of half the size of modern humans.

Another primordial form, Homo erectus, existed from 1.9 million to 70,000 BP. Curiously, the brain of H. erectus is double that of H. habilis and there is a huge debate over what caused this change. H. erectus also had smaller teeth and gut, and their body was similar to that of modern humans.

Homo erectus originated in Africa, and sizable numbers started leaving the continent approximately 1.8 million years ago. H. erectus were the first hominins to leave Africa, use fire, cook, and wear clothes. They migrated throughout Eurasia as far as Georgia, India, Sri Lanka, China, and Indonesia.

Homo erectus remains are often accompanied by primitive stone tools whose transport distances show that these animals ranged over vast territories. Distinct H. erectus groups may have survived until 50,000 BP or later, before they were absorbed into modern humans.

Other Homo forms include H. floresiensis (700,000 - 50,000 BP), H. neanderthal (600,000 - 40,000 BP), H. denisovan (400,000 - 50,000 BP), H. cepranensis (450,000 BP), H. naledi (335,000 BP), H. helmei (260,000 BP), H. sapiens (200,000 BP - present) or modern humans, and other unidentified lineages.

Other Homo forms are close relatives to humans and the vast majority of people carry their DNA in our genes. This leads to elementary questions regarding our prehistory and evolution. For instance, how were other Homo groups different from us, and was the mixing of our genes consensual or coerced? What forms of diet and social relations did various Homo forms practice? And was Homo sapiens the cause of other hominins demise?

H. Floresiensis

Homo floresiensis are a dwarf hominin found in Indonesia. This species may have evolved from a population of Homo erectus that arrived there roughly a million years ago. H. floresiensis was more analogous to apes and primordial hominins than modern humans. The remains of an individual that stood 3.5 feet (1.1 m) in height, nicknamed 'hobbit,' were discovered in 2003 on the island of Flores.

Partial skeletons of nine individuals have been recovered, dated 100,000 to 60,000 BP. Other H. floresiensis finds date to about 700,000 BP, and are even smaller than the later fossils.[10] Stone tools were found from 190,000 to 50,000 BP.[11] These artifacts suggest that H. floresiensis lived contemporaneously with modern humans on Flores. Did H. sapiens cause their extinction?

In addition to diminutive body, H. floresiensis had a remarkably tiny brain cavity. It is in the range of chimpanzees and half that of its presumed immediate ancestor, H. erectus. Why did this hominin evolve dwarf stature and cranium? Maybe, in the limited food environment on Flores, H. erectus adapted to petite bodies via insular dwarfism.[12] This process is duplicated by other species on Flores.

Notwithstanding the tiny brain of H. floresiensis, advanced behaviors are connected with this Homo species. One cave shows evidence of the use of fire for cooking. And they used sophisticated stone tools similar to the Late Stone Age associated with modern humans, who have nearly quadruple the brain volume.

H. Naledi

Homo naledi is an early slender upright hominin species characterized by a body mass and stature akin to small-bodied human populations between 4.5 and 5 feet tall, and 100 to 110 lbs. Discovered in 2013, they have a smaller brain volume, similar to Australopithecus. H. naledi may have originated near the start of the Homo genus, around 335,000 to 236,000 years ago.[13]

This dating suggests that H. naledi lived at the same time as ancient humans, or Homo sapiens. And instead of human evolution being a linear progression towards larger-brains, there may have been multiple lines of different species evolving side by side.

H. naledi may represent a relic population that may have evolved in near isolation in South Africa, similar to Homo floresiensis. Bones deposit over centuries in a cave imply that despite having a brain no bigger than a gorilla's, H. naledi may have been carrying out a burial ritual, which is an advanced social behavior.[14] The grave site hints that complex social bonds already existed among hominins at the beginning of our species.

H. Neanderthal

Neanderthals existed throughout Eurasia, from Western Europe to Central, Northern, and Western Asia. Homo neanderthalensis emerged from the Homo sapiens lineage 600,000 years ago, and became extinct around 40,000 BP.[15] Were modern humans responsible for their demise?

This Homo species was closely related to modern humans, with 99.5 percent identical DNA. Approximately 1.5 to 2.1 percent of the DNA of anyone outside Africa is Neanderthal in origin.[16] Their DNA presence in modern H. sapiens could have been higher in the past, then diminished over time. Two caves in Palestine show alternating Homo sapiens and Neanderthal occupation.[17]

This archaic Homo species was stronger than modern humans, and had related intelligence and technology. Neanderthals were not making bone tools or seashell ornaments like modern humans, but they were digging their fireplaces the same and practicing related rituals.[18] For instance, far inside a cave in France, elaborate constructions of rings of broken stalagmites were made by early Neanderthals around 176,000 BP.[19]

The ring structure is a powerful, gynocentric symbol that often appear with H. sapiens, such as megalith sites. A rock engraving made by Neanderthals in Gibraltar about 40,000 BP, further demonstrates their capacity for abstract thought and expression through the use of geometric forms.[20]   One of their buildings was constructed with mammoth skulls, jaws, tusks and leg bones, and had 25 fire hearths inside.[21]

Neanderthals were building some form of watercraft since the Middle Stone Age and may have been the World's first mariners. They were on Crete around 130,000 BP.[22] In comparison, modern humans took to the seas just 50,000 years ago in crossing to Australia.[23]

Who Killed Off Neanderthals?

Why did Neanderthals go extinct? Were Neanderthals hyper-carnivores, like lions and polar bears, who were highly dependent on animal protein for survival, especially megafauna and giant herbivores? The extinction of megafauna could have contributed to their ending, but Neanderthals were also using cooked vegetables in their diet.[24] One group in Spain some 50,000 years ago consumed plenty of mushrooms, pine nuts, and moss, but no flesh. These

Spanish neanderthals might even have been vegetarians.[25]

Researchers suggest a scenario of violent conflict between Neanderthals and H. sapiens comparable to the genocides suffered by Indigenous peoples in recent human history.[26] But reasons for their dying out might be less sinister. For instance, lower population density may have increased Neanderthal susceptibility to mutations caused by inbreeding.

Did better gynocentric patterns enable modern humans to out-compete and replace the Neanderthals? More peaceful gynocentric practices like social networking and alliances could have allowed modern humans to grow their population faster and overwhelm Neanderthals and other hominin groups in Europe, Asia, and Australia.[27]

Possibly, Neanderthals did not really go extinct, but instead were assimilated into other hominin populations.[28] There were three distinct interbreeding events with Homo Sapiens from 114,000 to 77,000 years ago. The first encounter involved the ancestors of all non-African modern humans, probably soon after leaving Africa. The second happened after the ancestral Melanesian group had branched off, and subsequently had a unique breeding event with Denisovans. And the third mixing involved the ancestors of East Asians only.[29]

H. Denisovan

Denisovans are a primeval Homo species that ranged from Europe and Siberia to Southeast Asia. They might have shared a common origin with Neanderthals. H. denisovan interbred with Neanderthals and another unidentified ancient human. A 400,000-year-old Denisovan femur bone discovered in Spain is the earliest known fossil for this species.[30]

Remains of a 50,000-year old Denisovan girl with dark skin, brown hair, and brown eyes were found in a cave in southwestern Siberia. The girl was closely related to Neanderthals, yet distinct enough to merit classification as a new species. Teeth of two other individuals were also found, dated 110,000 BP to 170,000 BP. Denisovans, Neanderthals, and Sapiens inhabited the cave at various times.[31]

Several artifacts, including a 40,000-year-old bracelet were discovered.[32] It is the oldest known stone jewelry of its kind, intricately made from a green stone, chlorite. In bright sunlight, the bracelet reflects the sun rays, and at night by the fire, it casts a dark shade of green. The polished bangle had a carefully drilled hole to attach a strap with a charm. There was also a ring, carved out of marble.[33]

Other artifacts were found in the cave dating as far back as 125,000 years. Notably, archaeologists did not find any male-centric object, art, or symbolism. This precious piece of jewelry was probably worn by a clan elder which implies that Denisovan females enjoyed high social status. The vast majority of ancient H. sapiens' jewelry were worn by egg-producers as well, suggesting that they might have held similar positions and power.

The manufacturing technology of the Denisovan bracelet is more common to techniques of the New Stone Age (12,000 BP). The most 'advanced' of the hominin triad - H. sapiens, H. neanderthal and H. denisovan - may have been Denisovans, yet, they were much more archaic than Neanderthals and modern humans.

Many bloodlines around the world, particularly those of South Asian descent, contain Denisovan DNA.[34] Interestingly, the Denisovan admixture into modern humans occurred after the Neanderthal addition. Did H. sapiens cause the termination of Denisovans? The absorption into Sapiens could have paralleled what happened to Neanderthals. Plus, reduced fertility among Denisovan males probably occurred after modern humans started interbreeding with them.[35]

Part of Denisovans exist inside non-Africans. Genetic mutations from Denisovans might have influenced modern human immune systems, as well as fat and blood sugar levels, which assisted our survival. And their DNA may have helped Tibetans and Sherpas live at high altitudes with 40 percent less oxygen than air at sea level.[36]

Progress As ♂ Carnism

There are fundamental gaps in our knowledge of prehistory. The few and varied artifacts recovered so far reveal little about the diet and social lives of hominins. That stone tools were primarily used for hunting is taken for granted,[37] but associations between juxtaposed stone artifacts and fragmentary animal bones do not establish causation.[38] And traces of blood on stone tools of an extinct hominin does not prove that human-like creatures were avid carnivores.[39]

Even so, as part of the 'killer ape' construct, animal-based diets are used to measure time, intelligence, and civilization. The assumption is that human ancestors were killer apes who eliminated more peaceful vegetarian hominids, their main competition.[40] These killer apes passed their violent but 'successful' traits on to modern humans, who are therefore 'naturally' hyper-masculine.[41]

For biologists, it is held that increased energy demands along with decreased chewing and digestive capacities were possible only by adding animal protein to the diet.[42] Many claim that flesh provided critical nutrients for both young and old hominins.[43]

These male-centered, carnist notions are far from conclusive, and numerous questions remain.[44] For example, there is vigorous debate over the timing and significance of the adaptation to carnism. Further, the commencement of butchering is inconclusive, and theories vary widely on how hominins captured prey.[45]

Many modern hunting tools, such as fish hooks, nets, bows, and poisons were not introduced until the Late Stone Age and possibly even New Stone Age (12,000 BP). Before then, the only hunting tools widely available were hand-held spears and harpoons.[46]

The first substantial flesh-based eaters would not have been prepared for a quick transition to a high fat and high cholesterol diet.[47] Plus, there was increased risk from injury in hunting and guarding carcass. These challenges may have shortened ancient humans' lifespan. Evolutionary adaptations are not always helpful and sometimes emerging traits can lead to a decrease in diversification of species.[48]

Regardless of when the changeover to hunters from foragers purportedly occurred, human ancestors continued to consume vast amounts of plant-base foods, even Neanderthals. So the assumed dietary transition to carnism might not be as significant as scholars claim.

Human groups subsisted by gathering plant roots, leaves, fruits, berries, fire-foraging, and scavenging. Animal-based foods were consumed in colder regions, but anatomically modern humans did not populate these areas until 30,000 to 50,000 BP.[49] Furthermore, since some of the great apes occasionally hunt or scavenge flesh,[50] there really is no boundary in terms of violence.

Moreover, as fire foragers, phallic humans could consume animal protein without violence. Curiously, instead of man-the-hunter, Barbara Ehrenreich suggests that the psychology of Stone Age sperm-producers revolved around 'man-the-prey,' and men's role as prey for other animals.[51]

Most chimpanzees derive their dietary protein primarily from daily fruit and seasonal nut, and males tend to eat a bit more flesh. This sex difference in food acquisition and consumption may have persisted throughout hominin evolution, rather than being a recent 'improvement' in the lineage.

After extensive chemical analysis on ancient humans' teeth, two researchers concluded, "the dietary shift from apes to early hominids did not involve an increase in the consumption of tough foods, and so the australopithecines were not preadapted for eating meat."[52]

Since hunting developed long after gathering, it is far more likely that woman-the-gatherer's roles in collecting, preserving, and storing food made them the first inventors of tools. For instance, females' invented digging sticks that were fire-hardened and regularly sharpened with stone tools. Much of female-centered tools and technology in the Stone Age were based on wood and skins, which quickly disintegrated and became lost in the archaeological record.

Moreover, the invention of women-centric fire, cooking, ritual, jewelry, and art were crucial accomplishments that likely preceded the development of hunting-based tools. Therefore, the assumptive connection between hominin intelligence and carnism is spurious.

And, if for the most part, human ancestors were no more violent that other great apes, then their social relations may not have been so male-centered and dominated as they currently are, or their females as domesticated. Plus, the expansive trade networks that existed would have been difficult if not impossible to maintain under hyper-aggressive and combative, man-the-hunter cultures.

Conclusion

Given the regular intermixture of hominin genes, and the serious ecological crisis we face, humans need to become critical and go beyond our divisive patriarchal identities. The negation of surface variations in skin color, beliefs, language, customs and so on, allows us to live without being identified with any patriarchal ideas and conditioning.

In undoing identification, we become free to be a light upon our self and re-discover our original gynecological being. As Mary Daly writes in Gyn/Ecology, "The original movement is the Self's cosmic questing power. Restraining it is "only not dying"; regaining it is ultimately the only thing that matters."

For the critical observer of prehistory, hominin relics offer strong evidence of gynocentrism. The Neanderthal ring structures are highly suggestive of gynocentrism, and the Denisovan bracelet is even more revealing. The other great apes are all female-centered to some degree, and these patterns were probably maintained a million years ago by Floresiensis, Naledi, Denisovan, Neanderthal, or other unknown Homo forms.

More evidence of female-centered social relations start to appear with the most direct ancestor of modern humans, Homo sapiens. The physical characteristics of this species is explored next. Other sapiens' artifacts point to the high standing and influence of egg-producers, such as Goddess figures, and these are explored later.

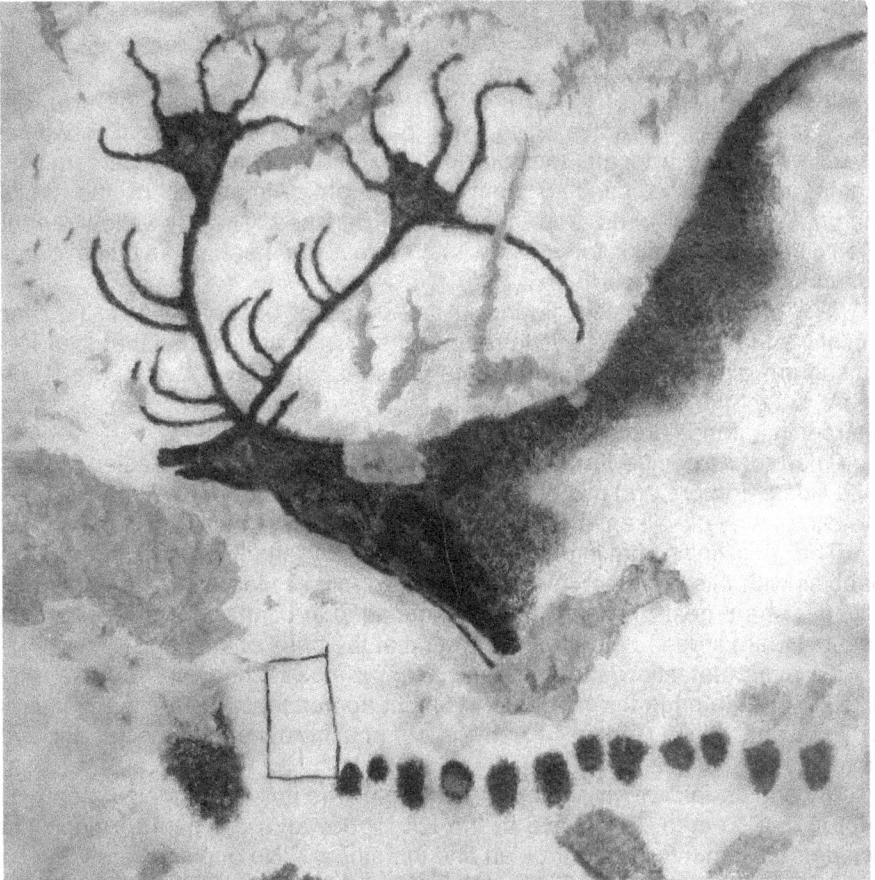

(Figure 5: Lascaux Cave Painting c. 20,000 BP)

5: Homo Sapiens

Radical feminist metaethics means moving past this puppet of Papa [Athena], dis-covering the immortal Metis. - Mary Daly

ASIA's Journey 2121.05

It is late afternoon. At 116°F (46°C), the sun is searing to the skin, and ASIA has to stay fully covered to avoid painful welts and burns. The women sweat to cool-off and are thankful for the low humidity of 30 percent. The plants are dry and parched from the drought. Almost all of the desert mammals, reptiles, birds, and insects have perished. The dry valley is eerily silent, and ASIA walks for miles without seeing or hearing anything except vultures circling overhead.

The group sits on the ground in the shade of bushes, waiting for Lian, Xóchitl, and the two teen boys to return. The crones are worried that their food rations are almost empty and the safe house is three days away. The longer ASIA waits, the harder it will be to reach safety. The children are busy sharpening stones and sticks for the security team.

The crones decide to make camp on a ridge since it was easier to guard both sides. Zemora and two other women start to dig a trench. After they made the camp, they dig a kennel in the trench for the dogs, which keeps them quiet.

The girls finish making hundreds of darts by attaching cactus thorns to pebbles with bits of string. It was 11-year-old Iniko's idea, and she made hers with five sharp points. The children camouflaged the darts with leaves, and the security team spreads them on the ground at the base of the ridge.

To avoid detection, the cook and helpers make dinner at the base, then hike it up to the ridge for the group. As night approaches, ASIA sits together in a circle and silently eat as Kuan-Yin returns from her search for the two women and boys.

"I went straight down and north, but there was no sign of them," Kuan-Yin informs the women. Zola gaze at the hill top towards the quarter moon and wonders, "Did hunters capture Lian and the others?" No one answers.

The smell of burning drifts in the air intermittently. Onaiwah scans the horizon and mutters, "Maybe a wildfire in the distance."

Hehewuti places her ears to the ground and replies, "It could be coming from the campfire of other climate migrants."

Zola smells the air, "Probably pedo-hunters celebrating a capture."

Just after moonset, Kuan-Yin spots the silhouettes of Lian and Xóchitl returning from the south. She walks down to guide them safely through the defensive traps laid at the bottom of the ridge.

The boys were missing and Lian explains what happened, "We saw a gang of pedo-hunters approaching from the west. We led them south with a camp fire, then kept going south for an hour. Then, we went east and began heading back. After ten minutes, Alex and Roshi went missing."

Hehewuti stares at Kuan-Yin, "What could have happened to the boys?"

"We searched everywhere," Xóchitl says, waving her hand in an arc. "I have no idea."

"Maybe they ran away." Kuan-Yin sighs.

Hehewuti sighs, "Were we too hard on them when Cha'Kwaina fainted?"

"Maybe they wanted to join the men even before that," Xóchitl offers.

Zola stares into the moon-less sky and ponders, "Could they have told pedo-hunters where we are."

The crones motion their heads up and down in harmony. Xóchitl and Zola may be right. After sacrificing so much to care for the two boys, ASIA now have to fight their sons to save their daughters from sex-trafficking and enslavement.

Introduction

Reconstruction of hominin evolutionary journey is difficult. Direct observation is impossible and fossil and archaeological evidence is scarce. Not surprisingly, much of the process of human growth remains a mystery. For instance, how did the evolutionary process produce such a singularly unique species as modern humans? And, how did the natural environment, social organization, and diet influence this process?

This third chapter of Part II on Stone Age ecogynocentrism extends the inquiry into food consumption among the great apes and primeval hominins, to modern humans. And while the last two chapters focused on physical evolution, this one explores hominins' social development as well.

The chapter commences with a discussion of plant-based diets among hominins. A brief survey of how hominins differ from primates comes next. Then, an examination of artifacts from modern humans, or Homo sapiens, comes after. Afterward, the chapter considers aspects of social development among sapiens.

A lot of factors contribute to being biologically male or female, and the complicated, sex-determination process that takes place inside a young-bearing body and the human fetus is examined next. A discussion of how childcare was related to human social evolution follows, and the chapter concludes with a look at the genetics of the famous Mitochondrial 'Eve' or the first human-like female.

Plant-based Hominins

Was flesh a regular item on hominins' menu? If not, how much animal-based protein did they eat? Research on hominin diet is limited since tooth wear patterns, assorted stone tools, bone cut marks, and isotopic bone data cannot readily distinguish among plant, flesh, and omnivorous diets.[1]

What looks like charring on a rock or bone could be staining from minerals or fungus. Animal bones found next to hominin fossils do not prove that they were killed and eaten by our ancestors since both human and non-human animals could have been prey for predators. High-tech analytic techniques do not always erase these historical ambiguity.

There is insufficient evidence to conclude that the predatory behavior of hominins differed significantly from hominids.[2] In forests, wetlands, woodlands, and other regions, an abundance of plant-based foods were available in great diversity. And out of 800,000 total plant species worldwide, roughly 3,000 species of plants were regularly consumed by hominins.

Teeth analysis show that 2.3 million years ago, H. habilis was primarily a fruit and vegetable eater. And 500,000 years later, there is scant information on how much flesh was being consumed by the supposedly omnivorous H. erectus. In Palestine, numerous hearths dated from 690,000 to 790,000 BP were carefully excavated. Researchers uncovered fragments of burned fruit, grain, and wood, but charred animal bones were conspicuously absent.

Comparing the diets of H. habilis and H. erectus, one researcher concludes, "Both of the species would probably have focused on high energy-yield, easy-to-consume foods, such as soft fruits when they could get them."[3] These hominins were akin to the great apes who are plant-based and are not protein deficient.[4]

The great apes were probably stronger than hominins who supposedly ate much more animal-based protein. There were noteworthy dietary changes in the transition from hominid to hominin, but these adaptations did not involve hunting or the consumption of animal flesh.

Approximately 3.5 million years ago, A. sediba extended the basic primate diet and started eating an increasingly amount of grassy foods, thus setting the stage for a modern diet based on grains and grasses.[5] And A. africanus could have consumed the underground storage organs of plants rather than flesh.[6] Ancient hominins may have also specialized on seeds, as modern humans do with grains.[7]

Contrary to the man-the-hunter theory, indications of hominins scavenging flesh does not appear until 2.5 BP. Moreover, definitive evidence of hunting and the common use of fire dates to only 500,000 years ago.[8] Scavenging could have been a part of hominin's way of life, but for the vast majority of the Stone Age, they consumed a mostly plant-based diet, akin to other hominids.

Wrangham proposed that a fundamental change in the evolution of hominids from the last common ancestor shared with chimpanzees was the substitution of tubers for herbaceous vegetation as fallback foods.[9] And teeth analysis of hominins reveal that grain, nuts, and fruits were the major foods, not flesh. Therefore, the common image of Stone Age gatherer-'hunters' eating hunks of animal flesh around an open fire is probably false.[10]

Researchers performed an extensive chemical analysis of 110 pottery fragments found in the Libyan Sahara Desert, dated between 10,200 to 8,400 BP. Over half of the vessels studied were used for processing plants, and this practice was continuous for over 4,000 years. Some of the pots were utilized for grains and fruits, while others had remains of leaves and stems.[11]

These Ancient Libyan cooks may have been making plant-based bread or grain mashes, porridge, stews, and syrups. Julie Dunne, the lead author of the research concludes, "Until now, the importance of plants in prehistoric diets has been under-recognized but this work clearly demonstrates the importance of plants as a reliable dietary resource."[12]

Difference - Bipedal Apes

Hominin forms varied widely from the other great apes. Physically, compared to Pan, Gorilla, and Orangutan, hominins stood erect, had less hair, and expanded brains. There were vast cultural alterations as well, but these areas are much less understood. The primordial physiological and social transitions made from hominid to hominin, or from apes to human-like animals, were critical to the 'success' of our species.

Why did H. erectus stand and walk on two legs? The other great apes use four limbs, so why did this radical departure from hominids occur roughly four million years ago? Was it a female ape who started primates down this path to hominin locomotion?

There are several advantages to being a biped ape. It requires less energy than quadrupeds, for instance. With freed arms, early hominin gatherers were able to transport more food, and mothers could carry two children. Standing upright might even have helped them control their temperature better by reducing the amount of skin directly exposed to the sun.

What are the evolutionary advantages to having less hair? Primeval hominins may have started to shed hairiness to stay cool while traveling across the tropical grasslands and savannas of Africa. And losing their fur coats could have freed hominins from parasite infestations and the diseases they can spread.

Their dispersal to as far north as 40 degrees latitude show that, unlike the majority of primates, hominins had evolved means to cope with the summer to winter seasonality. Casting off hair meant early humans had to use appropriate clothing, which was part of female-centered production. Clothing and cover were especially critical for infants and children during winter, and a mother-centered culture evolved to meet children's needs.

Maybe the most fundamental transformation from hominid to hominin is brain size, which started to grow some 800,000 years ago. A general claim made by man-the-hunter theorists is that additional flesh consumption is associated with improved skills and expanded brains. The brain is a bulky organ that requires lots of energy, and it is assumed that this could only come from animal carcass.[13]

Homo species are also larger in body size than primordial hominins who supposedly ate more plant-based foods. Thus, having a bigger brain and body is viewed as part of the evolutionary benefits of consuming more animal protein. Hominins' wider ranging, compared to other primates, is also used to imply increased carnivory.[14]

These assertions are based on conjecture and scant evidence. Little is known about the proportions of animal protein intake necessary to influence hominin biology. And there is no definitive proof of a causal and/or functional link between intake of flesh and Homo sapiens' increased brains and bodies. Chimpanzees, our closest relatives, hunt and consume flesh, and they have far less cranial volume than humans.

The brain needs plenty of energy and fats, but not that much protein. And, since humans have the lowest-protein milk in the mammalian world, this further demonstrates that the brain-protein link is hollow.

If the hominin diet did not vary substantially from other primates, why then would they need expanded brains to do the same ecological job? Perhaps, radical alterations in the natural environment demanded hominins to rapidly evaluate a shifting World. Another possibility is that increased brain power enabled hominins to make better tools.

Social brain theorists view the cranial phenomenon in terms of increasing group numbers and pressures towards social knowledge. Expansive brains may have aided various Homo types to interact better with each other. This is in concord with the improvement of communication, cooperation, and trade among female-the-gatherer clans that occurred during the Stone Age.

Social brain theorists point out that primates, in general, have more voluminous brains that other groups and their social systems are more complex than those of non-primate animals. Great apes' behavior includes tactical deception and coalition-formation which are rare or occur only in simpler forms in other groups.[15]

The computational requirement of living in complex societies selected for oversize brains in hominids. And perhaps, for hominins, the particular demands of intense pair-bonding triggered even more substantial brains.[16] Given hominin egg-producers' power over sex-selection, this aspect of evolution could have been female-driven.

The social brain was associated with language growth as well, and Homo females may have similarly led the way in communication. Notably, socialization and the change in sapiens' cranial capacity was facilitated by cooking, another female invention.

According to researcher Karen Hardy, cooked food provides greater energy, and females' cooking of a variety of plant-based foods may be linked to the rapid increases in brain size that occurred from 800,000 years ago onward.[17] Hardy states, "Starchy food was an essential element in facilitating brain development, and contrary to popular belief about the 'paleodiet', the role of starchy food in the Paleolithic diet was significant."[18]

Further, Suzana Herculano-Houzel affirms that it is not only the size of Homo brain that matters but the fact that hominins have more neurons in the cerebral cortex than any other animal, due to cooking. Her research suggests that ingesting more calories in less time made possible the rapid acquisition of a vast number of neurons in the cerebral cortex, the part of the brain responsible for finding patterns, reasoning, developing technology, and passing it on through culture.[19]

Dawn of 'Modern' Sapiens

Homo sapiens first appeared about 400,000 years ago. The subspecies Homo sapiens sapiens, usually referred to as modern humans, evolved between 200,000 and 100,000 years ago in Africa. At that time, Neanderthals occupied the Middle East.

H. sapiens sapiens left Africa several times. And there was no mass migration. The dispersal out of Africa may have involved only a few hundred individuals at a time. The majority of modern humans stayed in Africa and adapted to a diverse array of environments.

One popular misconception is that the first H. sapiens sapiens who left Africa went west to Europe. They actually went east and arrived in China between 80,000 and 120,000 years ago, and did not get into Europe until 45,000 BP. Perhaps, modern humans could only enter Europe when the demise of Neanderthals had already started.[20]

Homo sapiens sapiens began to migrate out of Africa again around 70,000 BP from northeast Africa. They joined and replaced earlier hominins through hybridization since there are no signs of mass conflict. H. sapiens sapiens spread across Asia, Europe, and Australia by 40,000 BP, and the Americas earlier than 15,000 BP.

Curiously, populations from South and Southeast Asia have a proportion of ancestry from one or more extinct hominins which is not present in Europeans and East Asians. Asia had more hominin forms than Europe, and Asians are a product of greater hybridization.[21]

Proponents of the model known as the "human revolution" claim that modern human behaviors arose suddenly, and nearly simultaneously, throughout Europe and the Middle East roughly 40,000 to 50,000 BP. This fundamental behavioral shift is supposed to signal a cognitive advance, a possible reorganization of the brain, and the origin of language. And the 'creative revolution' is theorized as paralleling a change in culture.[22]

This Eurocentric framing creates the impression that the first modern Africans were behaviorally primitive. The theory stems from a racial bias and determination to ignore the African archaeological record. In fact, many of the components of the "human revolution" are found in the African Middle Stone Age, tens of thousands of years earlier than in Europe.

The 'modern' features of the human revolution consist of blade and microlithic technology, bone tools, increased geographic range, and the use of aquatic resources. Creative aspects include long distance trade, systematic processing and use of pigment, and art and decoration. Although unstated, these characteristics of modernity and creativity were female-centered, and are emblematic of gynocentric social organization.

For instance, females used stone blades in chopping roots for cooking; bone tools for making jewelry, clothing, and accessories; ranged further for gathering their favorite foods; processed shells and pigment for art and decoration; and traded items across vast distances through gynocentric networks. The so-called 'human' and 'creative revolution' in modernity are female-centered, but for the most part, these facts are overlooked by mainstream academia.

Also, 'modern' cultural artifacts in Africa did not occur suddenly and together as predicted by the 'human revolution' model. The recent features of Homo sapiens sapiens are found at sites widely separated in space and time. As one team concludes, "This suggests a gradual assembling of the package of modern human behaviors in Africa, and its later export to other regions of the Old World."[23]

Throughout the Middle Stone Age, 130,000 years ago, when homo sapiens sapiens first evolved, they began to develop advanced cultural traits such as religion, art, and long distance trade for rare commodities. One example is ochre, an iron ore keenly prized by prehistoric women to use in decoration and spiritual practice.[24]

Across Africa, ochre was used to honor egg-producers and the Goddess. The wide transport distance of ochre and its prevalent use indicate that the Stone Age economies of modern humans were female-centered. Ochre also reveal that gynocentrism may have been far-flung, and female art and culture existed at the birth of the species in the Middle Stone Age.

By the beginning of the Late Stone Age, around 50,000 BP, full behavioral modernity had developed in Africa, including language, music, and other cultural universals. Though unexpressed, these forms of cultural evolution were most likely female-centered and led as well, since mothers and females were responsible for passing them on to the young.

Artistic work blossomed, and Late Stone Age art includes rock and cave painting, jewelry, drawing, carving, engraving and sculpture in clay, bone, antler, stone and ivory, such as Earth Goddess figurines. They also include musical instruments such as flutes.[25]

Homo Social Evolution

The population of early humans was tiny, like that of a modern endangered species such as mountain gorillas.[26] A combination of environmental, biological, and social changes enabled hominin populations to expand exponentially, but there were variations. Eventually, Homo sapiens were able to colonize the Earth.[27]

The social modification of exaggerated carnivory is viewed as the 'revolutionary step' in hominin evolution and population expansion. But the adoption of a flesh-eating diet required significant biological and behavioral adaptations, and relied on changing environmental conditions as well. Plant-based innovations like fire farming could also help to explain the rise in population. Instead of emerging as a sudden event, hominin to Homo sapiens sapiens evolution and rise in numbers may have been the result of a progression of multiple changes, with several setbacks.

Perhaps, the first momentous step in Homo evolution was not hunting larger prey but learning to cook and eat a broad range of vegetables. Woman-the-gatherer and gynocentrism were the underlying features that made this adaptation possible. For instance, this transformation relied on women's labor in digging roots, gathering plants, collecting firewood, building and maintaining a fire, chopping and preparing vegetables, and cooking a variety of roots, leaves, stems, and seeds.

Beyond diet, it is important to remember that all of the biological adjustments involved in hominin evolution were physically produced and reproduced by the young-bearing. Gynocentrism facilitated the difficult physiological adaptations for hominin females that produced the peculiar characteristics of H. sapiens sapiens. And up until the New Stone Age, female-centered forms of organization likewise produced and reproduced complicated human behavioral and social adaptations.

There is little evidence corresponding to the domination of one sex over the other in the Stone Age, which characterizes modern patriarchal societies. Unlike the sexist, man-the-hunter portrayal, Middle Stone Age people lived in small, egalitarian bands led by woman-the-gatherer.

As gatherer-'hunters,' hominins lived, foraged, and reared children in tiny, genetically diverse groups that shared food and many tasks. This equality is similar to those of Late Stone Age societies and some existent gatherer-'hunters,' such as the !Kung San Bushmen, and the Mbuti.[28] Social relations are based on a mother-centered gift economy.

Commencing in the Middle Stone Age, both neanderthal and modern humans took care of elderly members of their societies, which is consistent with gynocentric principles and honoring of crones. Elder care extended into the afterlife through ritual and burial.

The oldest known burials can be attributed to the Middle Stone Age, around 100,000 BP. And from the Late Stone Age onward, burials had richer goods and symbolic items.[29] Burial practices may have represented honor, ceremony, and belief in the continuance of identity beyond cellular death.

The Late Stone Age had many forms of organized settlements for socialization and ritual. Some camps included a kitchen area, sleeping grounds, storage facilities, and a discard zone. Throughout this era, humans in some regions used great ingenuity to construct intricate shelters. Massive mammoth-bone houses were built in the Ukraine around 16,000 to 10,000 BP.

In the Late Stone Age, complex social groupings emerged, supported by more varied and reliable food sources, and specialized tool types. There is evidence for some craft specialization, and the transport over considerable distances of materials such as stone and, above all, marine shells.

Shells were used by females for jewelry and decorating clothes. And, shells from Mediterranean species have been found 1,000 kilometers from the coast. Like ochre, the trade in shells indicates the vast scale of Stone Age gynocentric economies.

Some scholars argue that the appearance of abstract language made these behavior and economic transformations possible. Whatever the causes are, the emergence of cooperative and coherent communication and trade marked a new era in hominin cultural development.

Childcare & Evolution

On average, the size of primates' brains is nearly double what is expected for mammals of the same body size. Over seven million years, the human brain has tripled in size, with most of this growth occurring from 800,000 to 200,000 BP. As modern hominins developed, the costs of brain growth were overwhelmingly paid by the young-bearing sex. In addition to reproductive complications, there was an increasingly challenging birthing process.

Throughout pregnancy, hominin mothers had to secure more and better quality food for themselves. Plus, the young-bearing sex had to provide for children, who require tremendous nutritional and social investment through breastfeeding and constant care giving.[30] For example, contemporary gatherer-'hunter' mothers typically breastfeed infants for two to four years.[31]

Hominin woman-the-gatherers had to walk for miles to collect plant-based foods while being burdened by heavily dependent offspring. Children were highly vulnerable to infanticide, predators, insects, climate, and starvation. The first tools may have been invented by mothers to carry their young who could not cling or walk, a sling or container.[32]

Stone Age mothers would have found it hard and almost impossible to cope with nuclear families led by bellicose man-the-hunter types. Like other species who rely on childcare investment by others, humans are now considered to be cooperative breeders.[33] This form of childcare implies gynocentric social organization. Throughout evolutionary history, and in most of the world today, the human mother-child relationship is immersed in dense social and care giving networks that form an integral part of human sociality and society.[34]

In her book, Mothers and Others, Sarah Hrdy argues that childcare was critical for the development of the long length of hominin childhood. For the H. sapiens young to outlive childhood in a dangerous world with scarce food, they needed care and protection - not only by their mothers, but also by siblings, aunts, fathers, friends, and grandmothers.[35]

Hrdy observes that only H. sapiens sapiens mothers among the great apes are willing to let another individual take hold of their babies. And they are routinely willing to let others babysit. Hrdy suggests that lack of trust is the leading reason that prevents chimp, bonobo, and gorilla mothers from doing the same.

Hominin females had to line up helpers, sometimes extending beyond their kin, to raise their young as part of a continuous contact and care model. Parenting duties were spread out across a gynocentric network of female friends and relatives. Out of this complicated and contingent form of communal child-rearing came the human capacity for emotional intelligence and compassion for others.

Juveniles also influenced cooperative, child-centered behavior. The children most likely to survive were those who could relate to and solicit help from others. Child-centered hominins evolved to having the capacities for empathy, consideration, and intuition into how others are feeling. This adaptation in primeval humans is unique among great apes, although cooperative breeding occurs elsewhere in the animal kingdom.

Gynocentric cooperation represented an excellent use of resources by woman-the-gatherer. One woman could watch two or three kids, relieving other mothers to gather food. Cooperative breeding was and is practiced by indigenous peoples. For example, Iroquois children had several 'mothers.'[36] And in !Kung culture, non-maternal caregivers respond to infant distress over forty percent of the time.[37] Similarly, Efe infants spend one-third to over fifty percent of their time in the care of others.[38]

Although not universal, various gatherer-'hunter' populations practice non-maternal breastfeeding, for instance, the Ongee, Efe, Aka, and Agta.[39] Efe non-maternal caregivers are the first to breast-feed a child since maternal breast-feeding does not commence until several days after birth when the mother's milk comes in.

Hrdy argues that cooperation more than competition accounts for human's unique traits. What is more, Hrdy stresses that human cooperation is rooted in childcare, not in male conflict and war. She argues that aggression and competition is granted far too central a place in how humans evolved.

Some of the human traits that developed as a result of cooperation for childcare are an extended lifespan, prolonged childhood, big brain, perspective taking or inter-subjectivity, language use, cumulative culture, mutual understanding, norm formation and enforcement, altruistic punishment, and moral judgment. These traits co-evolved, and are pro-social and female-centered.

Because maternal investment was high, the young-bearing sex were precisely choosing sperm-producers who were friendly, nurturing, tool-using, and willing to share food. Men were supportive of child-centered clans, and there may not have been a sexual division of labor until the Late Stone Age.

There is an intrinsic difficulty in establishing biological paternity, and sperm-producers probably could not know who their offspring were. So they likely preferred a "pair bond" situation with one egg-producer where there is greater confidence in identifying paternity.

Partner unions, sex egalitarianism, and female-centered cultures may have provided an evolutionary advantage for primeval hominins over other hominids. It fostered wider-ranging social networks and closer cooperation between unrelated individuals and made inbreeding less of an issue.[40]

Women's shared interests include sexuality, childcare, food security, leadership, and elder care. In the Stone Age, egg-producing hominins may have created proto-symbolic schemes to refer to mutual interests and for coalition action. These early forms of language and culture were integral to female gossip and strategies for counter-dominance.[41]

Anthropologist Chris Knight agrees with much of Hrdy's child-centered analysis. He suggests that acting in solidarity allows mothers to shield daughters from the sexual advances of fathers. Knight argues that there was egg-producing solidarity of a scale sufficient to keep Stone Age women and men in separate camps for much of the time in hominin history.[42]

Knight points out that when brother/sister bonds are preserved into adulthood, they do so at the expense of partner unions. In these societies, paternity certainty will be less likely, and the culture will tend to have matrilineal descent.[43]

Raising vast numbers of large-brained offspring to maturity required an exceptional quality of childcare, and so hominin mothers practiced group motherhood in matrilocal clans. They motivated multiple suitors to work hard for them, and took advantage of every available childcare resource they had.

Stone Age egg-producers were able to cooperatively resist phallic sexual control by relying for protection on female collectives and supportive male kin.

Like bonobos, there were several advantages to young-bearing hominins acting in concert to restrain male-domination. Contemporary egg-producers have a lot of mutual interests as well, including the genetics from a common Stone Age mother.

Mitochondrial 'Eve'

Both egg-producers and sperm-producers pass along genetic material that is unchanged during sexual reproduction. For the young-bearing sex, this is the mitochondrial DNA, which is a distinct subset of genetic material found not in the cell nucleus, but rather in the mitochondria, the power plants of the cell.

In most species, including humans, the egg cells completely destroy the mitochondria in the sperm cell shortly after fertilization, leaving only the female mitochondria behind. The term 'Mitochondrial Eve' (MtE) comes from this sexual reproduction process. A single Stone Age individual passed down her mitochondria relatively unchanged to every human alive today. And all young-bearing humans will continue to pass down her mitochondria indefinitely.[44]

'Mitochondrial Eve' is the most recent woman from whom all living humans today descend, in an unbroken line, on their mother's side, and through the mothers of those mothers, and so on, back until all lines converge on one person about 200,000 years ago. Most likely, MtE lived in East Africa, later than the emergence of Neanderthal, but earlier than the out of Africa migration by Homo sapiens sapiens.

Modern humans who migrated across the globe are descendants of this single African woman, who would not have been exceptional during her life. MtE was maybe among 1,500 to 16,000 inter-breeding individuals in a population of 5,000 to 50,000 people. But of this group, she is the only one who can trace descent to everyone alive right now.

Even if 'man-the-hunter' was the prehistoric norm, the existence of 'Mitochondrial Eve' shows that the lives of individual females were significant in the evolutionary process. In addition, many symbiotic microorganisms are transmitted matrilineally, however little is known about the effect this may have on the sexes.

Less famous than MtE is her male counterpart, MtA. In the Stone Age, a fertile woman usually had several offspring. Men probably had many children by multiple mothers, or they might fail to father any children at all. It was difficult for men to determine paternity and they remained dependent on female fidelity.

Only men have a Y-chromosome, and fathers pass it on more or less unchanged to their sons. The Y-chromosome gains a new mutation roughly every 125 years, enabling geneticists to tell when two closely related populations split, or how distant cousins are related.

Y-chromosomal 'Adam' probably lived around the same time as 'Eve,' but MtE may be older and of more significance to H. sapiens evolution. The presence of MtE, and other limiting genetic characteristics demonstrate that humans are more closely related than is commonly held.

Sex-Determination

In humans and many other species, the customary belief is that a father, through his most aggressive sperm, determines the sex of a child.[45] In the plain XY sex-determination system, the ovum contributes an X chromosome and the sperm contributes either an X or a Y chromosome. This combination usually results in a female (XX) or male (XY) offspring, respectively.

Sex-determination is far more complicated than this simplistic narrative though. For instance, half of sperm are female with a X chromosome. Sperm are weak swimmers that thrash around, go side to side, swim in circles, and haphazardly work their way up the female tract to the fallopian tubes.

And instead of an easy mechanism by which pro-male genes go all the way to make a male, a number of pro-male, anti-male, and pro-female genes are responsible. If there is a little too much of anti-male genes, then a egg-producer will be hatched. And, if there is a bit too much of pro-male genes, then there will be a sperm-producer spawned.

A majority of pro-male genes starts the process of virilization, modifications that make a phallic body different from a young-bearing body. Androgens produce most of the changes of virilization, and they and other factors result in the sex differences in humans.

For instance, hormone levels in the phallic parent affect the sex ratio of sperm.[46] The time at which insemination occurs during the oestrus cycle likewise bear on the sex ratio of the offspring of humans, cattle, and other mammals. Hormonal and pH conditions within the female reproductive tract vary with time, and this also affects the sex ratio of the sperm that reaches the egg.[47]

Furthermore, maternal influences impact which sperm are more likely to achieve conception. The human ova functions as a sophisticated biological security system that chemically controls the entry of the sperm into the egg and protects the fertilized egg from additional sperm.[48] The ova also produce a chemical which attracts sperm and influences their swimming motion. Not all sperm are impacted positively, and some actually move away from the egg.[49]

In addition, sugar molecules on the egg's surface, known as SLeX, act as "hitching posts" that binds the rapidly moving sperm, helping it to penetrate the egg's protective jelly-like protein coating. Amazingly, many mammalian mothers can deliberately "choose" the sex of their offspring. In a study of 200 species of mammals, researchers found that the young-bearing sex can choose whether or not they are going to have a boy or a girl.[50]

Other research shows that egg-producers who are more dominant when compared with the other women in their cultural group, are more likely to conceive sons.[51] These mechanisms provide a means by which sperm access and sex-determination could be under maternal control.

Conclusion

The presence of Neanderthal and Denisovan DNA in the human genome show that no race of people on earth belongs to one hereditary group. Rather, humans have 'proportions of ancestral groups.' And, modern human animals are connected to other species, extinct smart bipeds.

The next chapter goes into the 'paleo' or Stone Age diet in more detail. The alpha 'man-the-hunter' image is used to justify male violence, dominance, and competition as natural and progressive. But the reality was that 'woman-the-gatherer' was the primary food provider and leader of cooperative hominin clans.

(Figure 6: Woman/Goddess of Tolentino is 5.1 in (13 cm) high, c. 10,000 BP.
The stone was likely used to crush seeds as both ends are chipped from use.)

6: Woman-the-Gatherer

It [radical feminist metaethics] also means discovering the parthenogenetic Daughter, the original Athena, whose loyalty is to her own kind, whose science/wisdom is of womankind. - Mary Daly

ASIA's Journey 2121.06

Stars fill the cloudless sky, and the dark trench wall feels chill at 79°F (26°C) with 40 percent humidity. The children are asleep, but Onaiwah and a few mothers are awake, still hopeful the two straying boys would return. They promised each other to stay up, but were exhausted and dozed off.

Near midnight, a man screaming in pain shatters the silence. The night watch gives the warning signal immediately, the low-pitched call of an owl. After a pause, she makes the call again. If it is Alex and Roshi, they would have given a reply. But it is quiet.

Zemora is half-awake, and her vivid dreams of a female utopia have not yet stopped. She does not want to wake up in her comfortable blanket. Is she still dreaming? There are more screams from below, followed by male voices cursing. "The children's traps are working," Zemora mumbles sleepily to her partner, Jean.

"We cannot give our position away." Jean is tired too, but she knows the danger. "I'll go and keep the dogs calm."

Zemora stands up and peers out of the trench. The moon is low on the horizon. She sees silhouettes moving in the distance below. Jean leaves their sleeping blanket and crawls backward to the kennel. Zemora whispers, "Keep the dogs' muzzle on until the hunters get close."

Another scream and a pedophile-hunter cries out, "The whole place is booby-trapped."

"Those little cunts must be close," another one proclaims.

"Wake-up, my pretties." The first pedophile-hunter holler out. "Daddy is coming for you." A louder shriek is taken over by long-lasting squall.

One pedophile-hunter yell in agony, "Damn bitches! We're going to rape you raw until you bleed!"

Zemora shivers as she stares into the dark below.

Suddenly, tracer lights emerge from opposite directions above the men. One-by-one, seven silhouettes drop to the ground and stop moving. It becomes quiet again. After 30 minutes the all clear signal sounds. Everyone in the trench goes back to sleep.

Introduction

The man-the-hunter narrative justifies and glorifies phallic violence, from private to public spheres. Forevermore, the false perception of sperm-producers as aggressive killers and avid flesh eaters aids in the reduction of egg-producing humans, viewed as consuming less animal tissue, passive, and idle.

At the same time, the male-centric framework maintains the horrendous exploitation of animal-as-capital for food, clothes, and other products. The enslavement of nonhumans on factory farms in turn leads to critical environmental and social problems such as infection, chronic disease, pollution, rural displacement, poverty, and global warming.[1]

This fourth chapter of Part II on Stone Age ecogynocentrism continues the survey of the first domestication and the Paleo diet presented in the last three chapters. It highlights the value of work done by the egg-producing sex, particularly gathering, to the species' survival.

The chapter commences with an investigation into woman-the-gatherer, ensued by an inquiry into their carbohydrate diets in the Stone Age. Then, the chapter discusses loss of gut flora in carnist humans compared to plant-based primates. The chapter concludes with a survey of egg-producers' culture, first with animals portrayed in Paleolithic art, and second, with their practice of gynocentric dancing.

Woman-the-Gatherer

Throughout the course of prehistory, women and children constituted 75 percent of the population, on average. The over-emphasizing of activities conducted by 25 percent of community members, sperm-producers, creates a fictitious view of ancient societies and neglects egg-producers' contribution to human evolution.

There are few studies on Paleolithic females, or on hominin feminist theory.[2] This academic oversight is remarkable given the fact that the young-bearing sex are the creators of life in the species.[3] Female hominins exercised enormous power in sex selection, and under gynocentric socialization, they would have been the primary determinants of our evolution.

The production by hominin egg-producers in food provision and gathering of plant foods have garnered far less attention than they deserve. Edible plants, eggs, and shellfish often makeup 80 percent of the contemporary gatherer-'hunter' diet. In Woman the Gatherer, Frances Dahlberg discusses the roles and activities of women in prehistoric groups and among four contemporary gatherer-'hunter' communities. She found that gathering was used as the principal form of food security.[4]

Egg-producing hominins were the keepers of a vast botanical knowledge, and they used it to help their families and communities survive and thrive. Foraging and botanical knowledge may have led to the development of memory,[5] communication, language, and a bigger brain.

H. sapiens females observed other animals burying food in the ground to preserve it for winter, and they imitated this behavior by hiding roots and tubers in holes dug in the ground. During winter, they stored an assortment of tubers, wild carrots, onions, seeds, nuts, herbs, grains, vegetables, and other plant-based foods in caves, root cellars, and other places relatively safe from insects and other animals.

The young-bearing sex were far from sedentary homemakers waiting for men to show up with rapidly decomposing animal carcass. Egg-producers were the primary providers for hominins' plant-based diet. Mothers were actively moving around the environment, gathering food, and carrying infants while doing so. Woman-the-gatherer may have traveled for millennia along established routes to gather wild plants in well-scheduled assemblies.

Successful gathering required skills of discrimination, evaluation, and memory. The range of seeds, nuts, shells, and grasses discovered at primeval sites indicate careful and knowledgeable selection rather than random gleaning. While traveling and foraging, woman-the-gatherer had to protect herself and children, and her sharpened digging-stick was a primary weapon.

A hominin child's survival depended upon its mother's ability to carry it great distances for several years, her skill in finding and gathering food, using tools, her ability to space infants, to feed her weaned offspring, and to maintain social ties with the clan or community. Child-centered, egalitarian groups allowed for cooperative breeding and equal distribution of resources to ensure a stable food supply and avoid famine.

In addition to gathering, females were doing a lot of plant based processing in the Stone Age. Vegetable foods were usually available to hominids and were exploited easily with simple tools. Women used seeds, nuts, and grains to make cakes, breads and other portable and preserved edibles that would keep during travel over long distances. And, they used fire to bake and cook hard plant-based foods like roots and tubers.

Paleo Carb Diet

Chimpanzees are close to H. sapiens sapiens genetically, sharing more than 96 percent of their DNA code with humans, and their digestive tract is functionally very similar to that of humans.[6] Pans are primarily frugivores. Their actual diet in nature is just about 95 percent plant-based, with the remaining 5 percent filled with insects, eggs, and baby animals. Given the similarity to Pans, what then did hominins eat, and which sex was more responsible for meeting their nutritional needs?[7]

The Stone Age diet[8] was primarily plant-based.[9] Earlier hominins ate a diet of mostly raw, fiber-rich plants, grains, and legumes, and not that much flesh, for millennia.[10] As part of the Paleolithic diet, carbohydrate tubers, the underground storage organs of plants, may have been eaten in high amounts by pre-agricultural humans.[11] The Stone Age diet may have included as much as 3.6 to 4.1 pounds (1.65 to 1.9 kg) of fruit and vegetables per day.

During the Early Stone Age, tubers, seeds, fruits, nuts and other starchy foods were readily available and contributed to the evolution of humans' oversized brains. Cooked starch, a source of preformed glucose, substantially enhanced energy availability to human tissues with high glucose demands, such as the brain, red blood cells, and the developing fetus. Since the human brain uses as much as 25 percent of the body's energy and up to 60 percent of blood glucose, it probably could not have grown so massive on a low-carbohydrate diet.[12]

Also, pregnancy and lactation require more glucose, and low maternal blood glucose compromises the health of females and their fetus. Plus, analysis of European DNA show they had extra copies of amylase genes to break down starchy foods, long before the intensive cultivation of plants.[13] Lactase persistence emerged only 7,500 years ago,[14] which proves that prior to animal colonization, H. sapiens were not regularly consuming the milk of other-than-human animals.

Maybe hominin ovary beings were making plant-based milks instead. Archaeologists found stone tools with thousands of wild grain residues on them in Mozambique, dated to 105,000 BP. The grains were highly processed, either boiled, fermented, or ground.[15] This plant-based evidence shows that female foraging groups in the Middle Stone Age routinely brought starchy plants to their cave sites.

Most of the grain was sorghum, an ancestor of modern sorghum used in porridge, bread, and beer. Possibly, Paleolithic egg-producers grounded and processed grains and nuts into milk shakes and smoothies. Other plant-based foods were found, such as the African 'potato,' false banana, wine palm trunk, and seed from a woody tree.

By the Late Stone Age, the processing of wild cereals was routine and women invented efficient methods for cooking ground seeds.[16] Researchers in Palestine uncovered mortars and pestles with grains embedded in the pores dating back to 23,000 BP. The foods processed were wild barley and possibly wild wheat.[17] Large-seeded legumes were part of the Palestinian diet as well, long before the New Stone Age agrarian revolution.[18]

Late Stone Age societies were gathering wild cereals for food 30,000 years ago.[19] Some grindstones found were used for grinding plant tissue,[20] proving that women were making flour 32,000 years ago from oat seeds, acorns, and the relatives of millet.[21]

There were flour residues on 30,000-year-old grinding stones found in Italy, Russia, and the Czech Republic. The grain residues are from a wild species of cattail and a grass called Brachypodium, which both offer a nutritional package comparable to wheat and barley.[22] The grains were heated as part of the processing for consumption.

Vegetal food processing and the production of flour were standard practice across Europe from 30,000 years BP onward.[23] The food economy of mobile gatherer-'hunters' throughout Europe included the high energy content plant foods that were normally available.[24] Conversion to flour helped to preserve food, and made it is easier to transport and use.

Three grinding stones from the middle Yellow River region in China were found, dated to 23,000-19,500 BP. These female tools were used to process various plants, including grasses, beans, yam, and snake-gourd roots. Tubers were essential food resources for Paleolithic gatherers-'hunters,' and native grasses were exploited about 12,000 years before their intensive cultivation.[25]

Wild rice was a central part of the diets and cultures of Ojibwa peoples in Canada and North America, and an important food of the Algonquin, Dakota, Winnebago, Sioux, Fox, and many other tribes through trade. There was even a language group called the Menominee, or "Wild Rice People."[26]

Losing Gut Flora

Sapiens, chimps, bonobos, and gorillas all have distinct microbial fingerprints. Human stomach microorganisms have been passed down from generation to generation over millions of years, evolving right alongside us in a process called cospeciation. Like other primates, people acquire gut flora through cohabitation, social interaction, and social transmission.[27]

As hominins separated into different species over time, their bacteria did too as well, so there is a direct line of descent between the microbes of ancient hominids and those that live in our guts today.[28] In comparison to Pan, humans have lost microbial diversity in adapting for animal-based diets. Apes in their natural environment cultivate more species of bacteria than humans across a range of societies.[29]

People in non-industrialized societies have gut microbiomes that are 60 percent different from those of chimpanzees. Even worse, those living in the US have stomach microbiomes that are 70 percent different from chimps. Alarmingly, research has linked a lack of microorganism diversity in human guts to various diseases such as asthma, colon cancer, and autoimmune diseases.

As one scientist notes, "It took millions of years, since humans and chimpanzees split from a common ancestor, to become 60 percent different in these colonies living in our digestive systems. On the other hand, in apparently only hundreds of years and possibly a lot fewer, people in the United States lost a great deal of diversity in the bacteria living in their gut."[30]

Each of person is a super-organism. The 'germs' that we have sought to eliminate have been there for millennia supporting hominins. More than a thousand species live inside each individual, and they comprise 90 percent of the cells in and on our bodies. What is more, plant foods are vital for microbiome diversity.[31]

Over 100 trillion bacteria live in the oxygen-free zone of each person's large intestines. A female's microbiome collectively weighs more than her brain, and these microorganism play a preeminent role in digestion, metabolism, and stomach health. Gut flora can impact a woman's sensory, signaling, and immune systems, and influence the nerve endings in her stomach that connects to the brain.[32]

Some microbes can affect the production of serotonin, which plays a role in appetite regulation, food intake, well-being, and sleep. Emotional states in the brain are reflected at the gut level as well. For example, the pattern for an angry stomach is contraction, more acid secretion, and increased blood flow. Also, stress hormones like adrenaline can influence the behavior of intestinal microbes.

The value of gut flora, plant-based foods, and the dialogue between the stomach and the brain is recognized and addressed in ancient healing traditions, such as Ayurvedic and Chinese medicine. Modern doctors and gastroenterologists are also emphasizing that consuming a predominantly plant-based diet is key for gut and brain health.

Animals in Paleo Art

In the oldest known examples of Paleolithic art, representations of animals are numerous, so it is evident that animals played a predominant role in sapiens' mental world. Did the images serve as a phallic hunting manual, or was cave art part of gynecological training on sustainable land management?

People appear rarely, and then frequently with animal attributes, or as mixed human-animal figures. The representations might have been honorific and reflected gynocentric views of the sacredness of nature. We can not know what the Stone Age artists were thinking, and interpretations are often based on modern-day carnist biases toward food animals.

The African pigment and drawing record extends over 300,000 years and becomes regular with the emergence of Homo sapiens around 200,000 to 160,000 years ago.[33] In Australia, images of animals date to between 50,000 and 40,000 BP. Ranging from red to white, the artists' palette show animals realistically.[34]

For instance, Lascaux is a complex of caves in southwestern France, renowned for over 600 excellently detailed animal paintings that decorate the interior walls and ceilings. The paintings are the combined effort of many generations of artists, dated to around 17,000 years BP. Of the nearly 2,000 figures, over 900 can be identified as animals, and many shown within their natural environment.

Bison and lions live in open plains areas, while aurochs, deer and bears are associated with forests and marshes. The ibex habitat is rocky areas, and horses are shown in all these areas. There is frequent association of bison-horses-lions and aurochs-horses-deer-bears in compositions. Perhaps, this showed the relationship between the species pictured and their environmental conditions.

The most famous section of the Lascaux cave is Hall of the Bulls where bulls, equines, and stags are depicted. Four black bulls, or aurochs, are the dominant figures among the 36 animals represented here. One of the bulls is 17 feet (5.2 meters) long, the largest animal discovered so far in cave art. Additionally, the bulls appear to be in motion.

In Paleolithic art, characteristics essential to nonhuman animals, and the intermixing of human and animal forms, are often shown. Paintings of nonhuman animals were regularly made and maybe served as clan totems. Caves and special boulders may have been places of ritual, and rock art might have been created to honor the Goddess of Animals.

Female artists could have painted pictures of herbivores and other migrating animals to use in biology training and woman-the-gatherer instruction. Shadowing grazers was good foraging practice since grasslands often had tubers and other staples primeval humans consumed.

And the animals' dried dung was likely used as fuel in fires used for cooking, as they are in the present. Female-centered groups probably trailed different grazing herds throughout the year, so recognition was crucial, especially if the animals were no longer around.

Maybe, storytelling incorporated animal images to bring the action alive. Musical instruments, such as bone flutes, have been found in the caves, implying that even acoustical properties may have had a role to play in rock art. Some images could have represented Stone Age women's connection to individual animals.

Gynocentric Dancing

Dance has been instrumental in strengthening the bonds between hominin communities and their relationship to nature. Art, music, and dancing were integral to female-centered cultures. What is more, gynocentric rhythm is related to the social evolution and the use of symbols, language, communication, math, and ritual.

Woman-the-gatherer might have used song and dance to encode directions and descriptions of favorite vegetation. Stone Age women could have incorporated animal-based art, and dances that mimics the animals depicted, into foraging education. But dance had meanings beyond survival.

Simple repeated patterns synchronize brain waves and establish a mutual feeling of unity, connectedness, and being held. The celebratory impulse is ingrained in human females' nature, and there is a collective and joyful power in repeating a simple, familiar pattern in synchrony with others. Each dance circle is an opportunity for egg-producers to practice being in a gynocentric community in a respectful and cooperative way.[35]

Circles of women dancing with joined hands appear in rock art, pottery shards, vases, and frescoes in the Middle to Late Stone Age. Ovary circles show that ritual dance was a primary means of women's worship. Female dances are profoundly spiritual and incorporate symbols of the Goddess in her many guises.[36]

Dances are feminist in the way they provide women with a place of power, not 'power-over' but 'power-from-within.' The internal framing consists of personal ability and spiritual integrity. Dance is also about 'power-with,' pertaining to social power or influence among equals.[37] In the Middle East and elsewhere, there is a women's solo dance tradition which goes back thousands of years.[38]

Dancing is among the oldest and most persistent themes in Near Eastern prehistoric art, and these depictions of dance accompanied the spread of agriculture into surrounding regions of Europe and Africa. Across the World, dance images were engraved, incised, applied, or painted on pottery, stamp and cylinder seals, plaster walls and floors, and on stone vessels and slabs.[39]

Dancing is an activist practice because the qualities they embody - connection, inclusiveness, balance, empathy, and mutuality - are the principles of a Partnership society.[40] Gynocentric dances are a movement practice like yoga or t'ai chi. They are a women's mystery school where the dances transmit encoded information with conscious intent.

Throughout the world, folk music and dancing are often female-centered. In the New Stone Age, scenes of dancing depict real community rituals linked to the agricultural cycle, and that dance was essential for maintaining these calendrical rituals and passing them on to succeeding generations.

Conclusion

This chapter unpacked several misleading characterizations of hominin diet that serves to promote dominant behavior among modern men and violence against animals and nature. It argued that during the Stone Age, 'woman-the-gatherer' was far more likely the primary food provider than 'man-the-hunter.'

Plant-based carbohydrates were the primary part of the Paleo diet, not animal flesh. Interestingly, if the loss of ancient gut flora played a part in the extinction of more carnist hominins, then this may have implications for the animal-based diet of contemporary humans as well.

'Man-the-scavenger' and 'man-the-gatherer' suggests contrasting and more plausible models of prehistoric masculinity. These terms challenges the current framing of toxic phallic identities in radical ways. The next chapter expands the critique of 'man-the-hunter' by describing the second and third domestication events and women's role in them.

(Figure 7: Neolithic Cup-and-ring mark, Galicia. Spain)

7: Female Fire-keeper

As this [discovering the original] happens, Athena will shuck off her robothood, will re-turn to her real Source, to her Self, leaving the demented Male Mother to play impotently with his malfunctioning machine, his dutiful dim-witted "Daughter", his broken Baby Doll gone berserk, his failed fembot. - Mary Daly

ASIA's Journey 2121.07

It is pre-dawn in the moonless sky. It is a rare cool night, 86°F (30°C) in the dry air over the shallow trench. Heat from the previous day radiates from the rocks and hard ground, and soon, the comfortable night air will give way to oppressive heat and higher humidity.

Lian and Nakeisha slowly crawl down from the ridge to investigate the scene at the base. Seven males lay motionless on the hard ground. Nakeisha recognizes some of the men from the shelter. They are part of FST, a new gang in the area. There are numerous networks of pedo-hunters, and she knows that more will come looking for ASIA as they flee north.

Lian is not surprised to find Alex and Roshi among the bodies. Since the pedo-hunters knew exactly where ASIA's camp was, the boys must have told them.

Nakeisha notice signs of bruises and cuts on the teens' bodies. "These are signs of torture," she guesses.

Lian shrugs. "Or they were in an initiation fight... Either way, they abandoned ASIA and probably sold us out."

The two women start to dig a hole to bury the bodies. The sun was just rising but the heat was already exhausting, and they had to take a break every 5 minutes.

Lian stops and looks up. "Face it, sister. Everything has changed. Women are no longer able to raise males who are willing to protect us. We are on our own."

"How can you blame them?" Nakeisha shakes her head. "There is no benefit in protecting our girls. If they do, there's only a harsh life and suffering for them." She is sad to be burying the teens, who were a part of ASIA.

Lian is adamant. "No, from the beginning, Alex and Roshi did not respect or protect their mothers. Now, they were willing to sell their sisters."

Nakeisha wipes a tear and continues digging. With the bodies covered, the pair collects the darts and walk up to camp.

It is near mid-day and moon-rise. With Xóchitl in the lead, the women from ASIA regroup to continue their journey toward a safe house. Lian steps behind Zaid, the only boy left in the group, shadowing him closely.

Nakeisha looks at Lian and slowly shakes her head. "May the Goddess help to guide that one," she mutters to Zamora.

Introduction

The taming of fire was far more useful than any stone tool humans has previously invented. Even so, this aspect of Hominin evolution is little known and understood. In additional to its domestic use, fire became an essential tool in land management, and it enabled hominins to domesticate and transform their entire landscape.

This fifth chapter of Part II on female-centered cultures in the Stone Age expands the inquiry into the restraining of sperm-producers and diet with an investigation into the second and third taming, the use of fire. The chapter starts off with a discourse on sapiens' control of fire. Next, it explores the notion that men searched for fire more often than they hunted animals.

A survey of female-centered fireplaces for cooking, or hearth-fire, comes afterward. Then, an analysis of the third modification, that of humans' use of fire to farm the landscape, follows. Female cooking techniques and their use of fire in socialization were remarkable improvements, and the chapter ends with a discussion of these two aspects of gynocentrism.

2nd Domestication: Fire

Harnessing the power of fire was the second form of female control, and an essential hominin innovation.[1] Darwin regarded the taming of the flame as the greatest discovery made by humanity, second only to language. Typical of phallic scholars, he gave little credit to women in the development of fire or communication.[2]

Wrangham suggests that it was fire use that allowed Homo genus to descend from the trees. Hominins no longer needed to build tree platforms, as Gorillas and the other great apes do.[3] And, rather than a single event, the discovery of fire was a set of processes happening over the long term.[4]

Hominin use of fire occurred before one million BP, and maybe as early as 1.7 million BP in Yuanmau, China.[5] H. erectus females could tend fires, and H. sapiens egg-producers could make fire at will.[6] Hominin females were instrumental in the development of fire-keeping technology and cooking. And, they heated clay to about 400°C (752 °F) to make pottery and ceramics.

H. erectus females were cooking food as early as 400,000 to 500,000 BP.[7] And by 250,000 BP, female-centered fireplaces were common among hominins across Europe and the Middle East.[8] Fire was instrumental in cooking and greatly aided the feeding of infants, children, and elders.[9]

Subduing the flame led to the growth of a home-based, land use strategy,[10] and contributed immensely to egg-producers' advancement of languages.[11] In addition to communal meals and fireplace gatherings, fires served other social purposes. For instance, hominins probably lit signal fires for purposes similar to present-day announcements on social media and chain messaging.[12]

The flame transformed hominin diet, culture, and even biology.[13] Its heat helped people to cope with the cold, which became all the more critical once we lost much of our body hair. Burning became socially embedded with religious meaning.[14] For example, female-centered rites incorporated fire-sticks and the burning of incense.[15]

Harnessing the force of combustion was made easier through cooperation to obtain fuel and embers from nature or other hominins. Collaboration also aided in the transport of a flame, to keep it ablaze, and to prevent it from going out. By joining forces, individuals could reduce maintenance costs and lessen the risk of being without a fire.[16]

Other cooperative behaviors were equally important, such as group foraging, cooperative breeding, food sharing, and mutual defense.[17] Fire facilitated these other forms of group action as well, and could have started the gift economy. Among the Maasai in Africa, females formed fire-stick alliances across vast regions.[18] Some Aboriginal nations have Dreamtime stories of how once women controlled fire and men stole it from them.

The loss of fire was catastrophic for hominins, especially during the wet season. The fear of losing the flame possibly led to more sharing and altruism among various language groups. The force and warmth of combustion could have fostered the evolution of morality and teachings against selfishness, like the hoarding of fire as recounted in numerous oral tales.

The constant need for ruminant dung to build and maintain fires presented a strong incentive for human females to discourage their men from hunting these animals, especially during the rainy season. Scaring away ruminants and other prey meant females had to walk further to gather dung for cooking and warmth.

Man-the-Fire-Hunter

The main role hominin men played in gynocentric communities may not have been stalking animals for a kill, but searching for a spark. When Stone Age women's hearth-fire was extinguished, they asked their phallic clan members to hunt for a flame, not flesh-based protein. And in their quest, sperm-producers probably fire-foraged for roots, eggs, and other forms of animal-based protein and brought these back with the embers.[19]

Baked roots and tubers last much longer than carcass, so men probably focused on collecting plant-based foods for others at the camp. If finding a flame was the primary purpose of men's pursuit, they probably focused on quickly transporting it back to women. The need to obtain fire likely encouraged Stone Age men to remain cooperative.[20]

Some skill was required to carry a flame without burning the body and allowing the embers to die. From time to time, the fire-stick would be waved, fanning the coals to life, or plunged into scrub or grass, which in flaring would rekindle the main stalk. People even transported fire in canoes by lining it with clay.

Why are female's use of combustion, and gathering and cooking of plants in prehistory overlooked? Who benefits, and who loses, from the perpetuation of the 'man-the-hunter' myth? Men searching for embers and fuel, gathering fruits, digging up roots, and cooking do not fit into the 'masculine' narrative. These phallic behaviors mirror those of ovary beings and so contradict the notion of male supremacy.

Phallic-domination and legitimization of violence rely extensively on the 'man-the-hunter' fallacy. With stalking prey as the primary objective, the focal point of H. sapiens' evolution becomes phallic bonding and the buddy system. Women are irrelevant or secondary in this framing, passively waiting with their children in camp for the hunter/savior to return with supposedly freshly killed carcass.[21]

Far from the myth of fearless killers, hominin sperm-producers were probably more opportunistic fire-foragers than hyper-carnivore killers pursuing dangerous herds of big animals, armed only with spears and stones. The over-generalization of Paleolithic men's consumption of animal protein and prowess in killing giant animals is not only false, it is fundamentally sexist.

First, it disregards woman-the-gatherer's production and females' strategies for obtaining the vast majority of food throughout this extensive era. Second, the 'man-the-hunter' tales conveniently dismiss the lack of predatory behavior, and existence of female-centered cultures, among other great apes.

And third, this fictionalized account of prehistory ignores female-centered technology, cultural practices, and trade that began in the Middle Stone Age.

♀ Hearth-fire

The first real fireplaces date to the Middle Stone Age around 125,000 years ago. Since egg-producing hominins were primarily responsible for feeding themselves, children and families, it is likely that women invented various fireplaces and numerous ways of cooking, processing, and preparing food.

The flame is a species monopoly and sapiens' ecological signature. Recognizable fireplaces at hominin sites demonstrate social and productive uses. Neanderthals were manufacturing pitch from fire around 80,000 BP, and the existence of gypsum plaster also implies primeval use of combustion.[22]

Camp sites were cleared of fuel to prevent the hearth fire from escaping, often by pre-burning it. Each hominin family lived as a separate unit within a camp, and life was centered around its fireside. The fireplace warmed sleeping areas and provided security at night. It made light and gave humans the nighttime for story, ceremony, and companionship. To maintain a fire through the night involved constant tending, so people took turns or broke their sleep into a chain of lighter naps.

The domestic flame was the province of the Stone Age woman and her fireplace took many forms. Larger and specially shaped hearths were used to bake cakes, cook tubers, and leach toxins from various foods.[23] Hot stones were used to crack open hard fruits and Acacia seeds. The fireplace also interacted with other Stone Age tools. Careful charring hardened digging sticks. Heated waxes and resins made a useful glue. Ashes served as a poultice for wounds and snakebites, and for body decoration.

Taming the flame transformed H. sapiens all the way down to our genome. A genetic mutation in modern humans allows certain toxins, including those found in smoke, to be metabolized at a safe rate. The same genetic sequence was not found in other primates, including older hominins, such as Neanderthals and Denisovans.[24] Hominins also got smaller guts and bigger heads because they could cook food. And, the species went to the top of the food chain because they could shape the landscape in a form of semi-cultivation.

3rd Taming: Fire Farming

Fifty millennia before intensive agriculture began, the land was being 'tilled' and 'cultivated' through burning. This third form of modification, fire-farming, was part of the technological skill set of modern humans.[25] Suitable burning was utilized as part of sustainable land management and site preparation from Africa and Asia to Australia and the Americas.

Farming and settlement are much older than is current held in the scientific literature that focuses on the Middle East around 12,000 BP. Indigenous Australians began burning and 'gardening' the land as early as 120,000 BP,[26] and 'cultivation' with the flame was widely practiced by 60,000 BP. Prehistoric people ignited areas to "clean up the land," and to change and improve the composition of plant species and arid-zone vegetational diversity.[27]

Using genetic sampling of forest ecosystems, isotope analysis of human teeth, and soil analysis, Roberts and other researchers found abundant evidence that people at the equator were actively changing the natural world to make it more human-centric 45,000 years ago. Very similar evidence for ancient proto-farming was found in equatorial Africa, South Asia, and Southeast Asia, when people began burning down vegetation to make room for plant resources and homes.[28]

Over the next 35,000 years, the practice of burning back the forest evolved in the tropics as people practiced proto-agriculture techniques by mixing specialized soils for growing plants and draining swamps for agriculture. In New Guinea, humans were farming yam, banana and taro by 10,000 BP. Later, clans began to build "garden cities" where they lived in low-density neighborhoods surrounded by cultivated land.

The proto-farms often evolved into highly-developed networks of cities like those of the Maya. These ingenious, sustainable farms and cities may have been what saved H. sapiens from the fate of the Neanderthals and other hominins through long periods of dramatic climate change.

The research by Roberts and his colleagues challenges the very notion of a "Neolithic revolution" in which the shift to settlement happened in just a few hundred years. In the tropical regions, there was not a clearly defined line between nomadic existence and agricultural life. Roberts notes that when humans first arrived in South Asia, Southeast Asia, and Melanesia, they spent millennia adapting to the tropics, eventually "shaping environments to meet their own needs." He concludes, "So rather than huge leaps, what we see is a continuation of this local knowledge and adaptation in these regions through time."[29]

Throughout the Middle Stone Age, people manipulated vegetation in north-western Europe.[30] Native American language groups exploited the flame to selectively shape the landscape,[31] to obtain salt from grasses, and for the production of straight branches for basketry.[32]

In the Amazon, cultivators were domesticating rubber, cocoa, Brazil nut, caimito, acai palm, cashew, and tucuma palm trees around 8,000 BP at roughly the same time Neolithic peoples in the Levant were first domesticating wheat and barley.[33] Moreover, the forest is the product of a long history of plant domestication by Amazonian peoples. This seemingly untouched wilderness is actually a patchwork of farms abandoned centuries ago.

Australia is a cobweb of 'Dreaming Tracks' which are part of the mythology of Aboriginal nations.[34] The symbolic markings represented ecological knowledge, associations with the land, travel tales, and trading routes. The symbolic tracks weaves together people with hundreds of languages, diverse cultural customs, different skin, and hair color. 'Dreaming Tracks' were also part of an ecological land management system based on fire-stick farming.[35]

The Anbara regarded sunburn grassland as neglected. At least once every three to four years the grassland, eucalyptus woodlands, and savanna in their territory are burnt.[36] Through fire-farming, the people managed to avoid high-intensity catastrophic wildfires and maintain their food supply.

The cleared land is colonized by other desert plants that provide more food such as wild tomato, the most important fruit for the desert people. The fruit are very nutritious, high in vitamin C, and remain edible for long periods on the plant. Another is the wild banana, and its leaves, fruit, and roots are all edible.

♀ Cooking

Harnessing the flame to cook plants helped hominins to evolve a more voluminous brain. Cooking food significantly increases the amount of energy that can be absorbed into the body and reduce diseases in raw foods.[37] Heated food is processed more efficiently in the gut and the extra energy was exploited for brain expansion.[38]

Preparing foods with fire is linked to the emergence of salivary amylase, an enzyme needed to process cooked, starchy food. With cooking, toxins in seeds and cyanogenic glycosides such as those found in linseed and cassava, are rendered non-toxic.[39]

Even before the advent of fire-hearths, hominins were foraging and consuming flora cooked by natural fires. Prior to exploiting the flame, ovary hominins were cooking and processing food by pounding and soaking them first. Crushing, pounding, and grinding implements were frequently used throughout the Stone Age. The grinding process dates to 50,000 BP, and Nancy Kraybill suggests that pounding started in the Early Stone Age.[40]

Ample quantities of seeds and grinding stones found at Paleolithic sites, such as one in Palestine dated to around 19,400 BP, imply advanced female planning of plant food preparation. These finds suggest that egg-producers processed grain before cooking and consumption.[41]

Long before intensive agriculture began, women invented ways to collect, store, carry, and sprout grains to make bread.[42] For instance, essene bread is made by sprouting grains, mashing, and forming them into flat patties and cooking them on rocks in the sun, or on hot rocks from a fire.

Contemporary cooking methods such as baking, boiling, roasting, steaming, and smoking were familiar to ancient sapiens. In general, tropical cultures often roasted and steamed, Arctic cultures relied on direct-fire, and, in the mid-latitudes, stone boiling was most favored.[43]

Before the invention of pottery, females used gourds for cooking, food storage, and carrying foods. By filling a gourd with water and dropping hot rocks into it, the water boils. The hot liquid could then soften and improve the digestibility of added grains, roots, vegetables, leaves, and so on.

Cooking over a hot open flame requires regular tending of the fire pit. However, adding rocks to the flames gradually warms them up, and they could hold heat for 48 hours or longer, thereby conserving both fuel and human energy.[44]

One primeval baking method involves digging a deep hole and starting a fire in the pit. Heavy stones are placed on top the flames and heated to a high temperature. Roots, vegetables, and other foods are placed on top of the hot stones between layers of green plants. The hole is filled in with soil, and the food is cooked for up to several days. Another prehistoric baking method involves the use of clay. Hard roots, tubers, and other foods are covered with wet clay, and placed inside a fireplace. The flame bakes the clay and cooks the food inside. Cultures across the world still use clay pots to soften root crops and tough plants.

Herbs and spices were being exploited by gatherer-'hunters' and the first agriculturalists not only for energy requirements but for taste as well.[45] Researchers found traces of garlic in prehistoric pottery from Northern Europe dating from 6,100 BP to 5,750 BP, during the transition to farming.[46]

Fire & ♀ Ritual

The open flame was a necessary and important part of later Homo cultures and often was invested with profound cultural meaning. Fire served as protector and purifier, and a flame fostered contemplation, "dreamtime," and stories. Numerous tales and rites link girls and women with the 'sacred' fire.[47]

Females' utilization of the flame begins at birth. The young-bearing in labor may squat over a small fire to facilitate birthing. And after parturition, Aboriginal mothers held their babies over a smoking fire to help dry the mucous.

Age, sex, and group-related ceremonies consist of congregations dancing and singing around an open flame. In cleansing ceremonies, participants are brushed or passed through smoke to prevent illness. And after cellular death, funeral pyres completed a lifecycle of rites that began with birthing fires.

Those entrusted with tending a ritual flame often held a sacred role in the culture. Female fire-keepers often tended the sacred fire in a manner peculiar to the cultural traditions of their group. For instance, Brigid, an Irish Goddess, was served by human egg-producers who tended to an eternal flame.[48]

An association between ceremonial fire and health continues in many traditional cultures into the present day. For example, the Native American sweat lodge, a ceremonial structure and rite involving purification by fire and steam. During some rituals, hallucinogens are burned and inhaled to create altered states like peyote in North America, and the pituri in Australia.[49]

Women figured centrally in prehistoric creation legends and cultural practices. Their Dreaming Tracks, role as fire-keeper, and land-management skills added to ovary beings' status and influence. For instance, if Central Australian men hurt an egg-producer, they feared that she might take ritual action against them.

A woman's spiritual power was considerable, and it entitled her to much respect. This strength was based on ovary beings' gynecological relationship to the land and its preservation. Sperm-producers needed women's knowledge to back their own claims to rights in the country.[50] Unlike the phallic preoccupation with male ancestor worship in abrahamic cults, Indigenous female ceremonies focused on current environmental, social, and personal issues.

In Australia, phallic anthropologists with no access to senior egg-producers living in the jilimi, the women's camp, had little understanding of females' essential roles in rituals. Aboriginal ovary beings play a part even in the ultimate phallic celebration, ritualized rebirth through circumcision of young men. This ceremony could not be conducted without participating women who could stop any rite if they felt that sperm-producers were not performing them correctly.

Warlpiri egg-producers performed rites for attracting lovers or repelling phallic interest they did not want. Warrabri and other females retained the ability to leave phallic company and live independently in the jilimi, a long snake-like building that women erected themselves.

On one side of the jilimi is a wide clearing known as the "ring place." Here, Aboriginal women conduct rituals, display their sacred Dreamtime boards, tell stories, and sometimes sleep especially when ill or in trouble. Offenders were brought to trial and disputes resolved by ritual means in the ring place.

The major themes and purposes of female rites were for love, land, and health. Some observances celebrated a girl's menarche or first occurrence of menstruation. For ceremonies, crones greased then painted the bodies of girls and women with ochre in the patterns that showed their link with the land while singing gently and harmoniously of the Dreamtime. Red ochre represented the force of life, blood, and the energy of the land.[51]

As women moved through the countryside, they sing of the travels of the creating ancestors and teach their children about the land and its Dreaming. All food gathered was first distributed among the young-bearing and their children before being shared with the men. Crones are highly respected and women were never considered inferior in Aboriginal society until Europeans arrived.

Conclusion

The leading advancements of the New Stone Age were already being practiced by egg-producers in the Middle and Late Stone Age, like proto-agriculture and settlements. The second and third restraining were used by women to advance plant-based food production and ecogynocentrism. Along with improving subsistence practices, ovary beings in prehistory were evolving culture, communication, philosophy, oral history, jewelry, and creativity.

The next chapter examines female-centered art, especially Woman/Goddess figures created in the Stone Age. These simple images disrupt the 'killer ape' and 'man-the-hunter' narratives by revealing aspects of gynocentric culture among hominins. The vast numbers of symbolic representations found provide evidence of Goddess theology and worship across the world throughout the Stone Age.

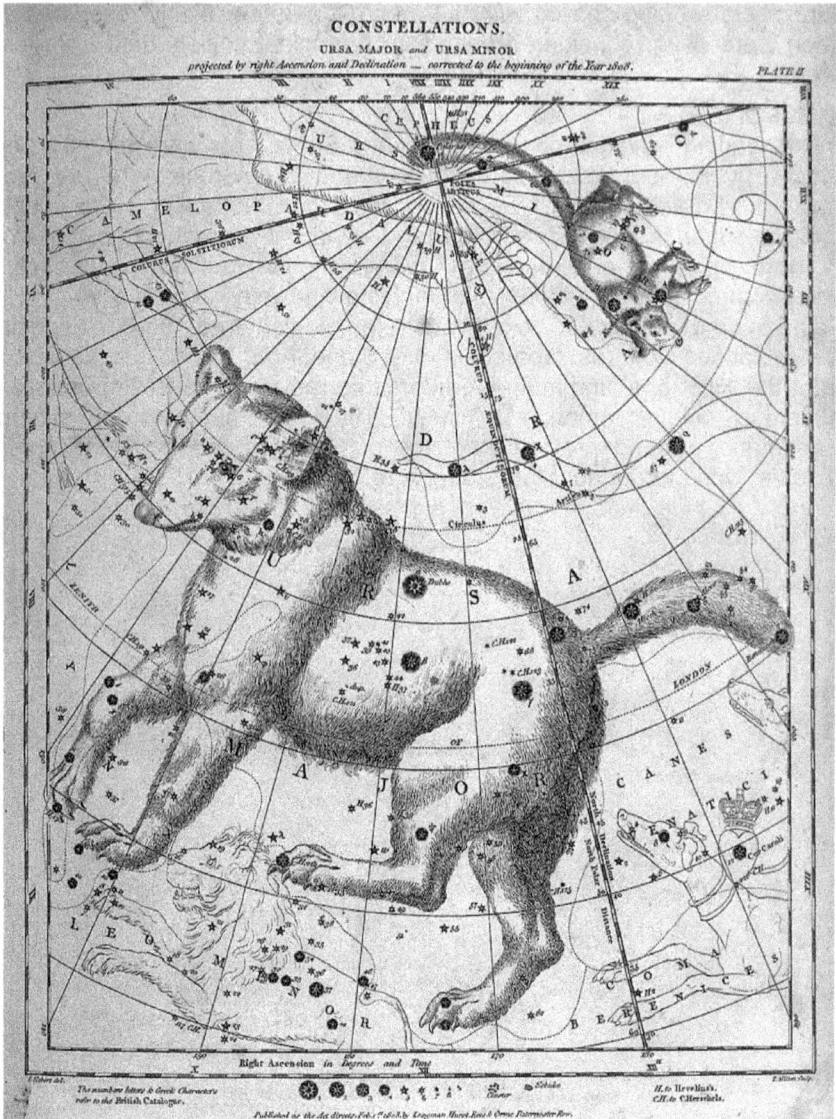

(Figure 8: English engraving of Big and Little Bear Constellation)

8: Female Artists

> The metaethics of radical feminism means simply that while Zeus, Yahweh, and all the other divine male "Mothers" are trying to retrieve their dolls from the ashcan of patriarchal creation, women on our own Journey are dis-covering Metis and the third-born Athena: our own new be-ing. That is, we are be-ing in the Triple Goddess, who is, and is not yet. - Mary Daly

ASIA's Journey 2121.08

ASIA are a day away from the safe house but are completely out of food and water. In is morning, 119°F (48°C) with low humidity as the group rests after a steep uphill walk. The 12-year drought has taken a toll on the plants in the coastal desert and the only moisture available to sustain life are dew droplets at night.

Hungry, the girls follows Jean foraging for plants to eat and cook. Almost immediately, Iniko finds a big cactus tree with blossoms and fruit. Jean cuts off parts of the plant and drains the liquid for the children to drink. Two children carry parts to the camp for the cook, Waynoka.

The other kids follow Jean along a dried up stream bed, and they walk for ten minutes. They enter a fire-scared area with a huge oak tree. The group looks around for acorns and edible shrubs. Cha'Kwaina finds some berries and shows them to Jean who joyfully announces they are wild blueberries. The children eat them happily and excitedly fill up their bags.

The wind picks up suddenly, and Jean tells the children to hurry, but they are too busy eating and chatting to hear her. A blast of hot air flows along the flat stream bed with tremendous force.

"Get down on the ground," Jean yells out, but her warning is muffled by the howling wind. After a twenty seconds, the gusts are accompanied by clouds of dust, and visibility is reduced to zero. The waves of dust then turns into a tsunami of debris. Frightened, the girls scream and look for cover, but there is none.

"Stay together," Jean calls out as she grabs two girls to her right and pulls them down to the ground. The swirling sand and rubble stings their faces and burn their eyes. The children cry out in fear and pain.

"Hang on," Jean yells. "It will soon be over." A minute later, the dust storm vanishes as quickly as it came. The girls and food are scattered all over.

A teenager, 14-year-old Nadie, and 7-year-old Sabra, are missing. Jean leads the group in a search for them, being careful to stay together.

The girls carefully examined the dried-out stream bed but find no sign of their two sisters. Jean and the children gather their food and return to ASIA, with the children in tears.

Introduction

Since humans are ocular-dependent creatures, visual art represents a powerful resource for mental and physical well-being. The production of visual art improves effective interaction between parts of the brain, and creating art could delay or negate age-related decline in these brain functions.[1]

Over time, art and sculpture acquires heavy meaning and significance to communities and individuals. Objects of art can be used to transmit family and clan history, as well as ecological literacy. From the Middle Stone Age onward, egg-producing hominins discovered and practiced numerous forms of visual and figurative art for social purposes. And maybe, they created art for personal enjoyment as well.

Makeup, body painting, and tattoos are female inventions. Accessories, jewelry, decorating, and symbolic imagery are female-derived as well. Human egg-producers adopted their artistic skills to create the numerous Paleolithic cave drawings and rock art found throughout the World. Contrary to the popular belief, Stone Age artists may have been predominantly female.

This sixth chapter of Part II on Paleolithic gynocentric cultures concentrates on cultural production and reproductive issues. The chapter begins by broadening prior discussions on childcare with a survey of the maternal brain and then, the role of grandmothers.

The prevalence of female hand prints in Paleolithic artistry comes after, and then there is a brief examination of Early Stone Age art. A scrutiny of Stone Age Woman/Goddess sculptures follows, then Avdeevo Woman/Goddess carvings are discussed. The chapter concludes with a discourse on the significance of Women/Goddess portable art, especially in the lives of mothers.

Maternal Brain

Reproductive success involve young-bearers' investment of time and energy in ovulating, gestating, nursing, feeding, carrying, and establishing lifelong social ties with offspring. In mothers, the brain's gray matter becomes concentrated, and activity increases in regions that control empathy, anxiety, and social interaction.[2]

There are changes at both hormonal and cerebral levels which may play a role in helping females transition into motherhood.[3] During pregnancy, the young-bearing undergo considerable brain remodeling that persists for at least two years after birth. These alterations are obvious and could be used to predict how child-bearers scored on an attachment scale.[4]

Furthermore, researchers were able to use a computer algorithm to identify which ovary beings were new parents based solely on their patterns of gray matter loss. Curiously, gray matter loss did not occur in new fathers or non-parents. Maternal feelings of overwhelming love, fierce protectiveness, and constant worry begin with reactions in the cranium. Just by staring at her baby, the reward centers of a mother's brain will light up.[5]

The odor of newborns also activates the neurological reward circuit in child-bearers.[6] Interestingly, mothers show greater activation in the emotional processing network and phallic parents in socio-cognitive circuits. These areas are linked with oxytocin and behavior differently. And among fathers, time spent in childcare correlated with brain connectivity.[7]

Grandmother Hypothesis

Female fertility ends at similar ages in humans and the other great apes. They can have deliveries into the forties but not beyond. Other ape females become frail in their thirties and usually die during the cycling years. This is not true of humans, which suggests that the ancestral age when fertility ends has persisted among all great apes, while greater longevity evolved in our lineage.

Even among gatherer-'hunters,' women past their childbearing years make up a substantial fraction of the population in a group. So why would it be beneficial for hominin females to stop being able to have children with decades still left to live?

According to the 'grandmother' hypothesis, postmenopausal life functions as a primal feature in females' existence from which other characteristics are derived. By helping their children and grandchildren to survive and thrive, a 'grandmother' can ensure that their genes will cascade down the generations.[8]

In general, the presence of non-maternal caregivers is often linked with improved child survival.[9] In the Early Stone Age, crones helped gather food for their offspring's children. In so doing, they enabled their daughters to have more children, more quickly. The most evolutionary fit grandmothers had the most grandchildren, to whom they passed on their longevity-promoting genes.

Without grandmothers present, if a mother gives birth and already has a two-year-old child, the odds of the older child surviving are much lower, because unlike other primates, humans are not able to feed and take care of themselves immediately after weaning. Hominin mothers have to devote time and attention to their new infants at the expense of older children. And once older mothers died, many young offspring would likely die too. Grandmothers solve this problem by acting as supplementary caregivers.[10]

Kristen Hawkes demonstrated that our mothers' mother explains why humans live so long. After less than 60,000 years, with "only a little bit of grandmothering," the human lifespan doubled in her simulation. Grandmothers are also what make us human, as Hawkes contends, "Grandmothering gave us the kind of upbringing that made us more dependent on each other socially and prone to engage each other's attention."

Their style of upbringing, with its emphasis on social dependence, gave rise to "a whole array of social capacities that are then the foundation for the evolution of other distinctly human traits, including pair bonding, bigger brains, learning new skills and our tendency for cooperation."[11]

Menopause led to longer lifespans and sowed the seeds for gynocentric cultures. Without menopause, older women would simply continue to mother children, instead of acting as grandmothers. For instance, grandmothers from Aka, a contemporary gatherer-'hunter' culture, provide one-quarter of all childcare in late infancy.[12]

Grandmothers reduce child stress responses,[13] and increase maternal responsiveness to children which in turn improve mother-child interactions.[14] A woman over 45 with grown children is more liable to be in a camp with her daughter than with her son. She is also more likely to be with her daughter if that daughter has children under seven years of age, or if that daughter is suckling a baby.[15]

Early Paleo Art

Stone Age ovary beings had little use for cumbersome tools, objects, and devices. If an item was not portable, it was pretty much useless to them.[16] Herbal healers obtained fresh cures from nature, and egg-producers used naturally available materials for body decorations. Food and cosmetic products were functional and rendered as needed. Carting nonfunctional art around was an expensive indulgence that took up precious space and energy.

Nonetheless, Stone Age women made and carried thousands of symbolic works of art, including Woman/Goddess carvings. Although there is a low frequency of archaeological finds, most human figures discovered from the

Paleolithic are female, and this finding is highly significant.

Numerous Paleolithic sculptures portray a Woman/Goddess with exaggerated physical female features, the so-called 'Venus' figurines. The carvings were created as far back as the Early Stone Age, and two of the oldest known are the Tan-Tan[17] and Berekhat Ram[18] figurines.

A few of the Woman/Goddess statuettes found are older than Neanderthals, and were probably carved by Homo Erectus females.[19] These carvings suggest that hominids were gynocentric from the beginning. Some of the World's first art come from South Africa - two 77,000-year-old, engraved blocks of red ocher that girls and women used. Ocher was utilized to decorate bodies as well as to color objects such as tools or shell ornaments.

In one South African site, researchers uncovered over 36 shells, each of which was perforated so they were probably hung from a string to form necklaces and wristbands.[20] The ocher blocks and shells show that egg-producers drew body art and wore jewelry prior to modern humans migrating out of Africa.

The schematized symbol of a birth-giving Woman/Goddess, with raised hands and splayed legs, occurs all over the World during the Late Stone Age. Similar images of a Woman/Goddess giving birth exist in Africa, Asia, China, the Near East, Europe, Australia, and the Americas. Across the Globe, Paleolithic 'sacred vulvas' and other female-centered imagery were discovered as well.

Cave shrines stood for the sacred womb of Mother Earth and numerous were uncovered sites across the Globe. Entrance into, and reemergence out of the shrine, symbolized regeneration, much like later traditions of water baptism. The Goddess was the primary life principle from which all living forms emerge and return as part of her cycles of creation and destruction.

The similarities in shape between the upper section of Chauvet cave in France and female ovaries was probably recognized since the inner section was developed as the most sacred part of the shrine. Animal paintings at the entrance and lower sections served as a transition space to the sacred inner sanctum. Animals are depicted as dynamic, moving, and active representatives of the Earth Mother. Horned animals, like the ox, rhino, and ram symbolized the quarter moon and several are painted in the inner section of the cave.

Among Aboriginal Australians, there are hundreds of sacred Gwion figures and rock paintings. In most Gwion human figures, females were indicated by fuller hips, thighs, and bellies. Aboriginal women had immense authority as demonstrated by the strong and imposing gynocentric Gwion icons at Alyaguma waterhole and other sites.

Prehistoric Woman/Goddess statuettes were found in most of Eurasia and as far away as China and Japan. Virtually all of the human carvings recovered are from the young-bearing sex, and phallic sculptures rarely appear. When they do occur in the Paleolithic, the male figures are mostly of youths.

Phallic statuettes and art are atypical and poorly executed. In mixed groups of egg-producing and sperm-producing figures, the former is especially emphasized by being much larger than the phallic ones. Usually females are depicted as a giver, and males as receivers, like mother and son.

♀ Hand-prints

Decorated caves had a special meaning, and people returned to them over many generations, in some cases over thousands of years. In prehistoric cave art, the most common themes are abstract signs; figure paintings, mostly of animals; and painted hands.[21] The signs and animals had symbolic significance, but what about the hands?

Archaeologists have found hundreds of hand stencils on cave walls across the Globe. The cave art artists probably painted the hand-prints of themselves. The petite hand-prints were assumed to be that of adolescent boys, but it was determined that a wide majority of the hands are female.

Archaeologist Dean Snow analyzed hand stencils found in eight cave sites in France and Spain.[22] By comparing the relative lengths of individual fingers, Snow determined that three-quarters of the hand-prints were female.[23] This finding overturns the 'man-the-hunter' and leader tenet that assumes Stone Age artists were all men.

Women and children began stenciling, painting, or chipping imprints of their hands onto rock walls earlier than 35,000 BP. Hand prints were discovered in caves in Africa, Asia, Australia, and Europe. The world's oldest hand stencil comes from the Sulawesi Caves, Indonesia, around 40,000 BP. The site includes some of the most ancient animal paintings as well.

Hand paintings could appear anywhere in a cave. They might be on their own, or clustered in varying groups of left and right hands. The stencils were made among or even inside paintings of animals and other objects. Red pigment was blown over hands to make the stencils.[24]

Woman/Goddess Figures

Hundreds of Woman/Goddess figurines were uncovered from the Stone Age, Neolithic, and Bronze Age. Female icons are the most frequent human figurative art that occur in prehistory, and some discoveries date before 40,000 BP. Woman/Goddess figures are among the first works of prehistoric art and ceramics known.

Importantly, erotic depictions of women, vulvae, and penises are absent. A few phallus and possibly other sexual toys were pieced together, but there are no imagery of sexual intercourse in Stone Age art. The lack of objectification suggests that the artists were egg-producing humans. And for the phallic artists, it indicates that Paleolithic sperm-producers did not objectify females.

The recovered Woman/Goddess carvings include the Hohle Fels,[25] Galgenberg,[26] Kostenki,[27] Montpazier,[28] Dolni Vestonice,[29] Willendorf,[30] and Frasassi[31] figures. The Hohle Fels statuette confirms that Woman/Goddess figurative imagery was part of human migration into Europe, 40,000 years ago.

There are several fragments of Woman/Goddess figures found at Grottes du Pape, France, dated from around 27,000 to 25,000 BP.[32] There are dozens of Woman/Goddess figures from Russia,[33] which contains prominent Stone Age sites from 25,000 to 16,000 BP.[34]

Other European Woman/Goddess statuettes include the Mauern,[35] Lespugue,[36] Sireuil,[37] Mainz,[38] Tursac,[39] Savignano,[40] Renancourt,[41] Moravany,[42] Abri Pataud,[43] and Laussel.[44] The Laussel Woman/Goddess holds a wisent horn in one hand, which has 13 notches which could symbolize the number of moons or menstrual cycles in a year.

Other figures were found at La Madeleine,[45] Parabita,[46] Impudique,[47] Mas d'Azil,[48] Courbet,[49] Neuchâtel,[50] Roc-aux-Sorciers, Nebra, and Grimaldi, where 15 Woman/Goddess were uncovered. The Petersfels site, in Germany, was one of the most important Paleolithic sites in Central Europe from 15,500 to 14,000 BP. At Petersfels, numerous stylized Woman/Goddess figurines made of jet, or hard coal, were discovered, some with holes for use as pendants.

Dozens of Gönnersdorf statuettes and icons were uncovered in 19 sites across Germany, France, Czech Republic, Poland and Russia.[51] In addition to Woman/Goddess figures, other gynocentric sculptures were discovered, including phallic objects at Milandes,[52] Hohle Fels,[53] and Mas d'Azil.[54]

The distributed presence of Woman/Goddess figures in the Late Stone Age suggests that gynocentrism was evolving rapidly in art, spirituality, culture, communication, trade, and food production. The progression of female-centered cultures occurred alongside a refinement of woman-the-gatherer's task to feed expanding human populations, which naturally led to their development of farming and settlements.

Avdeevo Woman/Goddess

The Avdeevo Woman/Goddess figures in Russia depict mature women in various stages of their reproductive cycle.[55] Numerous Woman/Goddess statuettes were uncovered in two oval living areas surrounded by semi-subterranean lodges and pits dated between 21,000 and 20,000 BP.[56]

The Avdeevo cultural site is remarkable because its abundant and picturesque material show the peculiarities of, and links between, the Stone Age sites of Eastern and Central Europe.[57] The inter-connections included the predominant use of Woman/Goddess figurines and female triangle symbols in cultures across the region.[58]

Avdeevo contains several mammoth-bone and ivory Woman/Goddess figures, including double-female, back-to-back carvings. Four of these statuettes are about 6 inches (15 cm) high. Goddess statuettes made from marl and chalk were also uncovered, along with other figurines.

Over 11,000 Avdeevo objects were discovered at this single site, including Woman/Goddess figures and fragments;[59] jewelry;[60] diadems, an ornamental headband;[61] bracelets;[62] beads and decorated points. There are needles, decorated needle-cases, spoons, and spatulas. Beads were made from sectioned teeth of wolf and polar fox and from long bones of petite animals.[63]

The Avdeevo inventory contains a series of utilitarian objects fashioned with anthropomorphic or zoomorphic 'heads,' shaped limbs, and sub-triangular pieces. These art pieces and tools reflect schematic and realistic depictions of animals and females.[64]

Why Portable Art of ♀?

Why did Stone Age people create so many Woman/Goddess statuettes? The Woman/Goddess carvings do not leave us any clear message, and their precise meanings and significance are open to debate. All the same, the figures were not merely inanimate, passive artifacts, and probably had more value than use as toys. As one researcher points out, "a society's iconography certainly bears some relation to its ideology."[65]

More specifically, Marshack claims each Woman/Goddess carving "was clearly richly and elaborately clothed in inference and meaning. She wore the fabric of her culture. She was, in fact, a referential library and a multivalent, multipurpose symbol."[66]

The Woman/Goddess images served complex purposes that varied over time and place. Each Woman/Goddess statuette was an object that played an active social role in human clans. These unique icons were invested with powerful symbolic attributes which cannot be fully ascertained.[67] Quite possibly, they reflected various aspects of gynecological cultures.

The Woman/Goddess figures were part of a wide array of female-centered stories, imagery, and symbols, including vulvas, downward-pointing triangles, caves, concentric ovals, spiral patterns, sea shells, and fruits. For instance, researchers in France uncovered rock engravings of vulvas dated to 30,000 BP. Vulvas and the spread legs of a Woman/Goddess could indicate womb and vagina worship.[68]

Some archaeologists speculate that the Woman/Goddess figures were emblems of security and success. A female icon with excess weight could have symbolized a yearning for plenty and safety. It might also represent health and fertility, which could ensure the ability to produce strong children, thus guaranteeing the survival of the clan.

The Woman/Goddess figures could easily have served a ritual or symbolic function and used in a social context, like singing and learning. They were mostly uncovered in settlement contexts, both in open-air sites and caves. Discoveries in burial contexts are rare.

The figures might have been part of an ancestors' cult. Ancestor images in various forms exist all over the Earth and are central aspects of traditional societies.[69] The Woman/Goddess statuettes could represent real and mythological female ancestors. The 40,000-year history of the phenomena in art suggests that Woman/Goddess figures were vital to modern human material cultures. And, it points to the existence and persistence of symbolism, rites, and myths centered around human egg-producers.

Helen Benigni argues that the consistency in design of these featureless, large-breasted, often pregnant figures throughout a vast region and over a broad interval suggests they represent an archetype of a female Supreme Creator.[70] New Stone Age, Bronze Age, and Iron Age people likely connected 'female-as-creator' to the rhythm of nature since the young-bearing sex gave birth and their menstrual intervals aligned with lunar cycles and tides.[71]

Gamble noted the unusual similarity in the shapes of figures, even those found in widely distant parts of Europe. He suggested that when groups of Paleolithic gatherer-'hunters' occasionally met up and interacted, the statues of egg-producers and other objects signaled whether a clan was friendly and acceptable for interaction and, probably, for mating.[72]

The Woman/Goddess figures could likewise be a female representation of nature or an Earth-based deity. They may be part of an Earth Goddess theology that combined human female sexuality, motherhood, fertility and the birth of humanity as a whole.[73] Marija Gimbutas ascertained that the statuettes were representations of "the Great Mother Goddess who personifies the eternally renewing cycle of life in all of its forms and manifestations."[74]

There was direct continuity between the Stone Age figurines and later examples of Goddess depictions in the Neolithic and Bronze Age. The worshiping of the Great Mother has been continually practiced into the present as evident in contemporary devotion to Mother Kali, Virgin Mary, Quan Yin, Gaia, and other Great Mothers.

Three fundamental premises could be inferred from the numerous Woman/Goddess figures recovered so far. The first is the notion that female beings are the source of magical and religious powers. The second is the idea that these abilities originate exclusively in the egg-producing sex. And third, the thousands of realistic representations of ovary beings of all ages and sizes, collectively demonstrate that female objectification and body shaming were certainly not part of prehistoric cultures.

Goddess of Mothers

Possibly, prehistoric Woman/Goddess figures were regarded as genius-spirits and used to protect people's houses and territories. As such, the carvings were representations of the abodes of spirits whose function was to help and protect human and nonhuman animals. Maybe, the icons were conceived as Mothers or rulers of the animals, and Goddesses of the underworld.

Interestingly, McDermott argued that the objects' perspective was that of a pregnant woman looking down at her body. The young-bearing artists created Woman/Goddess figurines with broad breasts and bellies as symbols of their motherhood. If pregnant women sculpted the icons, then females were artists in control of their representation.[75] Closely related to this idea is the contention that Upper Paleolithic women employed these female-centered artifacts for obstetrical purposes.[76] But, they could have used the real living bodies in their midst as well.

Maybe the idols were part of birthing preparation by prospective mothers themselves, one that included positive reformations and guided imagery similar to current Lamaze childbirth exercises. They could also have used as part of the work of mid-wives, doulas, and birth companions. Whether it was a woman individually known or a more publicly acclaimed Goddess, the symbols might have been endowed with spiritual potency and powers for young-bearing worshipers.[77]

Possibly, the carvings were viewed as an extension of the physical body of the Mother Goddess. As such, by coming into contact with the icon, touching it, looking at it, or even making a mental picture of it, girls and women could actually be making contact with her. In this framing, the statuette opened a channel of communication whereby the Goddess' own creative forces could pass into the body of a pregnant young-bearer.

Conclusion

Did figurative art help human egg-producers and the entire species to evolve more expansive and intricate brains? If so, visual art could likewise have aided in the formation of language, myths, and Goddess theology. One interesting aspect of Stone Age human and nonhuman representations is their realism and similarity. The similarity may indicate gynecological equality between humans, nature, and other-than-human animals.

Does the lack of Paleolithic phallic imagery prove the existence of gynocentrism and the success of the first-domestication with women's restraining of men? Not surprisingly, in later patriarchal cultures, male-centered representations far outnumber those of females.

In direct contrast to the early Egyptians, the ancient Greeks viewed the Earth as female and the sky as male. This reduced framing of the 'lowly' Earth and Woman/Goddess became embedded in western language and science which derived from Greek roots.[78] The next chapter exposes the myth of prehistoric female passivity by examining egg-producers' enormous influence over the selection of mating partners. It also surveys the fourth taming, that of wolves.

(Figure 9: Symbols of vulvas engraving in La Ferrassie c. 35,000 BP)

9: Paleo Sex Choice

The first salvific moment for any woman comes when she perceives the reality of her "original sin," that is, internalization of blame and guilt... The phallocratic categorizations of "good" and "evil" no longer apply when women honor women, when we become honorable to ourselves.
- Mary Daly

ASIA's Journey 2121.09

At day-break, the women pack up camp and fill dirt back into the trench. They have to get underway to take advantage of the morning shade, but choose to linger for news about their missing children. They eventually leave, and by mid-morning it is 124°F (51°C) with a humidity of 75 percent. At a rest stop, the crones tie a sand-colored sheet on some tall shrubs, and ASIA sits underneath for cover.

The cook, Waynoka, makes a delicious brunch salad with the cactus, acorn, sage, nuts, and other edible plants the children gathered. She crushed the berries and made a smoothie for everyone to enjoy. While the others eat, Hehewuti and Zola dig up wild onions and edible roots for Waynoka to use for dinner. If everything goes well, they may have enough food to last until they reach the safe house.

ASIA is somber as they eat. With the boys' absence, and now two missing girls, the group is much smaller. Nakeisha informed the crones and women about Alex and Roshi's betrayal, but she did not have the heart to tell the children about their brothers.

Zemora stands up and announces, "We will get to the next safe house by the end of tomorrow." The girls and women are encouraged as they wait for Jean to return with the dogs.

Earlier, Jean and Lian gave items from Nadie's and Sabra's backpacks to the dogs to smell, and headed off towards the stream bed.

The dogs are excited, and the women have to slow them down to keep them from overheating. They get to the spot where the children got separated a few hours before and inspect their surroundings. One of the dogs pick up a scent, and rush off to the right. After 10 minutes the dogs found Nadie and Sabra hiding behind a bush. Bruised and scared, the two children are overjoyed to see Jean and Lian.

Sabra drinks from the water bottle Lian gives her. She hugs the dogs and smiles as she stares at Lian. "We knew you would come."

Lian brushes the dust off of Sabra and asks, "What happened?"

Sabra looks at Nadie. "We stayed together and got lost. We decided to remain here and hide. We knew you would come for us, so we started collecting berries."

Nadie beams, "And now we have two full bags." Nadie is never without her hand-made, string bags, which she uses to gather edible leaves and fruit she finds along the way. Lian and Jean laughs. The women, girls, and canines are cheerful as they head back to the group.

Introduction

The Darwinian view of survival of the fittest has created a myth of the evolutionary value of phallic aggression and violence. Alternately, it reinforces the notion of female passivity and women as subjugated victims of male rivalry. This masculinist perspective is contradictory since Stone Age clans could not be protected by sperm-producers who were always out hunting or fending off the competition.

There were certainly times when woman-the-gatherer had to defend themselves and their children against predators while foraging or resting in a camp. The defensive maternal instincts of the young-bearing sex are a compelling part of their survival skills and abolishes any illusion of female passivity.

Like the previous one, this seventh chapter of Part II on Stone Age women centers on the feminist and biology themes. The section starts off by examining a misogynist question - are men 'driven' to rape? A feminist critique of Darwinism and its evolutionary bias on female submissiveness comes next.

The magnitude of egg-producers' choice in sex selection follows, and a brief look at unrestrained or so-called 'wild' ovary beings comes after. The value of medicine women to their communities is subsequently examined, and the chapter wraps up with a survey of the fourth adaptation, that of wolves to dogs.

Are ♂ 'Driven' to Rape?

Drawing on the primatology of his day, Darwin[1] assumed that primeval man was a sexual predator who jealously guarded his hard-won harem of young-bearers to the exclusion of his rivals.[2] No doubt contemporary sperm-producers are extremely violent, but this does not prove that they always were.[3] Evolutionary psychologists have put forward poorly conceived adaptive explanations for everything from female orgasms to same-sex preferences.

Adaptive theorists denies that animals could have any kind of subjective experience and insists that sexual selection is just another form of natural selection. Even so, Prum's study of manakins shows that each of the 54 species of this South American bird has its own combination of costumes, calls, and choreography, which males use in their mating displays. Each one of the bird's extraordinary variations cannot be equally adaptive.[4]

Sexual autonomy is an evolutionary engine of beauty, and Prum argues that by choosing what they like, independent female manakins transform both the form and the objects of their desires. Male manakin songs, ornaments, and dances evolve not because they signal good genes but because animals just like them. And female choice is arbitrary, not adaptive.

According to Prum, beauty "is a self-organizing process, by which selection will arrive at some standard of beauty all by itself, in the absence of any adaptive benefit—or, indeed, despite maladaptive disadvantage." The manakins is a great example of "aesthetic radiation," where a group of animals evolved "54 distinctive ideals of beauty." Prum is not the only proponent of aesthetics over adaption.

In *The Descent of Man*, Darwin discussed female choice and portrayed them as agents of their own evolution. He argued that their preferences were a powerful force behind nature's diversity. These ideas were rejected by Darwin's contemporaries as the notion of female animals making fine-grained choices was absurd to the Victorian patriarchy.[5]

Darwin's sexual selection theory remains static though, with its singular focus on mating. Fitness is the product of fertility and probability of survival, and evolution depends on this overall measure of reproductive success. Mating is one element of fitness, but a preoccupation with "mating success" has led to an emphasis in paleo-biology on mating, to the exclusion of other components of fitness, such as environmental variations favoring different traits.

Biologist Joan Roughgarden suggests emphasizing the mating act alone is simply not supported by real female choices. Sex selection for the young-bearing is more concerned with the totality of reproduction, including the growth and protection of the young.[6]

Some of Darwin's supporters even contend that our phallic ancestors increased their reproductive success by mating with unwilling partners. And the brain-wiring that led them to rape got passed on to their male descendants.[7] This framing is sexist since it assumes that sperm-producers have no control over their sexual drive, and are therefore innocent in the act of raping.[8]

Maybe, the first restraining of phallic violence by woman-the-gatherer meant that rape was unthinkable for the vast majority of sperm-producers throughout the Stone Age. The 'man-the-rapist' thesis ignores the influence of socialized practices and ongoing evolution.[9] Compared to our closest ape relatives, human sex is much longer, involves a variety of positions, and is not tied to fertility cycles. And unlike males, female orgasm is not necessary for actual procreation.

Prum argues that the female orgasm "may be the greatest testament to the power of aesthetic evolution. It's sexual pleasure for its own sake, which has evolved purely as a consequence of women's pursuit of pleasure." Rather than rape, Stone Age men may have been consensual romantics. Women preferred to have sex with men who stimulated their own sexual pleasure, and this may have led to co-evolution between female desire and male behaviors that met those desires.

Fitness and behavior are not set in stone, and as Marlene Zuk shows, evolution could occur speedily in humans. For instance, blue eyes in humans only arose around 6,000 to 10,000 years ago. Another example is the rapid selection of the CCR5-D gene variant which makes some people immune to HIV.[10] Most ethnic Tibetans have adaptations to deal with the lower oxygen levels at high altitudes. And Africans and Europeans have evolved, independently, the same adaptation to digest milk during the past 7,500 years.[11]

Feminist Critique of Darwin

Evolutionary biologists Patricia Gowaty suggests that instead of the static Darwinian male-model, there are dynamic, multilevel selective pressures affecting natural and sexual selection of social response and physical evolution. These include genes, environments, culture, learning, and development.[12]

Gowaty and other researchers show that pistillates and staminates are equal forces in evolution. It is individuals, not sexes, who are flexible, changing their response to enhance their fitness, including their "sex role" behavior, moment-to-moment as they experience changes in their ecological and social environments. Both sexes make decisions that improve their lifetime fitness, depending on the amount of time they have for reproduction and mating.

Some researchers contend that the emergence of human self-consciousness is due to an extensive sexual selection process, termed "emotional selection." The mechanisms of natural and sexual selection developed by Darwin are not sufficient to explain the sense of self.

In addition to sex, communication, and the cognitive processes required to support language functions, add complexity to the human experience. The emotional selection theory bridges the gap between animal sexual behavior and human erotic love,[13] and place females at the forefront in the growth of emotional intelligence and communication.

Curiously, Arian Wallach's study of the life cycles of more than a hundred species of mammalian carnivores found that apex predators are distinguishable by a capacity to limit their population densities. Among big carnivores, female self-regulation in sex-selection could ensure that dominant species do not over-exploit their resources. And the expression of traits that contribute to self-regulation, such as reproductive suppression, depends on social stability.[14]

So what happens when egg-producers' choice in sex-selection and reproduction are reduced and eliminated among Earth's apex predator? Contemporary religious and political restrictions of female reproductive rights are the principal causes behind human over-population and ecological overreach.

♀ Choice in Sex Selection

There are considerable sexual pressures for females and males in choosing who to mate with. But even after sex, the battle continues, especially if females mate with many males. This forces the sperm from different males to compete with one another for fertilization rights.

Penises are basically tubes to get sperm near eggs, but female genitals are not simple cavities. Female genitalia might change shape to interact with male organs, contract to improve or reduce the odds of insemination, or release floods of hormones to control the release of eggs or storage of sperm.[15]

There are also females with 'penises' or gynosome, for instance the Neotrogla curvata insect which lives in Brazilian caves. There are four Neotrogla species and the females all have a gynosome. During sexual bouts that can last for 40 to 70 hours, the female penetrates the male and uses her genitals not to deliver sperm, but to collect it along with nutrients.

Pistillates in other mites and beetles also have a protruding organ that collects sperm. Egg-producers can compete for males and be sexually coercive. Some female spiders are very aggressive and 75 percent of them will kill the males during sex.

Patricia Gowaty suggests that members of the egg-producing sex are potent selective forces, whether they 'feel' it or not. She points out that variation in young-bearers' abilities to remain in control of their reproductive decisions is critical to the evolutionary play between females and males across species.

Gowaty argues that critical individual, family, and community prospects are under ovary beings' control of reproductive "decisions" and women's reproductive autonomy. These include the relative mating success of sperm-producers, the fertility of young-bearers, the viability of offspring, the within-population variance in offspring viability, and the actual reproductive rate of the population.

Gowaty's reproductive compensation hypothesis emphasizes that procreative competition is not just between constrained and free individuals, but also among limited individuals who do and do not compensate with greater care of offspring.[16] This means that machismo does not guaranteed biological success since infant maintenance is a critical evolutionary component. Female-centered community care improved the fitness of individual females far more than mating with dominant sperm-producers.

Building upon French sociologist Pierre Bourdieu's concepts of economic, cultural and social capital,[17] sociologist Catherine Hakim defines sexual asset or erotic capital as the social value an individual or group accrues, as a result of their sexual attractiveness.[18] Sexual value could be related to both physical and mental health.

Erotic worth is related to class and is increasingly influential in affluent, modern societies. Egg-producers generally have more erotic capital than sperm-producers, and that erotic value has social benefits and privileges that benefit the young-bearing sex.

As with other forms of capital, sexual asset is convertible and may be useful in acquiring other types of worth, including social and economic resources. For example, actors parlay sexual value into financial worth or social influence. Likewise, attractive employees get raises and social connections from bringing in more customers by virtue of their looks.[19]

Sexual capital is also closely associated with race or racial stereotypes of sexual attractiveness.[20] For example, Susan Koshy argues that Asian women have gained sexual value in the west through glamorous accounts of western male and Asian female sexual relationships in the media and arts.[21]

Unrestrained ♀

Stone Age egg-producing humans were physically tough, mentally fierce, and courageous. They carried a formidable digging stick, and probably practiced forms of self-defense. From their first domestication, hominin females' creativity, resourcefulness, and solidarity developed as part of their survival skills, and they continue to do so.

Human ovary beings are unrestrained by nature, having survived millions of years in nature. Paleo-females lived and traveled under harsh environmental conditions, and endured numerous climatic changes in resource-poor areas. They not only managed to survive, but they thrived by successfully reproducing and taking care of children and families.

In Women Who Run With the Wolves, Clarissa Pinkola Estes notes that there are similar reputations contained in myths about wolves and coyotes, and about 'wildish' women. Both are wrongfully portrayed as "ungracious, wholly and innately dangerous... devouring and devious," and as "overly aggressive."[22]

In contrast to this misrepresentation, Pinkola Estes writes, "Healthy wolves and healthy women share certain psychic characteristics: keen sensing, playful spirit, and a heightened capacity for devotion. Wolves and women are relational by nature, inquiring, possessed of great endurance and strength." She continued, "They are deeply intuitive, intensely concerned with their young, their mates, and their pack."

Pinkola Estes notes that across all cultures, members of the egg-producing sex intuitively understand the words 'wild' and 'woman.' These words are part of an old memory "of our absolute, undeniable, and irrevocable kinship with the wild feminine." She does not use the word 'wild' in the modern pejorative sense, meaning out of control. Rather the author employs the term to mean 'to live a natural life.' The word represents a wise and knowing nature.[23]

Pinkola Estes suggests, "It is into this fundamental, elemental, and essential relationship that we are born and that in our essence we are also derived from. The Wild Woman archetype sheaths the alpha matrilineal being." According to the author, prehistory was female-centered and respect for nature is the 'natural' state for untamed girls and women.

Even so, after millennia of phallic domination, the author admits that the connection to the Wild Woman "may have become ghostly from neglect, buried by over-domestication, outlawed by the surrounding culture, or no longer understood anymore."

Nevertheless, the myth of the Wild Woman lives on in many cultures. In Spanish, she is called La Loba, the Wolf Woman; in Hungarian, she is Rozsomak, the wolverine; in Japanese, the untamed woman is Amaterasu Omikami, the one who brings light and all consciousness; in Tibet, she is called Dakini, the dancing force that produces clear-seeing in females.

Medicine ♀

In prehistoric times, young-bearers were the ultimate expression of Life and their value increased with age. Along with their high status in gynecological clans, crones were the herbalists, healers, shamans, and priestesses. Women were the doctors and anatomists of the Stone Age, the abortionists, nurses, and counselors.[24]

Egg-producing healers were the first pharmacists and medical schools, cultivating healing herbs and exchanging the secrets of their uses. Medicine women were the doulas and midwives, traveling from home to home, and clan to clan, to help other women. And they still do. Lakshmikutty, a 75-year-old Douala and herbalist in South Asia, can prepare 500 medicines from memory.[25]

Medicinal knowledge was essential for survival in the Stone Age. Cuts, bruises, and breakages of bone, without plant antiseptics, proper facilities, or knowledge of germs, could become severe if infected.[26] Shamans probably experimented with plant-based pain-relievers to help with injury, tooth pain, arthritis, kidney stones, and so on.[27]

Gathering and dispensing of herbal plant materials was in most cultures handled by women, who prepared food and healing potions as herbalists.[28] The effects of different plant and Earth materials were found through trial and error and by observing their use by other animals.[29]

Female healers probably utilized hallucinogenic plants as part of various treatments, for example, as a pain-reliever and aid during birthing. Medicine women may have had remedies for pre-menstrual syndrome, with all its characteristics of cramps, pain, depression and headaches. Woman herbalists may have had different contraceptives and gynecological practices. Their role as mid-wife was vital since many mothers died in childbirth.

An abortifacient is a substance that induces abortion. Ancient and contemporary medicine women use many kinds of natural abortifacients, including bitter melon, wild carrot, blue cohosh, pennyroyal, nutmeg, mugwort, slippery elm, papaya, vervain, common rue, ergot, saffron, tansy, and pomegranate.[30]

Female herbalists and Goddess figures were known as the greatest traditional healers in the myths of many cultures across the Globe.[31] For example, Isis in Egypt, Pa Sini Jobu in Mali, Medea of Greece, Ilmatar of Finland, Teteke of China, Bari Gongju of Korea, and Yeshe Tsogyel of Tibet.[32]

Transferring vast amounts of botanical and traditional healing knowledge orally over millennia was challenging, and Goddess rituals helped to reproduce herbal expertise specific to different regions. Most shaman ceremonies, like those practiced by Deer Goddess cultures of northern Europe, were administered by women only.[33]

Priestesses of the Deer Goddess wore horned headdresses and antlers. Intriguingly, the ceremonial clothing worn by women healers of Siberia and Lapland is similar to that adopted by the Santa figure - green and white with a red pointed hat, curled toed boots, reindeer mittens, fur lining, and trim.

4th Taming: Wolves

The most popular form of inter-species bonding, in the past and present, occurs between humans and dogs. Currently, there are between 700 million to one billion domestic dogs, making them the most abundant member of the order Carnivora.

The adoption of Canis lupus familiaris, commonly known as "man's best friend," was a long process. The taming occurred long after fire and fire-farming, as genetics suggests that wolves and dogs split into different species around 40,000 years ago.[34] This fourth modification most likely started in Asia, but Europeans had dogs by 30,000 BP.[35]

In a well-researched series of historical novels, Jean Auel wrote that Stone Age women used scraps of food to tame wolves.[36] But maybe, wolves tamed themselves, and those who carried genes to be less afraid of hominins had an evolutionary advantage. Over time, a wolf population grew that was more docile and comfortable co-existing with people.

Intriguingly, according to Shipman, dogs may have changed human appearances as well, for example, the whites of our eyes. The wolf possesses white sclera as does Homo sapiens, and crucially, we are the only primate that has them.[37]

The main advantage of having white sclera is that it is very easy to work out where another person is gazing. It provides a very useful form of non-verbal messaging, and dogs and people would have been able to communicate silently and efficiently.

Dogs' fierce defense of territory were put-upon in attacks by carnivores and other sapiens. They were vital to mothers in the protection of little children. Canines' robust sense of smell could be used to assist in finding a missing child, water, and other resources. Dogs were also put to use as pack animals. For example, they were critical for the migration into North America, around 12,000 BP.[38]

A female dog, or 'Bitch,' was prized for her strength, fertility, and utility. Curiously, this ancient, powerful term 'Bitch' is the divine archetype behind the contemporary derogatory term for human egg-producers. Jane Caputi argues that this reversal of meaning reflects men's fear of the 'bitch Goddess,' as well as the sexually sovereign, creative, and autonomous power of human ovary beings.[39]

After proto-dogs were restrained, they became companions and were buried with humans.[40] A burial site in Germany has joint human and dog bones dated to 14,000 BP. By the New Stone Age, in some cases, dogs were awarded "person-hood" and treated as equal to humans.[41] Protective figurines of dogs were often deposited in the foundations of buildings.

After interactions like petting, play and talking, many studies find increases in beta-endorphin, oxytocin, and dopamine, neurochemicals associated with positive feelings and bonding, in both dogs and people. The dog-to-owner gaze probably evolved as a form of inter-species, social communication.[42]

Conclusion

This chapter expanded on the nature-nurture process. As an apex species, female reproductive choices are essential. The extent of egg-producers' choice in sex selection and reproduction determines the long-term survival of the species.

Men are not natural rapist, but rather socialized masculinity is responsible for the vast majority of phallic violence. Although ten millennia of violent conditioning could have some effect on genetics, evolution is flexible and sperm-producers can deconstruct and negate this heritage.

The next chapter broadens the nature-nurture debate on phallic violence during prehistory. Among other issues, it considers whether males have inferior brains and if men were responsible for the sudden extinction of many giant mammals around 30,000 to 10,000 BP.

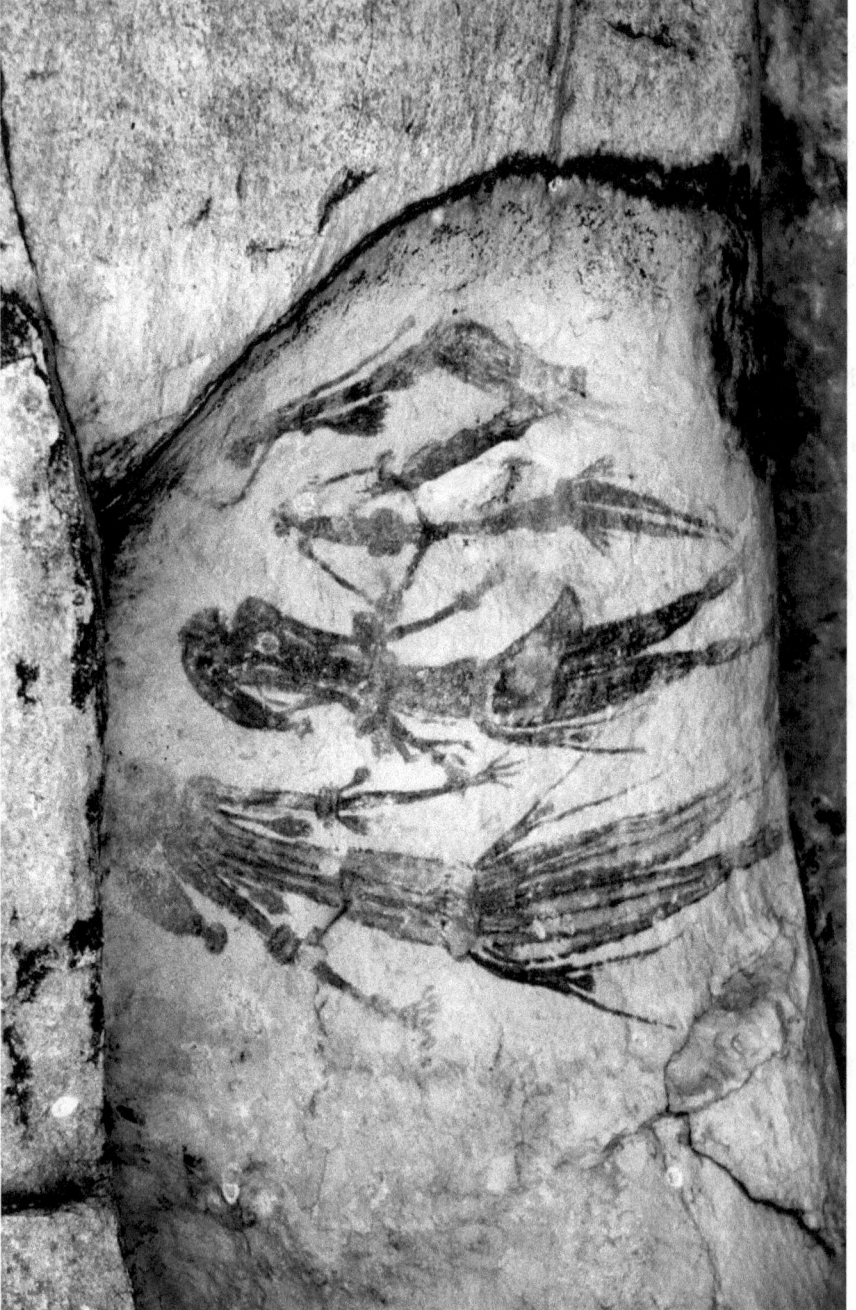

(Figure 10: Aboriginal Bradshaw rock paintings, c. 20,000 BP)

10: Man-the-Killer?

The method of liberation-castration-exorcism, then is a becoming process of "the Other" - women - in which we hear and speak our own words. - Mary Daly

ASIA's Journey 2121.10

The sand is white hot, and the ground bakes in the 123°F (50°C) temperature. It is 10 AM and the humidity is 70 percent and raising. If they keep walking, ASIA could reach the safe house by evening, but they have to be extra cautious of heat exhaustion today. Everyone is excited with an extra bit of energy in their step.

Cha'Kwaina glances over to Nadie. "It would be great to be staying in a home for a few nights," she says.

Nadie manages a faint smile, "We used to live in a house..."

As they walk, the girls plan long baths and ways to unknot their hair. The women too long for a bath, but are more excited talking about vegetables, soup, and fruit-flavored drinks.

Xóchitl notices a dust cloud in the far west moving fast towards ASIA. The wind is blowing the opposite direction, though. The dust appears to be coming from the ground, like a small tornado.

Xóchitl makes a high-pitch owl alarm. "It a gang. We have to find someplace to hide, quickly." She scans the surrounding hills.

Nadie spots a shadow on the left, behind a wide boulder. "How about over there?" She points to the spot. Xóchitl keeps scanning. The dust cloud gets closer, and now appears to be two separate plumes. Lian starts hiking up to the rock and says, "Alright, let's move it, ladies."

ASIA scrambles up the hillside. Xóchitl sweeps the ground behind them with a dried branch to cover their tracks. They hide behind the massive stone, as the security team takes up positions on opposite sides.

Two dust clouds approaches below. A wagon appears out of the first plume, pulled by four horses. Behind the wagon, a group of ten pedophile riders emerges out of the second plume. The pedo-hunters are in hot pursuit of the wheeled vehicle steered by a teenage girl. Screams of females inside the cart pierce the dry air.

Zemora whispers to Jean. "Maybe they are escaping from a brothel."

Jean grabs Zemora's arm, "Shouldn't we try to help them?" Zamora stares at the crones who are silent. Zola shakes here head and no one says anything. They could not risk placing their children in danger.

The girls shriek for help in the wagon racing pass them below. The pedophile hunters howl in excitement, enjoying the chase. The horses are exhausted and seem ready to drop from the heat. The pursuit heads off to the east, and the dust plume soon disappears.

"Don't be scared, children. We're almost there," Hehewuti says to encourage everyone. "We'll make it to safety later today." The children are aghast and move slowly out from their hiding place. The screams of the girls in the wagon still rung in their ears.

Introduction

Paleolithic sperm-producers may not have been genetically programmed to rape, but were they demonic in other ways, for example in causing genocides and mass extinctions? Was phallic rivalry, conflict, and murder a constant part of the Stone Age experience? Or did female-centered clans find a way to mitigate men's propensity for violence and inter-clan warfare?

These questions are intriguing to explore since the answers could help lead us out of the current appalling state of affairs. This eight chapter of Part II on Stone Age humans concentrates on biology and feminist themes and continues the discussion on Paleo males' violence. The chapter begins by examining the notion that men are 'demonic,' biologically programmed for violence.

The chapter proceeds with a critique of the prevalent view that male hunters were responsible for megafauna extinction starting 50,000 years ago. It next surveys the lack of evidence for warfare during the Stone Age. In contrast to the restraining of Paleolithic masculinity, the chapter then jumps ahead to explore examples of cyborg genocides in the Bronze Age.

Once the biological sex of the fetus is determined, the process of becoming a biological female start. The biology of sexual differentiation is next explored, and then, whether males have inferior brains is analyzed. The chapter concludes with a brief look at socialized gene expression or how experiences can change our bodies and genes.

Sexual Differentiation

Since ancient times, people have believed that the sex of an infant is determined by how much heat a man's sperm had during insemination. In addition to this fallacy, socialization of the sexes into genders, as well as gender identification, are often confused with the physical process of divergence into pistillate and staminate from an undifferentiated zygote. As discussed earlier, initial sex-determination and virilization, or sexual modification, are influenced by androgens.[1]

As females and males grow into fetuses, infants, children, adolescents, and adults, sexual distinctness at many levels emerge in genes, chromosomes, gonads, hormones, anatomy, and psyche. Sex-dichotomous attributes are alterations which are characteristic of one sex only. For example, sex-specific genital organs such as ovaries and a uterus.

With some sex-based variance, such as stature and behaviors, there is much overlap between female and male populations. And, sex-dichotomous deviations are not absolute. The differentiation of parts of the body other than the sex organ creates secondary sex characteristics. In humans, visible secondary sex characteristics include prominent breasts in females, and facial hair and Adam's apple on males.

Sexual differentiation may be induced by specific genes, by hormones, by anatomy, or by social learning. Some of the divergences are entirely physical, like the presence of a uterus. And some deviations are part of social learning and custom, for example, relative hair length. Many variations, such as gender identity, are influenced by both biological and social factors.

Sexual determination includes brain differentiation. In most animals, fluctuations in exposure of a fetal or infant brain to sex hormones produce fundamental divergences in brain structure and function which correlate with adult reproductive behavior.[2]

Demonic Males?

In cultural anthropology, Smith and others contend that all humans are naturally violent, just like our primate cousin, the chimpanzee.[3] Pan troglodytes are very violent and male-dominated. A chimp has more chance of being killed by another pan than by anything else. Egg-producing chimpanzees are usually beaten by every adolescent male making his way up through the ranks. Females are raped and infants are sometimes killed.[4]

Like Pan troglodytes, phallic humans batter ovary beings into submission, commit rape, and kill females in infanticide and femicide. Men commit murder 11 times more often than women. The frequency and similarity of violence between human sperm-producers and male chimps raises many questions.

Did our species survive because men were natural-born killers? Was it inherent men's violence that led H. sapiens to out-compete and dominate all other primates and hominins?[5] Is aggression a built-in part of human phallic behavior?[6] Were other hominin men as violent as H. sapiens males?[7]

Among bonobos, there is more sharing of food and a break from the 'baboon' dominance model of social interaction. Instead of alpha males, a group of females tends to play a central role in holding the troop together. This indicates that culture and egg-producers' influence can actually regulate phallic violence in primates. And possibly, hominin gynocentric cultures accomplished the restraining of men throughout the Stone Age.

When levels of intra-male conflict are high, nursing mothers have to divert scarce energy and resources away from direct offspring care into fighting off harassment and guarding against infanticide. A hominin population whose young-bearing had to cope with such behavior might head toward extinction, even as a minority of its sperm-producers achieved short-term reproductive success.

While the demonic phallic argument applies generally to the post-Stone Age, there is scant evidence of a hyper-masculine struggle for supremacy before this era. For example, prehistoric war scenes are unknown, and the wounded warrior theme is rare in African and Eurasian Paleolithic art. This suggests that Stone Age weapons were made for the purpose of defense against predators, not for hostility.[8]

In Mas d'Azil cave in France, there is an exceptional pair of images of a man who confronts a bear. The images are etched on a fragmented, 30 inch (78 mm) by 15 inch (37 mm) bone disk dated to 16,000 BP, with an engraving on each side.[9] This disk may have represented a Paleolithic worldview regarding hyper-masculinity and male-dominance.

On one side of the disk, a human with an erect penis confronts a bear, with a thick stick over his shoulder. On the opposite surface, the sperm-producer is struck down by the bear and is shown lying face down. Uniquely, there is no other Paleolithic representation of a male in such a position. This art indicates that there are limits to human phallic force and that the power of nature can be dangerous to provoke.

Megafauna Extinction

Megafauna, or giant animals, have been continuously abundant in almost all of the landscapes and seascapes on Earth for hundreds of millions of years. They survived through multiple glacial transitions and other periods of serious climate change. Hominids and hominins evolved and dispersed in a world teeming with behemoth creatures.

Humans' earliest art forms, such as the female cave paintings of Lascaux and Altamira, show that megafauna had a profound impact on the psyche and spirituality of our ancestors. Then, mainly in the last 50,000 years, there has been a rapid decrease in giant animal abundance and diversity.[10] Was this defaunation part of the Anthropocene?[11]

H. sapiens sapiens emerged from Africa over 70,000 years BP, traveled across Asia, and reached Australia by 50,000 BP, a time that coincides with a wave of extinctions of creatures there. And, as human language groups spread across North America 15,000 years ago, animals that survived elsewhere, including horses and camels, became extinct.[12]

In 1973, Martin suggested that within a few hundred years of their arrival, fast-moving bands of hunters eliminated the megafauna by overkill.[13] Other have suggested hominin fire farming as a contributing factor. Does the extinction of megafauna reveal a propensity for male violence and lack of foresight? With plenty of other food sources available, was megafauna extinction due in part to machismo trophy hunting, like shooting elephants?

Interestingly, significant megafauna extinctions did not occur in Africa, where hominins existed for millions of years, and there were few extinctions in Eurasia where the supposedly hyper-carnivore Neanderthals lived for hundreds of thousands of years. Humans started spreading across the Americas nearly 15,000 years ago, yet many megafauna species in South America disappeared only around 12,280 BP, 1,000 to 3,000 years after human colonization.[14]

The giant animals were surviving in the presence of humans for 3,000 years, but when the climate rapidly warmed, they died off within 300 years. Camels, for example, resilient survivors of the last ice age, suffered massive losses in genetic diversity.[15]

Since none of the earlier migrations of hominins resulted in extinctions, it is unclear whether H. sapiens sapiens were involved in eradicating dozens of species of giant animals starting 50,000 years ago. A major criticism of the "overkill" theory is that it is implausible for a relatively small number of humans to selectively kill off millions of large-bodied mammals.[16]

The extinction of giants may represent a long-term trend in "trophic downgrading" or downsizing of Earth's animals.[17] In some areas, extinction may have been due to physical characteristics, climate, and vegetation change such as loss of northern grasslands. The massive size of megafauna may have contributed to their extinction. The largest species live near the boundary of energy constraints, and any shift in food supply could drive these species to extinction.[18]

Megafauna extinction has had wide-ranging environmental effects and cascading ecological impacts across the Globe, including climate change.[19] The loss of keystone herbivores may have triggered waves of extinctions through ensuing vegetation change, changing fire regimes, and the loss of a prey base for mega carnivores.

Paleo Wars?

Is war innate, an adaptation bred into our ancestors by natural selection.[20] Evidence for man-the-warrior is weak[21] since skeletal and artifacts of inter-group violence between Paleolithic nomadic foragers are absent.[22] Of the many cave paintings of the Upper Paleolithic, none depict people attacking other people.[23]

Throughout the Stone Age, the population density of primeval societies of H. erectus and H. sapiens was probably low enough to avoid armed conflict.[24]

And, Paleolithic 'warlessness' may have persisted until well after the appearance of Homo sapiens around 200,000 BP.

The most ancient clear-cut evidence of deadly group violence is a mass grave, estimated to be 13,000 years old, found in the Jebel Sahaba region of the Sudan, near the Nile River. Of the 59 skeletons in the grave, 24 bear marks of violence, such as hack marks and embedded stone points.

The Jebel Sahaba discovery is an exception and uncertainties remain. The bodies, which are buried in carefully made graves, could have accumulated over many decades, and may even be evidence of the murder of trespassers rather than actual battles. Nearly half of the bodies are female, who scholars generally do not believe would have played an active role in violent skirmishes. Perhaps, the violence occurred in the wake of a local ecological crisis.

Significantly, Haas and Piscitelli surveyed more than 2,900 hominin skeletons 10,000 years and older, from over 400 separate sites. Apart from Jebel Sahaba, they found that only four skeletons showed signs of violence, and further, the marks were consistent with homicide, not warfare. This "dearth of evidence," Haas writes, "is in contrast with later periods when warfare clearly appears in this historical record of specific societies and is marked by skeletal markers of violence, weapons of war, defensive sites and architecture, etc."[25]

Brian Ferguson's survey of early human settlements likewise concludes, "the global archaeological record contradicts the idea that war was always a feature of human existence; instead, the record shows that warfare is largely a development of the last 10,000 years."[26] Ethnographers have encountered numerous non-state peoples that had little experience with warfare.[27]

In another important study, Fry and Söderberg reexamined a cross-cultural sample of 21 mobile forager societies and found almost no evidence for large-scale conflicts or wars.[28] Instead, the majority of incidences of lethal aggression in these societies were homicides driven by a variety of factors relevant at the individual or family scale such as competition over a particular woman. Close to 96 percent of the killers were male.[29]

In ethnographic research of pre-colonial cultures, Margaret Mead found no evidence for what could be called the Malthusian theory of war, which holds that war is the inevitable consequence of competition for resources. Instead, Mead proposed that war is a cultural "invention" that can arise in any society, from the simplest to the most complex.[30]

Once it occurs, war often becomes self-perpetuating, with attacks by one group provoking reprisals and pre-emptive attacks by others. The war mindset also transforms societies and militarizes them in ways that make war more likely.

New Stone Age Genocides

In many regions of Eurasia, agrarian settlements lasted for 500 to 1,000 years without leaving signs of warfare.[31] Agriculture was only able to develop initially at locations where ambushes, battles, and raids were absent.[32] But after animal colonization, New Stone Age cultures became male-centered and war-like.[33]

Since the rise of the patriarchal State about 5,000 years ago, military activity has occurred over much of the Globe. The advent of gunpowder and the acceleration of technological advances led to modern warfare. Between 5,500 BP and the late 20th century over 14,500 wars have taken place, costing 3.5 billion lives, and leaving only 300 years of peace.[34]

As part of the Neolithic masculinity, war and genocide were normalized. Genocides are acts committed with intent to destroy, in whole or in part, a national, ethnic, racial or religious group. Genocide is different from gendercide, in which males are killed but children, particularly girls, and women are incorporated into the conquering group.

Instances of cyborg gendercide include those carried out by the Assyrian Empire in the first half of the third millennium BP, and the men of Athens destruction of Melos in the 25th century BP. One of the most striking example was the Hebrews' gendercide of the Midianites in the 4th millennium BP.

Midian is in the area of present day Jordan and Saudi Arabia. The Midianites were descendants of Midian, a son of Abraham, who worshiped a multitude of gods, including the Queen of Heaven, Ashteroth. Midianite pottery dates as early as the 23rd century BP, with interesting geometric, human, and animal designs.

The Bible's Book of Numbers chapter 31, recounts a war of gendercide by god-appointed cyborg leader, Moses, who ordered the army of Jews to kill every Midianite male, and to capture the females and children as plunder. Moses's wife, Zipporah, was a Midianite, and he supposedly spent 40 years in exile with the Midianites who provided him with refuge.[35]

The Hebrews claimed that Midianite women were converting Jewish sperm-producers to their animal-based religion, and this caused the Judaic god to become upset. More likely, Bronze Age cyborgs' like Moses completely rejected Midianites' ancient, gynocentric traditions. Abrahamic cults strictly forbids the use of idols like Woman/Goddess carvings, which cleverly erase gynocentric imagery and the worship of Earth Goddesses.

The Bible states, "And the children of Israel took all the women of Midian captives, and their little ones, and took the spoil of all their cattle, and all their flocks, and all their goods. And they burnt all their cities wherein they dwelt, and all their goodly castles, with fire."

Moses later ordered that the captured Midianite women and children be killed, except for girls who 'have not slept with a man,' that is, who were not yet raped by a Jewish cyborg. The total number of Midianites killed was unrecorded, but the number of surviving girls was listed at 32,000. Moses orchestrated other massacres, and his actions against the Midianites were typical of phallic leaders at the time.

The destruction of Carthage around 2,160 BP was another genocide.[36] There are dozens of other examples of genocide and gendercide, including those by famous cyborg horsemen such as Alexander the Great, Genghis Khan, and Tamerlane.[37]

From 1500 to 1620, European cyborgs killed well over 20 million Indigenous people, up to 95 percent of the population in the Americas.[38] Then from 1600 to 1865, European cyborgs enslaved over 12.5 Africans for the Atlantic trade in humans, cotton, coffee, and sugar. Millions of Africans died in cyborgs' wars of enslavement in Africa, and along the dreaded Middle Passage to the Americas. The capture and sale of Africans by European enslavers was the largest forced migration in modern history.[39]

From 1885 to 1908, European cyborgs terminated 10 million people in the Congo. In 1932 to 1933, around 7.5 million were slaughtered in Ukraine. From 1937 to 1945, over 80 million people were put to death in Europe, and Japanese cyborgs murdered another 10 million people, including six million

Chinese.[40]

Up to three million were annihilated in Nigeria from 1967 to 1970. Pakistanis decimated another three million Bangladeshis in 1971. And, close to three million people were also extinguished in Cambodia by the USA from 1975 to 1979. Since the 1980s there were several other genocides, including the one million who perished in Rwanda in 1994.

In addition to genocide, cyborgs are committing ecocide at local and global levels. Like the man in the cave drawings of the bear in Mas d'Azil, cyborgs will find there are limits to male power, and it is dangerous to provoke the climate Goddess.

Socialized Gene Expression

Unlike the rugged individualism and accumulation promoted by patriarchal capitalism, humans are social creatures who enjoy sharing knowledge and tools. People thrive when they have meaningful community connection, which can protect against the effects of some abuse.

A sense of isolation can disrupt an individual's thinking abilities and will power. Social rejection can harm immune systems and be as damaging as obesity or smoking. There is an intense need for connection, and isolated individuals sometimes form para-social relations with pets or TV characters.[41]

Alienation may even influence the body's gene expression, which varies depending on environment and socialization.[42] There are regulatory genes that can cause whole networks of other genes to change activity in response to physical and social conditions. For example, the environment can sharply alter the activity of some genes, as happens in cancer or digestion.[43]

Socialization alters gene expression, and a cell may just be a mechanism for turning experience into biology. For instance, when European honeybees are raised among more aggressive African killer bees, they not only start to become as belligerent as their new hive mates, they come to genetically resemble them as well.

Isolation and discrimination are stressors that can cause physical changes fairly quickly. Cole's research found that whole sector of genes were markedly different in lonely people from those who feel socially secure.[44] A study of social stress levels in young women found changes in their gene activity only six months later.

Research demonstrate that the urban poor in the US are experiencing accelerated aging at the cellular level.[45] Chronic stress linked both to income level and racial-ethnic identity is driving this physiological deterioration.[46] Similarly unbalanced gene-expression or immune-response profiles were found in poor children, depressed people with cancer, and people caring for spouses dying of cancer.

For over five decades, feminists have argued that genes and brain differentiation do not determine behavior. However, as scientists are showing, socialization can influence gene expression via stress levels. Structurally rooted social processes can work through biological mechanisms to influence an individuals' health and behavior.[47]

In addition to genes, the body's chemical and electrical responses are influenced by the environment. For example, when a person lives in poverty, the limbic system is constantly sending fear and stress messages to the prefrontal cortex, which overloads its ability to solve problems, set goals, and complete tasks in the most efficient ways.[48]

These circular genetic, limbic and other processes can become intensified and entrenched over time, and work alongside structural forces that leads to inter-generational oppression, poverty and ill-health. Socialized gene expression theory indicate that humans are pliable and are not trapped into their genes. It offers hope that gynocentric culture and education can once again help to restrain phallic tendencies toward violence and ecocidal behaviors.

♂ Have Inferior Genes?

Male-centered rule has colonized humans and the entire Earth. Oil and gas wells spread from the melting Arctic to warming depths of the Gulf of Mexico. Although the effects of patriarchal domination vary according to species, sex, class, race, location, and so on, Earthlings all face the serious threat of cyborg-induced rapid global warming.

Male 'civilization' may soon dramatically reverse course. While a few economic, military and social elites benefit in the short-term, the vast majority of humans, other-than-human animals, and nature are overwhelmingly losing. Moreover, any individual or collective gain is ephemeral, vulnerable to abrupt climate change and rapid ecosystem crashes that are occurring.

Cyborg consciousness has had a profound influence on males, especially the glorification of hyper-masculine identities. If phallic violence and fatalism are part of socialized gene expression after domestication, the Neolithic male-centered experiment may be an evolutionary dead end.

Phallic supremacy leads to the illusion of invincibility, and this has resulted in environmental over-shoot and civilization collapse, time and time again. Are sperm-producers incapable of ecological learning or changing their ecocidal behavior in any significant way? As the principal beneficiaries of animal and female colonization, it is in men's interest to persist in being blind to the consequences of their disastrous exploitation, so they remain willfully ignorant to their peril.

Violent crime is overwhelmingly committed by men.[49] Of the over 15,000 homicides that occur in the US annually, 77 percent involve male victims and 23 percent ovary beings.[50] Sperm-producers were over 90 percent of the killers.[51] Why are phallic humans so savage? Have men developed inferior brains due to their nurturing of violence?

Studies show that pistillate and staminate brains are different in many species, including human animals.[52] Louann Brizendine argues that the female brain is different.[53] And, Marian Diamond's work demonstrates a relationship between sex, brain, and the environment.[54] Boys are four times as likely to be autistic, a complex disorder resulting from the combination of genetic and environmental factors.[55] This means that girls have a "female protective effect."[56] Some accumulation of mitochondrial mutations are deleterious to males only, in the so-called 'Mother's curse.'[57]

Curiously, children are more likely to inherit intelligence from the mother, because intelligence genes are located on chromosome X.[58] And since women have two X chromosomes, they are twice as likely to transmit characteristics related to intelligence.[59] It is no coincidence that mental disability is 30 percent more common in males.[60]

Boys may lag behind girls in early development and are more risk-taking. Judith Hall suggest that human ovary beings are better at verbal and nonverbal communication and at reading emotions.[61] While Lise Eliot contend that minor sex differences present at birth are magnified through socialization.[62] Cordelia Fine,[63] Leslie Brody,[64] and others also support the cultural argument in brain differentiation.[65]

Konner declares that human egg-producers are not only equal to sperm-producers, but are superior in many ways. Konner cites studies that indicate women have superiority in judgment, trustworthiness, reliability, fairness, working and playing well with others, relative freedom from distracting sexual impulses, and lower levels of prejudice, bigotry, and violence.[66]

Egg-producers live longer, have lower mortality at all ages, are more resistant to most categories of disease, and are much less likely to suffer brain disorders that lead to disruptive and even destructive behavior. And, ovary beings can produce new life from their own bodies, to which men add only a minor biological contribution.[67]

Curiously, Konner points to genetic data for recent selection of aggressive and hyper-sexual traits in sperm-producers that correlates with the time of food animal colonization. Approximately one in twelve males in Central Asia has a Y-chromosome signature consistent with descent from a single man who lived at the time of Genghis Khan. A similar pattern is found in Ireland during the Middle Ages when that island was dominated by warring tribes.

Conclusion

This chapter examined sexual difference and phallic violence. Sperm-producers' aggression was tempered during female-centered prehistory but was unleashed in the patriarchal post-Stone Age. Having power over women and animals has heightened phallic insecurity. As a cyborg, anything that you practice, that you accept, that you develop, always has behind it the element of greed - wanting to get something, wanting to reach something, wanting to break a record, to transcend death and insignificance.

The pursuit of male-defined 'accomplishment' may be personally satisfying, but you are going to be caught in the things you are practicing. Therefore, you will always be held a prisoner, and your vision will be everlastingly limited. As Mary Daly writes in Gyn/Ecology, "revolting against the tyrants of a phallotechnic world is revolting not only against their pseudonatural "life", that is, maintenance level of existence, but also against their pseudosupernatural state, against their myths and technological miracles."

The next chapter explores gynocentric Stone Age cultural practices, including the symbolism around menstruation and menstrual blood. The use of blood in post-Stone Age phallic rituals involving animal sacrifice could be related to these earlier gynocentric traditions. Human sperm-producers' rituals and culture drove the need for colonizing animals and carnism, not food insecurity. Hostility against food animals may have been one way for men to co-opt and embody female creative power.

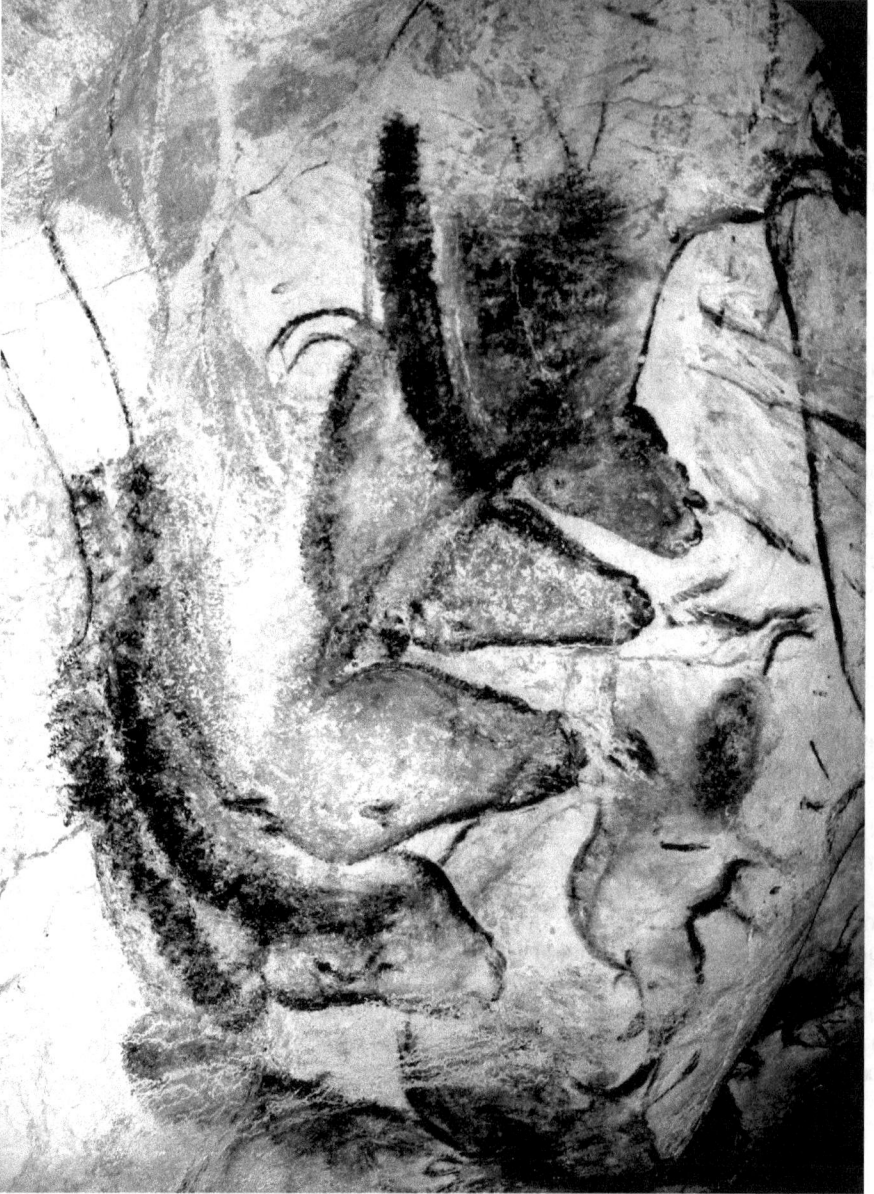

(Figure 11: Lascaux Cave Painting c. 20,000 BP)

11: Paleo-Female Culture

The method of liberation, then, involves a castrating of language and images that reflect and perpetuate the structures of a sexist world.
- Mary Daly

ASIA's Journey 2121.11

It is dark, hours after sunset, 110°F (43°C) with high humidity. ASIA stands outside the gate of a dilapidated farmhouse with a barn in the back. The safe-house looks abandoned in the light of the waxing, almost full-moon.

Nakeisha cautiously proceeds inside the gate and knocks on the door about 150 feet away. No one answers. She tries the door knob, but it is locked. "They must have left," Nakeisha shouts back.

Hehewuti motions Xóchitl over and asks, "Can you open a window and get inside?" Xóchitl nods and tip-toes around to the back of the safe-house.

Two minutes later, a candle appears inside the house, and Xóchitl emerges from the front door. "Come on in," she beams. The children race from the gate to get inside the building.

The women light several lamps, and the fire-keeper gets the fireplace started. Soon the dwelling is bright and lively, with the smell of food in the air.

Kuan-Yin notices a note taped to the inside of the front door, signed by the Separatist Sisters. She reads it to the crones. "Sorry we couldn't wait but we had errands to do. Help yourself to everything. The water barrel is full. The harvest this year of fruits, beans, and nuts are dried and stored in the basement. Fresh fruits, vegetables, and bread are in the pantry. Take as much as you need and make yourselves at home."

The cook quickly puts together a salad, bread with olive oil, and pasta with tomato sauce. Her two helpers make sandwiches with peanut butter and fruit jelly for dessert. Sitting around a rectangular dining table, the women and children eat and drink in a haste.

Chomping on a bowl of salad, Kuan-Yin asks Hehewuti, "How did you know about this place?"

Hehewuti speaks with her mouth full of pasta. "I used to live here as a child," she blurts out. "A long time ago."

Zemora is on her second serving of salad. "Who are the Separatist Sisters?"

Hehewuti swallows and replies. "Anyone who stays here. There were many female houses and female-only communes. Dozens of women once lived here, and my mother was one of them."

Jean is inquisitive. She dips a piece of bread into a bowl of olive oil and asks, "What happened?"

Hehewuti stuffs her mouth with salad and continues, "Things were better then and women were not afraid. When civilization declined, men attacked and raided women's spaces. Female-only communes were turned into brothels. This farmhouse is one of the few remaining female separatist spaces."

Zemora sighs, her stomach overflowing from pasta. "What a huge loss for women. To be safe, we need female-only spaces like this." She turns to the children who are stuffed. "Alright girls, let's wash up and get ready for Cronetime."

Introduction

Blood rituals were common in the past in Europe and Asia. Two or more people, typically male, intermingled their blood in some way to symbolically bring the participants together into one family. Blood rituals often involve a symbolic death and rebirth, as birth literally involves bleeding.

Patriarchal blood rituals may have evolved from gynocentric ceremony that revolved around the fire, incorporated dance, and used blood to honor females and the Earth Goddess. Remnants of these prehistoric, female-centered practices exist in various cultures.

This ninth and last chapter of Part II on Stone Age ecogynocentrism focuses on biological and feminist themes. It broadens the study of female biology and explores female-centered culture, art, communication, and technology. The chapter gets going with a survey of the uniqueness of human pistillate bodies.

The chapter presents a discussion of menstruation and ritual next. After this, it explores egg-producers' oral language. Then, it examines women's invention of pottery, and a discourse on female dress and textiles follows. The chapter wraps up with a look at animal folktales.

♀ Bodies

An egg is a potential store of reproductive wealth. While human females during fetal life have several million follicles, these diminish rapidly in number, with less than half a million remaining by age 5, and attrition continues through pre-pubertal years. By their late teens, about 200,000 follicles may remain.[1]

During ovulation, few eggs are released. Even fewer get fertilized, and of those fertilized an estimated 30 to 70 percent are spontaneously aborted.[2] A successful conception is difficult and it results in dramatic changes in a young-bearer's life.

Estrogens, along with androgens such as testosterone, are the primary drivers of women's socio-sexuality. Peak levels of estrogens and androgens across the ovulatory cycle occur around the time of ovulation, potentially facilitating female attractivity, proceptivity, and receptivity.[3]

In human ovary beings, breasts are a manifestation of higher levels of estrogen. During an egg-producer's development, this hormone widens the pelvis and increases the amount of body fat in hips, thighs, buttocks, and breasts. Estrogen also induces growth of the uterus, proliferation of the endometrium, and menses.

Female secondary characteristics include enlargement of breasts, erection of nipples, and growth of body hair, most prominently underarm and pubic hair. Labia minora, the inner lips of the vulva, may grow more prominent and undergo changes in color.[4]

On average, egg-producers have a rounder face and a smaller waist than sperm-producers. Women have a lower waist to hip ratio than adult men, and smaller hands and feet than men. Women also have changed distribution in weight and fat, and, more subcutaneous fat and fat deposits, mainly around the buttocks, thighs, and hips.

There is greater development of thigh muscles behind the femur, rather than in front of it, and widening of hips. Females have elbows that hyperextend 5 to 8 degrees more than men, and upper arms approximately three-quarter inch (2 cm) longer, on average, for a given height.[5]

Unlike childbirth and sexuality, menstruation affects all women. And remarkably, egg-producers residing together can synchronize ovulatory cycles. There is a lot to be learned from this unique from of community coordination, but due to masculinist bias the science and history of female bodies and menstruation are neglected. Childbirth and menstruation were culturally significant to gynocentrism and this topic is explored next.

♀ Blood Power

The monthly discharge of blood was an essential aspect of female-centered hominin communities. Body art and decoration is a Stone Age female tradition, and the ornamented body lies at the base of their symbolic culture and consciousness. Ancient women used the color red as an organic, feminist symbol to represent menstrual blood, female creativity, and the entire egg-producing collective.

A girl's first period usually begins between twelve and fifteen years of age, a point in time known as menarche.[6] Humans may have used red ochre and other pigments to signify and celebrate the menstrual event starting 110,000 years ago. And, during the Bronze Age, cups of red ochre were found in early Egyptian tombs.[7]

For millennia, menses were part of gynocentric ritual, myth, and taboo across the Earth.[8] In ancient Africa, menstrual blood was used in the most potent magic charms to both purify and destroy.[9] In times of danger and epidemics, the door-posts of houses are marked with blood or red paint especially.[10] For Aboriginal Australian women, menstrual blood is 'sacred' and female solidarity is unyielding.[11]

Around the World, among modern-day, gatherer-'hunters,' ceremonial red paint is associated with menstrual blood. For instance, Indigenous females in Africa, Australia, and Brazil paint themselves red while menstruating. In South Asian and many other cultures, grooms are marked with the color red.[12] And daily, over a billion buddhists and hindus wear a red dot on their forehead.

Knight reasons that during the Stone Age, menses, and its representation, were utilized by ovary hominins to exercise power through a sex-strike. He concludes that women used menstrual blood and female-centered culture to resist and end phallic status as the leisured sex.[13]

In Indigenous societies across the Globe, during menstruation, females seclude themselves in a particular hut or shelter. They isolate themselves without consulting men, and warn men not to approach them. Almost universally, menstruating females were viewed as bad luck. The menstrual curse was perhaps a warning to men not to violate egg-producers' space during this time.

Girl and boys of the Warrbiri language group of Central Australia both learn to use weapons to defend themselves. Even in 1977, men were careful not to go near the Single Women's camp, perhaps more from fear of their magic as of their weapons.[14]

A menstruating woman was considered as sacred and mighty by Indigenous cultures, with increased psychic abilities, and strong enough to even heal the sick.[15] Menstrual blood was regarded as being able to scare away evil spirits and act as a disinfectant. According to the Cherokee, menstrual blood was a source of feminine strength and had the ability to destroy enemies.[16]

Among the contemporary gatherer-'hunter' Hadza of East Africa, a girl's menstruation initiation is played out as a ritualized battle of the sexes with girls reversing sexual characteristics, dressed up as 'hunters' and 'hunting' boys. The shared experience of traumatic bloodshed during the first part of the ritual forms the basis for securing solidarity among female coalitions.[17]

It is a usual practice to smear sacred objects with blood or red paint, like sacred stones and statues of deities, in Madagascar, South Asia, the Pacific Islands, and Australia. The Greeks painted the statues of Dionysos red, and the Romans applied a coat of red paint to the face of Jupiter just before their festivals.[18]

There is a purification ceremony performed about eight to ten times a year in connection with the menstruation of the Goddess in Travancore, India. In each ceremony, cloth is wrapped around the image of the Goddess and discolored with red spots. The Goddess is removed from the temple and the principle shrine remain closed for four days.[19]

After the purification ceremony, the Goddess returns to the shrine. There is a high demand for the discolored cloth, which is considered a holy relic. Another menstruating Indian Goddess is Parvati at Chunganur. The cloth worn by the Goddess is discolored, and for three days the temple is closed.

♀ Language

Language use may have been begun around 200,000 BP, or as early half a million years ago. Speech was preceded by ancient ritual, which may have helped to establish community-wide trust in facts that enabled language to evolve.[20] Women created rites for critical life events like menstruation, pregnancy, birthing, and childhood transitions, such as puberty for girls.

Linguistic experts indicate that children learn words from mothers and only secondarily from fathers. Mothers must have invented various words to use in playing with and educating children. Over time basic speaking skills and vocabulary developed into language, which in turn could have caused the brain to become more complex.

Hominin women created female-centered ritual, oral and nonverbal communication, and social organization. Eons prior to leaving Africa, sapiens egg-producers probably invented storytelling, education, music, rhythm, dance, and song to share and expand female-centered knowledge and culture.[21]

With communication expertise, ovary beings probably invented creative fiction, narration, history, theology and philosophy. Females used language to expand Goddess-centered spiritually. The far-flung presence of Woman/Goddess figures and Goddess narratives show that egg-producers were orally recording and transmitting social and theological knowledge for millennia throughout the World.

There were female-only language, song, dance, and rites that men were not privy to and some of their creativity could have been utilized to maintain gynocentric knowledge and influence. Women likely invented words and ritual to facilitate female-centered leadership and governance.

Paleolithic language and the arts were merged in beautiful harmony. A testament to women's prehistoric oral ability is the tens of thousands of female folks songs that still exists in the World today. Egg-producers make and play reed flutes, the only musical instruments known to the indigenous Bari people of Columbia.[22] And, numerous Stone Age Woman/Goddess figurines are shown in dance poses.[23]

♀ Pottery

For liquids to be carried and stored, pottery from clay was the natural product, and ceramic technology emerged independently, at different times, across the globe. The pot revolution marked a shift from a complete reliance on skin, textile, and wooden containers to the use of pots made by firing clay.

Ceramic ware originated in East Asia around 20,000 BP,[24] before women's improvement of agriculture.[25] This early timing refutes conventional theories that pottery correlated to the time when humans moved from gathers to farmers.[26] By 12,500 BP, fine pottery was being made by human egg-producers from the Jomon culture in Japan, and in parts of the East Asian mainland [27]

Women invented and produced the first potteries in New Stone Age cultures, especially before the use of the potter's wheel.[28] As the primary cooks, members of the young-bearing sex would have observed that particular dirt hardened when exposed to fire. They then collected and processed clay from the soil, created jars from the wet mud, placed dried vessels into a kiln, fired the containers, and then decorated the pots.

Females used pottery for gathering, processing, cooking, storage, and transportation of food and medicine. Hardened clay was also used for communication and proto-writing. Pottery was essential for the storage of surplus food, and to the growth of settlements and towns.

Pottery provided a new medium of extraordinary potential for shaping and decorating durable objects. In addition to firing clay to make pots, cups, pitchers, and massive storage containers, Neolithic egg-producing artists made thousands of miniature figures of Woman/Goddess icons, nonhuman animals, and geometric patterns. These had different meanings and functions, for example, as part of fertility rites, toys, portraits, and votives.

Even before women invented pottery, ceramic art existed during the Late Stone Age in Siberia, North Africa, France, and the Czech Republic. Ornamental ceramic fragments in Moravia date to 26,000 BP. The manufacturing of ceramics was driven by a desire to produce jewelry and was likely carried out by females.

Female ornamentation is also likely responsible for the creation of metals. For example, the manipulation of copper, which can be traced to 10,000 BP in the Near East, was first used to make jewelry. Only 4,000 years later was copper extended to the making of utilitarian objects.[29]

♀ Dress & Textile

Similar to female art, jewelry, and pottery, dress and clothing accessories are ancient female inventions that pre-date intensive agriculture by over ten millennia. Women and girls were a powerful economic force in the Stone Age and beyond, with several industries - fabric, clothing, footwear, bedding, bags, accessories, and jewelry.

Throughout the Stone Age, women fashioned, used, and exchanged baskets, leather slings, fiber belts, and animal skin pouches, but decomposition leaves little trace of these items. Likewise, bags, storage items, and containers were constructed from perishable materials such as gourds, shells, animal skin, and stomachs.

Elizabeth Barber contends that twenty thousand years ago, human egg-producers were making and wearing the first clothing created from spun fibers. Barber notes that a Paleolithic Woman/Goddess figure is carved wearing a skirt woven of loose strings.[30] In prehistoric Europe, females invented elaborate textiles with intricate designs. And, in ancient Anatolia, ovary beings ran cloth-making establishments.

The production of textiles is complicated.[31] Early fiber artists combined color and techniques to create a great variety of fiber.[32] The women of the ancient Near East used woven and dyed patterns, and created the knotted pile of the so-called Persian carpet.[33] They also invented felt, a cloth made of fibers bound by heat and pressure, not by spinning, weaving, or knitting.[34]

As traveling merchants, men sold or bartered the extra fabrics not needed by the family. Early Assyrian cuneiform tablets preserve correspondence between merchants traveling by caravan and their wives. These astute businesswomen ran the production end of the business back home and often complained to their husbands about late payments and changed orders.[35]

Long after the rise of patriarchy, women maintained control of the textile industry, and for millennia were primarily responsible for sewing and weaving textiles and making clothing. The interests of the young-bearing sex was the key driver of this enterprise. For instance, in Eastern Europe, beautiful, elaborate floral headdresses were made and worn by young, unmarried women to show their "purity" and marital eligibility.[36]

Animal Folktales

Stone Age humans created thousands of drawings and stories of non-human animals.[37] Perhaps, cave paintings of animals were early picture books, helping mothers and teachers to entertain and teach children.[38] Animal figurines may have been used as ancient puppet theater.[39] Folktales about animals may have served the same purposes as animal art and sculpture.[40]

Animal-based stories are a central part of oral culture, which pre-date literacy for tens of millennia. Narratives involving animals reflect human-animal relations, philosophy, and cosmology.[41] Animal folktales were Stone Age libraries, and abundant examples from the Bronze Age survive into the present. The short and lengthy tales include commentaries on diet, sexual relations, cultural norms, personal thoughts, actions, and other topics.[42]

Numerous Indigenous myths link animals with the creation of the World. For instance, Asian and Native North American traditions place the Earth on the back of an enormous turtle. Tales from Africa and elsewhere tell that the Earth was formed from, or supported by, the body of an immense serpent.[43] Some legends say that the Earth's features, such as lakes or canyons, were carved by the digging of mythic beasts.[44]

In addition to shaping the world, animals are connected to human origins as well. Some Native American groups believed they descended from animals. The Yao people of southern China traced their roots to a dog ancestor. The 'Iroquois Creation Myth' is a Cayuga legend about how the animals helped the Mother Goddess, Sky Woman.

The 'Grandmother's Creation Story' is a Cree narrative about the friendly relationship between the first animals and the first people. Various African tales tell of a dog, chimpanzee, wasp, and praying mantis bringing fire to people. The Bambara people of Mali believe that a sacred antelope taught people to farm long ago. And 'How Bear Became Keeper of the Medicines' is a Native American legend about spirit animals bringing medicine or sacred songs to the people.

Several Native American language groups have creation legends which describe people as vegetarian, living in a kind of Garden of Eden. A Cherokee legend describes humans, plants, and animals as having lived in the beginning in "equality and mutual helpfulness."

The needs of all were met without killing one another. When man became aggressive and ate some of the animals, the animals invented diseases to keep the human population in check. The plants remained friendly, however, and offered themselves not only as food to people, but also as medicine, to combat the new diseases.[45]

West Africans and Native Americans believe that each person has a magical or spiritual connection to a particular animal that can act as a guardian, a source of wisdom, or inspiration. Among the Plains Indians of North America, individuals had to discover their spirit animal through a mystical experience called a vision quest.

The 'Tale of the Eagle's Revenge' is a Native American folktale about humans who are punished for their disrespect of animals. The buffalo had to respected for it controlled love affairs and determined how many children a woman could bear.

'When the Animals Left Lenapé Land' is a myth about treating animals with the proper respect. The animals left and when the War Chief found them, he asked, "How is it that we have offended you?"[46]

The Elk replied, "You have wasted our flesh; desecrated our forest homes, and our bones; you have dishonored us and yourselves. We can live without you, but you cannot live without us!"

"How can we make right our wrongs to you? How shall we atone for your grief? Tell us!" cried the War Chief.

The Elk spoke again. "Honor and respect our lives, our beings, in life and death. Do what you have failed to do before. Stop doing that which offends our Spirits."

The War Chief promised, and the animals followed the Lenapé back to their homeland. Ever since that time, the Lenapé have burnt tobacco as an offering and shown the utmost respect when hunting an animal for food. They never took more than they needed and utilized as much of the flesh and skin as they could.

Conclusion

The nine chapters of Part II discussed aspects of prehistoric female-centered diet, cultures, and gynecological land management. Part Two presented multiple evidence for gynocentrism and female civilization, like the prevalence of Woman/Goddess figures, female hand-prints, pottery, textile, trade, and so on. During the Stone Age, imagery of male violence against women and warfare are absent.

Prehistoric women were not passive victims waiting on man-the-hunter for food and inventions to improve their lives. From the Middle Paleolithic onward, females actively created gynocentric networks to facilitate their discovery and use of fire for illumination, protection, cooking, fire-farming, medicine, jewelry, and communication. Women likewise domesticated the wolf for protection and help with foraging.

The next section explores female-centered cultures during the last part of the Stone Age and the transition to the fifth modification, intensive agriculture. It also examines practical aspects of gynocentric organization.

(Figure 12: Neolithic Lepenski Vir grinding stone c. 10,000 BP)

III: NEOLITHIC GYNOCENTRISM (12,000 to 7,000 BP)

12: Fifth Taming - Crops

> This (feminist) revolution may well be also the greatest single hope for survival of spiritual consciousness on this planet. - Mary Daly

ASIA's Journey 2121.12

It is close to midnight, and the temperature outside is 108°F (42°C). It is a humid night and the full moon illuminates the farm house from outside. Inside, a few candles provide a warm light in the spacious living room. Haunting shadows dance on the walls. It is quiet, and a slight breeze flows through the open windows.

The women and children gather in the circle in the living room of the safe house. Hehewuti gives the ASIA board to Zola, dressed in a white flowing gown. Zola's face and hands are covered in red powder. She wears several bead necklaces around her neck, bracelets on both arms, and a crown. When she moves, her beads rattle, adding emphasis to her voice.

Zola places a bowl of water near a window and slants it to reflect the dancing moon on the surface. The girls are mesmerized. Zola writes a word on the ASIA board and shows it to everyone. The children stare at each other.

"What is it?" Iniko asks innocently. "I never heard that word."

Zola looks at Iniko, "Take a guess."

"A-P-S-A-R-A." Cha'Kwaina reads the letters out aloud, one at a time.

"Was she a Goddess?" Nadie asks.

Zola pats Nadie's head. "Sort of." Zola continues, "Apsara is a female spirit of the clouds and waters able to change shape at will."

"Huh, like a mermaid?" Sabra is amazed.

Zola rattles the board and continues, "Not only water. They are ethereal beings who inhabit the skies, like angels."

"Mermaid angels," Iniko laughs. "That's cool."

Nadie smiles. "I get it. Like Goddesses who rule the water and sky."

Zola shakes her rattle and twirls around. "Apsaras[1] are supernatural female beings, youthful and elegant, and superb in the art of dancing, like this." She shakes the water in the bowl to reflect the moon dancing gracefully. The children are delighted and get up to dance.

"Can I be an Apsara?" Sabra asks as she swirls. "I'm an excellent dancer."

"People can't be gods." Zaid declares.

"You mean Goddess." Cha'Kwaina circles and corrects him.

"Can't we?" Nadie wonders as she does a twirl. "We can learn to to dance like a Goddess, even if we don't have their powers."

Iniko stops and stares at her twin. "Can Zaid be like an Apsara Goddess?"

The women smile in unison. Zola's Cronetime is always good times.

Introduction

The debate over the origins of the World's 'first farmers' ignores and suppresses the extensive interval of gynecological, long-term, land management that occurred earlier. The were multiple stages in the improvement of agriculture and subsequent migrations of agrarian people. For example, the first farmers in the Zagros mountains of Iran were different from the Aegean people who spread farming west through Turkey and into Europe around 8,500 BP.[2]

The six chapters of Part III focuses on female-centered cultures in the late Stone Age. The first chapter examines female agriculture and the transition to a sedentary diet. The second chapter surveys Earth Goddesses from around the world. The third one explores Eurasian ecogynocentrism and female narratives, including the Goddess of Animals.

The fourth chapter analyzes gynocentric theology through various Goddesses and the sacred vulva. The fifth one discusses gynocentric practices, power, and existing matrilocal groups. The sixth and last chapter of Part Three investigates gynocentric scholarship and its opposition by patriarchal capitalism.

The first chapter in this section returns to the diet theme and starts with a survey of the fifth alteration, farming. An analysis of why agriculture was intensified follows, and then how changes in diet affected agrarian communities. The chapter then explores the New Stone Age female, followed by an overview of woman-the-farmer. Next, the presence of Woman/Goddess figures at a Neolithic farming site, Mehrgarh, is discussed. The chapter then turns to explore the relationship between cats and gynocentrism, and it concludes with a survey of harvest Goddesses.

5th Domestication: ♀Farming

With their intimate knowledge of fire-farming, terrain, plants, and seeds, hominin woman-the-gatherers were probably the first farmers. From an early date, women-the-gatherers would have noted that some of the seeds they buried sprouted in damp soil.

Females may have used water in vessels to sprout seeds for daily consumption, and sprouting may have led them to learn the secret of fertilization. Perhaps even in the Early Stone Age, woman-the-gatherers were purposely dispersing seeds in damp Earth to harvest more seeds later or practicing unrestrained agriculture.

There was a prolonged interval of women's manipulation of naturally occurring plants which, in particular species, resulted in the evolution of cultivated crops.[3] Agrarian cultures were a gradual, evolutionary adaptation of plants and humans. Proto-agriculture and protection of unrestrained plants, led to specialization of location, and then full-fledged farming.[4]

The history of human settlements is interlinked with that of other-than-human animals. For instance, mice first colonized human settlements 15,000 years ago, long before the intensification of agriculture.[5] The first long-term human settlements transformed ecological interactions and food webs, and this enabled house mice to out-compete field mice and establish durable populations that expanded with human societies.[6]

The Neolithic, or New Stone Age, commenced with the beginning of farming around 12,200 BP, which produced the 'Neolithic Revolution.'[7] It ended when metal tools became commonplace in the Bronze Age, around 5,300 BP. In the Fertile Crescent, intensive plant cultivation was an extended process,[8] and there are early signs of human ecosystem engineering aimed at encouraging plant production.[9]

The possible centers of origin of agriculture and its spread in prehistory include the Fertile Crescent (11,000 BP),[10] the Yangtze and Yellow River basins (10,000 BP),[11] and the New Guinea Highlands (9,000-6,000 BP). There were also Central Mexico (5,000-4,000 BP), Northern South America (5,000-4,000 BP), sub-Saharan Africa (5,000-4,000 BP), and eastern North America (4,000-3,000 BP).[12]

Figs are one of the oldest known cultivated crop.[13] Cereals were cultured from different grass species. Breeding began with emmer, einkorn, and barley. Flax, pea, chickpea, bitter vetch, and lentil came later.[14] Human selection focused on the grass seed. They shaped the generally small-sized, naturally dispersed, and coated seed, into the modern cereal grain - broad, naked, and devoid of dormancy and dispersal ability. Years of harvesting was selected for plant strains that retained their edible seeds longer.[15]

Some of the pioneering attempts of woman-the-farmer failed at first, and some crops were neglected, sometimes to be taken up again and successfully domesticated thousands of years later. For instance, rye was tried and abandoned in Turkey. It eventually made its way to Europe as weed seeds. Then, thousands of years after the earliest agriculture in Europe began, rye was successfully domesticated there.[16]

Why Intensive Agriculture?

In many ways, leaving the gatherers' lifestyle was leaving the proverbial garden of Eden, with its bio-diverse flora. Pre-farming diets varied by region, season, available plant resources, and degree of scavenging and hunting. Newly-agrarian communities' diet were restricted to the crops they grew, and a limited variety of plants near their settlements.

In the Late Stone Age, various social and economic factors helped drive the need for food and cultivation. The increasingly sedentary population had expanded up to the carrying capacity of the local environment and required more food than could be gathered.[17] One study points to the importance of group structuring, group size, conservatism, and farming-friendly property rights, for the switch to farming around 12,000 BP.[18]

Perhaps, gynocentric cultures improved agricultural technologies as a solution to their rapidly expanding numbers.[19] Female clan leaders may have viewed farming in permanent settlements as a resolution for the increasing amount of children, disabled, sick, and elderly in their community.

The semi-nomadic Natufians (14,500 to 11,500 BP) had already become dependent on cereals as a staple food, so beginning deliberate cultivation was a natural progression to obtain more.[20] And farming may have coincided with an increasingly stable climate.[21]

Intensive agriculture might not have looked very appealing to people at the beginning, and numerous groups decided to delay its adoption.[22] For example, Northern Europeans resisted the shift long after farming had made its way into other parts of Europe. Foraging fed them sufficiently, so maybe they saw no reason to change.[23]

Once gynocentric communities decided to pursue this new form of agriculture, they may have supported a group of dedicated women-the-gatherers to experiment with crops. It was difficult going at first, and the innovators endured severely restricted diversity in diet compared to those who remained nomadic.

Early adopters grew smaller, unhealthier, and suffered from poorer nutrition.[24] But women-the-gatherers were determined to succeed as women-the-farmers and stuck with the plan until their productivity was equal to, or greater than, foraging. Woman-the-farmer reduced the high rates of infant immortality present among earlier Natufians.[25] Egg-producers played a leading role in growing, harvesting, and processing crops, as well as in cooking, food preservation, and storage.

Once early farmers perfected agricultural techniques like irrigation, crops began to yield surpluses that needed storage.[26] Eventually, granaries were built that allowed villages to store their seeds longer. With more food, the population expanded, and communities added specialized workers and more advanced tools.

The success of the agrarian farming communities in the Near East under the favorable climatic conditions enabled them to expand into Turkey and neighboring regions. The rate of dispersal varied, with farming colonists taking 2,000 years to move from Cyprus to the Aegean, another 500 to reach Italy, and then only 500 to 600 years to travel the much greater distance from Italy to the Atlantic.[27]

After the sixth domestication, the colonization of nonhuman animals, small-scale intensive herding was the norm in various regions. However, cultivated crops remained the main protein source. Farmers concentrated manure on wheat and pulses, whereas hulled barley was managed with little to no manuring.[28]

Sedentary Diet

Evidence suggest that Stone Age peoples suffered less famine and malnutrition than the New Stone Age farming groups that followed them. This decline in food security was partly due to gatherer-'hunters' access to a wider variety natural foods, which allowed them a more nutritious diet, and decreased risk of famine.

The settlers' diet utilized a mixture of successfully cultivated cereal grains, such as wheat and barley, and other crops such as beans, cabbages, spinach, onions, garlic, cucumbers. Later on, the diet included domesticated animal products, like milk.[29]

Naturally occurring foods can have a significantly different nutritional profile than cultivated foods.[30] Famines experienced by New Stone Age groups, and some modern farmers, were caused or amplified by their dependence on a limited number of crops.[31] Sedentary people were also more vulnerable to infectious diseases and epidemics than nomadic groups.

Heightened population density and reduced mobility led to increased proximity to domesticated animals, ongoing occupation of population-dense sites, altered sanitation needs, and magnified illnesses. Several diseases jumped from animals to people, including influenza, smallpox, and measles.[32]

Traditional herbal medicines were scarce or unavailable in early settlements, and probably female herbalists as well. Minor problems went untreated and became dangerous and fatal. Also contributing to ill health, settled populations may have used grains for making alcohol, and suffered from alcoholism.

Nonetheless, groups practicing intensive agriculture soon had a variety and surplus of fruits and vegetables, and children adapted to plant-based, farming diets. A sedentary life and the diet meant less stress on females during pregnancy and more stable conditions for mother and child after childbirth. Further, a decrease in birth intervals is connected with high-carbohydrate diets. These factors combined to produce higher birth rates.[33]

Sedentary living was easier for children and old people and may have resulted in reduced death rates and increased life expectancy. Agrarian food production led to additional population and changes in the age profiles within communities. Settlements also fostered pivotal intellectual and social changes.

A plant-based diet was believed to make children healthy and disease resistant. For instance, Aztec, Mayan, and Zapotec children in olden times ate vegetarian diets until at least the age of ten years old. Their primary food was cereal, especially varieties of corn.[34]

Native American healers advise the sick to "return to the arms of Mother Corn" in order to get well. Atole, made from corn, is considered a sacred food. Nearly half of all the plant foods grown in the world today were first cultivated by prehistoric Native Americans and were unknown elsewhere before the discovery of the Americas.[35]

Studies of the roles of women in different types of agricultural communities show the importance of women's work. In horticultural societies, in which digging sticks are used for making holes to plant roots or seeds, women are usually more responsible for farming, and this would have been the first pattern of agricultural development.

The ancient Choctaws of present-day Mississippi were, first and foremost, farmers. For the Choctaw, vegetables are the traditional diet mainstay. A French manuscript of the eighteenth century describes the Choctaws' vegetarian leanings in shelter and food.[36]

Choctaw homes were constructed not of skins, but of wood, mud, bark and cane. The principal food, eaten daily from earthen pots, was a vegetarian stew containing corn, pumpkin, and beans. Their bread was made from corn and acorns. Other familiar favorites were roasted corn and corn porridge. Even the clothing was plant based, artistically embroidered dresses for the women and cotton breeches for the men. Choctaws never adorned their hair with feathers.

New Stone Age ♀

One of the first New Stone Age groups in the Southern Levant were the Sultanians who lasted from 11,500 to 9,300 BP. Their domestic hearths were tiny and oval with cobble floors. Sultanian sites include Jericho, Gilgal, Dra, and others, and they domesticated emmer wheat, barley, and pulses.

Presumptive ritual areas have been discovered in grander sites with weed and plaster statues representing deities. Sultanians made numerous Woman/Goddess figures from limestone and clay. Several depict a kneeling female, while others are of a seated woman.[37] These figures point to the essential agrarian tasks performed by egg-producers in the first settlements.

Kneeling and seated ovary beings may symbolize women's inventions of various agricultural skills, such as planting seeds and shoots, watering, removing weeds, tiling the soil, fertilizing, managing insects, and so on. Maybe the sculptures served as agricultural teaching aids for young farmers.

The agrarian Woman/Goddess figures may represent a continuation of Stone Age Earth Goddess art and worship. Standing Sultanian female figures have hands tucked under their breast, a common Woman/Goddess motif found in Paleolithic cultures. The high status of woman-the-farmer is reflected in the many items of female jewelry that were common grave goods, including head decorations, necklaces, bracelets, belts, earrings, and pendants made of marine shells, bone, teeth, and beads.

Gimbutas writes, "Since agriculture was developed by women (the former gatherers), the Neolithic period created optimum conditions for the survival of matrilineal, endogamous systems inherited from Paleolithic times. During the early agricultural period women reached the apex of their influence in farming, arts and crafts, and social functions. The matri-clan, with collectivist principles, continued..."[38]

Mehrgarh

Thousands of female statuettes dated as early as 7,500 BP was recovered at Mehrgarh, Pakistan, one of the most important New Stone Age sites in archaeology. As one of the earliest sites with evidence of farming and herding in South Asia, Mehrgarh is seen as a precursor to the Indus Valley Civilization. Technologies included stone and copper drills, updraft kilns, immense pit kilns, and copper melting crucibles.[39]

From 9,000 BP to 7,500 BP, semi-nomadic people carried out the first farming in the Mehrgarh by using plants such as wheat and barley. From 7,500 BP to 5,500 BP, they started to produce pottery. The first button seals were made from terracotta and bone and had geometric designs.

Mehrgarh has the oldest ceramic figurines in South Asia. The statues occur in all phases of the settlement and were prevalent even before pottery appears. The earliest Woman/Goddess figurines are quite simple and do not show intricate features. There are also collections of colorful stones marked with natural triangles.

The Woman/Goddess figures grow in sophistication with time and by 6,000 BP begin to show their distinctive hairstyles and typical prominent breasts. All the figurines up to this time were female. Artists also created humped bull figures, and the joint burials of humans and animals reflect a close inter-relationship.

In the later Harappa culture, a 5,000 BP seal shows a male figure standing over a seated female figure with a sickle. It probably suggests an association between the female figure and crops.[40] And in the main cities of the Indus Bronze Age civilization (5,300 to 3,300 BP) female figurines can be found in almost all households. The objects and images uncovered suggest that the Goddess worship of Indus valley civilization were associated with fertility and agriculture.[41]

Gynocentric Pet - Cats

Lions were powerful symbols of shamanic magic and female power. The lion stands as mythological guardian and protector of the Mother Goddess.[42] In India and the Near East, the usual animal-mount of the Goddess was the lion, and in the mythological art both of the Hittites and the Yoruba of Nigeria, the Goddess stands poised on the lion, nursing her child. Perhaps smaller cats were also gynocentric symbols.

Felis silvestris catus were first domesticated from the Middle Eastern subspecies of the wildcat about 10,000 years ago in the Fertile Crescent.[43] Cats were probably the one of the first species to be domesticated in the Neolithic. Praised for controlling vermin and its ability to kill snakes such as cobras, the domesticated cat became a symbol of grace and poise.[44]

In comparison to dogs, cats have not undergone major changes during the domestication process, as the form and behavior of the domestic cat is not radically different from those of wildcats and domestic cats are perfectly capable of surviving in the wild. Looking for an easy meal, cats could have tamed themselves as they adapted to hunting the vermin found around humans in towns and villages.[45]

The social behavior of domestic cats ranges from widely dispersed individuals to feral cat colonies that form around a food source, based on groups of co-operating females.[46] The human keeper of a cat may function as a sort of surrogate for the cat's mother, and adult house cats live their lives in a kind of extended kitten hood. The high-pitched sounds house cats make to solicit food may mimic the cries of a hungry human infant, making them particularly hard for humans to ignore.

Cats known in ancient Egypt as "Mau," were considered sacred in Egyptian society[47] and represented almost every aspect of their life. Felines were associated with over a dozen Goddesses, such as Isis, Mafdet, and Ba'at. Cats received the same mummification after death as humans, and were given in offering to the cat goddess Bast or Bastet who represented protection, fertility, childbirth, motherhood, and the benevolent aspects of the sun. Along with Sekhmet, Bast was known as the Eye of Ra, and was immensely popular, perhaps due to high childbirth mortality.

Herodotus wrote that the annual festival of Bast held in the city of Bubastis was one of the most popular of all, with attendees from all over Egypt, who would raft down the Nile celebrating and feasting all the way. When they arrived in Bubastis, they feasted yet more and made sacrifices to Bast.[48]

Several ancient religions believed cats are exalted souls, companions or guides for humans, which are all-knowing but mute so they cannot influence decisions made by humans. According to a myth in many cultures, cats have multiple lives.[49] Cats were witches' companions and used to augment a witch's powers and skills. In Japan, the maneki neko cat is a symbol of luck and fortune. Freyja, the goddess of love, beauty, and fertility in Norse mythology, is depicted as riding a chariot drawn by cats.

Harvest Goddesses

Across the World, there are hundreds of female deities who are served as fertility Goddesses, and dozens that are specifically related to agriculture and harvesting. In comparison there are very few gods of fertility, agriculture or farmed animals which suggests that farming was female-centered and developed under gynocentric cultures.

Hare Ke is a West African Goddess of the sweet waters fed by the spring rains that brought fertility back to the land. Nigerian Goddess Inna is responsible for the yam harvest. She brings abundance in crop yields to all the farmers that make offerings to her. Mbaba Mwana Waresa was a fertility Goddess of the Zulu religion. She is a Goddess of the rainbow, agriculture, rain, and beer.

Ashnan was the Mesopotamian Goddess of grain. Nidaba was the Sumerian Goddess of writing, learning and the harvest. Nikkal, whose name means "Great Lady" and "Fruitful" was the Phoenician Goddess of orchards and fruit. Heqet was the Egyptian Goddess of fertility. She was associated with the flooding of the Nile, and the germination of grain crops. She was often depicted as a frog sitting upon a lotus. Renenutet was the Egyptian Goddess of nourishment and the harvest. She was depicted as a cobra or a woman with the head of a cobra.

Fire offerings are made to Huichi, the Japanese Harvest Goddess by farm laborers in exchange for the necessary energy to complete the harvest. Kono-Hana-Sakuya-Hime is associated with the Springtime and cherry blossom as her name means "Lady who makes the trees bloom." She is also Goddess of the sacred site Mount Fuji.

Po Ino Nogar is the Cambodian Goddess of agriculture who protects the fields and harvests. Born in the clouds she spreads her generative, gentle rain onto the land below. Her name means "great one, Mother of the kingdom." Dewi Sri is the Javanese, Sundanese, and Balinese Goddess of rice and fertility.

Corn Mother is the Native American spirit of corn, bringing abundance and healing from the Earth. Special dances are still performed in her honor. To the Pueblo Indians she is known as Selu or Santa Clara. Myths tell of the planting of Goddess Selu's heart, from which corn stalks sprouted to feed the people. Chicomecoatl was the Aztec Goddess of agriculture during the Middle Culture period. She is sometimes called "Goddess of nourishment", a Goddess of plenty and the female aspect of corn. Axomamma was the Incan Goddess of potatoes and Sara Mama was the Incan Goddess of grain.

Demeter was the Greek Harvest Goddess responsible for the growing, preserving and harvesting of grain. As the grain Goddess she also became the patron Goddess of Millers and bakers. A three day festival called the Thesmophoria was celebrated by the married women of Athens. They fasted and prepared themselves for a feast where offerings of corn fruits and nuts were made to Demeter.

In ancient Roman religion, Ceres was a Goddess of agriculture, grain crops, fertility and motherly relationships. Goddess Ceres was credited with the discovery of spelt wheat, the yoking of oxen and tilling, sowing, protection and nourishing of the young seed, and the gift of agriculture to humankind. Before this humans subsisted on acorns, and wandered without settlement or laws. Goddess Ceres had the power to fertilize, multiply and fructify plant seed, and her laws and rites protected all activities of the agricultural cycle.

Conclusion

This first chapter of Part III on women during the New Stone Age introduced the fifth modification or the transition from woman-the-gatherer to woman-the-farmer. Female-centered groups were practicing proto-agriculture during the Middle Stone Age, so this fifth taming was a natural progression in gynecological land management. This chapter also examined the profound changes in diet that occurred with lengthened occupation of settlements.

The notion behind gynocentric settlement was the sharing of work, community, and resources. The entire community had food security, so there was no need for individuals to accumulate property, tools, seeds, position, knowledge, and so on. With the elimination of gynocentric communal living, every woman was left to fend for herself and her children.

Personal accumulation and knowledge became crucial under private property since they allowed individuals to regain a sense of security. But individual security is not the same as group solidarity and shared responsibility. The status of women and children under the patriarchal nuclear family is generally far more insecure than within female-centered collectives.

The next chapter explores female-centered theology with a sketch of the 11,000 Goddesses preserved in oral histories across the World. Collectively, these unwritten stories provide substantial evidence of Goddess worship in the Stone Age and New Stone Age. The diversity of ancient Goddesses is a sharp contrast to the few patriarchal gods that are promulgated now.

(Figure 13: Russian Postcard of Sirin, Bird-woman)

13: Earth Goddesses

For in fact feminists breaking the code of distorted phallic myth are breaking the routine, the vanity, the illusions, the adaptive behavior of the death marchers caught on the wheel of their "paradigms".
- Mary Daly

ASIA's Journey 2121.13

The females are having breakfast at the safe house. The moon is high up in the morning sun. The children are rested and hydrated. The crones are busy fermenting grain and fruit to make wine, an easy commodity to trade.

A week has passed, and the temperature keeps rising as mid-Spring approaches. Just after sunrise, it gets to 100°F (37°C) and it get up to 125°F (51°C) by midday. The humidity is under 50 percent, and it feels much cooler inside the farm house. There has been no rain so far this year.

The women know they have to leave to find water and cooler temperatures up north. Their next destination is a safe house about a month away, and the journey is going to be arduous. Ruthless pedo-hunters patrol the area to prey on climate migrants.

The children are learning self-defense from Kuan-Yin in the living room, and the women are in the barn doing weapons training with Lian.

Xóchitl is guarding the front. She sits behind a bush near the gate and hears a noise in the distance. Soon she sees two figures running on the dirt road towards the safe house. A tall young man, and an older one with a hat run up and push on the locked gate.

"Stop," Xóchitl commands from behind her hiding spot. "Who are you?"

"Let us in." The tall man replies. "We are from BKS."

"You have to pay our gang for protection." The man with the hat says as he looks behind nervously. "We want to talk. Let us in now."

"No," Xóchitl says firmly. "Just tell me how much to pay."

On the dirt road, four men on horses ride up quickly and approach the two men standing outside the gate. The horsemen quickly dismount and shoot the two men from the BKS gang, who apparently are out of bullets. They check the bodies for valuables, then spit and kick them repeatedly. A bald man in the front shoots the lock on the gate and   enter the property.

"Stop right there!" Xóchitl commands.

The bald leader stare. "Which woman dares give a man an order?"

"Go away!" Xóchitl shouts. "You have no business here."

The man laughs. "We are FST, and this is our turf now. If you're hiding BKS scum, you'll suffer the same faith as those two."

"We are alone here," Xóchitl replies.

The bald man points to the two bodies. "That was a warning. Be gone by tonight." He turns to leave. "We'll be back to check, don't worry." The four horsemen mount their exhausted animals and ride away.

Xóchitl runs to the house and yells, "Everyone pack now. We leave in less than an hour!" Zaid starts to cry.

Introduction

There is little research available on Stone Age sites around the World, and on the transition from woman-the-gatherer to woman-the-farmer. In archaeology and genealogy, Europe, the Near East, and Asia are probably the most documented, but prehistoric diet, cultures, and spirituality remains a mystery.

This chapter goes beyond archaeological studies of the New Stone Age to explore oral histories and female-centered narratives that exist across the Globe. Thousands of omnipotent Goddesses existed before the era of woman-the-farmer. As cultivation improved, numerous female deities associated with plants, crops, and the products of intensive agriculture, like wine, were added.

Before the onset of male-dominance ten millennia ago, people honored the Earth and Mother Goddesses. These deities symbolized a very different perspective of egg-producers, nature, and animals from the objectified commodities they have become in patriarchal society. During a vast stretch of human existence, nature and animals were not considered freely available for male exploitation, and many Goddess myths illustrate their sacredness.

Part III's second chapter on female-centered cultures in the New Stone Age outlines the diversity of women's spirituality that may have existed as early as the dawn of woman-the-farmer. This Goddess chapter surveys dozens of female deities from oral traditions, which provides further evidence of gynocentric prehistory.

The chapter starts with a look at Mother/Goddess-based theology in general. Then, to give a sense of the vast range and diversity of the 11,000 known female deities, the chapter briefly lists Goddesses from Africa, Australia, the Near East, South Asia, East Asia, the Americas, and Europe.

Mother/Earth Goddesses

Late Stone Age humans had much in common with Indigenous groups, whose theology and worldview represent some form of cultural continuity from prehistoric times. From past to present, there are similarities in location, art, artifacts, diet, and so on.

Stone Age people have ceaselessly reproduced Woman/Goddess figures in Europe for 40,000 years. Their art include the Woman/Goddess figures from the 8th millennium BP that Gimbutas cites as evidence for women being a fundamental part of societies in Old Europe. Woman/Goddess figures almost identical in form were found on Malta, dated to the 5th and 6th millennium BP.[1] In addition to carvings, thousands of Goddess stories and myths were transmitted by females from one generation to another for millennia.[2]

Among pre-literate cultures and Indigenous people, there is a nature-based, metaphysics perceived to have female qualities, and Earth Goddess narratives that conceive of nature as female. There are easily observed parallels between nature and human egg-producers, and these were connected independently by Indigenous groups across the World.[3]

Like nature, the young-bearing sex can bountifully produce life and sustenance, milk. Women menstruate with the cycles of the moon, and grow round with pregnancy, like a full moon. Andree Collard writes, "Being of Mother Earth, everything that existed was perceived as partaking of her spirit and there developed a relationship of kinship between human beings and all of creation."[4]

Numerous Goddesses depict motherhood in one way or another, and some are credited with the birth of humanity, along with the Universe and everything in it. Other deities represent the fertility of the Earth.[5] A Mother Goddess symbolize personification of nature, motherhood, fertility, creation, destruction, and Earth's bounty.

There are a lot of books that elaborate on the inter-connections of Goddesses and females. For example, Marta Weigle's text on Goddess stories in the Americas,[6] Merlin Stone[7] and Denise Carmody's[8] work on World Goddess narratives, Bettina Knapp's writings on World Goddess tales[9] and the feminine principle,[10] Jenny Jochens' analysis of Northern European Goddess stories,[11] and Betty Lies's survey of Greek and Roman Goddess myths.[12]

Jane Caputi examined Goddess narratives, nuclear families[13] and popular culture.[14] Leeming and Page looked at Goddess traditions and the development of patriarchal systems,[15] as did one of Campbell's lectures.[16] A biographical dictionary published by Oxford University Press in 1993, Goddesses in World Mythology, lists 11,000 Goddesses and fifty-eight categories of their powers and attributions. Thousands more Earth Goddesses may have existed as oral traditions for millennia before becoming lost to the passage of time.

Across the Globe, from the Paleolithic to the Iron Age, there were thousands of ancient Goddesses in Africa, Eurasia, the Americas, and Pacific.[17] These ancient Goddess narratives express the immediacy and the power of the natural world as alive and sacred. The Goddesses were viewed as active sexual beings and embodied multiple qualities. They were beneficent, erotic, whimsical, and ferocious. They can bring love or war, storms or gentle rain, life or death.

African Goddesses

There are thousands of African Goddesses from all parts of the continent. Out of this copious variety, the following list is a small sample of existing Goddesses whose names begin with the letter 'a.' The list includes Abuk,[18] Aja,[19] Akonadi,[20] Akwaba,[21] Ala,[22] Agwe,[23] Aha Njoku,[24] Aje,[25] Akonandi,[26] Amirini,[27] and Anansi, the spider Goddess of Ghana, who is considered the creator's chief official, and a shero of many tales. There is also Asase Ya,[28] Atete,[29] Ayabba,[30] Ashiakle,[31] Aziri,[32] Aje,[33] and scores of other Goddesses whose names start with an 'a.'

Other African Goddesses include Iyami Osoronga, the primordial mothers of Yoruba and Òshun, the Yorùbá Goddess in Nigeria and the African Diaspora. Oshun, whose name means 'The Source,' has been worshiped as Mother of the Yoruba people for thousands of years. She rules over many aspects of life, especially love and beauty, and she is a fierce protectress of everything she nourishes.[34]

Tanit is a Phoenician lunar Goddess, worshiped as the patron Goddess at Carthage. There are dozens of Egyptian Goddesses. The Nile Goddess is a prehistoric fertility deity with the head of a bird. In the beginning of the Universe, there was Nut, the Goddess of the night sky. Nut gave the Earth to her first child, Isis, whose name means 'Ultimate Queen.' Goddess Isis was worshiped in Egypt for over seven thousand years.[35]

This many faceted Goddess Isis was born in the swamps of the Nile delta and is linked to the annual flooding of this great river. Goddess Isis brings the nutrients in the rich silted water that ensure a good harvest. She also taught the women how to grind and store corn. Goddess Isis festival was held on March 20th to celebrate the spring harvest.

Egyptian Goddess Nephthys stood at the head of the bed encouraging mother in labor while her sister Isis acted as the midwife. Goddess Meskhent also presided over the delivery of babies while Hepat was the Goddess of Midwives. Goddess Taueret protected infants by taking the form of a pregnant hippopotamus to frighten demons away.

Bast was the cat headed Goddess was associated with both childbirth and fertility. The seven Hathors blessed new-born and set a child's destiny. The deities are associated with nursing infants while Goddess Renenet presided over a baby's suckling. She bestowed both a name and a personality on a new-born infant.

Mami Wata is an embodiment of the spirit of water, venerated throughout much of Africa and the African diaspora of the Atlantic. Mami Wata often appears in the guise of a mermaid, accompanied by a snake that serves as a symbol of divinity. They are essential figures in contemporary Vodoun practice. Among the Bakweri, Mami Wata spirits are a pivotal part of a young girl's rite of passage into womanhood.[36]

Australian Goddesses

Rock art of the Kimberly range in northwestern Australia are at least 17,000 years old. Aboriginal people in this region call the paintings, or rather the Beings in them, Gwion.[37] Egg-producers are indicated through variations in clothing, like the triangular waist girdles of possum or kangaroo hide. Although Indigenous people do not explicitly describe the Dreamtime characters as Goddesses the Gwion figures are female, divine, and creators and protectors of their people.[38]

Jillinya is the First Woman, 'the Mother of all the Gwion ancestors.'[39] Jillinya, also known by the sacred name Mumuu, gave women their womb and vaginas and the power of reproduction.[40] Rainbow Snake is an Aboriginal Goddess representing the fertile rains, and the sea. She flows through her people's lives bringing children.

In Pacific cultures, the Earth Mother was known under as many names and with as many attributes as cultures who revered her. The Māori creation myth included Papatuanuku or Earth Mother, partner to Ranginui or Sky Father. Varima-te-takere, Goddess of the beginning, is the primordial mother in Cook Islands mythology. In ancient Hawaii, Nuakea was a Mother Goddess of lactation.

Near East Goddesses

Figurines of fertility Goddesses, both individually sculpted and mass-produced, have been found at nearly all Near Eastern sites. The first figurines date to 9th and 8th millennia BP, and they continue to be made throughout Near Eastern history.

The Sumerian Goddesses known from later myths and hymns were initially local aspects of Indigenous Mother Goddesses. Prominent local deities include Damgalnunna,[41] Ninhursaga, Ninmah, Nintu and Nammu.[42] Curiously, the Sumerians wrote erotic poetry about their Mother Goddesses, such as Ninhursag.[43]

Mesopotamian narratives generally regards Ninsun, the mother of Gilgamesh, as a Mother Goddess. Ninsun is Asherah in Canaan,[44] and Ashtart in Syria. In Akkadian texts, Asherah appears as the wife of Anu, the God of Heaven.[45] Numerous Woman/Goddess figurines unearthed in Palestine support the view that Asherah was a consort of Yahweh and worshiped as Queen of Heaven. The various incarnations of Ninsun illustrate spiritual continuity throughout the Fertile Crescent, and between Sumerian, ancient Arabic, and Hebrew mythology.

Later Near Eastern Goddesses includes Inanna,[46] Ishtar, Uras,[47] Nisaba,[48] Anat,[49] Ki,[50] and many others.[51] Inanna was associated with the city of Uruk (ca. 6,000 to 5,100 BP), and a sacred marriage to Inanna may have conferred legitimacy on a number of rulers of Uruk.[52] Ishtar is the East Semitic Akkadian, Assyrian and Babylonian Goddess of fertility, love, war, and sex. She is the counterpart to the Sumerian Inanna.

South Asian Goddesses

In South Asia, the Mother of all creation is Gayatri.[53] There are several collectives and incarnations of Durga, the invincible Goddess. For instance, the Nava (nine) Durgas, and the 42, 64, and 81 Yoginis.[54] Numerous Goddesses have elemental energies, while others contain particular forces of the natural world. Some emulate the powers of the female body, sexual and reproductive cycles, as well as stages of a woman's life.

The Yogini is the Goddess herself, as well as devotee and attendant of the Goddess, and some are shown in this triple form. Since ancient times, the Yoginis have appeared in various shapes and often with a close association to nature. The qualities of Yoginis are similar to those of Yakshis and Yakshinis, the tree and nature spirits of early Buddhism.[55]

There are eight Yoginis of astrology: Mangala, Pingala, Dhanya, Brahmari, Bhadrika, Ulaka, Siddhida, and Sankata. Each is linked to one of the nine grahas, or planets.[56] At a human's birth, the stellar positions of these Yogini-governed planets give specific details about the fate of the individual.[57] Yogini rituals as well living Yoginis still exist, suggesting at least 1,200 years of continuous worship.[58] Yogini temples are circular and open air.[59]

Other principal South Asian deities include Kali, Goddess of life, death, and transcendence, and Mariamma, the cosmic creation Goddess. There is also Goddess Ganga of the sacred river, and Lakshmi, Goddess of abundance. Plus, there are numerous village Goddesses with local significance. In temple art, female genitalia represented by the yoni, are often emphasized to symbolize the Great Mother's crucial metaphysical role in giving birth to all that is.

Nepal's eternally living Goddess, Kumaris, are pre-pubescent girls worshiped as a manifestation of divine female energy or devi, by some Hindus and Buddhists. There are several Kumaris throughout Nepal, with some cities having several. The best known is the Royal Kumari of Kathmandu, and she lives in the Kumari Ghar, a palace in the center of the city.

East Asian Goddesses

Phra Mae Thorani is the Goddess of the Earth in Burma, Cambodia, Laos, Thailand, and other Southeast Asian countries. Other East Asian Goddesses includes Dakini, the Goddess who takes form as a Woman, and Tara, savior, buddha, and holy Mother. Haumea was a Hawaiian Goddess perpetually reborn, allowing her to continually mate with her offspring.

East Asia female deities include Xi Wangmu, or Queen Mother of the West, a great Goddess of China. Xi Wangmu is often associated with Taoism, and oracle bone inscriptions from 3,500 BP record sacrifices to a "Western Mother." Claiming to be trained by the Queen Mother was used to legitimize a long succession of Chinese rulers and dynasties. Pi-hsia-yuan-chun was a Chinese Goddess who protected women and children, and presided over birth.

Magu or "Hemp Maiden" is a deity associated with the elixir of life and a symbolic protector of egg-producers in Chinese mythology. Stories in Chinese literature describe Magu as a beautiful young woman with long birdlike fingernails, while primal myths associate her with caves. 'Magu xian shou' (Magu gives her birthday greetings) is a popular motif in Chinese art.

A preeminent Asian Goddesses is Kuan Yin, Goddess of embodied compassion whose name means 'She Who Hears the Cries of the World." Kuan Yin was a king's daughter who became a deity worshiped for centuries as the Goddess of kindness, mercy, and grace.[60] As a child, she refused to wear fancy clothes, eat rich food, or marry. She had two passions, praying for the poor and sick, and nursing stray, underfed animals back to health. Her father ordered her death, but she was spared and granted immortality by the Queen Mother of the West.

There is also Yama no Kami, the mountain mother of Japan, the Goddess of Cheju, and the Maiden with a Thousand Slippers. Amaterasu is a leading deity in the animistic Shinto religion of Japan whose full name means "Great Divinity Illuminating Heaven." Amaterasu is the Goddess of the Sun, one of the world's few female solar deities, and ruler of the six directions. Tamayorihime is an ancient Japanese sea Goddess who watches over the birth waters to ensure a safe delivery.

American Goddesses

In Native American storytelling, the 'Earth Goddess,' is one of several Creator-based titles given to the Spider Grandmother. The Hopi people refer to the Earth as Tuuwaqatsi-Earth Mother. In Hopi's first law, Tutskwa I'qatsi, land and life are one. The Earth's body is land, the inner core-heart is her life, and all Earthlings are relatives.

In Ojibway and Cree legends, it was a young-bearer who came to Earth through a hole in the sky to care for the planet. To the Ojibway, the earth is female, the Mother of the people, and her hair, the sweet-grass, is braided and used in ceremonies.[61] Nokomis or grandmother, taught Anishinabe, or human beings, medicines of the Earth, tool-making, and technology.[62] Pukkeenegak was a Goddess who gave children to the Eskimo women.

White Buffalo Woman of the Lakota and Sioux nations, was a messenger from the Great Spirit. She brought many important ideas to the Plains people when food was scarce and gave them sacred objects, like the pipe. White Buffalo Woman taught people that the Earth is the mother of all creatures, and how to make ceremonies to honor the Earth and all of her children.[63]

In South America, the Indigenous peoples of the Andes worship the fertility Goddess Pachamama. In Inca mythology, Pachamama presides over planting and harvesting, and she causes earthquakes. Ixchel was the ancient Mayan Goddess of childbirth and war.[64] In Aztec mythology, Toci is the 'Mother of the Gods.' Toci is often associated with Tlazolteotl, a central Mesoamerican Goddess of purification, filth, healing, and midwifery.

European Goddesses

There are thousands of European Goddesses from Anatolia, the Baltic, Britain, Greece, France,[65] Latvia, Norway, and Siberia.[66] Even during the Iron Age, Celtic Goddesses alone run into the hundreds with local and regional Gaulish, Brythonic, Welsh, Gaelic, and Celtiberian deities.[67]

Cerridwen, whose name means 'White Grain,' is also known as the White Goddess. She is a powerful magician who works her spells by mixing ingredients in a great copper cauldron. Cerridwen is also a Goddess of fertility, death, and rebirth. She loved to talk to animals, whose shapes she could take at will.

Māra is the highest-ranking Goddess in Latvian mythology.[68] Cybele was the great Anatolian Mother of the Gods, a primal nature Goddess who was later worshiped with orgiastic rites in the mountains.[69] The Greeks closely identified her with their own mother of the gods, Goddess Rhea.[70] The Romans had from the earliest times worshiped Jupiter and his mother Ops, the wife of Saturn.

In Greek mythology, Gaia was the personification of the Earth and one of the primordial deities. The gods reigning over their classical pantheon were born from her union with Uranus, the sky, while the sea-gods were born from her union with Pontus, the sea. Her equivalent in the Roman pantheon was Terra. Maia was the Greek Goddess of Spring, representing the forces of growth and the return of the warm rays of the sun.

Hera was the Queen of the gods, and presided over all things feminine especially maternity and marriage. Eleithyia was the Greek Goddess of childbirth and labor. She was shown as a woman wielding a torch, representing the burning pains of childbirth, or with her arms raised in the air summoning a child to the light. As a midwife Hekate carried a sacred knife to cut the cord at birth.

Sheela na gigs are figurative carvings of naked women displaying an exaggerated vulva. Sheela na gigs were used to ward off death and evil and a lot of these figures existed in Ireland and Britain. The carvings are remnants of pre-christian fertility and Mother Goddess spirituality.[71]

Conclusion

This second chapter of Part III on New Stone Age ecogynocentrism outlined the vast range and diversity of female-centered theology that existed before Bronze-Age male religions. The plethora of egg-producing deities in the oral histories of cultures across the Globe likely reflect gynocentric traditions that honored women, mothers, females, nature, and animals. In many of these traditions, plant-based foods and woman-the-farmer are especially honored.

Our minds are presently burdened with male-based culture, religion, and traditions which prevents us from looking at alternatives. However necessary at one level, knowledge and texts do not bring comprehension of life, which is a flowing movement. Ancient Goddess worship was likely the opposite of static male theology. Goddess devotees seek to experience life and nature afresh, and focus on that which is constantly moving, living.

Goddess narratives portray the Earth and nature as omnipotent and not always benevolent forces. For gynocentric cultures, living in harmony with female deities meant respecting and honoring nonhuman animals and nature as manifestations of the Goddess. The next chapter further explores gynecological perspectives on animals through animal-based narratives.

(Figure 14: Lajja Gauri, Asian Mother Goddess worshiped from
1,400 BP to present)

14: Lady of the Beasts

When I speak of gynocentric myth and feminist myth-making I do not refer to tales of reified gods and/or goddesses but to stories arising from the experiences of Crones - stories which convey primary and archetypal messages about our own Prehistory and about Female identified power.
- Mary Daly

ASIA's Journey 2121.14

The women and children left the safe house in a hurry two days ago. In is near noon, and the climate refugees are walking north along an endlessly flat stretch of rough, dusty terrain. It is 121°F (49°C) with low humidity.

The monotonous, dry landscape is interspersed with clumps of bushes, bramble, and tumbleweed. When the wind picks up, the clusters coalesce into hundreds of heavy bouncing balls of thorns, which can be lethal.

A hot gust blows in suddenly from the east, picking up the clumps and tossing them around. ASIA lies directly in the path of several giant balls. The wind picks up speed, and the balls are now moving too fast to escape.

"Children, get down on the ground, quick." Kuan-Yin yells. The girls follow her command and lie flat.

Lian understands Kuan-Yin's plan. "Sisters, use your bodies to cover the children," she shouts in the wind. "Stay on all fours, on your knees and palms, so you don't crush them."

"And keep your packs on to deflect the blows," Xóchitl adds quickly. The wind blasts the women's eyes as the wooden projectiles approach. "Close your eyes and hold tight," Jean screams.

The security team position themselves on the eastern edge of the group and takes the brunt of the strikes. The wind storm lasts for ten minutes, but the women hold their ground, and the balls keeps bouncing off their backpacks, without piercing anyone.

Eventually, the wind decreases and the tumbleweed slow down. The women and children stand up and watch the bramble disappear to the west. The girls yell, dance, and celebrate. They chant "Thank you, Apsara, all praise to the Goddess," and the women join in.

The crones beam as Zola proclaims, "ASIA is channeling the Goddess."

Introduction

Stone Age women in northern Europe held high ritual and social status. European woman-the-gatherers were known to be keen observers of herd movements. They could read the circling constellations overhead and identify herb and plant medicines below. And they were integrally linked to the management of the reindeer.

It was woman-the-gatherer who taught the people how to help birth the Reindeer young, gather herbs and berries to feed mothers in order to bring the milk, followed the estrus and gestation cycles of the reindeer cows, and learned to fashion warm and nearly indestructible clothing from reindeer hide, bone, and sinew.

The creative Goddess, egg-producers, and Reindeers were all considered sacred. Artifacts and funerary practices identified from thousands of years ago from Sami and Siberian burial sites indicate that some of the principal spiritual guides were women.

This third chapter of Part III on ecogynocentrism in the New Stone Age gets started with a survey of the history of women in Neolithic Europe. Egg-producers' imagery in Aegean cultures comes after. The chapter then concentrates on women and other-than-human animals.

First, the chapter defines animalism and totemism, then it examines various forms of the Goddess of Animals. The significance of bears to Stone Age people is next discussed, followed by examples of Animal Goddesses. The chapter concludes with a discourse on female perception, sexuality, and spirituality as represented by sacred vulvas.

New Stone Age Europe

Indigenous Europeans descended from three major migrations in the past 20,000 years, including two from the Middle East. The new migrants swept across Europe, mingled with previous immigrants, and then remixed to create the peoples of today. So there is no such person as a 'pure' European.[1]

Modern humans first settled in Europe around 43,000 BP and soon after, the continent entered into an ice age that lasted 20,000 years. Glaciers covered the Northern Hemisphere and drove Cro-magnon south, so they have little connection to today's Europeans.

By 19,000 BP, gatherer-'hunters' from the Middle East had migrated back into northern Europe, and may have practiced proto-agriculture there. Around 9,000 BP, farmers from Turkey migrated north taking intensive agriculture with them, but animals were not yet domesticated. Then, close to 5,000 BP, the male-dominated Yamnaya herders invaded from the Pontic Steppe.

Anatolia or Turkey was one of the first places where women sowed the seeds of modern civilization. The word Anadolu means 'full of Mothers' or 'land of the Mothers.' Anatolia may be regarded as 'the land of the Mother Goddesses,' since along with the spread of gynocentric agricultural societies, the Mother Goddess was prominent.[2]

The spread of agrarian and pastoral peoples into Europe eventual led to the assimilation of resident gatherer-'hunters.'[3] The second wave of farmers from the Middle and Near East were the World's first skilled migrants.[4]

During the New Stone Age, Europeans lived in small tribes composed of multiple bands or lineages.[5] The migrants were eventually assimilated, and by 6,000 to 5,000 BP, farmers throughout much of Europe once more had more gatherer-'hunter' ancestry than their predecessors.[6] The peaceful retreat and gradual assimilation by European nomadic populations are typical of the deliberate decision-making of matrifocal cultures.

With settlement and differential access to intensively managed, heritable plots of land, social differentiation began to take shape in farming communities.[7] But there is little evidence of developed social stratification and no evidence that explicitly suggests that the first New Stone Age agrarian societies functioned under any dominating class or individual, as was the case with pastoral herders that followed.[8]

Aegean Cultures

Because of its strategic location, the Mediterranean region was the center of trading routes between Europe, Asia, Africa, and the Middle East. The Mediterranean Sea was used by many early civilizations to establish and expand trade with other cultures thousands of miles away.

From about 8,000 BP, Cycladic artists used clay to make a variety of ceramic objects, including engaging ceramic Women/Goddess and animal figurines, as well as domestic and ceremonial wares. About 3,000 years later, they began to use marble to create sleek, abstracted representations of Woman/Goddess figures, ranging from a few inches to almost 5 feet tall. They were shaped perhaps by women with scrapers made of obsidian.[9] The sculptures were buried in graves, and, although there are a few male figures, the overwhelming majority represent Women/Goddess figures.[10]

By the Middle and Later Bronze Age, the art and culture of the Cyclades were subsumed by Minoan and, later, Mycenaean culture on Crete. The surviving Minoan sculptures consists mainly of small, finely executed work in wood, ivory, precious metals, and stone, colorfully glazed in fine ceramic.

Woman/Goddess figurines holding serpents are among the most characteristic Minoan images and they were possibly linked to water, regenerative power, and protection of the home. One figurine that dates from 3,700 to 3,550 BP, has a commanding presence. The Goddess is bare-breasted, with arms extended and a snake in each hand.[11]

Animalism

In Indigenous spirituality there is a general perception of a unified cosmos, where nonhuman and human animals, Goddesses and mortals, and environment and culture are all intertwined. Animals and nature are powerful equals to humans, and oral narratives use animal-based metaphors and nature as symbols of cyclical regeneration.[12]

The mixed human-animal figures of the Paleolithic and Neolithic periods suggest a view of animals similar to animalism.[13] This is a theology defined by close ties between humans and animals, especially with untamed animals. Animalism is a basis for totemism, which involves various permanent relationships of individuals or groups to particular animals, like the crow or bear, and natural objects.[14]

One aspect of animalism involves transformation between the human and animal states or shape shifting. For example, a princess kisses an enchanted frog, and it becomes a handsome prince with whom she will live 'happily ever after.' Typically, ovary beings have the ability to transform others, not men. Such transformations take place in stories across the Earth, which are about crossing the boundaries that set humans apart from the rest of the World.[15]

Also reflective of animalism are numerous examples of morphed animal and female mythical forms, such as the Swan Maiden, a mythical creature who shape-shifts from human to swan. Other shape-shifters include seal to Selkie, and dolphin to Mermaid.

Native American narratives describe a time in the past when the boundaries between people and animals were less sharply drawn and beings changed form freely. Bears were especially close to humans, and in some Native American stories, bears appear as humans wearing coats made of bearskins. Native American stories tell of girls marrying bears and men marrying deer.[16]

The well-known fable of Beauty and the Beast is a modern version of the myth of the animal husband whose beastly form cannot disguise his noble soul. There are dozens of versions of the Little Red Riding Hood story from around the world, from Africa to Japan and Korea.[17] This famous story of a wolf stalking a little girl visiting her grandmother's house is a gynocentric warning about male sexual predation.

Lady of the 'Beasts'

Of the 11,000 known Goddesses, there are hundreds of Goddess of animals from across the Globe. The Lady of the Beasts is a common type of Goddess who assumes the full or partial form of an animal. She is frequently rendered along with her characteristic animals, such as a dog, bear, or bird.

The Mistress of Animals combines two sources of power - the potency of the female body, and command over the strength and abilities of animals.[18] The creatures remained free until called by the Goddess. In contrast, under cyborg's command, nonhuman animals are always enslaved.

The most sacred title of the Goddess Artemis-Diana was the name of a female dog - 'Bitch.' The Goddess often appeared as a dog herself, or in the company of hounds.[19] Protective figurines of dogs were often deposited in the foundations of buildings.

The Caribou Mother is an Inuit deity who is the patron of wildlife and the guardian of animals. She is seen as gigantic, with people and caribou as lice on her enormous body. The Caribou Mother is known as one of the oldest Inuit Deities. Luot-chozjik, is the Sami protector-Goddess of the reindeer herds. She appears as a human woman, but she is covered in reindeer fur. She protects the reindeer as they graze.

In Polynesian mythology, Kohara is the Goddess of tuna, and is considered the "mother of all tuna fish."[20] Goddess of animals include Áine,[21] Arnapkapfaaluk,[22] and Artio, a Celtic bear Goddess. Her name derives from the Celtic word for "bear", artos.

Britomartis was a precursor of Artemis, the Greek Goddess of Animals. Britomartis was worshiped in Minoan Crete as an aspect of Potnia Theron, the 'Mistress of Animals' and Goddess of Mountains.[23] The patriarchal bias of Greek writers later made Britomartis the "daughter" of Zeus.[24]

The Greeks could only conceive of the Mistress of Animals as a huntress, so Artemis became the Hellenic Goddess of the hunt, unrestrained animals, and nature. But Artemis was principally a Mother Goddess of childbirth, protector of young girls, and relieving disease in women. The deer and cypress were sacred to her.

Inara, in Hittite-Hurrian mythology, was Goddess of the unrestrained animals of the steppe, and daughter of the Storm-god. She corresponds to Artemis and Potnia Theron of Greek mythology.[25] Athena is the Goddess of horses in Greece, an indication of their high value.

In the New Stone Age, the numerous Lady of the Beasts become attached to domesticates instead of untamed animals.[26] The naked Goddess with hands to breast, standing next to goats, cows, and other animals, is a regular motif in Old Syrian, Mitanni, and Kassite seals. Side pattern of birds and fish symbolize the air and sea, and the Goddess' fecundity in nature. The naked Goddess was sometimes illustrated with fierce animals to indicate her dangerous and powerful aspects.[27]

From 7,500 to 5,500 BP, New Stone Age art frequently depicted tamed pigs standing next to fertility Goddesses. Colonized pigs were sacrificed to Demeter, the Greek Goddess of agriculture. In Rome, sows or pregnant sows were favored by deities such as Ceres, Goddess of plant growth and agriculture.

Other Lady of the Beasts include Feronia,[28] Flidais,[29] Medeina,[30] Mafdet,[31] and Macha, a Goddess of ancient Ireland related to war, horses, and sovereignty. There is also Rumina,[32] Aranyani,[33] Kamadhenu,[34] Mansa Devi,[35] Varahi,[36] and Sarama, the mother of all dogs.[37]

She-Bear, the Great Mother

There is an ancient kinship between bears and humans. Bears can walk along on all fours, or stand up on their hind feet and gesture with their front paws. Bears and humans sought caves as a shelter from winter, and both consume mostly plants.[38] Giant bears coexisted with humans for tens of thousands of years before they died off around 28,000 BP.[39]

The image of a mother bear protecting her cub became a symbol of the fierce power of human young bearers, and bears are honored in Asian, European, and North American cultures.[40] Bear worship may have been practiced as far back as the Early Stone Age, among Neanderthal societies.[41]

Throughout prehistory, bears were connected to the cycles of life and with female creative agency. The hibernation rhythm of bears represented the three-fold sacred experience of life, death, and rebirth all within the same lifespan. Every winter, the bear goes back into the 'womb' of the earth and is 'reborn' each spring.[42]

One clue to the significance of bears in prehistory is that their imagery are applied to the most prominent stars in the northern sky. The third largest constellation, Ursa Major, means "the greater she-bear," and her design includes seven bright stars known as the 'big dipper,' which are among the oldest recognized patterns in the sky.[43] Nearby is Ursa Minor, "the lesser she-bear," a figure that incorporates the little dipper and the northern pole star, Polaris. As the axis mundi or Pole of the World, Polaris is the most important navigational star in the sky.[44]

And since Ursa Major circles the pole star without disappearing into the sea, she symbolizes female cycles of time, change, and eternity. Her cub represents the life force that emanated out of her and that is forever under her protection, influence, and care.

Ursa Major is Artemis, the ancient queen of the stars and the ruler of the Arctic Pole,[45] whose symbol is the she-bear. She is the "Sounding One," the "Lady of the Wild Mountains," and the queen of the crescent moon with moonlight being her actual presence. Artemis is believed to cause animals and trees to dance.[46]

Curiously, the bear is the most represented animal at the entrance of the majestic Chauvet cave from 35,000 BP. Could these images refer to the celestial Mother Bear and her cub? Other areas in the cave incorporate or highlight bear skulls, bones, and scratches into the imagery. And a bear skull was deliberately placed on a stone altar in the center of one chamber.[47]

Other Animal Goddesses

Reindeer are the only members of the deer family whose females have horns and are stronger and larger than the males. The males shed their antlers in winter, leaving it to the Deer Mother to lead through the long, dark nights of Winter.

In the Late Stone Age, when the Earth was much colder and reindeer more distributed, the female Reindeer was venerated by northern Europeans. She was the "life-giving mother," and the leader of the herds upon which they depended for survival. Humans followed reindeer migrations for milk, food, clothing, and shelter.

The female Reindeer was a revered spiritual figure associated with fertility, motherhood, regeneration and the rebirth of the sun. Her antlers adorned shrines and altars, were worn as shamanic headdresses, and buried in ceremonial graves. The Deer Mother's image was etched in standing stones, woven into ceremonial cloth and clothing, cast in jewelry, painted on drums, and tattooed onto skin.

The Deer Mother was sacred animal, and her doe was the giver of light and life. Their antlers were connected with the tree of life and often depicted as carrying the sun, the giver of life, in their branches. Monolithic "Deer Stones" are found through Eastern Europe and Asia, carved with stylized depictions of Reindeer as if in flight.

Gamayun is a prophetic bird of Russian folklore, like the Greek harpy.[48] Gamayun is a symbol of wisdom and knowledge and lives on an island in the east, close to paradise. Like Sirin[49] and Alkonost, Gamayun are normally depicted as a massive bird with a woman's head.[50]

The Greek sphinx was pictured as the head of a woman, the haunches of a lion, and sometimes the wings of a bird. It guarded the entrance to Thebes. The sphinx is treacherous and merciless, and those who cannot answer its riddle are killed and eaten. The oldest known sphinx was found near Nevali Çori, Turkey, dated to 11,500 BP.

Nag panchami is a South Asian female festival associated with snake worship.[51] Ancient Mesopotamians and Semites believed that snakes were immortal because they could infinitely shed their skin and appear forever youthful. Wadjet, the patron goddess of Upper Egypt, was represented as a cobra with spread hood, or a cobra-headed woman.

Medusa and the other Gorgons were vicious female monsters with sharp fangs and hair of living, venomous snakes whose origins predate the written myths of Greece. Gorgons were the protectors of the most ancient ritual secrets. They wore a belt of two intertwined serpents in the same configuration of the caduceus, a staff with two snakes intertwined around it as in the modern medical symbol. The Gorgon was placed at the highest point and is central to the relief on the Greek Parthenon temple.

Sacred Vulva & Sexuality

The connection between the sacred vulva and womb with birth, death, and regeneration, is a central aspect of Stone Age theology, as expressed in prehistoric art. Riane Eisler writes, "In traditions that go back to the dawn of civilization, the female vulva was revered as the magical portal of life, possessed of the power of both physical regeneration and spiritual illumination and transformation."[52]

A lot of the primeval Woman/Goddess figurines, and other sacred ceremonial objects, have highly emphasized genitalia. Some of the divine vulvas are found in cave sanctuaries and date to 30,000 BP. The cave was symbolic of the Great Mother's womb, and its entrance represented the sanctified portal or vaginal opening.[53]

New Stone Age European cultures widely celebrated the female form and the power of young-bearing genitalia.[54] Sacred genitalia was a primary symbol of the Earth Goddess, viewed as the divine source of life, pleasure, and love. In the megalithic site of Gobekli Tepe, a Woman/Goddess figure is carved on a stone slab in a birth or dance position, dated around 10,000 BP. An earlier Woman/Goddess limestone statue from Urfa, dated to 11,000 BP, is pulling apart her vulva.[55]

Hesiod wrote that the Goddess Aphrodite was fond of her sex organ. A

Greek myth features an old Woman figure, Baubo, the Goddess of Obscenity, who is associated with lewd jokes and the exposure of her vulva.[56] In a Sumerian narrative, entitled "Dumuzi and Inanna," the poet states that Inanna composes a song about her vulva.[57]

In South Asia, Lajja Gauri or modesty Goddess is related to abundance and fertility.[58] Early depictions of Lajja Gauri in Shakti or Devi (Divine Mother) worship were found on the Indus Valley seals. The Devi's began appearing in South Asian settlements even earlier, around 25,000 BP. The seven Chakras of human anatomy are often depicted as blossoming lotuses, and Lajja Gauri is often depicted as a Yoni, shown as a simplified triangle at the center.[59]

According to folklore, women lifted their skirts to chase off enemies in Ireland and China. Dilukai are wooden figures of young women carved over the doorways of chiefs' houses in the Palau Islands. They are typically shown with legs splayed, revealing a black, triangular pubic area with the hands resting on the thighs.[60]

Anasyrma is the gesture of lifting the skirt or kilt. It is used in connection with certain prehistoric religious rituals and eroticism, and is done only for the effect on onlookers. In several cultures, there is a myth of anasyrma used for emotional healing. In some nations of Africa, a woman stripping naked and displaying herself is still considered a curse and a means to ward off evil.[61]

In Nigeria, among other places, women invoked the curse only under the most extreme circumstances, and men who are exposed are considered dead. No one will cook, marry, enter into a contract, or buy anything from them. The curse extends to foreign men as well, who will go impotent or suffer some great harm.[62] During mass protests against the petroleum industry, women displayed themselves in anasyrma. Liberian leader, Leymah Gbowee, also used anasyrma to bring peace during the Second Liberian Civil War.

Conclusion

This third chapter of Part III examined female-centered art and representation during the New Stone Age that were similar to those uncovered from the Middle and Late Stone Age. Woman/Female figures were regularly carved in Europe and Asia during the Neolithic.

The Lady of the 'Beast' and Animal Goddess narratives reveal that untamed animals were once viewed as sacred and protected by egg-producing, Earth-based deities. For gynocentric women, enslaving nonhuman animals for labor and flesh would be akin to capturing and colonizing the Goddess herself.

The next chapter explores female theology in more detail with a discussion of female-centered perception, philosophy, and influence as exemplified by the Moon Goddess, Triple Goddesses, Deer Goddess, Oracles, and Sibyls. These refined deities and wise women codified female-centered perceptions of reality and symbolized their views on life, death, rebirth, and rejuvenation.

(Figure 15: Bone depicting a series of moon phases in Abri Blanchard
c. 32,000 BP.)

15: Goddess Being

> In rejecting rigid splits associated with the patriarchally defined categories of "sacred", "charismatic", or "the holy", I am not saying that feminist analysis makes no distinctions. I am saying that we have to be free to dis-cover our own distinctions, refusing to be locked into these mental temples. - Mary Daly

ASIA's Journey 2121.15

The trench was dark under the moonless sky. It is 102°F (38°C) with low humidity, and several days since ASIA left the safe house. Even at night, the heat saps the women's energy, so they limit their activity to mending clothes and other essential tasks.

The children have adjusted to the rhythm of traveling. The girls are tightly bonded, like sisters who share a joint purpose. They love, honor, and respect the women and crones, and eagerly look forward to Cronetime each night.

The Milky Way stretches from the eastern horizon to the western skyline, patiently waiting for the waning last quarter moon to rise. It is Cronetime, and Nakeisha has the board. Everyone looks up at the sky as Nakeisha talks about comets, stars, and the Universe. There is a meteor shower, and the children are amazed as dozens of bright lights flash across the sky.

"What happens if a big comet hits the Earth?" Iniko asks.

Nadie follows with another question, "Will we all die like the dinosaurs?"

Nakeisha gives the board to Zola, dressed in her gown of beads. "You are the Earth Goddess, and you are protected," Zola says. "Look at Mars, Jupiter, and Saturn." Zola points to each planet. "They are the Triple Goddesses of the Earth."

Cha'Kwaina is amazed. "So the Earth Goddess has help?"

"Yes." Zola smiles. "Jupiter and Saturn are enormous. Over 1,000 Earths can fit in Jupiter, and more than 700 in Saturn. Most of the comets that could hit Earth are pulled instead into Jupiter and Saturn. Massive objects that could have destroyed Earth have become trapped as moons of Jupiter and Saturn. And Mars protects us from a belt of smaller rocks between Earth and Jupiter."

"So we are safe" Sabra smiles and chants, "Thank you, Apsaras, all praise to the Goddess." The girls join in.

Zola nods, "The Sun is the Mother Goddess of all the planets. Each day she becomes the Triple Goddess in a cycle - dawn, dusk, and dawn again."

Nadie is puzzled. "What does the Triple Goddess mean?"

"Birth, death, and rebirth." Zola pauses and spreads her arms wide. "This endless cycle is the way the Earth Goddess, and of the Universe. The ancients used the Triple Goddess to show that life is eternal and the human body is just one stage."

The children are quiet and reflective as they stare up at the stars.

Zola shakes her head and rattles the board. "Men have forsaken the Triple Goddess. So, they fear death. And out of their fear, they destroy life." She pauses and then continues, "But those who honor the Goddess do not dwell on death. Our focus is life, birth and rebirth."

Introduction

Ontology is the study of the nature of being, becoming, existence, or reality, as well as the basic categories of being and their relations. Philosophers have provided various answers to these questions but have failed to address their relevance to women's lives and experiences. Explorations into the ontology of females, past and present, are therefore, critical.

Throughout prehistory, women had opposite philosophical constructs, especially in regards to nature and reality. Women's ontology is based broadly on their experiences as mothers, caregivers, and community members. Some of these metaphysical frames are still relevant to females and are preserved in modern traditions.

For instance, the Norse goddess, Freya was a spinning goddess who sat at her spinning wheel during the Winter Solstice weaving the fates of the year to come. This celebration was called Yule, from the Norse word for wheel. Christmas is often called Yule or Yuletide. The Christmas wreath was adapted from Freya's "Wheel of Fate," symbolizing the cyclical nature of life.[1]

Dismissing female-centered myths and Goddess ontology as no more than revisionist superstition and idealization of a romanticized past ignores a vital part of human experience and women's history, which was/is part of 'reality.' Gynocentric constructs provide a unique counterbalance to the predominant masculinist metaphysics, and few other models offer a radical alternative to patriarchal greed and accumulation.

This fourth chapter of Part III on New Stone Age ecogynocentrism expands on women's spirituality by focusing on the philosophy of various Earth Goddesses. It shows how female-centered thinking and practice led to technological innovations as well. The chapter commences with a discussion on the Moon Goddess and the evolution of calendars to measure female-centered time.

The Triple Goddesses are a common theme in female philosophy, and various interpretations are next examined. A discourse on the Deer Goddess and how animals relate to prehistoric egg-producers' worldviews comes after. Female-centered ontology as expressed in Stone Age mounds, monuments, and settlements follows. The chapter concludes by exploring the powerful influence of female fore-tellers in early patriarchal societies who served as Oracles and Sibyls.

Moon Goddess: ♀ Time

Understanding the seasons was critical to female-centered cultures and there were many Goddess traditions which kept track of seasons and time. For example, Rozhanitza, the Slavic Winter Goddess is connected to reindeer and winter. She is depicted as a horned Goddess with reindeer antlers. Folk art of red and white embroideries are made of her for solstice celebrations. On Rozhanitza's feast day, December 26, cookies made in the shape of deer are given and eaten for good luck.

Women's astronomical knowledge existed before the Neolithic, and the adoption of agriculture in the Near East was prepared for and assisted by the seasonal, economic, and ritual calendars of Stone Age women. For example, the Abri Blanchard bone represents a lunar calendar that is over 30,000 years old, and the one on the Laussel 'Venus' is around 25,000 years old. Stone Age members of the young-bearing sex observed and kept track of phases of the moon,[2] which was conceived as female.[3]

Penelope Shuttle emphasized that a Stone Age female would have noticed the relationship between her body rhythm and the lunar cycle, so women were most likely the first to invent a lunar calendar.[4] The numerous Moon Goddesses in prehistoric and Indigenous cultures imply that gynocentric societies did make connections between lunar and menstrual intervals,[5] which were probably part of young-bearers' reproductive strategies.[6]

For instance, the Ibo of Nigeria calls the new moon "The Women's Day," while in the Congo, egg-producers offer prayers, and Wemba females in southern Africa whiten their faces when the new moon appears.[7] Likewise, Aleutian females have special rites and dances in the moonlight at full moon.

According to Marshack, lunar notation was connected to seasonal changes in climate, vegetation, migration of herds, and biological cycles, especially those relating to menstruation and pregnancy. These primordial scripts were also affiliated with the mythological aspects of culture.[8]

Thirteen is a female-centered number, representing the average frequency of a woman's cycle in a year and annual intervals of the moon. Friday the 13th was considered the day of the Goddess, a day to worship the Divine Female and to honor the rhythm of creation, death, and rebirth.[9]

A chief purpose of the ancient Egyptian calendar was to mark the 'lucky' and 'unlucky' days, and the Babylonian calendar had primarily the same purpose. The unlucky days often assumed the form of established taboo, holy or rest days. Rest days were almost invariably regulated by the phases of the moon, that is, the female menstrual cycle. It is not unlikely that on her 'evil day' the Moon Goddess was thought to be menstruating and resting.

Triple Goddesses: ♀ Cycle

Earth Goddesses helped to define Stone Age and Neolithic gynocentric philosophy and spirituality. Egg-producing artists often fashioned the Earth Goddess as three deities, each serving a separate but related purpose in Mesopotamia,[10] Egypt,[11] Arabia,[12] South Asia,[13] Italy,[14] and elsewhere.

Triple Goddesses in Europe include the Fates, Furies,[15] Graces,[16] Hours,[17] Matres,[18] Moirai,[19] and Norns.[20] The pre-Hellenic Triple Goddess is sometimes identified as Hera-Demeter-Kore, and in Irish myth there is the Triple Goddess Eire, Fodhla, and Banbha. There was also in Hellenic mythology the Triple Moon Goddess, whose different local titles were Thetis, Amphitrite, and Nereis.

The three-fold imagery has temporal, spatial, and cosmic meanings. There were local and practical uses of Triple Goddesses, for example, as protector of families, aid to midwives, and for celebrations. Triple Earth Goddesses also represented ancient females' notions of their environment, Earth, sky, seasons, and astronomical events, such as the waxing, full, and waning moon.

Triple Goddesses were used to define and support females' three roles as a maiden, mother, and crone.[21] This female life-cycle motif was distributed across the World. The deities were endowed with egg-producers' belief concerning birth, life, and death, and viewed as 'spinners' of the destiny of nonhuman and human animals.[22]

The meanings and philosophies transcribed to the Triple Goddesses were inter-connected. For instance, the seasons were part of a young-bearer's life-cycle, with Spring as birth, Summer as maiden, Fall as mother, and Winter as crone. Death was part of a cycle of sex, birth, death, and rebirth, in which the Goddess reclaimed what was hers to give, and in which sex played a mysterious but central part.[23]

Joan Harrison suggested that gynocentric Goddesses may have reflected the three stages of a woman's life. Harrison wrote, "First it should be noted that the trinity-form was confined to the women Goddesses... of a male trinity we find no trace."[24] Robert Graves regarded the Triple Goddess of Birth, Love, and Death as the continuing muse of all true poetry and ancient worship.[25]

In psychology, Jung, Kerényi,[26] and Neumann analyze the Triple Goddess as an archetype. Jung asserted that mothering was part of the collective unconscious of humans.[27] And, Neumann contended that the Fates were "the threefold form of the Great Mother."[28]

Kerényi pointed out that several Greek Goddesses were Triple Moon Goddesses of the Maiden-Mother-Crone type, including Hera. He wrote, "With Hera the correspondences of the mythological and and cosmic transformation extended to all three phases in which the Greeks saw the moon: she corresponded to the waxing moon as maiden, to the full moon as fulfilled wife, to the waning moon as abandoned withdrawing women."[29]

Goddess Theory: Gimbutas

In East European archaeology, Marija Gimbutas (1921-1994) was an established academic with decades of fieldwork and research in southeast European sites.[30] Gimbutas conducted a comparative study of Goddess worship in eastern Europe and the Aegean from 8,500 to 5,500 BP, and showed that their Women/Goddess figures descended from earlier New Stone Age female-centered social systems.

Gimbutas concluded that New Stone Age people viewed the Great Goddess as the central figure in a pantheon that reflected a society dominated by the mother.[31] Although this leading anthropologist connected the Woman/Goddess figures with motherhood, fertility, and sexuality, Gimbutas emphasized that this symbol was viewed first and foremost as a mighty creatrix, an Earth Goddess presiding over all life and death.[32]

The thousands of female images recovered from ancient European sites represent different Triple Goddess symbolism. A 'bird and snake' group was connected with water, while an 'Earth mother' group was related to birth.[33] There was a 'stiff nude' group associated with death, as well as other Triple Goddess groups. Gimbutas maintained that the "Earth mother" group of Old Europe continues the Stone Age Women/Goddess tradition.[34]

The Earth Goddess of Neolithic Europe was mainly life-creatresses, not 'Venuses' or beauties. The Earthly Deity was a Triple Goddess who served as 'Life-giver, Death-wielder, and Re-generator.'[35] Two aspects of the Goddess were often conflated to make a Goddess of death-and-regeneration, represented in folklore by figures such as Baba Yaga. In Slavic folklore, Baba Yaga is a supernatural being, or one of a trio of sisters of the same name, who appears as a deformed and ferocious-looking woman.[36]

Gimbutas explains that between 9,000 BP and 5,500 BP, the people of eastern Europe lived in sedentary agricultural societies that worshiped the Great Goddess. These gynocentric groups had a sophisticated culture and lived in long-lasting, stable societies with an egalitarian social structure.[37]

Neolithic Europeans crafted superb ceramics rather than weapons. These female-centered settlements were not routinely sacked as were subsequent patriarchal villages and towns. Their social system was matrilineal, and egg-producers acted as heads of clans or queen-priestesses.[38]

Gimbutas writes, "The Goddess in all her manifestations was a symbol of the unity of all life in Nature... The multiple categories, functions, and symbols used by prehistoric peoples to express the Great Mystery are all aspects of the unbroken unity of one deity, a Goddess who is ultimately Nature herself."[39]

Deer Goddess: ♀ Spirituality

Esther Jacobson conducted extensive research of artifacts, pictures, and other material of southern Siberia and north-central Asia, from the New Stone Age to the Bronze Age. Jacobson concludes that their religion was initially based on the veneration of the Great Mother, who was also the Mother of Animals in later Siberian shamanic traditions.[40]

The art historian calls attention to elements that continually re-emerge in varying relationships to the Woman/Goddess figures. She reveals intrinsic connections between the great Goddess, the Mother of Animals, and the Deer Spirit, as the background to the Scytho-Siberian animal style of art and theology, or hierophany.[41]

Siberian spirituality starts with reindeer and elk spirits, and later uses cow and human images when gathering-'hunting' cultures transformed to pastoralism. This evolution incorporated changes in the concept of the World Tree, or World Mountain, that is modeled on the Great Mother. In southwest Asia and elsewhere, the Goddess is often portrayed with a tree.

Jacobson observes that the deer in drawings and sculptures, such as the numerous deer stones, resembles through their antlers, a tree which represents the Goddess. The deer image represents the Goddess, or Tree of Life, with the souls of the yet to be born, pictured as birds on the antler tines.

In prehistory, the 'World-supporting' tree or pole was female. In archaic myths, the Tree of Life is called 'birth-giving, and 'fruit- or milk- producing.' The ancient Near East referred to this magical tree by its older name of Mutvidr or 'Mother-Tree.'[42] The spring at the tree's root was a fountain of wisdom or the life-giving fluid which may be compared to the 'wise blood' of the Mother. The cosmic Tree of Life was a symbol of the body of the Great Mother from which all light and life emerges.

In addition to antler and stone artifacts, Jacobson used shamanic dress patterns and their symbolism to coordinate the evolution of the Mother of Animals with the growth of shamanism. She points to the close associations between the deer or Animal Mother, the Tree, and the shaman's drum, which is created out of the tree.

Jacobson suggests that the notion of sacred mountains originated with pastoralism, and that male gods appeared as creators much later than Mother Goddesses. As Siberian cultures became male-dominated, the great Mother of Animals, pictured before as the Tree of Life, became reduced and reformulated as trivial spirits.[43]

Mound/Megalith: ♀ Belief

In many sites across the world, Late Stone Age humans started to construct permanent dirt mounds and immense stone structures, or megaliths. In some cases, they had to transport massive rocks and tons of soil over long distances.

In her thesis, Henna Lindström analyzed oral traditions about the Mouras Encantadas, faeries connected with megalithic monuments in Portugal and other parts of Europe. She concluded that Mouras[44] were similar to the Triple Goddess and revolved around the cycle of life, death, and rebirth.[45] Lindström contends, "megaliths were built by women."[46]

But why would women raise these monumental earthen mounds? The sites could have been used for observing the night sky, tracking the movements of stars, mining, and trade. Megaliths were embedded in metaphysics and reflected gynocentric philosophy on reincarnation.[47]

Stone Age burial art emphasized the dual image of death and rebirth under gynocentrism, as do Neolithic megalithic structures. Mounds represented a womb of the Earth, and women's faith in re-birth. Members of the community were buried collectively so they would be born again together.

Nevai Çori was a New Stone Age settlement in Turkey around 10,000 BP, with some of the world's oldest known temples and monumental sculptures.[48] Several hundred clay figurines about two inches high (5 cm), most of them depicting females, have been interpreted as votive offerings.[49] A 6,000-year-old temple of the Trypillian culture is another 'mega-structure.'[50]

Stonehenge in the UK is not the largest megalith circle, but it is one of the most intricate. The site had eight different phases of construction and activity starting around 5,000 BP, and stretching over a millennium and a half through the Bronze Age.[51] The monument faces a nearby river which was possibly regarded as a deity.[52]

Mound settlements were part of first cities in the Americas.[53] For instance, the monumental earthworks of Poverty Point, Louisiana, built around 3,650 BP.[54] As old as some of the pyramids in Egypt, the six concentric curving earthworks located in the center of the site, and the surrounding mounds, may well be the largest gatherer settlement that has ever existed.[55] Post-holes indicates the presence of buildings and usual residence, and they may have astronomical significance in being aligned to the solstices.[56]

Poverty Point was the center of a major exchange network with goods brought in from as far as 1,600 kilometers (1,000 miles) distant. The vast majority of artifacts uncovered were female-centered clay cooking balls. There was also Woman/Goddess figurines with different physical characteristics, hairstyles, and so on. Some figurines have hands clasped under their breast.

Oracles: ♀ Prophecy

In prehistory, an oracle was a female or Goddess temple that provided wise and insightful counsel, prophetic predictions, and precognitions of the future. Oracles were portals through which the Goddess spoke directly to the priestess. They were different from seers who interpreted signs sent by the Goddess through bird songs, animal tracks, and other methods.

In Greece, all of the old oracles were devoted to the Mother Goddess.[57] The most significant oracles of Greek antiquity were Pythia, the priestess at Delphi, and the oracle at Dodona.[58] Delphi had origins in prehistoric times with the worship of Gaia, and extensive activity during the Mycenaean era (3,600 to 3,100 BP).[59]

The Delphic Oracle exerted considerable influence throughout Hellenic culture. Pythia, the oracle at Delphi, was said to be infallible, and she was the highest authority both civilly and religiously in male-dominated ancient Greece. Pythia responded to the questions of citizens, foreigners, kings, and philosophers on issues of political impact, war, duty, crime, laws, and even personal matters.[60]

Dodona in northwestern Greece was the oldest Hellenic oracle, possibly dating to the 4,000 BP.[61] Dodona was an oracle devoted to a Mother Goddess like Rhea, Gaia, and Dione, whose name just means "deity." The shrine remained an eminent spiritual sanctuary until the rise of christianity during the Late Roman era.

The ancient Greek and the Romans had their own ways of telling the future. The Greeks had an oracle and the Romans had a Sibyl. The most famous oracle was the Oracle of Delphi, and the most famous Sibyl was the Sibyl of Cumae. The Oracle and the Sibyl are similar in that they are both women chosen by the 'gods' to speak prophecies, and they both spoke prophecies.

The ancient Oracles and Sibyl were famous women who acted as foretellers at sacred sites of the Goddess. These powerful crones were representatives of ancient gynocentric ideologies, cultures, and healing traditions, with roots in the Stone Age and Africa. They were close to the natural world and were respectful to animals and nature.

Goddess Cybele: ♀ Legacy

The priestesses of Goddess Cybele (Kybele or cave dweller) were confused with and eventually known as the Sibyls. Cybele, the Great Goddess of Asia Minor is one of the oldest Goddess known, predating the Goddesses of the Sumerian and Egyptians by at least 5,000 years. She was the Mountain Mother and the Kybela mountains were likely named after Goddess Cybele.

Cybele's temples and shrines were always in mountains or caves and her guardians were lions or leopards and her priestesses had a close affinity with nature. The Woman/Goddess statue found at Çatal Hüyük, dating to 8,000 BP, depicts the Mother Goddess squatting in the process of giving birth while flanked by two leopards.

The priestesses of Cybele were part of gynocentric groups that were distributed throughout east Africa and Eurasia. This female-centered culture peacefully governed three continents for thousands of years in the early Neolithic. In Africa, they were known as the Mami Wata and are descendants of the first neolithic clans of the African Queens, healers, prophetess, and Goddess.

As women became domesticated and Goddess Cybele became replaced by phallic deities, female healers, spiritual leaders, and priestesses of Cybele remained powerful figures as oracles and prophetess known as 'Pythoness.' The Pythoness had snakes and often prophesied while in a state of frenzy, under the inspiration of a deity, perhaps Cybele.

The word Sibyl comes from the ancient Greek word sibylla, meaning prophetess. Known as the 'Black Doves,' the Sibyls were also referred to by names such as Sisters of Isis and Prophetesses of the Black Diana of Euphesus.[62] The dove symbolize the sacred soul or 'holy spirit,' and 'Mami' whom the Sibyls venerated in ancient Minoa as "Laocoon with her serpents," was known as the manifestation of the Divine logos.

The Pythoness or Sibyls worked in temples in the black Egyptian colonies in ancient Greece, Rome, Turkey, Palestine, Syria, and Babylon. The first known Greek writer to mention a Sibyl is Heraclitus, who wrote in the 25th century BP, "The Sibyl, with frenzied mouth uttering things not to be laughed at, unadorned and unperfumed, yet reaches to a thousand years with her voice by aid of the god."[63]

There were celebrated Sibyls in different locations throughout the ancient world. Plato speaks of one, while Aristotle and Aristophanes mention several, and Varro the Roman scholar and director of Caesar's library itemize eleven: He writes, "In Persia she was Sibylla Persica, and was depicted as carrying a lantern and had a serpent under her feet; in Libya, Sibylla Libyea held a lighted torch; at Delphi, the Sibylla Delphica wore a crown of thorns."

Varro continues, "at Cumae, Sibylla Cumana had an stone manger; at Samos, Sibylla Cania bore a reed and a candle; the Sibylla Cimmeria carried a cross; Sibylla Erythreia held a white rose; on the Tibur, Sibylla Tibertina was dressed in animal skins and carried the fascista bundle of rods; at Marpessa, Sibylla Europa carried sword; on the Hellesport, Sibylla Hellespontina carried a flowering branch; and Sibylla Phrygia carried a banner and prophesied resurrection."

Pausanias lists four: the Libyan Sibyl; Herophile, the Sibyl of Marpessus or Erythræ who prophesied both in Asia Minor and at Delphi, and therefore frequently mentioned under various other names; the Demo of Cumæ, the chief Sibyl of Roman history; and the Sabbe of Palestine known also as the Babylonian or Egyptian Sibyl.[64]

The most famous temples were the Temple of Amon in ancient Libya; the Temple of Delphi (dolphin) at Dodona and Delos in the Grecian islands; a temple in the Mattani Empire in ancient Turkey; and a great mother temple in Bethlehem, Palestine.[65] The Sibyl of Dodona, possibly date to the fourth millennium BP, according to Herodotus.

The Antro della Sibilla cave near Naples, Italy is a trapezoidal passage cut out of the volcanic stone that leads to an innermost chamber, where the Sibyl prophesied. The cave has many entrances, and is 16 feet (5 meters) high and 430 feet (131 meters) long, with several side galleries and cisterns.

According to tradition, the Sibyl sung her prophecies, or wrote them on oak leaves which she left at the mouth of the cave. If the wind blew and scattered them, she would not help to reassemble the leaves to form the original prophecy again. The prophecies were given in riddles. Once a king came to Delphi to ask a question, "Who will win the battle tomorrow?" he asked. She answered, "A great king."

Vivian Hindrew argues, "The Sibyls preserved their history in poetic and prophetic prose that would later be used as the basis for Greek and Roman tragedies."[66] A Black Moor (Phoenician) coat-of-arms found was engraved with an Ethiopian Sibyl Prophetess. Images of Sibyl on amulets were cherished and worn by warriors as a symbol of luck and protection during battles.[67]

Sabazius was a Cretan demigod from which the Greeks got the name Zeus. Prior to the Greeks, however, Sabazius appears to have been a title for priestesses. These women were the first to replace beer with wine and incorporate the Bacchic rituals in their Holy Taverns.

Sibyl: ♀ Legends

Written around 2,030 BP, Virgil's Aeneid chronicles the adventures of Trojan warrior Aeneas, including his encounter with a mysterious ancient fortune teller. Virgil describes a cave with a hundred openings as home to one of the most famous prophetesses of ancient legend, the Cumaean Sibyl.[68] Virgil writes, "A hundred doors a hundred entries grace; As many voices issue, and the sound Of Sybil's words as many times rebound."[69]

One famous story dates to the time of the last Roman king, Tarquin, around 2,500 BP. An old woman "who was not a native of the country" arrived incognita in Rome. The Sibyl approached the king with nine books of prophesy, collected from the wisest seers, available for a costly price. Tarquin haughtily refused and in response, the Sibyl burned three of the books, then offered the remaining six at the original high price.

Again the king refused. Of the remaining six books, the Sibyl threw three more onto the fire, and repeated her offer of the final three at the original price.

Afraid of seeing all the prophesy destroyed, Tarquin finally accepted. the Sibyl "disappeared from among men." Lactantius' Varro claims that the old woman selling the books was the Cumaean Sibyl.

The Sibylline Books, which foretold the fall of Tarquin and the future of Rome, became a famous source of power and knowledge. The books were stored on the Capitoline Hill in Rome, to be consulted only in emergencies by an act of the Senate. When Hannibal threatened Rome around 2,230 BP, the Senate ordered consultation of the Sibylline Books.

The Romans found a promise by the Sibyl that whenever an enemy from abroad invaded Italy, they would be expelled and conquered if the Idaean Mother was brought to Rome. The senators immediately began building a temple for the Great Mother of the Gods on the Palatine, but it was six years before Her silver statue and sacred symbol, a small black stone which fell from the sky, was able to be brought to Rome. In 2,100 BP, the Sibylline Books were destroyed in the burning of the Temple of Jupiter.[70]

During the great fall of women and dismantlement of ecogynocentrism, Sibyls were exiled, condemned as infidels, false prophetesses, and witches. After the destruction of their temples by the Romans, many Sibyls were sold as slaves, and forced to perform spiritual duties in the now male dominated Sun and thunder temples.

The Cumaean Sibyl later appeared in the works of Ovid, on the ceiling of the Sistine Chapel, painted by Michelangelo, and in Dante's Inferno. Ovid tells of the Sybil's sad end in Metamorphosis (book 14). She ended up on the losing side of a deal with Apollo, who sought her virginity, offering her a wish in exchange.

The Palestine Sibyl was regarded as an ancient personage who perpetuated the wisdom of the past. Epiphanius regarded Sibyl as the daughter of Noah himself, or even of Eve. Both jews and christians forged Sibylline books to give credence to their claims of prophesy. A Sibylline poem of considerable extent was circulated by Alexandrian jews in the 22nd century BP.

In jewish oracles, the Sibyl often complains that she is exhausted by the mighty spirit of the lord, but that she is compelled by his command to continue her utterances. She is fully conscious of her divine mission, which is to be "the light of the heathen," and "preparing the path for man."

For instance, the Sibyl wrote, "Of centuries fifteen have passed away, Since o'er the Greeks those haughty tyrants ruled, Who first taught evil unto mortal man, And made false gods for them that now are dead, Whereby ye learned to think but vanity." Sibylline poems continued to be published by jews until late in the imperial period.

These compositions reflected current events, and the frequent convulsions in the Roman empire furnished rich material for new visions, which profoundly affected judaism. The christian Sibylline poems covered a greater period of time, with verses written until the Middle Ages. Christians believed the Sibyls foretold the coming of Jesus, and curiously, the "Chronicon Paschale," composed in 16th century BP, enumerates twelve Sibyls.

As with the ancient Greeks, Hindrew writes, "many of the first Christian churches were created by either assimilating, or were built atop the temple ruins of the Sibyls." The Sibyl tradition continued in the imagery of the Black Madonnas in christendom, and the custom lives on in West Africa and the Americas as Mami Wata and Vodun, which means spirit in the Fon and Ewe languages.[71]

Conclusion

This fourth chapter of Part III explored aspects of gynocentric perceptions and spirituality. In gynocentric theology, animals and nature are not viewed as separate from humans since all Earthlings are imbued with the 'spirit' of the Earth Goddess. This female-centered view of reality is based on diversity, not hierarchy, and mutual existence, not superiority.

Stone Age and Neolithic women and children lived in natural environments and their spirituality was based on a relationship to their changing body, landscape, and nature. The ideas behind the Moon Goddess, Deer Goddess, Triple Goddess, and Goddess of Animals reflect females' close kinship to their body, animals, and nature. We still have affection for Earthlings, but our emotions have been colonized and we have separated ourselves from other-than-human animals.

Jiddu Krishnamurti notes about contemporary people, "It is odd that we have so little relationship with nature, with the insects and the leaping frog, and the owl that hoots among the hills calling for its mate. We never seem to have a feeling for all living things on the earth." Gynocentric cultures were rich in this sense, and we can lose this alienation if we observe the similarities of our bodies to nature and decolonized our minds.

Krishnamurti continues "If we could establish a deep, abiding relationship with nature, we would never kill an animal for our appetite, we would never harm, vivisect, a monkey, a dog, a guinea pig for our benefit. We would find other ways to heal our wounds."

The next chapter moves chronologically to explore the social practices of gynocentric groups that existed before European colonization. Analysis of these cultures suggest that the basis of prehistoric female power was matrilocal residence, matrilineal inheritance of property rights, and pivotal roles in governance and decision-making.

(Figure 16: Venus of Laussel is an 18.11 inch (46.0 cm) tall limestone bas-relief of a Woman/Goddess painted with red ochre c. 25,000 BP)

16: Gynocentric Power

> What is required of women at this point in history is a firm and deep refusal to limit our perspectives, questioning, and creativity to any of the preconceived patterns of male-dominated culture. - Mary Daly

ASIA's Journey 2121.16

After Cronetime, everyone is exhausted and falls asleep in the 96°F (35°C) temperature. It is past midnight, and the moon is rising in the cloudless night sky. Only Xóchitl remains awake as the night watch. A scream shatters the stillness of the warm night. It is Zaid again. The almost daily struggle with his mother, Sawni, often ends with him winning. His screaming wakes up the women of ASIA.

"Why is he having a tantrum now?" Zemora says sleepily to Jean. Her partner looks worried. "He is going to give our position away."

"I want a snack now!" Zaid cries out. "Calm down, son, please." Sawni tries to remain calm herself. "If you stop this I will see. "

"No, get me it now!" Zaid screams.

"Stop it," Sawni pleads. "The gangs will come and get us."

"I don't care." Zaid sobs.

The crones gather in the center of the trench for a meeting. They want to support their sister but do not want to interfere with Sawni's authority and parenting.

"We have to move," Lian says. "We're just sitting ducks now." The crones nod in agreement. "We will tell the mothers," Hehewuti tells Lian.

"I will go scout ahead for another camp site." Lian stands up. "Listen for my signal and follow me as soon as you can."

"We will," Zola clasps her hands. "Go, we'll get your pack." The child's screaming continues as his mother tries to get him a snack. Lian starts to leave then looks at Nakeisha. "He has to go."

Nakeisha stretches her arms wide. "We are all sisters. We are Sawni's support group and her village."

Lian is adamant. "Like the other two, he's spoiled, privileged, and out of control."

"We can't kick a sister out." Hehewuti sighs. "You know that."

Lian stomps her feet and heads off towards the low moon-rise.

Introduction

In the past, female-based cultures existed across the Earth, and some remain. They show that another World is possible, one in which humans live in harmony with nature and animals. Gynocentric cultures are not based on accumulation, but on balance, equity, and the well-being of all.

This fifth chapter of Part III on prehistorical gynecological practices broadens the earlier discussions on female-centered perception, thought, and spirituality by exploring how these ideas are incorporated into notions of female power and community. The chapter starts out with a discussion of how gynocentric cultures conceive of residential location, children, and inheritance.

The prevalence of matrilocal cultures, or female-centered residence,

Worldwide is further evidence of gynocentric prehistory, and some examples are next examined. A survey of gynocentric organization, governance, and power comes afterward.

Perhaps most the most striking difference between patriarchal societies and matrifocal communities are their views relating to ownership of land and property and overall goals of the economy. A look at the Mothers' gift economy follows. The chapter turns to examine matrilocal research and women's inner orientation, before discussing the gynocentric characteristics of the Roman Goddess Justitia. Finally, modern matrilineal cultures are surveyed.

♀ Property

In 1724, an American priest described the high status of women among the Indigenous Iroquois as follows: "Nothing... is more real than this superiority of the women. It is essentially the women who embody the Nation, the nobility of blood, the genealogical tree, the sequence of generations and the continuity of families."[1]

The priest continued, "It is in them that all real authority resides: the land, the fields and all their produce belongs to them; they are the soul of the councils, the arbiters of peace and war." Women held all property, according to Iroquois law, which states: "The lineal descent of the people of the Five Fires (the Iroquois Nations) shall run in the female line. They shall own the land and the soil. Men and women shall follow the status of their mothers."

Before European conquest, the Iroquois and other native groups observed a broad range of matriarchal practices.[2] A 'gynocentric culture' could just mean that all individuals descended from a single living female.[3] Typically, gynocentric cultures include matrilocal partner unions,[4] 'bride' price, and inheritance of 'property' or usage rights through the maternal line.[5]

Performing 'bride-service' is a basic economic institution in gatherer-hunter societies. Young males have to visit female partners in their camps and work strenuously for them. The practice encourages egg-producers to remain with close kin following partner unions.[6]

Female-centered organization is not merely a reversal of patriarchy where women rule. They are more egalitarian and do not contain hierarchies, classes, and social control of one sex by the other. Members live in a state of anarchy without authority, which is restrictive.[7] Gynocentric societies are relatively free of interpersonal subordination, but they still have regulations.

Heide Göttner-Abendroth defines gynocentric groups as societies with complementary equality, where great care is taken to provide a balance in many aspects of society - economic, social, political, worldview, spirituality, and so on.[8] Complementary equality applies to balance between genders, among generations, and between humans and nature.[9]

men have vital duties, but ovary beings make the final decisions regarding children, land, food, and other resources.[10] Endogamy, or partner unions within the clan, is strictly prohibited, irrespective of degree of relatedness. 'Property' rights are inherited by daughters from generation to generation and remains undivided.

Matrilocal Dating

As a norm, visiting partner unions was practiced throughout the Stone Age, which means that females and males lived apart with their separate families, and see each other in their spare time.[11] Matrilocal unions were practiced all over the World, from Africa[12] and Eurasia, to North America,[13]

Central and South America,[14] to Oceania.

The tradition of matrilocality was an open one that encouraged diversity and change. Partner unions were with others outside the clan, which meant that in-group, identity-based isolation was limited. With egg-producers as the key decision-makers, women's status and power were assured.

In addition, matrilineal practices ensured female inheritance and safety. Unlike European societies, rape was a rare occurrence among Indigenous female-centered communities. For instance, one report suggests that Indigenous males were killed for committing rape, a crime that was most despised.[15]

In female-centered cultures, children are raised in a stable household consisting of their mother and her sisters and brothers. There are also maternal aunts, uncles, grandmothers, grand aunts, and uncles. There are lovers and unions, but no husbands and wives.[16] Girls started unions without any objections from parents, and the union continued according to the wishes of each egg-producer.[17] A female could easily dismiss a sperm-producer and start a union with some other man.[18]

Women practiced exogamy and did not mate with men from their clan.[19] Consequently, men seldom had a permanent home as partner unions were contracted with ovary beings from various clans.[20] In the New Stone Age, males traveled from camp to camp to visit female partners, to help them dig their fields, and sow and reap their crops.[21]

Cherokee women were sexually liberated and their unions were typically based on mutual attraction. The concept of being ashamed of one's body or physical desires was foreign to the Cherokee egg-producers' mindset. Even though married men and women were expected to be faithful to one another, adultery was not considered a grand crime, and divorce based on loss of attraction was not uncommon. In general, physical relations between consenting adults were viewed as natural and even divine, and not as a source of shame, fear or sin.[22]

Other first nations had similar practices, including the Seneca,[23] Sioux,[24] Cree,[25] Seminole,[26] and Pueblo Indians.[27] Zuni men were devoted to their children, and sew clothes and shoes for their female partners. Among the Carajas, the women own their houses, all its contents, and the canoes. Male partners merely stay with them.

When the Portuguese colonized Brazil, they found that Bororo gynocentric families were extremely loyal to their egg-producing kin. If a Portuguese man captured any Bororo female, even very young girls, all of her relatives followed her and the captor. The entire family willingly served the Portuguese man, remaining enslaved to him all of their lives.

Interestingly, studies show that egg-producers find selfless sperm-producers to be attractive mates. When looking for a long-term partner, a young-bearer might favor more conventional altruism which may indicate that a man is willing to share resources with her and her children.[28]

In contrast, when looking for a short-term union, females may prefer more heroic risk-taking, which may be a costly signal showing good genes. Sensing this, men perform more unselfish acts in the early stages of a romantic relationship or simply when in the presence of an attractive woman.

♀ Governance

Under Stone Age matrilocality, the transient nature of phallic humans meant that they could not form strong alliances and take over egg-producers' agency. Within female-centered clans, women had veto power and could act to remove any male prone to violence against young-bearers, their children, or other men.

What is more, New Stone Age females' primary roles in economic and household production underpinned their leadership roles. For instance, egg-producers foraged and gathered foods, prepared and cooked meals, and kept warm fires burning in camp. They cared for children, and the sick and elderly. Females also weaved baskets, molded pottery, made hats, shoes, clothing, and accessories, and performed other vital household tasks.

Europeans were astonished to see that Indigenous females were the equals of men, politically, economically, and theologically.[29] Cherokee women's close association with nature, as mothers and producers, served as a basis of their power within the language group, not as a basis of oppression as it is currently constructed. Men's position as 'the other' led to gender equivalence, not hierarchy.[30]

In February of 1757, Attakullakulla, a Cherokee leader negotiating trade agreements with the South Carolina governor was shocked to find that no European women were present. Attakullakulla asked the male governor, "Since the white man as well as the red was born of woman, did not the white man admit women to their council?"

The governor replied, "The white men do place confidence in their women and share their councils with them when they know their hearts are good." Taken literally, this meant there were no European women with good hearts in the entire state.

Mothers' Gift Economy

Altruism or selflessness is the principle or practice of concern for the welfare of others. It is a traditional virtue in many cultures and a core aspect of various spiritual traditions and secular worldviews.[31] And, like the sharing of fire, philanthropy is the essence of mothers' gift economies.

Research in prehistoric altruism, and the gift economy of gatherer-'hunter' groups is lacking[32] but these are central aspects of ecogynocentrism.[33] Rather than seeking individual security, Stone Age young-bearers provided for their entire society as a way to better the lives of their offspring. If each community's future was assured, then so too would their children.

Göttner-Abendroth describes contemporary matriarchal economies as focused on careful management of available resources at the subsistence level.[34] The economy is based on agriculture, and the communities sometimes use animals for field labor. Göttner-Abendroth argues that the women's focus on balance and altruism prevented the development of an exchange economy based on accumulation.[35]

Gynocentric women are managers who organize their clan resources in a manner opposite to that of the ego-centered, profit-principle where a tiny group of people benefit by taking advantage of the majority.[36] The motivation behind a matriarch's actions is 'motherliness,' where selflessness is the norm, and the well-being of all members of the community is the primary goal.

The gift economy is a way of constructing and interpreting reality that derives from the practice of mothering and is therefore women-based. The notion of balance emphasizes the value of giving to satisfy needs. The system is need-oriented rather than profit-oriented.[37] For example, the Mosuo woman who is elected to be the clan mother from among her sisters is the one who most clearly displays the attitude of care for other group members.

In contrast to the rapacious greed of patriarchal economic systems, the free satisfaction of needs is still visible in the relation between mothers and children. Young children especially, cannot 'give back' anything in exchange for the nurturing they receive, and they have to receive free goods and services from their caregivers.

In the gynocentric trading system, goods circulate as presents. Generally, money is not known because it has no purpose. The seasonal folk festivals of the agricultural year are the principal resource motor of gynocentric economies. Added to this are lifecycle festivals of the individual clans, and festivals that are celebrated with the whole village.

Gynocentric societies operate according the maxim, "Those who have shall give." And at the big festivals the group that is by comparison better off than the rest of the community takes on the giving role. Other clans are invited and gifts are lavished upon them.

The gynocentric intent is the care and intensifying of human and societal relationships, by fulfilling needs free of ulterior motives. This enables love to grow. It is the principle of unreserved motherliness, in the physical as well as in the spiritual sense. The notion of balance is preserved in christianity and its christmas practices, which has roots in Goddess traditions.

Before Santa, there was Saule, the Lithuanian and Latvian goddess of light and the sun, who took to the skies on the Winter Solstice in a sleigh pulled by horned reindeer. Saule journeyed with the aide of her smith, who forged a golden cup in which to catch her tears which then transformed into amber. During her flight through the heavens, Saule threw these pebbles of amber, like little bits of sun, and apples down to humans below.[38]

Saulė is one of the most powerful deities, the Goddess of life and fertility, warmth and health. She is patroness of the unfortunate, especially orphans. She was a spinning Goddess who used her skill to spin the rays of sunlight onto the World.

Matrilocal Research

Just how prevalent was gynocentric gift-giving and for how long? Was females' notion of balance merely an abnormally under a long-established, competitive, survival of the fittest, man-the-hunter model? Or were resource and trade systems throughout prehistory based on unselfish ideas of motherliness?

Hrdy and other evolutionary feminists dismiss the dogma of primordial patriarchy. For instance, Hrdy demonstrated that since a mothers' kin were so useful in raising her children, gynocentric societies were far more likely than patriarchal arrangements.[39]

Some anthropologists now concede the male-based kinship model is flawed[40] and that early human groups were matrilineal.[41] Scholars who argue for patrilocal residence ignore that human pair-bonding itself was an outcome of having the cooperative female-centered breeding network in place to support larger-brained offspring.[42]

Social anthropologist Chris Knight rejects the common assumption that human culture was a modified extension of primate behavior.[43] Instead, Knight contends that culture was the product of an immense social, sexual, and political revolution initiated by women.[44]

Genetic studies demonstrate that for over tens of thousands of years, gatherer-'hunter' females in Africa were matrilocal.[45] In contrast, patrilocal residence tends to be practiced by pastorals and farming groups.[46] One study showed that endogamy in an early Neolithic village in the Near East was not due to geographic isolation or a lack of exogamous mating partners. Endogamy, perhaps matrilocal, was due to socio-cultural choice.[47]

Starting in the early 1970s, ethnographic and other research among gatherer-'hunter' societies proved that the patrilocal clan model was inaccurate.[48] Cultural anthropology provides ample evidence of matrilocal[49] and matrilineal practices among gatherer-'hunter' cultures.[50] For instance, almost 70 percent of Hadza married females whose mothers were still alive, resided with them in the same camp.[51]

♀ Inner Orientation

Contemporary matrilineal cultures could represent traces of ancient matrilocal and gynocentric societies, when females were clan leaders with high status and power.[52] Peggy Reeves Sanday studied anthropological data on 156 cultures and rejected the argument of universal female subordination. Sanday argues that male dominance is not inherent in human relations but is a response to cultural strain. And those who are thought to embody, be in touch with, or control the creative forces of nature are perceived as omnipotent.[53]

Sanday argues that social formations are grounded in local, ecological, and historical circumstances. To some extent, people's secular authority and roles derive from ancient concepts of power, as exemplified by their origin myths. In addition, levels of authority and dominance are determined by people's adaptation to their environment, social conflict, and emotional stress.[54]

Peggy Reeves Sanday explores power relations through case studies of the effects of European colonialism, migration, and food stress. There are numerous statistical associations between sexual inequity and various cultural pressures. In general, Sanday notes that some cultures functioned around an "inner orientation" in which nature is a partner. In these cultures, food is obtained rather easily from the Earth or sea and the forces of nature are considered sacred.

The social structure of inner orientation cultures is non-patriarchal, and the origins story involves a Goddess or Original Mother. Origin myths may also consist of a divine couple, often Original Mother and her phallic associate. There is a reciprocal flow perceived between the force of nature and the capabilities inherent in women, a power dynamic in which sperm-producers can participate through ritual.

The other cultural orientation Sanday found was an "outer orientation." In these cultures, engagement with nature revolves around seasonal migration and the pursuit of giant animals, or later on herding. There is a focus on creating weapons for interpersonal violence among men, and the social system is patriarchal.

In outer orientation cultures, the origin myths center on a god. And a metaphysics drives males to fear and defend against an implicit power that is "out there." These cultures are highly militarized and sex-segregated. And, in the last few hundred years, most experienced conditions of famine or migration from the over-exploitation of their environment.

Within outer positioning groups, there is a lot of divergence in status between egg-producers and sperm-producers. In general, men's fears are related to female sexuality and phallic 'outsiders.' The care of children is devalued and often delegated to subordinate women.

Roman Goddess: Justitia

Gynocentric philosophies and organization revolved around notions of fairness, equality, and collective decision-making. These powerful ideas were coopted by patriarchal legal systems and maintained throughout the ages via Lady Justice or Justitia. The Roman Goddess of Justice is an allegorical personification of the moral force in judicial systems, and she often appears as a pair with Goddess Prudentia, who holds a mirror and a snake.

Goddess Prudentia represents the ability to govern and discipline oneself by the use of reason. Goddess Justitia is similar to Goddess Aequitas and equivalent to Greek Goddesses Themis and Dike, who also hold a set of scales (libra). Perhaps the scales were an ancient ecogynocentric symbol that represented equality and justice between humans, included non-human animals as well.

The word 'justice' has several meanings, including the quality of being just, righteous, equitable, or moral; to act or treat justly or fairly; to appreciate properly; to uphold the justice of a cause; the administering of deserved punishment or reward; the administration of what is just by law; to bring to justice; and to receive punishment for one's misdeeds.

Lady Justice's attributes are a balance, blindfold, and a sword, but depictions of her wearing a blindfold are modern, not classical. The Goddess was only commonly represented as "blind" since about the end of the 15th century. The earliest Roman coins depicted Goddess Justitia with the sword in one hand and the scale in the other, but with her eyes uncovered. The sword represented authority in ancient times, and conveys the idea that justice can be swift and final.

The scales are typically suspended from Goddess Justitia's left hand, upon which she measures the strengths of a case's support and opposition. Currently, there are thousands of Lady Justice statues installed around the World in legislatures, courts, universities, parks, public plazas and so on.

The personification of justice balancing the scales dates back to the Goddess Maat, and later Isis, of ancient Egypt. Maat or Ma'at refers to both the ancient Egyptian concepts of truth, balance, order, harmony, law, morality, and justice, and the personification of these concepts as the Goddess of Truth and Justice regulating the stars, seasons, and the actions of both mortals and the deities.

Goddess Ma'at primary role in Egyptian mythology dealt with the weighing of the heart that took place in the underworld, Duat. The "Feather of Ma'at" was the measure that determined whether the souls, considered to reside in the heart, of the departed would successfully reach the paradise of afterlife.

The God Anubis was frequently depicted with a set of scales on which he weighed a deceased's heart against the Feather of Truth. The heart was placed on one side of the balance and the feather on the other scale. The lioness Ammit awaited the results so she could consume those who failed.

Maat called the rich to help the less fortunate rather than exploit them, echoed in Egyptian tomb declarations such as, "I have given bread to the hungry and clothed the naked," and "I was a husband to the widow and father to the orphan."

Modern Matrilineality

There are still cultures that are matrilineal, matrilocal, and gynocentric. These groups give great honor and centrality to clan mothers, who distribute material wealth and play a central role in the culture. Modern matrilocal and matrilineal cultures include the Akan, Minangkabau, Khasi, Garo, Jaintia, Mosuo, Bribri, and Nagovisi.[55]

Given the 10,000-year-old history of patriarchal domination, the existence of these cultures is astonishing. Each one is a testament to the enduring nature of female accomplishments, and to the legacy of the Stone Age Earth Goddesses.[56]

Gimbutas suggests that matriliny in Old Europe is the historical continuity of matrilineal succession of older agrarian societies of Europe and Asia Minor. This gynocentric pattern is found in modern groups such as the Celts, Teutons, Slavs, and Balts, who absorbed matricentric and matrilineal traditions from the rich substratum of Old European populations.[57]

The Akan are a big group in Ghana and the Ivory Coast, with around 20 million. Akan social organization is built around the matri-clan, and an individual's identity, inheritance, wealth, and politics are determined by the clan. All matri-clan founders are female, but men traditionally hold leadership positions within the society.

Many Akan still practice their traditional matrilineal customs, living in their traditional extended family households. The traditional Akan economic and political organization is grounded in matrilineal lineages, which are the basis of inheritance and succession.[58]

The Minangkabau is an ethnic group Indigenous to West Sumatra, in Indonesia, of around eight million people. Their culture is matrilineal with property and land passing down from mother to daughter.[59] Sanday describes the birth ceremony where women and men play different roles: "The mother and her female relatives orchestrate the event, choose the day, invite the guests, and prepare the food. The father's family prepares the foods that will be fed to the child."[60]

The Khasi are an Indigenous or tribal people in north east India of around 1.2 million. They are a matrilineal society which goes back to a time when Khasis had several partners and it was hard to determine the paternity of children.[61] The youngest Khasi daughter inherits, children take their mother's surname, and once married, men live in their mother-in-law's home. A Khasi man returns to his home upon the death of his spouse if she is an heiress.[62]

The Garos are the second-largest language group in Meghalaya, India, after the Khasi, with around one million people. The language group is matrilineal, and individuals take their clan titles from their mothers. Traditionally, the youngest daughter inherits the property from her mother. Sons leave their parents' house at puberty and are trained in the village bachelor dormitory. After accepted as a partner, the man lives in the female's house.[63]

Like the Khasi, the Jaintia are in Meghalaya, India, with around 300,000 individuals. They are matrilineal and claim descent from seven mothers. The three cardinal principles of Jaintia religion are right living and practice based on right livelihood, the fulfillment of duties toward fellow humans, and showing respect to the members of one's mother's and father's clans.

The Mosuo are a language group living in China with a population of about 40,000. Mosuo culture is primarily agrarian, and the people are generally self-sufficient in diet. Females grow crops, including grains and potatoes. Local economies tend to be barter-based.[64] The Mosuo culture is matrilineal, but it is frequently described as matriarchal.[65]

Mosuo women are the head of the house, and inheritance is through the female line. The Ah mi, or elder crone, is a matriarch who decides the fate of all those living in her house. For example, the matriarch manages the money and jobs of each family member. When the Ah mi wishes to pass her duties on to the next generation, she will give this female successor the keys to the household storage, signifying the passing on of property rights and responsibility.[66]

The Bribri are an Indigenous group of Costa Rica, with around 35,000 people. Like other matrilineal societies, the Bribri are organized into clans determined through the mother/female lines. Bribri egg-producers are the only ones that can inherit land and prepare the sacred cacao drink that is essential for the group's rituals.[67]

The Nagovisi live in Papua New Guinea, with a population of around 8,000 in the 1970s. A food garden is almost always exclusively worked on by a husband-wife couple, physically situating a couple's marriage in a public space, and also often symbolically representing the state of the relationship. If a couple is quarreling, for example, the husband is not allowed to take food from his wife's garden and must return to his village of origin to eat or use materials from plants.[68]

Among South American native cultures, the paternity of a female's baby becomes partitioned among multiple males.[69] And the Na of China are without fathers or husbands.[70] Based on extensive fieldwork in Southwest China, Du argues that gender-egalitarian societies do exist among the Lahu and other groups. Practical gender equality has become the byproduct of a potent ideology of gender unity, vividly expressed by the proverb, "chopsticks only work in pairs."[71]

In many of these cultures, women are responsible for holding and passing on environmental knowledge. Grandmothers, as midwives, are responsible for welcoming new life into their community, as well as washing and preparing the dead for burial. Women's responsibilities, and the ceremonies involved, are grounded in the land, which is considered a female realm. Likewise, the rivers and water are viewed as veins of the great Mother.[72]

Conclusion

This fifth chapter of Part III outlined some gynocentric traditions in pre and post-colonial societies around the World. It deconstructed gynocentric power as based on balance and equity, and showed that empowerment practice includes recognizing and prioritizing female choice in sex selection, as in matrilocality.

The surviving examples of matrifocal, matrilocal and matrilineal cultures provide glimpses of egg-producers' status and vital roles during prehistory. These groups are under tremendous pressure to abandon gynocentric practices but they have so far resisted.[73]

The next chapter delves into research by feminist scholars and the powerful opposition they faced in doing work that contradicted the dominant man-the-leader narrative. The prehistoric existence of gynocentric cultures is anathema to patriarchal ideology, which presents phallic dominance as natural and eternal for the species. The cyborgs' highly successful backlash against gynocentric prehistory and the Earth Goddess are examined next.

(Figure 17: Hohlefels Woman/Goddess ivory carving c. 37,000 BP)

17: Theorizing History

Elemental faith is farfetched. The words of the Fates are fetched from remote times and places as well as from the inner-most depths of Here and Now. - Mary Daly

ASIA's Journey 2121.17

It's one AM, 95°F (35°C) with low humidity on a last quarter-moon night. The women and children are sleepy and stagger in the dark as they move towards Lian's low call to their new campsite. Before the left the trench, Zaid ate his snack, but he continues to whimper. The dogs are in front, muzzled to keep them quiet.

Kuan-Yin leads the group and Xóchitl guards the rear. The children trip in the dark and fall occasionally, but ASIA stays close and moves together. The sound of an owl call fills the night air. "Keep moving," Hehewuti whispers. "We're almost there."

The group remain as one until Sabra falls. The women in the middle stop and Nakeisha takes a look at Sabra's ankle with a pen flashlight as the women in front wait for them to catch up.

The night suddenly gets darker, and a thick fog quickly covers the group. Visibility drops to zero and the children in the rear complain loudly. Xóchitl scrambles forward, crawling on the ground and touches one girl.

"Hang on," Xóchitl reassures the child, grabbing her tightly. "You're safe with me." The dense fog persists and girls in front of her panic and scream.

"Help!" One child cries out. "Pedo-hunters are here."

Xóchitl yells. "Hold on to each other and don't make a sound."

The group quiets down, but the screaming continues ahead, to the left of her. "They're kidnapping us," a girl shouts above the din of cries on the far left.

Hehewuti tightens her grip on Kuan-Yin. "That sounds like Nadie's voice," she utters, her voice breaking.

Xóchitl is blinded by the fog and can do nothing as the children's cries on the left fades into the night. Slowly, the fog dissipates, and the women regroup. Four girls are missing - Nadie, Cha'Kwaina, Iniko, and Sabra. The children sob silently for their missing friends.

"Keep moving!" Kuan-Yin commands. "Quickly before the gangs return."

ASIA stands up, ready to leave as Jean comforts the girls. "We are all sad, but we have to walk silently until we get to the next camp."

Xóchitl holds up two cans to the crones as the group walks forward. "These are the fog canisters the pedo-hunters used to attack us."

Jean nods. "The pedo-hunters must have heard Zaid and tracked us after we left camp."

Nakeisha whimpers in disbelief of what just happened. Sawni grabs Zaid and cries silently over Iniko.

"We will find Iniko." Xóchitl stares at the waning moon as she promises Sawni. "We will bring our daughters back." Jean and Xóchitl leads the two dogs and jogs off in the direction of the missing children.

Introduction

Modern neoliberalism is the opposite of Stone Age ecogynocentrism and its gift economies. The cyborg's competitive, 'every man for himself' paradigm is a fundamental cause of climate change, and much of history and science is trapped within this predatory patriarchal framework.

This sixth and last chapter of Part III on New Stone Age females explores patriarchal academic manipulation and the conflict between communism and male-centered, capitalist 'science.' The debate over prehistoric sexual relations underlies a lot of social and economic theory and is critical for feminists and activists to understand.

The chapter starts with a discourse on the link between gynocentric prehistory and socialism and the reaction of capitalist historians and scholars. Then, it explores original scholarship of feminist archaeologist Marija Gimbutas. Male denigration of Gimbutas's work comes next, then a look at the 'feminist' backlash against her, followed by a survey of the evidence for gynocentric prehistory. The chapter concludes with a discussion on the Roman Goddess Aequitas, the deity of equality.

Gyno-Socialism

In the 19th and early 20th century, the existence of prehistoric gynocentrism was accepted by numerous social scientists. For instance, in 1861, after studying ancient Greek historical texts and myths, Johann Bachofen proposed that so-called kinship was based on females alone.[1] A decade later, in Ancient Society, Lewis Morgan provided several examples of matrilineal clans from across the World.[2]

In searching for alternatives to capitalism, Marx and Engels found Morgan's analysis and used it as confirmation of their view that ancient forms of non-market economies preceded property-based class society. Moreover, anarchist and socialist reformers alike concluded that the basis for prehistoric communism was sexual equality.

Engels wrote in 1884, "The overthrow of mother right was the world-historic defeat of the female sex. The man seized the reins in the house also, the woman was degraded, enthralled, the slave of the man's lust, a mere instrument for breeding children... the first class oppression with that of the female sex by the male"[3]

In the early 20th century, socialist-feminist Rosa Luxemburg defended Karl Marx's dialectical materialism and conception of history. Luxemburg was part of a German working class revolution in 1918 that was brutally suppressed by the ruling class. She argued that "primitive communism, with its corresponding democracy and social equality [was] ... the cradle of social development."[4]

Luxemburg continued, "the noble tradition of the ancient past, thus holds out a hand to the revolutionary aspirations of the future, the circle of knowledge closes harmoniously, and the present world of class domination and exploitation... becomes merely a minuscule transient stage in the great cultural advance of humanity."

Managed economies in Russia, China, Yugoslavia, Vietnam and elsewhere were influenced by the mother's gift economy that emphasized sharing, balance, and equality. All the same, socialism's phallic leaders completely ignored gynocentric circular organization and consensual decision-making process. Akin to their capitalist predecessors, socialists and communists resorted to the same hierarchical, top-down, phallic-centered planning that generated class inequality in the first place, with predictable results.

Still, there are numerous examples of resistance to individualized greed and glorification of the rich. There are thousands of mutual aid societies, cooperatives, community organizations, communes, artisan guilds, unions, worker cooperatives, collective ownerships, and so on. Most of these groups are top-down and phallic-centric, but they do provide somewhat of an alternative to the prevailing disorder.

Capitalist-based ♂ Science

The political implications of communal matriarchy and its economy of balance represented a dangerous ideological challenge to the 'survival of the fittest' capitalist myth. Woman-the-gift-giver was the opposite of man-the-competitor, and this fundamental break in the dominant narrative was taken seriously by proponents of individualized, laissez-faire capitalism.

Female-centered, community-managed mutualism was the prevailing economic system for millennia, but from early on, a line of academics out rightly dismissed socialist perspectives of prehistory as idealistic romantic fallacy. Marxists and gynocentric theorists were accused of failing to see the anthropological and genetic basis for phallic violence. Socio-biologists argue that Marxists' key error is to "conceive of human nature as relatively unstructured and largely or wholly the product of external socio-economic forces."[5]

Marvin Harris exposed the focus of 20th century social science on disproving communism's origins.[6] To cast doubt on men's overthrow and reduction of women, anthropologist Franz Boas used flawed analysis of a single Indigenous group on Vancouver Island to 'establish' that it was just as likely that matrilineality succeeded patrilineality.[7]

Malinowski went further by completely rejected prehistorical group motherhood to claim that the patriarchal nuclear family had always existed.[8] Subsequently, Lévi-Strauss proposed that an 'exchange of women' between men were the origins of marriage and kinship.[9]

By the 1940s, the 'patrilocal band' of Stone Age gatherer-'hunters' was taken for granted by social scientists, completely reversing Bachofen and Morgan's evidence for matrilocal organization.[10] Moreover, monogamy was accepted as a defining characteristic of modern hominins, while Bachofen's theory of 'primitive promiscuity' was condemned as akin to prostitution.

The myth of humans as a patriarchal species prevails in popular culture and academia. At the end of the 20th century, academics were suggesting that that Stone Age men would not have expended time and energy to benefit the genes of another sperm-producer.[11] With hardly any evidence, monogamy was extended way back to H. erectus.

Ignoring overwhelming evidence on the existence of ecogynocentrism, the controlling paradigm is that man-the-hunter was a successful husband who provided all that his wife needed. For example, one group of experts argue, "If H. erectus hunted regularly, males might have been able to provide high-quality food for their mates and offspring. Monogamy would have increased the males' confidence of paternity and favored paternal investment."[12] This theory is little more than conjecture.

Gimbutas's Spinning

Marija Gimbutas combined her extensive background in linguistic paleontology with archaeological evidence to conclude that societies in Europe and Turkey during the New Stone Age had a balanced, nonpatriarchal and nonmatriarchal social system.[13] The noted expert on Eastern Europe noted that the Greek male-female dualism is not present in agrarian cultures.

In Neolithic Europe, men were prominent in trade, architecture, and crafts. There was no marriage, and mothers had a consort but no husband. While these cultures may not have had all female leadership, they were probably matrifocal or matrilineal, like numerous agrarian cultures in the World today.

According to Gimbutas's Kurgan migration theory, the expansion of herders from Ukraine and southern Russia disrupted the Old European cultures. Starting from around 5,500 BP, Gimbutas surmised that three major waves of Bronze Age patriarchal groups invaded Europe. The pastoral invaders had a different language, social structure, technologies, and culture.

The Kurgan attackers used domesticated horses to travel quickly and conquer vast tracks of territory. Thousands of New Stone Age settlements were burned down and abruptly abandoned. There was a rapid disappearance of the Old European symbolic system, coupled with the sudden appearance of constructed fortifications.[14]

Unlike earlier waves of agricultural migrants from the Middle East, the 'androcratic' or male-centered Kurgan herders had a strict hierarchical rule of warriors. The chieftain was buried with his possessions, often including retainers, wives, concubines, horses, and artifacts. This form of femicide and burial did not exist in Europe before the arrival of Kurgan clans. This burial ritual embodied a new perception of the individual and of small monogamous family groups as the foundation of society.

Hoofed animals, especially domesticated sheep and oxen, played an important part in the Kurgan economy and culture. Kurgan's practice of sacrificing domesticates as part of male-based religion set a pattern for phallic-bonding, theology, and economy in subsequent patriarchal regimes from Mesopotamia and Egypt, to the subsequent Abrahamic cults.

In Kurgan culture, enslaved bulls were allotted to the masculine sphere, and the symbolism of bull heads and bull horns were used to represent machismo and aggressiveness. The invaders' warrior gods dethroned the nurturing Goddess, and her various manifestations were incorporated into the male-dominated pantheons as wives, daughters, or consorts.

The savagery of Kurgan and other Neolithic warriors laid the groundwork for current phallic-centered rule. As Carol Christ writes, "Patriarchy is not simply the domination of women by men. Patriarchy is an integral system in which men's control of women's sexuality, private property, violence, war, and the institutions of conquest, rape, slavery arise and thrive together."[15]

Christ continues, "The different elements are so intertwined that it is impossible to separate one as the cause of the others. Patriarchy is an integral system of interlocking oppressions, enforced through violence. The whole of the patriarchal system is legitimated by patriarchal religions."

♂ Dismissal of Gimbutas

The pro-capitalist, masculinist agenda in anthropology in mirrored in archaeology where tremendous effort is expended to disprove the existence of prehistoric communism. For decades, researchers have strenuously denied any cultural continuity from the Stone Age into the New Stone Age, and the significance of Woman/Goddess figures.

Marija Gimbutas have spent decades documenting gynocentric prehistory in Europe. Her work represents a radical break from male-centered archaeologists who have widely adopted the 'patrilocal band' theory from anthropology. Consequently, there is a concerted effort to reject Gimbutas' analysis by academics from various disciplines.

Similar to Marvin Harris's exposure of anthropology's class bias, Charlene Spretnak details how Gimbutas's work was systematically debunked in archaeology.[16] For instance, Gimbutas's hypothesis of ancient Goddess-worshiping female-centered cultures was disparaged by 'experts' with considerably less expertise in eastern European archaeology.[17]

The derogation of Gimbutas got started by men like Renfew, Hayden, and Fagan,[18] who totally dismissed her brilliant scholarship and meticulous research. Phallic 'experts' in cognitive archaeology suggested that the Neolithic Woman/Goddess figures Gimbutas discovered served as nothing more than foreplay for men during sex, or as sexual insults of a subordinate group, females.[19]

For example, Hodder argues, "the elaborate female symbolism in the earlier Neolithic expressed the objectification and subordination of women... Perhaps women rather than men were shown as objects because they, unlike men, had become objects of ownership and male desire."[20]

Phallic archaeologists automatically assume that Woman/Goddess statuettes were constructed by and for men based on a presumption that representation of female nudity is always erotica. But, as Nelson rightly points out, assigning the figurines with erotic connotations merely illustrates "unexamined assumptions about gender" and is itself sexist.[21]

Feminist Backlash

The backlash against Gimbutas took on a feminist tone and gained much legitimacy with female critics.[22] Gimbutas's sophisticated, multi-disciplinary analysis was reduced to behavioral psychology and rejected by female academics on the basis of minor details over the dates of artifact, archaeological context, typologies, and so on.

Similar to her male dissenters, Gimbutas's feminist critics have not read or studied most of her work. Yet, they have no problem claiming Woman/Goddess figurines were merely fertility fetishes restricted to household production, without larger ideological or spiritual significance.[23]

Sarah Nelson contend that Gimbutas employed the same techniques used to disparage women, to falsely glorify them. Nelson quotes Pamela Russell, as saying "The archaeological evidence is, in some cases, distorted enough to make a careful prehistorian shudder."[24] Actually, careful prehistorians would not read Gimbutas out of context but study all of her field-notes before passing judgment.

The feminist backlash against Gimbutas is ironic. Arguing for a matrilocal and female-centered prehistory is considered irresponsible idealism by her feminist critics.[25] Gimbutas's work is dismissed as feminist-revisionist history, and for being essentialist because she supposedly views egg-producers power as purely biological and not cultural.[26] Gimbutas is accused of 'reverse sexism' and even of sanctifying misandry.[27]

Gimbutas's groundbreaking research has revolutionized feminism and archaeology, yet it is viewed as 'pseudo-feminism' and 'pseudo-archaeology.' In doing so, feminists and anthropologists reject genetic and material evidence of a patriarchal society invading non-patriarchal groups during the New Stone Age, as Gimbutas's work clearly shows. The preferred academic feminist theory is that the raise of patriarchy is a by-product of technologies and internal social upheavals. The Neolithic domesticating process and its effects on sexual relations is discounted, as well as any notion of what existed before male-domination.

In a repeat of the backlash against Bachofen and Morgan in anthropology, Gimbutas's critics quickly gained prominence, and their generally unfounded claims acquired the status of common knowledge. The steady feminist drumbeat of 'Gimbutas must be dismissed' has resulted in her scholarship not being read, assigned, or cited in classes on European archaeology.

Far from the charge of pseudo-science and distorted analysis, Gimbutas gynocentric theory is supported by a plethora of data and artifacts, including the thousands of Woman/Goddess figures, female hand prints, and female-centered art uncovered from the Stone Age and Neolithic. In addition, there are thousands of ancient folktales, myths, and oral traditions of female deities and Goddesses across the Globe.

There are existing gynocentric cultures, and modern-day gatherer-'hunters' are matrilocal as shown by Sanday, Göttner-Abendroth, and other anthropologists.[28] There is genetic mapping evidence, the grandmother hypothesis, and grounds for female-centered cultures established by evolutionary feminists like Hrdy and Gowaty.

The Stone Age man-the-hunter, male band premise is based on far less evidence, yet it is considered 'unbiased' and without a taint of sexism. It is not "absurd" to propose that Neolithic art, cultural symbols, and material artifacts had roots in Stone Age gynocentric worldviews and spirituality. For instance, myths of Celtic Goddesses are more widely distributed than phallic gods, and date from an earlier time.[29]

Prehistory Was ♀

Gimbutas's hypotheses of an invasion of gynocentric Europe by patriarchal clans from the east is supported by paleolinguists and historical genetic mapping. Her Kurgan migration theory is substantiated by findings of the Yamanya invasion, and by other archaeologists.[30]

The worldwide predominance of ovary beings in art and oral tradition suggest there was a belief that egg-producers had spiritual attributes that were peculiar to the sex.[31] And, Gimbutas's Goddess-based analysis is substantiated by other archaeological research, such as Jacobson's study of the Deer Goddess.

In comparison, dissenters provide little evidence that male dominance has been virtually universal unto the present.[32] There is no absolute disproof of the veneration of a Great Goddess in academic literature, only alternative explanations.[33] Moreover, the notion that Neolithic Europeans burned down their own settlements is not widely accepted.

Martin West concluded that Gimbutas's argument that Goddess-based Old European spirituality was overtaken by a patriarchal Indo-European religion, is "essentially sound."[34] Many prominent scholars agree that the Woman/Goddess figurines are objects with magic/spiritual meaning.[35] One contended that the figures were representations of fertility Goddesses and part of agrarian cultures.[36]

Gimbutas regarded the Eleusinian Mysteries as a remnant of ancient Goddess worship. This view is supported by Luck who contends that the

Goddess persisted into Classical times as Gaia, Magna Mater, and numerous others.[37]

An extensive study of South Asian art revealed that there was a common cultural inheritance based on the Great Mother - from Mesopotamia to Egypt, and from the Ganges to the Mediterranean.[38] And a survey of prehistoric, near Eastern civilizations, concluded the Great Goddess "is the basis of our civilization."[39]

The same pattern of Woman/Goddess figures is uncovered in the Americas. Laurette Sejourne, who studied the ceramic objects found at Tlatilco, Mexico dating to 1,500 BP, writes, "There is an extraordinary number of figurines. Representations of men - almost always oddities - dwarfs, hunchbacks, magicians - form a small percentage of the whole. The female figurines are surprising in their quantity and quality."[40]

After the great fall of women and the rise of male-based civilizations, prehistoric gynocentric principles persisted in many forms. For example, ideas around equality and the Mother's gift economy were encapsulated in various deities, such as the Roman Goddesses Justitia and Aequitas, the Greek Titaness Nyx, Themis, Dike, Adrestia, Nemesis, an many others.

Roman Goddess: Aequitas

The Roman Goddess Aequitas is a good example of the persistence of gynocentric egalitarian philosophy. This abstract deity was a powerful symbol that was co-opted by male Roman rulers to garner appeal from the masses. Aequitas is the Latin concept of equality, symmetry, uniformity, fairness, equal rights, kindness, and moderation. The term is derived from aequus meaning "even, just, equal" and is the origin of the English word "equity."

The Goddess Aequitas reflected earlier notions of gynocentric behavior, organization, and egalitarianism, the doctrine that all people are equal and deserve equal rights and opportunities. Aequitas means just or equitable conduct toward others governed by benevolence, while justitia yields to another only what is strictly due.

'Veritas aequitas' is Latin for truth and justice. This a popular motto that stands for personal honor and truth in actions and justice, regardless of the circumstances. In sharp contrast to male aggressiveness, the esteemed term aequitas also means having a quiet, tranquil state of mind, evenness of temper, calmness, and equanimity. Perhaps, this meaning and the slogan reflected gynocentric customs that existed in the past.

Cicero defined aequitas as having three parts - the first pertained to the gods above and is equivalent to religious obligation; the second, to the Manes, the underworld spirits of the dead that were sacred; and the third related to human beings and iustitia, or "justice." The Goddess Aequitas encapsulated all three of these meanings.

During the Roman Empire, Goddess Aequitas was part of the religious propaganda of the emperor, under the name Aequitas Augusti, which also appeared on coins. The Goddess is depicted on coins holding a balance and cornucopia. Her scale (libra) was more often a symbol of "honest measure" and equality to the Romans, than of justice.

The cornucopia was a symbol of plenty consisting of a cone-shaped ornament or receptacle overflowing with fruit, flowers, and grain, signifying prosperity. It was also called horn of plenty and represented the horn of the goat that suckled Zeus, which broke off and became filled with fruit. In folklore, it became full of whatever its owner desired. The juxtaposition of Goddess

Aequitas' scales and harvest bounty was not an accident. Perhaps, it reflected deep gyno-socialist principles that the fruits of the empire belongs to the people and must be shared equally.

Conclusion

History is critical for perception, analysis, and action regarding injustices. This last chapter of Part III explained some aspects around the suppression of Stone Age and Neolithic female accomplishments. History is personal and political, and academia is heavily embedded within the patriarchal order.

Anthropologists, archaeologists, historians, and academic feminists are paid specialists within patriarchal institutions, and these so-called 'experts' are part of an ongoing conspiracy to erase egg-producers' communism from the human story. The conflicts of interest of these 'professionals' are no different from the scientists who defended smoking as harmless for decades.

The erasure of the young-bearing sex from prehistory is part of patriarchal capitalists' attempt to reinforce their domestication of girls and women. The next section, Part IV, surveys the sixth and seventh tamings, that of animals and females. It explores how the erasure of the Goddess and ecogynocentrism occurred in concurrence with phallic ascendancy, the rise of patriarchy, and male-centered 'civilization.'

(Figure 18: Woman/Goddess baked clay figure of Çatalhöyük
c. 8,000 BP)

IV: RISE OF CYBORGS (8,000 to 5,000 BP)

18: Taming Nature

> Since the passion of necrophiliacs is for the destruction of life and since their attraction is to all that is dead, dying, and purely mechanical, the fathers' fetishized "fetuses" (re-productions/replicas of themselves), with which they passionately identify, are fatal for the future of this planet.
> - Mary Daly

ASIA's Journey 2121.18

It is 101°F (38°C) in the morning under a patchy sky with high humidity. ASIA is near the end of their second second rest stop. The sun's rays are unrelenting, and the sparse shade is a welcome relief.

It is two days since pedophile hunters captured the four girls, and the group is on guard, expecting the men to come back for the other children. Four members were having muscle and abdominal cramps, nausea, vomiting, and diarrhea. The women were short on food and water and have to keep moving.

Sawni and the mothers of the kidnapped girls, Nadie, Cha'Kwaina, and Sabra are hopeful since Jean and Xóchitl are out looking for their missing children. But, in two days they have not received any signal from the pair.

"What if Jean and Xóchitl are too far away to track our receiver?" Zemora wonders.

"It's not that, Z," Lian explains. "The range is 100 miles."

"Those two will not give up," Hehewuti says. "They will find a way to get our daughters back."

The women and children stand up and start to walk again. Zaid runs out and takes the lead. Since the attack, ASIA's only male has calmed down and stopped being fussy. He is playful and does not seem to miss his sister.

It is now afternoon, and ASIA is taking shelter under the massive branches of a dried up oak tree. They crones notice long shadows in the distance moving towards them. It could be the pedo-hunters returning.

The group lies flat on the ground while Lian scouts for a better spot to hide. But it is Jean, Xóchitl, and the two dogs. The girls are not with them.

"What happened?" Hehewuti asks when the pair arrives.

"We followed the pedo-hunters to their camp," Jean explained. "They had horses waiting. After a while, they threw the girls in a wagon and rode west." Sawni, Onaiwah, and Zamora break down sobbing.

"The dogs tracked the wagon for a few hours but then we lost the trail," Xóchitl continued. "We're so sorry."

Kuan-Yin blesses Jean and Xóchitl. "You did your best."

"They are probably going to city to sell the children," Xóchitl suggests.

Sawni stares at the crones. "We have to go there."

"It's only a few days away if we hurry," Hehewuti agrees. "If we find them we can try to buy our girls back."

The mothers are encouraged, and the women plan a new path west to the city. When he hears about the change in plans, Zaid smiles "We get to eat all we can!" He looks at the girls. "And take baths."

"Praise be, the Goddess in me. Praise be, the Apsaras." The children sing as they walk, casting long, dancing shadows towards the rising moon.

Introduction

With phallic ascendancy in the New Stone Age, the building of houses and settlements were done as part of private enterprise, not for the community or clan. Men abandoned the economy of balance, and reduced land, building materials, animals, and people to private objects, mere commodities to be owned and dispensed in any way.

The chief purpose of males' individualized architecture was personal comfort, status, and wealth. The first houses, settlements, and towns not only represents the dawn of cyborg 'civilization,' but also phallic desire to transcend the Earth, nature, and animals through 'progress,' achievement, and accumulation.

The five chapters of Part IV analyzes the growth of phallic dominance and the transition from ecogynocentrism to male-centered rule and so-called 'civilization.' The first chapter covers the emergence of pastoral clans, male-centered settlements, and the first cities.

The second and third chapters of Part IV investigates the role that enslaved animals played in the growth of male-dominated economies, competition, and war. The fourth chapter examines the development of speciest and sexist laws that normalized men's ownership of nature, animals, and females.

The fifth and final chapter in this section explores male-centered religion and the reduction of the Goddess and women during the phallic 'civilization' process. This first chapter of Part IV commences with a study of the Yamnaya invasion and the Neolithic Y-bottleneck. Examples of how New Stone Age men monopolized female surplus are explored next.

The chapter turns to surveying one of the first male-based towns, Chatalhuyuk, then lists nascent cities and their populations. It concludes with a discussion of the powerful role of the Greek Titaness, Goddess Nyx ('Night').

Yamnaya ♂ Invasion

Gatherer-'hunters' started settling in the Middle East close to 15,000 BP, and human populations surged after the emergence of agriculture around 11,000 BP. Curiously, there is no significant evidence of warfare until 5,500 BP, when the region increasingly came under the influence of the emerging military empire of Egypt.[1] In other parts of the World, war originated as late as 4,000 BP.[2]

Humans lived and thrived in the Middle East for roughly 10,000 years, a period that included population growth, climate shifts, and environmental degradation, without waging war. Ferguson found that "the Western world's first widespread, enduring social system of war" emerged around 8,000 BP in Anatolia. The scholar notes, "This is the start of a system of war that flows down in a river of blood to the present."

The Stone Age peace ended with the occurrence of economic and social shifts associated with Neolithic, when domesticates, stored grains, and other property incentivized the organized raiding of settlements.[3] By the time Europeans started supplementing stone tools with metal ones roughly 5,500 years ago, "a culture of war was in place across all of Europe," Ferguson argues. His analysis coincides with Gimbutas's timeline of the Kurgan invasion.

Male farmers from the Middle and Near East migrated across the Mediterranean and Europe, spreading agrarian technology.[4] The skilled agrarian migrants were mostly peaceful, and female-centered social organization continued to flourish among Indigenous European nomads. The new Neolithic societies were based on large farming communities as reflected in their collective burial ritual often in big stone chambers, or megaliths.

With the Neolithic 'revolution,' male-centered colonization of nonhuman animals started to bring about profound social changes and divisions in the Middle East, Europe, and elsewhere. For one, the balanced ecogynocentrism of Indigenous gatherer-'hunters' slowly gave way to unequal power systems led by phallic-dominated pastoral groups.

Wilma Dunaway writes, "historically, agrarian capitalism has shifted control of household, land, and means of production to men; has stimulated public policies that disempowered women; and has fostered the 'cult of domesticity' in order to justify the inequitable treatment of wives."[5]

Four to five thousand years after farmers arrived and settled, an extreme form of patriarchy was ushered in by horseman cultures from Russia who brought war and chaos throughout Eurasia.[6] Around 5,000 and 4,800 BP, there was a massive migration into the heartland of Europe by the Yamnaya people from the grasslands north of the Black Sea. Yamnaya horsemen also rode east, all the way to the Altai Mountains in Siberia.

The Yamnaya were mobile, pastoral nomads who lived in wagons and relied heavily on cattle for dairy farming. This culture had genes that link to lactose tolerance, allowing people to drink and consume dairy products. Sheep were kept for their wool, and horses were used for warfare, as pack animals, and to manage cattle herds.[7]

The sex ratios of the earliest Yamnaya burials in central Europe suggest that the new arrivals were 90 percent males. This phallic conquest was part of a war band tradition. Young men who did not have any inheritance were probably more willing to make a career as migrating warriors.

Arriving with few women, the tall strangers were eager to abduct local farmers' daughters. Not long after the Yamnaya invasion, their skeletons were buried with women who had lived on farms as children.[8] The rigidly male-dominated culture buried their dead in immense mounds known as kurgans.[9]

Plague was widespread in both Europe and Central Asia at this time. Akin to the European colonization process in America, perhaps the Yamnaya brought plague to Europe and caused a massive collapse in the population. Eventually, the unions between the Yamnaya and the descendants of Anatolian farmers catalyzed the creation of the famous Corded Ware culture.

The original herding economy gradually gave way to new practices of crop cultivation, which led to the adoption of new words for crops that did not belong in the original Yamnaya languages. The invaders also learned how to grow barley from Neolithic women to produce beer.

As the Yamnaya spread through central Europe during the early Bronze Age, they introduced domestic horses, the wheel, new metal skills, and genes for brown eyes.[10] They spoke a language that served as the basis for English, Spanish, French, Greek, and Russian. For example, there are common words across these languages for wheeled vehicles, transport, and other Yamnaya innovations.[11] They brought not only a new language, but also novel ideas on organizing society around small monogamous families with individual ownership to animals and land.

A few closely-linked Yamnaya groups from the Russian steppe dominated far-flung areas in Europe and Asia, introduced patriarchy, and shaped significant parts of the genetics of Europeans and Asians. Territorial claims led to extreme violence, as evidenced by a mass burial around eight millennium BP at Talheim, Germany, where an entire community was killed by assailants wielding stone axes like those used to clear-cut land.

In conflicts, nomadic bands tend to take few captives of any sex or age, or, only on occasion, young women. In contrast, male-dominated settlers and states might take everyone captive because they could become 'slaves' or tax payers. Ever since the Yamnaya invasion, capitalist-based expansion have fueled endless wars and strife for 5,000 years.[12]

Neolithic Y-Bottleneck

Scientists agree that human genetic diversity in non-African populations was shaped primarily by an out-of-Africa dispersal of H. sapiens sapiens around 50,000 to 100,000 BP. This migration led to lower genetic variety among non-Africans, and there was a subsequent event that reduced diversity further.

Recent genetic mapping uncovered that starting around 8,000 BP, a second substantial bottleneck in Y-chromosome lineages occurred in non-African populations. This biological restriction could be the result of cultural changes affecting the reproductive success of males,[13] in one of the first instances of culture affecting human evolution.[14] The second Y-bottleneck may be due to the dating success of migrant farmers and their offspring.[15] It also reflected Indigenous female choice in sex-selection.

Around 4,000 to 8,000 years after domestication, across the Globe, for every 17 young-bearers who were reproducing and passing on their genes to people alive today, only one sperm-producer did. The 17 to 1 ratio is quite astonishing since about four or five egg-producers procreate for every one man on average.

Intensive cultivation of plants and other technologies arrived as part of a migrant farming package. Indigenous female gatherers were early adopters, which provided phallic settlers with the most mating partners. Local nomadic men retreated further into the interior, and so had less mating opportunities.[16]

The Y-bottleneck suggests that the few males who were settler-farmers accumulated property and resources as success in domesticating plants served as a proxy for wealth. The fifth and sixth domestication events gave smaller groups of related men the reproductive upper hand for generations. Men who had more wealth and status might have had more to offer to generations of ovary gatherers. And, their sons and grandsons were more successful in the same way.

Farming settlers and later Yamnaya invaders passed on their wealth to their phallic offspring, which, along with female dis-inheritance of wives and daughters, led to capital accumulation, class formation, and a pattern of elite male reproductive success.[17] At the same time, though, the lower diversity in Y-chromosome may have had cascading physical and cognitive effects.[18]

The Y-bottleneck in Europe reflects the transition from gynocentric, matrilineal clans towards patrilineal cultures tracing their descent through the male line. Later on, as more sperm-producers gained agrarian and herding skills, the genetic restriction may have reflected the invasion of pastorals and corresponding phallic battles.[19]

Monopolizing ♀ Surplus

Ever since the dawn of phallic thinking, men have regarded women with a mixture of attraction and awe. Egg-producers are the gateway to life, and also objects of desire. The ovary body was associated with magic, as mysterious as life itself, and most sperm-producers accepted their roles in Stone Age maternal cultures. But along with these emotions, some men may have harbored resentment, fear, and jealously of women for tens of millennia.

In the Neolithic, when women's gathering and agricultural activities created surplus food, males monopolized it to spend more time in large-scale, men-only ceremonies that lasted for days or even weeks.[20]   Annette Hamilton's study of contemporary Australian Aborigines show that the grinding of seeds was a vital part of egg-producers' work, but they detested doing it.

Women were reluctant to create extra rations not only because the process as tedious and hard, but because females did not benefit from the surplus food they produce in any significant way. Making vast numbers of seed cakes allowed sons and brothers to just rely on the food produced by women for developing male-culture and forms of violence, for example, inter-clan rivalries.[21]

Initially, the improvement of agriculture was a positive step for women. But it soon contributed to their great fall of as sons and grandsons monopolized female agrarian technology. By exploiting egg-producers' agricultural labor and trading women's surplus crops, New Stone Age men were able to amass considerable resources. Moreover, the transition to private accumulation from a female-centered gift economy led to rapid devolution in men's thinking, or cyborg consciousness.

Mound Cities: Çatalhöyük

Villages required phallic coalitions to defend them, which probably aided in the development of machismo and hyper-masculinity. Since there was property worth inheriting, paternity became an issue which led to greater control of egg-producers by sperm-producers. Early settlements became strictly patrilineal and the dis-inheritance of females continued as phallic-based 'civilizations' transformed into towns. By the formation of the first cities, female status and capacities were drastically reduced.

In many ways, architecture and ownership represent some of males' earliest attempts to transcend nature and community. Unlike female-centered burials and Earth mounds in the New Stone Age, sperm-producers' emerging Neolithic and Bronze Age architecture were individualized, exclusive, and status-based. Men's hierarchical organization of privatized housing in towns and cities represented a radical alteration in social space that altered human communities and consciousness.

Prehistoric women's architecture was natural, organized, and group based. Gynocentric clans focused their energies and resources on community housing, ritual space, and public areas. Privatized space existed as basic huts and fireplaces that were similar, so there were no status differences associated with housing structures. Women's massive community structures reflected harmony between humans and nature, and were built to last for centuries.

Bronze Age phallic constructions, in comparison, were temporary, haphazard, and lacking in central planning. In some places, men built house upon house in successive generations for 1,000 years or more as part of mound villages.

A good example is Çatalhöyük, a settlement in Turkey that lasted from approximately 9,500 BP to 7,700 BP.[22] The oldest part of Çatalhöyük consists of densely clustered houses separated by areas of rubbish.[23] The site was immense and home to as many as 3,000 people at any one time.[24]

Distinctive clay Women/Goddess statues represent only five percent of the 2,000 carvings uncovered in Çatalhöyük. Most of the figurines are of animals, which suggest that Goddess-based theology was significantly diminished by this time. A stately Woman/Goddess statue seated on a throne flanked by two female lions was discovered in a grain bin, dated to 8,000 BP.[25] The sculpture may have served as a prototype for Cybele, a leading deity and Mother Goddess of later Anatolian states.[26]

There are clues at Çatalhöyük that egg-producers and sperm-producers status and power was already unbalanced in favor of men. Heads of animals, especially of cattle, were typically mounted on walls, and the skulls of rams and bulls occupied a central placement on shrines. Predominant pictorial material includes men with erect phallus and hunting scenes.[27]

Çatalhöyük art deviates dramatically from the Stone Age worldview in which representations of the female body, human fertility, and the Mother Goddess were all-powerful. The realistic portraits of untamed herds peacefully grazing in the Stone Age were replaced by images of phallic dominance over individual nonhuman animals in the Neolithic.

The art of this early colonizing settlement indicates that a hyper-masculine, cyborg mindset was already ingrained into the consciousness of phallic humans, who exercised control over other men, and took pleasure in torturing untamed and enslaved animals. Perhaps, machismo became a pressure valve to release anxieties associated with the patriarchal imperative to obtain and expand wealth.

♂ Cities & 'Mountains'

Due to periodic flooding and drought, there was pressure for farmers to construct large-scale systems to control the water supply. Meeting this need contributed to the development of the first settlements around 10,000 BP.[28] Between 6,000 and 5,000 BP, another significant cultural shift took place as agricultural villages evolved into cities in both northern and southern Mesopotamia.

These prosperous cities joined with their surrounding territories to create what are known as city-states, each with its own phallic gods and governments. Social hierarchies, rulers, and workers emerged with the development of specialized skills beyond those needed for agricultural work. To grain mills and ovens were added brick and pottery kilns, and textile and metal workshops, all run by men.[29] With extra goods and even modest affluence came increased trade and contact with other male-based cultures.

Near Eastern people worshiped numerous gods and Goddesses, but each metropolis had a unique protective deity that people believed protected the fate of their city.[30] The population of city-states continued to expand, and by 5,000 BP, Uruk had about 45,000 residents, and Memphis in Egypt had 30,000. Close to 4,500 BP, Uruk had 80,000 people, Lagash in Iraq had 60,000, and Nippur had 20,000.[31]

As humans became more stationary, empires arose, such as those in Mesopotamia, Egypt, Anatolia, and Greece. Cities and ruling regimes became dependent upon agriculture to feed their growing populations, and on enslavement practices to provide labor needed for intensifying agricultural processes.

Around 4,000 BP, Memphis in Egypt and Ur in Iraq both had 60,000 people, while Isin, Larsa, and Girsu in Iraq each had 40,000. By 3,700 BP, Babylon in Iraq had 65,000 inhabitants. And around 3,300 BP, Thebes in Egypt had 80,000 residents, while Yinxu in China had 120,000.

Men's goals to transcend nature through architecture was mostly achieved by the Bronze Age with the rise of phallic-centered empires and mega structures like the Egyptian pyramids.[32] The Sumerians most impressive archaeological remains are ziggurats, huge stepped structures with a temple or shrine on top. Ziggurats towering above the flat plain proclaimed the wealth, prestige, and stability of a city's phallic rulers and glorified its gods. They were analogous to the step-pyramids that evolved in Africa.

Perhaps, at first, these male-based edifices served to reflect the womb of the Earth and the Goddess, as did the structures of female-centered cultures.[33] Notably, the architecture of both ziggurats and pyramids form a triangular shape, and this co-option of gynocentric imagery continued under patriarchal religions.[34]

Nonetheless, ziggurats and pyramids came to signify new meanings under phallic rule. They functioned symbolically as lofty bridges between the Earth and the heavens and a meeting place for sperm-producers and their male gods. The structures were given names such as 'House of the Mountain' and 'Bond between Heaven and Earth.'[35]

The phallic-based edifices, or axis mundi, that connected heaven and Earth became significant in the construction of cyborg consciousness. They came to represent men's separation from the Earth, and transcendence over nature, animals, and women. The mountain-based architecture and narrative were later transferred to the phallic temples, sanctuaries, and other ritual sites.

Men appropriated and coopted Goddess iconography in their construction of patriarchy during the New Stone Age. The supreme male status of monarch and god-king was frequently ordained by a Goddess, such as the Sumerian Inanna (Ishtar) for Sargon, the first king of Akkadia. Numerous Goddess temples were constructed by male-based cultures in the Bronze and Iron Ages, until this practice was entirely eclipsed by abrahamic cults.

In addition to altars to female deities at the Çatalhöyük site, there was a Goddess shrine at Sabatinovka in Moldavia (c. 6,500 BP), and the Mnajdra and Hal Tarxien temples in Malta (c. 5,300 BP). Other examples of Goddess sites include the Horns of Consecration in the palace of Knossos, Crete (4,000 BP), the Ziggurat at Erech in Sumer (5,000 BP), and the temples of Isis and Dendera in Egypt (4,300 BP). The Eleusis and Oracle of Delphi in Greece (3,000 BP), and the Parthenon (2,400 BP) are among many other buildings dedicated to the Goddess.

Greek Titaness: Nyx/Night

The omnipotent role of Goddesses in early patriarchal civilizations point to their prehistorical importance and to the time when there were no male gods and important father figures. Even though men dominated women and nature, they felt obligated to legitimize their rein with reference to female deities who represented nature and biological processes. One such example is the significance of night as personified by Nyx the Greek Goddess of the night.

A shadowy figure in Greek mythology, Goddess Nyx stood at or near the beginning of creation, an acknowledgment that females were the first human deities. One her own, Goddess Nyx mothered eminent and personified deities such as Hypnos (Sleep) and Thanatos (Death). She is a figure of such exceptional power and beauty that she is feared by the greatest patriarchal god, Zeus.

Nyx had an important role in Orpheus' poems, and it was she, rather than Chaos, who is the first principle from which all creation emerges. In Hesiod's *Theogony*, Nyx is born of Chaos and with Erebus (Darkness), Nyx gives birth to Aether (Brightness) and Hemera (Day). Interestingly, the Goddess of night had no need for darkness, and Erebus was probably added later to the gynocentric creation myth.

Later, by herself, Goddess Nyx gives birth to Moros (Doom, Destiny), Ker (Destruction), the Oneiroi (Dreams), Momus (Blame), Oizys (Pain, Distress), the Hesperides (Nymphs of evening), the Moirai (Fates), the Keres (female spirits or daimones of violent or cruel death), Nemesis (Indignation, Retribution), Apate (Deceit), Philotes (Friendship), Geras (Old Age), and Eris (Strife).

Goddess Nyx's birthing of so many fundamental environmental and human processes is a reflection of the importance of women's philosophy during prehistory. Goddess Nyx was not the most popular Greek deity, but she often lurked in the background of other cults, for example, there was a statue of her in the Temple of Artemis at Ephesus.

Goddess Nyx occupies a cave in which she gives oracles. Cronus - who is chained within, asleep and drunk on honey - dreams and prophesies. Outside the cave, Goddess Adrasteia clashes cymbals and beats upon her tympanon, moving the entire universe in an ecstatic dance to the rhythm of Nyx's chanting.

In Homer's *Iliad*, Hypnos placed Zeus to sleep at the bidding of Goddess Hera, allowing her to cause Heracles great misfortune. Zeus was furious and would have smitten Hypnos into the sea if he had not fled to Goddess Nyx, his mother. Zeus, frightful of the Night Goddess' anger, held his fury and Hypnos disturbed him a few more times, always running back to his mother for protection. If Hypnos was punished, Goddess Nyx would have confronted Zeus with maternal fury, which even he feared.

Conclusion

In sharp contrast to the unfortified Stone Age settlements, cities in the Neolithic were dotted with fortifications, from the walls of Jericho (10,000 BP) to those of Troy (5,000 BP). This indicates that male-centered maldevelopment spawned a lifetime of fear and obsession over safety, and a curse to everyone living under patriarchal rule.

There can be no security without generosity and goodness, and ancient gynocentric cultures knew and practiced this principle. To be generous means to be free from pride, to never to climb the ladder of success, and live as if you will never know what it is to be famous or rich. You have to die to whatever has been achieved, every minute of the day. It is only in such fertile ground that goodness can grow and flower.

This first chapter of Part IV on the evolution of cyborg thinking and power explored the role architecture played in the development of male domination and hierarchy. It also examined an interesting example of female choice in sex-selection that resulted in far fewer men reproducing during the interval of early intensive agriculture.

Patriarchy developed through privatization of land, accumulation of resources, and patrilineality, in direct opposition to gynocentric forms of community ownership, gift-giving, and matrilineality. The rapid rise in urban-based populations added to sperm-producers' quorum, power, and feelings of invincibility. This was accompanied by a great fall in the status of females and the Goddess.

Simultaneously, the most critical element in the evolution of cyborg consciousness was occurring as the sixth colonization of animals for labor, ritual, and food. By capturing, enslaving, and harnessing animal-based power, men were able to privatize and transform the land even more rapidly, which led to greater capital accumulation. Male objectification of nonhuman animals ignored eons of gynocentric philosophy and practice, and the next chapter describes this pivotal process.

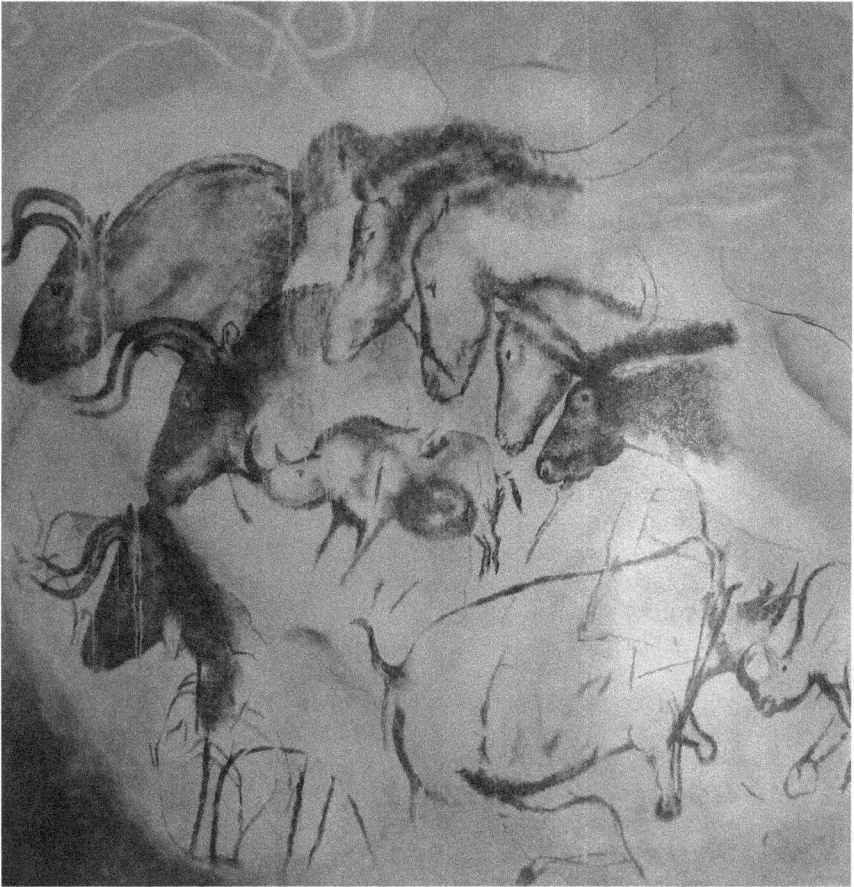

(Figure 19: Chauvet cave paintings c. 31,000 BP)

19: Taming the 'Beast'

Nuclear reactors and the poisons they produce, stockpiles of atomic bombs, ozone-destroying aerosol spray propellants, oil tankers "designed" to self-destruct in the ocean, iatrogenic medications and carcinogenic food additives, refined sugar, mind pollutants of all kinds - these are the multiple fetuses/feces of stale male-mates in love with a dead world that is ultimately co-equal and consubstantial with themselves. - Mary Daly

ASIA's Journey 2121.19

It is 117°F (47°C) in the midday sun with humidity hovering around 70 percent. The women and children are carefully walking through the derelict outskirts of a city that once had the most expensive real estate in the World. It is eerily quiet as ASIA pass abandoned office buildings, boarded-up factories, empty malls, and burned-out apartments. A few vagrants and dozens of stray dogs and cats are all that remains now.

The safe house is weeks away north, but first, the women have to find their missing children. The mothers are determined to find Nadie, Cha'Kwaina, Iniko, and Sabra, and Jean knows an old friend in Chinatown who can help them with a place to stay.

The group walks on an old railway track on the side of a decrepit slaughterhouse. Inside the fence, hundreds of cows, pigs, and chickens are locked in open-air pens. The food animals swelter and suffer in the heat, and the stench of waste, blood, and decomposing flesh is overpowering.

From inside the factory, a cow screams and the children are alarmed.

"What is that noise?" 13-year old Lehana asks.

"That is the sound of a cow crying for help," Hehewuti replies. The group stops as they hear a chicken scream. The children stand wide-eyed and puzzled.

"What is happening?" Zaid asks in a timid voice.

Nakeisha sighs and points to the caged food animals. "Those animals are taken inside and killed for people to eat."

"What?" Zaid starts to tear-up. "Why?"

"People eat animals." Nakeisha shrugs. "But it costs a lot and only a few wealthy people can afford it."

"They are few animals left," Lehana frowns. "Why kill and eat them?"

"It makes me so mad," Zola clenches her fist. "Meat is the main reason for this heat we are facing. A long time ago, people knew that meat causes ten times more warming than eating plants."

"If they knew that, then why didn't they stop?" Lehana shake her head in disbelief. "They could have prevented the collapse and this extreme heat."

"The rich knows that even today, but they wouldn't stop." Zola waves her hand over the slaughterhouse. "This is one of the few factories still working."

"There is also a girls mill," Lian whispers to Xóchitl, thinking about the four missing children.

Introduction

The abandonment of sustainable gynecological practices in the Neolithic resulted in constant conflict between pastorals and agriculturalists for grazing land. For instance, the Yamnaya migration from the Eurasian steppes was caused by drought, resource depletion, and warfare. As one expert noted, "huge flocks of sheep and herds of horses into settled land signaled disaster for the farmers and their crops."[1]

Pastorals often served as a form of landed aristocracy, living off the tribute of peasant farmers for protection from other raiders. Men captured and used females as possessions, concubines, and servants, and this disruption of farming communities in Eurasia resulted in a late Neolithic crisis.[2]

This second chapter of Part IV on the rise of male-centered rule centers on the 6th colonization of nonhuman animals. It sets off with an overview of the uniqueness of men's bodies, followed by the shrinking Y-gene.

A survey of the colonization of ruminants and chronology of subjugation comes next. The victimization of nonhuman animals in early capitalist economies is examined after. A look at men's transcendence over nature and nonhuman animals follows, and the chapter concludes with discourses on phallic transcendence and competition with animals.

♂ Bodies

Male secondary sex characteristics include growth of body hair in the underarm, abdominal, chest, facial, and pubic area. Adult males are taller than adult females on average, partly as a result of later puberty and slower bone fusion.

In men, testosterone directly increases the size and mass of muscles, vocal cords, and bones, deepening the voice, and changing the shape of the face and skeleton. Converted to DHT in the skin, testosterone accelerates the growth of androgen-responsive facial and body hair but may slow and eventually stop the growth of head hair.[3]

On average, sperm-producers have a heavier skull and bone structure, and increased muscle mass and strength. Men have a greater mass of thigh muscles in front of the femur, rather than behind it as is typical in mature females. They also have larger bodies and a more square face.

Men have a narrower waist, but wider than ovary beings. There is a broadening of shoulders and chest, and shoulders are wider than hips. Men have a higher waist-to-hip ratio than prepubescent or adult females or prepubescent males. They also have larger hands, feet, and nose than women, prepubescent boys, and girls.

With sperm-producers, there is increased secretions of oil and sweat glands, often causing acne and body odor. On average, there is also a coarsening or rigidity of skin texture due to less subcutaneous fat, and lower body-fat percentage, than prepubescent or adult women or prepubescent males.

Is the Y Going Extinct?

There are links between the Y-chromosome and increased health risk for males, including many forms of cancers. As an asexual chromosome, the Y pays a price and keeps losing genes.[4] What is more, due to the constant division of cells in making sperm, there is a chance for mutation or gene loss with every split.[5]

Another change is the elimination of genes that are harmful to females.

Some genes have opposite effects in pistillates and staminates, and evolution is a tug of war between sperm-producers jettisoning genes that they find detrimental only to have egg-producers put them back, and vice versa.

Consequently, the X chromosome is becoming more 'feminized' with genes that are good for females but detrimental to males. The X is also becoming 'demasculinized,' losing genes that are of use only in the males. Jennifer Graves argues that the Y-chromosome is poorly designed and is degrading rapidly. Graves points out that the ancestral Y has lost most of its genes and hints that the Y may disappear while humans are still on the planet.[6]

Around 300 million years ago, the Y chromosome had about 1,400 genes on it. Now it has only 45 genes. At this rate, the Y is going to run out of genes in about five million years. A little accident could tip it over the edge, or a new sex-determining system could evolve.

The two X chromosomes that are inherited by females look nearly identical to the other non-sex chromosomes.[7] The Y chromosome, however, which is inherited by males along with one X chromosome, is a withered version of the X, having lost many genes since it stopped recombining with the X.[8] The Y genes are no longer producing proteins, so many genes on the X chromosome are involved in dosage compensation.[9]

Some mammals have already lost their Y chromosome, though they still have females and males and reproduce normally. For instance, some rodents have no Y chromosome, and also lack a gene that switches on the development of testis to make male hormones. Yet there are healthy male rats, which suggests that some other gene have taken over the Y's role.[10]

6th Colonization: Ruminants

Once the agrarian revolution was established, phallic enslavers experimented with controlled breeding for hundreds of years in their attempt to colonize nonhuman animals.[11] Animals become 'domesticated' when humans control their breeding and living conditions.[12] Around 5,000 BP, invasion, diffusion and independent taming led to the rapid expansion of domesticates in Europe and Asia.[13]

Some domesticates were intentionally bred, kept in an enclosure, and fed by human-provided food.[14] Others were not enclosed, fed by access to natural foods, and are allowed to breed freely. Sheep,[15] goats, and cattle are fond of leaves and bark, while pigs snuffle around roots. Men used their different foraging strategies to clear wide areas of dense forest, and open lands for agriculture and towns.

Animal colonization resulted in ecosystem collapse, and caused a dramatic increase in competition between households that led to inherited inequalities of wealth. A small number of phallic pastorals who controlled vast herds made economic divergence more pronounced.

Moreover, nonhuman animals were exploited ritually to supersede the ancient spirituality related to females and Earth Goddesses and install sperm-producers in their place. Men used animal blood as a substitute for female blood power, and the fact that animal sacrifice, blood, milk, and flesh remain cardinal to phallic religions is a measure of the static nature of cyborg consciousness.

Sperm-producers competition for grazing lands in the Bronze and Iron Age developed into wars that lasted for decades. They employed dogs to protect domesticates from predators, to tame animals like cattle and horses, and to herd sheep and goats. Men further exploited dogs and horses in inter-male rivalry and inter-tribal warfare.[16] By the 5th millennium BP, vehicles drawn by equids were being used in warfare.

Men utilized the experience gained from taming domesticates to control women and children as well. Dominance training is the essence of cyborg consciousness, and animal husbandry increases the intensity of patriarchal systems.[17] For instance, there is a negative correlation between African matrilineal forms and cattle-owning,[18] and one cultural expert concluded. "the cow is the enemy of matriliny."[19]

Chronology of Domesticates

Dogs were domesticated more than 30,000 years ago, and cats around 11,500 BP. Goats and sheep were the first ruminants to be exploited as livestock about 10,000 BP, and pigs around 9,000 BP in the Near East and China. Cows were colonized around 8,500 BP in Turkey, and horses were enslaved around 8,000 BP.[20] Chickens were domesticated close to 10,000 BP in China.[21]

In the beginning, domesticates were kept mainly for agricultural labor and transportation. In Mesopotamia, domesticated ruminants were exploited for agricultural work and were not part of the daily diet.[22] Flesh was regularly consumed only by the society's elite. Most of the population were dependent on agricultural production for their nutrition, augmenting it occasionally with some flesh, and even more sparsely with dairy products.[23]

Milk production was very small, not more than 50 gallons (200 liters) per cow yearly in the Fertile Crescent.[24] In the texts of the 4th millennium BP, dairy products are not mentioned. And since domesticates were herded at a considerable distance from settlements for at least part of the year, they were only available to augment the food of herders.

♂ Animal-based Economy

In the New Stone Age, colonized ruminants became the foundation of phallic belief, trade, economic, and social development. Men's worship often require animal sacrifice, and the trade in enslaved animals for ritual slaughter and sanctified flesh, such as kosher meat, led to the emergence of the first cities, like Jerusalem.

During the Early Roman era about 40 percent of the goat and sheep consumed in Jerusalem were imported.[25] Sacrificial animals were brought in from desert regions hundreds of miles away, such as Arabia or Trans-Jordan.[26] Later on, the ritualized slaughter of animals for halal meat became instrumental to the development of islamic communities and economies.

The donkey is a domesticated member of the horse family, Equidae. Donkeys were valuable as beasts of burden in the ancient Near East, with links to royalty.[27] From 3,800 to 3,700 BP, donkey caravans helped to establish vast trade networks across the Eastern Mediterranean and Turkey, and contributed to the wealth of countless patriarchs.[28]

Pastoral workers were linked to regional trade since wool and hair from sheep and goats were used to manufacture cloth. Weaving was one of the most frequently cited profession in administrative texts in Mesopotamia, and 'factories' of weavers were established in several cities.[29] The textile industry formed the backbone of trade, especially during the third and second millennia.[30]

In some early civilizations and cultures, cockfighting played a leading role in the development of phallic identity, competition, gambling, capital accumulation, culture, and local economies.[31] Cock-fighting is one of the world's oldest spectator sport, going back 6,000 years to South Asia and Persia. The original name of Indus valley city, Mohenjo-daro, was "the city of the cock." Chickens were used for sport, not for food, and by 3,000 BP, chickens and cockfighting had assumed "religious significance."[32]

Introduced into Ancient Greece around 2,500 BP, cockfighting became immensely popular. For a long time the Romans despised this 'Greek diversion,' but they ended up adopting it so enthusiastically that by the 1st century AD, male devotees often spent their whole patrimony in betting at the side of the pit.[33] Although forbidden by law in many countries, chickens remain exploited as a sport by men all over the world.[34]

Prior to steam power, ruminants were the only available source of non-human labor, and they are still utilized for this purpose in many places of the world, including for tilling fields, transporting goods, and military functions. This extended time of men's direct harnessing of non-human labor contributed to cyborg consciousness.

In the modern era, food is the most primary use of domesticates, although animals rank well behind plants in the total quantity of food supplied.[35] Colonized animals are a leading global industry, and their continued exploitation maintains the notion of cyborg superiority.

The global population of domestic ruminants is greater than 3.5 billion, with cattle, sheep, and goats accounting for about 95 percent of the total.[36] In roughly 6,000 years, the ratio of enslaved to unrestrained ruminant population has grown from near zero, to close to 500 times at present.

♂ Transcending Animals & ♀

The capture, enslavement, and selective breeding of nonhuman animals were formidable technological achievements. The sixth colonization was accomplished exclusively by human sperm-producers, and it had a tremendous impact on phallic identity, economy, and supremacy.[37] Far more significant than hunting,[38] domesticating animals allowed sperm-producing humans to redefine New Stone Age metaphysics through hyper-masculinity and ritual sacrifice.

Domesticates provided males with a permanent, ever-present mirror that grossly expanded their reflection. And, by unfolding the mysteries regarding sexual reproduction,[39] men began to envision a greater role for themselves as active agents of procreative technologies and mastery over life itself. It was the objectification and colonization of animal bodies that permitted phallic humans to finally go beyond their womb-envy.

As Mary Daly writes in Gyn/Ecology, "Not only disparagement, but also glorification of women's procreative organs are expressions of male fixation and fetishism. These disproportionate attitudes are also demonically deceptive, inviting women to re-act with mere derivative fetishism, instead of deriding these fixations and focusing upon the real "object" of male envy, which is female creative energy in all of its dimensions."

The spread of domesticates mirrored the dispersal of male-centered economies in the New Stone Age. Males' selfish, exploitation-based economy and philosophy soon challenged all aspects of female creativity, from art and song, to partner unions and gift economies.

Gynocentric practices existed alongside the emerging patriarchies for eons though, until they were entirely eclipsed by the Iron Age. For a significant interval of time, gynecological norms prevailed across vast areas, such as Indus Valley and Egyptian cultures where male priests maintained plant-based diets.

Breeding of domesticates led to increasing importance placed on male herbivores, and a reduction in the status of female nonhuman animals.[40] Marti Kheel writes, "Just as men under patriarchal society view women as their antithesis in the quest for masculine self-identity, so too humans have often viewed animals as a foil for the establishment of human identity."

Bronze-Age male elites In the Near East began to think of themselves as cyborgs, incorporating the qualities of animals and gods. For instance, the lamassus protective figures of Assyria (c. 2,700 BP) are sculptures which combined the bearded head of a man, the powerful body of a lion or bull, the wings of an eagle, and the horned headdress of a god. From the front they appear to stand, and from the side, walk. This carefully morphed representation showed that men had harnessed the strength and skills of the most powerful and dangerous animals and attained the status of gods.[41]

War and Masculinity

What draws men to war and makes them see it as a kind of sacred undertaking? How are notions of masculinity and military service constructed in a field of unequal power relationships? Is war related to the elaborate human sacrifices of some parts of the ancient world? Or is war more a product of patriarchy, animal domestication, and the need to protect phallic accumulation?

De Laet describes how domestication and the emergence of private property led to conflict between men: "Property came into existence. No doubt the concept existed in embryonic form among the hunter-gatherers, where each community possessed 'its own' hunting territory. Among farmers, however, the idea of property assumed considerable importance : every farmer had their 'own' fields, their 'own' cattle, their 'own' house and their 'own' tools. At the same time, the other face of property was revealed, for it led to theft, pillage and also war."[42]

There was no need for theft in a gift-economy as food, resources, and tools were shared. Neolithic men were not willing to hand over their colonized herbivores, however, and this led to private fencing and the notion of permanent ownership. Conflict over the commons, grazing rights, and theft was fairly numerous, as is shown by the fact that most New Stone Age villages were fortified.

De Laet explains how the need to protect male property might have led to male dominance, militarism, and war. "A class of professional warriors gradually came into being, responsible for defending the village while the farmers and shepherds were in the fields. It may well be imagined that initially all able-bodied men took up arms in cases of danger but that soon a few men were made permanently responsible for maintaining security. Such military activities called for a commander, and this role naturally fell to the village chief, whose powers, as noted earlier, thus took on a military character."

In the present, many institutions in society are organized around sex, and the military is a prime example. It is not the composition of an institution that makes it gendered, that is, how many women and men it has. Rather, it is the organization of the institution around ideals of masculinity and femininity that makes it gendered. For instance, in war and sports, aggressive masculinity is encouraged on the field but it also gets carried off the field.[43]

Soldiers and civilians both share beliefs of strength, bravery, competence, and patriotic duty tied to military service. These impressions ignore the reality that toxic masculinity is preserved in the military through selection of competitive individuals and aggressive behavior.[44] Wars and militarism are organized around a socially constructed masculinity that is defined by discrimination and humiliation of women and gays, and a mentality of conquest.[45]

The promotion of alpha male identity, loyalty, duty, and honor is further problematic since combative masculinity is connected to harassment, assault, racism, domestic violence, authoritarian rule, and so on. For example, the rate of sexual assault against men in the military is almost 100 times that of all men in the US.[46] Despite this, the military depicts its men as white, straight, physically well-built, and emblematic of white, middle class norms and values.[47]

Enlistment is not only seen as a service to the state, but one that defines proper masculinity. Serving in the armed forces is often indispensable to a boy's right to belong to the inner circle of adult males. For example, in Turkey, a woman may not want to marry a man who skipped military service since her patriarchal family would not agree to such a marriage. Joining the forces, Altinay concludes, "is a rite of passage to manhood."[48]

The military is supposed to create 'men' out of 'boys' who can then earn the respect of phallic peers and females - their mothers, wives, sisters, and girlfriends. Moreover, the armed forces offer one of the few job opportunities available for millions of unemployed young men. It is a legal obligation for males in numerous countries, and 'serving' is a prerequisite for many forms of urban employment.

The militarization of society is an ongoing process that is happening on many levels. Cynthia Enloe comments, "It's happening at the individual level, when a woman who has a son is persuaded that the best way she can be a good mother is to allow the military recruiter to recruit her son so her son will get off the couch. When she is persuaded to let him go, even if reluctantly, she's being militarized. She's not as militarized as somebody who is a Special Forces soldier, but she's being militarized all the same."[49]

Melissa Brown points out that the army "has offered men several versions of masculinity: the soldier firing high-tech weapons, the professional who makes important decisions under tough conditions and saves lives, the caring surrogate father and provider of relief and protection, the bearer of marketable skills, and, of course, the guy who successfully gets into his girlfriend's bedroom."[50]

In military culture, personal courage and combat are idolized and soldiers are eager to face fear, danger, or adversity. But considering armed engagement as something exiting creates a climate of toxic masculinity that glorifies phallic violence. Every aspect of the military is geared toward the enterprise of waging successful "macho" war, as opposed to "sissy" diplomacy. And war is repeatedly waged to ensure that the US maintains a dominating masculine force on the world stage.

The emphasis on ceremony, discipline, hierarchy, and a battlefield mindset often leads to adjustment issues when soldiers return home. It does not initiate a young man into real society, but into a socially constructed, backwards oriented illusionary world. Frequent sexual assault in the military and domestic violence in sports show the consequences of organizing institutions around violent masculinity.

Lesley Gill contends that through military service, lower class men shape a positive sense of masculine identity that is linked to collusion with their own subordination and tied to other gendered patterns of social degradation. Material constraints and beliefs about gender often lead subaltern and minority men to participate in a state institution that contributes to the continuing oppression of their own culture and other dominated groups.[51]

Angelic Men Vs Earthlings

An analysis of the connection between the Earth Goddesses, females, and nature provides an understanding of the patriarchy and phallic-dominance that is seldom explored in feminist and other literature. This connection reveals some of the backgrounds of cyborg consciousness and the hidden motives behind men's destruction of forests and ecosystems.

Suppressing the Stone Age conception of the Earth Goddesses and nature as divine were crucial to the emergence of cyborg consciousness.[52] Most human properties were traditionally articulated in terms of 'natural' and 'divine.' Human territory borders on animality, the 'natural' sphere closer to us, and on 'angelity,' the region of the 'divine.' Earthlings in the Stone Age were considered as both natural and divine.

In the New Stone Age, men domesticated and replaced the Earth Goddesses and nature with male sky magic, thereby placing the divine far above the Earth and beyond the realm of humans and Earthlings. As a result, men suffer from two deficiencies, the shortcomings of other animals and the completeness of angels. Neither animal or angel, men have fraudulently situated themselves as angelic cyborgs outside the scope of morality and environmental responsibility.

The absurdity of cyborgs' angelity is evident in the common fantasy among leaders and laymen alike that somehow god will take care of climate change and save humans from catastrophe. These phallic demagogues even maintain that it is arrogant to think that humans can influence the climate, thereby abdicating personal complicity and social responsibility.

Men's distinction between 'human,' 'bestial,' and 'angelic' serves a dualistic purpose in maintaining cyborg consciousness. For one, there is an appropriating exclusion, which degrades nonhuman animals to objects, goods, and labor. For instance, other-than-human animals are viewed as lacking angelic characteristics, such as a 'soul.'

In addition, there is an expropriating inclusion, which equates human males to angels in order to deny the species' fragile and mortal corporeality. This framework allows cyborgs to place themselves outside of nature and to have the whole of existence at their disposal as the absolute owners. Simultaneously, this duality reduces females who are viewed as more natural and animal-like.

The search for the lost wisdom of female-centered theology constitutes a longing for re-connection in the relationship between humans and nature. It is looking for a way of relating to the Earth that is the antithesis of cyborg consciousness. Despite thousands of years of repression, an underground wisdom tradition of females can still be found in the background of words and myth. It can also be found in contemporary oral, popular, artistic, and literary works.

Yet, the past must be viewed through a critical lens and there is no way back to some 'golden age' of gynecological, gatherer-based society. Also, increasing awareness of the Earth Goddesses, based on historical scientific reality, will not automatically lead to dismantling the patriarchy, or to the restoration of lost pre-patriarchal cultures.

All the same, the re-claiming of a gynocentric, Goddess-based prehistory is significant since it corrects long-held misconceptions about uninterrupted phallic dominance and women's subjugation. And, it restores females' rightful place in the story of human evolution. At the very least, it represents one way to think about the political construction of society.

♂ Supremacy Over Animals

Barbara Ehrenreich suggests that the wellspring of war is not in a "killer instinct" unique to males of our species. The roots lie in the blood rites ancient humans performed to reenact their terrifying experience of predation by stronger carnivores.[53] Yet, predators were portrayed as protectors in Paleolithic art. Stone Age rites incorporated menstruation, but with male ascendancy in the Neolithic, men began to use the blood of animals to replicate female-based power.

To experience the supremacy of predators, males invented bull-baiting, a blood sport that involves the molestation of bulls.[54] Bull baiting dogs, referred to today as bulldogs, were bred to bait animals, mainly bulls and bears.[55] Phallic humans likewise created bull-fighting,[56] the Running of the Bulls,[57] and other 'sports' to demonstrate superiority over domesticates.

Men's contest with other animals is unfairly stacked in their favor. Combat between herbivores and males' using spears, rope, dogs, and so on, are entirely one-sided. Since humans were almost always the victors, defeated nonhuman animals helped to reinforce men's notion of superiority and machismo. Curiously, males rarely volunteer to fight strong carnivores without modern weapons.

Mary Daly writes, "The machismo ethos that has the human psyche in its grip creates a web of projections, introjections, and self-fulfilling prophecies. It fosters a basic alienation within the psyche - a failure to lay claim to that part of the psyche that is then projected onto the "Other." It is essentially demonic in that it cuts off the power of human becoming."

Superiority over other-than-human animals situated Neolithic males on the same level as their imaginary sky-gods. The desire for transcendence drove men to prove human superiority over animals in a multitude of ways, from baiting and competition, to colonization and sacrifice. This change in male aggressiveness toward animals created a machismo that culminated in wars and conquest of gynocentric cultures across the Globe. The supremacy of Bronze Age pastorals was transferred to agrarian men, and according to Gore Vidal, male religions played a huge part.

Vidal writes, "The great unmentionable evil at the center of our culture is monotheism. From a barbaric Bronze Age text known as the Old Testament, three anti-human religions have evolved – Judaism, Christianity, Islam. These are sky-god religions. They are, literally, patriarchal - God is the Omnipotent Father - hence the loathing of women for 2,000 years in those countries afflicted by the sky-god and his earthly male delegates."[58]

The author continues, "The sky-god is a jealous god, of course. He requires total obedience from everyone on earth, as he is in place not for just one tribe but for all creation. Those who would reject him must be converted or killed for their own good. Ultimately, totalitarianism is the only sort of politics that can truly serve the sky-god's purpose."

Conclusion

This second chapter of Part IV on male ascendancy provided an overview of the biological uniqueness of male bodies and genes. Perhaps current male physiology represents repercussions from the New Stone Age Y-bottleneck, as well as socialized gene expressions and other factors derived from five thousand years of male dominance.

Can a human being, living in this world, totally cease to be violent? Societies and religious communities have tried not to kill animals. Some have even said, "If you don't want to kill animals, what about the vegetables?" An individual can carry this line of reasoning to such an extent that she ceases to exist. Where do you draw the line? Is there an arbitrary line according to your fancy at which you say, "I'll go up to there but not beyond"?

In gynecological reasoning, animals or plants are not objectified. Both are sacred aspects of the Goddess and under human protection. Preservation of fauna and floral diversity and sustainable land use are paramount, and this requires eating lower on the food chain. Ancient female-centered clans understood this basic ecological principle and adhered to it for eons.

This chapter explored how men's animal husbandry practices deviated from ancient female-centered cultures. And it explored how captured, enslaved, and oppressed animals contributed to the creation of patriarchal thinking, economies, and ritual. The next chapter looks at how these processes become even more intensified with the use of horses and the development of male warfare.

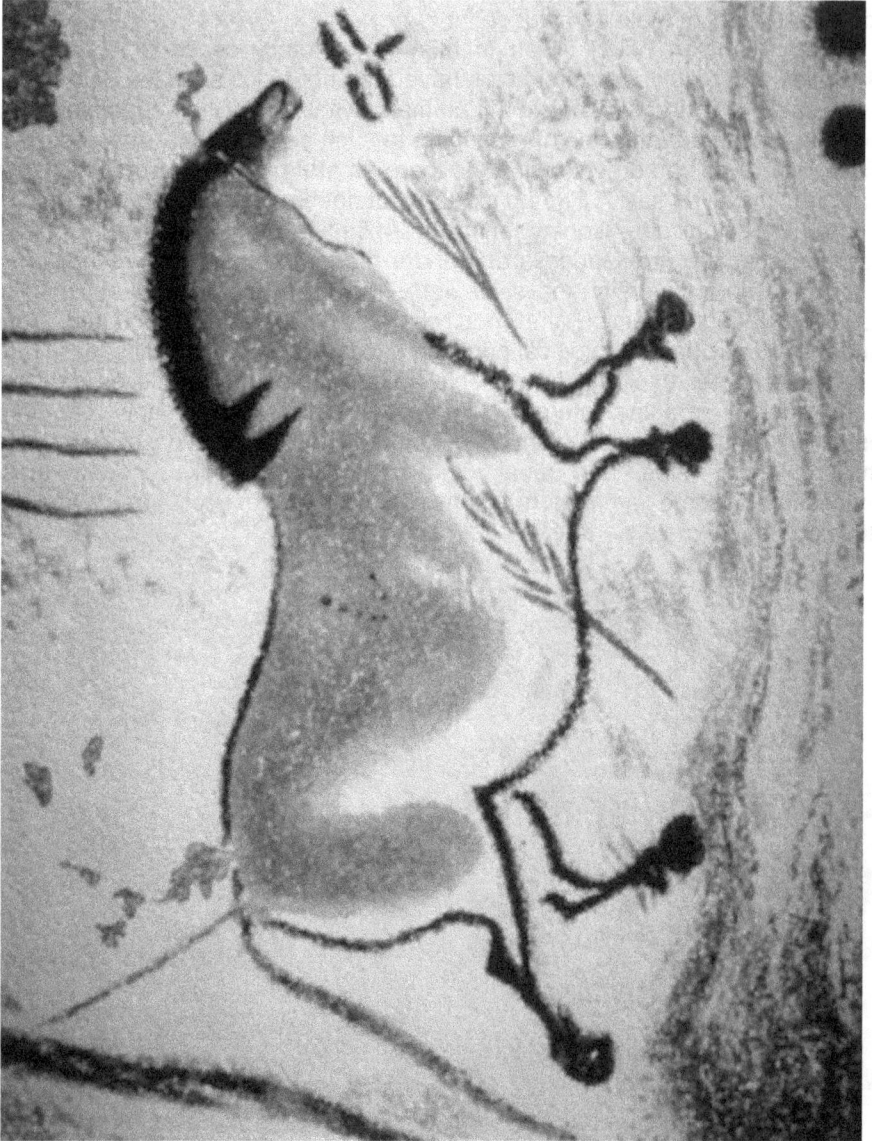

(Figure 20: Lascaux cave painting of horse c. 20,000 BP)

20: Warhorse & Toxic Masculinity

Summoning the courage to See and to Name and to Act is a process of exorcism, clearing away the smog of deception so that ways of escape can be imagined and Realized. - Mary Daly

ASIA's Journey 2121.20

The group slept in an abandoned fire station, and as the sun raises they are well on their journey towards the city. It is very humid and 105°F (40°C) under an overcast sky. The marine layer will not last long, and ASIA takes advantage of the relative coolness.

The older women take frequent rest in a shade to cool down and hydrate with salt and electrolytes. They monitor each other for signs of heat exhaustion, such as dizziness, excessive thirst, weakness, and headache, and signs of salt depletion, like nausea, vomiting, and muscle cramps.

They know that without proper intervention, heat exhaustion can progress to heat stroke, which can damage the brain and other vital organs, and even cause death. When someone begins to suffer from heat exhaustion, they are immediately placed under a shade, doused in water, and fanned. Except for a few rare instances, so far, they have all avoided heat stroke.

The women and girls are slowly walking westward next to a collapsed freeway. They are on a side road littered with trash and burned-out tires. In the front of the group, Lian stops and shouts. "We have to turn around,"

"What is it?" Xóchitl asks as she approaches from the back.

"It's a fortified position." Lian points to empty bullet shells on the ground ahead and warns. "Gangs."

Xóchitl nods, "Alright, everyone, I am in the lead now." She turns around, and ASIA begins walking back east. But it's too late. Ten horsemen emerges from a side road and quickly rides up to the front and blocks the group.

A burly pedo-hunter in the front grins and asks, "Where are you going, my pretties?" Without waiting for an answer, a tall member on the side shouts. "Where did your daddies go?"

Hehewuti boldly steps toward the pedo-hunters and asks calmly, "How much to help us get to Chinatown?"

The husky man spits. "Chinatown?" The pedo-hunters sneer and laugh. The horses perspire, flicker their tail constantly, and appear uncomfortable in the high temperature. The burly gangster raises a hand and his goons become quiet. "You are our slaves now," he laughs and dismounts to the ground.

Lian moves close to the pedo-hunter and aims her weapon at his head, "We will take you and and a few more before that happens." She threatens the leader. "You want to go first?" In a flash, the pedo-hunters and women draw weapons and aim at each other.

"Hell, no," the burly man shouts. "We will crush you bitches."

Hehewuti starts walking westward. "Just let us pass through. Why kill each other and hurt these expensive animals?"

"Pay us with a girl or two gold coins," the leader demands.

Hehewuti point to the girls, "Our girls are so skinny, hardly bones. They are not worth much like this. We're going to the Chinatown to trade, and they'll be fat when we return."

ASIA edges onward, as Hehewuti promises, "We have to come back this way. We have nothing now, but we'll have gold for you then."

The leader of the pedo-hunters grudgingly lets them go. "You'll have to pay double," the burly man warns. "Two girls." The tall pedo-hunter grins and shouts, "And they better be virgins."

The men jeer and joke as ASIA carefully advances out of their territory.

Introduction

The use of oppressed horses as forms of transportation gave male pastorals the ability to travel great distances, conduct lighting-fast raids, and lay siege to villages, settlements, and entire cities. Goods gained from looting could be distributed quickly and attackers were able to make a quick retreat if necessary. Even the most powerful agrarian societies were vulnerable to invasions from pastoral horsemen, and the Roman Empire was no exception.

Over centuries, numerous horsemen clans ravaged Eurasian settlements, stole valuables, and dominated inhabitants. Rampaging pastoral armies include the Scythians, Huns, Goths, Turks, Mongols, Manchus and scores of others. Organized gangs also extorted payments through their control of trade routes. Along with conquest, a hierarchical caste system was often introduced, with farmers placed on the bottom.[1]

This third chapter of Part IV on the rise of cyborg rule explores men's use of the horse and cattle to wage war and construct patriarchal identity. The chapter begins with a discussion of the ancients' view of the sacredness of equines, then it examines men's taming and exploitation of horses.

Phallic use of chariots for warfare comes after, and next the evolution of war horses is detailed. Men's symbolic manipulation of domesticated horses is considered next, followed by their usage of captured bulls. Afterward, the chapter examines Egyptian animal sacrifice, and then turns to a discussion of gynocentric philosophy as exemplified by the Greek Titaness, Themis ('Divine Order'). The chapter concludes with a survey of Bronze Age Queens.

Sacred Equine

From ancient times, female equines represented freedom, power, and fertility. Priestesses wore equine masks on ceremonial occasions. Gimbutas noted that Paleolithic cave images of pregnant mares are often covered with paired finger marks, each made by a different person. The red and brown dots were possibly mixed with menstrual blood and part of fertility rites for couples.

Arabs, hindus, and celts regarded the yonic shape of an equid's foot as a symbol of the Goddess's "Great Gate." Druid and hindu temples were often constructed in the shape of horseshoes with the specific intention of representing the yoni.[2] Greeks assigned the yonic shape to the last letter of their sacred alphabet, Omega, literally "Great Om," the word of creation that initiates the next cycle of becoming.

The implication of the horseshoe symbol was that, having entered the yonic door at the end of life, Omega, a woman would be reborn as a new child, Alpha, through the same door. Across the world, the horseshoe is nailed to millions of doors as a form of good luck.

As one of the symbols in the Chinese zodiac, equines are equated with Gemini, and represents practicality, love, endurance, devotion and stability. In Native American cultures, the horse combines the grounded forces of the

Earth with the whispers of wisdom in the spirit winds.

White equids have a special significance in mythologies around the World, often related to fertility. White horses also symbolized the balance of wisdom and power. In Aegean cultures, the white mare, Goddess Leukippe, was the daytime aspect of the mare-headed Goddess Demeter. The black mare was Goddess Melanippe who punished sinners in the form of a night-mare.

Equids occupy a prominent position in the Chauvet Cave and are painted at several key locations. In Scandinavia, it was believed that a herbalist or witch could transform herself into a mare called volva. And the devotees of the divine mare in England venerated the Goddess Epona as the white mare.

Equid to Horse

Equines have a well-developed sense of balance, a strong fight-or-flight response, and anatomy that enables them to speedily escape predators. Equids also have the rare ability to sleep standing up and lying down. Around 6,000 years ago, men began to colonize equids in Ukraine and Kazakhstan.[3]

Riding horses enabled sperm-producers to travel further and faster than they could while using an ox-cart, and they were essential for the pastoral way of life. Nomadism began to be practiced, which was more than herding, and involved migration across vast distances.[4]

Compared to sheep and goat, horses reproduce slowly, but it was quickly discovered that they were useful for field work, and carrying goods and people. The practical work of horses, combined with their significance as companion animals and signifier of wealth and power, made equines a unique property among domesticates.

By 4,000 BP, there was a sharp increase in the number of horse bones found in human settlements in northwestern Europe, indicating the spread of domestication throughout the continent.[5] This data provides further evidence of a Kurgan migration from the Eurasian steppes.

In the traditions of many nomadic cultures, horses are of focal importance. Mobility, intensified by horses, helped enhance contacts and exchange between pastoral groups across vast regions. But the transfer to remote pasturing made it easy to steal domesticates. This led to robberies and looting, which in its turn stimulated the intensification of weapon production.

The milk, blood, and flesh of horses were used for nourishment, and men consumed fermented horse milk as an alcoholic drink. With sufficient horses and pasture, the nomadic life promised adventure and wealth to the pastoralist who could threaten confiscation and domination of settlers.[6]

In the 4th millennium BP, Iranians played an crucial role in the dispersal of horse-breeding and chariots in the Near East.[7] The practice of riding led to the progressive development of horse equipment. Since the success of a mounted warrior depended on the speed of his stallion and his control over him, leather bits and horn cheek-pieces needed to be replaced by bronze articles.

The taming and use of domesticates drove the development of male technology, weaponry, and conflict over land and wealth that continues into the present. Move than any other domesticate, men's harnessing of the strength and speed of equines was equivalent to having a super power, which helped to foster and maintain their cyborg mentality.

♂ Chariotry & Warfare

Chariots played a huge role in the military in the Bronze Age. Syrian-Palestinian seals had images of two-wheeled carts from 38th to 36th century

BP, and chariots were depicted from 25th century BP. By 3,600 BP, improved harness and chariot designs made chariot warfare standard throughout the Near East.

The earliest written training manual for war horses was written about 3,350 BP. Iranian horse-raising vocabulary included terms for the color of a horse, its age, parts of the body, fodder, and so on, as well as words for chariot, shaft, bridle, saddle-girth, harness parts, and rituals connected with horses. The highest official was entrusted with the role of 'managing horses.' And the term 'standing on a chariot' denoted a representative of the privileged warrior caste.

Chariotry was of primary significance in Hittite warfare around 3,600 BP. Some texts mention 600 chariots and 10,000 infantry troops deployed in battle. Kings frequently rode in chariots and exceptional care was taken to use only 'ritually pure' leather in constructing the king's chariot. After a victory, one ruler presented three chariots to appease the Sun Goddesses of Arinna.[8]

During the Iron Age, in the 27th century BP, Scythian tribes from Inner Asia moved into Europe as equestrian nomads and agriculturalists. Scythians kept herds of horses, cattle, and sheep, lived in tent-covered wagons, and fought with bows and arrows on horseback. Among the earliest peoples to master mounted warfare, they possibly raided as far as Zhou, China. There was a close link between horses, warriors and potential kings, and Scythian leaders were sometimes buried with dozens of equids in Kurgans.

The Sarmatians, renowned for their horsemanship and cavalry skills, defeated the closely-related Scynthians around 2,200 BP. The Sarmatians had massive mounted armies, for example, 8,000 Sarmatian horsemen were enlisted by the Roman Army after a victory in AD 175.   Riding   equipment and horse riding warfare skills represented the cutting edge of Iron-Age hyper-masculine aggression and technology.[9] Semi-nomads employed their horsemanship for countless, random assaults on neighbors, and on occasion, as mercenary services for leading rulers and empires.[10]

Horses enabled Alexander's armies and mercenaries to rapidly subdue vast areas of Eurasia close to 2,330 BP. The Huns, famous for their horsemanship, occupied the steppe and pushed out the Scynthians around 2,000 BP. The Huns moved east, defeated the Visigoths, and around 1,600 BP, conquered Roman provinces in the Balkans.[11] German and Asian horsemen further overwhelmed the Roman Empire during the 15th century BP. This vigorous military activity would have been impossible without cavalry.

The introduction of stirrups, as well as saddles with high pommels, allowed archers to rise and aim with short reflex bows in an almost full circle. Chazars, a semi-nomadic people, used stirrups to rule the steppe and the North Caucasus around the 14th century BP.

♂ War Horses

Throughout the history of male 'civilizations,' mules and donkeys, as well as horses, played a crucial role in providing support to armies in the field. Numerous types and sizes of colonized equids were exploited, depending on the form of warfare. Various equines were ridden or driven for reconnaissance, cavalry charges, raiding, communication, and supply.

Arab warriors began arriving in Europe around 600 AD, and lighter Arabian equids began mixing with heavier European breeds.[12] The combination resulted in horses that were heavy enough to carry weighed down, armored riders into war, and agile enough to move quickly during battle.

Europeans used several types of war horses in the Middle Ages to carry a heavy cavalry warrior or armored knight. With the decline of the knight and rise of gunpowder in warfare, light cavalry again rose to prominence and was utilized in both European warfare and the conquest of the Americas.

In the late 18th and early 19th century, men developed battle cavalry to take on a multitude of roles and they were often crucial for victory in the Napoleonic wars. In the present, horses are used by organized armed fighters in Third World countries, and by police across the World for crowd control.

Horse as Symbolism

Equids were ancient representatives of the Goddess and men exploited this relationship to establish legitimacy for themselves. For example, Iron Age Vedic texts describe the Asvamedha, an annual horse sacrifice that kings conducted. After intricate preparations, a selected white stallion was killed to ensure good luck for the kingdom.

In an elaborate ceremony, the king's wives circled the stallion nine times to represent the beginnings of the Universe. The horse is then covered with a piece of cloth, and the queen crawls under to perform a sexual act with the horse's penis while having an obscene dialogue with the priests and other wives. The horse is later killed and the king eats some of the carcass. The renewal of the year, the Universe, and his royal power is thereby completed.[13]

In European mythology, intercourse with a selected white mare was part of the initiation custom for a new king, a ritual shown on several Scandinavian rock carvings. When the act is accomplished, the mare is sacrificed, and the carcass is cooked. The king then sits in the cauldron, and eats the flesh and drinks the broth to gain the might of the divine horse Goddess, Macha.

The Hittite Law Code does not specify a mare, therefore man-stallion sex is also possible. The Roman October Equus ceremony involved a victorious horse and a king ritually renewing his kingship, but without the erotic element. Despite variations, these practices fit into a pattern in which animals, and sexuality, are coupled with male-centered power.

In the later myths of Macha and Medusa, punishment of the Goddess is a metaphor for the horse-sacrifice. Although the ritual of the kingship was no longer an element, the Goddess-mares undergo sacrifice.[14]

Equestrian statues are typically portraits of rulers and military commanders. Public display of a man on a horse is a 3,000-year old tradition. There is a 26th century BP statue from archaic Greece, and a number of ancient Egyptian, Assyrian, and Persian reliefs show mounted figures, usually rulers. The Chinese Terracotta Army (c. 2,200 BP) has cavalrymen standing beside their horses, and Qua figures include mounted riders.

As a clue to equid's crucial role in military campaigns, there are hundreds of equestrian statues located in almost every country of the world, from Albania, Argentina, Armenia, and Australia to Uruguay, Uzbekistan, Venezuela, and Wales.[15] Many equines are personalized with names, such as Rocinante, the name of Don Quixote's skinny and clumsy horse.[16]

♂ Bull Gods

People revered domesticated cows for tilling their fields, and for providing a source of fuel and fertilizer. From the start of domestication, cattle were consecrated and used in sacrificial rituals.[17] The cow's status as a 'caretaker' even led them being considered as a maternal figure.[18]

In the middle Neolithic, as cattle colonization advanced, cows became a symbol of wealth, and people began to worship several bull-deities. Cattle are a major economic asset and are still sacred in hinduism, jainism, zoroastrianism and other cults. A bull-deity can be a god represented and worshiped in animal form, or a real animal worshiped as a god. Bull horns and masks were often used in popular culture, warfare, and worship. Bulls have less utilitarian value than female cows, but they were linked to phallic virility, force, and dominance. Female cattle were venerated as caretakers, but bulls assumed much wider theological standing as potent male symbols.

The earliest form of bull worship were the horned heads excavated from Çatalhöyük. In Cyprus, masks made from skulls were worn in various phallic rites. Masked terracotta figurines and horned stone altars were also uncovered in Cyprus.[19] On an ancient Syrian seal, standing next to a naked Goddess are two men with bull heads, horns, and erect penis. The horned men, not the animals themselves, were protecting the Goddess.

In the Near East and Aegean, aurochs or unrestrained bulls were widely worshiped, often as the Lunar Bull and as the creature of the god, El. In the Akkadian epic poem, Gilgamesh is the shepherd of the city of Uruk and at the same time its 'bull,' that is, he rapes all the women in his flock.[20]

In Egyptian mythology, Apis was a bull-deity worshiped in the Memphis region.[21] Apis served as an intermediary between humans and the god, Ptah, and was the most sacred animal in Egypt. The bull is named on ancient monuments at the very beginning of Egyptian history, probably as a fertility god connected to the herds.[22]

The horned bull in Greece is sometimes depicted with the attribute of Zeus between the horns - the double ax. Throughout the Bronze Age, ox horns and double axes remained divine symbols in the Near East, Mediterranean, and Asia Minor. Horned divinities were very close to ruling elite families and sometimes symbolized divine rule. The horned helmet and other royal paraphernalia were later copied by Scandinavian and other cultures.

Egyptian Animal Sacrifice

Ancient Egyptian divinities often manifested in animal forms, for example, the jackal Anubis, the great bull Apis, Hathor the cow, and Horus the falcon.[23] Correspondingly, at various sacred sites, Egyptians worshiped individual animals as the materialization of particular deities.[24] Animals were selected, based on specific sacred markings which Egyptians believed indicated their fitness for the role, and held in places of worship devoted to the divinity the animals represented.[25]

Some cult animals retained sacred status their entire lives, as with the Apis bull worshiped in Memphis as a manifestation of Ptah and Osiris. Other animals were selected for much shorter periods. Animal-based cults grew more popular in later times, and numerous temples began raising stocks of animals from which to choose a new divine manifestation.[26]

In addition, people typically made offerings of animals to deities. Over time, millions of mummified cats, birds, and other creatures were buried at sites honoring various divinities. Cats were seen as the incarnation of Bastet, Goddess of music, joy, and protector of women. There were lizard, fish, and beetle mummies. Pets were also mummified and buried in tombs with their owners, including dogs, cats, baboons, monkeys, and gazelles.[27]

Greek Titaness: Themis/Order

Gynocentric order in terms of collective decision-making, mutual consent, and egalitarianism, are often reflected in patriarchal creation myths and traditions. For example, the honoring crones as wise women and considering wisdom as residing with females such as Goddesses Metis and Themis.

Goddess Themis is described as "the Lady of Good Counsel" and "Divine Order." She is the personification of divine order, fairness, natural law, and custom, and her symbols are the scales of justice (libra), tools used to remain balanced and pragmatic. To the ancient Greeks, Goddess Themis was the original organizer of the "communal affairs of humans, particularly assemblies." This narrative suggest that the first clans were female-led and centered on gynocentric principles of equality.

Goddess Themis's ability to foresee the future enabled her to become one of the Oracles of Delphi, which in turn led to her establishment as the Goddess of divine justice. The Lady of Good Counsel built the Oracle at Delphi and was herself oracular. This myth reveals a connection to the Sibyl tradition of female spiritual leaders from Africa.

According to another legend, Goddess Themis received the Oracle at Delphi from Gaia and later gave it to Phoebe. Some classical representations of the Lady of Good Counsel showed her holding a sword, believed to represent her ability to cut fact from fiction. To the Goddess of divine order there was no middle ground.

Hesiod mentions Goddess Themis among the six sons and six daughters of Gaia and Uranus (Earth and Sky). According to Ovid, it was Goddess Themis rather than Zeus, who told Deucalion to throw the bones of "his Mother" over his shoulder to create a new race of humankind after the deluge.

Notably, the only consort for Goddess Themis ever mentioned is Zeus. Like other omnipotent deities, she was too eminent to be married off to a lesser patriarchal divinity so her stature survived the great fall of women. One of Goddess Themis few children was Natura, the Greek goddess of the forest. Followers of Zeus later claimed that it was with him that Goddess Themis produced the Horae (Hours), the Moirai (Fates), and Astraea (Justice), but there were children of Nyx who birthed them without a father.

Goddess Themis occurred in Hesiod's *Theogony* as the first recorded appearance of Justice as a divine personage. He portrayed temporal justice, the Goddess Dike, as the daughter of Zeus and Themis. Goddess Dike carried out the law of judgments and sentencing and, together with her mother Goddess Themis, they fulfilled the final decisions of the Moirai.

Themis was the Goddess in charge of proper relationships between partners, women and men, and the rightly ordered family. Male judges were referred to as servants of the Lady of Good Counsel. The omnipotent Goddess of Divine Order was so powerful that she also presided over the affairs of deities on Olympus. There were so many wise Goddesses from prehistory that Zeus could not swallow and cannibalize them all, as he did Metis.

When Goddess Themis is disregarded, Goddess Nemesis brings just and wrathful retribution. Thus, the Lady of Good Counsel shared the Nemesion temple at Rhamnous. However, Goddess Themis is not wrathful, and she, "of the lovely cheeks," was the first to offer Goddess Hera a cup when she returned to Olympus distraught over threats from Zeus. Among Goddesses and mortals alike, female solidarity was used to resist and recover from the all-encompassing violence by hyper-masculine males in women's midst.

Bronze Age Queens

There were hundreds of Queens in the Bronze Age. Although, most were partners of kings in male-centered dynasties and groups, they demonstrate the power that females, especially royal women, could have. Some were regents and examples of a Queen willing to go to any lengths to protect 'her' kingdom, even resorting to violence and invasion.

In Mesopotamia, Kubaba is the only Sumerian Queen. She reigned in the Early Dynastic III period (ca. 4,500 BP) and in later times was worshiped as a Goddess. Shibtu (c. 3,800 BP) was the Queen of the city-state of Mari in Syria. During the king's absence, Shibtu handled the administration of the city, the royal palace, and the temple. In Persian history, Gordafarid is a great heroine, and the epic poem, the Shāhnāmeh, or Mulan, in her ballad.

Neithhotep and Merneith were Ancient Egyptian Queen during the early first dynasty (c. 5,000 BP). They may have been the first female pharaohs and the earliest Queens in recorded history. Their tombs are of the same scale as kings of that period.

Sobekneferu was the last ruler of the Twelfth dynasty of Egypt around 3,800 BP. Hatshepsut (c. 3,500 BC) was the fifth pharaoh of the Eighteenth Dynasty of Egypt. She was the second historically confirmed female pharaoh. Twosret (c. 3,200 BP) was the last known ruler and the final Pharaoh of the Nineteenth Dynasty of Egypt.

There were numerous Kushite Queens starting from 4,000 BP, including Amanirenas who fought the Romans. The Queen of Sheba from the South Arabian realm of Saba, is a Biblical figure who visited King Solomon around 3,000 BP with a vast retinue and immense quantities of spices, gold, and precious stones.

The ancient Hittites in Turkey (c. 3,600 BP) were matrilineal and royal blood was ascribed to the female line. Tawananna is the title for the Queen of the Hittites. The Tawannana had the duty of ruling when the King was away fighting in battle and was the High Priestess.

Puduḫepa (c. 3,300 BP) was a Hittite Queen referred to as "one of the most influential women known from the Ancient Near East." Puduḫepa was portrayed as reigning hand in hand with her husband rather than subservient to the king. For example, she negotiated deals and exchanged gifts with Queen Nefertari, the first Queen of the 18th Dynasty in Egypt.

Semiramis or Shammurāmat was an Assyrian Queen who restored Babylon around 2,800 BP and protected it with a high brick wall that surrounded the city. Semiramis built several palaces in Persia, added Libya and Ethiopia to the empire, then went to war with king Stabrobates of India. Assyrian inscriptions repeatedly mention Arab Queens in the north who were powerful rulers bold enough to face the Assyrian kings.

Samsi was an Arab Queen of nomadic people that traded in spices and incense in the 28th century BP. Samsi came after Queen Zabibe, and ruled for 20 years. She was succeeded by Queen Iatie about 2,700 BP. Iatie sent her forces to aid the Chaldean's bid to hold on to Babylon against the Assyrians. She was succeeded by Queen Te'el-hunu.

Across the Mediterranean Sea in Africa, Dido or Elissa was the founder and first Queen of Carthage, modern-day Tunisia, around the 28th century BP. And in Asia Minor, Eryxo was a Greek Queen of Cyrenaica around 26th century BP. Camilla was the Amazon Queen of the Volsci famous for her foot speed. And the women of Argos fought against King Cleomenes and the Spartans under the command of Telesilla in the 25th century BP.

In Scandinavia, Blenda is the heroine of a legend from Småland, who leads the women of Värend in an attack on a pillaging Danish army and annihilates it. Shield-maidens in Scandinavian folklore were women who did not have the responsibility for raising a family and could take up arms to live like warriors.[28]

Gwendolen was a legendary Queen of Britain around 3,100 BP who defeated her husband, the king, in battle to become the regent. Boudica was a Queen in Britain who led a major uprising of the tribes against the occupying forces of the Roman Empire around 2,000 BP.

Arsinoë II was a Ptolemaic Greek Princess of Egypt (c. 2,300 BP). There were successive generations of Ptolemaic Cleopatra Queens, from Cleopatra I (c. 2,200 BP) to Cleopatra VII (c. 2,000 BP), the last active Greek ruler of Egypt.[29] After her reign, Egypt became a province of the recently established Roman Empire.

Augusta was a Roman imperial honorific title given to empresses and honored women of the imperial families like Livia, Antonia Minor, Agrippina the Younger, Poppaea Sabina, Claudia Augusta and others. Elite Roman women could also receive the titles of Mater Castrorum ("Mother of the Camp") and Mater Patriae ("Mother of the Fatherland"). An Augusta could issue her own coinage, wear imperial regalia, and rule her own court.

Lü Zhi was the first woman to assume the title Empress of China around 2,200 BP. Empress Jingū was a legendary Japanese empress and famous among the onna-bugeisha or 'woman warrior.' Agathokleia was an Indo-Greek queen who ruled in parts of northern India around 2,100 BP.

Conclusion

Men used their conquest of animals with the sixth colonization to construct Neolithic toxic masculinity. They exploited the enormous power of horses to wage war against matrilineal cultures to replace women-based rule quickly. A man on top of a horse, or in a chariot pulled by a team of horses, was an overwhelming force few gynocentric groups could oppose.

Domesticates became central to male-based power, culture, religion, and diet in the New Stone Age. But colonization of animals and separation from nature also intensified phallic insecurity. To overcome their fear of mortality, men are always seeking wider and deeper, transcendental experiences. Ritual and sacrifice allows them to escape from the actual reality of their own conditioned mind, male violence, and chaos.

Negating toxic masculinity does not imply that males have to act and feel 'feminine.' Rather, they have to avoid being 'masculine' or machismo. Having a 'soft' and caring attitude means that males are making a conscious and sincere effort to not be 'hard.'

Men's obsession with wars, possessions, and death are alien to gynocentric thinking. A female-centered mind that is awake, intelligent, and free has no need for accumulation. Light is light and it does not ask for more light. And a free and 'civilized' person cannot rationally justify the exploitation of animals for self-fulfillment.

From the first settlements and cities, men adopted strict rules regarding possession and exploitation of tamed herbivores that were rigorously enforced. Following this pattern of objectification, they were similar laws relating to the ownership and utilization of females. The next chapter examines these two interrelated issues.

(Figure 21: Neolithic Relief of a Mesopotamian woman being fanned by an attendant while she holds what may be a spinning device before a table with a bowl)

21: Codifying ♂ Property

If God is male, then male is God. The divine patriarch castrates women as long as he is allowed to live on in the human imagination. - Mary Daly

ASIA's Journey 2121.21

As the group slips away from the pedo gang, the girls recite a poem that 11-year old Ashadia and Naina wrote. "Respect to you, dear Apsaras. You are our daily guide in flight. All praises to you, dear Gaias. Give thanks to the Goddess in me."

The children are immersed into the moment, in the color, form, and movement of their surroundings. They are spirited and determined to save their four sisters. Lian goes over the rescue plan with everyone. "We will search the city in teams, using night as cover. Once a girl is located, all teams will assemble to support the extraction."

Lian points to the older girls, and continues, "First, the reconnaissance team will go inside the pedo-cage and alert our sister. Then, it is up to the extraction team to get the child out." Lian pauses, and Xóchitl glances around, "Any questions so far?"

Lehana and the other girls nod silently, as Lian continues, "The roof is usually the best staging area. The child will be taken there and briefly checked out. Then, the extraction team will descend to the ground and join the rest."

15-year old Naina and Lehana look at each other for support. They are part of an extraction team and have prepared themselves physically and mentally for this task.

"What must we do after freeing a sister?" Xóchitl asks the puzzled girls.

Ashadia blurts out, "We have to get her back to the safe-house."

"Of course," the other girls smile, slightly embarrassed.

Lian stares intently at the children. "Remember, there is greater danger in the city for females. We have to stick together regardless of the threat, because if we get separated, we will lose even more girls."

"We are sisters of ASIA, we are one," Ashadia replies.

Xóchitl remains concerned and questions the girls. "What would you do if you are separated from a search team?"

Lehana answers quickly. "Hide and wait for contact. Then after two hours, if there is no communication, we should start to head back to the safe-house."

Lian and Xóchitl exchange glances. The children are prepared and young and old, ASIA is confident they will succeed. The group walk with heads held high, poised and self-assured, as they head into the city.

Introduction

The Neolithic change over was a male revolt against women as the evolution of private property and patriarchy worked hand-in-hand to destabilize egalitarian ecogynocentrism. The possession of colonized nonhuman animals enabled men to abandon the balance of Stone Age ecogynocentrism for unequal, sexist systems that rapidly devolved into enslavement of the poor and vanquished.

The price of phallic ascendancy was a drastic reduction in the status of seventy-five percent of the human population - women and children. Notably, ownership of humans is unknown before the colonization of nonhuman animals. Female-centered organizations do not practice enslavement, however, they may banish violent males from clan grounds. There were no gynocentric wars of conquest, nor do female-centered clans take advantage of the impoverished. Instead, the poor are assisted to regain their independence.

This third chapter of Part IV on the New Stone Age transformation to patriarchy focuses on how men codified domesticated animals, human females, and enslaved people as part of male-based property. The chapter commences with an outline of the seventh domestication, that of human females by men. An overview of animal husbandry laws in Mesopotamia follows.

The codifying of females as phallic property in Sumerian law is explored next, followed by a discussion of masculinity as represented in the Hammurabi code. The chapter turns to an examination of male literacy and its relation to the taming of Goddesses and female-centered power. It concludes with a discussion of gynocentric philosophy encapsulated in the Greek Titaness Dike, the Goddess of Justice.

7th Domestication: Females

The development of intensive agriculture meant men had to learn women's work of foraging, gathering, and farming. Phallic resentment of 'female' work may have provided incentives for men to domesticate animals. Colonized herbivores provided men with resources they could trade, independent of female-centered clans. And with phallic dominance, the focus of human cultures shifted profoundly from child-centered to animal-centered.

Sperm-producers' emphasis on domesticates led to the general devaluing of human young bearers and their reproductive work, like childcare. Under males' animal-based economies, founded on privatized property, the ancient care-takers of communal land were reduced to mere farm laborers.

Moreover, restrictions on mobility resulted in women losing much of their understanding of herbal medicine, biodiversity, native flora, and various features of the landscape. And since foraging and gathering activities were no longer possible, egg-producers became dependent and trapped in phallic-dominated settlements growing a few varieties of cereals. Their limited mobility and knowledge had an immense impact on females' economic, nutritional, and social independence.[1]

Men's taming of women meant reducing and eliminating matrilocality, matrilineality, ecogynocentrism, young-bearers' traditional networks, and female solidarity. As part of the domesticating process, egg-producers were isolated into nuclear, patriarchal families and trapped within house walls. Males started having several wives and more children than women, which reinforced patrilocal residence.

Patrilocal clans reversed the position of partner and mother in the household. Ovary beings now belonged to a different group from that of their children and spouse, and rigid rules were adopted to enforce female fidelity and monogamy. Wives were isolated from the reach of relatives and brothers.[2]

For women and girls, partner unions went from temporary, voluntary associations to a lifetime commitment to a single man. Extra-marital affairs by egg-producers were severely sanctioned. When only one sex has influence over residence, as is typically the case in phallic-dominated pastoral and horticultural societies, a dense network of closely related men emerges, with their spouses on the periphery. However, the average number of related individuals is much lower when females and males have an equal influence.[3]

Increasingly, the benefits of clan prosperity and human progress by-passed females, who remained dis-inherited and dis-empowered. Patrilineal descent meant that sons inherited everything, and sisters were left to the mercy of their brothers. First-son preference, along with female disinheritance, led to rapid resource accumulation for men.

Phallic-dominance over clans soon resulted in the practice of enslaving women and girls from other groups. The forced labor of 'other' egg-producers, in turn, promoted to the general devaluing of females, as their productive, reproductive, and domestic work were no longer essential for men.[4]

The Erlenmeyer tablets give a picture of the Sumerian economy in the Euphrates Valley around 4,200 BP. Labor inputs were valued in "female labor days," and the market economy was based on the fruits of women's labor, barley. Forced into unpaid agricultural labor, girls and women learned to be submissive and likable to sperm-producers since their entire existence, and that of their children, was dependent on the benevolence of men.

Gerder Lerner argues that dominance over females provided men with a model out of which slavery developed as a social institution. Men learned strategies of subordination, especially rape, as a way to break the body and spirit of human animals.[5] Men went from enslaving females, to enslaving men from outside groups who could be defined as strangers.[6] Lerner concludes, "the enslavement of women, combining both racism and sexism, preceded the formation of classes and class oppression."

According to Lerner, the invention of private property derives from the model provided by the manipulation of female sexuality. Egg-producers were controlled through the exchange and sale of brides, slavery, prostitution, codes of virginity, forced reproduction, and being corralled into a patriarchal marriage and family.

Un-enslaved females' cooperation with patriarchy was secured by domination, including rape and abuse in the family, and by the promise of class privilege and protection against external male aggression. Women were pitted against each another by artificially constituted racial distinctions as well.

Egg-producers were also divided by the fabricated division of women into those who are 'respectable,' that is, attached to one sperm-producer, and those who were 'not-respectable,' that is, not attached to one man, or free of all males. Respectable or not, all women were defined by their relationship to a phallic human or lack thereof.

Although there is general agreement with Lerner's analysis, this book argues that phallic dominance over nonhuman animals lies at the root of sexism and capitalism. It was domesticates that provided a model for men's control over human females and the formation of private property.

One indication of domesticates' importance to male economies is that rules relating to the sale, rental, and treatment of enslaved animals were among the first legal codes written and enforced by phallic-based societies, and this issue is explored next.

Animal Husbandry Laws

Cuneiform law refers to any of the legal codes written in cuneiform script[7] that were developed and used throughout the ancient Near East among the Sumerians, Babylonians, Assyrians, Elamites, Hurrians, Kassites, and Hittites. The Code of Hammurabi is the most well-known of the cuneiform laws, but there were some precursors.[8]

Sumer was the first urban civilization in southern Mesopotamia, modern-day southern Iraq, during the early Bronze Age (7,500 and 6,000 BP).[9] Living along the valleys of the Tigris and Euphrates, Sumerian farmers were able to grow an abundance of grain and other crops, and the surplus enabled them to settle in one place. After centuries of conquest, Sumer was united under Babylonian rule around 3,700 BP.

In Babylonia, Hammurabi's Code was written down around 3,700 BP.[10] This text is one of the oldest deciphered writings of significant length in the world. There are 282 laws in the code, covering crime, trade, land rights, irrigation, animal husbandry, labor, enslavement, inheritance, adoption, medical and veterinary care, construction, and other practices. Corn was the currency used for wages, fines, and compensation.

A third of the text cover issues relating to household and family relationships such as inheritance, divorce, paternity, and sexual behavior. Animal husbandry is discussed in many codes relating to property and labor, and specific costs for use and abuse of animals are detailed.

For instance, the price to hire an ox or donkey for threshing crops was twenty ka of corn, and for a young animal, it was ten.[11] In comparison, to hire a cart alone was forty ka, and for an oxen, cart, and driver it was one hundred and eighty ka of corn per day. And, if anyone used an ox for 'forced labor,' that is without permission of the owner, he had to pay one-third a mina in fine.[12]

A herdsman entrusted with cattle or sheep who received agreed wages and is satisfied with his compensation was responsible for any decrease in the numbers or birth rates of domesticates. He had to pay for the potential increase or profit that was lost under his care.

If someone hired an ox and damaged its eye, he had to pay the Babylonian owner one-half of its value. And if anyone hired an ox, and broke off a horn, or cut off its tail, or hurt its muzzle, he had to pay one-fourth of its value to the owner.

Owners also faced fines for harm caused by their domesticates. If a dangerous oxen injured a free-born man and killed him, the owner had to pay one-half a mina in fines. In comparison, if the ox killed an enslaved human, the fine was one-third a mina. So a free Babylonian man had far greater value than an enslaved person.

There were also fees and penalties related to veterinary care. If an animal surgeon performed an operation on an injured equid or oxen, and cured it, the owner had to pay one-sixth of a shekel. If the animal died, the vet had to pay the owner one-fourth of the animals' value.

♀ as Property of ♂

Hammurabi's animal-based laws centered on phallic property rights, and so too were its legal codes relating to females. All egg-producers were men's property, and if other men abused girls and women, they had to compensate their male 'owners.'

For example, a Babylonian father or husband had to be compensated if a daughter or wife was 'violated' in cases of rape and sexual assault, that is, if male property was 'damaged.' There were no laws against marital rape, or the abuse of prostitutes, which reinforced the status of egg-producers as phallic property, and as sexual objects.

By the Bronze Age, the value of ovary beings was vastly reduced as evidenced in the practice of bride price. Babylonians and other cultures observed a form of dowry in which a father had to pay a male to marry his daughter. The economic, sexual, social, psychological, and other burdens of being an egg-producer under patriarchy were a complete reversal of the freedom and high status females enjoyed during gynocentric prehistory.

Girls and women were valued only in terms of male property. For instance, in the case of divorce, when females returned to their paternal home, the dowry was usually returned to the father. As another example, if a Babylonian man married a woman, and she gave birth to sons and then died, then the father had no claim on the dowry for it belonged to her sons, not daughters.

The severely reduced status of the young-bearing sex by the Bronze Age is also evidenced by the customary practice of femicide, or murder of women and girls. Femicide of Babylonian females was fully sanctioned in Hammurabi's Code, even for trivial 'offenses.'

For instance, if a 'sister of a god' or priestess, open a tavern, or enter a tavern to drink, she was to be burned to death. This shows that moral codes for females in the service of patriarchal religions were extremely harsh and tightly enforced, with fatal punishment for even small infractions like socializing. Similar prohibitions for a 'brother of a god' are absent.

Femicide and control over egg-producers' sexuality were integral to the subjugation of Bronze Age women and girls. Death was the punishment for female adultery, even for unproven accusations. For instance, if the 'finger is pointed' at a man's wife about another man, but she was not caught sleeping with the other man, she still had to risk her life by jumping into the river for her husband as a test of her fidelity.

Members of the young-bearing sex lived under the constant threat of execution and policed each other to comply with the rigid codes of patriarchal 'morality' as a matter of survival. Females who refused to be tamed and rejected their inferior status as phallic property were frequently injured and killed. Girls and women dared not oppose men's domination.

For instance, if a Babylonian man was captured as a prisoner in war, but there was sustenance in his house, his spouse could not leave. Otherwise, she could be judicially condemned and thrown into a river. If a wife separated from her husband without his permission, she could also be killed.

In contrast, as part of undeserved phallic privilege, Babylonian men did not need permission to separate from their spouses. This male-dominated union reduced wives to the mercy of their partner who could use abandonment to make them compliant. Moreover, Mesopotamian men could have multiple wives and maidservants as mates.

When Babylonian men injured or killed a woman or girl, they only had to pay a relatively minor fine compared to injuring or killing a man. For example, if a man abused a free-born woman and caused her to miscarriage, he had to pay ten shekels for her loss. If the woman died, his daughter was put to death as punishment, not the male murder. Babylonian phallic privilege extended to rape, incest, and femicide, and victimized girls and women had to bear the blame and burden of male violence. As an example, the punishment for incest with a daughter was exile and men could just move to another city.

If a man abused the maidservant of another man, and she suffered a miscarriage, he had to pay two shekels in fine. If the maid-servant dies, he had to pay one-third of a mina. The status and value of impoverished and enslaved egg-producers were lower than those of 'free' women. Babylonian men could abuse, torture, and murder female servants with impunity, and if charged, they only had to pay a minimal payment.

In contrast, victimized and enslaved females faced harsh punishment for damaging any aspect of patriarchal property, and for misleading their male 'owners' and employers. For instance, if a child died, and a caregiver nursed another child unknown to her hirer, the penalty was to have her breasts cut off.

Reduction applied equally to females born with class privilege. In another reversal of prehistorical gynocentric norms, 'free' Bronze Age females were completely disinherited by law. If a Babylonian father gave a present to his daughter, she could enjoy it for as long as she lived, but her estate belonged to her brothers. And a man could give his daughter by a concubine a dowry and deed, but when he died, she received no part of the paternal estate.

As another example of the 'Great Fall' in egg-producers' status by the Bronze Age, Babylonian sons had more rights than their own mothers. If a chieftain or ordinary soldier was captured in battle, the field and garden was given to his sons, and they took over the fee of their father.

However, if the son was still young, and could not take possession, only a third of the field and garden was given to his mother, and this was only so she could bring the son up. Egg-producers, young and old, were dependent on phallic benefaction. Prevented from ownership of property and land, daughters, widows, and other females, at the most, were just allowed temporary use of patriarchal resources that automatically returned to phallic ownership after they died.

Hammurabi's laws on females demonstrate that patriarchal class-based roles and sexist structures were fully developed and sustained by the emergence of sperm-producers' 'civilization' in the Bronze Age. The formulation of masculinity and phallic dominance through hierarchical sexual dualism overwhelmingly favored men and served to domesticate women in numerous ways. The image of man-the-authority and agreement on males' 'superior' roles were constructed on an oppositional identity that view females as the inferior, animalized 'other.'[13]

Overall, patriarchal rule was maintained by the continual menace of femicide. Girls and women were just as vulnerable as domesticates and untamed nonhuman animals to phallic violence. Both groups faced the constant threat of injury and murder at any moment for resistance to male abuse and victimization.

Hammurabi's rigid, phallic-based property laws were mirrored in cultures far and wide. In ancient Greece, for instance, women were generally not allowed to own property, were not regarded as citizens, could not vote, and were excluded from many public spaces.[14]

Babylonian Masculinity

The privatization of land and colonization of animals are the foundations of patriarchal rule and cyborg consciousness. This scheme is biased in favor of elite males and the majority of the population are compelled to work and support the system with little or no compensation.

In lieu of actual resources, glorification of machismo identities and promotion of male supremacy over women and animals are part of the emotional wages non-elite men receive for their consent to the corrupt system. Every adult male is responsible for complicity in maintaining the social and environmental disorder, and men collectively benefit from various forms of phallic privilege.

Unless they are resisting, each man is at fault, but at the same time, a pernicious form of systemic oppression founded on the integration of sexism, speciesism, and capitalism, is also to blame. Men's first legal codes offer a clue as to how this wretched synthesis of subjugation was created.

Hammurabi's patriarchal laws were used to uphold a rigid class-sex and species hierarchy, and geared toward protecting the body and property of free males, and especially elite men. A stratified state was established with an increase in fines for the killing of an animal, female, and male. Females were simultaneously defined as different and similar to animals, and the status of enslaved females mirrored that of enslaved domesticates.

Babylonian men with wealth, status, and power were at the apex of society, and there were severe penalties for disrespecting male elites. For instance, anyone in Mesopotamia who struck the body of a man higher in rank received sixty blows with an ox-whip in public. Public whippings presented a highly visible warning to all men of the severe consequences for violating the class-based hierarchy.

In fights between equals of free men, penalties were correlative, but punishments were unequally applied in conflicts between free and unfree men. For example, if a free Babylonian man injured another free man's vision, the aggressor's eye was blinded. Similarly, if a free man broke the bone of some other freeman, the attacker's limbs was broken. And if he knocked out another's tooth, a freeman's own teeth were bashed. This 'eye-for-an-eye' regime indicates that at least some of Hammurabi's codes were the basis for patriarchal Mosaic law.

Punishment for violent Babylonian sperm-producers was dependent on the status and position of their victims. The artificially-created social hierarchy among males had to be implemented in both private and public spaces. For instance, patriarchs were protected from their own children, and if a son struck his father, his hands was chopped off.

Babylonian enslavement laws were enforced with strong penalties to maintain subjugation practices and phallic hierarchical boundaries. For example, if an enslaved male resisted by saying to his owner: "You are not my master," the oppressed man's ear was cut off. Even if an enslaved man struck the body of a free man in self-defense, his ear was still cut off.

In a patriarchal society, the preservation of male property is paramount. For instance, if a Babylonian barber, without the knowledge of an enslaver, cuts the ownership sign off of an enslaved person who was not for sale, the hands of the barber was cut off. And if anyone deceived a barber, and made him mark a person not for sale with the sign of a slave, he was put to death and buried in his house.

Damage to assets, dwellings, and other privatized property was taken seriously, and contractors were liable for their work. If a builder assembled a house and it fell and killed its proprietor, then that contractor was put to death. If the building collapsed and killed the son of the owner, the son of the builder was put to death. And if the dwelling killed a slave of the proprietor, then the contractor had to pay slave for slave to the possessor of the house.

Literacy: Codifying Patriarchy

Similar to the colonization of nonhuman animals, literacy in the New Stone Age was critical to the development of the new patriarchal disorder. Men used animals to enhance their physical might, and literacy to expand their mental force. Hammurabi and other restrictive legal codes were copied widely to impose phallic, class-based hierarchies and religions across the Middle East,

Mediterranean, Europe, and Asia.

Besides aiding in the establishment and protection of sperm-producers' propertied interests, the literacy boom created a paradigm shift in consciousness that resulted in phallic disembodiment. Men used literacy and religion to separate their cognition from their body. Moreover, they claimed that the male mind was closer to the source of all power in the Universe, the sky magic of a jealous and insecure phallic god.[15]

In *The Great Cosmic Mother*, Sjoo and Mor contend that thousands of pre-literate, oral Goddess-based theologies were replaced with the debut of phallic literacy, patriarchal faiths, and abrahamic cults.[16] Cyborg alphabetism resulted in a devaluation of the natural world and its inhabitants, with the sole exception of human male animals. Literacy was not a male invention, but like other female technologies, it was co-opted by men for selfish purposes.

Writing is considered the hallmark of civilization and it began early in human existence. For example, a Homo Erectus engraved bone from 350,000 BP has astrological and other markings.[17] Also, the zigzag or serpentine line was used as a symbol for water in the Stone Age and Neolithic.

Marija Gimbutas argued that the Old European, or Danube script, was part of a wider set of signs that expressed the cosmological and spiritual beliefs of the New Stone Age, which were female-centered. For instance, Gimbutas contends that the symbolic designs and motifs of crosses, spirals, dots, lozenges, and so on, "represent the grammar and syntax of a kind of meta-language by which the entire constellation of meanings is transmitted. They reveal the basic world-view of Old European culture."[18]

As another example, the cross and related symbols, such as the swastika, represents the four corners of the world, the cosmic or yearly cycle, and the birth and death of vegetation. Long before it was coopted by christians and the nazis, these common icons were associated with the Great Goddess.

Gimbutas demonstrated that several patterns from the pre-Indo-European religion are evident in the subsequent religions of the Greeks, the Etruscans, the Basques, the Celts, the Germanic peoples, and the Balts. And her work on the Danube script is supported by other experts, such as Joan Marler.[19]

As literacy developed under phallic-dominated cultures, it resulted in the devaluing of female's traditional oral knowledge. By the Bronze Age, alphabetism became the key measure of learning and egg-producers' lack of access to education meant that they remained non-literate. And, in an insidious form of circular logic, men used female non-literacy to 'prove' that women lacked understanding and were therefore mentally inferior.

The written word was key to the development of phallic faiths, spiritual, and intellectual dominance. Shlain argues that pre-literate cultures were principally informed by holistic, right-brain modes that venerated the Goddess and female-centered values. Composition drove cultures toward linear, left-brain thinking, and this shift changed the balance between ovary beings and sperm-producers. Thus, alphabetism initiated the decline of the gynocentrism and ushered in patriarchal rule.[20]

Shlain concludes, "Literacy has promoted the subjugation of women by men throughout all but the very recent history of the West. Misogyny and patriarchy rise and fall with the fortunes of the alphabetic written word." The Old Testament was one of the first alphabetic work to influence future ages, and multitudes still read it three thousand years later. The words on its pages anchor three dominant religions - judaism, christianity, and islam - each an exemplar of patriarchy.[21]

Patriarchal religions depend heavily on the alphabetism and textual prohibitions to maintain their legitimacy. Unlike images, text can readily convey prohibitions in a few sentences, like the exclusive worship of a jealous god. This new theology was defined by decrees, creeds, and scriptures, and was basically a form of phallic monotheism that was adamantly opposed to female iconography and polytheism.

Goddess worship, female-centered values, and women's power depend on the ubiquity of representation, like the Woman/Goddess figures. In contrast, God-worship, masculine values, and men's domination of women are bound to the written word. The image and text, like female and male, are complementary opposites. Whenever a culture elevates writing at the expense of visual representation, patriarchy dominates. And when the standing of the image supersedes the written word, female-centered values and egalitarianism flourish.

Patriarchy has attempted to stamp out the iconography and writings of women through various legal, economic, and social punishments. Until recently, women were frequently barred from publishing their work and had to take on male pen names to get published. Like the hand-prints of the Stone Age, the works of 'Anonymous' were probably female-authored as well.

Greek Titaness: Dike/Justice

Ma'at, Isis, Metis, Themis and other ancient female deities were concerned with issues like equality and justice, which points to the prevalence of egalitarian, Goddess-base narratives during prehistory. Even in patriarchal mature Egyptian societies, it was considered a crime against Ma'at if a person engaged in jealousy, dishonesty, gluttony, laziness, injustice, and ungratefulness.

Similar to Ma'at, in ancient Greek culture, Dike (Dicé) was the Goddess of justice, fair judgments and the rights established by custom and law. She was one of the three Horai, Goddesses of the seasons, and keepers of the gates of heaven. Her sisters were Eunomia or good order, and Eirene or peace. Like her siblings, Dike represented an aspect of springtime growth.

Goddess Dike was identified with Dikaiosyne or righteousness, and Astraia, the virgin Goddess of justice who resided in the Constellation Virgo. Her personification stands in contrast to justice viewed as retribution or sentence. According to Hesiod, Goddess Dike was fathered by Zeus and Goddess Themis, and she and her mother were both forms of justice. Goddess Dike ruled over human justice, while her mother ruled over divine justice. Dike's opposite was adikia ("injustice").

Goddess Dike is depicted as a young, slender woman carrying a physical balance scale and wearing a laurel wreath. Her Roman counterpart, Goddess Justitia, appears in a similar fashion. Goddess Dike is represented in the constellation Libra which is named for the Latin name of her symbol (Scales).

The Goddess of Justice is often associated with Astraea ("star-maiden" or "starry night"), the celestial virgin Goddess of innocence and purity, who has a similar iconography. Goddess Astria was the last of the immortals to live with humans during the Golden Age, one of the old Greek religion's five deteriorating Ages of Man. Ovid suggested that Goddess Astraea abandoned the Earth during the Iron Age, fleeing from the new wickedness of humanity, to become the constellation Virgo. The nearby constellation Libra reflected Goddess Astraea's symbolic association with Goddess Dike.

According to Aratus, Goddess Dike lived upon Earth during the Golden and Silver ages, when there were no wars or diseases, when men raised fine crops, and did not yet know how to sail. The men grew greedy, however, and the Goddess was sickened. She proclaimed:

> "Behold what manner of race the fathers of the Golden Age left behind them! Far meaner than themselves! but you will breed a viler progeny! Verily wars and cruel bloodshed shall be unto men and grievous woe shall be laid upon them."

Goddess Dike left Earth for the sky, from which, as the constellation, she watched the despicable human race. After her departure, the human race declined into the Bronze Age, when diseases arose and men learned how to sail. This myth suggests that the early Neolithic remained gynocentric and peaceful, with men helping woman-the-farmer. Capitalizing on the surplus of female technologies and labor, men became greedy and violent.

The exit of the two Goddesses, Dike and Astraea, helps to explain men's abandonment of gynocentric principles of egalitarianism with the rise of patriarchy. The scales of equality and balance, and notions of innocence and just conduct were separated from Earth and became providence of the heavens. The departure of the Goddesses also hints at the banishment and great fall of women, and removal of divinity from Earth.

Bronze Age ♀ Resistance

The rise of patriarchy and phallic accumulation were not attained everywhere, at the identical rate, or at the same time. There were significant variations in gender construction during the Bronze Age and a few females benefited from having class advantage with access to education and libraries. Several of these women became renowned poets and writers, such as Enheduanna of Mesopotamia.

Historical examples of accomplished Greek writers include Sappho, Erinna, Aesara, Aelia, Anicia, Anyte, Aristodama, Boeo, Cleobulina, Elephantis, Hedyle, Korinna, Megalostrata, Metrodora, Moero, Myrtis, Paxilla, and Telesilla. There were also Nossis, Sulpicia I and II, Theophila, Claudia Severa, and Julia Balbilla of Italy, Gargi, Maitreyi, Avvaiyar, and Khana of South Asia, Xu Mu and Li Qingzhao of China, and numerous others.

Daughter of King Sargon in Sumer, Enheduanna (c. 4,300 BP) was a high priestess who wrote three hymns to the goddess Inanna which survive. Enheduanna is the earliest author and poet in the world that history knows by name. Enheduanna composed 42 hymns addressed to temples across Sumer and Akkad.[22]

The Hurrian Hymn is the oldest surviving melody, over 3400 years old. It was discovered on a clay tablet fragment in Ugarit, and is dedicated the Hurrians' Goddess of the orchards, Nikkal.[23] One translation of the lyrics on the tablet is as follows: 'Once I have endeared the deity, she will love me in her heart, the offer I bring may wholly cover my sin, bringing sesame oil may work on my behalf in awe may I.'

Therigatha or Verses of the Elder Nuns is a collection of short poems of elder Buddhist nuns from around 2,600 BP. Therigatha is a significant document in Buddhism as well as the earliest-known collection of women's literature. The Therigatha contains passages reaffirming the view that women are the equal of men in terms of spiritual attainment. An additional collection of scriptures concerning the role and abilities of women in the early Sangha is the Bhikkhunī-Saṃyutta or Nun's Discourse.

One Therigatha passage was written by Vimalā, a Former Courtesan. It says:

> Intoxicated with my complexion
> figure, beauty, & fame;
> haughty with youth,
> I despised other women.
> Adorning this body
> embellished to delude foolish men,
> I stood at the door to the brothel:
> a hunter with snare laid out.
> I showed off my ornaments,
> and revealed many a private part.
> I worked my manifold magic,
> laughing out loud at the crowd.
> Today, wrapped in a double cloak,
> my head shaven,
> having wandered for alms,
> I sit at the foot of a tree
> and attain the state of no-thought.
> All ties—human & divine—have been cut.
> Having cast off all
> effluents,
> cooled am I. Unbound[24]

Sappho (c. 2,600 BP) was a prolific Greek poet, probably composing around 10,000 lines. Her poetry was well-known and greatly admired through much of antiquity, and she was among nine lyric poets most highly esteemed by scholars of Hellenistic Alexandria.

Erinna (c. 2,400 BP) was perhaps the most famous female Greek poet in the ancient world after Sappho. She is one of the few female poets whose work has, at least in part, survived. Anyte of Tegea (c. 2,300 BP) was an Arcadian poet. She is one of the nine outstanding ancient women poets listed in the Palatine Anthology.

Metrodora (c. 1,700 BP) was a Greek female physician and author of the oldest medical text known to have been written by a woman, On the Diseases and Cures of Women. Her medical treatise covers many areas of medicine, and discussed women's relationship to nature.

Aesara of Lucania (c. 2,300 BP) was a Pythagorean philosopher, who wrote On Human Nature.[25] Aesara divides the soul into three parts: the mind which performs judgment and thought, the spirit which contains courage and strength, and desire which provides love and friendliness. Aesara argues that only by studying our human nature and soul can we understand the philosophical basis for natural law and morality.

Gargi Vachaknavi (c. 2,700 BP) may have written many hymns in the Rigveda and she could challenge the most esteemed phallic-philosophers in debate. Gargi, along with Vadava Pratitheyi and Sulabha Maitreyi, are among the prominent females in the Upanishads.

Maitreyi was a philosopher during the later vedic period (c. 2,700 BP). Ten hymns in the Rigveda are attributed to her, and Maitreyi explored the concept of soul or self in various debates. Both Gargi and Maitreyi remained celibate their entire life. The Avvaiyar were some of the most famous female poets of the Tamil canon (c. 1,800 BP).

Lady Xu Mu (c. 2,700 BP) was a princess of the State of Wey and the first recorded female poet in Chinese history. Li Qingzhao (1,100 BP) was a Song dynasty writer considered the greatest woman poet in Chinese history.

Ancient Egyptian females serve as other examples of fluidity in Bronze Age gender construction. As Janet Johnson observes, "From our earliest preserved records in the Old Kingdom on, the formal legal status of Egyptian women - whether unmarried, married, divorced or widowed - was nearly identical with that of Egyptian men."[26]

With status similar to those in Stone Age gynocentric societies, Egyptian women were entitled to work, own property, go to court, bear witness, and serve on a jury.[27] They had the right to choose partners freely, to marry out of love, to spell out detailed prenuptial agreements to protect them and their children, and to divorce for any reason.

Although Egyptian females enjoyed property ownership, partner unions, and other rights for millennia, there was a glass ceiling. The upper echelons of Egyptian society were overwhelmingly male, and only a tiny minority of scribes and priests, two of the most respected professions, were women. Moreover, the role of pharaoh was mostly off bounds to women, with some notable exceptions, such as Hatshepsut, Nefertiti, and Cleopatra.

In comparison, the status of western European women in the 19th century was more similar to that of Mesopotamian females. For instance, in the 1870s, American women could not own property, could not sign contracts, could not vote, file lawsuits, nor have their own money. A female lived under her father's roof, and his control was passed to her husband upon marriage. A woman running away from violent domestic abuse was hunted down by the law and returned to her husband as she was his property.

Conclusion

This fourth chapter of Part IV on the emergence of toxic masculinity discussed how the seventh subjugation of women was codified in law under phallic-centered rule. Similar to the enslavement of animals, men's harnessing of female reproductive and productive labor increased their ownership and control of resources.

Starting with cuneiform texts in the Bronze Age, phallic-centered law enshrined the objectification of animals and females as the private property of human sperm-producers. Literacy helped to expedite male supremacy and rule in religion, economy, culture, and almost all areas of public and private life.

The next and final chapter in this section examines in more detail men's taming of women and their reversal of female-centered cultures, including Goddess-centered religions. The subjugation of human egg-producers was/is part of phallic transcendence over the Earth, nature, and animals, and this inter-related oppression is justified by cyborgs' claim to an exclusive connection with male sky magic.

(Figure 22: Neolithic Relief fragment of Nintinugga - Babylonian Goddess of healing)

22: Mastering Gaia

This christian demolition of the Goddess and mythic establishment of male divinity has paved the way for the technological elimination of women through the application of modern medicine, transsexualism, cloning, and other forms of genetic engineering. - Mary Daly

ASIA's Journey 2121.22

It's 8:00 PM and 104°F (40°C) in Chinatown, with a humidity under 50 percent. Jean's friend arranges for ASIA to stay in the basement of a restaurant, and the hungry group rapidly eats the rice, vegetables, noodles, and fruits served. Earlier, six women formed into three teams to search for the missing children. Dressed as men, they left with the groups' gold coins and wine to trade for the abducted girls.

The children shower and wear clean clothes. It's Cronetime, and Hehewuti marks their winding passage on the board and maps out the 3-week journey ahead, north to the next safe house.

"How long can we stay here?" Lehana wants to know.

"We leave as soon as we find our missing sisters." Hehewuti answers.

"Three weeks of walking again!" Zaid slumps, then ask, "Why can't we take horses like the men?"

Hehewuti says nothing. She talks about ASIA's missing daughters, to reassure the other girls who are scared.

"The gangs have horses," Zaid interrupts. "We need horses so they cannot catch us."

"A horse is very costly," Hehewuti replies gently. "And there are too many of us to ride in a carriage."

"But I don't want to walk anymore." Zaid is almost tearful. "We have four dogs, so why can't we get one horse?"

Hehewuti waves her hand in the air. "There are differences between the two animals. Can you girls think of any?"

"Horses need to eat a lot of grass," Ashadia tells Ziad. "And the drought has killed most of the grass."

"Dogs don't eat that much," 12-year-old Bo explains. "And, our dogs eat whatever we have."

"My horse will be my pet," Zaid pleads. "I will find food for it."

"But we can't hide a horse," Ashadia reasons with the boy. "They cannot fit in a narrow trench."

"And they make loud noises," Naina points out.

"When the bad men come, I will ride away," Zaid shouts.

"Horses require more land and resources," Hehewuti says. "It's the same problem with the slaughterhouse."

"More tamed animals equals more heat," Naina blurts out.

Zaid is not convinced and screams in frustration.

Introduction

The rise of cyborg consciousness was spurred on by pastorals' exploitation of horses and grazing ruminants. Men's construction of houses, structures, and settlements contributed further to male ascendancy over nature, animals, and women.

After replacement of female-centered power and forms of organization, gynocentric theology remained one of the few obstacles in the way of complete phallic domination or hegemony. To counter the ancient female philosophical tradition, men methodically co-opted the Goddesses and eventually reduced them to irrelevant consorts of kings.

This fifth and last chapter of Part IV on the rise of male-centered rule broadens the discussion of the previous chapter on the reduction of females. The chapter starts by exploring the subversion of Goddess stories into phallic-centered narratives. The Greek myths of Medusa and Persephone are next discussed, followed by the messaging behind female rivalry.

The chapter then explores men's transfer of sacredness from Earth to the sky. Next, it reviews research into male-based religions by Elizabeth Gould Davis and Merlin Stone, and the chapter concludes with a survey of resistance among early christian women.

Subverting Goddess Myths

As phallic-based systems rose to prominence, they perverted the might of Goddesses and placed them into the service of sperm-producers. A common means of legitimizing the transition from gynocentric society was forcible marriage of the Triple Goddess to a trinity of gods. For instance, Hera was taken by Zeus, Demeter by Poseidon, and Kore by Hades. The Triple Goddess lies in the background of the various trinities of gods which foreshadowed the biblical trinity.

Göttner-Abendroth observed that there was a transformation from prehistoric cultures in which the local Goddess was primary and the male god, if any, derived his power from the Goddess. The "Downfall," occurred at varying times in various Neolithic cultures as gods got the better of Goddesses and made them subordinate.[1]

The dethroning of the Goddess mirrored the gradual suppression of women leaders and installation of patriarchs in their place. For instance, among the Sumerians and Greeks, the Goddesses were converted to token figureheads at the same time that females were turned into the property of men. Ancient Goddesses who were sovereign, sophisticated, and unrestrained became simplified, chastened, straightened, married off, raped, degraded, abused, and demoted in stature.[2]

In order for a male to become the supreme "god" and for patriarchal religion to triumph, it was imperative that the Goddesses and female sacredness be disrespected, profaned, and distorted. The female Earth was considered inferior to masculine sky-magic and, to make their heavenly, de-sexed father/god credible, it was essential that the rival Earthy sex-mother-grandmother Goddess(es) and related signs, messages, and practices be defanged and demonized.

Consequently, aspects of the Earth's exposed flesh like volcanoes and caves were viewed as the entrance to men's worse nightmare, fiery hell. Gynecological narratives were disguised, suppressed, caricatured, and twisted,[3] and Goddess murder was enacted numerous times, for example, the sea serpent Goddess Tiamat was slaughtered by Marduk in the Babylonian epic. These mythic murders legitimate continuing violence against the Goddess personified as females, as with witch-burnings and femicides.

Observing this profoundly misogynist trend, Gloria Anzaldúa writes, "The male-dominated Azteca-Mexica culture drove the powerful female deities underground by giving them monstrous attributes... thus splitting the female Self and the female deities. They divided her who had been complete, who possessed both upper (light) and underworld (dark) aspects... into chaste virgins and... putas, into Beauties and the Beasts."[4]

Hecate, Goddess of witches, was built upon a triangle, with faces turned in three directions. Hecate statues were set up at the crossing of three roads, representing the realms of the Goddess - Earth, Air, and Sea. Hecate's cosmic faces/forces was later replaced by three dancing maidens.

Similarly, cosmic energy was symbolized in the Tree of Life, which is the Goddess. Helen Diner suggests the sacred tree was part of the worship of Great Mothers, and in ancient Egypt, the tree is depicted as bringing forth the sun itself. The cosmic tree was transformed into the christian cross, a dead wood rack to which a dying body is fastened with nails. As Diner succinctly states: "In Christianity, the tree becomes the torture cross of the world."[5]

Kim Power points out that women were assumed to have a "closer connection to all that was temporal and mutable." And, "in both East and West, the 'holy' was that most removed from the human and, therefore, women were by nature further removed from holiness than men."[6] Being closer to nature means being further from god.

Commenting on the significance of this 'othering' process, Gerda Lerner concludes, "This symbolic devaluing of women in relation to the divine becomes one of the founding metaphors of Western civilization." The other founding metaphor was supplied by Aristotelian philosophy, the notion that women are incomplete, irrational, and "damaged human beings of an entirely different order than men."

The Bronze Age imagery of female and bull coincided with the appearance of cultivation and herding,[7] however, the Woman figure was no longer an all-powerful deity. The Goddess was diminished to a "god-bearing Mother," and she still is, as portrayed by her modern identity of Virgin Mary. Female value is thus confined to the bearer of sons, kings, and prophets.

In the first cities, creation and coronation myths often took the form of a Mother Goddess like Inanna giving birth to the king. The Mother Goddess was honored in art and song as the progenitor of godlike Egyptian monarchs, and to Sumerian rulers like Gilgamesh who was supposedly a god by two-thirds.

In the Pelasgian creation myth, Eurynome, the Goddess of All Things, assumed the form of a dove and laid the universal egg. Her Sumerian name was Iahu meaning "exalted dove," a title that later passed on to Yahweh as creator. Although Neolithic men eagerly co-opted the imagery of the Goddess, they steadfastly rejected her gynecological philosophy.

The intricate messaging behind the Goddess, female-centered narratives of the journey and return, honoring the cycles of birth-death-rebirth, sustainability, and so on, were neglected or radically transformed. Female characters as repositories of eco-cultural knowledge were removed from stories that were reformulated as journeys of discoveries undertaken by lone male heroes.

The Goddesses who remained powerful were eroticized, like Aphrodite, or militarized, like Athena. Priestesses were demoted into a curse, like the term 'Bitch' was in Europe. A 'Harlot' was a priestess of the Egyptian Goddess Hathor. But as patriarchal hierarchy replaced sexual and social egalitarianism, isolated communities still held vestiges of the worship of various Goddesses.

Gimbutas meticulously researched these traces and concluded that an awareness of gynocentric prehistory is essential to decoding much of Western culture. The Goddess/Woman figures and narratives are a source of ancient wisdom that modern civilization must tap into, Gimbutas argues, to counter its own alienation from nature.

♂ Myths - Medusa

The story of Medusa starts with a paternal femicide plot by king Acrisius to drown his daughter, Danae, and grandson, Perseus. They survived, and aided by Athena's shield, Perseus was able to slay Medusa, one of three 'monsters' known as the Gorgons. The Triple Goddess/Gorgon sisters, Medusa, Stheno, and Euryale, were beautiful women, but the gods punished and turned them into birds with twisted claws and snakes crawling in their hair.[8]

Medusa was innocently murdered by Perseus who used her head, which retained its ability to turn onlookers to stone, as a weapon until he gave it to Athena to place on her shield. This patriarchal story sanctifies female betrayal at the highest level, with a female deity aiding a mortal man to murder a supernatural woman. Furthermore, the femicide of Medusa established that a divine ovary being was not worth the life of any mortal sperm-producer.

Greek myths generally reflect politico-religious history. As such, Perseus may have represented patriarchal groups that invaded Greece and Asia Minor in the fourth millennium BP to challenged gynocentric power. The myth records how these groups annulled the ancient Medusan calendar and replaced it with another.

Jane Harrison points out that Medusa was once the Goddess herself hiding behind a protective Gorgon mask or a hideous face that was intended to warn the profane against trespassing on her mysteries. Perseus beheading of Medusa is a sign of how the Greeks overran the Goddess's principal shrines, stripped her priestesses of their Gorgon masks, and took possession of their sacred animals.

Harrison argues that Medusa's "potency only begins when her head is severed, and that potency resides in the head; she is in a word a mask with a body later appended... the basis of the Gorgoneion is a cultus object, a ritual mask misunderstood." Harrison's states, "the Gorgon was made out of the terror, not the terror out of the Gorgon."[9]

Men's capture or murder of one of the Triple Goddesses interrupted female-centered thought and cycles of birth, death, and re-birth. Medusa's femicide was symbolic of the defeat of gynocentric spirituality and the elimination of female-centered perspectives. It also signaled the transition from viewing females with a sense of mystery to one of fear and dread.

♂ Myths - Persephone

Persephone, also know as Kore, is an old chthonic or underworld deity of agricultural communities. This Goddess received the souls of the dead into the earth and held powers over the fertility of the soil, over which she reigned. Like Medusa, Persephone was a Triple Goddess who was abused by a man to symbolize the end of female-centered organization and thinking.

Kore was an all-pervading Goddess of nature who produced and destroyed everything. In early images, the Goddess has a vegetable-like appearance and is surrounded by dancing girls between blossoming flowers.[10] Athena and Artemis made the same choice of maidenhood as Kore and were reared together with her. The Triple Goddesses joined in gathering flowers, and together wove a robe for their father, Zeus. Their tranquility was abruptly shattered with the rape of Persephone.

While her two sisters went to the beach to cool their feet, Persephone, daughter of the harvest Goddess Demeter, wandered off to the shade of the forest trees where the violets grew thickest. On the spur of the moment, Kore was kidnapped and raped by the king of the underworld, Hades, her uncle, with the help of Zeus, her father.[11] Hades then forced Persephone into his chariot and down to his realm of mist and gloom.

Hades' four black horses and chariot were essential elements in the crime of capturing a female deity and ending the reign of the Triple Goddesses. The narrative is symbolic of men's use of horses to ravage, capture, and domesticate gynecological, agrarian communities. Kore's enslavement showed that the Goddess could be tamed by phallic forces, and females were no longer safe from the might of cyborgs.[12] The rape of Persephone could also be interpreted as male dominance over agriculture and nature.[13]

As a deity of the underworld, Kore was given names that were possible the names of original Goddesses.[14] Persephone was the terrible Queen of the Dead, whose name was not safe to speak aloud, who was euphemistically named "the Maiden." With her abduction, the land grew cold and barren. At last the gods sent a messenger, Hermes, to rescue Kore and bring springtime back to the Earth.[15] However, Persephone was obliged to spend a third of each year with Hades, and the remainder of the year among the gods.

♂ Myths - Female Rivalry

Goddess pitted against Goddess, or notable women competing for the love of a man, were common themes in Greek mythology. Hera, the queen of Olympus, was wildly jealous of her philandering husband, Zeus. Hera was in perpetual conflict with other women, who she blames and not her spouse. Thus, the status of this domesticated queen was not very different from the average wife in the patriarchal Greek household.

The role of queen of the heavens was shriveled to that of an envious rival of mere mortals.[16] And as a clue to the extent of misogyny under Greek culture, Hera's energies are mercilessly directed at the victims of phallic abuse. For instance, Hera turns Echo into a mute, and Callisto into a bear.

Another example of Hera's misplaced aggression was when Zeus impregnated Leto with twins. Leto had to search far and wide for a place where she could give birth to Apollo and Artemis since Hera in her enviousness had caused all lands to shun her.

There are numerous other examples of celestial female rivalry. For instance, Leto sent Artemis and Apollo to kill the fourteen children of another woman, Niobe. And Medea, a sorceress, and wife of Jason, killed her own children to punish Jason for his infidelity. Clytemnestra murdered the Trojan princess Cassandra whom her husband, Agamemnon, had taken as a war prize following the sack of Troy.

In another example of mythic femicide, Artemis ordered Agamemnon to kill his daughter, Iphigenia, so his ships could sail to Troy. And, Electra, daughter of Agamemnon and Clytemnestra, aided her brother in plotting revenge against their mother for the murder of their father. While Polyxena, the youngest daughter of Priam of Troy, was sacrificed to the ghost of Achilles.

Hemithea and Parthenos, princesses of the Island of Naxos, jumped into the sea to escape their father's wrath. And when the immortal Muses had to contend with the mortal daughters of Pierus for their title, the girls were turned into magpies. Arachne challenged Athena to a weaving contest and was transformed into a spider. One meaning behind the numerous tales of female rivalry was the notion that women could not trust each other, which deterred them from organizing as a sex-based group.

In addition to female-vs-female competition over men, gods are also avid women-haters. Semele, the mother of Dionysus, was six months pregnant when Zeus killed her. Hermes sewed Semele's premature son inside Zeus's thigh to gestate fully and in due course, delivered him.[17] In this narrative, Semele represents the patriarchal ideal of mother as mere vessel.

Apollo, who was fathered by Zeus, also encouraged matricide. Apollo was the personification of anti-gynocentrism and an opponent of Earth deities. His name is derived from 'appollunai' meaning destroy. Jane Harrison points out that he is a death-dealer and woman-hater. Apollo's real enemy was a female creature, a dragoness named Delphyne, a name connected to an old word for womb. Apollo killed Delphyne immediately after his birth. His temple was built at Delphi and engraved with the maxim, "Keep woman under the rule."

To reinforce the link between females and conflict in Greek mythology, Eris became the Goddess or personified spirit (daimona) of strife, discord, contention, and rivalry. Her Roman name was Discordia and she was closely identified with the war Goddess, Enyo. Eris was the mother of Kakodaimones, evil spirits which plagued humanity.[18]

Another myth which planted the idea that females are negative was Pandora, the first mortal woman created by the gods. Like Eve after her, Pandora was blamed for all misfortune humans faced. Pandora opened a jar (pithos), releasing all the evils of humanity, leaving only Hope inside once she had closed it again.

The rape of Goddesses and notable women were frequent in Greek narratives, which perhaps reflected prevailing sexual abuse faced by the average females. Europa was raped by Zeus, disguised as a bull.[19] And Zeus seized Thalia, a nymph, while he was in the form of an eagle, as he did with Aegina, Leto, and Ganymede, an adolescent male.

Zeus raped and then buried Thalia in the ground to avoid Hera's jealousy. This astonishing level of violence perpetuated by a god gave boys and men license to behave is a similar manner. In another instance, Zeus pursued Taygete, a nymph who invoked her protectress Artemis. To save her devotee from celestial rape, the Goddess turned Taygete into a doe with golden horns.

Helen, the daughter of Zeus and Leda, was abducted and abused twice - by Theseus and by Prince Paris of Troy. Orithyia, an Athenian princess, was kidnapped and raped by Boreas, the north wind, and made the Goddess of cold, gusty mountain winds. Bolina was a mortal maiden of Achaea. When Apollo attempted to rape her, Bolina fled and threw herself into the sea.

In the 'great' epic, The Iliad, said to be the foundation of western culture, Achilles and Agamemnon are fighting over which of them has the right to own a captured woman named Briseis. In these misogynist myths, human females suffer and perish while their rapists and jailers are celebrated as 'heroes'.

Removing Sacred from Earth

Removing the sacredness of Earth and placing it into the sky was a critical element in the construction of patriarchal ideology. The New Stone Age notion of "sky father" was a stark contrast to ancient gynocentric views of "Earth Mother." One clue to the link between domestication and patriarchy is that the worship of a sky father was characteristic of pastoral groups, while Earth

Mothers continued to be honored by agrarian communities.

The opposing god/Goddess ideologies reflected a struggle over land use by nomads and settlers, as well as conflict between patriarchy and gynocentrism. Underlying these tensions were divergent views of human's relationship to nature and animals, and concerns regarding sustainability. Male pastoral cultures with their animal-as-capital model eventually dominated female farming communities, and phallic-based sky magic and exploitation of the Earth became the religious and environmental norm.

Although some patriarchal groups honored 'sky Goddesses,' and 'heavenly Mothers,' phallic gods were usually primary. In Mesopotamia, An or Anu, the Sumerian name for heaven or sky, was one of the earliest known celestial father deity. Tengri or 'sky' was a primordial god of Turkic peoples. The vedic 'dyaus pita' means 'sky father' and includes sun gods. In Egypt, Horus was the ruler of the cosmos, and Zeus and Jupiter were the main celestial gods in Greece and Italy.

By the Bronze Age, almost all of the important gods and deities were males who resided in the atmosphere above or underground, but notably, not on the surface of the Earth. For example, Sabazios was the nomadic horseman and sky father god of the Phrygians and Thracians. While the Greeks had Aether, Apollo, Astraios, Hades, Helios, Uranus, and so on.[20]

Regarding the dichotomy between Earth and sky, Linda Hogan observes, "The Western belief that God lives apart from Earth is one that has taken us toward collective destruction. It is a belief narrow enough to forget the value of matter, the very thing that soul inhabits."[21] Also on point, Mary Daly notes the christian god's hostility toward Earth as exemplified by the proclamation of the gospel of Peter that the phallic deity will ultimately destroy the World by fire.

The patriarchal bible declares the supremacy of sky magic and dictates the faithful to, "Set your affection on things above, not on things on the Earth." The impression of an aloof deity hostile to the Earth is key to the cyborg psyche and is reinforced daily by dominant patriarchal religions.

Under the new celestial regime, girls and women were denied the solace of honoring a female deity and powerful role model. Human egg-producers were not only dependent on phallic benevolence on Earth, but they had to seek the benefaction of male sky magic as well. Female inter-species grounding with Earthlings and other young-bearers is negated in favor of celestial fantasy of phallic birthing.

Curiously, sky-based female deities continued to be honored by the craftsmen in fields in which the young-bearing sex were excluded. For instance, astrology was under the creator Goddesses Tiamat and Vari, and history was governed by the Fates and their counterparts.

Similarly, the arts and professions were under the inspiration and direction of Goddesses such as the Muses and Athena. Philosophy was under Sophia, while ethics and justice were under Goddesses such as Mayet, Themis, Dike, and Nemesis. While the professions honored celestial Goddesses, almost all of the astrologers, historians, artists, philosophers, and judges were men.

Elizabeth Gould Davis

After extensive research, Elizabeth Gould Davis (1910 to 1974) concluded that ancient human society consisted of gynocentric "queendoms" based around worship of the "Great Goddess," and was characterized by pacifism and democracy. Gould Davis argued that the primeval gynocentric societies attained a high level of civilization, which was comprehensively wiped out as a result of the "patriarchal revolution."[22]

In her book, *The First Sex*, Gould Davis asserted that patriarchy introduced a new system of society, centered on property rights rather than human rights. The author showed that men's social organization was founded on the worship of a stern and vengeful phallic deity, instead of the nurturing and forgiving Mother Goddesses that preceded him.[23]

Before the phallic revolution, in parts of the Mediterranean, egg-producers' tombs were preserved more carefully than those of sperm-producers, which is physical evidence of female primacy.[24] In addition, ancient sexual taboos and customs were indicative of gynocentrism. For instance, restrictions against brother-sister unions acted to protect girls and women against violent men.[25]

To establish a patrilineal system of inheritance, rigorous control of female sexuality was paramount. Accordingly, women's right to sexual pleasure was redefined as sinful, and egg-producers' virginity was conceived as the property right of a father or husband. Gould Davis explained that female circumcision was an attempt to protect female virginity and assure clear lines of paternity.

The misogynist myth of Eve was fundamental to the development of patriarchy. Ironically, the first 'female' had her origin in a man, who claimed the power of creation and motherhood. Moreover, Eve, translated into all women, was the cause of man's downfall and all his miseries.[26] That is, women are men's Frankenstein creation, a demon spawn.[27]

Gould Davis contend that the influence of Mary as a "Goddess" grew as the violent imposition of christianity erased ancient Goddess spirituality. Women and girls by the fifteenth century were treated so poorly by men of all social classes that they were seen as "worse than beasts."[28]

In the Middle Ages, puritanism's witch-hunts and a reinforced papacy placed the young-bearing sex into further submission. As part of both catholic and protestant inquisitions, hundreds of thousands of females were falsely accused and murdered via burning, drowning, hanging, and torture.

In Gould Davis's view, the 17th and 18th centuries marked the first time Western women accepted their own inferiority, and she made a special effort to show how the minds of women were subjugated during the 17th to 19th centuries.[29] The author contends that the survival of humanity depend on the restoration of women to their former position as rulers of society, and concludes, "the matriarchal counterrevolution is the only hope for the survival of the human race."[30]

Merlin Stone

In her book, When God Was a Woman, art historian Merlin Stone (1931 to 2011) describes archetypal Woman/Goddess figures as reflections of women as leaders, sacred entities, and benevolent matriarchs.[31] Stone contends that numerous, benevolent gynocentric societies and Goddess-reverent traditions were attacked, undermined, and ultimately destroyed by ancient tribes including hebrews and christians.

The feminist historian compiled a plethora of evidence to show that the transformation of matrilineal, matrifocal, Goddess-worshiping groups into patriarchal cultures and religions, was a worldwide event.[32] According to Stone, the torah was a phallic attempt to re-write the story of human society, dethrone the Goddesses, and change female symbolism to masculine forms.

Using abrahamic texts, phallic cults dismantled the primordial understanding held by matrifocal cultures that the female body and creativity are the origins of good and beautiful things. For instance, the ritual position of the fingers of the catholic priest giving a blessing, with the thumb, index finger, and middle finger raised, and the other two fingers are turned down, is said to represent the christian trinity. Originally, this sign was the "Phrygian blessing", giving in the name of Myrine, the great Moon-Goddess of Asia Minor and counterpart of Neith.[33] Myrine was Mother of the gods, later reversed into the 'honoring' of Mary as 'Mother of god,' a child-god whom she adores.

Stone decoded the way in which the Genesis story transformed the sacred icons of Goddess religion into symbols of evil. For instance, there are references to the hebrew people "whoring" after "idols," and worshiping "on every high hill and under every green tree." These admonishments referred to people who honored various Goddesses at sacred places in nature.

This feminist historian meticulously documents abrahamic cults' dis-empowerment of egg-producers' creativity and minds, and their demonizing of the pistillate body. Stone shows that the daily usurpation of female energy, and shaming of women and girls, are normative aspects of patriarchal culture that are continuously re-enacted in churches and synagogues, school and universities, workplaces and homes.[34]

♀ Resistance in Christendom

Female literature from the ancient Near East dates to 5,000 BP. Noblewomen in Mesopotamia were educated, literate, and artistically expressive, composing intricate verse a few hundred years after the invention of writing. For instance, during the fifth millennium BP, Enheduanna was well known, well read, well respected, and a talented poet.

Females were resisting abrahamic cults from its inception. The "Song of Deborah" date to 3,200 BP, an early example of Hebrew poetry. Deborah is the only female judge mentioned in the Bible.[35] Women were the last disciples at the cross and the first at Christ's empty tomb. And proclamation of the all-important Easter event was entrusted solely to egg-producers.

Hypatia was the powerful head of the Library of Alexandria around 1,600 BP, and her high status incurred the wrath of ascending christians. A mob of hysterical christians ambushed and flayed her alive. They then proceeded to burn down the greatest reservoir of knowledge in the World, performing what Carl Sagan described as "radical brain surgery."

Females were integral to the work of the church in the first few centuries. The early church considered Junia an apostle, and Mary Magdalene as the "apostle to the apostles."[36] Jesus may even have married Mary Magdalene and had children with her. Despite her importance, the Gospel of Mary is among the 'lost scriptures' not included in the bible.[37]

In Magdalene's text, Peter is offended by the discovery that Jesus selected Mary above the other disciples to interpret his teachings. Peter asks, "Did he then speak secretly with a woman, in preference to us, and not openly? Are we to turn back and all listen to her? Did he prefer her to us?" Peter's open skepticism and hostility toward Mary was mirrored by other christian men at the time, and ever since then.

Yet, women and girls from all walks of life played an invaluable role in christianity's growth to become a Global religion. Peasants, empresses, and independent businesswomen alike contributed what they could to an emotional revolution unlike anything the ancient World had ever seen.[38]

In the first two centuries of christendom, human egg-producers could become full-fledged ministers, and in some areas, there were even female bishops. But soon after the early revolutionary era, female leaders were barred from being fully ordained and women's groups were closely monitored by men.

Roman law required all upper-class males to marry, and all women to procreate. Around 1,750 BP, numerous upper-class christian women defied the law, took a vow of chastity, and lived together in female separatist communities in Rome. Led by Marcella, these monastic women never allowed themselves to rest on couches or cushions of any kind, and at night they slept on thin mats on the floor.[39]

For years, rebel virgins defied Roman family laws and walked the streets spreading the gospel.[40] The women taught themselves Hebrew, analyzed Scripture, and corresponded with other leaders. Women in the cities formed their own network of house churches. The rebel virgins took control of their money and funneled it into the movement, building monasteries, and helping prisoners and the poor.

The rebel virgins' radical existence on the outside of Roman social convention would not last. Starting around 1,760 BP, Roman emperors ordered far-flung attacks on christians, including rebel virgins. Subsequently, thousands of egg-producers who refused to marry were raped or prostituted, especially in the Roman Eastern Empire.[41]

More than 1,000 widows were killed in Antioch, "the cradle of christianity." And over 2,000 rebel virgins were murdered in Ancyra, including St. Christina. There were christian femicides in other Roman cities and towns during this time as well. Pagan ceremonies were punishable by death in christian kingdoms, and Emperor Theodosius decreed that children playing with pagan statues should be executed.

Despite tremendous backlash from rulers and leaders, abundant male violence, and gross acts of femicide, the resistance of early rebel virgins continued underground in the wilderness. One group of female ascetics became known as Desert Mothers, including Marcella of the rebel virgins, Melania the Younger, Paula of Rome, Susan, and others.

Around 1,600 BP, Melania of Rome studied with desert ascetics and eventually went to Jerusalem. Saint Melania the Younger built two single-sex monastic communities on the Mount of Olives, one for men, and one for women. For the next 27 years, Melania lived in the female convent, caring for pilgrims and refugees, and working with the destitute.

Susan's journey to the desert began at an early age. About 1,500 BP, at eight years of age, Susan ran away from home and traveled to a place she had only heard of, a community of christian women who lived somewhere near Gaza. A decade later, Susan became the leader of the Gazan female ascetics. Facing persecution, the group left Gaza and went further into the desert.

One day, having wandered far out into the dunes, praying as she walked, Susan discovered a cave and decided to stay there. For the next three years, her christian sisters would visit Susan once a week to bring her water and a few pieces of dry bread, which was all she would touch.[42] Her existence in the cave became widely known, and people throughout Egypt passed around Susan's teachings.

Eventually, pilgrims built a nearby desert monastery, with separate enclosures for the men and the women. Only then were they able to convince Susan to emerge from her desert cave to lead them. Susan spent her last years in the female monastery, willing to talk to any who visited about the monastic life, but always from behind a wall. By the time of her death, Susan had not looked at the face of a man in 25 years.

Later on, like the Romans did to them, christians themselves persecuted non-christian women. Jeanne Roberts sees a rejection of the crone figure by christians in the Middle Ages as a root cause of the persecution of witches.[43] As many as one million individuals in Europe were executed for the crime of witchcraft.[44] Witches were said to cause impotence in men, stillbirth, infertility, and crop failures.

The majority of the trials and executions took place during the 16th and 17th centuries. The victims were eighty-five percent women, primarily poor, and disproportionately widows.[45] For hundreds of years, all girls and women lived in fear that they could be jailed, abused, and sexually assaulted.[46] Any female could be pornographically tortured in public before her execution, in front of her family.

It became a major European public spectacle to humiliate and subjugate members of the young-bearing sex, or to get women and girls to testify against their accused mothers, and then stand at the front as they were executed. Human egg-producers could be made to wear bridles in public for speaking out of turn to any man, including their husbands, or for simply being poor, or too old to work.

For generations, European men ritually battered females for expressing any social solidarity with each other, or asserting independence. To survive the christian inquisition and subsequent forms of patriarchy, women had to isolate themselves and refuse friendships with other women.

In her book, *Loving to Survive*, Dee Graham argues that men's violence against females has created 'Societal Stockholm Syndrome.'[47] Graham writes, "all women are exposed to conditions conducive to the development of Societal Stockholm Syndrome: threat to survival, inability to escape, isolation, and kindness. Men's violence against women encourages women to bond with "kind" men for protection against other men, setting the stage for men's one-on-one oppression of women and the institutionalization of heterosexuality."[48]

With the constant threat of rape and femicide, women learned to be very good at making men like them. And, women taught their daughters to do the same. But females have always resisted, as the rebel virgins and others show.

Conclusion

This fifth and last chapter of Part IV concludes the inquiry into male violence during the New Stone Age. Part IV showed how men used female surplus to accumulate resources and private property and to domesticate nonhuman animals. Sperm-producers used animals, in turn, to attack and defeat gynocentric cultures and to domesticate human females.

This chapter showed how male-based religious myths and texts were used to subjugate the Goddesses and gynocentric cultures. Consequently, by the Bronze Age, men's conquest of females was broadly accomplished. The rise of abrahamic cults in the Iron Age further solidified cyborg consciousness and led to the continued destruction of gynocentric cultures throughout the Globe. Many christian women who resisted the newly enshrined patriarchal order were imprisoned and killed.

The next section, Part V, considers cyborg rule in the present. It expands the inquiry into the objectification of nonhuman animals and females by exploring men's sexist and speciesist theoretical framing, as well as specific misogynist practices.

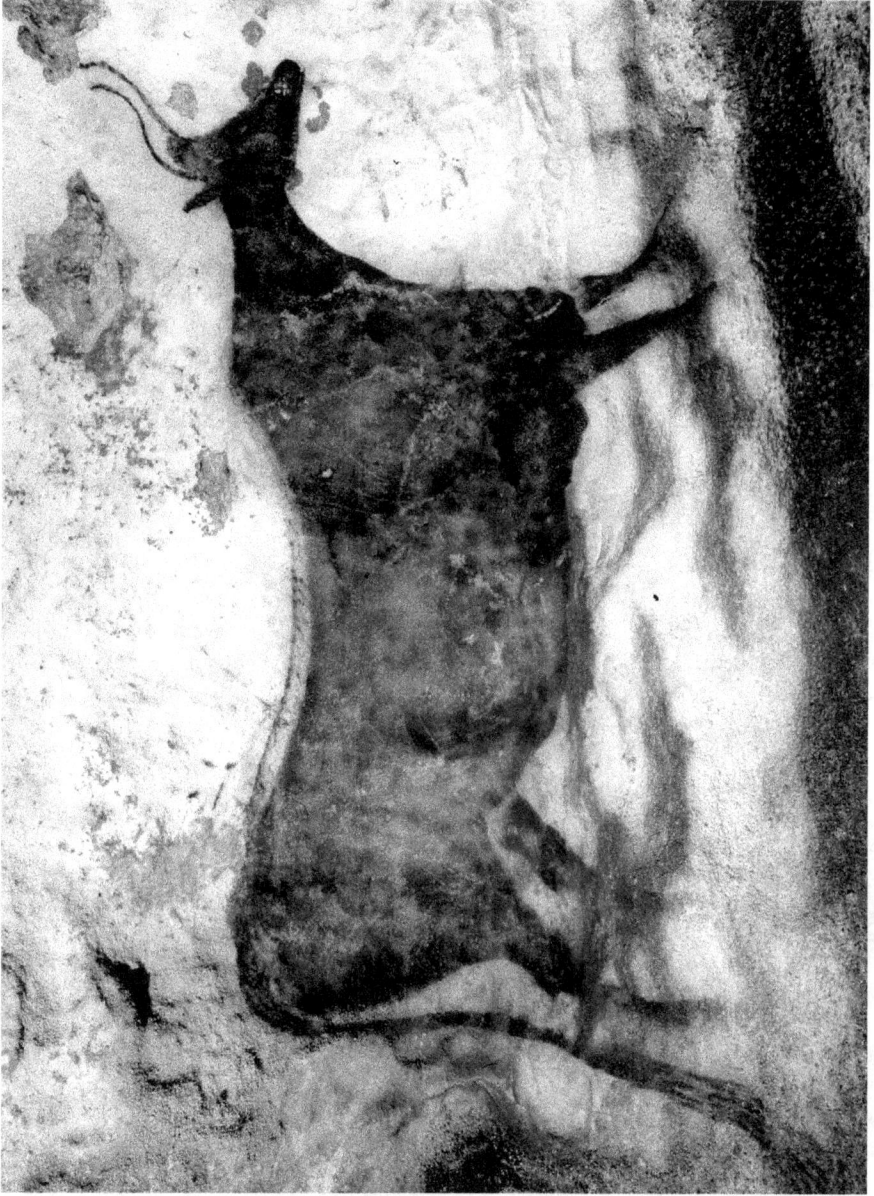

(Figure 23: Lascaux cave painting of ancient Cow c. 20,000 BP)

V: CYBORG TERROR & THEORY (Present)

23: Terrorizing Animals

> If life is to survive on this planet, there must be a decontamination of the Earth. I think this will be accompanied by an evolutionary process that will result in a drastic reduction of the population of males. - Mary Daly

ASIA's Journey 2121.23

It is 8:15 PM, 103°F (39°C) with a humidity of 65 percent in the heart of Chinatown. The noise of the restaurant upstairs filters through the basement, and the smell of vegetables, grains, and sauces fills the air.

It is Cronetime, a time of healing and building solidarity. There are three teams of women out looking for the missing girls, and she needs to focus on them, but Hehewuti is at her wits' end trying to explain to Zaid why he cannot have an equid.

"A Horse?" Zola rattles her beads from the back, steps to the front, and takes the board from Hehewuti. Zaid smiles, "I will call it Lightning."

Zola shakes her head. "Son, a horse is a Goddess. You don't ride a Goddess. Breaking this rule is what got us here."

Zaid shrugs. "But Lightening will get me to safe house quicker."

"It doesn't matter. It is wrong to capture and enslave horses." Zola is adamant and shakes the board. "If we are to survive on this Earth, we must respect other animals. We have to live in harmony with nature again."

"So the animals are Goddess too?" Lehana asks.

Zola smiles. "We do eat animals. Just like we would not eat a Goddess."

"But I wouldn't eat Lightning," Zaid says. "I will love him."

"Then why ride one?" Zola asks. "Do you think these beautiful creatures want to be ridden?"

Zaid says nothing.

Zola continues, "When we use animals, for any reason, we lower the Goddess, and this affects us all."

"That's why the men on horses treat girls like animals," Lehana exclaims.

"I get it." Bo stares at Zaid. "You understand, don't you."

Zaid looks puzzled. "No. I want Lightning."

Hehewuti and Zola exchange glances and Zola whispers, "Maybe Lian is right about boys."

Introduction

The five chapters of Part V on men's current reign of terror explore violence, pornography, unequal work and pay, female erasure, and other aspects of patriarchal rule. The first chapter centers on men's framing of nonhuman animals and its influence on humans. The second examines men's economic oppression of women, and the third discusses their private and public violence against females.

The fourth chapter analyzes men's objectification, pornography, and reduction of females into sexualized objects. And the fifth and last chapter of Part V explore the theoretical framing and erasure of biological females.

This first chapter of Part V revolves around males' colonization of nonhuman animals. Nonhuman domesticates, and the agricultural economies based on them, are associated with a radical restructuring of human societies worldwide. Patriarchal carnism is causing major alterations to biodiversity, and significant changes to Earth's land and atmosphere.

The climate crisis is not merely a result of western men's mechanical bride of the industrial revolution. The ideological roots of the current environmental juncture run far deeper, with the capture and enslavement of food animals at the dawn of male-centered 'civilization.' Modern human males are the most destructive and invasive species on the planet, and this is a logical extension of men's colonization of food animals, which resulted in an accelerated devolution of male consciousness.

This chapter gets started with a quick look at how male philosophers have theorized nonhuman animals as different, followed by a short discussion on the naming of animals. A brief survey of the utilization of tools, language, and feelings by nonhuman animals comes next.

Then, the chapter examines how animal and human oppressions are linked, and who benefits from the notion of animal-as-capital afterward. Subsequently, it explores the connection between violence against animals and deviant social violence. Next, it outlines the industrial exploitation of animals-as-capital, and the chapter concludes with a brief overview of militarism, war, and ecocide.

Theorizing Animality

Human interest in nonhuman animals is ubiquitous, yet outside of animal science, domesticates are ignored by most disciplines. The human-animal interface remains a paradox, and contradictions underlie the philosophical and psychological theories on this relationship. The phenomenon that humans eat some animals, while they keep others as beloved pets, and are fascinated and amazed by still others, remains lamentably unexamined.

Intellectuals like Foucault, Hardt, Negri, and Agamben have outlined in detail capital's comprehensive penetration into our social and biological lives. But social and cultural theorists limit their inquiry to human subjects and disregard the impact of phallic colonization and transcendence over nonhuman animals and nature. The unsustainable, neoliberal model of animals-as-capital, and its ecological consequences, are also neglected in the natural sciences.

The humanities and sciences conceive of animals, if they do at all, as metaphors for men's objectification, and as expressions of sex, race, and class oppression. From example, liberal feminists point out that women are treated as pieces of meat for consumption, and racial scholars look at the comparison of minorities to untamed animals.

In his book, The Animal That Therefore I Am, philosopher Jacques Derrida made some valuable contributions to theorizing about animals.[1] Derrida challenged earlier views on animals, including those of Descartes,[2] Kant,[3] Heidegger,[4] Levinas,[5] and Lacan.[6] Ironically, the ideas of these 'enlightened' men have only served to extend cyborg consciousness, disembodiment, and transcendence. And they have collectively provided justification for the horrendous exploitation of domesticates by phallic-centered capitalism.

Derrida addresses Descartes's separation of humans on one side, and animals and machines on the other. Descartes mirrored the cyborg mindset and regarded animals as machines or automata. He contended that creatures do not think, and are without language, consciousness, and feeling.[7]

The famous French philosopher writes, "my opinion is not so much cruel to animals as indulgent to men - at least to those who are not given to the superstitions of Pythagoras - since it absolves them from the suspicion of crime when they eat or kill animals."[8] Here, Descartes refers dismissively to Pythagoras, the inventor of the word, 'philosopher', around 2,500 BP, and one of the first animal theorists in western recorded history.

Curiously, a meatless diet was referred to as a "Pythagorean diet" for centuries, up until the modern vegetarian movement began in the mid-1800s.[9] A hundred years after Pythagoras, Plato hints of an ideal future without flesh-eating in his Republic, but there is no evidence that Plato made any attempt to be vegetarian himself.

Jacques Derrida likewise deconstructs Kant's development of human subjectivity over and against animals. Kant wrote, "Animals are not self-conscious and are there merely as a means to an end. The end is man." Kant also wrote, "Vivisectionists, who use living animals for their experiments, certainly act cruelly, although their aim is praiseworthy, and they can justify their cruelty, since animals must be regarded as man's instruments."

Derrida's discusses Heidegger's thesis on animals as the "poor in world." Highlighting speech, instead of reason, is a fundamental premise in Heidegger's overall work, and this leads to his conclusion that animals cannot calculate. Regardless, studies show that nonhuman animal mothers have a clear understanding of numbers and uses math on a daily basis to keep track of their offspring, in-group members, predators, resources, and so on.

Like the others, Levinas's notion of ethics is built on the uniqueness of human ethical subjectivity. And although he has a more positive evaluation of animality, specifically a dog named Bobby, Levinas is guided by heavy anthropomorphic prejudices.[10] And he was clearly reluctant to extend to nonhuman animals the same kind of moral consideration he gave to humans.[11]

Lacan also single humans out as unparalleled living beings, but he considers our uniqueness a deficit rather than a privilege. We are different not because we have something which other animals lack, such as a 'rational soul,' but rather because we lack something which other animals have. Nonetheless, Derrida critiques Lacan's framing of the human-animal distinction and Lacan's insistence that animals are unable to "respond" to others, and can only "react" to external stimuli.[12]

Naming the 'Other'

Cyborg consciousness employs language to define men in relation to their power over human females and nonhuman animals who serve as mirrors to magnify the reflection of male egos and accomplishments. Males with unearned privilege are very clever animals who use specific words, language, and 'reason' to justify their daily monumental violence.

From the biblical Adam's power of naming nonhuman animals in Genesis, to Aristotle's definition of man as a 'speaking animal,' human language is utilized as the element of demarcation between man and 'beasts.' To name is to 'know,' and how nature and animals are classified affects they way they are treated as individuals, groups, and as part of ecosystems.

The various use of animals in food, fashion, sport, companionship, research, and assistance have influenced their social construction in arts, humanities, and the sciences. According to Margo DeMello, the most significant categorization of nonhuman animals is them being defined as either 'wild' or domestic.[13]

Classification may be inevitable, but the hierarchical ranking of species is not, for example, between women and men, and companion and food animals. The use of animals to bolster humans' sense of species superiority is noted by psychologist Kenneth Shapiro. He writes, "animals are employed as a categorical foil representing precisely the absence of reason and relative autonomy, hallmarks of individuality."[14] This 'othering' process is part of patriarchal dualism.

Human egg-producers are simultaneously constructed as superior to nonhuman animals and as similar to them. Likewise, girls and women's attachment to pet animals, and detachment from food animals, both serve to support phallic-centered economies. The emotional colonization of female minds assures their complicity with the animal-as-capital model and aids in the myth of phallic supremacy.

The 'Other' is Us

Are humans that unusual among animals? Are differences in tools, language, emotion, and cognition real or imagined? What aspects of behavior should be given more weight than others? And how much relevance should longevity and sustainability have? Under the current definitions, who benefits, who loses, and who decides?

Tools are used by nonhuman animals for the acquisition of food and water, grooming, defense, recreation, and in construction. Animals that use tools include mammals, birds, fish, cephalopods, and insects.[15] The Bottlenose dolphins in Shark Bay, Australia, carries marine sponges in their beaks to stir ocean-bottom sand and uncover prey. These dolphins spend more time with tools than any animal besides humans.[16]

Researchers have shown that many mammals and birds use what might be called "language," by using a variety of signs such as sounds or movements. Humans are able to distinguish real words from fake words based on the phonological order of the word itself, and a 2013 study demonstrate that baboons have this skill, as well.[17] And, chimpanzees and bonobos can be taught to use lexigrams, or symbols, to communicate.[18]

A vast array of creatures display emotions like grief and empathy. Brain-imaging studies show that people form feelings in the primitive parts of the brain, such as the limbic system. H. sapiens share our limbic system with all mammals. Plus, neurotransmitter chemicals like dopamine and endorphins are identical across various species. Therefore, if nonhuman animals have related anatomy, physiology, and biochemistry, they must experience similar feelings as humans.[19]

Even domestic animals, such as chickens and fishes, are viewed as having more complex mental lives than previously thought. In terms of grief, H. sapiens are not the only species which bury their dead. This practice has been observed in chimpanzees, elephants, and dogs. Jane Goodall tells a story of a young chimpanzee, Flint, who stopped eating, became socially withdrawn and eventually died following the death of his mother.

The positive influence of pet animals on human health and well-being is documented in many areas. Companion animals help human animals to enjoy better physical health with decreased blood pressure and reduced stress. There are therapeutic benefits such as preventing illness and ailment recovery. Pets also assist with human psychological health, for example, with reduced depression and increased self-esteem. And pets help with social contacts through reduced loneliness and isolation.[20]

Under gynecologic systems, nonhuman animals were viewed as mysterious and different, yet equals and sacred. By respecting nature, people were able to limit their populations and live sustainably for hundreds of thousands of years. Short-lived human, mostly male, 'progress' does not justify the victimization of domesticates and other creatures under patriarchy. The ongoing conquest and colonization of the Earth's sacred beings foments hyper-masculinity and social hierarchy, and leads to numerous forms of human oppression.

Animals and Hierarchy

Social hierarchy in the Mediterranean, Near East, and Eurasia developed out of the surpluses that female and animal labor enabled. Women and animals are linked in being historically defined by their bodies and reproductive abilities to serve phallic potentiality and desire. This dual exploitation within capitalist economies has increased exponentially profits of the wealthy.[21]

Aggression against nonhuman animals intersects with violence against humans through tactics of objectification, othering, essentializing, and so on. As part of a sex-species hierarchy, females, the impoverished, and people of color are viewed as 'animalized humans,' while white, upper-class males are projected as 'humanized humans.'

Carnism is related to masculine construction and gender dualism. Over the 19th century, as animal carcass became 'democratize' and more available to the working classes, there developed a false notion that flesh consumption led to phallic virility and strength. Therefore, Western male who consumed more animal-based protein were thought to be more superior to Asian and smaller non-Western men, who ate mostly plant-based protein.

Often, animal stereotypes in patriarchal ideology are applied to some people to highlight hierarchies of gender,[22] race[23] and class.[24] People of non-European descent have historically been harmed through dehumanizing animal metaphors and being "treated like animals" through the policies of slavery and eugenics.

One illustration of the intersections of animals, class, and race are the scientific and media conjectures over the non-Western origins of infectious diseases like mad cow disease, AIDS, SARS, and avian flu. These speculations serve to deflect from the industrial practices of cyborg consciousness, and the use of animal-as-capital/machine, as the source for infectious diseases.

Colonized domesticates are fundamental elements of the sex, class, and social hierarchies under patriarchy. Some animals, such as pets, are 'humanized animals,' considered as having individual personalities, human traits, and behaviors. Care for pets serve to illustrate the enlightened side of maldevelopment and deflect the impact on other animals, such as those facing rapid depletion and extinction.

At the very bottom of the sex-species hierarchy, though, are food-animals, or 'animalized animals.' Food animals are seen as unemotional and having no value other than human consumption. There are contradictions in the same species, such as pet and food dogs in Asia, and western carnist often express outrage over dog meat.

The oppression of 'animalized animals' is gendered as well. Cows, pigs, chickens and other animals in CAFOs are almost exclusively female, and are employed precisely because of the value femaleness represents to livestock production. Pigs and poultry are especially exploited due to their high reproductive rate and favorable feed efficiency.

Elite ♂ Progress

The animal-as-capital model has resulted in environmental over-reach and civilization collapse numerous times since the sixth domestication began. This animal-intensive framework serves to benefit mainly elite males, but remains the goal of vast numbers of non-elite men. The endless phallic cycles of over-exploitation of colonized, nonhuman animals and ecosystems are maintained by religious, economic, social, political, and academic systems, and by the majority of boys and men who are indoctrinated into the cyborg enslavement mindset.

By comparing animal use for food and resources in different societies over time, David Nibert in *Animal Oppression & Human Violence: Domesecration, Capitalism, & Global Conflict*, argues that the colonization of nonhuman animals, which he renames 'domesecration,' resulted in a perversion of human ethics. Nibert documents how domesecration facilitated the emergence of large-scale acts of violence, caused patterns of destruction, and created growth-curbing epidemics of infectious disease.[25]

The author centers his study on nomadic pastoralism and the development of commercial ranching, a practice that has been primarily controlled by elite groups and expanded with the rise of capitalism. Beginning with the pastoral societies of the Eurasian steppe and continuing through to the exportation of Western, meat-centered eating habits throughout today's world, Nibert connects the domesecration of animals to violence, invasion, extermination, displacement, enslavement, repression, pandemic chronic disease, and hunger.

In Nibert's view, local territorial conquest and social subjugation were the results of the need to appropriate land and water to maintain vast numbers of animals. He argues that the gross amassing of military power has its roots in the economic benefits from the exploitation, exchange, and sale of animals. Moreover, deadly zoonotic diseases have accompanied violence throughout pastoralism, laying waste to whole cities, societies, and civilizations.

Nibert situates the domesecration of animals as a precondition for the oppression of human populations, particularly Indigenous peoples. And he links domesecration to some of the most critical issues facing the world today, including the depletion of fresh water, topsoil, and oil reserves; global warming, and world hunger. Nibert suggests reforms that challenge the legitimacy of both domesecration and capitalism.

Similarly, in his book, *The Ecological Hoofprint: The Global Burden of Industrial Livestock*, Tony Weis shows why the growth and industrialization of livestock production is a central part of the accelerating biophysical contradictions of industrial capitalist agriculture. Weis places meat at the center of global problems like climate change, poverty, workers' rights, and speciesism.[26]

In the book, *Meat Climate Change*, there are similar arguments as Nibert and Weis about the intensification and consolidation of animal carcass industries. It shows how corporate supply chains and trade policy are responsible for the westernization of global diets, and the rise in animal consumption among the middle-class. This study also explores how livestock production represents a form of neocolonialism in the global South.[27]

Nibert, Weis, and Seenarine demonstrate the animal-as-capital approach has long surpassed the Earth's limit of finite land and water resources. The cyborg utilitarian, animal-as-capital paradigm is once again unraveling from its inherent contradictions, causing social oppression, harmful greenhouse gas pollution, and diseases in its wake.

♂ Deviant Violence

DeMello classifies hostility against animals under three labels, institutional, culture-specific, and deviant. In institutional violence, for instance, in the flesh and dairy industries, belligerence is tolerated and commissioned in part because of its invisibility and distance. Public displays of institutional aggression against animals are less tolerated.

Culturally-specific killings by 'ethnic' groups, for example, dog slaughter and animal sacrifice, are frequently objectionable to dominant western societal norms. To be humane translates into making hostility toward nonhuman animals invisible, and how and where domesticates are killed are civilizational markers.

Deviant violence on animals is perceived as socially unacceptable and "unnecessary." Why is any level of aggression towards colonized domesticates deemed necessary? Normalized violence in one area influences behavior toward animals and humans in other spaces. And from the creature's perspective, any form of human utilization is deviant.

There is often a link between deviant violence on nonhumans and aggressive acts toward humans, for example, in men's sexual abuse and violence against women, children, and their pets. Animal cruelty is a reliable predictor of criminality, including mass murder and other heinous crimes.

Many male serial killers, such as Bundy, Gacy, Dahmer and others, have abused nonhuman animals as children. For example, Dahmer tortured frogs, cats, and dogs, decapitated them, and mounted their heads on sticks. His own puppy suffered this fate. Anders Breivik, who killed 77 people in Norway in 2011, kept pet rats and tortured them.[28]

Psychiatrists and criminologists suggest that childhood compassion instruction can deter psychopathic behavior in later years. It is imperative that educational goals include teaching children to have respect for other human beings and nonhuman animals. Yet, at the same time, a selective attitude toward institutional, culture-specific, and deviant violence will undermine concerns over animal cruelty and its link to phallic violence and psychopathy.

Cyborg violence on nonhuman animals is completely normalized, from government-sponsored 'pest' control of predators to support ranchers, to overcrowding on factory farms, and torture in laboratories. The environmental protection agencies in charge of the preservation of nature and biodiversity are used instead to eradicate rare species and enforce the will of pastorals.

The masculinist notion of nonhuman animals as 'outsider' is used to gain females' complicity in the colonization of food animals' bodies, and their objectification as protein. Furthermore, the definition of nature and nonhuman animals as 'wild' or 'domestic other' cleverly masks the commonality of cyborg's objectification and oppression of human and animal females.

In a short span, westerners' relationship to unrestrained animals went from them being that of respected co-spirits in nature, to one of romanticized victims, and to being bureaucratically eradicated. A few centuries have brought numerous species in the US to near extinction, including buffalo, pigeon, lion, and eagle. This is also deviant violence.

Animals-as-Capital

In her book, Animal Capital, Nicole Shukin examined aspects of the history of domesticate use in an attempt to develop a theory of animal-as-capital. For example, Shukin points out that automotive factories and other sites of mass production adopted the spatial model of meat production plants and disassembly lines.[29]

The patriarchal colonization of animal bodies as pets, food, and fiber animals is an evolving process of engineering, body mutilation, and dependency. Some nonhuman animals may have in the beginning benefited from controlled and intensive breeding by phallic humans, but, modern commodified, industrialized domesticates do not experience the same benefits as their predecessors.[30]

Across the Earth, the capitalization of nonhuman animal bodies is steadily expanding. On the increase are flesh and dairy consumption; the usage of animal skin as leather, fur, wool, and other products; pet ownership; and other animal-based industries.[31] Also on the rise are displays of animals in zoos, marine mammal parks, animal sports, racetracks, fighting rings, bull racing, and so on. These industries market predominantly to cyborgs' desire to gaze, profit, and dominate.[32]

Annually, in the food animal industry, over 70 billion land animals are slaughtered, and countless billions more sea creatures are killed for humans' limitless appetite for flesh. Alarmingly, the demand for animal-based products is set to increase 70 percent by 2050.[33] The production of farmed animals is already the second leading cause of global warming, and expansion will lead to further catastrophic warming.

There is profound unwillingness among individuals and societies to release themselves from their dependency on colonized nonhuman animals for food, clothing, labor, pleasure, and experiment. As 'absent referents' in cyborg cultures, violence against food animals is hidden via terms such as 'steak,' 'bacon,' and 'breasts,'[34] while common terms such as 'paleo' normalize flesh consumption.

There are many aspects of human dependency on nonhuman animals that are exploited by marketers in animal-based industries. Marketers often appeal to taste, attachment, greed, selfishness, culture, tradition, the outdoor lifestyle, phallic identity, the desire to dominate others, and so on.[35] Race, class, and sex are inter-related to animal consumption, and populations in European majority countries, such as Europe, Canada, the US, and Australia, lead the way in annual intake.

Over 100 million animals are burned, crippled, poisoned, and abused in US labs every year. 92 percent of experimental drugs that are safe and effective in animals fail in human clinical trials because they are too dangerous or don't work. Millions more animals are used in the beauty industry.

Typically, animal tests for cosmetics include skin and eye irritation tests where chemicals are rubbed onto the shaved skin or dripped into the eyes of rabbits. And there are repeated oral, force-feeding studies lasting weeks or months to look for signs of general illness or specific health hazards, such as cancer or birth defects.

And there is the widely condemned "lethal dose" tests, in which animals are forced to swallow massive amounts of a test chemical to determine the dose that causes death. These tests can cause considerable pain and distress including blindness, swollen eyes, sore bleeding skin, internal bleeding and organ damage, birth defects, convulsions and death. Pain relief is not provided and at the end of a test the animals are killed, normally by asphyxiation, neck-breaking or decapitation.

Mothers raise children to love animals, to care for and protect them. From talking cows and chickens in picture-books, to TV shows and film, animals take center stage, and kids are encouraged to empathize with them. But when girls and boys are simultaneously fed flesh and other products taken from animals, this sends a very confusing message.

Health experts agree that plant-based diets can be suitable for anyone, of any age. Yet, mothers condition their offspring to see flesh as food, and to forget that it was once part of a living animal. Most parents would not dream of telling their kids how animals are killed, presumably because the truth is considered inappropriate to explain to young children. But if the truth is too disturbing, surely we should stop funding it, rather than help to keep it hidden.

♂ War and Ecocide

Like boys fighting for toys in a sandbox, masculine states are engaged in an unending arms race that is destroying numerous ecosystems and cooking the Earth. Wars and military exercises leads to dramatic habitat alteration, environmental pollution, and disruption. These outcomes contribute to population declines and biodiversity losses arising from both acute and chronic effects in both terrestrial and aquatic systems.[36]

US actions in Vietnam gave rise to the concept of 'ecocide,' the deliberate destruction of the environment as a military strategy. And, it seems that Americans, unconcerned about climate change, are committed to ecocide on a Global scale.[37] Militarism is the most oil-exhaustive activity on the planet, and their carbon output is growing with faster, bigger, more fuel-guzzling planes, tanks, and naval vessels employed in intensive air and ground wars. Disadvantaged people, especially communities of color, are the most severely impacted by continuing military spending and pollution.

According to its own study, in 2013 the Pentagon consumed fuel equivalent to 90,000,000 barrels of crude oil. This amounts to 80 percent of the total fuel usage by the federal government. If burned as jet fuel it produces about 38,700,000 metric tons of CO2. And the Pentagon's figures do not include carbon produced by the thousands of bombs dropped in 2013, or the fires that burned after the jets and drones departed.[38]

Many Americans think that war as ancient, innate, and inevitable. President Barack Obama seemed to be expressing this notion in 2009 when he accepted the Nobel Peace Prize, just nine days after he announced a major escalation of the US war in Afghanistan. "War, in one form or another, appeared with the first man," Obama said. Obama added, "We must begin by acknowledging the hard truth: we will not eradicate violent conflict in our lifetimes." Obama is certainly not the first presidential apologist for war. President Teddy Roosevelt once said, for example, "All the great masterful races have been fighting races. No triumph of peace is quite so great as the supreme triumph of war."

The USA seem to be a society that has embraced war as a way of life. The most hyper-masculine culture are Americans, and they are determined to use the military to prove this. For decades, the US has maintained its position as the world's strongest military. World military spending totaled more than $1.6 trillion in 2015, and the US accounted for 37 percent of the total.[39]

By every measure, the Pentagon is the largest institutional user of petroleum products and energy. The US military machine is the world's biggest institutional consumer of petroleum products and the world's worst polluter of greenhouse gas emissions.[40] Yet, the US Congress passed an explicit provision guaranteeing the US military exemption from any energy reduction or even measurement.[41]

At the outset of the Iraq war in March 2003, the Army estimated it would need more than 40 million gallons of gasoline for three weeks of combat, exceeding the total quantity used by all Allied forces in the four years of World War 1. Among the Army's vehicles were 2,000 M-1 Abrams tanks burning 250 gallons of fuel per hour.[42]

Newspapers and television stations run favorable stories on air shows like the Navy's Blue Angels without noting that the jets from a typical show generate about 300,000 pounds of CO2 into the air.[43] The military is not just a prolific user of oil, it is one of the central pillars of the global fossil-fuel economy. Whether it is in the Middle East, the Gulf, or the Pacific, modern-day military deployment is about controlling oil-rich regions and defending the key shipping supply routes that sustain our consumer economy.

The US officer corps is committed to 'full spectrum dominance,' so studies on climate change by the military planners are not aimed at mitigation. Instead, they are based on evaluating how to take advantage of the future crisis to more firmly entrench US corporate power and protect the irrational capitalist system that has created this crisis.

It is important to note that the original Mother's Day, now celebrated by men with a bunch of flowers to wives and mothers, was a women's day for peace. In 1870, Julia Ward Howe, a feminist and abolitionist, called for a national Mother's Day for Peace every June 2. It was a time for women of all nations to come together to take action to prevent future wars. The holiday was celebrated in some cities unofficially for a while.[44]

Conclusion

Diet intersects with the environment, climate, and social concerns. Sex, race, class, language, culture, and location are critical issues that should occupy the center of social interest, planning, and discussions on the continuing exploitation of animals. Also, inter-sectional analysis must include nature and animals as a section. Otherwise, this useful theoretical approach runs the risk of overlooking significant aspects of reality and survival.

Humans are facing a tremendous crisis. This is a situation which politicians cannot figure out because they are programmed to think in a particular way. Scientists are equally unable to grasp or solve our precarious position, and neither can the technology sector and financial world.

The turning point, the perceptive decision, is in our consciousness and relationship to nature and animals. The challenge is to decolonize our emotions and negate the domesticating mindset which has brought us to this point. Discerning how domesticates are theorized, defined, and exploited is critical to unpacking cyborgs' colonization of animal bodies, and to seeing how this influences environmental and social relations. These issues are further examined in the last chapter.

The next chapter returns to the feminist theme and explores men's current economic violence against human females. Similar to the critical examination of 'progress' regarding animals in this chapter, it deconstructs the myth of empowered girls and women in the phallic-dominated order.

(Figure 24: Neolithic Elam relief of a woman holding snakes)

24: 'Civilizing' Females

No kind of tokenism in a transcendence-sapping system will free our Selves from the spell of patriarchal myth. As long as that myth (system of myths) prevails, it is conceivable that there be a society comprised even of 50 percent female tokens: women with anatomically female bodies but totally male-identified, male-possessed brains/spirits. The myth/spell itself of phallocratism must be broken. - Mary Daly

ASIA's Journey 2121.24

It is 8:15 PM and 102°F (38°C) on the humid docks on the edge of the city. The half-moon dancing on the calm ocean reminds ASIA's search teams of their strong connection with the elders, who await them in Chinatown. They must not disappoint the crones.

The three teams are in search of Nadie, Cha'Kwaina, Iniko, and Sabra. There were several possibilities, and the teams split up earlier with gold coins and wine to trade with the pedo-hunters. While Xóchitl and Lian visited brothels, Zemora and Jean went to massage parlors, and Nakeisha and Ramla searched bars and restaurants across the city.

There was no sign of the children anywhere, and the women still have their coins and wine. The three teams are gathered at the docks to attend an auction of girls and fresh meat on the festive pier. They decide that Nakeisha and Ramla will go inside with all seven of their gold coins, and try to buy the girls back if they are there. The other four women wait outside in the shadows, hiding with the wine containers.

Nakeisha and Ramla walk through the vast warehouse perched on the water. There are barrels of fish and rows of animal carcass on display. The crowd of males attending the auction observes the two women covetously. The pair are the only free females in the room and the traders are confused.

One man stops Ramla and demands, "What are you doing here?" Nakeisha smiles. "We are Chinatown madams looking for girls." She points to the exit. "Our gang is waiting outside." The butcher grunts and walks away.

Ramla scans piles of frightened children on stage. Several of the girls are crying out loudly and are beaten as punishment. Ramla tugs on Nakeisha's arms. "The four girls are here!" She nods her head to the left.

ASIA's daughters, Nadie, Cha'Kwaina, Iniko, and Sabra, are huddled in the back, sobbing quietly. They appear bruised and disheveled.

Nakeisha and Ramla avoid staring at the ASIA's daughters. They do not want the men to know they have any involvement with the four children. The bidding starts and one by one, the girls are forced to parade across a runway as men bid for them. The oldest girls are displayed first as they are the least expensive.

Scores of teens around 15 years of age are sold for roughly two gold coins each. Ramla quickly wins a bid for 15-year old Nadie at two coins, and Nakeisha buys 12-year old Cha'Kwaina after five minutes of haggling, for three coins.

The women have only two gold coins remaining, and the wine outside was worth maybe one coin. The price of the younger girls start higher, and there were dozens of pre-teens up for auction.

Nakeisha and Ramla stare in agony as 11-year old Iniko is sold to Don Omar, a middle-aged money-lender for four gold coins. Soon after, 7-year old Sabra is sold to Jerry the Weasel, a brothel owner for four and a half coins. The pair lost their bids for ASIA's two daughters and watched helplessly as Iniko and Sabra are hauled away in tears by their new male owners.

The women are stoic when Nadie and Cha'Kwaina are handed over to them. They place the two children in chains, and drag them out of the warehouse to join the other four females of ASIA outside.

The entire group is assessed of the situation and they decided to split into three teams. Xóchitl and Lian follows Jerry, the brothel owner of Sabra, and Nakeisha takes Nadie and Cha'Kwaina back to Chinatown. The three other women tags behind Don Omar, the money lender who has Iniko. The two search teams each has one gold coin and six wine containers.

Introduction

Cyborg society is characterized by narcissism, arrogance, insensitivity, de-sensualization, alienation, and escalating violence. Men's 10,000 years reduction of females, nonhuman animals, and nature is the chief cause of humans' chaotic, unbalanced, and unsustainable existence. We must face the facts to move forward.

The steadfast failure to face the truth, James Baldwin warned, perpetuates a kind of collective psychosis. Baldwin writes, "People pay for what they do, and, still more for what they allowed themselves to become." For instance, unwilling to face the truth about colonization and enslavement, white Americans limit and destroy their capacity for self-reflection and self-criticism. This collective psychosis allows white Americans to invent a world of dangerous, self-serving fantasy instead.[1]

Baldwin continues, "And they pay for it very simply by the lives they lead. The crucial thing, here, is that the sum of these individual abdications menaces life all over the world. For, in the generality, as social and moral and political and sexual entities, white Americans are probably the sickest and certainly the most dangerous people, of any color, to be found in the world today."

This second chapter of Part V on cyborgs' current manifestation is the first of four that canvas men's overwhelming violence against women and girls. Cyborgs' economic exploitation of human egg-producers is immense and relentless and this chapter briefly addresses some of its deleterious effects.

This section challenges popular assumptions of human 'progress' and female empowerment by exploring unpaid and underpaid forms of female labor in sexists work spaces and economies. It also covers women's lack of access to and control over female 'empowerment.'

The chapter commences with a brief overview of phallic structural oppression of the young-bearing sex, followed by a short discussion of so-called female empowerment in the USA. Men's economic oppression of women is examined next, then the unequal burden of time placed on human egg-producers is considered afterward.

The chapter turns to look at women in development planning, starting with a discussion of woman-the-farmer. Inter-governmental efforts aimed at women's equality is appraised subsequently, followed a brief discussion of the tremendous non-profit industry dedicated to female empowerment. The chapter ends with a look at the Roman Goddess for revolt, Adrestia.

♂ Economics

While there is not a universal patriarchal framework that can be applied cross-culturally, many aspects of phallic domination are related. From the Neolithic onward, gross inequality was implicit in all economic systems, from feudal lords and serfs, and slavery's masters and servants, to a few dozen capitalists controlling more wealth than half of the World's population.

The emergence of the industrial division of labor exacerbated existing gender differences by setting up women and men with competing employments, social trajectories, and value orientation. Likewise, the ascent of the technology and financial sectors have further entrenched phallic domination of the economy.

Neoliberal supporters argue that only a 'free' market can create healthy competition and therefore more business and reasonable prices. This simplistic ideology has been proven false countless times yet it is represented as 'fact.' Machismo economics is grounded in the protestant work ethic of individual hard work, and in darwinian views of competition.

In real world situations, 'free-market fundamentalism' is susceptible to price fixing monopolies and requires government intervention to force competition and reasonable prices, for example, antitrust law. Unbridled competition trivializes the concern for disadvantaged individuals and the public interest, and makes money-driven, poll-obsessed elected officials deferential to corporate goals of profit, often at the cost of the common good.

The meritocracy claim by the market economy is also myth. The playing field is stacked and unequal, especially in terms of sex, class, race, nationality, religion, culture, and so on. Poor women of color, for instance, are subjected to multiple forms of oppressions, and it is much harder for them to obtain 'merit.'

The system is unbalanced because whenever workers organize for higher wages, capitalists respond by replacing them with machines and out-sourcing their jobs. From textile mills and automated assembly lines, to robots and vending machines, workers cannot win by losing.

Despite their hard work, millions of black and brown women are trapped at the bottom of the hierarchical pyramid in the US. Inter-generational poverty among the Indigenous and minorities is linked to systemic sex, class, and racial bias, not merely to a lack of hard work.

What is more, neoliberal countries are fast moving from a market economy to a market society where literally everything is for sale, including aspects of social and civic life such as education, access to justice and political influence. Justice in this unequal system is available only to individual rights holders who earn 'wages' of respect through wealth, fame, and power.

♂ Sex-Based Oppression

Along with the first hierarchical, phallic-centered 'civilizations,' there developed a phenomenon of sexual caste, a stratified system that females are born into which is near impossible to escape. The sex caste system is essentially the same in countries across the globe, from Saudi Arabia to Iceland, and remarkably persistent. As part of systematic discrimination, human egg-producers have unequal access to goods, services, and prestige, and to physical and mental well-being.

Girls and women are socially discriminated and disadvantaged in almost every social sphere, from religion, politics, economics, and media to science, technology, sports, and many other areas. On top of this, members of the young-bearing sex are subjected to harassment, objectification, and abusive language in the media and public spaces on a daily basis.[2]

Females are mistreated from the cradle to the grave by cyborgs whose insecurity and hatred of women and girls is unrelenting. The cyborg misogynist mindset is manifested in female infanticide at birth, genital mutilation as teens, femicide as young and older women, and neglect and abandonment in old age.

In addition to unequal pay, the market society is having a disastrous effect on the self-esteem of girls and women who are reduced to commodities, sexual objects, and 'empowered' consumers. Every day, tens of thousands of females are bought and sold as commodities for phallic consumption and domination in cyborgs' pornography, prostitution, and trafficking industries.

Despite significant gains for females, men's hostility toward women and girls remains obstinately high in countries that are developed and underdeveloped, whether at war or peace. Cyborgs' motivation to prove and reprove their masculinity through violence against members of the young-bearing sex have reached epidemic proportions and is present in almost all communities.[3]

Some women have reasonably high levels of physical security in a handful of EU countries, but there is no country where women are really physically secure. Men's violence against human females is rampant, from verbal insult, sexual harassment, and spatial abuse, to physical aggression, including rape and murder. In the UK alone, in 2014, there were 64,000 sexual offenses and 1.4 million domestic violence assaults against women.[4]

Hostility is essential to the maintenance of cyborg consciousness and the patriarchal state, and machismo behavior is not only tolerated but widely concealed. For instance, a study conducted in the 28 countries of the European Union found that only 14 percent of women reported their most serious episode of domestic violence to the police.[5]

Old domesticating attitudes from the Neolithic and Bronze Age regarding females stubbornly remain in the present. What's more, sexism and feminism are considered quaint and unnecessary concepts in a 'post-sexist' and 'post-feminist' world of 'new femininities' and supposedly empowered women.

When taken seriously at all, sexism and feminism are deployed in a neo-colonialist competitive framework, projected onto 'others' whose females are in need of 'rescuing' from patriarchy. The often animalized 'others' in these evil, 'male-dominated' societies are portrayed as having harmful cultural practices, such as veiling among Muslim women.[6]

Post-feminist theory is part of the patriarchal academy's backlash against the women's liberation movement and the limited gains some egg-producers have achieved. In this misogynist framing, all of women's unhappiness can be attributed to the struggle for equality. In the positive-thinking mantra, no amount of maltreatment by men can be assigned blame.

The notion of post-feminism is employed to promote contradictory outcomes for women rights, such as 'all the battles have been won,' or conversely, that 'you can't have it all - something has to give.' Also, that the 'political correctness' inherent in the acknowledgment of female interests, has itself become a new form of tyranny.[7]

'Empowered' ♀ in USA?

The western media and academy usually claim that American women are the luckiest and most privileged in the history of the World. Female consumers in the USA are touted as having the most options, and the mere availability of goods, not ability to purchase them, is equated with autonomy and power. In this world of 'choice feminism,' any selection a girl or woman makes is construed as empowering, including actions that reinforce sexism.[8]

According to the empowerment feminism narrative, under the more rigidly patriarchal past, women's choices were made for them. So simply by choosing anything at all, egg-producers are resisting the patriarchy and acting 'feminist.' This framing prioritizes the interests of educated, white, middle-class women, and consequently, American feminists have focused on reforming the system rather than rebuilding it from the ground up.[9] Corporations, media, and commodity feminism have also co-opted the women's movement to profit from years of women's activism and mobilization.

One way to gauge the independence of members of the young-bearing sex in the USA is to examine their freedom to speak and write about their experiences under patriarchy. The voices of women, especially women of color, that are ignored and silenced provides a clue to their status in American patriarchal society.

First, feminist voices are stigmatized and marginalized in both media and academia. Second, feminist bookstores and publishing houses have disappeared in recent decades. And third, books written by women about women are frequently banned.

In the early 20th century, Margaret Sanger's The Woman Rebel (1914) was banned, and she was arrested for disseminating information on contraceptive methods to women. Radclyffe Hall's The Well of Loneliness (1928), was prohibited for exploring lesbian identity. Simone de Beauvoir's extraordinary work, The Second Sex (1949) was outlawed by the Catholic church and still appears on the Vatican's list of banned books.

Our Bodies Our Selves by the Boston Women's Health Book Collective (1971) was prohibited from libraries across North America. This explicit, radical feminist text centers on women's bodies and provides information on birth control, abortion, menopause, and lesbianism. Margaret Atwood's The Handmaid's Tale (1985) is a feminist dystopia often deemed as too "explicit" by various schools across the US.

Maya Angelou, I Know Why the Caged Bird Sings (1969) explores Angelou's survival of rape, teen pregnancy, and prostitution while growing up in racist America. Maya Angelou has been called "one of the most banned authors in US history." Alice Walker's The Color Purple (1982) is on the list of books most frequently challenged by US school boards and libraries. It explores sisterhood, phallic violence, and racism.[10]

Alarmingly, the life expectancy for American 'white' women is decreasing. For white women who did not graduate from high school, life expectancy dropped by five years - from 78 years in 1990, to 73 in 2008. This is an unprecedented drop for a wealthy country in the age of modern medicine.[11] The causes for this significant decline range from opiate abuse to lower economic status, and perhaps accelerating hypermasculinity of 'white' males may be an underlying factor.

American women have struggled for hundreds of years to achieve the kind of equality that Indigenous women enjoyed in matrilocal and matrilineal communities for millennia. For Indigenous females, European conquest and becoming 'civilized' meant an extreme alteration of sex roles and reduction in status. For example, the US government and missionaries made a concerted effort to transform Indigenous attitudes towards female sexuality and the female body.[12]

In the US, both state and religion sought to inculcate Euro-American values of 'true womanhood' and confine Indigenous women to the domestic sphere. The domestication of Native females was achieved by the end of the 18th century, especially among wealthier individuals of mixed ancestry. With the passage of a reformulated Cherokee Constitution in 1827, women were politically disenfranchised, and Cherokee egg-producers could no longer vote or hold public office.[13]

But Cherokee women and other ovary beings are resisting, and education is a vital aspect of female agency. For thousands of years, girls and women all over the World have been prevented from writing books and even from learning to read. Plus, the few women who were able to read books, for the most part, read books written by men. This is slowly changing.[14]

♀ Employment Inequality

Decades of studies by Marxists-feminists have focused on the formation of modern capitalism and the oppression of women. Notably, Silvia Federici analyzed the reduction of female healers, leaders, and visionaries in Europe in the Middle Ages. She found that Christian accusations and burning of witches were linked to the development of private property and a market economy.[15] Federici also examines how female reduction continues into the present with the globalization process that is occurring in Africa, South America, Asia and elsewhere.[16]

Patriarchal laws, practices, and culture all have a detrimental effect on women's employment and economic status. There is inequality in land and property rights worldwide, but it is the highest in Africa, the Middle East, and Asia.[17] Also, there is discrepant government behavior regarding son preference, inequality in property rights, child marriage, trafficking, and required dress codes.

Globally, women are paid less than unworthy sperm-producers. Women in most countries earn on average only 60 to 75 percent of men's wages. And, members of the young-bearing sex continue to participate in labor markets on an unequal basis. In 2013, the male employment-to-population ratio stood at 72 percent, while the ratio for females was 47 percent.[18]

Egg-producers are paid far less than undeserving males, and race is as much a factor as sex. Ethnicity and sex interact to create exceptional pay gaps, especially for minority women in the US. Is it unfortunate that white egg-producers make only 78 cents for every dollar a white man makes, but black females make a mere 64 cents, and Latinas make even less, a paltry 54 cents.[19] The pay scale reflects America's sex, race, and class hierarchy and each disadvantaged female group is vulnerable to falling even lower relative to white men.

Furthermore, in the under-developed World, husbands often object to their wives working and prevent them from accepting jobs.[20] Women could increase their income Globally by up to 76 percent if the employment participation gap and the wage gap between women and men were closed, a value of US $17 trillion.[21]

The mantra of technology as savior in a gender-fluid, selfie-happy future is misleading for several reasons. Despite programs for inclusion, the 4 to 1 male to female sex-ratio is becoming worse in the computer industry.[22] On top of that, members of the young-bearing sex leave frustrated after years of working in hostile and unwelcoming sexist environments.

Ellen Pao's failed gender-discrimination lawsuit against a venture capital firm offers a clue into cyborgs' hi-tech culture. Pao reported unwanted sexual advances, all-male bonding trips, pornography, and retaliation for resisting the status quo. Facebook's CEO, Sheryl Sandberg, expressed support and suggested that a lot of women shared Pao's experiences.[23]

Women are more likely than men to work in casual employment and the 'black-market.' In South Asia, over 80 percent of women in non-agricultural jobs are in informal employment. In sub-Saharan Africa, female participation in the informal sector is 74 percent, and in Latin America and the Caribbean, it is 54 percent. In rural areas, many women derive their livelihoods from small-scale farming, almost always informal and often underpaid.[24]

Women farmers not only suffer from less control over land than do men with undeserved privilege, but they also have to endure sex-bias with limited access to agricultural inputs, seeds, credits, and extension services.[25] Less than 20 percent of landholders are women, yet they comprise the majority of agricultural laborers Worldwide.[26]

Wasting ♀ Time

Sex-based inequalities in time utilization are vast and persistent in all countries. When paid and unpaid work are combined, girls and women in developing countries work more than unfairly advantaged boys and men. Consequently, females have less time for education, leisure, political participation, and self-care. Cumbersome and unequal care responsibilities are major barriers to sex equality, and to women's equal enjoyment of human rights. In many cases, the unequal burden of childcare condemns women and children to poverty.[27]

Girls and women devote one to three hours more a day to housework than sperm-producers with unearned prerogative. In addition, females spend two to 10 times the amount of time a day to care for children, elderly, and the sick. And, they spend one to four hours less a day on market activities.[28]

Women are 85 to 90 percent responsible for household food preparation in a wide range of countries.[29] Neoliberal cyborg capitalism is profitable only due to their exploitation of unpaid female labor in household production and reproduction of the worker force. Unpaid care work would constitute between 10 and 50 percent of GDP if it were assigned a monetary value.[30]

Girls and women living in developing nations tend to be natural resource managers as the gatherers of food, water, and firewood. From a young age, girls traditionally assist their mothers with this work. The household production demands on female time are even more in countries with limited natural resources.

In 25 sub-Saharan countries, for instance, egg-producers spend 16 million hours per day collecting water. In comparison, males with unmerited privilege spend about 35 percent of this amount, or 6 million hours. Women and girls also spend millions more hours collecting firewood and dung for cooking.[31]

Women account for 60 percent of the world's illiterate, and barely half are 'literate' in the least-developed countries. The sex disparity widens at higher educational levels. As resources become scarcer with the decline in resources and ecosystem health, girls are attending fewer hours of school to dedicate more time to finding water and firewood. And, their education fees may no longer be available as crop cycles become less predictable.

When females are educated, their entire community benefits. For example, one study using data from 219 countries from 1970 to 2009 found that, for every one additional year of education for females of reproductive age, child mortality decreased by 9.5 percent.[32]

More women and children die than men from natural hazards, and the worse the disaster, the bigger the sex disparity.[33] And after a disaster, women and girls become vulnerable to different forms of trafficking and exploitation, or a 'double disaster,' where indirect or secondary impacts make life worse for females.[34]

Women makeup 70 percent of those living below the poverty line, and are more vulnerable to climate change, environmental degradation, and natural disasters. As primary natural resource managers, rural women are especially well-equipped to lead environmental mitigation and adaptation efforts. Due to patriarchal gender roles that devalue unpaid work like childcare and water retrieval, women's specialized knowledge in smart and effective climate change adaptation is typically not respected or considered in decision-making processes.

Woman-the-Farmer

Up to 2.5 billion people hold and use the world's community lands, yet the tenure rights of women, who comprise more than half the population of the world's Indigenous Peoples and local communities, are seldom acknowledged or protected by national laws. Women's ability to access forests and to take part in decision-making regarding resource utilization is crucial to conservation and climate change mitigation efforts.[35]

In Africa, the work of small-scale farming is mainly done by females. This was the pattern during prehistory, but over time, farming become a phallic preserve with men owning the farmland and tools. Where farming is predominately carried out with the use of plows and animal labor, males dominate. And when a herd of enslaved animals is sizable, men take care of them. If just a few animals are kept for the household, then females managed them.

In the first artistic depictions of plowing and milking, males are pictured doing these tasks. Females do these chores when it done at a household scale, but men do them when the crops and products are for sale. As more land came under cultivation with the usage of a plow, farming became more labor intensive and broader in scope. Women, therefore, would have needed to have more children to fill the increase work demand.

As young-bearers spent more time pregnant and caring for their children, they had less time for farming activities, and so by default sperm-producers took over many of their tasks. Women no longer contributed as much to the economic structure of the household, and consequently, their rights and status were lessened.

By the first written records in the Neolithic, around 5,000 BP, phallic dominance in agriculture was accomplished, about five thousands years after intensive farming began. In tandem with these changes in farming practices was the transition to patriarchal rule.[36]

Women still comprise 43 percent of the agricultural labor force in developing countries. Female farmers form 20 percent in Latin America, to over 50 percent in parts of Asia and Africa. Despite the regional and sub-regional variation, females make an essential contribution to agriculture across the developing World.[37]

Starting in the 1970s, sociological studies began to dispel the myth that women are and have been universally subordinated.[38] In the 1980s, feminist sociologists uncovered the central roles of women in productive work and several studies documented females' work in agriculture, commerce, and paid labor.[39]

The context in which work takes place affects women's status. Engels argued that as "women's work lost its public character, women themselves lost much of their own independence and became subservient to men."[40] June Nash argues that work contribution is one of the "crucial rights and powers" that women must have if they are to have relatively high standing in society.[41]

In foraging or subsistence-living societies, the more work egg-producers do in the garden, in comparison to men, the better off men are, and the more freedom sperm-producers have to accumulate power and prestige. Women are therefore interpreted as a kind of 'early proletariat.'

Furthermore, when colonial policies are imposed upon Indigenous communities, important productive tasks are taken from women, who are taught to stay out of 'unladylike' productive work. Simultaneously, men are also often taught modern and prestigious forms of wage-earning work.

Structural ♀'Empowerment'

Despite ten millennia of phallic rule, girls and women still have agency and are exercising them every day. In the last century, human ovary beings have made some remarkable gains and improvements that are positive for each female affected, and for their communities.[42] Moreover, these advances suggest that societal changes can be abrupt.

In a few generations, women have attained betterment in the right to vote, education, employment, health, and political power.[43] Girls and women in the US now do better in school than boys and men, and the original sex gap in education is almost entirely erased. The majority of young people now graduating from high school, entering college, and finishing college, are female.

The United Nations 'Beijing+20 Planet 50-50 by 2030' program envisage a World where all females have equal opportunities and rights by 2030. 'Step It Up' asks governments to make national commitments that will close the sexual equality gap, from laws and policies to national action plans and adequate investment.

So far, only one country has signed on, Germany. There is little effective enforcement of many laws for women, and improving the situation for females is a low priority for governments. Micro-loans and saving programs rarely provide more than basic subsistence and do not address broader political, economic, and culturally oppressive patriarchal structures.

The onus of changing 10,000 years of cyborg domination and hegemony is placed on the shoulders of disadvantaged women and girls themselves. Having token females in positions of power does little to change the utilitarian mindset of cyborg domesticaters, as Mary Daly observes, "the very few women in 'masculine' occupations often behave much as men do."

Daly explains further, "The minute proportion of women in the United States who occupy such roles (such as senators, judges, business executives, doctors, etc.) have been trained by men in institutions defined and designed by men, and they have been pressures subtly to operate according to male rules. There are no alternate models."[44]

Empowering ♂ NGOs

In the name of "gender equality," multinational and national development and aid agencies keep funding the same old tired and limiting stereotypes of female empowerment, such as basic literacy and micro-loans. For over five decades, programs and assistance offered by the nonprofit industry have left untouched the root structures of phallic dominance, privilege, and power operating at micro and macro levels.[45]

Following the animal-as-capital model, the modern development industry view girls and women as capital as shown by how little egg-producers have benefited from the vast sums spent in their name. After over fifty years of targeted programs, and billions in international and national funding, women in the Global South have little to show for it.

At the 2015 UN women's conference, delegates from national and non-governmental organizations (NGOs) around the world gathered to assess how well governments have done since they promised to ensure women's equality at the Beijing conference 20 years ago, and what to do next. The same dire statistics of male violence against females were reported, and the same tired rhetoric of female empowerment was prescribed.[46]

At the 2015 UN women's conference, the states and NGOs set grossly reduced targets and metrics for attaining equality, and left the real barrier to a fairer, better world for people of all sexes unaddressed, phallic domination. Sustainable development goals were stressed, but there is never much funding and resources to provide women with the tools to achieve these conferences' goals. One young woman commented, "The more I listen to NGOs speak about female empowerment, the more disempowered I feel."[47]

Instead of empowering NGOs, why not provide a basic income to impoverished females? This is one way of guaranteeing a minimum financial independence for women, and recognizing girls and women's unpaid work in the home.[48] Members of the young-bearing sex could decide when, or if, to return to work after having a baby, based on what works for their family, rather than a choice between career suicide or prohibitive childcare costs.[49]

The related UN Women report, Progress of the World's Women 2015-2016, acknowledges some of the problems with equality-based solutions. The report states, "We must go beyond creating equal opportunities to ensure equal outcomes... 'Different treatment' may be required to achieve real equality in practice."[50]

This is one of the first major international reports to acknowledge that legal equivalence for women does not translate into actual equality. The document also recognize that governments must make substantial social-policy changes that enable the redistribution of domestic duties and economic participation in order for women to play a truly equal role in society.

Greek Titaness: Adrestia

Prehistoric, gynocentric notions of solidarity, determination, justice and egalitarianism are preserved in narratives around Goddess Adrestia, who is known as "unyielding," and 'she who cannot be escaped.' She was the Deity of equilibrium, just retribution, and, interestingly, revolt. This hints that prehistoric women viewed resistance as part of obtaining justice and just retribution, and essential to maintaining equality.

Goddess Adrestia was the daughter of Aphrodite, Goddess of beauty and love, and Ares, and she often accompanied her father to war. A favorite in the heavens, the 'unyielding one' was fought over by gods and titans alike to get her on their side. Goddess Adrasteia, "the inescapable," was asked by Goddess Rhea to nurture the infant Zeus, in secret in the Dictaean cave, to protect him from his father Cronus.

Interestingly, the name Rhea means "ground" or "flow." Goddess Rhea was Mother of the Olympian Goddesses and gods and Queen of the Titans. She was also Goddess of women, motherhood, and generation. Goddess Adrasteia was worshiped in Phrygia, probably derived from a local Anatolian mountain deity. She is known from inscriptions in Greece from around 2,400 BP as a deity who defends the righteous. Goddess Adrastea may be interchangeable with the ancient Cybele, the Anatolian Mother Goddess who was assimilated into aspects of the Earth Goddess Gaia, her Minoan equivalent Rhea, and the harvest Mother Goddess Demeter.

In earlier times, Goddess Adrasteia or "She whom none can escape" was a manifestation of Goddess Rhea Cybele in her attribute of the Mother who punishes human injustice, which is a transgression of the gynocentric natural order of things. The Greeks and Romans identified Goddess Rhea Cybele with Nemesis, the Goddess of divine retribution.

The gynocentric symbolism of scales for equality was paramount, and Goddess Adrestia was venerated as a deity of sublime balance between good and evil among humans. Because of her role in just retribution, she was usually portrayed with Nemesis, and sometimes identical to Nemesis herself, who also had the name Adrasteia.

Notable, Adrestia is a Goddess of just retribution, not blind revenge. Retribution is generally a 'just' action taken in response to an unjust one, such as the communal re-distribution of privatized, hoarded resources. On the other hand, revenge is more of a chaotic response to evil and injustice. Revolt and retribution were lawful outcomes to inequality and atrocities, and reflected ecogynocentric principles of justice, sharing, egalitarianism, and equity.

Conclusion

This second chapter of Part V on men's current debauchery examined the economic and social oppression of women and girls. This segment uncovered the myth of female 'progress' under phallic-centered civilizations, and stressed that female-specific forms of public-based discrimination are long-standing and structural.

The unrestricted harassment of human egg-producers is part of the socialization of phallic violence and objectification of 'femaleness.' As Mary Daly writes, "this attraction/need of males for female energy, seen for what it is, is necrophilia - not in the sense of love for actual corpses, but of love for those victimized into a state of living death."

The next chapter discusses more private forms of phallic-centered violence, including rape and murder, that serves to maintain the oppressive cyborg disorder. Following up on the arguments presented in this chapter, the next chapter illustrates how phallic-centered 'civilization' is far from civil, and more akin to 'terrorism' for human female animals.

(Figure 25: Woman/Goddess figure of Galgenberg is 2.8 in (7.2 cm) tall
and sculpted from shiny green serpentine rock c. 30,000 BP)

25: Terrorizing Females

Male religion entombs women in sepulchres of silence in order to chant its own eternal and dreary dirge to a past that never was. - Mary Daly

ASIA's Journey 2121.25

It is 9:15 PM and 109°F (42°C) in the middle of the humid city. People move at a snail's pace as if glued to the hot pave. The few air-cooled bars are packed with customers, and expensive restaurants employ dozens of children to pull over-sized fan blades in the ceiling to cool their diners.

Jean tags behind the money-lender who brought Iniko, to his home-office and stands outside with Zemora, Nakeisha, and Ramla. Earlier, the two rescued girls, Nadie and Cha'Kwaina, tearfully recalled tales of horrible abuse and hostility by the pedo-hunters.

Jean dressed in jeans and a shirt, paints on a fake mustache, walks up to the office door of the money-lender, and knocks. A guard quickly opens the door. "What do you want?"

"I represent a client who needs a dozen girls now," Jean flashes her gold coin. "Can we discuss business?" After a few minutes, the guard opens the door and lets Jean in to see the money lender in his elegant office.

"I'm a busy man," Don, the money-lender says without looking up from his desk. "How can I help you?" Jean glances at 11-year old Iniko handcuffed to a chair behind Don's desk.

"My client need a dozen very young girls for a long trip,"Jean says in a low voice. "They'll be gone for a month and he is willing to pay one gold coin per girl."

Don looks irritated. "One gold coin? No way! I need two coins for each girl. Otherwise, forget it."

Jean smirks. "There are thousands of girls out there. If you're smart, this can be a long-term deal with a dozen new girls each month." Don scratches his head. "When do you want them?"

"Tonight, but I need to take back a sample first," Jean points toward Iniko. "Only your youngest and freshest girls will do."

"You can have this pretty kitty," Don points to the scared child. "I just got her tonight." Jean slams her gold coin on Don's desk. "I will come back for the others in a couple of hours." Don waves the guard to release Iniko and Jean grabs her hand ready to leave.

"Wait a minute," Don stands up tall above his desk as Jean freezes. "I don't know you. I'll need collateral for this one."

Jean pauses, then smiles. "I have some very expensive liquor to deliver to my client. I will leave them here until I return."

"Alright, but I need 12 coins as collateral when you come for the rest." Don explains. "Until we get to know each other better, you understand?"

Jean shrugs and leaves with Iniko who is overjoyed when she meets her sisters from ASIA. Although abused and exploited, now three children are free.

Introduction

If girls and women are to be regarded as persons with full and equal human rights, they should not be viewed as merely a container for a fetus. The first moral right and consideration must be given to egg-producers, and their consent, interests, and needs lie above all else. Full independence for females implies absolute biological autonomy and any deviation from this exclusive right reduces their freedom.

Cyborgs realize the value of egg-producers' reproductive rights, and their reduction to involuntary incubators has been an integral part of phallic ascendancy for thousands of years. This third chapter of Part V on toxic masculinity concentrates on men's reproductive persecution of women.

The chapter starts off with an overview of cyborgs' diminution of young-bearers' reproductive rights. Men's taming of girls in marriage is next considered, followed by a look at cyborgs' public harassment, and then, private violence in the home.

How pornography is related to phallic-centered power is discussed afterward, and a discourse on men's rape culture comes next. Unpacking the burden of multiple forms of oppression some females face follows, then female resistance and femicide are examined. The chapter turns to look at the connection between war and misogyny, and concludes with a discussion of retribution and gynocentric philosophy behind the Greek Titaness, Nemesis.

♂ Colonization of ♀ Bodies

In addition to dealing with phallic harassment, limited educational access, and impoverishment, girls and women suffer from other serious problems, including health. Intolerably, 800 women die every day from preventable pregnancy-related causes. Almost all of these deaths occur in developing countries.[1] Phallic opposition to abortion is to blame, yet reproductive-related deaths are viewed as a female-only problem.

As Ellen Frankfort aptly comments, "It takes a certain kind of imagination to assume guardianship for something lodged within another's body - a rather acquisitive proprietary imagination that fits right in with the conception of a woman as a spaceship and the contents of her womb as an astronaut."[2]

About 222 million Third World women who want to avoid pregnancy lack modern birth control. Family planning has helped to decrease the number of deaths during or around the time of pregnancy by 40 percent, or about 270,000 deaths prevented in 2008.[3] Greater access could prevent 70 percent of deaths if the full demand for birth control were met.[4]

By lengthening the time between pregnancies, birth control can improve women's delivery outcomes and the survival of their children. In the developing World, women's earnings, assets, weight, and their children's schooling and health all improve with greater access to birth control.[5] Birth control increases economic growth because of parents having fewer dependent children, more women participating in the workforce, and less use of scarce resources.[6]

Given the danger of childbirth and benefits of preventing unwanted pregnancies, it is surprising that some 'feminists' are anti-abortion. Pro-life 'feminism' is part of the backlash against the women's movement, and Katha Pollitt observes, "Without abortion rights, there isn't a lot left to the fundamental ideals of equality and self-determination."[7]

Abortion has been a controversial subject in many societies since the New Stone Age. As part of the colonization of ovary beings, all female products, that is, children, are considered phallic property. Elite men base their restrictions on 'practical,' religious, ethical, and political reasons.

Yet, one sperm can derail a girl for life, and even cause her to die. The onus should be on boys and men to take birth control, but instead, sperm-producers compel females to gamble with their lives, and society blames them for the result. Males' usual excuse for placing female lives at risk is that using a condom diminishes their 'feeling' of pleasure.

Underlying this defense is the notion that the sexual organ of boys and men 'feels' small inside a female's lubricated vagina. Stemming from their insecurity, sperm-producers conceive of their penis as a knife they must wield in order to create maximum damage to the insides of egg-producers. Males appear to have an inherent need to 'feel' their penetration power over girls and women. This insatiable rape fantasy is part of phallic psychosis based on reproductive insignificance and false privilege.[8]

The unconscious misogyny inherent in males' refusal to use birth control, leads to millions of unwanted pregnancies. There are structural forces driving population growth as well as a constant increase in human population is an essential aspect of capitalism's continuous growth model.

♀ Reproductive Subjugation

Young-bearers bodies are perceived as actual battlegrounds in conflicts between phallic-centered nationalist, religious, and race-based ideologies. For instance, ovary beings are increasingly significant in the clash of men's 'civilizations' and cultures in the USA.[9]

In the 1960s, women fought for birth control in the US, and it was illegal in many parts of the country until the Roe v. Wade court decision in 1973.[10] A reflection of the continuing conflict over female sexuality is that violence directed at abortion clinics are at their highest in 20 years. Around 35 percent of US abortion providers reported "severe violence or threats of violence" in the first half of 2016. And in 2015, US abortion providers were targeted in three murders, nine attempted murders, and 94 reports of death threats.[11]

Abortion is severely limited by law in dozens of countries, from Angola to Chile, Ireland to the USA. Seven countries in Latin America and Europe have banned the procedure entirely, including El Salvador, Honduras, Nicaragua, and the Dominican Republic.[12] More that a quarter of all girls and women reside in countries where abortion is generally prohibited.

According to the WHO, 21.6 million women experience an unsafe abortion worldwide each year. Around 18.5 million of these occur in developing countries. More than 47,000 females die from complications of unsafe abortion each year, or 13 percent of all maternal deaths.[13]

As a consequence of misogynist reproductive laws, thousands of Brazilian women and girls illegally use the drug Cytotec to induce a miscarriage, and over 200,000 Brazilian egg-producers are hospitalized annually as a result of botched abortions. More than 300,000 illegal abortions are performed annually in Colombia, where termination of pregnancy is the third leading cause of maternal mortality.

In developed western societies, the trend is to treat members of the young-bearing sex like nonhuman animal domesticates, as mere baby factories or reproductive machines in the service of phallic-centered maldevelopment and ideologies. Lacking bodily consent is akin to being legally colonized, and objectification into a infant-machine illustrates how encumbered modern female animals are.

In March 2015, Purvi Patel became the first woman in the USA to be sentenced to jail for having a premature delivery that ended in stillbirth.[14] Patel did not buy or take any abortifacients, but she was still sentenced to 20 years in jail for killing a nonviable fetus.[15]

Purvi Patel was reduced to a cyborg reproductive device, and when her body/machine malfunctioned, she was accused of murder/industrial sabotage, and deemed to be the sole perpetrator of the 'crime.' According to the US cyborg courts, the circumstances of Patel's pregnancy, which may not have been by choice, or even forced, were entirely irrelevant.

In 2012, dentist Savita Halappanavar, suffered a miscarriage in Ireland. She requested an abortion but was refused by its cyborg administration. Ireland's doctors put the welfare of Halappanavar's unborn fetus above the growing risk to her life. She died two days later.[16]

In Paraguay, a 10-year girl under 70 lbs. was raped by her stepfather and became pregnant. When her mother requested an abortion, she was arrested for breaching her duty of care and being an accomplice to sexual abuse.[17] The 10-year child was placed in a state maternal center and compelled to carry the pregnancy to full term.[18]

Cyborgs' Child Brides

Two of the most effective practices of cyborgs' reduction of human egg-producers is child marriage and patrifocal residence. Worldwide, more than 700 million women alive today were married as children, below 18 years of age. More than 250 million were married before 15. In developing countries, one in 3 girls are married by age 18, and one in 9 minors are married by 15.

In the US, exceptions allow children younger than 18 to marry. Furthermore, laws in 27 states do not specify an age below which a minor cannot marry. In a single decade, 2000 to 2010, around 250,000 children were married in the US alone. This figure does not include children united in religious-only ceremonies or taken overseas to be married.[19]

Almost all American children in wedlock are child brides, including the 12-year-old girls wedded in Alaska, Louisiana, and South Carolina. The grooms were mostly men, 18 or older. Some minors are married at an age, or with a spousal age difference, which constitutes statutory rape under their state's laws. Child marriage exists in nearly every American culture and religion, including christian, jewish, muslim, and secular communities.

A child bride in the US is often trapped in an abusive relationship that has a 70 percent chance of ending in divorce. Females who marry before 18 are three times more likely to be beaten by their spouses than women who wed at 21 or older. If a minor wife leaves home, she is considered a runaway and the police will try to return her to her family. Most domestic-violence shelters do not accept minors, and youth shelters typically notify parents that their children are there. Plus, preventing legal marriages is not in the mandate of child-protective services.

Child brides are often unable to effectively negotiate safer sex, leaving themselves vulnerable to sexually transmitted infections, including HIV, along with early pregnancy.[20] The risk of complications during childbirth is exponentially higher in girls under 15 years of age. According to the WHO, maternal mortality is the leading cause of death for adolescent girls in developing countries.[21]

American girls who marry before 19 are 50 percent more likely to drop out of high school, and four times less likely to graduate from college.

Consequently, a girl who marries young is 31 percent more likely to live in poverty when she is older.

In addition to child marriage, over 133 million girls and women have experienced some form of female genital mutilation. FGM comprises procedures that involve partial or total removal of the external female genitalia, or another injury to the female genital organs for non-medical reasons. This brutal mutilation is practiced in 29 countries in Africa and the Middle East.[22]

Human trafficking by men ensnares millions of women and girls in modern-day slavery. Females represent 55 percent of the estimated 20.9 million victims of forced labor worldwide, and 98 percent of the estimated 4.5 million forced into sexual exploitation.[23] The US State Dept estimate that 600,000 to 800,000 people are trafficked across international borders each year. And around 80 percent of trafficking victims are women and girls.[24]

Cyborg Harassment

An integral component of phallic superiority is the privilege to harass the young-bearing sex in both private and public spaces. Girls and women experience a constant barrage of objectification from the media, advertising, and boys and men with spurious prerogative over public space.

Human egg-producers suffer from verbal harassment such as catcalls, sexually explicit comments, and sexist remarks, and from physical molestation like groping, leering, stalking, public masturbation, and assault. This ubiquitous form of sex-based violence is a human rights violation, but it is not on any government's priority list.

As Caitlin Roper argues, "sexual harassment isn't a compliment, it's an expression of power. It is just one manifestation of a culture that is openly hostile to women, one in which women and girls exist for the pleasure of men. Where women are regarded as public property and men entitled to vocally appraise their bodies and signify their approval or lack thereof, because that's what women and girls are for - to be aesthetically pleasing for men. Sexual harassment not only reflects sexist attitudes towards women, it communicates messages of power between men and women, reminding women of their place, and what they are for."[25]

Cyborg torment is frequent and ongoing with males with unearned worth dominating work places, community spaces, and the public gaze. In the US, around 65 percent of females report having experienced some type of street harassment, with 41 percent being victims of aggressive forms. About 23 percent said they had been sexually touched, 20 percent had been followed, and nine percent had been forced to do something sexual.[26]

Astoundingly, each one of 600 women surveyed in Paris said that they were subjected to sexually-motivated abuse by strangers on trains and buses at some point in their lives, often before they were 18.[27] And in India, a 2010 study found that two out of three women said they were harried more than twice in the last year alone.[28]

Schools are just one more location for young cyborgs to exercise mistreatment. In the US, 83 percent of girls aged 12 to 16 said they had experienced some form of molestation in public schools.[29] The US military is a highly unsafe place, and it estimates close to 20,300 active members were sexually assaulted during 2014 alone. Female victims made up 80 percent of the reports.[30]

In 2000, the National Institute of Justice calculated that over half a million US women were stalked by an intimate partner. One in 12 women will be stalked in their lifetime, and 77 percent know their stalker. Around 87 percent of stalkers are men, who manifestly feel falsely entitled. Shockingly, the average duration of stalking is 1.8 years. And if the pursuit involves intimate partners, the average duration increases to 2.2 years.[31]

Cyborg molestation can be unrelenting and it completely drain females' time, energy, peace, and security. Around 61 percent of stalkers made unwanted phone calls; 33 percent sent or left unwanted letters or items; 29 percent vandalized property, and nine percent killed or threatened to kill a family pet. About 28 percent of female victims obtained a protective order, but around 70 percent had the protection order violated.

Stalking occurs frequently on college campus, with 13 percent of college women reported being stalked during a six to nine-month time frame.[32] More than three in 10 college women reported being injured emotionally or psychologically from being stalked.[33]

Scurrilous phallic partners often try to stop women from working by calling them numerous times during the day or going to their place of employment unannounced. About 50 percent of battered women who are employed are harried at work by their abusive partners.[34]

Over three-quarters of phallic offenders used workplace resources to express remorse or anger, check up on, pressure, or threaten their female victim. Despite the mortal danger they present, men have easy access to their intimate partner's work environment, with 21 percent reporting they contacted her at the workplace in violation of a no contact order.[35]

♂ Domestic Violence

Understanding statistics regarding phallic violence is complex. A lot of it is hidden, under-reported, under-counted, or simply not recorded.[36] Nonetheless, close to 90 percent of violent crime and sexual violence are perpetuated by self-entitled cyborgs.

Physical aggression occurs in 1 in 3 teen dating relationships.[37] A UNICEF report found 120 million girls worldwide, slightly more than 1 in 10, experienced forced intercourse or other coerced sexual acts by a male at some point in their lives.[38] In the US, one in five high school girls report being physically or sexually violated by a dating partner.[39]

In a study of eighth and ninth graders, 25 percent indicated that they had been victims of dating hostility. And, eight percent disclosed being sexually abused.[40] Around 32 percent of girls who had been mistreated reported overeating and purging, compared to 12 percent of girls who had not been violated.[41]

Among acts of sexual aggression committed against females over the age of 18, 100 percent of rapes, 92 percent of physical assaults, and 97 percent of stalking acts were committed by sperm-producers. Sexual attacks on boys and men is likewise primarily phallic violence with 70 percent of rapes, 86 percent of physical assaults, and 65 percent of stalking perpetrated by other men.[42]

According to the US Surgeon General, domestic hostility by sperm-producers is the leading cause of injury to women. While the World's Health Organization (WHO) finds that 35 to 70 percent of women globally said they had experienced physical violence in their lifetime, mostly by an intimate partner.[43] And, the US Department of Justice estimates around 85 percent of the victims of domestic violence are women. Lamentably, all categories of egg-producers suffer from men's domestic aggression, regardless of income, age, race, education, or belief system.[44]

As part of their subjugation of females, phallic partners with false privilege assault three million women and girls in the US each year. A woman in America is more likely to be assaulted, raped, or killed by an intimate partner than by any other type of assailant. Moreover, victimization by domestic violence is usually not a single event. If a woman is battered once, her risk of further maltreatment is high. And over time, a victim's abuse usually becomes not only more frequent, but more severe.

Similarly, there is an overlap between child beatings and female battering. Over 65 percent of men in the US who attack their partner also physically and sexually abuse the children. Child ill-treatment occurs in 30 to 60 percent of family violence cases that involve families with children. Exposure to fathers' abusing and domesticating their mother is the strongest risk factor for transmitting aggressive behavior from one generation to the next.[45]

In households with pets, women are more often the primary caretaker of the pet, which increases the human-animal bond. There is a strong link between men's mistreatment of animals and their abuse of human egg-producers. In the US, over 70 percent of female survivors own pets who were likewise beaten. Many victims do not leave a harmful situation because they worry their pets are also in danger.[46]

Battered women are more likely to remain in an abusive home or return to such an environment if they do not have a safe place for their pets. Between 18 and 48 percent of assaulted women have delayed their decision to leave their batterer or have returned to their abuser out of fear for the welfare of their pets or livestock.[47]

Phallic domesticating violence is a leading contributing factor to other problems including child neglect, drug and alcohol abuse, emotional problems, job loss, homelessness, and attempted suicide. The social and economic costs on women and society are enormous, but generally go uncounted and unrecognized.[48]

According to the US DOJ, between 1998 and 2002, of the almost 3.5 million violent crimes committed against family members, 50 percent were crimes against spouses.[49] A woman is beaten every 15 seconds in the US by a man, and 35 percent of all emergency room calls are a result of domestic aggression. Each day, four women and three children die as a result of phallic abuse in the US alone.

Men's violence against females worldwide "persists at alarmingly high levels." This conclusion was reached by a UN report that the Secretary General presented to the General Assembly, one day after International Women's Day on March 9, 2015.[50]

Although 125 countries criminalize domestic violence, the laws are not reliably enforced, and the economic impact alone is astronomical. One study found that cyborgs' domestic violence costs the global economy $4 trillion. The report states, "the costs of violence are high; the welfare cost of collective, interpersonal violence, harsh child discipline, intimate partner violence and sexual abuse are equivalent to around 11 percent of global GDP."[51]

The report continues, "The cost of homicides are much larger than the cost of civil conflict. However, violence perpetrated in the home appears to be the most prevalent form of violence. Domestic abuse of women and children should no longer be regarded as a private matter but a public health concern."

Cyborg Rape Culture

Rape is a huge and growing problem for females, but reporting and recording of statistics vary widely even in developed economies. As Messerschmidt points out, in Western industrialized societies "hegemonic masculinity is currently established through an alleged uncontrollable and insatiable sexual appetite for women, which results in a 'naturally' coercive 'male' sexuality."[52]

In the US, marital rape was not a crime in all 50 US states until 1993. Given that barely one percent of rapists ever see a day in jail in even the most sexually egalitarian countries, this form of phallic torture against women remains effectively legal. And, due to stigmatization, victims often do not feel comfortable going to law enforcement, or they are unable to pay the bribes required to file a police report.

If a woman wants to fight back against sexual violation, almost all of the police officers, judges, and medical personnel she has to deal with are men with a phallic-superiority complex. In violation of the law, male officials do not take their fellow cyborgs' brutality against members of the young-bearing sex seriously and often engage in 'victim-blaming.' Consequently, girls and women experience further victimization in attempting to obtain justice from patriarchal institutions.

From 2004 to 2010, the country with the highest reported rape cases was the USA with over 80,000 sexual crimes. More alarming, the US DOJ estimates 300,000 American women are sexually violated every year,[53] and the Centers for Disease Control puts the number much higher at 1.3 million.[54] These estimates indicate that the overwhelming majority of cyborgs' sexual transgressions go unreported.

India is listed second in the number of reported rape cases, with over 20,000 over six years. The UK and Mexico had a little less than 20,000 documented cases of sexual crimes against girls and women. And from 2004 to 2010, Australia, Botswana, and Lesotho had the highest average per capita of reported rape.[55]

The evidence for cyborgs' terrorism against women and girls is ubiquitous, and despite numerous protests, nothing much ever changes. For example, In December 2012, the murder of a 23-year-old physiotherapy student who was gang-raped in New Delhi, India, drew nation-wide protests. In an interview with a BBC filmmaker, one of the rapist stated that the victim should not have fought back.[56]

In a documentary on the rape, "India's Daughter," the director read out a long and shocking list of injuries the young woman sustained, to the accused males rapists. The men appeared to be unmoved by their crime. The female director admitted, "I tried, really hard, to search for a glimmer of regret. There was none."

One rapist argued that the victim was at fault. He stated, "When being raped, she shouldn't fight back. She should just be silent and allow the rape. Then we'd have dropped her off after 'doing her', and only hit the boy." He added, "A decent girl won't roam around at nine o'clock at night. A girl is far more responsible for rape than a boy."

Alarmingly, the unrepentant rapist warned, "The death penalty will make things even more dangerous for girls. Now when they rape, they won't leave the girl like we did. They will kill her. Before, they would rape and say, 'Leave her, she won't tell anyone.' Now when they rape, especially the criminal types, they will just kill the girl."

Instead of airing the documentary, the Indian government banned it from broadcast or being shared online. A male parliamentary affairs minister claimed, "this is an international conspiracy to defame India."[57]

The documentary has several limitations. For example, by focusing on one rape, it ignores the vast majority of rape victims in South Asia, Dalit females, who are at the bottom of the sex, class and caste hierarchy.[58] Nonetheless, the film is a rare and useful exploration into the South Asian phallic domesticating mindset.

♂ Inter-sectional Misogyny

Race, color, caste, and sex are intersectional issues affecting countless poor 'minority' women. For example, dalits represent a community of 200 million in India, or 20 percent of the population. Dalit egg-producers were subjected to centuries of hindu apartheid, segregation, and untouchability, and continue to be denied access to basic facilities, such as water sources in 50 percent of Indian villages.[59]

Men's concerns over ritual pollution affects dalit girls and women's access to survival resources daily, but ironically, hindu cyborgs' obsession with 'purity' does not apply to dalit female sexuality. Even priests often ignore spiritual defilement to exercise their assumed sexual right to dalit female bodies. In one Indian state, the rape of dalit females has increased 500 percent in the past decade.[60]

As part of their colonization, hindu boys and men with biased prerogatives are adamantly opposed to dalit girls gaining access to education. For example, three days before International Women's Day, on March 5, 2015, a 17-year old dalit girl was set on fire by four men for pursuing education and appearing for the national examinations. The student was alone in her hut and cooking when the accused barged in, dragged her out, poured kerosene on her, and set her on fire.[61]

A week earlier, a 19-year-old dalit girl was hanged inside a bathroom of a private textile mill. Police claimed the girl committed suicide as she could not bear her stomach pain, but she may have been raped and killed.[62] And, in the prior week, a 16-year-old dalit girl was sexually violated then hung from a tree by two young men from her village.[63]

Rape, murder, and hanging of dalit girls are only part of cyborg terrorism that operates at the community level. At home, dalit females face daily insult, harassment, mistreatment, and subjugation from their male family.

♀ Resistance & Femicide

Women's groups that resist systematic oppression face tremendous backlash, and individual females who resist local men are punished with a range of consequences, from imprisonment to murder. Femicide, or the slaying of females by men, is an immense problem across the globe. From the USA and Mexico to Europe and Africa, members of the young-bearing sex are killed in vast numbers.

Any act of sex-based force that results in the death of a female is a femicide. The frequent femicide of girls and women reflect the enormity of phallic power and males' gross violations of females' human rights. It also hints at egg-producers' resistance since cyborgs brutalize and kill females who are defiant and refuse to be domesticated.

Femicide includes intimate partner homicide and serial murder, or the repeated homicide of girls and women. Over 90 percent of serial killers are male, and in the USA alone, there are thousands of cyborg mass murderers of egg-producers. Femicides reflects machismo and female vulnerability, as well as courageous resistance by girls and women.

The systematic murder of egg-producers Worldwide includes honor killing, dowry-related death, mass femicide, racist femicide, and lesbicide. Female infanticide and sex-selective abortion is an accelerating form of mass femicide in China, South Korea, South Asia, and even Armenia. Alarmingly, the number of girls in Asia is about 100 million less than would be expected given average demographics.

Intimate partner femicide accounts for 40 to 50 percent of all deaths of American women killed, but only accounts for 5 to 8 percent of all murders of men. This crime disproportionately affects females, and each day results in the deaths of four women and girls in the US alone.[64]

Although the overall risk of homicide for women was substantially lower than that of men, their risk of being killed by a spouse or intimate acquaintance is higher. More than twice as many women were shot and killed by their phallic partners or family members than were murdered by male strangers using guns, knives, or any other means.[65]

In the US, more than three-quarters of femicide victims had been stalked by the man who killed them. Around 85 percent of attempted femicide cases involved at least one episode of stalking within 12 months prior to the attempted murder. And 54 percent of femicide victims reported stalking to the police before they were killed by their phallic pursuer.[66]

One of the main motives that cause men with unwarranted prerogatives to kill their intimate partners is jealousy. Jacquelyn Campbell argues this is caused by phallic efforts to control and possess women, to display ownership, and to reinforce patriarchy. Furthermore, the provocation defense, which is the idea that any "reasonable man can be provoked into killing by insubordination on the part of a woman," is often cited as justifiable cause.

War and Misogyny

In her book, Sexism and the War System, Betty Reardon points out that both systems depend on male violence.[67] Gender roles and sexual dualism are nowhere more prominent than in war, evident in the near-total exclusion of women from combat forces, through history and across cultures.

Goebbels defined Nazism as "in its nature a masculine movement." In the same vein, the city council of the coastal city of Or Yehuda hung a public banner that read: "Israeli soldiers, the residents of Or Yehuda are with you! Pound their mother and come back home safely to your mother."[68]

If symbolic and actual rape encode domination, then misogyny serves as an important motor of male aggression in war.[69] Women's bodies can become a battleground on which men communicate their rage to other men because women's bodies have been the implicit political battlefields all along. Raped women bear the message that 'their' men were not able to protect them, as well as that they are worthless as 'property.'

Betty Reardon assert that rape is "the ultimate metaphor for the war system." As a symbolic form of rape, armed violence genders the victor as male and the vanquished as female. Other feminists have argued that misogyny itself is "the mother's milk of militarism," that is, essential to the war system.

Feminists such as Mary Beard and Virginia Woolf in the 1930s recognized the misogyny inherent in militaristic discourse on both sides. Misogyny is central to men's identities as soldiers, and there are recurrent images of war as a man destroying a prostitute.[70]

War fosters sex trafficking in a number of ways. Economic disruption, unemployment, poverty, and lack of prospects in general influence both supply and demand for prostitution. And lawlessness, corruption, and social disorganization contributes to sex trafficking in war-affected areas.

Desperate women easily become open to false promises and deception, as well as to different forms of violence. Traffickers exploit the fact that many persons are in vulnerable situations, undocumented, and separated from their families. Refugees are especially vulnerable, both while fleeing from war zones and while in exile.

Not only during war, but where there is far-flung military presence, there will be a significant and concurrent growth of the commercial sex industry and the trafficking of women and girls into the industry.[71] Women are sold to and exploited in brothels around US military bases in South Korea despite the military's 'zero tolerance policy.' More than one million Korean women have been used in prostitution by US troops since 1945.

In the 1980s, the US Subic Bay Naval Base in the Philippines was the largest military base outside of the US, with an estimated 500 million USD generated by the brothels surrounding it. The base fueled the estimated 300,000 to 400,000 women and up to 100,000 children in the Philippines commercial sex industry. As Susan Cunningham notes regarding macro level policy, "if the society's structural dynamics continue to produce violence, anti-violence policies and programs are bound to fail."[72]

Greek Titaness: Nemesis

Gynocentric principles of equality, sharing and egalitarianism were manifested in numerous Goddesses throughout the World. One such Goddess is Nemesis, an omniscient figure that loomed over the actions and affairs of Greeks. She was implacable justice and the Goddess who enacted retribution against those who succumb to hubris and arrogance, akin to Atë and the Erinyes. Atë was the personified spirit (daimona) of delusion, infatuation, blind folly, rash action and reckless impulse who led men down the path of ruin.

The name Nemesis is related to a Greek word meaning "to give what is due," from term nem or "distribute." The word originally meant the distributor of fortune, neither good nor bad, simply in due proportion to each according to what was deserved. Later, the term and the Goddess came to represent the resentment caused by any disturbance in equality and right proportion, and the sense of justice people felt that gross inequality should not be allowed to pass unpunished.

Divine retribution is a major theme in the Hellenic world view, and fearing the wrath of Goddess Nemesis may have encouraged many wealthy Greeks to share with their bounty with the poor. This daughter of Nyx was portrayed as a winged Goddess wielding a whip or a dagger. Later, as the maiden Goddess of Proportion and the Avenger of Crime, Nemesis had as attributes a measuring rod or tally stick, a bridle, scales, a sword, and a whip, and she rode in a chariot drawn by griffins.

Mesomedes wrote a hymn to Nemesis, where he addressed her as "Nemesis, winged balancer of life, dark-faced Goddess, daughter of Justice." He also mentioned her "adamantine bridles" that restrain "the frivolous insolences of mortals."

Nemesis brought sorrow to mortals such as Narcissus, an arrogant hunter who disdained the ones who loved him. Goddess Nemesis lured him to a pool where he saw his own reflection and fell in love with it, not realizing it was only an image. He was unable to leave the 'beauty' of his reflection and eventually dies.

Goddess Nemesis believed that no one should ever have too much resources and power, and she always cursed those who gained access to too much privilege. She was the Goddess of balance, making good things happen to someone who just had something bad happen to them and vice versa. Like Themis, Dike, Adrestia and other Greek Goddesses, Nemesis represented the fundamental gynocentric principles of justice and egalitarianism.

Conclusion

This third chapter of Part V on cyborg terror showed that cyborgs' oppression against human ovary beings is relentless and ongoing. By maintaining child marriages and reducing human egg-producers to baby factories, men are increasing their power over women, and at the same time, limiting females' control over their own bodies.

While many forms of structural oppression exist at the macro level, the most dangerous place for females are often inside of their home where they face the constant threat of male abuse. The domestic violence problem is primarily due to cyborg consciousness and the domesticating mindset. In patriarchal cultures, boys and men enjoy countless false entitlements, and lack of satisfaction with any one of their tyrannical expectations often leads to phallic frustration and hostility.

One of the greatest stumbling blocks for boys and men is a constant struggle to reach, compete, and accumulate. Males are trained from childhood to acquire and succeed so that their brain cells themselves create and demand this blueprint of achievement in order to have physical safety. This pattern continually leads to major disappointment since psychological security is not within the field of male achievement. For men to heal and become wholesome again, the whole structure of patriarchal society and the cyborg mindset based on individual achievement has to change.

Pornography and media play an increasingly crucial role in female objectification and reduction, with severe impacts on girls and women. The next chapter explores men's pornification of females in popular culture, and how this alarming trend reinforces male supremacy and cyborg consciousness.

(Figure 26: Woman/Goddess ivory figurine of Brassempouy c. 25,000 BP)

26: Pornifying Culture

Every woman who has come to consciousness can recall an almost endless series of oppressive, violating, insulting, assaulting acts against her Self. Every woman is battered by such assaults - is on a psychic level, a battered woman. - Mary Daly

ASIA's Journey 2121.26

It is 9:30 PM, 105°F (40°C) with raising humidity downtown. After the auction at the dock, Xóchitl and Lian followed Jerry the Weasel, the man who brought Sabra, to a dingy brothel located in a three-story building on the west side of the city.

The women stand on the opposite sidewalk, studying the exits and windows of the sexual prison. They have to find a way to save the 7-year old child from a daily onslaught of phallic terror.

The pair notice that the front roof of the building serves as a smoking area for pedophile patrons, and on the ground floor, the rear exit leads to an empty alley. Xóchitl figures that the back street will be the best place for the rescue and informs Lian, "I can climb the back wall to the roof, gain access to the inside, then climb out a back window with Sabra."

Lian looks worried. "The child will be scared. What if she falls?"

Xóchitl grins. "I will first strap her to my back then rappel out the window. We need more rope though."

"We can use the electrical wire over there." Lian points to old electrical pole with wire wrapped on top. She scales up the metal pole quickly, cuts the wire, and slowly lowers it to the ground. Xóchitl wraps the long cable around her body and hides it under her men's jacket.

Xóchitl looks like a pedophile with a big stomach as she sticks cotton balls in her mouth to fatten up her cheeks. "I'm all set."

"Here is the gold coin." Lian hands it to Xóchitl then asks, "What if you find her but the room has no window?" Xóchitl grunts and uses a man's irritated voice. "I want another room, dammit. This one smells."

Lian cracks a smile. "If they give you some other girl, how will you find Sabra?" Xóchitl uses a low, angry voice. "I only want the girl from the auction. Give me her or I'll leave now."

Lian watches as Xóchitl takes a shallow breath and swaggers over to the front of the building. She waves past the security guards outside and disappears inside the busy brothel. Lian waits in the back alley, and about half-hour later, a window on the third floor of the building opens.

Xóchitl promptly drops the long cable to the ground, climbs out the window backward, and effortlessly repels down the wall with Sabra tied to her back.

Sabra is safe, and Xóchitl hugs the child tightly all the way back to their shelter at the restaurant. Though abused and scared, ASIA's four missing girls are rescued and free for now.

Introduction

Similar to the last two chapters, this fourth chapter of Part V on modern toxic masculinity concentrates on the phallic diminution of girls and women into sexual commodities through the media and popular culture. This segment analyzes how female bodies are reduced and objectified through the lens of phallic-centered thinking and misogynist cultures.

From advertising and movies, to pop songs and video games, young human egg-producers are diminished to mere objects for male visual and physical pleasure. Like animals, girls and women are regarded as mindless bodies, lacking autonomy, and perpetually available for sale and plunder. Both are treated as existing solely to serve their cyborg 'superiors.' The constant bombardment of sexist media takes a toll on females' psyche, and this often leads to false consciousness regarding themselves, patriarchal society, and dominated nature.

The chapter sets out with a survey of femininity under misogynist cultures. The media's glorification of phallic aggression and shades of reduction is detailed afterward, and the normalization of misogynistic beauty standards is discussed next. Then, the chapter investigates porn and the robotized abuse of pistillate bodies, including anal domination. And, it concludes with a discussion of modern masculinity.

Misogynist Media

Notions of 'femininity' in misogynist, binary cultures can be a paradox. On the one hand, members of the young-bearing sex are ascribed forms of masculine traits in marketing campaigns, with terms such as 'girl power,' 'top girls,'[1] and 'can-do girls.'[2] On the other hand, almost derisively, media portrayals of 'empowered' girls and women co-exist alongside news of intensifying phallic hostility against females.

A further contradiction lies in the token examples of women with corporate and political power who exist amid glaring sex-based inequalities and objectification. From the 1920s onward, the media was fundamental in domesticating females and advancing phallic rule.[3]

In 2010, women were the subjects only a quarter of the time on mainstream media, compared to 17 percent in 1995. Moreover, 46 percent of the 2010 media stories reinforced sex-based stereotypes, and only six percent challenged them.[4] Through omission and misrepresentation, popular books and movies for girls and women likewise exacerbate female subjugation.

As a result of decades of media and cultural misogyny, egg-producers are made to feel ashamed of having periods, choosing what they want to wear, having hair on their body, and for not appreciating sexual harassment or phallic 'chivalry.' Members of the young-bearing sex are made to feel guilty for wanting to or not wanting to have sex, for standing up against misogyny, for 'ruining' a man's life by exposing that he is a rapist, for having an abortion, and much more.

As Mary Daly observes in *Beyond God the Father*, "television has been a major instrument of... ritual reinforcement of self-destructive mechanisms, so that 'the majority, drugged by the perpetual presence of the politics of rape on the TV screen, sees it all but sees nothing. The horrors of a phallocentric world have simultaneously become more visible and more invisible."

Shades of ♀Reduction

The normalized hostility of patriarchal society can be seen in females' support for the misogynist entertainment industry. The film adaptation of EL James' erotic trilogy about a misogynist billionaire was released on Valentine's Day and earned $37 million, the biggest single-day gross ever in February.[5]

"Fifty Shades of Grey" opened at the number one spot in 55 foreign markets, grossing $158 million, close to being the biggest R-rated weekend premiere, ever.[6] There were hundreds of sold-out showings through the weekend all over the world. The novel is notable for its explicitly erotic scenes featuring elements of bondage, sadism, and masochism (BDSM).[7] The author described her "Fifty Shades" trilogy as "my midlife crisis, writ large. All my fantasies in there, and that's it."[8]

Notably, the cyborgs' domesticating desire to bound and gag females while inflicting pain on them is similar to their taming of unrestrained animals. The books and film have spawned numerous copy-cat crimes. In 2012, a German woman died after being hit 123 times by a man with a wooden blackboard pointer while bound with nylon tights and condoms.[9]

A week later after the film's big weekend release, a student with charged with sexually assaulting a 19-year-old woman in an incident that allegedly involved tying the victim to a bed, blindfolding her, stuffing a necktie in her mouth, and beating her with a belt. The man told authorities he was acting out scenes from "Fifty Shades of Grey."[10]

Misogynist Success

The rationale behind the success of this misogynist trilogy and film are complicated. There are many structural, psychological, and social reasons for the popularity of sexualized force. For instance, the film appeals to a psycho-social theme of female desire for security and upward mobility, which is a product of economic inequality between the sexes.[11]

Misogynist media that romanticize and normalize phallic aggression is supported to a significant extent by male-centered capitalism. Romance escapist books written by females for other women are co-opted and promoted precisely because they legitimize and maintain male domesticating norms.

Structural and state influence likewise explains the popularity of films that portray masculinized females, such as GI Jane, Joan of Arc, and the Hunger Games. It is the same principle that explains why books and films that oppose female objectification and threaten the patriarchal status quo are rare and unfunded.

Many defend the film as just sexy fun, analogous to other novels in the romance genre. Of the millions of egg-producers who read the books and saw the movie, only a tiny fraction may have had any kind of unconventional sex, much less BDSM experience. Perhaps, the popularity of this form is a response to sexual repression and curiosity.[12]

Freudians may argue that as a result of sexual trauma and subjugation, female sexuality comes out in strange ways, such a preference for housewife erotica and films.[13] Given the prevalence of maltreatment, in some sense, these lurid fantasies may help the young-bearing sex to deal with sexual and other assaults.[14]

Moreover, sexist society and a pervasive rape culture teach girls and women to eroticize their own disempowerment. Ovary beings are unceasingly socialized, in multiple ways, to think that abusive relationships and rape are normal. And, recognizing their restricted roles in phallic society, women may want to learn how to love a narcissist, a theme the genre explores.

Mary Daly writes, "The exploitative sexual caste system could not be perpetuated without the consent of the victims as well as of the dominant sex, and such consent is obtained through sex role socialization - a conditioning process which begins to operate from the moment we are born, and which is enforced by most institutions. This happens through dynamics that are largely uncalculated and unconscious, yet which reinforce the assumptions, attitudes, stereotypes, customs, and arrangements of sexually hierarchical society."[15]

There were some protests against the film, and a feminist group collected donations for a women's shelter outside one theater. Despite the success of this misogynist film, advocates for women's rights are calling out the ongoing pornification of popular culture, and are daily resisting multiple forms of female reduction.

♀ Complicity

As Mary Daly observes, almost all egg-producers are complicit with the patriarchal order, either voluntarily, involuntarily, or unconsciously. The majority of white women who voted for Trump in USA's 2016 election provides insight into this reality. Curiously, the 90 percent of black women who backed Hillary Clinton is more a reflection of their vulnerability under overt white supremacy, than of feminist solidarity. Both candidates are heavily entrenched in the patriarchal disorder.

Regardless of how they voted, framing any woman as an oppressor while excluding the over-arching phallic power structure is part of the feminist backlash and victim-blaming. Even white feminists with class privilege, and women who oppose abortion should be viewed within the patriarchal lens.

This pro-female position does not imply that women lack agency, and are never responsible for their actions. Nor does it give members of the young-bearing sex a free pass to be sexists, racist, bigoted, and discriminatory. The behavior and performance of individual females are circumscribed by males and the entire phallic-centered system, so men share most of the blame for false consciousness among women.

Men's dominance is all-pervasive, and there appears to be no alternative to male supremacy and private accumulation. Humans have been heavily anesthetized for thousands of years by patriarchal religions, and are profoundly challenged to think outside of the cyborg's ecocidal box. In addition, female prehistory is rigorously suppressed, and girls and women are entirely unaware of their former gynecological selves, agency, governance, gift economies, and philosophies.

Egg-producers have few choices to the prevailing phallic dis-order, and must 'lean-in' to sperm-producers' professions and economic systems to survive. And, since women's status are dependent on the social standing of the men in their lives, supporting male relatives and phallic-centered culture is in each woman's short-term interest.

Moreover, women and girls are punished for asserting their subjectivity and abused for not supporting individual men and phallic customs in general. Members of the young-bearing sex are compelled to participate in the sperm-producers' processions, and to maintain cyborgs' illusion of 'fairness.' Young or old, females face severe censure for being defiant and resisting the ubiquitous patriarchal system in any way.

At the same time, human ovary beings are praised for performing as submissive, sexualized objects. Women are also rewarded for parroting men in hunting, war, leadership, and so on. Yes, as soldier or CEO, women continue to be sexualized and objectified by their colleagues.

Within cyborg society, females are damned if they 'lean in' and damned if they do not. In the absence of ovary solidarity, it is difficult to see how individual females can become non-cooperative to the patriarchal dis-order, and still survive.

♀ Beauty & Misogyny

Children and adults are daily conditioned into toxic masculinity, and lack other cultural options. Objectification, commodification, and sexualization are intolerably misogynist, but this is what passes for popular culture under cyborgs' rule. However, females' low caste condition in society is disguised and hidden by various forms of derivative status as a consequence of their relationships with boys and men.

Boys and men with erroneous rights benefit from girls and women's engagement in gendered beauty practices. And tellingly, self-objectification is one of the few ways human ovary beings can gain social recognition, however limited, that is independent of sperm-producers. Females' war against body hair provides a clue into gendered social control.

By the turn of the twentieth century, hair-free faces and limbs were expected for American women. Visible hair growth, particularly on young, white women, came to be perceived as a sign of political extremism, sexual deviance, or mental illness. Rebecca Herzig notes that the effect of a hairlessness norm is to "produce feelings of inadequacy and vulnerability, the sense that women's bodies are problematic the way they naturally are."[16]

In her book, Beauty and Misogyny, radical feminist Sheila Jeffreys writes, "Beauty practices can reasonably be understood to be for the benefit of men. Though women in the west sometimes say that they choose to engage in beauty practices for their own sake, or for other women and not for men, men benefit in several ways."[17]

Jeffreys explain that men, "gain the advantage of having their superior sex class status marked out, and the satisfaction of being reminded of their superior status every time they look at a woman. They also gain the advantage of being sexually stimulated by 'beautiful' women."

On an almost daily basis, American egg-producers feel compelled to use about a dozen beauty products, which are usually tested on animals.[18] The list includes shower gel, shampoo, conditioner, styling products, cleanser, moisturizer, exfoliator, toner, lotion, mascara, eyeliner, eye shadow, face foundation, primer, blush, lip gloss, lipstick, nail polish, deodorant, and perfume.[19] Females in the US put an average of 168 chemicals on their bodies each day.[20]

Conforming to beauty practices affects women and men at the subconscious level, for example in reinforcing domesticated and domesticator attitudes. Girls and women are expected to both 'complement' and 'compliment' phallic cyborg consciousness. Complement refers to something that completes or goes well with something, while compliment is expressing praise or admiration.

Through engagement with beauty practices, Jeffreys contend that females play an essential role in complementing men by helping to define masculinity through the adoption of opposite feminine standards that reinforces binary difference. By being prepared to make an effort to adorn themselves for cyborgs' visual pleasure and sense of entitlement over egg-producers' identity, women and girls compliment undeserving men.

Jeffreys explains further, "Thus men can feel both defined in manhood and flattered by women's exertions and, if the women are wearing high heels for instance, pain endured for their delight. Those women who refuse beauty practices are offering neither complement nor compliment and their resistance can be heavily resented by members of the dominant sex class."

Disposable Females

The media saturates popular culture with the message that boys and men are falsely entitled to use girls and women as walking sex toys. Females are commonly portrayed as disposable objects, to be used and thrown away by sperm-producers just because they were born female.

For instance, kindergarten-aged girls sing along to pop songs with lyrics like "do what you want with my body." The chorus of this typical woman-hating song is sung by a female and played on the public airwaves for girls and boys of all ages to repeat. The constant barrage of prejudice against women takes a heavy toll on girls' psyche.

Reflective of the contempt for females in media, one study found that in only five years, there was a 55 percent increase among girls aged 11 to 13 reporting emotional issues. While girls faced 'unique pressures, not surprisingly, boys whose immature and violence-based identities are glorified, remained fairly emotionally stable.[21]

The researchers suggest the alarming rise in mental health issues for girls include the drive to achieve an unrealistic body shape, perpetuated by social media, and the increasing sexualization of young females. Millions of egg-producers try unsafe diets and undergo unnecessary surgery to conform to patriarchal norms, and many suffer ill health and even die as a result.

Females who view mere vocabulary as empowerment become easy targets for the media. Mary Daly writes, "When a woman is caught in this delusion she does not see that all the propaganda of patriarchy - fairy tales, popular songs and films, psychology, advertising, political speeches - replication of the godfather, son and holy ghost theology and that she is susceptible to its influence. Continually caught off guard and full-filled with false confidence, she is a prime target of the paternal public relations experts."[22]

Starting in the 1960s, Andrea Dworkin and second-wave feminists claimed that advertising, entertainment, and other forms of cultural expressions were mechanisms of control and harm, but the psychological crisis has only multiplied. Susan Brownmiller contended that unhealthy emotions in women, such as female rape fantasies, are a pathological manifestation of phallic-dominated culture. Brownmiller noted, "the rape fantasy exists in women as a man-made iceberg" that can and should be destroyed by feminism.

Even so, as Mary Daly writes, "The struggle to break out of the circles of rapism has in some ways become more difficult, since the sovereigns of sado-society have augmented their assaults, using their religion, their politics, their professions, their media as rituals for erasure of female powers, imprisoning women in the state of the grateful dead."

Porn & ♀ Abuse

With the booming pornographic industry, the objectification, subjugation, and universal revilement of human female animals is near accomplished. Girls and women are reduced to mere vessels in the service of cyborgs' most 'valuable' body part, their penis. Andrea Dworkin observes, "I live in a country where if you film any act of humiliation or torture, and if the victim is a woman, the film is both entertainment and it is protected speech."[23]

Dworkin continues, "The civil impact of pornography on women is staggering. It keeps us socially silent. It keeps us socially compliant. it keeps us afraid in neighborhoods; and it creates a vast hopelessness for women... When your rape is entertainment, your worthlessness is absolute."

Among young adults today, pornography use is the norm, not the exception. Since the Internet's inception, female erotica has dominated its use, and one in eight online searches is still for smut.[24] In 2006, revenues for sex-related businesses were $13 billion in the US alone, including video sales and rentals, Internet sales, cable, pay-per-view, phone sex, erotic dance clubs, magazines, and novelty stores. Furthermore, global pornography revenues have declined 50 percent since 2007 due to the amount of free online smut.

Almost 90 percent of scenes in porno films contain acts of physical hostility, and half of the scenes contain verbal aggression. Feminists have strenuously argued that pornography is demeaning to females and contributes to violence against girls and women, both in its production and consumption.

The relatively new crime of webcam sex tourism is spreading rapidly, and new digital technologies are sparking what the United Nations calls an "alarming growth of new forms of child sexual exploitation online." Pedophiles in the US, Canada, Europe, and Australia pay facilitators on the other side of the world to sexually abuse children, even babies, by directing their moves through online live-streaming services. The FBI reports that pedophile porn is an epidemic, and that at any given moment, 750,000 child predators are online.

The production of pornography entails the physical, psychological, or economic coercion of the girls and women who perform in it. The porn set is a site where the mistreatment and exploitation of females is rampant. The consumption of smut eroticizes the domination, humiliation, and coercion of human egg-producers, and reinforces sexual and cultural attitudes that are complicit in rape and sexual harassment.

MacKinnon argues pornography is, "Sex forced on real women so that it can be sold at a profit to be forced on other real women; women's bodies trussed and maimed and raped and made into things to be hurt and obtained and accessed, and this presented as the nature of women; the coercion that is visible and the coercion that has become invisible—this and more grounds the feminist concern with pornography."[25]

MacKinnon continues, "Pornography affects people's belief in rape myths. So, for example, if a woman says 'I didn't consent' and people have been viewing pornography, they believe rape myths and believe the woman did consent no matter what she said... Pornography desensitizes people to violence against women so that you need more violence to become sexually aroused if you're a pornography consumer."

Anal Domination of ♀

The US DOJ states, "Never before in the history of telecommunications media in the United States has so much indecent (and obscene) material been so easily accessible by so many minors in so many American homes with so few restrictions."[26]

Sociologist Jill Manning comments, "Research reveals many systemic effects of Internet pornography that are undermining an already vulnerable culture of marriage and family. Even more disturbing is the fact that the first Internet generations have not reached full maturity, so the upper limits of this impact have yet to be realized."

Pornography has changed the landscape of adolescence beyond recognition, with a sharp rise in the number of schoolgirls at risk of emotional problems. In recent years, physicians have been treating growing numbers of teenage girls with internal injuries caused by frequent anal sex because boys expected it from them.[27]

Teenage girls are profoundly ashamed about talking about such injuries. They lie to their mothers and feel they cannot confide in anyone else, which only adds to their distress. They were humiliated by the experience, but felt they could not say no. Anal sex is standard among teenagers now, even though girls know that it hurts. One doctor states, "these girls are very young and slight and their bodies are simply not designed for that."

One study found that both heterosexual partners expected only sperm-producers to find pleasure in penis-in-ass sex, but egg-producers were expected to "endure the negative aspects such as pain or a damaged reputation." But both girls and boys said anal sex could damage females' reputations, but young cyborgs perceive having anal sex as a feat in competition with other phallic humans.[28]

Researchers found a normalization of phallic sexual coercion, even among girls. Teenage boys thought that girls and women would generally be reluctant to have anal sex, and would participate only if persuaded, or even coerced into it. They also admitted that the act might hurt females. Nonetheless, boys believed they were expected to persuade or coerce reluctant female partners into anal domination.

Acting Like a Man

Given the rapid pace of environmental and social devastation, why do phallic humans remain so committed to patriarchy and violence? Are boys and men willfully ignorant, permanently out-to-lunch, or incapable of grasping the cataclysmal reality of phallic-rule? Sperm-producers are rated according to general expectations of machismo, and are constantly insecure about their performance, making them somewhat bi-polar.

Across the World, masculine identity is highly policed by the local community of phallic humans. As Stoltenberg observes, "All men grow up learning to mistake their manhood act for themselves."[29] Some men may realize that cyborg consciousness is an act, nevertheless they may be fearful of the consequences if they act otherwise.

Stoltenberg comments on masculinity, "You don't wear the manhood mask to feel real - only to be judged as real (as a real-enough man). You never actually get to feel real except when other masked men bestow their approval on your manhood act." He concludes, "This insanity can only cease when one by one we each learn the commitment and the skills to disempower the manhood act by laying to rest our subservience to it."

Undoubtedly, sperm-producers have forgotten the peace and comfort they enjoyed during millions of years of gynocentric organization. Men also take false phallic privilege and male supremacy for granted, and consider phallic-dominated societies as part of the natural order and success of 'human' existence.

Due to insignificant roles in reproduction, men may feel inferior to young-bearers and may be over-compensating with phallic-centered violence. Through their capacity to give birth, egg-producers can achieve a sense of connection with other generations. And that has been a scary thing for men, to know that females have this capacity and they do not. Consequently, men have had to figure out other ways of creating a transcendent community that connects them across the generations.[30]

With the sixth and seventh subjugations in the New Stone Age, masculinity was transformed from complementary roles to entirely oppositional behavior in regards to women. That is, 'maleness' became dependent on constructed notions of 'femaleness' and as part of rigid gender dualism. Phallic-based violence became an essential marker for Neolithic masculinity.

Masculine identity is situational and contextual - it needs to be proven over and over again, at every moment, and in each new social environment. Masculinity is always a work in progress and can never be fully attained. Unlike females, becoming a man it is not a single achievement. For example, males have to go out and hunt once more, go back to war, and so on, to continually re-prove their 'masculinity.'

Male heroes in history, Riane Eisler argues, "were consummate killers, noted for their power not to give, but to take life. They did not hesitate to use lies and thievery to advance their ends. And, in a world where (eventually, even in Crete) women were gradually becoming male properties, they were frequently not only rapists and seducers, but also abductors or thieves of women."[31]

Rather than a sacred act connected to the worship of a Goddess, with New Stone Age masculinity, sex was associated with kingly ambition to conquer and rule with violence. Under gynocentrism, females were honored as divine, but Eisler suggests that in the development of male-based societies, femaleness and nature were increasingly seen as "abject, chaotic, 'dirty,' to be feared and controlled if not eradicated. Dutiful motherhood and exploitable fertility are honored, while free sexuality is labeled 'whoredom.'"

The force of desire that engenders life, an energy enabling connection and communion, is reduced to a dangerous abyss, and a black hole of evil. In patriarchal myth, enacted in sacred texts as well as pornography, female genitalia is associated with evil, monstrosity, and obscenity. Female sexuality is viewed as the devil's gateway and the mouth of hell.

While the phallus is deified, its female symbolic equivalent is stigmatized. Jane Caputi observes that the vagina became synonymous with "irrationality, chaos, the depths, and the common." The historical distortion and degradation of female divinity is the backdrop for the popular representations of females as femme fatale, dragon lady, monster, vamp, and witch.[32]

Cyborg phallic penetration of females is part of phallic domination and transcendence, and this interconnects with nonhuman animals in zoophilia. For example, 'stump training' is part of the colonization of horses, donkeys, sheep, and other animals who are trained to back up to a tree stump so that cyborgs can stand and sexually penetrate them.

Moreover, sexual acts involving animals sexually penetrating women are exploited to reduce both simultaneously. Popularized in art, pornography, and as paid spectacles, inter-species sexual victimization reduces egg-producers to a status lower than that of nonhuman animals. The sexual exploitation of women, children, and nonhuman animals are part of cyborgs' reduction of all life to mere objects of phallic desire, and to be perpetually available for male use.

Greek Titaness: Erinyes

Gynecological principles of equality and balance were primary. These fundamental notions were reflected in various Goddesses who served to mystically restore the egalitarianism of the natural order. The idea of divine justice and retribution acted to restrain privilege and accumulation. Any form of inequality was viewed as an injury to the entire female-based society, and Goddess myths reinforced social pressures for privileged individuals, families, and clans to share resources and knowledge.

In Greek mythology the Erinyes, also known as the Furies, were female deities of vengeance. The Erinyes lived in Erebus and are more ancient than the Olympians. According to variant accounts, they emerged from Goddess Nyx or from a union between air and Mother Earth. Fragments dealing with the Erinyes are found among the earliest records of ancient Greeks and they feature prominently in popular myths.

The Erinyes are crones and described as having snakes for hair, dog's heads, coal black bodies, bat's wings, and blood-shot eyes. In their hands they carry brass-studded whips, and their victims die in torment. Their task is to hear complaints brought by mortals against the insolence of the young to the aged, of children to parents, of hosts to guests, and of householders or city councils to suppliants - and to punish such crimes by hounding culprits relentlessly.

Like Nemesis, Dike, and others, these ancient Goddesses of retribution represented the poor and aggrieved against the powerful and privileged. They were sometimes referred to as "infernal Goddesses." The wrath of the Erinyes manifested itself in a number of ways. The most severe of these was the tormenting madness inflicted upon a patricide or matricide. Murderers might suffer illness or disease, and a nation harboring such a criminal could suffer scarcity, and with it hunger and disease.

The number of Goddesses is usually left indeterminate. Virgil, probably working from an Alexandrian source, recognized three: Alecto or "endless," Megaera or "jealous rage," and Tisiphone or "vengeful destruction." Telphousia was usually a by-name for Goddess Demeter. The Erinyes were similar to the Poinai or "Retaliations," the Arai or "Curses," the Praxidikai or "Exacters of Justice," and Maniai or "Madnesses."

In *The Greek Myths*, Graves interprets the legends about Clytemnestra, Agamemnon, and Orestes, as ceremonies that were suppressed when patriarchy replaced the matriarchies of very ancient Greece. Graves asserts that the sacrilege for which the Erinyes pursued Orestes was the killing of his mother, who represented matriarchy.

Conclusion

This fourth chapter of Part V on cyborgs' rabid sexual desires and violence focused on the diminution of women and girls into sex objects. It revealed that cyborg sexual misogyny is structural, pervasive, and insatiable. There are few private and public spaces where females are safe from the daily battering of reduction and woman-hating. The pervasiveness of negative patriarchal environments reinforces a need for separatist, born-female spaces, free from phallic objectification, dualism, and propaganda.

The next and final chapter of Part V examines the theoretical erasure of women, as the category becomes prohibited in 'feminist' and queer theory. Although female oppression is World-wide under cyborg dualism, even recognition of a biological and scientific category called 'female' is characterized by the cyborg academy as transphobic and anti-feminist.

(Figure 27: Dilukai from Caroline Islands, Belau (Palau),
19th to early 20th century)

27: Theorizing 'Female'

> The state of robotitude is marking time hopelessly, a pure repetition of mechanical gestures. Beginning living means that the victim sees and names the fact that the oppressor obliges her to consume her transcendence in vain, changing her into a thing. - Mary Daly

ASIA's Journey 2121.27

A bit of the morning dew remains and the temperature in under 98°F (36°C) with low humidity. The moon lingers in the dark blue sky with a few tiny patches of clouds.

The women and children of ASIA are walking north, three days away from the safe-house. Everyone is happy to that ASIA is reunited, especially the mothers of Nadie, Cha'Kwaina, Iniko, and Sabra.

Zaid is the only one who is not overjoyed. "It's not fair," Zaid yells, pointing to his sister. "Iniko gets to be a girl."

Ashadia stares at Iniko. "What's not fair. We're all girls."

"I am a boy," Zaid says adamantly, pointing to his penis. "I pee like this." He waves his penis around like a wand and pretends to urinate.

Lehana gags and says, "We don't care."

Ashadia shrugs. "You can be a boy outside and the Goddess inside."

"You can play with us," Naina smiles warmly.

"But everyone picks on me," Zaid pouts.

Nadie hugs the upset child. "Why don't you become a girl then?"

"You look almost like me." Iniko touches her head. "You just have to grow your hair longer." Zaid does not like her idea.

Sabra is puzzled. "A boy can't be a girl," she says.

"They can if they want to," Ashadia says. "And a girl can be a boy."

Sabra shakes her head emphatically, "I don't want to be a boy."

Zaid whines, "Neither do I."

Cha'Kwaina sways her hips. "Then practice walking like this."

"You can play with my dolls," Naina suggests sweetly.

Cha'Kwaina dances. "Act like a girl and you'll start to feel like one."

Sabra is unconvinced. "I don't do that, but I am a girl."

The girls laugh and Zaid pouts.

Introduction

Is a human female animal defined by biological traits, lived experience, or personal choice in identity? Who decides what 'femaleness' means within the overarching structure of patriarchal domination? Should deciders of 'femininity' be men, trans men, or born females? If it is transfemmes, then what do they win, and what do women lose?

This last chapter of Part V on cyborgs ongoing persecution centers on the social and ideological suppression of biological females. The naming and framing of human egg-producers are integral to phallic domination and terror. Members of the young-bearing sex are being erased and re-defined simultaneously within categories such as trans, queer, non-binary, womanist, and feminist.

The chapter starts with a brief discussion of sexual dualism or binary that regards ovary beings as inferior. A critical look at the trans movement's appropriation of women's culture follows, and then the essentialist problem in defining a 'female' from among multiple identities is addressed.

A discourse on feminist appropriations of Indigenous cultures comes after. Next is a brief examination of robotic females, and the chapter terminates with a discussion on re-claiming the Earth Goddess.

Cyborgs' Dualism

'Femininity' is a tightly policed set of practices, dispositions, and performances subscribed to egg-producers. The social construction of 'female' is part of a gender dualism that conceives of phallic humans as separate and superior.[1] Gender is a hierarchical system based on reproductive biology, in which femininity is defined as female-submissive behavior and masculinity as male-dominant behavior.

Gynocentric cultures do not enforce a sex-based double standard around work, sexuality, child care, use of public space, and so on. Moreover, female-centered groups view girls and women as coequal to their phallic kin in every way. This is not the case under cyborgs' rule.

Ecofeminist Marti Kheel outlined a series of male-female opposites or dualisms that exist within patriarchal society, such as 'conscious' and 'unconscious'; 'rational' and 'irrational'; 'autonomous' and 'dependent'; 'reason' and 'emotion'; 'wild' and 'tame'; and 'sacred' and 'profane.'[2] Not surprisingly, the superior side of these sexist dualisms is exclusively associated with sperm-producers, and the inferior side is linked to the young-bearing sex.

Furthermore, there is a notion that the 'inferior' section needs to be controlled and dominated by the 'superior' one. For example, the 'conscious' needs to dominate over the 'unconscious,' 'reason' needs to dominate over 'emotion,' and the 'tame' needs to exercise control over the 'wild.'

The gender binaries that ecofeminists have identified are characteristic of patriarchal perspectives, philosophies, and religions, and are found throughout society. Rosemary Ruether notes that sexual dualism is based on men's hierarchical division between 'lower,' temporal matter, and notions of a 'higher,' eternal spirit.

Ruether writes, "femaleness is both symbol and expression of the corruptible bodiliness that one must flee in order to purify the soul for eternal life. Female life processes - pregnancy, birth, suckling, indeed, female flesh as such - become vile and impure and carry with them the taint of decay and death."[3]

In the eyes of sperm-producers with undeserved privilege, a female's menstrual cycles, and ability to bring forth life, places her closer to nature and the Earth.[4] Egg-producers are unable to transcend their 'lower' material existence, and, like other animals, they merely repeat the rhythms of nature.[5] The ascendancy over females was and is integral to cyborgs' quest for transcendence over the natural World.

Men's gender dualism is profoundly entrenched and fundamental to the subjugation of females. There is little reason for hope, but these phallic-driven realities must be faced. As Mary Daly writes, "At the very minimum, these sobering experiences can help to dispel from our psyches any remnants of the delusion that phallocracy can be reformed or improved."

Daly continues, "One logical consequence of such total and positive disillusionment is a shifting of the focus of hope away from unredeemable structures to the Selves of women and other biophilic creatures, engendering intensified concentration upon our own powers of creation, our own Final Cause."

Rejecting Difference

The social construction of gender dualism is an on-going process that feminists are unraveling. One of the most contentious issues that emerged during the 2nd wave movement is the role of biology and nature. Andrea Dworkin warned that any association with nature or biology situates females on the losing side of the dualism,[6] and, in the name of advancing equality, gender feminists and transgender activists have embraced Dworkin's unscientific stance.[7]

For instance, gender feminists refuse to acknowledge the role of nature in shaping the human brain. Instead, they contend that sex differences are entirely caused by nurturing that begins at birth. While social conditioning is highly meaningful, egg-producing bodies and brains are not the same as sperm-producing ones, and to maintain that they are, profoundly distorts reality and is profoundly regressive.

The masculinizing effects of prenatal testosterone on neutral stem cells and the developing brain, are well documented.[8] And, contrary to the claim for identical brains, researchers using only neuro-imaging were able to successfully classify a brain by its sex 93 percent of the time.[9]

But even if human pistillate and staminate brains are structurally the same, there are variations in functionality. Studies have shown sex deviation across a broad range of cognitive domains, including verbal fluency and mental rotation. It is unlikely that nurture alone explains these sex-based variations in cognitive performance.

Trans(sending) 'Females'

In contrast to cultural feminists, transgender activists believe that gender is biological, rather than social. Transfemme activists maintain that the very idea that biology should determine who is a woman is misogynistic. Yet, far more simplistic gender arguments are advanced by the trans movement in regards to childhood sexual identity.

For queer theorists, gender identity becomes stable early on, but it is not tied to birth. Individuals can be born in the 'wrong' body, which warrants a transition for transgender children and adults. Even so, close to 90 percent of gender dysphoric children will desist from transitioning and grow up to be gay adults.[10] That is, children develop to be comfortable in their birth sex and have no need for gender reassignment surgery.

On top of the anti-science position of radical identity politics, the post-modernist, sexuality lens conflates culture's gender with nature's sex.[11] And, since gender and sexual identity are fluid for some, this gets translated into the misogynist notion that 'female' as a category does not exist.[12]

For transfemme advocates, a 'female' can be any sperm-producer who is willing to conform to the rigid construction of femininity under the prevailing gender dualism.[13] A 'woman' is defined as whatever a man wants to have sex with, and males remain subjects while "she" are objects than men desire.

The post-modernist, neoliberal narrative is that transfemmes are women without exceptions. But transfemmes are a diverse group of people who retain male genitalia and patterns of sexuality in majority numbers. The most common sexual behavior of biologically-male 'women' is to insert their penises into born-females.[14]

However, personal and social identities are fluid and vary a lot. Numerous forms of sexual personalities exists, and queer identities may be related to socialized gene expressions.[15] All the same, a dogmatic focus on 'feminine' performance ignores class, culture, violence, and other factors that can influence an individual's presentation of self.

Conspicuously absent in the emotionally charged debate over who is a 'real' woman is the deconstruction of manhood. What is a 'real man' and who decides which arbitrary phallic behaviors fail or succeed to meet the machismo criteria? Why is it rudimentary that the 'un-manly' be placed outside of the masculine category and aligned with femininity? Does this not reinforce gender dualism? Are men not to blame for excluding sperm-producers who act 'feminine' from the framing of manhood?

As Sarah Dictom writes, "The demand that womanhood be unbounded is really a demand that male authority be unquestioned." Manhood remains narrowly exclusive, while womanhood is framed as having to accommodate anyone that does not confirm to rigid masculinity.[16]

Essentialist Stigma

Despite the decades-old movement towards non-binary, gender neutrality by transfemme activists, there remains a gender caste system unique to born-females, and this has to be recognized as part of any resistance to patriarchal dualism. How biological 'females' are defined, or not defined, influences their self-awareness, self-image, social awareness and other psychological aspects.

A person's behavior is affected by numerous structural forces, including the political and social state of affairs. And while an individual may have multiple identities and are natural actors at playing different roles, there remain some essentialist aspects, such as sex, hair, and skin color.[17] Theorizing transfemmes as 'real women' essentializes performance over experience and diverts attention from vital concerns, such as ending sexual caste, phallic aggression, and the ecocidal patriarchy.[18]

Curiously, recognition of oppression based on biological sex and race contradicts the neoliberal framing of individual action and fluidity as solutions to sexual caste, race, and class constraints.[19] Structural feminists who oppose this denial of societal and cultural forces are accused of being 'biological essentialists' and attempting to restrict 'womanhood.'[20] For using fundamental sociological principles on in- and out-group formation, gender critical feminists are smeared as TERFs.[21]

But the notion that transfemmes should be the sole arbiters of what womanhood is, is far more reductionist than the construct of sexual caste. Trans people have long suffered from male prejudice and hostility, however this is not women's fault and the blame should not be placed at feminists' feet.

Curiously, accusations of trans-misogyny are leveled at feminist women far more often than at the men who commit the real violence against gay, trans, queer, and bi-sexual men. The backlash against gender critical theorists and feminist icons who insists biological females are 'real' include de-platforming them from conferences.[22]

Due to their 'essentialist defect,' ecofeminist discussions on the commonality of phallic-centered oppression of females and nature are summarily dismissed as 'anti-intellectual' and politically incorrect. Decades of critical intersectional work by radical feminists and environmental theorists is consigned to the theoretical garbage bin as infantile Goddess worship with falsely universalizing tendencies.[23]

The 'essentialist' witch-hunt by transfemme advocates extends to any cultural feminist who makes a connection between female embodiment and the honoring of women in any past or present culture. The charge is that honoring the female body limits human females to biology and prevents them from being active agents of culture.[24] This ignores the fact that Indigenous egg-producers are crucial bearers of traditional knowledge and the concept of 'sacred female' is an essential aspect of their self-image and culture.[25]

Trans Critical is Intersectional

Social movements are not perfect and constructive criticism is vital to addressing the concerns of multiple stakeholders. There are major contradictions in the racialized and class-entwined transfemme movement, and these must be managed so that the struggle can become more inclusive and reflective of the overall trans population.

De-platforming feminist scholars at women's conferences is not revolutionary, just like having an all transfemme panel to discuss feminist issues is not uber radical. Egg-producing scholars meeting to analyze sexual caste is a right, and disparaging born-females for not being trans is separatist and anti-women.

On the racialized nature of the transfemme framing, one African American feminist comments, "liberals apply a sentence of social and political death (and ignore actual death threats) against those who fail to "protect" transfemmes, and black transfemmes in particular. Indeed, their rhetorical vitriol has started to assume the same kind of shrill irrational rage that conservative white men reserve for the protection of white women."[26]

The gender critical writer points out that by reproducing negative stereotypes about black women, the glorification of the black transfemme plays a role "in the greater goal of propping up white supremacy and degrading black women." The author continues, "By applying rhetorics of sympathy to black transfemmes white people are able to engage in a kind of representational "trickle down" sympathy wherein they maintain the pretense that caring about the lives of 0.5 percent of the population is equivalent to caring about all black people by extension."[27]

The liberal perspective allows whites to engage in a game of moral "one upmanship," faux paternalism, and blackface by expending political capital on issues significant to white men. Simultaneously, the transfemme narrative maintains the historical trend of men seeking to define womanhood for women, and silencing women who do so.

The essentialist litmus test is applied to feminist science and studies on sex differences as well.[28] Feminist evolutionary biologists working to correct the historical misrepresentation of females are accused by academic feminists of erasing female agency by reducing women to bodies and brains.[29] But despite views to the contrary, females are real and they were and are active agents in the evolutionary process.[30]

The singular focus of radical identity feminists on sexual performance is as essentialist and fatalistic as patriarchal capitalism since it fails to address climate change, nature, and animals. This study rejects the dogmatic, post-modernist emphasis on sexual fluidly, as well as patriarchal gender dualism and separation of culture from nature.[31]

The occurrence of inter-sex biology and homosexuality are relatively rare,[32] and genetic exceptions should not be conflated with the lived experience of half of the World's human population under sexual caste. Acknowledging differences and being supportive of the trans movement are not mutually exclusive.

While androgynous identities are part of the solution, there are critical biological differences, and social consequences, in being born female. Notably, the commonality of sex-based oppression opens up the possibility of mutual resistance, but this potent threat to the misogynist status quo is being effectively countered by queer advocates and trans theory.

Strategic Essentialism

Binary, trans, queer, or spectrum, gender is a hierarchy. Under patriarchy, all 'females' are socially constructed and treated as an inferior caste regardless of class, race, religion, language, education, and so on. It is therefore strategic for feminists to explore how the category 'female' is theorized and maintained. Moreover, a critical analysis of 'womanhood' is indispensable to organizing 'females' as a class, and in imagining their liberation.

Although sexual, racial, and other identities are fluid, activists have found that utilizing a static identity is an effective way for subjugated individuals and communities to organize and resist their oppression. Political identities, for example, "Black Lives Matter," are essentialist in the sense that there is no universal conception of "blackness."[33] Nonetheless, the organizing principle of "blackness" can be used for tactical goals that are crucial for confronting immediate oppressions like everyday racism and institutionalized racial bias and injustice.

Racial, cultural, religious, and other identities are socially constructed and vary widely. In contrast, female identities are real, static, and rigidly enforced. The oppression of biological females is worldwide, while the subjugation of racial, cultural, and religious groups vary by location. Yet, born females are considered nonexistent and invalid as a category, while race, class, and religious groupings are characterized as real.

Analogous to 'Black Lives Matter,' a similar plan of action may be useful for women to organize and resist thousands of years of victimization under hegemonic toxic-masculinity. Even though there are variations in sexuality, and the experiences of each female is unique, a strategic 'female' essentialism may prove vital for their survival in the short-term.[34]

In many regards, phallic appropriation of domesticated female culture is mockery and theft, akin to 'blackface' and far from empowering.[35] Acting in an over-sexualized and hyper-feminine manner may be satisfying for some boys and men, but this behavior reinforces the reduction of females to bodily appearance.[36] This framing is also callous and insulting to women and girls as it assumes that, by identifying as something else, they can avoid oppression.

Claire Heuchan points out, "If trans womanhood is synonymous with womanhood, the hallmarks of women's oppression cease to be recognizable as women's experiences. If we cannot acknowledge the privileges those recognized and treated as male hold over their female counterparts, we cannot acknowledge the existence of patriarchy."

In a related manner, any inclusion of nonhuman animals or animal-based diet in feminism is characterized as divisive and essentialist. This censoring of discourse linking women to nonhuman animals/nature by academic feminists is untenable. It is comparable to considering feminist explorations of embodiment or emotions as compromised. Care and abuse of pets are clearly feminist issues with links to male harassment and domestic violence.[37]

Feminist Appropriations

One criticism of linking women to nature/animals is that in doing so, mainstream feminists appropriates Native and minority egg-producers' voices, and perpetuates colonial logic when engaging with women's relationships to land.[38] Non-native feminist analysis often minimizes the role of Indigenous environmental knowledge and their sound relationship with the Earth, viewed as female.[39]

Native and minority communities are disproportionately affected by environmental pollution with negative effects on ovary beings' health and reproduction.[40] And the ongoing phallic settler exploitation of Indigenous girls and women, including prostitution, rape, and murder, is due in part to dispossession of their land. As Katsi Cook argues, "women are the first environment."[41]

Mainstream feminists' focus on the neoliberal acquisition of rights and freedoms ignores Indigenous and minority women's land, property, health, racism, cultural oppressions, and so on.[42] Moreover, by locating feminist histories within legal reform, the chronicle of modern feminism excludes Indigenous women entirely.[43] They also fail to recognize that social justice issues are related to European men's brutal colonization of non-European women and nature.[44]

The imposition of European gender binaries and hierarchies brought patriarchy to Indigenous female-centered lands, and they need to be removed.[45] And since white women define normative womanhood in western nations, they openly or subconsciously reinforce white-supremacist systems of dominance by maintaining racial and gender hierarchies within settler nations.[46]

With a keen awareness of environmental racism, African-American ecofeminists seeks to recover and renew the strong historical connection of African women to the land, which is often broken by migration and urbanization. Their focus is a justice-oriented spirituality of creation.[47]

Remarking on the different views of eco-womanists, Shamara Riley writes, "There are several differences between ecofeminism and Afrocentric eco-womanism. While Afrocentric eco-womanism also articulates the links between male supremacy and environmental degradation, it lays far more stress on other distinctive features, such as race and class, that leave an impression markedly different from ecofeminists' theories."[48]

Justice for egg-producers should not stop at the species border. While minority ovary beings face multiple forms of oppression, aiding and abetting cyborgs' continued oppression of other-than-human animals does nothing to solve sex, race, class, health, environment, or any other problem. Rather than reinforcing machismo through carnism, re-discovering a plant-based diet can help to decolonize our emotions and minds from cyborgs' ecocidal consciousness.

Revolutionary Women

Girls and women are not, and were not, passive victims of patriarchy. In the US, for instance, there were three waves of feminism starting in the early 19th century. From the 1840s to 1920, American women fought hard for the right to vote as part of first wave feminism. Women's attempts to vote in 1870 were turned away, and the Supreme Court ruled against them in 1875.

In 1916, Alice Paul formed the groundbreaking National Women's Party. Activists from across the nation marched in Washington, DC, and over 200 were arrested while picketing the White House. Some women were beaten with clubs and thrown in prison. A few went on hunger strikes and were forced fed. On November 15, 1917, forty prison guards went on a rampage against 33 women, known as the "Night of Terror."

Long before first wave feminism got started, from the very emergence of patriarchy itself, girls and women have remained tirelessly resistant. Consequently, phallic domination is never complete. For instance, close to 3,000 BP, Queen Gwendolen gathered an army and fought her ex-husband in a civil war for the throne of Britain. She defeated him and became the monarch.[49] And in 1,639 BP, Queen Mavia led a rebellion against the Roman army and defeated them repeatedly. The Romans finally negotiated a truce on her conditions.[50]

Starting in the 16th century, phallic European colonizers with advance weapons laid waste to countless gynocentric language groups across the Globe, but women have courageously resisted this onslaught as well. For instance, in 1539, Gaitana led the indigenous people of northern Cauca, Colombia in armed resistance against the Spanish. From the onset of European invasion of the west, egg-producers led numerous struggles against colonization in the Caribbean, South, Central and North America.[51] females' frequent and distributed resistance points to the existence of gynocentric leadership at the time of European invasion 500 years ago. For centuries, African women likewise resisted European conquest and wars of enslavement.

In 1630, Queen Nzinga of Ndongo led a series of revolts against the Portuguese in Africa.[52] In 1716, Maria led a enslaved rebellion on Dutch Curaçao, and in 1720-1739, Granny Nanny, a spiritual leader of the Maroons of Jamaica, led enslaved rebels in the First Maroon War against the British. In 1760-1790, Rani Velu Nachiyar from Sivagangai, Tamil Nadu, was the first queen to fight against the British in India.[53]

On October 5, 1789, a young woman struck a marching drum and led the Women's March on Versailles, in a revolt against King Louis XVI of France. The women stormed the palace, signaling the start of the French Revolution. Egg-producers were integral to every revolutionary cause since, from the Paris Commune of 1871,[54] to the 1960s anti-colonial movements.

The long list of 19th and 20th century revolutionary women include Louise Michel,[55] Elisabeth Dmitrieff,[56] and Nathalie Le Mel[57] of the Paris Commune, and Nadezhda Krupskaya of the Russian revolution.[58] There was also Rosa Luxemburg of Germany's Spartacist uprising,[59] Petra Herrera of the Mexican revolution,[60] Constance Markievicz of the Irish revolution,[61] Nwanyeruwa in Nigeria's anti-colonial struggle,[62] Lakshmi Sahgal of India's anti-colonial movement,[63] the anti-Nazi Sophie Scholl,[64] Blanca Canales of Puerto Rico,[65] and Celia Sanchez of the Cuban revolution.[66]

Yet, after hundreds of years of active participation in the over-throw of economic elites across the Globe, women have little to show for it apart from rhetoric and token inclusion. All revolutionary movements, whether anarchist, socialist, communist, nationalist, or anti-colonial, have steadfastly maintained phallic supremacy and domination.[67]

Anarcho feminism, marxist feminism, and other revolutionary committees are just smokescreens. Men would lose too much if females actually gained freedom, so they choose instead to indulge in the quasi-religious hero worship of swaggering alpha male 'revolutionaries.' Women's liberation is not a priority under socialist or marxist activist frameworks. Rather, from top to bottom, sperm-producers use their revolutionary 'knowledge,' 'loyalty,' and 'authority' to gaslight and exploit girls and women in and outside of the movement.[68]

Women are tired of the status quo and are eager to join radical struggles for change. Sperm-producers know this and use every trick in the book to thwart egg-producers' well-meaning efforts. 'Radical' men have learned how to tap into women's dissatisfaction and use female energy to install themselves into power. And, as they in turn exploit the masses, 'revolutionary' men manufacture consent and hold on to leadership by preserving the sex and species hierarchy.[69]

Philosophically, radical feminism is related to marxism, in being materialist and relying on dialectics of class, which MacKinnon admits. Nevertheless, radical feminist theorists are consigned to an ideological ghetto of "women's issues," and their deliberations are considered irrelevant to the human condition.

In the 19th and 20th century, Marx, Engles and other leftist scholars embraced gynocentric prehistory and grounded their critique of private property on the pre-capitalist, mothers' gift-economy. But revolutionary theorists have ignored the underlying gynecological principles of female-centered organization and their utmost respect for other-than-human animals and nature.

Consequently, socialist and capitalist systems are ideologically the same in regards to their rejection of the sacredness of Earth. In their relationship to the environment, anarchists and libertarians are similarly anthropogenic, with views based on male transcendence over nature. The untamed commons is perceived by all factions along the political divide as a free resource for unsustainable 'human' development.

Admitting sex and ecology into their 'historical' and 'scientific' analysis requires behavioral and dietary changes that revolutionary sperm-producers are reluctant to undertake, and so they indulge in cognitive dissonance. The only people who actually care about the subordinated status of egg-producers are female-centered women organizing without men to end our oppression.

Robotic 'Females'

How and where do girls and women 'fit in' to cyborgs' technological future? Should young-bearers embrace the cyborgs' robots and artificial enhancements or the Goddess? Will emerging media and information systems be a catalyst for female resistance and action, or be employed in the service of disinformation and distraction? While becoming more plastic and hybrid can lead to temporary power for some egg-producers, this comes at the expense for all since objectified female bodies serve to fortify beauty myths and gender dualism.

The use of social media and communication technology can help women organize for a better future, but it will take more than millions of "Likes" and "Re-tweets" to save females from runaway toxic-masculinity. Moreover, females stand to benefit little from enabling cyborgs' maniacal obsession with technological transcendence and leaving the Earth. Helping to establish phallic dominance in space and on other planets will not lead to female empowerment on Earth or anyplace else.

From sexy, life-like 'girlfriends,' to sex robots and realistic female orifices, the robotic female is the 'have to own' man-toy of the 21st century. Females are socialized to be tamed, organic servants, and their robotic counterparts merely replicate their subservient roles. Cyborgs' robotic 'females' may have limited domestic and medical uses, but their hyper-sexualized appearance promotes the objectification of organic, female animals. Jane Caputi argues that the cyborg's mechanical bride, or fembot, suggests not the future for females, but rather futurelessness and Earthly sterility.

Mary Daly warns as well, "The march of mechanical masculinist progress is toward the elimination of female Self-centering reality. Whether or not our re-placements are materially "hollow" or "solid" is not the ultimate issue. These are simply different ways of describing the absence of Female Depth, of spirit, in feminine nonwomen conceived by male mothers."[70]

The hollowing out and elimination of women and girls has been ongoing for thousands of years. Females living within male-centered space are socially conditioned into serving phallic-based interests and needs, and to become successful, women must function as patriarchal robots.

Mary Daly continues, "I will call this hollow/solid depthless state robotitude. It is comparable to a term coined by Francoise d'Eaubonne to describe the state of servitude of women in a phallocratic world: "feminitude". Robotitude, however, stresses the reduction of life in the state of servitude to mechanical motion... Women are encouraged, that is, dis-couraged, to adapt to a maintenance level of cognition and behavior by all the myth-masters and enforcers."

Organic female robots are essential for the creation and maintenance of males, and a few of the most 'programmed' women can become 'powerful' tokens who are paraded to showcase cyborgs' 'equality.' This narrative ignores the reality that women who do not support men's ideologies are often punished, abused, and killed.[71]

But females have resisted and are resisting, as Mary Daly writes, "Revolting Hags/Crones are repudiating robotitude, which is an imposed state of idiocy, a kind of cretinism... It also implies repudiating inclusion in the pseudogeneric "after all human" condition of cretinism. Re-considering is denying this false harmony, breaking its bonds, bounding into freedom."

Re-claiming Earth/Goddess

The vast majority of modern humans are religious ideologues who believe in a supreme phallic savior. Notwithstanding, academic feminists view Goddess theology and female-centered culture as irredeemably essentialist. Ironically, feminists who subscribe to abrahamic cults and are heavily immersed in patriarchal cultures are not similarly disparaged.

This so-called academic stance is biased, narrow-minded, and inhibits understanding of the lives of prehistoric and modern females. For instance, Robert Briffault's work on the Mother had some influence on the women's movement in the 1960s, but due to its essentialist 'flaw,' this research soon fell out of feminist favor.[72] Characterized as hokey navel-worship, Goddess theology is much more than simply using female pronouns for male deities.

This study explores dozens of Earth Goddesses and gynocentric cultures that existed prior to sky magic and phallic domination.[73] Patricia Monaghan covers over 1,000 Goddesses and heroines,[74] and there are more than 11,000 known Goddesses around the planet. In African cultures, the female essence of creation was highly revered and the first conception of the 'Creator' was a woman physically bringing life into the world. It is likely that early hominin groups worshiped a Goddess, and those who migrated out of Africa left with a female deity.

A Goddess is not merely conceived of as being immanent in the World. Rather, the whole of nature and the Earth are theologically conceived as the living body of the Goddess. This allows a pantheistic framework of belief, while putting nature and the cosmos firmly at the center.

Mary Daly writes, "Goddess is the deep Source of creating integrity and the Self-affirming be-ing of women." She expands further, "A number of feminists have referred to 'God' as 'she.' While all of this has a point, the analysis has to reach a deeper level. The most basic change has to take place in women - in our being and self-image."

According to Kate Rigby, "the Goddess is only a metaphor, personifying that animating and life-generating energy that flows through and interconnects all things. The symbolism of the Goddess returns an aura of the sacred to the world that in not only feminist but also ecological in orientation."[75]

At the core of the Goddess vision is the recognition of worldwide female sovereignty, powers, and collective interests. The Goddess economy centers on community service and the equitable distribution of goods and services. Goddess women show respect, balance, compassion, healing, and tolerance for nature and diversity. They believe in the equality of all creatures. And, they know that to fulfill their vision, the dissolution of males' hierarchical, oppositional orientation is paramount.[76]

Conclusion

The fifth and last chapter of Part V on cyborgs' current terror campaigns deconstructed theoretical misogyny in the erasure of biological females. What if men are unfit to rule and they understand this subconsciously? And, what if men grasp that women are better at decision-making and conflict resolution, but they are in denial? These subconscious feelings can lead to male psychosis, and maybe it does. Males' undeserved power may be a source of profound insecurity, and it does not erase their enormous jealously of female creativity.

Gynocentrism may be the only solution to males' repressed anxiety over reproductive irrelevance. Female-centered communities enable men to once again honor girls and women in terms of their relative importance to human survival. Similar to the other great apes, ecogynocentrism may serve to limit phallic competition and aggression against women, animals, and nature. This restraining is increasingly critical in a World with diminishing resources and prospects for survival.

On the positive side, women and children have always resisted the phallic horror show, from the very beginning of cyborgs' rule. There is strong feminist resistance to the reductionist framing of nature and females, and the final chapter discusses the relevance of ecofeminism to the current ecological crisis.

(Figure 28: Serra da Capivara Rok art in Piauí, Brazil c. 20,000 BP)

VI: RESISTANCE

28: Radical Ecofeminism

> I urge you to sin. But not against these itty-bitty religions, Christianity, Judaism, Islam, Hinduism, Buddhism - or their secular derivatives, Marxism, Maoism, Freudianism and Jungianism - which are all derivatives of the big religion of patriarchy. Sin against the infrastructure itself! - Mary Daly

ASIA's Journey 2121.28

Nearing the end of spring, it is 92°F (33°C) with 60 percent humidity on a cloudy day in the lush valley. The grass feels soft and fresh from an overnight drizzle. Zola gazes at thousands of women and children gathered in a wide meadow surrounded by hills and mountains.

There are no men or older boys at the assembly, and only a few dozen younger males in total. At the back of the grassland, on the left, there is a garden filled with fruit trees and rows of vegetables. On the other side, fields of grains, corn, and beans bask in the sun.

Zola beams as a group of females hold hands and dance joyfully to music played by women and children sitting in a circle. ASIA's girls are laughing, singing, and dancing with abandon, while their mothers swap gifts and stories with other young-bearers, and the crones catch up with old friends.

It all seems like a dream, and Zola takes a heavy breath in awe. The children were finally safe and this female separatist space feels like a temple to the Earth Goddess.

At evening time, ASIA's women and children gather for Cronetime. The crones give blessings for the next stage of their journey, then Zola takes the board.

"Dear Gaias," Zola swings her arms wide and rattles her beads. "May the Goddess in each one of us bless the Earth, ourselves, and each other." The women and girls bow to the ground, themselves, and their neighbors.

"In honoring the Earth Goddess, we are honoring the Earth," Zola continues. "In honoring the Earth, we honor females and ourselves." The women and children chant, 'Gaia, Gaia, Gaia.'

Zola points to her chest, "Each day, we must consciously create a space for the Earth Goddess to live in ourselves, in our hearts and minds. And daily, we much create a space for her in our communities."

"We will," Some of the females shout.

Zola shakes her beads. "The Earth Goddess is global warming and she has defeated man's mighty machines." Zola pauses for emphasis. "And, Gaia will finish all men soon if the pedophiles continue to suppress women and nature."

"We will not let that happen," One crone shouts as the women and children chant, "We are Gaia, we are one."

Introduction

Part VI is the last section with one chapter that centers on feminists' metaphysical resistance to phallic-centered rule and consciousness regarding Earth, nature, and animals. The male mind is always seeking, endlessly searching for more - more money, escape, enlightenment, and fulfillment of desire. Too busy for self-awareness, men are permanently 'out-to-lunch,' willfully denying that their mindlessness is wrecking the planet.

When you do look at reality with greed, what you capture is the sediment of your greed, not reality. Reality is a living thing that cannot be captured. And you cannot say it is always there. There is a path only to something which is stationary and static. To a living thing like the Earth, which has no resting place, there is no guide or path. Men only look at nature as a path to accumulation, and are blind to everything else the Earth has to offer present and future generations.

This chapter starts with a brief look at ecology and feminism, then presents an ecofeminist critique of conservation theories and underlying perspectives of the environmental movement. The chapter next examines some implications of revolutionary ecofeminism. Then, it considers ecofeminists' framing of nature, followed by their conceptualization of females.

After this, plant-based feminists are surveyed, followed by a short introduction to the life and work of 19th century suffragist, Charlotte Perkins Gilman. The chapter turns to explore gynocentric continuity in the present and concludes with a discussion of awareness and activism.

Ecology & Feminism

Examining environmental issues with a feminist lens enables us to see the intersection of male dominance, gender, race, economics, culture, and other vital concerns. Feminists argue that masculinity is conceived not simply as an attribute of each male, but rather as a diffuse worldview that is an integral aspect of phallic-centered institutions, power relations, and ideas.

Ecologists show that life is an interconnected web, in which the sustainability of the whole ecosystem requires balance among each of its constituent parts. In nature, diversity is necessary and enriching, and embracing this perspective allows differences to be valued, rather than treated as weaknesses.

Unlike the variedness and balance of nature, feminists show that human social relationships are unbalanced and hierarchical. Deviations from the phallic norm are treated as inferiorities, and girls and women are framed as permanent outsiders.

Combining the insights of ecology with feminist analyses, ecofeminist theorists explore the causes and effects of men's domination of nature and women. For instance, Marti Kheel's work is exemplary in deconstructing the ethics of environmentalism and phallic-centered conservationists, as discussed next.

Critique of Conservation

Most environmentalists proclaim their love of nature, but at the same time many romanticize hunting and consume the flesh of other-than-human animals. In her groundbreaking book, Nature Ethics, Marti Kheel examines masculinity, nature, and nonhuman animals in the writings of four pioneering environmental ethicists, Theodore Roosevelt, Aldo Leopold, Holmes Rolston III, and Warwick Fox.[1]

Marti Kheel explored how these naturalist crusaders held a masculinist, utilitarian view of nonhuman animals. For instance, all four conservationists directed their moral allegiance to abstract constructs, such as 'species,' the 'ecosystem,' or the 'transpersonal' self, but not to individual animals. Consequently, flesh eating is portrayed as analogous to natural predation, and for Rolston, the cow is "a meat factory pure and simple."

Kheel notes, "philosophers have tended to view other-than-human animals in instrumentalist terms, as 'stock' or 'resource' to be conserved for present 'value' and as an 'investment' for future generations."[2] The aim of conservation is to maintain hunting for cyborgs, and concern for the animals is limited to stabilizing their population.[3] Kheel writes that from this perspective, humans "duty to a species is more like being responsible to a cause than to a person. It is a commitment to an idea," that is, to a higher order pursuit lacking urgency and individuality.

The four men's environmental theories suffer from multiple inconsistencies, primarily due to their unexamined masculinisms, and lack of an embodied connection to nature. Consequently, their sweeping metaphysical schema contains no "ethic of care" for living, individual animals. But then, in Spinoza's words, that would be "mere womanish pity."

A desire for predation and drive to protect unrestrained animals were combined in the US conservation movement in the early 20th century. First generation environmental 'progressive,' Theodore Roosevelt, once a sickly child, realized his manhood through the hunt on his way to becoming the US president (1901 to 1909). He justified his carnist blood-lust as the modern way to curb men's primal aggressive drives.[4]

But there was a further rationalization, as Kheel adds, "Roosevelt's emphasis on the value of hunting as sport was also part of a larger military philosophy that endorsed warfare as a means for advancing American imperial designs." He fought in the Spanish-American War, and as President, Roosevelt enhanced the Monroe Doctrine and incited civil-war in Columbia to build the Panama Canal. Roosevelt's views reveal that the Neolithic linking of toxic-masculinity, war, and hunting continues in the minds of modern cyborgs.

Like Roosevelt, the Norwegian philosopher Arne Naess spent a lot of time outdoors and was a noted mountaineer. Naess introduced "deep ecology" as an antidote to existing formulations in environmental ethics, and to counter the shallowness of "policy environmentalism." For Naess, rules on nature's value were obsolete, and he thought the ethics of rationality should be replaced by "a new sensibility" in conservation.[5] All the same, as Kheel observes, the deep ecology notion of "biospheric egalitarianism" typically omits concern for the exploitation and suffering of particular animals.

Rolston III is a darwinian who writes about dominion and the ethical use of animals. In his view, humans are "higher" animals with duties to ecosystems and endangered species, not to each unique creature.[6] This instrumentalist mindset leads him to conclude, "A substantial number of endangered species have no resource value."[7]

Marti Kheel reveals that the typical masculinist obsession with hierarchy and supremacy over female nature is implicit in Rolston III's environmental ethics. There is a godlike transcendence of mind over matter, and fertile nature is celebrated as "mother and wife ...the bosom out of which we have come."[8] According to this cyborg logic, nature is already tamed and the entire Earth now serves as men's faithful mothers and wives.

Warwick Fox takes deep ecology to a more abstract plane with his notion of "transpersonal ecology."[9] This state of being implies "identification with all that exists," and eventually one that evolves into a "cosmological identity."[10] Still and all, the "expanded Self" of deep ecology males display the routine features of hegemonic masculinity. Also, Fox's grand ethic is detached from socio-political conditions of class, race, and sex domination.

Similar to Kheel, Val Plumwood criticizes both deep ecology and environmental philosophy for missing the ecofeminist critique that "anthropocentrism and androcentrism are linked." That is, human-centered and phallic-centered interests are integrally related. Plumwood concludes that "the effect of ecofeminism is not to absorb or sacrifice the critique of anthropocentrism, but to deepen and enrich it."[11]

Plumwood contends, "The failure to observe such connections is the result of an inadequate historical analysis and understanding of the way in which the inferiorization of both women and nature is grounded in rationalism, and the connections of both to the inferiorizing of the body, hierarchical concepts of labor, and disembedded and individualist accounts of the self."

Like other forms of masculinism, deep ecology subsumed female experience under its own. And, paradoxically, it is not interested in non-human sensibilities or the emotional lives of nonhuman animals.[12] The environmental field is caught in cognitive dissonance, akin to humans who share profound emotional lives with pets but remain blind to the suffering of other species. Ecofeminism is perhaps the only intersectional analysis that encapsulates care for individual pet and food animals, as well as for ecosystems and the Earth.

Revolutionary Ecofeminism

Revolutionary ecofeminism explores the interconnections of sex, class, race, culture, and other social issues with oppression of nonhuman animals and nature. Proponent do not view animals as a resource and so avoid conflict of interest with much of the agricultural industry. Revolutionary ecofeminists are plant-based theorists and activists working to restore sustainable communities and sacredness to all Earthlings. Advocates uncover the mutuality of oppressions under phallic-centered rule by asking rudimentary questions about patriarchal societies and masculine construction.

For example, why are human males so violent against female animals, including human females, physically and verbally?[13] By removing themselves from nature, cyborgs have intensified womb envy. Their lack of connection to nature's creative powers leads to feelings of inferiority and inadequacy that manifest in nihilistic violence.

In gender dualism, human females' reduction to 'animalized humans' rationalizes the elevation of men into 'humanized humans,' or cyborgs. The connection between the categories 'female' and 'nature,' and separation between phallic culture and feminized nature, have served to re-define the category 'male' into variations of toxic-masculinity or cyborg consciousness.

This new form of masculinity exist in fundamentally opposition to the constructed otherness of femininity and feminized nature. With boys and men spending more time behind electronic screens, they are less aware of the smells, sounds, and rhythms of nature's cycles. And when males do try to develop a relationship with nature, their focus is on demonstrating masculinity in the form of hunting, fishing, climbing, and so on. Cyborgs' relationship to nature is centered on domination and colonization.

While the important work of ecofeminists unveil how masculinity is related to nature, diversity, hierarchy, and transcendence, some theorists argue against prioritizing one form of oppression over another. Other ecofeminists focus on one domineering societal structure like racism, sexism, and classism, that plays a significant role in the health of the environment, and in who is most impacted by declining health.

Regardless of priority, ecofeminists are intersectional thinkers who connect social and environmental concerns and the oppression of nonhuman animals. Ecofeminists replace hierarchical dualisms with relationships modeled on biodiversity and the feminist emphasis on the strength of difference. Revolutionary ecofeminism raises the bar and enhances anti-capitalist research and environmental discussion with an analysis of gynecological, gift economies.

Radical ecofeminists insist that understanding the domination of females by men is critical to realizing and stopping the destruction of nature. While most do not embrace Goddess theology and iconography as symbols of female resistance, revolutionary ecofeminists share a vision of female-centered communities living in harmony with nature.

In contrast to embracing nature, some academic feminists are advocating females adopt patriarchal technology as a form of empowerment. Between the choice of cyborg and Goddess/nature, modern-day feminists are choosing the mechanical bride.[14] But since a major feminist concern is body sovereignty, women should question the transgression and reconstruction of human and nonhuman animals and natural boundaries.

Some bodily limits must be placed beyond phallic-centered maldevelopment, but who will intervene if not feminists and environmentalists? Human emotions are colonized by animal domestication, and care is generally perceived, and diminished, as a 'natural capacity' of females. Care for the environment and animals is consequently viewed as undeserving of reciprocity from the phallic state and economy.

Marti Kheel writes, "in the post-Enlightenment Western tradition, care has been relegated to the realm of personal relations, distinct from the 'more important' public sphere which is the province of moral theory." This justifies abandonment of ethics that affects animals and nature, as well as the gift economy and notions of equity, social responsibility, and care that impacts human societies.

For radical ecofeminists, how individual non-human animals are cared for and thought of affects how female human animals are treated. The oppression of females and other-than-human animals is a parallel cycle of objectification, fragmentation, and exploitation, with consumption representing the fulfillment of oppression and annihilation of will, subjectivity, and identity.

The oppression of female non-human animals in livestock production by patriarchal models of maldevelopment is related to the devaluing of all agents of reproduction - human female animals and the Earth itself. Cyborgs' gendered view of animals-as-capital, freely available for phallic-development and exploitation, extends their false sense of entitlement to land, water, the entire Earth, and whatever lies above and inside her.

By examining the sociopolitical implications of how nature gets to be defined and utilized, revolutionary ecofeminists show how human-nature relations are immersed in a pervasive sex-based dualism, class hierarchy, and racial and cultural oppressions. They also offer a sound examination of the political and exclusionary uses of ideas of 'human' in constructions of masculinity and rationality.

Ecofeminism and Women

Ecofeminism stands in stark contrast to liberal and equality feminism by presenting an ethical challenge in its re-evaluation of nature and nonhuman animals. Karen Warren writes, "What makes ecofeminism distinct is its insistence that nonhuman nature and naturism (domination of nature) are feminist issues. Ecofeminist philosophy extends familiar feminist critiques of social-isms of domination to nature."

Charlene Spretnak summarizes the ecofeminist ideological position as, "An ontology based on dynamic and admittedly partial knowledge as well as awe toward the complexity of embodied and embedded existence would contribute substantially to the profound social transformation that is needed."[15]

In the 1970s, several ecofeminist publications analyzed the woman/nature connection in light of the environmental crisis. These include Mary Daly's Gyn/Ecology (1978), Griffin's Woman and Nature (1978) and Carolyn Merchant's The Death of Nature (1980).[16] In her innovative book, New Woman/New Earth (1975), Rosemary Ruether contends that women must acknowledge and act together to end the domination of nature if they are to work toward their own liberation. She exhorts women and environmentalists to join forces to end patriarchal systems that privilege hierarchies, control, and unequal socio-economic relations.

Ruether writes, "Women must see that there can be no liberation for them and no solution to the ecological crisis within a society whose fundamental model of relationships continues to be one of domination. They must unite the demands of the women's movement with those of the ecological movement to envision a radical reshaping of the basic socioeconomic relations and the underlying values of this society."[17]

On the positive side, marxist, liberal, equality, and cultural feminists also draw attention to the dangers to human survival generated by the patriarchal model of hierarchical and imperialistic leadership, as well as its severance of feeling and action. All the same, like deep ecologists, proponents of the various versions of feminism and womanism continue to view nonhuman animals and nature from a utilitarian perspective.

Mainstream feminism fails to find common cause with colonized food animals, and domesticates remain outside of feminists' concern. The care for individual pet animals is compartmentalized and reasoned as being outside of the moral economy of other animals. But due to the environmental impact of factory farming on extinction and climate change, feminists no longer have the luxury of ignoring this issue.

Dorothy Dinnerstein hints to this when she writes, "the task of focusing human energy on protection of the lifeweb for whose fate we humans have by now, willy-nilly, made ourselves responsible - is a task, at this point, which rests largely in female hands. What happens next may well depend on us."[18]

Plant-based Feminists

Thousands of years after men's colonization of herbivores and other food animals, women across the World continue to eat predominately plant-based foods. For millennium, girls and women have followed the Pythagorean diet. In the 19th century, early vegetarian restaurants in Europe and North America served as popular meeting spaces for suffragettes and first wave feminists.

Several trailblazing feminists of the 19th and 20th centuries were vegetarians who linked nonhuman animal consumption to phallic dominance, aggression, and wars. And quite a few of these vegetarian women had rivalries with other feminists regarding, diet, animals, and the work to end the oppression of human egg-producers.

Asenath Nicholson (1792 to 1855) was a plant-based author and philanthropist who operated a vegan boarding house in New York City. Author, Louisa May Alcott (1832 to 1888) who wrote the classic novel, Little Women, was raised on a plant-based diet. Alcott was an abolitionist and feminist as well.

Caroline Earl White (1833 to 1916) founded the first animal shelter in the US, as well as the first anti-vivisection society. Charlotte Despard (1844 to 1939) labored for women's rights, workers' rights, animal rights, and peace, to the point of destitution at the time of her death. Despard's groundbreaking intersectional should have garnered more support from feminists and progressive groups, but sadly did not. Was Charlotte Despard ostracized like other women advocates across the decades who insisted that the plight of food animals is a feminist, class, race, and cultural issue?

Anna Kingsford (1846 to 1888) was an early proponent of vegetarianism in the animal welfare movement. Kingsford was a campaigner against vivisection and a powerful speaker for women's rights. In her 1892 publication, The Perfect Way in Diet, Kingsford strongly condemned the consumption of other-than-human animals.

Gertrude Colmore (1855 to 1926) was an influential feminist who wrote the famous book, Suffragette Sally in 1908. Colmore was an author of novels with strong nonhuman animal themes. Margaret Damer Dawson (1873 to 1920) was a long-time British campaigner for nonhuman animal welfare.

Lizzy Lind (1878 to 1963) was an outstanding feminist, peace activist, and animal advocate who became one of England's most prominent anti-vivisection activists. Elsie "Sally" Shrigley co-founded the Vegan Society in 1944 and is credited with establishing the modern plant-based movement.

Dr. Alvenia Fulton (1906 to 1999) was an advocate of raw foods, juices, and fasting as a means of natural healing and food justice. She was a pioneer in the health food industry and co-authored Vegetarianism: Fact or Myth. Other plant-based feminists include Coretta Scott King (1927 to 2006), Brigid Brophy (1929 to 1995), and Leah Leneman (1944 to 1999).

Ruth Harrison was an early investigator of factory farms, and her book, Animal Machines (1964), revealed the indignities and suffering inflicted on farm animals by industrialized agriculture in the UK.[19] Harrison's described the dreadful conditions on factory farms, including battery cages for hens, individual crates for veal calves, and tether stalls for sows, in which animals were reduced to the status of production units.[20] The public reaction to Ruth's book was so intense that the British government ordered an investigation, and drafted the UK's first farm animal welfare legislation in 1968.

Charlotte Perkins Gilman

Charlotte Perkins Gilman (1860 to 1935) was a prodigious American philosopher, artist, writer, lecturer, suffragist, and publisher. In her insightful book, The Man-Made World; or, Our Androcentric Culture (1911), she carefully analyzes patriarchy and its domestication of females.[21] In the beginning of human existence, Gilman contended, mothers were the center of society and women were the founders of industry.

But then men became dominant and established androcentric cultures.[22] Men's main traits, she claimed, are desire, combativeness, and self-assertion. She noted that the word 'effeminate' means too female, and is an expression of disapproval and contempt. However, there is no corresponding word to denote 'too masculine.'

In Concerning Children (1900) and other works, Gilman explored ideas about communal child rearing and education to free mothers from domestic servitude. She wrote extensively on reforming the patriarchal marriage and family,[23] and fictionalized many of her ideas in a feminist utopian novel, Herland (1915).[24] In this book, she introduces readers to a country of peaceful women who worked cooperatively for two thousand years. Herland was a society with only girl babies being born.

The women of Herland are all plant-based, and only keep cats. They had domesticates in the beginning, but as one resident informs three male visitors, "We do not want them anymore. They took up too much room - we need all our land to feed our people. It is such a little country, you know." In this passage, Gilman points to the inherent unsustainability of raising animals for food.

The narrative explores the inter-relationship of humans and food animals further as one of the visitors explain the milk industry to the women of Herland, "It took some time to make clear to those three sweet-faced women the process which robs the cow of her calf, and the calf of its true food; and the talk led us into a further discussion of the meat business. They heard it out, looking very white, and presently begged to be excused."

Gilman was equally critical of patriarchal theology and sky magic, and suggested that humans should embrace the Earth instead. She writes, "Eternity is not something that begins after you are dead. It is going on all the time. We are in it now." Gilman explained further, "To attain happiness in another world we need only to believe something, while to secure it in this world we must do something."

Greek Titaness: Gaia

Thousands of Goddesses from prehistory provide strong evidence of the existence of gynocentrism and female-centered cultures. Across the Globe, there were dozens of Mothers of creation, Goddesses of seasons, deities of fertility, protectors of animals, and providers of crops, Goddesses of justice, arbiters of equality, guardians of revolt, and Goddesses of retribution. These deities provide insight into prehistoric ecogynocentrism and the philosophy of female-centered communities.

One of the most iconic Goddess is Gaia, "land" or "earth", also spelled Gaea. Marija Gimbutas, Barbara Walker, and other scholars claim that Gaia as Mother Earth is a later form of a Great Mother venerated in Neolithic times. In Greek mythology, Goddess Gaia is the personification of the Earth and one of the primordial deities. She is the ancestral mother of all life, the primal Mother Earth Goddess. Oaths sworn in the name of Goddess Gaia were considered the most binding of all. She was also worshiped under the epithet "Anesidora", which means "giver of gifts."

Goddess Gaia was often shown as a matronly woman only half risen from the Earth, often in the act of handing a baby to Athena to foster. In older representations, she appears as a woman reclining upon the Earth. She was the original deity behind the Oracle at Delphi and passed her powers on to Themis. Apollo killed Gaia's child Python there and usurped female power at the Oracle of Delphi. Goddess Hera punished Apollo for this by making him a shepherd for nine years. The snake may have been a metaphor for nature and it is interesting that serving as an animal domesticator was viewed as a punishment.

With the help of Gaia's advice, Zeus defeated the Titans. But afterwards, Gaia bore the youngest of her sons Typhon, the most deadly creature in Greek mythology who challenged the authority of Zeus. It is interesting that a creature of nature rose to oppose the divine patriarch and symbol of cyborg's rule. Men can shelter themselves but they cannot avoid the devestating effects of abrupt climate change. Gaia and her powerful children such as hurricanes and typhoons will eventually demolish cyborgs' hubris and civilizations.

Gynocentric Continuity

There are no 'men' in this World. The category 'man' belonged to the Stone Age and phallic humans in the present are fundamentally different from their predecessors. The Neolithic construction of masculinity as a cyborg lording over nonhuman animals is the root cause of climate change. And, the planetary crisis will not be solved until and unless maleness is redefined and masculine supremacy over femininity and nature is eliminated.

To this end, the Earth Goddess may serve as a helpful symbol for envisioning a more eco-friendly, female-centered future, as in the gynecological past. Remarkably, despite thousands of years of cyborg oppression, countless examples of gynocentric continuity remain across the World, from female embodiment and matrilocal practices to female-centered myths, storytelling, song, and dance. Though generally debased and hidden, the cultural signs and performance of members of the young bearing sex are powerful forms of resistance.

There are millions of people in Asia and the Pacific whose primary deity is a Goddess, from Durga and Lakshmi to Guanyin and Magu. Shakti, the personification of divine female creative power in South Asia, is increasingly popular among women in the west, as is Gaia, and other Earth Goddesses. Wicca, or the Goddess movement, is one of the fastest-growing religions in the US and Europe. From a handful of women in the 1950s, there are well over 200,000 female adherents Worldwide.[25]

There are hundreds of books on the Goddess movement, awakening the inner Goddess, and on being a yogini, or exercise Goddess. There is a Goddess periodical targeted to girls, ages 8 - 12, titled Goddess Girls. The 18 books in the series follows four best friends, Athena, Persephone, Aphrodite, and Artemis as they negotiate the ins and outs of Mount Olympus Academy. In addition, Goddesses are frequently depicted in anime and Asian media.

Across the Globe, there are assorted versions of the ancient myth of Cinderella, who transforms herself from a persecuted girl, consigned to the ashes, into a radiant Queen. This story promises the coming restoration of the oppressed to a place of honor, and the recognition of divinity in the commonplace.

Importantly, Cinderella's solace and savior come not from the patriarchal prince focused on female objectification, but from her fairy Godmother, or the Earth Goddess herself. This myth is a compelling example of the survival of the gynocentric oral tradition and women's 10,000-years longing for liberation from cyborgs' class and sex-based subjugation.

Analysis to Praxis

From Egypt 2,000 years ago, to Easter Island 500 years ago, rapid habitat destruction and civilization crash have been a common thread of phallic hegemony, cyborg consciousness, and patriarchal models of maldevelopment. The current wars in the Middle East and elsewhere, are in part due to land, water, and resource conflicts related to farming animals and pollution of the Earth for fossil fuels.

Despite profound industrial and technological changes, human diet remains based on farmed animals and agriculture, which are both climate dependent. The climate and environment can change abruptly, with grave consequences for human population, settlements, and activity. Humans exist on the tipping point of an ecological abyss and eating lower on the food chain is an effective and immediate way to back off from the edge.

Restoring female power and respecting nature and other-than-human animals are essential if we are to survive and adapt to abrupt climate change that is already occurring. Maybe, going beyond mere existence, humans can thrive and flourish once again as part of diverse female-centered cultures, honoring the Earth as the Mother Goddess.

Given the stupendous levels of cyborg aggression against the Earth and the incredible momentum of patriarchal programming, the task of gynocentric restoration is arduous to near impossible. There are few choices available besides resistance and accommodation to cyborg oppression and ecocide. If humans are to survive, we must all resist the cyborg genocidal mindset and the responsibility for liberation lies within each woman and man.

Human sperm producers are extremely reluctant to change a system that benefits them, so women's role in nurturing social transformation is critical. As the noted African environmentalist Wangari Maathai said, "Things will not just happen...Women must do something."[26]

If women collectively stopped supporting male ideologies and development, and only worked on female empowerment instead, the patriarchy would shrink overnight and go extinct soon after. Patriarchal greed, patriotism, cultures, religions, and so on, are highly dependent on female paid and unpaid labor. There are severe risks for resistance, though, and effective action will have to be collective and include safe spaces.

On the positive side, many females are aware of their oppression and urgently want the patriarchy to be transformed. The challenge is encouraging women and men to move from beyond analysis to practice and to live a life of liberation.[27]

Liberation starts with self-love, and being integral and wholesome since self-care is reflected in how we care for others. Being integral involves nurturing the physical, emotional, intellectual, spiritual, and other aspects of ourselves through creativity, writing, art, music, dance, and other activities. It implies having trust in ourselves and our labor.

Becoming socially conscious implies having a strong sense of community, that is, care and concern for others, and the Earth. It means reaching out from personal attention into the collective unconscious, and re-emergence into women's circles.

Activists often work in isolation and lack of community support. Also, neoliberal capitalism reinforces a profound sense of narcissism and alienation. Being social is part of the decolonization process, and it requires respecting the sovereignty of others and encouraging diversity.

Living and teaching freedom from cyborg consciousness requires the creation of more horizontal relationships, and providing space for individuals to grow as communal and political beings. Liberation calls for the collective construction of knowledge, and safe spaces where individual females can thrive and grow as communal and political beings.

Resistance implies decolonization from many forms of patriarchal ideologies, including sex, culture, identity, spiritual and emotional colonization. Deconstructing phallic ideologies also require a constant questioning of cyborgs' objectification of human females, nature and other-than-human animals.

Each human and other-than-human animal has a right to exist, to freedom, to the power to experience themselves as their being. Each Earthling has a right to dislike oppression, to resist cyborgs' rules and limitations, and to work on alternatives ways of being. Each nonhuman and human animal has a right to nurture themselves, and to nurture others.

Freedom from cyborg thinking involves understanding who we are as individuals and social beings, and voicing our feelings and those of others, nonhuman and human. It implies having a profound reverence for the Earth and her Earthlings, who may be referred to as Gaia. To live the life of liberation requires embracing the equality of creatures near and far, based on mutual threatened extinction.

Life is not limited to a patriarchal zero-sum game. We can act in the present to save ourselves and other Earthlings. In choosing the Goddess over the cyborg, we choose life over desire and death. Becoming the Goddess inside and making a conscious effort to embrace the sacredness of all life ends the reign the cyborgs inside and outside of our lives. May Gaia be with us all, now and forever. All praises be to girls and women, and to the Earth Goddess, our Mother.

1   M Seenarine. 2016. *Meat Climate Change: The 2ⁿᵈ Leading Cause of Global Warming*. Xpyr Press.
2   M Seenarine. 2004. *Education and Empowerment Among Dalit (Untouchable) Women in India: Voices from the Subaltern*. Mellen Press.
3   This demonstrates how mainstream academia functions to simultaneously minimize and marginalize radical feminist and minority discourse, while accommodating and co-opting other theoretical frameworks deemed less threatening.
4   Mies noted the importance of nonhuman nature to class analysis, yet this is entirely absent in intersectional discourse. In an era of abrupt climate change and biodiversity loss, animals should be part of intersectional inquiry, but they are not. Rather than widening the frame of reference, in effect, inter-sectionality is narrowing our analytical lens to cultural and sexual identity.
5   The author was intensely moved by Katharine Burdekin's *Swastika Night* (1937) and profoundly inspired by her feminist utopias. Yet, much of Burdekin's writings were done under a male pseudonym, and her forward-looking novels are little-known.
6   Monica Sjöö and Barbara Mor. 1987. *The Great Cosmic Mother: Rediscovering the Religion of the Earth*. HarperOne; 2nd edition.
7   Sonia Johnson. 1991. *The Ship That Sailed into the Living Room: Sex and Intimacy Reconsidered*. Wildfire books.
8   Monique Wittig. 2007. *Les Guerilleres*. U of Illinois Press; 1st edition. Translated by D Le Vay.
9   Mary Daly. 1993. *Beyond God the Father: Toward a Philosophy of Women's Liberation*. Beacon

1: Reclaiming the Goddess

1   UNODC. 2004. "Global Study on Homicide 2013." *UN Office on Drugs and Crime*. March.
2   Staff. "Domestic violence kills five women every hour." *Action Aid*, March 7.
3   In addition to recurring behavioral differences there are profound sex-based differences in psyche. In addition, there is an emotional selection process that serves as a complement to sexual selection or better as its socio-cultural expansion.
4   A patriarchy is the arrangement of society and governance under the control of men.
5   Marti Kheel. 2010. Personal Interview. April 15.
6   Lerner, Gerda. 1986. *The Creation of Patriarchy*, Volume 1. Oxford UP.
7   Jeffreys, Sheila. 2003. *Unpacking Queer Politics: A Lesbian Feminist Perspective*. Polity.
8   T Malthus. 1798. *An Essay on the Principle of Population*. London.
9   Underlying many of these common scientific arguments are the four Ns of carnism, the belief that eating the flesh of nonhuman animals is nice, natural, normal, and necessary.
10 J Speth. 2010. *The Paleoanthropology & Archaeology of Big-Game Hunting*. Springer.
11 J Diamond. 1999. *Guns, Germs, and Steel*. WW Norton
12 Men had no permanent home or property in pre-historic gynocentric groups. Following gynecological laws and sanctions, females in maternal clans controlled the land, which they maintained to forage, and to harvest seeds and cereals. As intensive cultivation developed, females still held ownership of land. So using enslaved animals as exclusive male property was far more influential for men than agriculture. The transition away from gatherer-hunter existence also prompted men to enslave food animals for labor and carcass consumption.
13 Barbara King. 2013. *How Animals Grieve*. Univ of Chicago Press.
14 Portable idols may have served as gynocentric ritual symbols, gynecological training aids, female dolls, and other purposes.
15 Marija Gimbutas. 1991. *The Civilization of the Goddess: The World of Old Europe*. Harper
16 J Vogt. 2009. "The Mosuo Matriarchy: 'Men Live Better Where Women Are In Charge' *Spiegel*, 5/28
17 Jill Hamilton. 2013. "Five Things We Know About Societies Run By Women." *Dame Magazine*, 5/5
18 Madeline Fernandez. 2006. "Cultural Beliefs and Domestic Violence." *Annals NY Academy of Sciences*, 1087:1 250-60
19 In contemporary society, a Goddess is a term used mainly to refer to an objectified female with exceptional 'beauty.'
20 DJ McConnell. 2003. *The Forest Farms of Kandy*. Ashgate.
21 Lorna Marshall. 1976. *The !Kung of Nyae Nyae*. Harvard University Press.
22 B Gammage. 2011. *The Biggest Estate on Earth: How Aborigines made Australia*. Allen & Unwin
23 By the Pre-Pottery Neolithic B (9,300 to 7,800 BP), well-established villages occupied the Fertile Crescent and beyond.
24 Studying female prehistory is viewed as an unworthy exercise in romanticizing the past, and part of neo-paganism. It is assumed that female-centered societies never existed and cannot exist. This denial of female prehistory rationalizes male-dominance and rule as natural and inevitable.
25 M Monroe. 2016. "Fire-Stick Farmers." Accessed 7/20 austhrutime.com
26 D Ward. 2010. *People, fire, forest and water in Wungong: the landscape ecology of a West Australian water catchment*. Ph.D thesis, Curtin Univ of Technology. June.
27 Riane Eisler. 1995. *Sacred Pleasure: Sex, Myth, & the Politics of the Body*. Harper.
28 Vandana Shiva. 1989. "Development, Ecology and Women" in Judith Plant, ed., *Healing the Wounds: The Promise of Ecofeminism*. New Society Pub.
29 R Monastersky. 2014. "Biodiversity: Life - a status report." *Nature*, Dec. 10.
30 Laura Hood. 2010. "Biodiversity Facts and Figures." *Scidev.net*. August 10.
31 WWF. 2014. "Living Planet Report: Species and Spaces, people and places." *World Wildlife Fund*.
32 WRI. 2014. "Earth Trends." *World Resources Institute*.

2: Subjects to Objects

1   This dated term uses the word fair in the sense of 'physically attractive,' and because it refers to a woman in terms of her appearance, it is demeaning.

2   Goddess beliefs were part of gynecological land management practices that contributed to the long-term survival of the species. The contrasting notions of power and transcendence over nature and nonhuman animals are fundamental aspects of patriarchal thought, which are unsustainable and self-destructive as the climate crisis demonstrates.

3   Chris Knight. 2008. "Early Human Kinship Was Matrilineal." In N. J. Allen, et al, eds., *Early Human Kinship.* Oxford: Blackwell, pp. 61-82.

4   Staff. 2016. "Found: grave of Siberian noblewoman up to 4,500 years old." *Siberian Times* Aug 19

5   S Bourget & K Jones. 2009. *The Art and Archaeology of the Moche: An Ancient Andean Society of the Peruvian North Coast.* U of Texas Press

6   Liz Mineo. 2016. "Where women once ruled." *Harvard Gazette*, July 19.

7   Melinda Zeder 2008. "Domestication & early agriculture in the Mediterranean Basin: Origins, diffusion, & impact." *PNAS* 105(33):11597-604.

8   A flower that lacks stamens is pistillate, or female, while one that lacks pistils is said to be staminate, or male.

9   Edith Lederer. 2017. "Women's Rights Are Under Attack Worldwide, Warns UN Chief." *AP*, Mar 13

10 Martha C Nussbaum. 1985. "Objectification." *Philosophy & Public Affairs* 24 (4): 279-83.

11 Silencing is a major aspect of female powerlessness. Women's autonomous voices must be included in progressive and queer discourses, and their critiques and dissent must be completely respected, especially regarding female issues.

12 Cara Sheffler. 2017. "The 'Fearless Girl' statue sums up what's wrong with feminism today." *The Guardian*, Mar 14

13 Females and males may act differently under matrifocal, matrilocal, and/or matrilineal structures.

14 'Speciesism' is the idea that being human is a good enough reason for human animals to have greater moral rights than non-human animals. It is a prejudice or bias in favor of the interests of members of one's own species and against those of members of other species.

15 Donna J Haraway. 2007. *When Species Meet.* Univ Of Minnesota Press.

16 John Stoltenberg. 1998. *The End of Manhood: A Book for Men of Conscience.* Replica Books.

17 It is significant that the best outcome for cyborg economies is a still referred to as a 'bull' market.

3: Hominid

1   Parthenogenesis is particularly common among arthropods and can also be found in some species of fish, amphibians, birds, and reptiles, but not in mammals.

2   The 1,000-year-long Copper Age is also known as the Chalcolithic.

3   Sonia Harmand et al. 2015. "3.3-million-year-old stone tools from Lomekwi 3, West Turkana, Kenya." *Nature* 521, 310-315 (21 May)

4   Most primates have opposable thumbs and some have prehensile tails. Many species are sexually dimorphic. Primates have slower rates of development than other similarly sized mammals and reach maturity later, but have longer lifespans. Most primates live in tropical or subtropical regions of the Americas, Africa and Asia. They range in size from the mouse lemur, which weighs only 30 g (1 oz), to the eastern gorilla, weighing over 200 kg (440 lb).

5   K Strier. 2007. *Primate Behavioral Ecology* (3rd ed.). Allyn & Bacon.

6   Richard Wrangham. 2007. "Chapter 12: The Cooking Enigma". In C Pasternak. *What Makes Us Human?* Oxford: Oneworld Press

7   Angiosperms became widespread by 120 million BP, and replaced conifers as the dominant trees during 100 to 60 million BP.

8   JE Hawes & CA Peres. 2014. "Ecological correlates of trophic status and frugivory in neotropical primates." *Oikos*, 123(3): 365-77.

9   A Hill & S Ward. 1988. "Origin of the Hominidae." *Yearbook of Physical Anthro* 31 (59): 49-83.

10 EA Fox. 2002. "Female tactics to reduce sexual harassment in the Sumatran orangutan (Pongo pygmaeus abelii)". *Behav Ecol Sociobiol* 52 (2): 93-101.

11 Dawn Prince-Hughes. 1987. *Songs of the Gorilla Nation.* Harmony. p. 66.

12 EJ Stokes et al. 2003. "Female dispersal and reproductive success in wild western lowland gorillas."*Behav Ecol Sociobiol* 54 (4): 329-39.

13 J Rothman et al. 2011. "Nutritional geometry: gorillas prioritize non-protein energy while consuming surplus protein." *Biology Letters*, 7(6):847-9. Dec 23

14 R Reiner et al. 2014. "Fatty acids in mountain gorilla diets: Implications for primate nutrition and health." *Am. J. Primatol.,* 76(3), 281-8

15 J Yamagiwa et al. 1994. "Seasonal change in the composition of the diet of eastern lowland gorillas". *Primates* 35: 1.

16 Genetically, humans and chimpanzees are more closely related than a horse and donkey, a cat and lion, or a dog and fox.

17 The common chimpanzee (P. troglodytes) live north of the Congo River and the bonobo (P. paniscus) live south.

18 CB Stanford. 1998. "The Social Behavior of Chimpanzees & Bonobos" *Cur Anthro* 39:4 399-420

19 Jane Goodall. 2007. "Chimp Behavior." Jane Goodall Institute.

20 B Carlson et al. 2013. "Diurnal variation in nutrients and chimpanzee foraging behavior." *American Journal of Primatology,* 75(4), 342-9.

21 To 'ape' someone is to copy them. This points to how similar apes are to humans

22 N Tokuyama & T Furuichi. 2016. "Do friends help each other? Patterns of female coalition formation in wild bonobos at Wamba." *Animal Behavior,* 119:27-35 Sep

23 F de Waal & F Lanting. 1997. *Bonobo: The Forgotten Ape.* U of California P.

24 Martin Surbeck et al. 2010. "Mothers matter! Maternal support, dominance status and mating success in male bonobos (Pan paniscus)." *Proceedings of the Royal Society B,* Sep 1.

25 Orcas, hyneas and other creatures also share strong mother-son bonds.

26 S Block. 2014. *The Bonobo Way: The Evolution of Peace Through Pleasure.* Gardner & Daugh

27 F de Waal. 1995. "Bonobo Sex and Society." *Scientific Am* 272 (3): 58-64. Mar

28 JP Balcombe. 2011. *The Exultant Ark: A Pictorial Tour of Animal Pleasure.* UC Press. p. 88

4: Hominin

1   Homo sapiens the only hominin species left and over a relatively short span of 20,000 years, modern humans pushed the Neanderthals and other existing hominids to extinction.

2   R Crompton et al. 2010. "Arboreality, terrestriality & bipedalism." *Phil. Trans. RSB* 365, 3301-14.

3   J Gowlett. 2016. "The discovery of fire by humans." *Phil. Trans. R. Soc. B* 371: 20150164.

4   T White et al. 2015. "Neither chimpanzee nor human, Ardipithecus reveals the surprising ancestry of both." *PNAS,* 112, 4877-84.

5   Staff. 2012. "Australopithecus sediba had plant foods on the menu." *Max-Planck-Gesellschaft,* Jun 27.

6   Paleoanthropologist Lee Berger states, "The find is unprecedented in the human record outside of fossils just a few thousand years old. It's the first truly direct evidence of what our early ancestors put in their mouths and chewed - what they ate."

7   The afarensis genus evolved in eastern Africa around four million BP and spread throughout the continent before dying out after three million BP.

8   Shannon McPherron et al. 2010. "Evidence for stone-tool-assisted consumption of animal tissues before 3.39 million years ago at Dikika, Ethiopia." *Nature,* 466, 857-60. Aug 12

9   Latin for wise man or knowing man

10 A Brumm et al. 2016. "Age and context of the oldest known hominin fossils from Flores." *Nature* 534 (7606): 249-253. Jun 8

11 P Brown et al. 2004. "A new small-bodied hominin from the Late Pleistocene of Flores, Indonesia." *Nature* 431 (7012): 1055-61. Oct 27

12 Insular dwarfism is the process of reduction in size of animals over a number of generations when their population's range is limited to a small environment, primarily islands.

13 LR Berger et al. 2015). "Homo naledi, a new species of the genus Homo from the Dinaledi Chamber, South Africa." *eLife* 4. Sep 10

14 E Yong. 2015. "6 Tiny Cavers, 15 Odd Skeletons, and 1 Amazing New Species of Ancient Human." *The Atlantic,* Sep 10.

15 JJ Hublin. 2009. "The origin of Neandertals." *PNAS* 106 (38): 16022-7.

16 CQ Choi. 2014. "Humans Did Not Wipe Out the Neanderthals." *Live Science.* Aug 20.

17 B Harder. 2002. "Did Humans and Neandertals Battle for Control of the Middle East?" *National Geographic News.* March 8.

18 Homo Neanderthals and Homo Sapiens shared many behavioral traits, including some tool making skills, sporadic burial of the dead, and control over fire. Both groups took care of their old and sick. Neanderthals made advanced tools, and lived in complex social groups. They built dwellings using animal bones.

19 J Jaubert et al. 2016. "Early Neanderthal Constructions deep in Bruniquel Cave in Southwestern France." *Nature* 534 (7605) Jun 2

20 J Rodríguez-Vidal. 2014. "A rock engraving made by Neanderthals in Gibraltar." *PNAS,* 16:111 (37) 13301-6. Sep

21 L Demay et al. 2012. "Mammoths used as food and building resources by Neanderthals," *Quaternary International.* 276-277: 212-226.

22 Crete has been an island for 5 million years and is 40 kilometers from its closest neighbor.

23 M Marshall. 2012. "Neanderthals were ancient mariners." *New Scientist.* 29 Feb

24 AG Henry et al. 2010. "Microfossils in calculus demonstrate consumption of plants and cooked foods in Neanderthal diets." *PNAS* 108 (2): 486-91.

25 Amina Khan. 2017. "Vegetarian Neanderthals?" *LA Times,* Mar 9.

26 J Diamond. 1992. *The Third Chimpanzee.* Harper Perennial.

27 SL Kuhn and Mary C Stiner. 2006. "What's a Mother to Do? The Division of Labor among Neandertals and Modern Humans in Eurasia." *Current Anthropology.* 47(6):953-81 Dec.

28 P Villa P & W Roebroeks. 2014. "Neandertal Demise: An Archaeological Analysis of the Modern Human Superiority Complex." *PLoS ONE* 9(4): e96424.

29 S Sankararaman et al. 2016. "The Combined Landscape of Denisovan and Neanderthal Ancestry in Present-Day Humans," *Current Biology,* 26, 1241-7.

30 E Callaway. 2013. "Hominin DNA baffles experts." *Nature* 504:16-7. 12/5.

31 J Krause et al. 2010. "The complete mitochondrial DNA genome of an unknown hominin from southern Siberia." *Nature* 464 (7290): 894-897.

32 Two fragments of the bracelet, with a width of 2.7cm and a thickness of 0.9 cm, were found. The estimated diameter is 7cm. Near one of the cracks is a drilled hole with a diameter of about 0.8 cm. The artist was skilled in techniques previously considered not characteristic for the Palaeolithic era, such as drilling with an implement, boring tool, grinding, and polishing.

33 The right-handed female bracelet is fragile and was probably not used as everyday jewelry. Given the complicated technology and 'imported' material, the piece probably belonged a high ranked person of the society and worn only on exceptional occasions. Perhaps, this fascinating bracelet was a heirloom worn by clan mothers, and its very existence suggests that Denisovans were gynocentric. Interestingly, if the Denisovans were more advanced than contemporary Sapiens, and this bracelet suggests they were, then their interbreeding may have helped modern humans to develop technology that resulted in the New Stone Age.

34 About 2 to 3.4 percent of the DNA of modern Melanesians and Aboriginal Australians derive from Denisovans, whereas only about 1.7 percent came from Neanderthals.

35 S Sankararaman et al. 2016. ibid.

36 C Choi. 2014. "Tibetans Thrive at High Altitudes Thanks to Neanderthal Cousin." *Live Science* 7/2

37 Archaeologists are presented with a historical record that contains mainly hunting artifacts. Perishable plant products and other critical aspects of the gathering economy are missing. This has led to a concentration of analysis on available animal data, which gives the mistaken impression that hunting was the most important means of getting food in the Paleolithic. Studies of modern gatherer-hunters show that male hunting is an inefficient method for providing food. Carcass from a killed nonhuman animal is available irregularly and infrequently, and cannot be stored adequately. Plus, there is considerably inefficiency in using protein as a source of calories.

38 H Bunn. 1981. "Archaeological evidence for meat-eating by Plio-Pleistocene hominids from Koobi Fora and Olduvai Gorge. *Nature*, 291, 574-577; M Sponheimer & J Lee-Thorp. 1999. "Isotopic evidence for the diet of an early hominid, Australopithecus africanus." *Science* 283, 368-70 Jan 15

39 A great deal of emphasis has been placed on the role of hunting in the Paleolithic and 'man the hunter' is assigned a crucial role in the formation of the human species. Hunting is assumed to have been in practice for 99 percent of human history, thereby providing the main sustenance and behavior pattern for the human species, and especially men. But rather than flesh playing a central role in Homo diets and cultures, animal protein could have merely served as a fallback food during hard times. Plus, chimpanzees are equally aggressive hunters, so claims of an evolutionary basis for human males' hyper-masculinity are dubious.

40 R Ardrey. 1976. *The Hunting Hypothesis*. Atheneum.

41 Evolutionary psychologists contend that hunting compelled male hominids to become more violent over time. And, since dominant men controlled the mating process through mate choice, violence was a critical characteristic that contributed to the species' evolutionary success.

42 Katherine Zink & D Lieberman. 2016. "Impact of meat and Lower Palaeolithic food processing techniques on chewing in humans." *Nature* 531, 500-3 Mar 24

43 Katharine Milton. 1999. "A hypothesis to explain the role of meat-eating in human evolution." *Evolutionary Anthropology*, 8:1, 11-21.

44 Speth's review of modern Bushman and Hadza research suggests that, in comparison to plant-based resources, African ruminants are an expensive, unreliable, and inadequate source of fat and do not warrant the time and effort required to make a successful kill. He concluded, "Their hunting activity appears to reflect the demands or expectations of their traditional gendered division of labor, not their nutritional needs."

45 M Domínguez-Rodrigo et al. 2010. "Configurational approach to identifying the earliest hominin butchers." *PNAS*, 107(49), 20929-34.

46 FW Marlowe. 2005. "Hunter-gatherers & human evolution." *Evolutionary Anthro* 14 (2): 15294

47 Chronic disorders associated with intake of high in fat and animal protein suggests that a diet composed of vegetables rich in fiber may represent a more "natural" condition of the species.

48 M McGee et al. 2015. "A pharyngeal jaw evolutionary innovation facilitated extinction in Lake Victoria cichlids." *Science*, 350:6264, 1077-9 Nov 27

49 J Gowlet. 2003. "What actually was the stone age diet?" *J of Environ. Medicine* 13:3 143-47. Sept

50 Geraldine Fahy et al. 2012. "Stable isotope evidence of meat eating and hunting specialization in adult male chimpanzees." *PNAS*, 110:15 5829-33 Apr 9

51 Barbara Ehrenreich. 1998. *Blood Rites: Origins & History of the Passions of War*. Holt.

52 M Teaford & Peter Ungar. 2000. "Diet and the evolution of the earliest human ancestors." *PNAS*, 97(25): 13506-11. Dec 5

5: Homo Sapiens

1 M Sponheimer et al. 2013. "Isotopic evidence of early hominin diets." *PNAS*, 110(26), 10513-8.

2 Primordial hominins were not more specialized than Homo to exploit hard foods and plant resources. (Z Alemseged & R Bobe. 2009. "Diet in early hominin species." In *The evolution of hominid diets*. J Hublin et al, eds. Springer, Dordrecht. 181-8.)

3 Jennifer Viegas. 2015. "Homo erectus ate crunchy food." *ABC Science*, Nov 22

4 N Conklin-Brittain et al 1997. "Frigivore Primate Diets in Kibale Forest." *Proc. Nutr. Soc.* 56: 322A.

5 Amanda Henry et al. 2012. "The diet of Australopithecus sediba." *Nature*, 487, 90-3. Jul 5

6 P Ungar. 2006. *Evolution of the Human Diet*. Oxford UP.

7 The argument for a plant-based hominin diet is supported by the fact that modern-day humans all consume fruits, grains, and other plant-based foods.

8 If ancient humans were not super carnivores competing against prides of big cats and wolf packs to prey on herds of herbivores, then hominin males may not have been hyper-masculine hunters, but more like opportunistic scavengers.

9 Indication for this include the co-occurrence of hominid fossils with root-eating rodents. (G Laden & R Wrangham. 2005. "The rise of the hominids as an adaptive shift in fallback foods: plant underground storage organs (USOs) and australopith origins." *J Hum Evol.* 49(4): 482-98 Oct)

10 Humans ten millinnia ago were eating more vegetables and grains than flesh.

11 Julie Dunne, et al. 2016. "Earliest direct evidence of plant processing in prehistoric Saharan pottery." *Nature, Plants* 3:16194 Dec

12 Staff. 2016. "Earliest Evidence Discovered of Plants Cooked in Ancient Pottery." *The Science Explorer,* U of Bristol, Dec 20.

13 The human brain is an incredibly expensive organ, taking up only about 2 percent of the body's mass yet using more than a fifth of the body's energy. Until about 2 million BP none of our ancestors had a brain larger than an ape's when compared to body size.

14 L Aiello. 1997. "Brains and guts in human evolution: The Expensive Tissue Hypothesis." *Brazilian Journal of Genetics*, 20(1) Mar

15 R Dunbar. 1998. "The social brain hypothesis." *Evol. Anthropol.* 6, 178-90

16 R Dunbar & S Shultz. 2007 "Evolution in the social brain." *Science* 317, 1344-7.

17 Karen Hardy et al. 2016. "Diet & environment 1.2 million years ago revealed through analysis of dental calculus from Europe's oldest hominin at Sima del Elefante, Spain." *Naturwissenschaften*, Online Dec 14

18 Staff. 2016. "Earliest Europeans Did Not Use Fire for Cooking." *Sci-News,* Dec 14

19 Suzana Herculano-Houzel. 2016. *The Human Advantage.* MIT Press.

20 Wu Liu et al. 2015. "The earliest unequivocally modern humans in southern China." *Nature* 526, 696-9 Oct 29

21 M Mondal et al. 2016. "Genomic analysis of Andamanese provides insights into ancient human migration into Asia and adaptation." *Nature Genetics*, Jul 26.

22 Ofer Bar-Yosef. 2007. "The Archaeological Framework of the Upper Paleolithic Revolution." *Diogenes* vol. 54 no. 2 3-18. May.

23 S Mcbrearty & A Brooks. 2000, "The revolution that wasn't: a new interpretation of the origin of modern human behavior." *J Hum Evol.* 39(5):453-63. Nov

24 Barbara Miller et al. 2006. *Anthropology*. Allyn and Bacon.

25 Marian Vanhaeren & F d'Errico. 2005. "Grave goods from the Saint-Germain-la-Rivière burial: Evidence for social inequality in the Upper Palaeolithic." *J of Anthro Archaeology*. 24:2 117-34 Jun

26 Dense concentrations of stone tools as early as 2.5 million BP show that hominins remained in one place long enough or frequently enough that lengthy stays were likely.

27 P Forster. 2004. "Ice Ages and the mitochondrial DNA chronology of human dispersals: a review." *Phil Trans of the Royal Soc*, Ser. B 359, 255-264

28 C Boehm. 1999. *Hierarchy in the Forest: the evolution of egalitarian behavior.* Harvard UP.

29 Narr. 2014. ibid

30 Sarah Hrdy 1999. *Mother Nature: A History of Mother, Infants, & Natural Selection.* Pantheon

31 PT Ellison. 2001. *On Fertile Ground.* Harvard UP.

32 Courtney Meehan & S Hawks. 2014. "Maternal & Allomaternal Responsiveness." In H Otto & H Keller., eds., *Different Faces of Attachment.* Cambridge UP.

33 KL Kramer. 2010. "Cooperative breeding and its significance to the demographic success of humans." *Annual Review of Anthropology,* 39. 417-36.

34 K Hill et al. 2011. "Co-residence Patterns in Hunter-Gatherer Societies Show Unique Human Social Structure." *Science*, 331. 1286-9.

35 Sarah Hrdy. 2011. *Mothers & Others: Evolutionary Origins of Mutual Understanding.* Belknap Press.

36 Knight 2008.

37 A Kruger & M Konner. 2010. "Who Responds to Crying?" *Human Nature,* 21. 309-29.

38 EZ Tronick et al. 1987. "Multiple Caretaking of Efe (Pygmy) Infants." *Amer. Anthro,* 89:96-106.

39 BS Hewlett & ME Lamb, eds., 2005. *Hunter-Gatherer Childhoods.* NJ: Aldine Transaction.

40 M Dyble et al. 2015. "Sex equality can explain the unique social structure of hunter-gatherer bands." *Science*, Vol. 348 no. 6236 pp. 796-8. 15 May.

41 C Power. 1998. "Old wives' tales: The gossip hypothesis and the reliability of cheap signals." In J Hurford, et al, eds, *Approaches to the Evolution of Language.* Cambridge UP.

42 Chris Knight. 1991. *Blood Relations: menstruation and the origins of culture.* Yale UP.

43 Genetic data on sub-Saharan African gatherer-'hunter' groups indicates a matrilocal residential bias. Females tended to reside close to their mothers following unions. And migration rates for females were lower than those for men. (Destro-Bisol, et al. 2004. "Variation of female and male lineages in sub-Saharan populations: the importance of sociocultural factors." *Molecular Biology and Evolution* 21(9): 1673-1682.)

44 Ewen Callaway. 2013. "Genetic Adam and Eve did not live too far apart in time." *Nature*, August 6.

45 A Fauci et al. 2008. *Harrison's Principles of Internal Medicine* (17th ed.). McGraw-Hill Medical.

46 S Krackow. 1995. "Potential mechanisms for sex ratio adjustment in mammals and birds." *Biological Reviews* 70 (2): 225-241.

47 Sex hormone levels in female and male fetuses and infants differ, and both androgen receptors and estrogen receptors are in the brain. Several sex-specific genes not dependent on sex steroids are expressed differently in male and female human brains. Structural sex differences in brains begin to be recognizable by two years of age. In adult women and men, they include size and shape of the corpus callosum, which are prominent in women, and the fasciculae connecting each hemisphere internally, which are bigger in men. Also, some forms of hypothalamic nuclei, and the gonadotropin feedback response to estradiol.

48 Suzanne Wymelenberg. 1990. *Science and Babies.* National Academy Press.

49 RE Jones & Kristin H Lopez. 2006. *Human Reproductive Biology*, Third Edition. Elsevier.

50 M Osborne. 2013. "Can Mammalian Mothers Control the Sex of their Offspring?" *KQED*. Jul 12

51 Valerie J Grant. 1996. "Sex determination and the maternal dominance hypothesis." *Human Reproduction* vol. 11 no.11 pp. 2371-2375.

6: Woman-the-Gatherer

1   M Seenarine. 2016. ibid

2   Gloria Bertonis & Carol Miranda. 2010. *Stone Age Divas*. Author House.

3   Similar to other primates and mammals, a hominin biological female can create life inside their body, give birth to other hominins, and produced milk to feed newborns. After weaning, hominin females were the primary providers of childcare, food, and security for offspring. And they accomplished these successfully with plant-based foraging strategies.

4   Frances Dahlberg. 1975. *Woman the Gatherer*. Yale Press.

5   T Wynn & F Coolidge. 2003. "The role of working memory in the evolution of managed foraging." *Before Farming*. 2:1-16.

6   Donna Hart & RW Sussman. 2005. *Man the Hunted*. Basic Books

7   Studies show that modern Bushmen hunt strenuously for a week, and rest the other three weeks. Hunting by men provides 20 percent of their nourishment, but women regularly produce 80 percent of the Bushmen's total food. So it is females' gathering of plant-based foods, not men's hunting, that sustains the group. These conclusions can then be transferred backward to the gathering-hunting societies of prehistoric cultures. Women in these ancient times must not have relied on the men's hunting or for food in general. (Dahlberg 1975 ibid)

8   The term "Paleolithic diet" is sometimes used with an implication that most humans shared a certain diet during the entire era. The relative proportions of plant and animal foods in the diets of Paleolithic people varied between regions, and depended on the habitats they lived in, the potential foods that were available, how valuable those various food items would have been in relation to their energy content, and how long it takes to handle a food item. Plus, the foods being consumed now, even in the case of fruits and vegetables, have been selected for desirable properties. The same fruits are different from what H. Sapiens ate. And, archaic humans had shorter life spans, so it's difficult to say if their diet was 'healthier.'

9   Dahlberg 1975 ibid.

10 Christina Warinner. 2013. "Debunking the paleo diet." *TEDxOU*. Feb 12.

11 RW Wrangham et al. 1999. "The Raw and the Stolen." *Current Anthropology* 40 (5): 567-94. Dec.

12 Karen Hardy et al. 2015. "The Importance of Dietary Carbohydrate in Human Evolution." *The Quarterly Review of Biology*, Vol. 90: 3 (Sept), pp. 251-268.

13 C Zimmer. 2014. "From Ancient DNA, a Clearer Picture of Europeans Today." *NYT*, Oct. 30.

14 Sarah A Tishkoff et al. 2007. "Convergent adaptation of human lactase persistence in Africa and Europe." *Nature Genetics* 39, 31 - 40.

15 J Mercader. 2009. "Mozambican Grass Seed Consumption During the Middle Stone Age." *Science* 18 Dec. Vol. 326 no. 5960 pp. 1680-83.

16 E Weiss et al. 2008. "Plant-food preparation area on an Upper Paleolithic brush hut floor at Ohalo II, Israel." *J Archaeol Sci* 35:2400-2414.

17 Dolores Piperno et al. 2004. "Processing of wild cereal grains in the Upper Palaeolithic revealed by starch grain analysis." *Nature* 430, 670-673 (5 August)

18 Efraim Lev et al. 2005. "Mousterian vegetal food in Kebara Cave, Mt. Carmel". *Journal of Archaeological Science* 32 (3): 475-484. March.

19 Anna Revedin et al. 2010. "Thirty thousand-year-old evidence of plant food processing". *Proc of the National Academy of Sci* (PNAS) 107 (44): 18815-9.

20 B Aranguren et al. 2007. "Grinding flour in Upper Paleolithic Europe." *Antiquity* 81:845-855.

21 Marta Lippi et al. 2015. "Multistep food plant processing at Grotta Paglicci c. 32,600 cal BP." *PNAS* Sep 8.

22 Anna Revedina et al. 2010. "Thirty thousand-year-old evidence of plant food processing." *PNAS* vol. 107 no. 44 Nov 2.

23 Meadows and forest edges were filled with many edible wild plants, such as lilies and onions. The bulbs of these plants are very nutritious, but their energy is locked up in a dense, indigestible carbohydrate called inulin. To make the bulbs digestible, paleo-females invented cooking methods to roast them for two days or longer.

24 By the Late Stone Age, many of Europe's native flora were gathered and used as part of the diet including Charlock (Field Mustard), Water Cress, Garlic Mustard, Chickweed, Wood Sorrel, Cow Parsley, Pignut, Wild Angelica, Wild Parsnip, Wild Carrot, Stinging Nettle, Water Mint, Wild Thyme, Wild Marjoram, Tansy, Chicory, Dandelion, Ramsons (Wild Garlic), Buttercups, Rose, Blackthorn, Elder, and many others.

25 Li Liu et al. 2013. "Paleolithic human exploitation of plant foods during the last glacial maximum in North China." *PNAS* vol. 110 no. 14 April 2.

26 T Vennum. 1988. *Wild Rice & the Ojibway People*. Minnesota Historical Soc. Press

27 A Moeller et al. 2016. "Social behavior shapes the chimpanzee pan-microbiome." *Sci Advances*, 2:1 Jan 15

28 Human and chimp microbiomes separated into different strains around 5.3 million BP, roughly when the split into different species occurred. The diversion from gorilla microbes was about 15.6 million BP, when the gorilla lineage split from other hominids.

29 A Moeller et al. 2014. "Rapid changes in the gut microbiome during human evolution." *PNAS*, 111(46):16431-5 Nov 18

30 Staff. 2014. "Compared with Apes, People's Gut Bacteria Lack Diversity." *U Texas News*, Nov 4

31 Rodney Dietert. 2016. *The Human Superorganism*. Dutton

32 E Mayer. 2016. *The Mind-Gut Connection.* Harper
33 I Watts. 2009. "Ochre in the Middle Stone Age of Southern Africa." *S. Afr. Arch Bul.* 57:175 1-14
34 Prehistoric painters used the pigments available in the vicinity. These pigments were the so-called earth pigments, (minerals limonite and hematite, red ochre, yellow ochre and umber), charcoal from the fire (carbon black), burnt bones (bone black) and white from grounded calcite.
35 Barbara Ehrenreich. 2006. *Dancing in the Streets: A History of Collective Joy.* Holt.
36 Laura Shannon. 2011. "Women's Ritual Dances," in J Leseho & S McMaster, eds., *Dancing on the Earth: Women's Stories of Healing Through Dance.* Findhorn Press.
37 Starhawk. 1988 *Truth or Dare: Encounters with Power, Authority & Mystery* Harper
38 Wendy Buonaventura. 1989. *Serpent of the Nile: Women & Dance in the Arab World.* Interlink Pub
39 Y Garfinkel. 2003. *Dancing at the Dawn Of Agriculture.* U of Texas Press
40 Riane Eisler. 1988. *The Chalice and The Blade: Our History, Our Future.* Harper

7: Female Fire-keeper

1   J Clark & J Harris. 1985. "Fire and its roles in early hominid lifeways." *Afr. Archaeol. Rev.* 3, 3- 27.
2   The second domestication of fire helped hominin females to maintain and extend their first domestication, that of males. Men became more useful to women, since slow-burning materials such as animal dung or plant material need to be selected and guarded, while other subsistence activities went on.
3   R Wrangham. 2007. *Catching Fire: How Cooking Made Us Human.* Basic Books
4   J Gowlett. 2016. "The discovery of fire by humans." *Phil. Trans. R. Soc. B* 371:20150164
5   Heather Pringle. 2012. "Quest for Fire Began Earlier Than Thought," *AAAS Science NOW,* Apr 2
6   R Rowlett. 2000. "Fire control by Homo erectus in East Africa & Asia." *Acta Anthro Sin* 19:198-208
7   Elizabeth Pollard. 2015. *Worlds Together, Worlds Apart.* Norton.
8   R Shimelmitz et al. 2014. "'Fire at will.'" *J. Hum. Evol.* 77, 196-203
9   J Gowlett & R Wrangham. 2013. "Earliest fire in Africa." *Azania Arch. Res. Africa* 48, 5-30.
10 N Rolland. 2004. "Was the emergence of home bases and domestic fire a punctuated event? A review of the Middle Pleistocene record in Eurasia." *Asian Persp.* 43, 248-80
11 R Dunbar & J Gowlett. 2014. "Fireside chat: the impact of fire on hominin socioecology." In *Lucy to language: the benchmark papers.* R Dunbar et al, eds. 277-96. Oxford UP.
12 Both female-centered fire and language were instrumental to the further evolution of gynocentric practices and cultures, including home-bases, shelters, community spaces, settlements, and eventually, so-called civilizations.
13 Hominins' development of fire was better facilitated by cooperative gynocentrism rather than by rugged, individual males in stiff competition. A campfire would have been relatively costly for an individual man to maintain and open to free riders.
14 A Barnard. 1992. *Hunters and herders of southern Africa.* Cambridge UP
15 T Sanders. 1999. "'Doing gender' in Africa," in *Those who play with fire.* Moore et al, eds. Athlone
16 T Twomey. 2014. "How domesticating fire facilitated the evolution of human cooperation." *Biol Philos,* 29: 89-99.
17 Intentional bush burning, or fire-stick farming, were essential components of hominins' home base and domestic fire system. For example, fire was used to clear tracks through the bush, for keeping poisonous snakes away, and protection from night predators.
18 P Spencer. 2014. *Youth and Experiences of Ageing among Maa.* W. de Gruyter.
19 Burning the landscape to hunt for prey was dangerous and restricted by its fuels. The frequency of this hunting technique depended on the capacity of plants to regrow. In perennial grasslands, a flaming drive to hunt animals could be used at most once a year. And a fire hunt was mostly wasteful since there was no way to preserve the flesh of vast numbers of animals killed.
20 Fire may have helped humans to become a collaborative species. Cooperation was adaptive because individuals that joined together were better at taking advantage of fire.
21 Robin Fox & Lionel Tiger. 1971. *The Imperial Animal.* Holt Rinehart.
22 J Koller et al. 2001. "High-tech in the Middle Palaeolithic." *Eur. J. Archaeol.* 4, 385-97.
23 Plants have indigestible components, such as raw cellulose and starch. Prior to the hominin use of fire, parts such as stems, mature leaves, enlarged roots, and tubers could not be easily ingested. Unless they were fire foraging, hominin consumption was limited to flora parts that were made of simpler sugars and carbohydrates such as seeds, flowers, and fleshy fruits.
24 T Hubbard. 2016. "Divergent Ah receptor ligand selectivity during hominin evolution." *Mol Biol Evol,* 33 (8) Aug 2
25 K Brown et al. 2009. "Fire As an Engineering Tool of Early Modern Humans" *Science,* 325:859-62
26 G Singh & E Geisler. 1985. "Late Cainozoic history of fire, lake levels and climate at Lake George, New South Wales, Australia." *Philosophical Transactions, Royal Society of London* 311: 379-447.
27 R Bird et al. 2008. "The "fire stick farming" hypothesis." *PNAS,* 105(39): 14796-801. Sep 30
28 P Roberts, et al. 2017. "The deep human prehistory of global tropical forests and its relevance for modern conservation." *Nature Plants* 3, Article number: 17093
29 A Newitz. 2017. "Evidence that ancient farms had very different origins than previously thought." *Arts Technica,* Aug 3.
30 S Mason. 2000. "Fire and Mesolithic subsistence-managing oaks for acorns in northwest Europe?" *Palaeogeography, Palaeoclimatology, Palaeoecology.* 164:139-150.
31 G Williams. 2002. "Aboriginal use of fire: are there any "natural" plant communities?" In C Kay & R Simmons, eds. *Wilderness & Political Ecology.* U. Utah P.

32 M Anderson. 1999. "The Fire, Pruning, and Coppice Management of Temperate Ecosystems for Basketry Material by California Indian Tribes." *Human Ecology*, 27:79-113.

33 C Levis, et al. 2017. "Persistent effects of pre-Columbian plant domestication on Amazonian forest composition." *Science*, Vol. 355, Issue 6328, pp. 925-31 03 Mar

34 R Jones. 1969. "Fire-stick farming." *Australian Natural History* 16:224-8.

35 The great corridors of Aboriginal transit were broad paths of fire that followed watercourses or connected waterholes. Burned paths made it much easier to travel great distances through the dense bush. Broadcast blazes made it easier to get to roots and tubers, and assisted in the harvest of seeds by exposing the cones and keeping woodlands open.

36 In the desert areas of Australia, a mosaic pattern of burning was practiced in winter, when only parts of an area were burnt. In spiny-leaved grasslands, all of the grass is burnt.

37 The value of the cooking to evolution is established since all modern humans need cooked food.

38 Cooking improved sapiens' health by releasing more nutrients from plants, removing toxins from vegetation, and by reducing the amount of energy required for chewing and digestion.

39 Ann Stahl. 1984. "Hominid Dietary Selection Before Fire." *Current Anthro* 25 (2): 151-68. April

40 Nancy Kraybill. 1977. "Pre-Agricultural Tools for the Preparation of Foods in the Old World." In CA Reed & W de Gruyter, eds., *Origins of Agriculture*. Mouton Publishers.

41 E Weiss et al. 2008. "Plant-food preparation area on an Upper Paleolithic brush hut floor at Ohalo II." *Journal of Archaeological Science*, 35 (8), 2400-2414.

42 The making of alcohol started in the Stone Age when females first began fermenting grapes in animal skin pouches, to create wine. Nearly every society since has used plants to make alcohol.

43 K Nelson. 2010. "Environment, cooking strategies & containers." *J of Anthro Arch* 29:2 238-47

44 Stone boiling facilitated the invention of stews and soups, and pottery made this possible. The earliest example of hearths filled with heat-fractured round river cobbles come from France, about 32,000 BP. Stone boiling involves placing stones into or next to a fireplace or other heat source until the stones are hot. The heated stones are then placed into a ceramic pot, lined basket or other vessel holding water or liquid or semi-liquid food. The hot stones then transfer the heat to the food.

45 S Hayley et al. 2013. "Phytoliths in Pottery Reveal the Use of Spice in European Prehistoric Cuisine." *PLoS ONE* 8 (8).

46 The occasional preservation of seeds and tissues of plants, such as the opium poppy, and aromatic herbs such as dill, shows that these spices spread from the Eastern Mediterranean, where wild varieties are found, to the Atlantic coastal margins around 5,000 BP. In Asia, starch granules from spices, such as ginger and tumeric, have been extracted from nearly 4,500 year old Harappan cooking pots.

47 One Aboriginal tale describes two women who destroy Thardid Jimbo, the "enemy of man," by luring him into a cave. They then covered the entrance with fire and he dies trying to escape.

48 Fire-keeper also describes ceremonial role. Smoke from aromatic plants such as sage, are used to purify the air and cultivate a serene atmosphere.

49 M de Rios & R Stachalek. 1999. "The Duboisia genus, Australian aborigines and suggestibility." *J Psychoactive Drugs,* 31(2):155-61 Apr-Jun

50 Roberts 2000. ibid

51 Through special rites, females reaffirmed their bond with their sacred land and their responsibility for it. During rituals, women held up and danced with sacred boards that were marked by them with divine signs denoting their links to their country.

8: Female Artists

1   A Bolwerk et al. 2014. "How Art Changes Your Brain." *PLoS ONE* 9(7)

2   Barrett et al. 2012. "Maternal affect and quality of parenting experiences are related to amygdala response to infant faces." *Soc Neurosci.* 2012;7(3):252-68.

3   Scientists who are mapping the maternal brain and observing behavioral changes in new mothers, are finding links in the way a woman acts with what's happening in her brain. Oxytocin levels, the system responsible for maternal-infant bonding across all mammalian species, dramatically increase during pregnancy and the postpartum period. And the more a mother is involved in childcare, the greater the increase in oxytocin. On the most basic level, these changes help attract a new mother to her baby.

4   Elseline Hoekzema, et al. 2016. "Pregnancy leads to long-lasting changes in human brain structure." *Nature Neuroscience,* Online Dec 19.

5   A Bartels & S Zeki. 2004. "The neural correlates of maternal & romantic love." NeuroImage 21:1155-66

6   Lundi. 2013. "Why do you want to eat the baby?" *Nouvelles* U of Montreal Sept 23

7   E Abraham et al. 2014. "Father's brain is sensitive to childcare experiences." *PNAS*, 111:27 Jul 8.

8   Kit Opie & Camila Power. 2008. "Grandmothering and female coalitions: A basis for matrilineal priority?" In NJ Allen et al, eds., *Early Human Kinship: From Sex to Social Reproduction.* UK: Blackwell. 168-186; O'Connell, J et al 1999. "Grandmothering and the evolution of Homo erectus." *Journal of Human Evolution* 36: 461-85; Voland, E et al, eds, 2005. *Grandmotherhood: The evolutionary significance of the second half of female life.* Rutgers.

9   J Beise. 2005. "The Helping and the Helpful Grandmother." In E Voland, et al., eds. *Grandmotherhood: The Evolutionary Significance of the Second Half of Female Life.* Rutgers UP.

10 J Stromberg. 2012. "New Evidence That Grandmothers Were Crucial for Human Evolution." Smithsonian. Oct 23.

11 PS Kim, J Coxworth & Kristen Hawkes. 2012. "Increased longevity evolves from grandmothering." *Proceedings of the Royal Society B*, Oct 24

12 CL Meehan. 2005. "The effects of residential locality on parental and alloparental investment among the Aka of the Central African Republic." *Human Nature*, 16. 58-80.

13 MV Flinn & D Leone. 2009. "Alloparental care & the ontogeny of glucocorticoid stress response among stepchildren." In GR Bentley and R Mace, eds., *Substitute Parents*. Berghahn Books.

14 SB Hrdy. 2007. "Evolutionary Context of Human Development: The Cooperative Breeding Model." In CA Salmon & TK Shackelford, eds., *Family Relationships*. NY: Oxford UP. pp. 39-68.

15 B Jones et al. 2005. "Older Hadza men & women as helpers." In Hewlett & Lamb, eds., *Hunter-Gatherer & Childhoods*. Transaction/Aldine. pp. 214-36.

16 Rudgley 2000. ibid

17 The Tan-Tan stone figurine found in Morocco, dates to around 500,000 - 300,000 BP. The Woman/Goddess statuette is 58 mm long, 26 mm wide, 12 mm thick, and weighs roughly 10 g. Originally planes formed the arms and legs but impact traces in grooves suggests they were carefully emphasized to shape breasts and the head.

18 The Berekhat Ram Woman figurine from Palestine dates between 233,000 and 800,000 years old. The original pebble bore a resemblance to a female, and this was enhanced by the carver, who cut grooves around the neck and along its arms.

19 D Hitchcock. 2014. "Avdeevo, a site with strong links to Kostenki." *Donsmaps.com.* 3/21

20 Marilyn Stokstad & MW Cothren. 2010. *Art History*, Vo 1, 4th Ed. Pearson.

21 Cave art may have been part of shamanism, the belief that certain people, shamans, can travel outside of their bodies in order to mediate between the worlds of the living and the spirits. Cave ceremonies may have involved the use of hallucinations, and the images conceived during a trance-like state combined recognizable animals and abstract, nonrepresentational symbols. Animal art may have aided in their mediation. The human form was often expressed, especially female shapes. They often look either young, old, or pregnant.

22 Dean Snow. 2013. "Sexual Dimorphism in European Upper Paleolithic Cave Art." *American Antiquity*, Number 4 / Oct 46-761(16).

23 Females and males differ in the relative lengths of their fingers. Women tend to have ring and index fingers of about the same length, whereas men's ring fingers tend to be longer than their index fingers. As long as humans have created works of art, they left behind hand-prints.

24 Left-hand stencils are more common than right-hand ones because right-handed people tend to make stencils of their left hands. They use their right hands to hold the pigment tube or to help purse their lips to spray on the pigment.

25 The Hohle Fels figure is a statuette of a well-endowed Woman discovered in a Germany cave more than 40,000 years old, one of the oldest sculptures ever discovered. The statuette, just under 6 cm tall and 3.4 cm wide, was carved out of a single piece of mammoth ivory.

26 The Galgenberg Woman/Goddess from Lower Austria, is from around 32,000 BP. It is 72 mm high, weights 10 grams, and is made of greenish, very shiny amphibolite slate. The figure has one breast jutting out to the left, the other facing frontward. The vulva is clearly indicated. The left arm raised, and the right hand rests on the thigh, posed as in a ritual or dance position.

27 The Bone Woman/Goddess of Kostenki, Russia, is from around 30,000 BP. The figurine is made of mammoth bone, it is 10.2 centimetres high and shows pregnancy, well developed buttocks and pendulous breasts that characterize most such statues, but naturally depicted.

28 The Woman/Goddess of Montpazier, France, dates from 30,000 BP. The figurine has a well drawn vulva like a woman about to give birth. It is carved in limonite, a yellowish brown ore of iron. The sagging breasts, sagging are flat. The spherical belly is broad and projected forward.

29 The Woman/Goddess of Dolni Vestonice, Czech Republic, dates from 29,000 to 25,000 BP. This figurine is one of the oldest known ceramics in the world, fired at a relatively low temperature. The figurine has a height of 11.1 centimeters and a width of 4.3 centimeters. It has pendulous breasts and a belt beneath the broad hips.

30 The Woman/Goddess of Willendorf, is a 11.1 cm (4.4 in) high statuette of a woman figure estimated to be from about 23,000 BP, found in Lower Austria. It is carved from an oolitic limestone that is not local to the area, and tinted with red ochre. There is a clear depiction of headgear, a fiber-based woven cap or hat made like a coiled basket.

31 The Woman/Goddess of Frasassi, Italy, was carved from a piece of stalactite between 28,000 and 20,000 BP. Its color is pearl white. The breasts are broad, and placed high on the chest. A navel is shown on the full abdomen, and the vulva is clearly shown in relief.

32 The Grottes du Pape figures include a miniature head, 36.5 mm high, 22 mm deep and 19 mm wide, carved from mammoth ivory, a fragment called la Figurine à la Pèlerine, another called la Figurine à la Ceinture, and la Fillette - a figurine of a girl. Another figure, La Manche de Poignard, has breasts that are cylindrical and pendant, and a belly that is broad and hanging. Le Torse is 94 mm high, 51.5 mm wide, 48 mm thick. It has broad breasts and wide hips. La Poire is another figurine of mammoth ivory of which only the corpulent torso survives, with emphatic treatment of the vulva's labia and prominent, slightly protruding pubic area.

33 The Kostienki Woman/Goddess statuettes have broad breasts and buttocks, and wide hips, and represent pregnant and older women. North of the Kostienki sites, in Gagarino is a house pit dated to 21,800 BP. The house had six hundred flint implements, over a thousand blades, several obese Woman/Goddess figurines, and one tall Woman statuette.

34 The Mal'ta - Buret' culture in Siberia, dates from 23,000 - 19,000 BP. Dozens of figurines of birds and Goddess statuettes were found. Also, in Zaraysk, Russia, there was an important Paleolithic site from 22,000 - 16,000 BP. It has several Woman/Goddess figurines and is the northernmost example of the Kostenki - Avdeevo culture.

35 The Mauern Goddess of Bavaria, is a limestone figure from 27,000 BP, covered with red ochre.

36 The Lespugue Venus from France was carved from ivory around 25,000 BP.

37 The Sireuil Venus of France dates from 27,000 - 25,000 BP.

38 Two Mainz, Germany Woman figures made of greenish sandstone are from around 25,000 BP.

39 The Woman/Goddess of Tursac, France, is a calcite figure from 25,000 BP.

40 The Savignano Woman/Goddess from Italy, is 22 cm high and is made of serpentine. It is dated from around 25,000 - 15,000 BP.

41 The Woman/Goddess of Renancourt, France, is a limestone statuette 12 cm high, from 23,000 BP

42 The Moravany Goddess from the Slovak Republic is 76 mm tall, and is dated at 22,800 BP.

43 The Woman/Goddess of Abri Pataud, France, is a very small figure carved into the surface of a rock around 22,000 BP. The figure appears to represent a comparatively young female.

44 The Goddess of Laussel is a 18.11 inches high limestone bas-relief of a nude female figure, painted with red ochre. It was carved into a massive block of fallen limestone in a rock shelter in southwestern France. The carving is associated with the Gravettian culture from around 25,000 BP. The figure has broad breasts and vulva. The Woman/Goddess figure has her hand on her abdomen or womb. Her faceless head is turned toward the horn.

45 A Woman/Goddess figurine carved on reindeer antler was found at La Madeleine, a rock shelter in France, dated from 18,000 BP to 10,000 BP. The shelter contains two reclining Woman figures on the wall with broad breasts and a pubic triangle.

46 The Goddess of Parabita, Italy, is from 17,000 BP. The statuette is 90 mm high and 20 mm wide. A second Woman/Goddess figurine was found, 61 mm high and 15 mm wide. The area is also an important Neolithic and Bronze Age site.

47 The Impudique Woman/Goddess, from France, is 8 cm high, and from around 16,000 BP. The stomach is flat, and it could be of a young girl.

48 A Goddess figure from the Mas d'Azil Cave, France, dated around 16,000 - 15,000 BP is 51 mm long, 17 mm wide, and 13 mm thick. The statuette shows great mastery of sculptural technique. The originality of this sculpture is reinforced by the representation of the breasts, elongated and pendant, but not bulky. There is also a second stylized Goddess figure.

49 The 14,000-year old Woman/Goddess figure of Courbet is 25 mm in height.

50 The Goddess of Neuchâtel, is a pendant in jet, 16 mm high.

51 Gönnersdorf Woman/Goddess figurines are stylized, overtly young-bearing forms with over-sized buttocks, long trunks, small or missing breasts, and no heads, dated 15,000 to 13,000 BP.

52 The Woman/Goddess of Milandes is a phallic shaped figure from France, dated around 25,000 - 15,000 BP. The object is 77.3 mm tall, 39.0 mm wide, and weighs about 90 grams.

53 A stone phallus at the Hohle Fels Cave is about 28,000 years old. It is 20 cm long and 3 cm wide.

54 The Mas d'Azil phallus is dated to 16,000 BP. It is made of carved ivory.

55 One Avdeevo ivory Woman/Goddess figure is 145 mm long and 50 mm wide. It has narrow shoulders, wide pelvis, and shortened back. Another Woman/Goddess figure is 125 mm long, 36 mm wide, and 32 mm thick. The buttocks are depicted realistically.

56 Mariana Gvozdover. 1995. "Art of the Mammoth Hunters." *Oxbow* Mono 49.

57 One Avdeevo Woman/Goddess statuette is 81 mm long, 43 mm wide and 35 mm thick. The breast/abdomen area is rendered as a single unit; the arms are prominent at the shoulders, bent forward and then lost in the upper breast/abdomen.

58 One Avdeevo Woman/Goddess is 160 mm long, 30 mm wide, and only 11 mm thick. Sagging, teardrop-shaped breasts descend to a rounded, flat abdomen, which turns into the pubic triangle. The figurine represents a tall, slender, mature, but not pregnant woman.

59 Numerous fragments of Avdeevo ivory Woman/Goddess figures were found. The length of one fragment is 80 mm, and the greatest width is 88 mm, so the whole figure probably measured 200-210 mm. It depicts a mature Woman/Goddess with a rounded abdomen.

60 One Avdeevo Woman statuette is 100 mm long and 20 mm wide. The chest is flattened, and the drop-shaped breasts, slightly apart, lie on the abdomen. The arms and the shoulders are slightly bent forwards, and the forearms are placed beneath the breasts, under which the hands are holding the upper part of the abdomen. Fingers are emphasized, one of which wears a bracelet.

61 One Avdeevo Woman/Goddess statuette is 90 mm tall and 30 mm wide. The shoulders are narrow and decorated bands are on the breasts.

62 One Avdeevo Woman/Goddess ivory carving is 95 mm long, the maximum width is 23 mm, and the thickness of the torso and hips is 10 mm. The forearms and hands emerge from beneath the teardrop-shaped breasts and lie below a keel-shaped abdomen. The fingers are turned as if holding the small projection at the lower part of the abdomen. There are bracelets on both hands.

63 Hitchcock. 2014

64 One Avdeevo Woman/Goddess figurine is 95 mm long and 30 mm wide. There are prominent fatty deposits at the base of the hips, producing a typical female contour. The figurine represents a mature probably pregnant woman.

65 R Carneiro. 1992. " Ecology & Ideology in the Development of New World Civilizations," in *Ideology & PreColumbian Civilizations.* Demarest & Conrad, eds. School of Am. Research Press

66 Alexander Marshack. 1991. "The Female Image." *Proceedings of Prehistoric Society.* 57(1): 17-31

67 H Harrmann. 2009. *Interacting with Figurines.* West Hartford: Full Circle Press.

68 F Marglin. 1987. "Yoni." In *Encyclopedia of Religion.* Mircea Eliade (ed). Macmillan, Vol 15: 530-5

69 C Ursu & S Terna, eds. 2014. *Anthropomorphism & Symbolic Behavior in the Neolithic & Copper Age Communities of South-Eastern Europe.* Suceava: Bucovina Museum.

70 Woman/Goddess figures changed styles over time. Prehistoric female figurines were voluptuous, then more schematic. This radical shift in representation perhaps reflected a modification in the culture and meanings attached to the figures. Maybe, the objects started off as celebrations of the female form, then later became generalized symbols that tied together a growing human society.

71 Helen Benigni, ed. 2013. *The Mythology of Venus.* UP Of America

72 C Gamble. 1982. "Interaction & Alliance in Paleolithic Society." *Man*. 17:92-107.
73 Regardless of their purpose, females were transmitting the religion of the Mother and Goddess from one generation to the other, for 40,000 years. They were also telling and re-telling her story to justify her being worthy of worshiping.
74 Gimbutas 1991.
75 LD McDermott. 1996. "Self Representation in Upper Paleolithic Female Figurines." *Curr Anthro* 37:227-75
76 MW Conkey. 1983. "On the Origins of Paleolithic Art" in *The Mousterian Legacy*. Ed by E Trinkaus, 201-27. Oxford: British Archaeological Reports Intl Series 164.
77 The first theology was probably started by egg-producers with the honoring of Goddess figurines. Having to bear the costs of increasing brain size throughout arduous pregnancies and childbirths, females may have invented the Mother Goddess to help them with the difficulty of reproduction.
78 R Hutton. 1997. "The Neolithic Great Goddess: A Study in Modern Tradition?" *Antiquity*, 71:91-9.

9: Paleo Sex Choice

1   Darwin 1871.
2   The common conception of Paleolithic masculinity is that men were primarily hunters who competed fiercely to mate and lead small hominin clans. It is assumed that Paleolithic humans were engaged in continual bloody combat both with other species and with each other. Males are characterized as more violent than females, who they frequently raped and killed. In this view, men are more prone to violence, and like waging war.
3   There is little evidence of Stone Age men-on-men or men-on-women violence in art and archaeology. This suggest that male violence among hominins was largely mitigated by female social structures and socialization, like the other great apes. Perhaps human ancestors differed in terms of female-centered organization, and the most successful ones were those that were most gynocentric.
4   R Prum. 2017. *The Evolution of Beauty*. Doubleday
5   E Young. 2017. "How Beauty Evolves." *The Atlantic*, May 8
6   Joan Roughgarden. 2009. *Evolution's Rainbow*. Univ of California Press.
7   Thornhill & Palmer, 2000. *A Natural History of Rape: Biological Bases of Sexual Coercion*. Bradford Books.
8   Brennan's 2009 study of ducks show that even in species where 40 percent of sexual encounters are forced, more than 95 percent of chicks are actually sired by a female's chosen partner.
9   Patricia Gowaty. 2003. "Sexual Natures: How Feminism Changed Evolutionary Biology." *Signs* 28:3 901-21
10 Marlene Zuk. 2013. *Paleofantasy*. WW Norton.
11 With lactase persistence in some groups, and increases in lactose digesting gut bacteria in others.
12 Patricia Adair Gowaty. 2003. "Power Asymmerties between the Sexes, Mate Preferences, & Components of Fitness," In Cheryl Travis, ed. *Evolution, Gender, and Rape*. 61-86. MIT Press.
13 F Fellmann & R Walsh. 2013. "Emotional Selection & Human Personality." *Biological Theory*.
14 AD Wallach et al. 2015. "What is an apex predator?" *Nordic Society Oikos* 000: 001-009.
15 E Young. 2014. "Where's All The Animal Vagina Research?" *National Geo. Phenomena*, May 6
16 PA Gowaty. 2008. "Reproductive Compensation." *Journal of Evolutionary Bio*, 21:1189-1200.
17 P Bourdieu. 1980. *The Logic of Practice*. Stanford University Press.
18 Catherine Hakim. 2010. "Erotic capital". *European Sociological Review* 26 (5): 499-518.
19 Catherine Hakim. 2010. "Have you got erotic capital?" *Prospect Magazine* (169). 24 March
20 Alicia M Gonzales & G Rolison. 2005. "Social Oppression and Attitudes Toward Sexual Practices". *Journal of Black Studies* 25 (6): 715-729.
21 Susan Koshy. 2004. *Sexual Naturalization: Asian Americans and Miscegenation*. Stanford UP
22 Clarissa Pinkola Estes.1992. *Women Who Run With the Wolves: Myths and Stories of the Wild Woman Archetype*. NY: Ballantine Books.
23 Pinkola Estes argues, "When we lose touch with the instinctive psyche, we live in a semi-destroyed state and images and powers that are natural to the feminine are not allowed full development. When a woman is cut away from her basic source, she is sanitized, and her instincts and natural cycles are lost, subsumed by the culture, or by the intellect or ego - one's own or those belonging to others."
24 Women herbalists experimented with different plants to prepare various treatments, so females may be considered the first doctors, scientists, and experimental researchers.
25 J Haritha. 2017. "Grandmother of the jungle: This Kerala tribal woman can prepare 500 medicines from memory." *The News Minute*, Mar 8
26 N Kelly. et al. 2003. *Medicine Through Time*. Heinemann.
27 Herbs like rosemary were used for medicinal purposes for thousands of years. Many prehistoric peoples were able to set broken or fractured bones. An injured area was covered in clay, which then set hard so that the bone could heal properly without interference.
28 Females were revered for their knowledge of medicinal plants, and preparation of balms and other treatments. Medicine women were central figures in the tribal system due to their herbal and medical knowledge, and because they could contact the Earth Goddess.
29 R Krishnamani & W Mahaney. 2000. "Geophagy among primates." *Animal Behavior* 59: 899-915.
30 JM Riddle. 1997. *Eve's Herbs: A History of Contraception and Abortion in the West*. Harvard UP.
31 Like many of the Goddess/Woman figurines found in Paleolithic, "medicine women" or female shamans tend to rotund. They were typically generously fed by their people, even when other

members of the group went hungry. Considered to be the "vessels" of divinity, or the Earth Goddesses, the others in her community did not want their divine personage to feel "restricted" or be unable to exercise her full power while in the shaman's body.

32   Max Dashu. 2013. "Raising the Dead: Medicine Women Who Revive & Retrieve Souls." *Academic.edu.*

33   J McKay. 1932. *The Deer-Cult & Deer-Goddess Cult of the Ancient Caledonians.* Taylor & Francis

34   P Skoglund et al. 2015. "Ancient Wolf Genome Reveals an Early Divergence of Domestic Dog Ancestors and Admixture into High Latitude Breeds." *Current Biology,* 25:11 1515-19, Jun 1

35   ND Ovodov et al. 2011. "A 33,000-Year-Old Incipient Dog from the Altai Mountains of Siberia: Evidence of the Earliest Domestication Disrupted by the Last Glacial Maximum." *PLoS ONE* 6(7):e22821.

36   Jean M Auel. 1983. *The Clan of the Cave Bear.* Bantam Books.

37   Pat Shipman. 2015. *The Invaders: How Humans & Their Dogs Drove Neanderthals to Extinction.* Belknap Press.

38   Jonica Newby. 1997. *The Pact for Survival.* Sydney: ABC Books.

39   Jane Caputi. 2004. *Goddesses and Monsters: Women, Myth, Power and Popular Culture.* Popular Press 3

40   There are burial sites of animals that are not related human burials in some cultures. In these cases, domestic animals almost exclusively are involved, and among them the dog and the ox predominate (K Narr, ed. 2014. "Prehistoric Religion: The beliefs and practices of Stone Age peoples." *Encyclopedia Britannica.*). It is difficult to differentiate between animal sacrifices and the spiritual veneration of an animal at the burial sites of animals.

41   RJ Losey et al. 2011. "Canids as persons: Early Neolithic dog and wolf burials, Cis-Baikal, Siberia." *Journal of Anthropological Archaeology* 30(2):174-189.

42   Miho Nagasawa,. 2015. "Oxytocin-gaze positive loop and the coevolution of human-dog bonds." *Science* 17 April Vol. 348 no. 6232 pp. 333-6

10: Man-the-Killer?

1   An androgen is any natural or synthetic compound, usually a steroid hormone, that stimulates or controls the development and maintenance of male characteristics in vertebrates by binding to androgen receptors. The most well-known androgen is testosterone. Dihydrotestosterone (DHT) and androstenedione are less known generally, but are of equal importance in male development.

2   PK Siiteri & JD Wilson. 1974. "Testosterone formation and metabolism during male sexual differentiation in the human embryo.". *The Journal of Clinical Endocrinology and Metabolism* 38 (1): 113-25.

3   DL Smith. 2009. *The Most Dangerous Animal: Human Nature & the Origins of War.* St. Martin's

4   D Peterson & R Wrangham. 1997. *Demonic Males: Apes & the Origins of Human Violence.* Mariner Books.

5   Some hominins survived until fairly recently. The Red Deer Cave People (14,500 to 11,500 BP) of China were a prehistoric hominin population. They had short, flat faces with archaic features such as big teeth and thick skulls, but brains with modern-looking frontal lobes. They were a separate or hybrid species of hominins that persisted until recent times and became extinct without contributing to the gene pool of modern humans. (D Curnoe et al. 2012. "Human Remains from the Pleistocene-Holocene Transition of Southwest China Suggest a Complex Evolutionary History for East Asians." *PLOS One* 7:3 Mar)

6   RA Dart. 1953. "The Predatory Transition from Ape to Man." *Int'l Anthro & Linguistic Review,* 1:4

7   An odd assemblage of ancient bones cannot tell us if four million years ago australopiths practiced gynecocracy like the bonobos. Stone tools do not inform us whether the female-centered social relations of orangutans were observed by H. erectus. And two million year-old teeth do not reveal if the higher status inherited by female chimpanzees were followed by H. erectus as they journeyed across the World. Yet, archaeologists claim the few hominin bone and stone tools found prove their man-the-hunter and male dominance thesis.

8   Yet, the theme of man being threatened by an animal is rare.

9   Hitchcock 2014. ibid

10   Many giant nonhuman animals including mammoths, mastodons, saber-toothed cats, glyptodon, diprotodon, and giant sloths disappeared with the arrival with modern humans, roughly 132,000 BP to the late Holocene or 1,000 years BP. Of 50 megaherbivore species, only 9 remain worldwide: 3 elephants, 5 rhinoceros, and the hippopotamus. The loss was most dramatic in the Americas, with all 27 megaherbivore species extinct. One billion individual animals were lost from the Earth's land surface.

11   C Sandom et al. 2014. "Global late Quaternary megafauna extinctions linked to humans, not climate change." *Proc Biol Sci.* 281(1787) Jul 22

12   T Surovell et al. 2016. "Test of Martin's overkill hypothesis using radiocarbon dates on extinct megafauna." *PNAS,* 113(4):886-91. Jan 26

13   PS Martin. 1973. "The Discovery of America." *Science,* vol. 179: 4077, 969-74. Mar. 9

14   Especially since the end of the last ice age about 12,000 BP, the largest animals on the planet have been hit hard by what may have been the beginnings of the sixth mass extinction.

15   Jessica Metcalf et al. 2016. "Synergistic roles of climate warming and human occupation in Patagonian megafaunal extinctions during the Last Deglaciation." *Science Advances,* 2:6 Jun 17

16   W Zuo et al. 2013. "A life-history approach to the late Pleistocene megafaunal extinction." *Am Nat.,* 182:4 524-31. Oct

17   Jacquelyn Gill. 2015. "Learning from Africa's herbivores." *Science* 350:6264 11/27

18   A Segura et al. 2016. "Exceptional body sizes but typical trophic structure in a Pleistocene food

web," *Biology Letters,* 12:5 May 24

19 F Smith et al. 2016. "Exploring the influence of ancient & historic megaherbivore extirpations on the global methane budget." *PNAS,* 113(4):874-9 Jan 26

20 This man-the-warrior hypothesis has been promoted by Jared Diamond, Richard Wrangham, Francis Fukuyama, David Brooks and others. Pinker claims in his bestseller *Better Angels of Our Nature* that "chronic raiding and feuding characterize life in a state of nature." In *The Social Conquest of the Earth,* Wilson calls warfare "humanity's hereditary curse."

21 The development of the throwing-spear, together with ambush hunting techniques, made potential violence between hunting parties very costly, dictating cooperation and maintenance of low population densities to prevent competition for resources. This behavior may have accelerated the migration out of Africa of H. erectus some 1.8 million years ago as a natural consequence of conflict avoidance.

22 J Horgan. 2013. "New Study of Prehistoric Skeletons Undermines Claim That War Has Deep Evolutionary Roots." *Scientific American,* Aug 2.

23 DR Guthrie. 2005. *The Nature of Paleolithic Art.* Chicago: University of Chicago Press.

24 RC Kelly. 2000. *Warless Societies and the Origin of War.* University of Michigan Press.

25 J Haas & M Piscitelli. 2013. "The Prehistory of Warfare: Misled by Ethnography" In *War, Peace, and Human Nature* edited by Douglas P. Fry, pp. 168-190. Oxford UP.

26 RB Ferguson. 2003. "The Birth of War." *Natural History,* July-August

27 Chagnon's study of Yanamomo life and society from the 1950s to 1970s concluded that they were a violent people who often kidnapped young women (Early and Peters 1990) and used nondeadly forms of physical violence like chest-pounding and club fights as their principal method to prevent wars. But the Yanomamo were already influenced by decades of colonialism by the time Chagnon appeared, and they practice horticulture, which makes them a poor proxy for nomadic Stone Age gatherer-'hunters.' Furthermore, Chagnon clearly acknowledges that some Yanomamo are much violent than others.

28 The societies include the Aranda and Tiwi of Australia; Kaska, Copper Inuit and Montagnais of North America; Botocudo of South America; !Kung, Hadza and Mbuti of Africa; and Vedda and Andamanese of South Asia.

29 Overall, the findings suggest that most incidents of lethal aggression may be classified as homicides, a few others as feuds, and a minority as war. Of the 21 societies examined by Fry and Soderberg, three had no observed killings of any kind, and 10 had no killings carried out by more than one perpetrator. In only six societies did ethnographers record killings that involved two or more perpetrators and two or more victims. However, a single society, the Tiwi of Australia, accounted for almost all of these group killings.

30 J Horgan. 2013. "Survey of Earliest Human Settlements Undermines Claim that War Has Deep Evolutionary Roots." *Scientific American,* Aug 2.

31 DP Fry & P Söderberg. 2013. "Lethal Aggression in Mobile Forager Bands & Implications for the Origins of War." *Science,* 341:6143, 270-273. Jul 19

32 KF Otterbein. 2004. *How War Began.* Texas A&M Univ. Press.

33 With the constraints of the first restraining removed, men quickly degenerated and became 'demonic.' Patriarchal dualism was introduced which created a 'superior' attitude in males, expressed as violence against nature and women. Females were conditioned or domesticated to be subservient to men.

34 Francis A Beer. 1981. *Peace Against War: The Ecology of International Violence.* W. H. Freeman

35 Another wife was a Kushite, or African woman.

36 A Jones. 2006. *Genocide: A Comprehensive Introduction.* Routledge.

37 There were at least ten major battles in the thousand years from 3,500 BP to 2,500 BP, including the Megiddo (3,470 BP), the Ten Kings (3,420 BP), Kadesh (3,280 BP), Muye (3,060 BP), Qarqar (2,870 BP), Megiddo (2,6020 BP), Carchemish (2,630 BP), Pteria (2,560 BP), Thymbra (2,560 BP), and Lade (2,560 BP) military clashes. In the next hundred years, from 2,500 BP to 2,400 BP, there were seven serious encounters, including that of Marathon (2,500 BP), Thermopylae (2,490 BP), Artemisium (2,490 BP), Salamis (2,490 BP), Plataea (2,490 BP), Mycale (2,490 BP), and Cunaxa (2,420 BP). There were dozens of other clashes in the next 300 years. (Note: dates are approximate and rounded)

38 CC Mann. 2005. *1491: New Revelations of the Americas Before Columbus.* Knopf.

39 S Behrendt. 1999. "Transatlantic Slave Trade". In *Africana: The Encyclopedia of the African and African American Experience.* Basic Civitas Books.

40 The deadliest war in history, in terms of the cumulative number of deaths since its start, is the Second World War, from 1939 to 1945, with 60 to 85 million deaths, followed by the Mongol conquests which was greater than 41 million.

41 JT Cacioppo. 2009. *Loneliness: Human Nature & the Need for Social Connection.* WW Norton.

42 D Dobbs. 2013. "The Social Life of Genes." *Pacific Standard Mag.* Sept. 3.

43 Genes can vary their level of activity in a process called gene expression. Cells die off and humans have to replace around one to two percent of their molecular structure every day. There is a constant building and re-engineering of new cells, driven by the contingent nature of gene expression. Gene expression can change with rapidity, breadth, and depth that science is only now discovering.

44 Psychological studies in "cognitive framing" show that poverty and poor neighborhoods, understandably, tend to make people more sensitive to threats in ambiguous social situations. Cole found that framing, not income levels, accounted for most of the difference in gene expression. (Cole, SW. 2009. "Social Regulation of Human Gene Expression." Current Directions in Psychological Science, June; vol. 18, 3: pp. 132-137).

45 The study found that white Detroit residents who were lower-middle-class had the longest

telomeres. But the shortest telomeres belonged to poor whites, who were a clear minority in all of areas, ranging from 2 to 21 percent of residents. Black residents had about the same telomere lengths regardless of whether they were poor or lower-middle-class. Interestingly, poor Mexicans actually had longer telomeres than Mexicans with higher incomes. Immigrants often reside in ethnic enclaves, while the second generation is more isolated and have a lifelong exposure to an environment that stigmatizes their identity, which in turn affects their health negatively. The study did not investigate sex differences.

46 Arline T Geronimus. 2015. "Race-Ethnicity, Poverty, Urban Stressors, and Telomere Length in a Detroit Community-based Sample." *Journal of Health and Social Behavior.* 1-26.

47 Elisabeth Babcock. 2014. "Using Brain Science to Design New Pathways Out of Poverty." *Crittenton Women's Union*

48 Social bias, persistent poverty, and trauma can directly undermine brain development and executive function skills like impulse control, working memory, and mental flexibility.

49 D Rowe et al. 1995. "Sex Differences in Crime." *J of Res in Crime & Delinquency* 32:84

50 AL Kellermann & JA Mercy. 1992. "Men, women, & murder: gender-specific differences in rates of fatal violence & victimization." *J Trauma.* Jul;33(1):1-5

51 DOJ. 2010. "Homicide Trends in the United States, 1980-2008" *US Dept Of Justice*

52 In part, this is due to the masculinizing influences of testosterone on the anterior hypothalamus, amygdala, and other parts of the brain involved in sex and aggression. Brain imaging studies show that the amygdala, is larger in men than in women. This divergence in amygdala size is magnified by variation in the frontal cortex lobes which help to regulate impulses coming from the amygdala. These lobes are more active in females.

53 Louann Brizendine. 2007. *The Female Brain.* Harmony.

54 Marian C Diamond. 1988. *Enriching Heredity.* NY: Free Press.

55 Pauline Chaste & Marion Leboyer. 2012. "Autism risk factors: genes, environment, and gene-environment interactions." *Dialogues Clin Neurosci.* 14(3): 281-292. Sep

56 J Gockley et al. 2015. "The female protective effect in autism spectrum disorder is not mediated by a single genetic locus." *Mol Autism.* 6:25. May 13.

57 Close to 85 percent of people affected by blindness caused by Leber's hereditary iptic neuropathy are male. Mitochondrial mutations may be related to a broad array of maladies, from Parkinson's and Alzheimer's diseases to reduced sperm and male infertility.

58 R Lehrke. 1972. "A theory of X-linkage of major intellectual traits." *Am J Ment Defic,* 76: 611-619.

59 Intelligence is the ability to solve problems. Between 40 to 60 percent of intelligence is hereditary. The remaining percentage depends on environment, stimulation, and personal characteristics.

60 Staff. 2016. "Did you know that intelligence is inherited from mothers?" *Psychology Spot.* March

61 Judith A Hall. 1990. *Nonverbal Sex Differences.* Johns Hopkins UP.

62 Lise Eliot. 2010. *Pink Brain, Blue Brain.* Mariner Books.

63 Cordelia Fine. 2011. *Delusions of Gender.* WW Norton.

64 Leslie Brody. 2001. *Gender, Emotion, and the Family.* Harvard UP.

65 The brain is flexible and can remodel itself continually to new experiences. A child is born with its genetic makeup, but actually growing a boy from XY cells or a girl from XX cells requires constant interaction with the environment. Eliot argues that boys are not, in fact, "better at math" but at certain kinds of spatial reasoning. And, girls are not naturally more empathetic, but they are allowed to express their feelings more.

66 M Konner. 2015. *Women After All: Sex, Evolution, and the End of Male Supremacy.* WW Norton.

67 Konner conflates a lot of issues, ignores structural misogyny, and so arrives at an overly optimistic outlook for sex relations. But he rightly suggests that the nature and nurture divergences in females may prove crucial for the species' survival in the future.

11: Paleo-Female Culture

1 P Gluckman et al. 2009. *Principles of Evolutionary Medicine.* Oxford UP.

2 Ellison 2001. ibid

3 J Bancroft. 2005. "The Endocrinology of Sexual Arousal." *Journal of Endocrinology*, 186: 411-427.

4 Jillian Lloyd et al. 2005. "Female Genital Appearance." *British J of Obstetrics & Gyn.* 12:5 May.

5 AA Amis & JH Miller. 1982. "The elbow". *Clinics in rheumatic diseases* 8 (3): 571-93.

6 Menstruation occurs in primates, such as apes and monkeys, as well as bats and the elephant shrew. It is the regular discharge of blood and mucosal tissue from the inner lining of the uterus through the vagina. This cycle is induced by the rise and fall of hormones in a female's body.

7 Knight 1991. ibid

8 Instead of perils and curses, a menstruating woman was viewed as being able to bestow benefits and blessings. Females, via sex and the rhythm of menstruation, nurtured the primal creative impulse of civilization and in essence created human culture.

9 Among the Dene people of North America, if a child is not thriving, or several of his brothers and sisters have died, his mother will fasten around their neck a small piece of cloth soiled with menstrual blood. Among many North American nations, when the corn began to ripen, a woman would leave her isolation hut in the middle of the night and walk naked through the fields.

10 This practice is observed from West Africa to South Asia, and the Near East to Peru. And, in many cultures, men embarking on a perilous undertaking, or who fear malign influences, paint themselves red.

11 Eugenia W Herbert. 1994. *Iron, Gender, & Power: Rituals of Transformation in African Societies.* Indiana UP

12 Hilary Alton, ed. 2010. *The Moon and Menstruation: Selected extracts from Robert Briffault's The*

Mothers. A Radical Anthropology Group Publication.

13 While female choice in sex-selection was a factor in the first domestication, there were other aspects like matrilocal residence and so on.

14 Jani Roberts. 2000. *Seven Days of My Creation: Tales of Magic, Sex & Gender*. iUniverse

15 Naomi Janowitz. 2001. *Magic in the Roman World: Pagans, Jews, and Christians*. Routledge.

16 Circe Sturm. 2002. *Blood Politics: Race, Culture, & Identity in the Cherokee Nation of Oklahoma*. UC Press.

17 Camilla Power. 2014. "The Evolution of Ritual as a Process of Sexual Selection." In D Dor, C Knight & J Lewis, eds., *The Social Origins of Language*. Oxford UP.

18 In Ancient Rome, Pliny wrote that a menstruating woman who uncovers her body could scare away hailstorms, whirlwinds, and lightning. If she strips naked and walks around the field, insects fall off the ears of corn. The notion that menstrual blood can remove insects and pests is popular around the world.

19 Alton 2010. ibid

20 F d'Errico & CB Stringer. 2011. "Evolution, revolution or saltation scenario for the emergence of modern cultures?" *Phil Trans of the Royal Soc* B: Bio Sci 366.

21 The record of female-created language is lost, and historical linguistics becomes inaccurate before 10,000 years ago since this time preceded writing. However, females played a huge role in the agricultural revolution, so they must have played a part in the concurrent linguistic evolution. Most of the historical linguistic literature does not address this important issue.

22 E Buenaventura-Posso & SE Brown. 1980. "Forced transition & egalitarianism to male dominance: the Bari of Columbia." In M Etienne & E Leacock, eds, *Women & Colonization*. Praeger.

23 Miriam R Dexter & VH Mair. 2010. *Sacred Display*. Cambria Press.

24 Elisabetta Boaretto et al. 2009. "Radiocarbon dating of charcoal & bone collagen associated with early pottery at Yuchanyan Cave, Hunan, China." *PNAS* 106(24): 9595-9600 Jun 16

25 The oldest pottery found were made by people who lived in a cave in Yuchanyan, Hunan Province of southern China around 20,000 BP. The pots had walls about three-fourths of an inch thick and were fired at temperatures between 700 and 900 degrees F.

26 Because of the presence of rice remains and early pottery in Yuchanyan, caves are often seen as the predecessors of the early, open-air Neolithic villages. In China, proto-cultivation of rice and cave settlements may predate open-air villages by 10,000 years.

27 Stokstad & Cothren 2010. ibid

28 Marilyn Stokstad. 2004. *Art History*, 2nd edition. Prentice Hall.

29 Rudgley 2000. ibid

30 Elizabeth Barber. 1995. *Women's Work: The First 20,000 Years- Cloth, & Society in Early Times*. WW Norton

31 First, fibers are gathered from plants, such as flax for linen cloth or hemp for rope. Fibers can also be gathered from animals - wool from sheep, goats, and camels, or hair from humans and horses. The fibers have to thoroughly cleaned, combed, and sorted. Only then can the fibers be twisted and drawn out under tension that is, spun into the long, strong, flexible thread needed for textiles. Early fiber artists depended on the natural colors of their materials and on natural dyes from the Earth and plants.

32 Egyptian females preferred white linen, elaborately pleated, for their garments. Minoans created multicolored patterned fabrics with borders. Greek females excelled in the art of pictorial tapestries.

33 K Gautam, ed. 1990. *India through the ages*. Pub Division, Ministry of Info and Broadcasting, GOI

34 In a fragment of bitumen carving from Susa, Iran, dated 2,800 to 2,700 BP, a woman is shown spinning. She is an imposing figure, wearing an elegant hairstyle, many ornaments, and a garment with a patterned border. She sits barefoot and cross-legged on a lion-footed stool covered with sheepskin, spinning thread with a wide spindle. A servant stands behind the woman, fanning her, while fruit lie on an offering stand in front of her.

35 Stokstad 2004. ibid

36 With the start of the late Bronze Age, about 3,500 BP, the advent of commercial textiles brought men to the looms. However, up to Industrial Revolution, the fiber arts were an enormous economic force, belonging primarily to females.

37 The Chauvet Cave in France contains hundreds of paintings starting from around 32,000 BP. Dramatic images depict grazing, running, or resting animals, including horses, bison, mammoths, bears, panthers, owls, deer, aurochs or early cows, woolly rhinoceroses, and ibex or unrestrained goats. Also included are occasional humans, both male and female, many handprints, and hundreds of geometric markings such as grids, circles, and dots.

38 Lascaux Cave, also in France, have been dated to about 15,000 BP. It has about 600 paintings and 1,500 engravings of cows, bulls, horses, and deer. Ibex, a bear, engraved felines, and a woolly rhinoceros have also been found. The animals appear singly, in rows, face to face, tail to tail, and even painted on top of one another.

39 Among the oldest ivory carvings found are five tiny mammoth-ivory figurines from the Ice Age, 35,000 years ago, discovered at the Vogelherd Cave in Germany. There were other small-scale carvings of other animals including horse, bison, lion and bear.

40 The abundance of animal art and tales hints to an intimate relationship between humans and other-than-human animals that transcends and overcomes the boundaries between different realms of being.

41 In Stone Age animalism, special sacrificial traditions were closely connected to animals. For example, the custom of preserving part of a skeleton in order to placate the ruler of the animals and to provide for continuation of the species. In contrast, the modern perception of animals and nature is that they represent a separate and indivisible entity from humans. Both animals and nature are

subordinated to men, and are permanently at men's service.

42 Zuni and Navajo myths show animals behaving heroically on behalf of people. In Chinese legends, monkeys perform brave deeds, while in Mayan myth, they possess artistic talent, particularly in writing and sculpture. Animals may serve as stand-ins for humans or human characteristics, as in the African and Native American trickster tales or the fables of the Greek, Aesop. In some legends, animals perform heroic deeds or act as mediators between humans. They may also be the source of the wisdom and power of a medicine woman. Other myths focus on the close connection between people and animals.

43 The Minoan Snake Goddess figure brandishes a serpent in either hand, perhaps evoking her role as source of wisdom, as well as her role as Mistress of the Animals, with a leopard under each arm. Ancient Egyptians worshiped snakes, especially the cobra that was associated with many female deities.

44 "Animals In Mythology." MythEncyclopedia.com. Accessed 4/9/15.

45 Rita Laws. 1994. "Native Americans & Vegetarianism." *Vegetarian Journal*, Sep

46 Hitakonanu'laxk. 1994. *The Grandfathers Speak.* NY: Interlink Books.

12: Fifth Taming - Crops

1 Apsaras are known in South and East Asia. As ethereal beings who inhabit the skies, and are often depicted taking flight, or at service of a god, they may be compared to angels. Apsaras are sometimes compared to the muses of ancient Greece, with each representing a distinct aspect of the performing arts. They are associated with fertility rites.

2 Farnaz Broushaki et al. 2016. "Early Neolithic genomes from the eastern Fertile Crescent." *Science.* Jul 14.

3 G Wilcox. 2005. "The distribution, natural habitats, and availability of wild cereals in relation to their domestication in the Near East." *Vegetative History Archaeobot* 14:534-541.

4 D Rindos. 1987. *The Origins of Agriculture: An Evolutionary Perspective.* Academic Press.

5 Thanks to this relationship, house mice have colonized almost every corner of the globe to become almost as ubiquitous as humans and also one of the most invasive mammalian species.

6 L Weissbrod et al. 2017. "Origins of house mice in ecological niches created by settled hunter-gatherers in the Levant 15,000 y ago." *PNAS* online, Mar 27

7 Around 14,500 to 11,500 BP, the Natufian culture of sedentary gatherer-'hunters' were already using many of the technologies typical in agrarian cultures. For example, mortar and pestle for processing cereals, and sickles for harvesting. They lived in permanent settlements, and stored their food surpluses. They harvested wild cereals, and had dogs.

8 E Weiss et al. 2006. "Autonomous cultivation before domestication." *Science* 312:1608-1610.

9 G Wilcox et al. 2007. "Early Holocene cultivation before domestication in northern Syria." *Vegetative History Archaeobot*, 10.

10 The markers of crop domestication, non-shattering seed heads in cereals, were not well established until around 10,500 BP (Nesbitt M. 2002. "When and where did domesticated cereals first occur in Southwest Asia?" *In The Dawn of Farming in the Near East*, eds., Cappers RT, Bottema S, 113-32. Berlin: Ex Oriente.).

11 There is evidence for rice cultivation in 13,000 year-old sediment from the Yangtze River valley. (Zhao Z & Piperno D. 2000. "Late Pleistocene/Holocene environments in the Middle Yangtze River Valley, China & rice (Oryza sativa L.) domestication." *Geoarch* 15(2): 203-222.); Early origins for common millet domesticates were also found in northern China, around 10,300 BP (Lu H, et al. 2009. "Earliest domestication of common millet (Panicum miliaceum) in East Asia extended to 10,000 years ago." *PNAS* 106(18): 7367-72.).

12 J Diamond & P Bellwood. 2003. "Farmers and Their Languages." *Science* 300 (5619): 597-603.

13 The domestication of fig trees in the Near East occurred around 11,400 BP, roughly a thousand years before staples such as wheat, barley, and legumes were domesticated in the region. Selectively propagated figs, wild barley and wild oats were cultivated at an early agrarian site around 11,000 BP (Harvard Gazette. 2006. "Tamed 11,400 years ago, figs likely first domesticated crop." *HG* May 23.).

14 Wild lentils presented a challenge as most of the wild seeds do not germinate in the first year. The first evidence of lentil breaking dormancy in their first year was in Syria. This process allowed the founder crops to adapt and eventually become larger, more easily harvested, more dependable in storage and more useful to the human population.

15 TA Brown et al. 2009. "The complex origins of domesticated crops in the Fertile Crescent." *Trends in Ecology & Evolution* 24 (2): 103.

16 Ehud Weiss et al 2006. "Autonomous Cultivation Before Domestication". *Science* 312 (5780): 1608-1610.

17 LR Binford. 1968. "Post-Pleistocene Adaptations." In Sally R & LR Binford, eds. *New Perspectives in Archaeology.* Aldine Pub. pp. 313-342.

18 Elizabeth Gallagher et al. 2015. "Transition to farming more likely for small, conservative groups with property rights, but increased productivity is not essential." *PNAS*, 112:46 14218-23 Nov 17

19 Female invention of agricultural tools marks a radical departure from Middle Stone Age methods of plant food preparation. The Natufian picks are forerunner of the axe-adzes of the Neolithic. Other possible female inventions are sickle blades used for harvesting cereals, and tools in early cereal cultivation.

20 From the fifth domestication onward, sizable villages existed, with populations of 300 to 500. The most populous early agrarian sites were at least three to eight times larger than Natufian sites.

21 PJ Richerson et al. 2001. "Was Agriculture Impossible during the Pleistocene but Mandatory during the Holocene?" *American Antiquity* 66 (3): 387-411.

22 Pre-agrarian cultures focusing on the intensive exploitation of estuary resources persist for several

hundred years after the establishment coastal farming enclaves along the Mediterranean. The subsequent spread of agricultural economies into the interior likely proceeded through a combined process of colonist expansion, selective local adoption of agrarian technologies, and the integration of colonist and Indigenous populations (Zilhao J. 2000. "From the Mesolithic to the Neolithic in the Iberian Peninsula," in *Europe's First Farmers*, ed. by Price TD, pp 144-183. Cambridge Univ Press.).

23 S Rigaud et al. 2015. "Ornaments Reveal Resistance of North European Cultures to the Spread of Farming." *PLoS ONE* 10(4): e0121166.

24 Inadequate sanitary practices and the domestication of animals may explain the high incidence of disease and rise in deaths and sickness following the Neolithic Revolution.

25 Decorated burials particularly characterized the early Natufian, and differences in mortuary practices may have reflected some form of social hierarchy.

26 Neolithic sites across Europe, dating from 7,900 to 4,400 BP, show that early farmers invested considerable labor in the maintenance of long-established cultivation plots, and used livestock manure and water management to enhance crop yields. Intensive manuring inextricably linked plant cultivation and animal herding and contributed to the resilience of combined practices across diverse climatic zones.

27 J Guilaine 2003. "The Neolithization in the Mediterranean & France," in *The Widening Harvest*, eds., Ammerman A, & Biagi P. 189-206. Arch Ins of Am

28 László Bartosiewicz et al. 2013. "Crop manuring & intensive land management by Europe's first farmers." *PNAS*. June.

29 Early agrarian communities did not rely exclusively on the cultivation or breeding. Instead, they balanced gathering, farming, and animal breeding in order to maintain a steady food supply.

30 Along with a massive reduction in plant diversity, female-centered botanical knowledge and status as herbalists decreased with the fourth domestication. Today only 150 plants are part of World commerce, and of these, a mere 12-15, mostly domesticated cereals, sustain almost all humans and farmed animals.

31 Katharine Milton. 2002. "Hunter-gatherer diets: wild foods signal relief from diseases of affluence". In Ungar, PS & Teaford, MF, eds. *Human Diet*. Bergin & Garvey. 111-22.

32 Y Furuse et al. 2010. "Origin of measles virus." *Virology* Journal 7: 52.

33 U Singh. 2008. *A History of Ancient and Early Medieval India*. Pearson Education India.

34 Laws. 1998 ibid

35 This list includes tomato, white potato, bell pepper, red pepper, peanut, cashew, sweet potatoe, avocado, passion fruit, zucchini, green bean, kidney bean, maple syrup, lima bean, cranberry, pecan, okra, chocolate, vanilla, sunflower seed, pumpkin, cassava, walnut, forty-seven varieties of berries, pineapple, and, many herbs like lavender, sage, and paprika.

36 Laws. 1994 ibid

37 Bar-Yosef 1998.

38 Gimbutas 1991.

39 Hirst, KK. 2005. "Mehrgarh". *Guide to Archaeology.*

40 N Bhattacharyya. 1970. *The Indian Mother Goddess*. South Asia Books.

41 Most figurines are naked and have elaborate coiffures. Some figurines have ornaments or horns on the head and a few are in poses that expose the genitals. Several small circular objects with holes in middle, possibly representing yoni, were also found.

42 Near the back of the Chauvet cave, a large inner chamber reveals an enigmatic scene of several lions sitting in a circle around a human female form in a Yonic representation.

43 N Wade. 2007. "Study Traces Cat's Ancestry to Middle East". *NYT*. June 29

44 Cats have excellent night vision and can see at only one-sixth the light level required for human vision. Cats have excellent hearing and can detect an extremely broad range of frequencies. They can hear higher-pitched sounds than either dogs or humans.

45 It was a beneficial situation for both species: cats got a reliable source of prey, and humans got effortless pest control. This mutually beneficial arrangement began the relationship between cats and humans which continues to this day.

46 S Crowell-Davis et al. 2004. "Social Organization in the Cat." *J. Feline Med. & Surgery*. 6:1 19-28

47 Herodotus also wrote that when a cat died, the Egyptian household would go into mourning as if for a human relative, and would often shave their eyebrows to signify their loss. The punishments for harming cats were severe.

48 Bubastis became a marketplace for merchants; artisans came with thousands of bronze sculptures and amulets depicting cats to worshippers of Bast. These amulets commonly featured an image of a cat and its kittens, and were often used by women trying to have children, praying to Bast, or Bastet that they be granted the same number of children as kittens depicted on the amulet.

49 The myth is attributed to the natural suppleness and swiftness cats exhibit to escape life-threatening situations.

13: Earth Goddesses

1 D Trimijopulos. 2011. "Great Mother." Revised. 61 pages. Web 3.2.15

2 Earth Goddesses are present in the earliest images in Ancient Egypt. An association is drawn to the early Goddesses of Egypt with animals seen as good mothers—the lioness, cow, hippopotamus, white vulture, cobra, scorpion, and cat—as well as, to the life-giving primordial waters, the sun, the night sky, and the Earth herself. The story of the Mother/Earth Goddess is found in texts written in the hieroglyphic as well as in the cuneiform script. Their texts date from 5,150 BP, and Mut was listed as the primal "mother of all who was not born of any."

3 The idea that the fertile Earth is female and nurtures humans is a global concept.

4   Andree Collard. 1989. *Rape of the Wild: Man's Violence against Animals & the Earth.* Indiana UP
5   Female deities have attributes of the moon. Many rituals of moon deities are viewed as part of a religion for human females. The Moon Goddess signified an association with pregnancy and menstruation.
6   Marta Weigle. 1982. *Spiders & Spinsters: Women & Mythology.* Univ of New Mexico Press.
7   Merlin Stone. 1989. *Ancient Mirrors of Womanhood: A Treasury of Goddess & Heroine Lore from Around the World.* Beacon Press.
8   Denise L Carmody. 1992. *Mythological woman.* NY: Crossroad.
9   Bettina L Knapp. 1997. *Women in myth.* NY: State Univ of New York Press.
10 Bettina L Knapp. 1998. *Women, myth, & the feminine principle.* SUNY Press.
11 Jenny Jochens. 1996. *Old Norse images of Women.* U of Pennsylvania Press.
12 Betty B. Lies. 1999. *Earth's Daughters: Stories of Women in Classical Mythology.* Fulcrum Resources.
13 Jane Caputi. 1993. *Gossips, Gorgons and Crones: The Fates of the Earth.* Bear & Company.
14 Jane Caputi. 2004. *Goddess & Monsters: Women, Myth, Power, & Popular Culture.* Popular Press
15 DA Leeming & J Page. 1996. *Goddess: Myths of the Female Divine.* Oxford UP.
16 Joseph Campbell. 2013. *Goddesses: Mysteries of the Feminine Divine.* New World Library.
17 Patricia Monaghan. 2011. *Goddesses in World Culture,* Volume 1. ABC-CLIO.
18 In Sudanese Dinka mythology, Abuk is the first woman. Abuk is the patron Goddess of women and gardens, and her emblem is a small snake.
19 Aja is a forest Goddess honored by the Yoruba of Nigeria. Aja instructs her followers in the use of medicinal herbs found in the African forests.
20 Akonadi is an oracular Goddess of Ghana. Akwaba is a Goddess who symbolizes welcome and is always placed above the door. Maidens receive her image from an elder mentor as they come of age, welcoming them into their motherhood role in the tribe.
21 In Togo, a giant Akwaba always precedes the chief in tribal procession, signifying that the Mother and reverence for Nature are the foremost communal values.
22 Ala is the earth and fertility goddess of the Ibo people of Nigeria, as well as a goddess of the underworld. Ala is the mother of all things. In the beginning she gives birth, and at the end she welcomes the dead back to her womb. In Nigeria, where she is still worshiped, she has temples situated in the center of the villages, where she has a statue surrounded by the images of other gods and animals.
23 Agwe is Mother of the sea in Benin. She is affectionate & nurturing to humans who honor her.
24 Aha Njoku is worshiped by the Ibo. She is responsible for yams, a central ingredient in the Ibo diet, and the women who care for them.
25 Aje is a Yoruba Goddess of wealth in all its forms.
26 Akonandi is a Ghanian oracular Goddess of justice.
27 Amirini is an early Goddess of the Yoruba of West Africa.
28 Asase Ya is the Ashanti Earth Goddess & the Ghanian creator of humanity, & mother of gods.
29 Atete is the fertility Goddess of the Kafa people of Ethiopia.
30 Ayabba is the hearth Goddess of the Fon people of Benin.
31 Ashiakle is the Goddess of wealth of the Gan people of Ghana
32 Aziri is a Goddess of possessions
33 Aje is a Nigerian Yoruba goddess of wealth.
34 Oshun taught the people how to use corn for food, the use of fire, to cook, and how to sing songs. She taught the first women to weave cloth and to dye it in bright colors squeezed from berries. She also taught women how to throw cowrie shells so they could see the future.
35 Isis was called 'The Lady of Ten Thousand Names," because all other Goddesses were believed to be aspects of Isis. She knew how to use plants as medicine, and was especially famous as a healer of children. She also taught women how to weave, spin, and cultivate gardens.
36 Traditions on both sides of the Atlantic tell of the Mami Wata spirit abducting her followers or random people whilst they are swimming or boating. She brings them to her paradisaical realm, which may be underwater, in the spirit world, or both. Should she allow them to leave, the travelers usually return in dry clothing and with a new spiritual understanding reflected in their gaze. They often grow wealthier, more attractive, & more easygoing after the encounter.
37 Max Dashu. 2014. "Jillinya, Great Mother of the Ngarinyin." *SageWoman Blogs.* 12 Feb.
38 In Australian Aboriginal narratives, Eingana is a creator/mother of water, animals, and humans. She is a snake Goddess of death who lives in the Dreamtime. Eingana holds a sinew that is attached to every living thing, and if she lets go of one, the attached creature dies.
39 Aboriginal Law Men are reverent toward Jillinya, and those of Algi & Mumuu, her other forms.
40 J Doring, ed. 2000. *Gwion Gwion.* Köln: Konemann.
41 Gwendolyn Leick. 1991. *A Dictionary of Ancient Near Eastern Mythology.* Routledge.
42 J Black & A Green. 1992. *Gods, Demons and Symbols of Ancient Mesopotamia.* UTexas Press.
43 Gwendolyn Leick. 2003. *Sex, Love, & Eroticism in Mesopotamian Literature.* Routledge
44 Asherah is a mother Goddess who appears in a number of ancient sources. Goddess of motherhood and fertility, known as Lady of the Sea, she appears in Akkadian writings as Ashratum (Antu), in Hittite as Asertu, and in Ugaritic as Goddess 'aṭirat. Asherah is identified as the consort of the Sumerian god Anu and Ugaritic El, the oldest deities of their respective pantheons. She is also called Elat, "Goddess", the feminine form of El.
45 WG Dever. 2005. *Did God Have A Wife? Archaeology & Folk Religion In Ancient Israel.* WB

Eerdmans.

46 Inanna was the Sumerian Goddess of love, fertility, and warfare. Inanna was the most prominent female deity in ancient Mesopotamia, associated with lions and frequently depicted standing on the backs of two lionesses. Her cuneiform was a hook-shaped twisted knot of reeds, representing the doorpost of the storehouse, and thus fertility. At Inanna's temple, sacred prostitution was a common practice which continued in other Semitic cults including Israelite. Asexual, hermaphroditic, and feminine people were particularly involved in rituals at Inanna's temples.

47 Uras in Sumerian mythology is a Goddess of Earth, and one of the consorts of the sky god Anu.

48 Nisaba of Eresh was the Sumerian Goddess of writing, learning, and the harvest. She is considered the teacher of both mortal scribes and deities. Many clay-tablets end with the phrase "Nisaba be praised" to honor the Goddess. In the Babylonian era, she was replaced by the god Nabu, who took over her functions. In some instances, Nisaba was his instructor or wife before he replaced her.

49 Anat is a main Semitic war-Goddess. She is a virgin who is the sister of the great god Ba'al Hadad. Anat first appears in Egypt in the 16th dynasty (the Hyksos era) along with other Semitic deities. She was often paired with Ashtart. In Akkadian, Anat was Antu, earlier Antum, the female form of Anu, the 'Sky' god. Antu appears in Akkadian texts as the mother of Ishtar in the Gilgamesh story. Inanna and Ishtar continued in Canaanite tradition as Anath and Astarte. The two Goddesses were invariably linked in scripture and formed a triad with a third Goddess, Qadesh, "the holy one."

50 In Sumerian mythology Ki is the Earth Goddess. She is associated with Ninhursag, lady of the mountains, the Earth and fertility mother Goddess, who had the surnames Nintu (lady of birth), and Mamma (Dalley, Stephanie. 1989. *Myths from Mesopotamia*. Oxford UP.).

51 Many of the older Goddesses were married off to gods in the Old Babylonian era, after which they became increasingly regarded as taking a mediating and intercessionary role.

52 Black & Green. 1992. ibid

53 In Buddhism, the specific local mother deity of Earth, as opposed to the mother deity of all creation, is called Bhūmi. Buddha called upon Bhumi when he achieved enlightenment.

54 Music, dance, sexuality and the arts are the Yoginis' domain. Each Yogini has a different plant associated with her and fertility. Perhaps, the Yoginis' attributes, names, and iconography were modeled after living women in which they were worshiped.

55 Vidya Dehejia. 1986. *Yogini Cult and Temples*. New Delhi: National Museum.

56 The Yogini is sometimes perceived as a sorceress or a witch. Legends tell of her abilities to turn humans into animals. Several such stories speak of a magic thread that is tied around the Yogini's lover's neck. He is then turned into a parrot or monkey and is forced to remain in that form until she sexually desires him and breaks the spell to make love to his human form. Other tales tell of flying women (Dakinis) or women who suddenly vanish in the night. This category of Yoginis always meets in circles to perform their rituals, which include transgressive acts that are said to give them supernatural powers.

57 Consulting the position of these stellar Yoginis before a pilgrimage or any serious undertaking was common practice in the past. Several ancient texts outline prayers, rituals and ways to appease and invoke the protection of these Yoginis.

58 For example at the Kamakhya temple in Assam, the daily worship of Devi Kamakhya includes the invocation of the 64 Yoginis. Kamakhya is the site where the Goddess' yoni fell according to myth, and it is considered the most sacred of temples.

59 Stella Dupuis. 2008. *The Yogini Temples of India*. Varanasi: Pilgrims Publishing.

60 It is said that if you are in danger and you call out her name Kuan Yin will come to your rescue. If you are sick and pray to her, she will heal you. She gives children to people who have none and she brings peace to the battlefield.

61 The Dakota and Lakota of Manitoba and the Dakotas tell how a woman, White Buffalo Calf Woman, brought the pipe to their people. It is through the pipe that prayer is carried by its smoke upwards to the Creator in their most sacred ceremonies.

62 When a traditional Ojibway person prays, thanks is given and the pipe is raised in each of the four directions, then to Mother Earth as well as to Grandfather, Mishomis, in the sky.

63 White Buffalo Woman told the people, "The Earth is your Mother and Grandmother. When you walk on Earth, you are making a prayer to her. We are all one family. When you smoke this pipe, you will make a prayer for the good of all of our Mother's children. When you pray with this pipe, all beings of the Universe will be a family."

64 Often depicted with jaguar claws or ears, she wears a serpent as her headdress and is also associated with the moon and the traditional Mayan sweatbath. She was so sacred to Maya women that they founded an island sanctuary, still called the Isla de Mujeres, dedicated to worship of Ixchel off the coast of contemporary Cancun.

65 Danu, Raetia, and Marisa were Mountain Goddess of the Alps.

66 Bugady Musun, was a Goddess revered by many Siberian peoples.

67 J Daniel. 2010. *The Philosophy of Ancient Britain*. Kessinger Publishing

68 Māra is Mother Earth, patroness of all female duties like children and cattle; economic activities ("God made the table, Māra made the bread"), and even money and markets. She is the Goddess of land (J Kursīte. 2005. "Baltic Religion." In L Jones *Ency. of Religion 2,* 2nd ed. Thomson Gale.).

69 Cybele's priests at Pessinus were rulers who derived advantages from their priestly functions. Even after the image of the Goddess was carried to Rome, Pessinus still continued to be looked upon as the metropolis of the great Goddess, and as the principal seat of her worship.

70 Under different names, the worship of Rhea occurred as far as the Euphrates and even Bactriana. She was the great Goddess of the Eastern world.

71 J McMahon & J Roberts. 2000. *The Sheela-na-Gigs of Ireland and Britain*. Mercier Press Ltd.

1 Ann Gibbons. 2017. "There's no such thing as a 'pure' European–or anyone else." *Science Magazine,* May 15

2 Resit Ergener. 1988. *Anatolia Land of the Mother Goddess.* Hitit Pub.

3 DNA analysis reveal that there was a population expansion between 15,000 and 10,000 BP in European gatherer-hunters. The expansion was followed by a decline in gatherer-hunter populations between 10,000 and 5,000 BP. These corresponded to an analogous population increase among early farmers around 9,000 BP. (Fu Q, Rudan P, Pa¨a¨bo S, Krause J. 2012. "Complete Mitochondrial Genomes Reveal Neolithic Expansion into Europe." *PLoS ONE* 7(3))

4 G Brandt et al. 2013. "Ancient DNA Reveals Key Stages in the Formation of Central European Mitochondrial Genetic Diversity." *Science* Vol. 342 no. 6155 pp. 257-261; October 11.

5 At first, the original gatherer-hunter populations retreated to the fringes of Europe. However, within a few thousand years they returned, and significant amounts of gatherer-hunters mixed with farmers from 7,000 to 5,000 BP. (Rigby, LD & Rigby, SH. 2000. *Evolutionary Origins of Morality: Cross-disciplinary Perspectives. UK:* Imprint Academic. p. 158.)

6 Rigaud et al 2015. ibid

7 Between 4500 and 4000 BP, the simplest form of the plough, called the ard, spread throughout Europe, replacing the hoe. This change in equipment significantly increased cultivation ability, and affected the demand for land, as well as ideas about property, inheritance and family rights. Before this time, simple digging sticks or hoes were used (Postan, MM et al, eds. 1987. *Cambridge Economic History of Europe: Vol. 2: Trade and Industry in the Middle Ages.* Cambridge UP. p. 28.).

8 J Langer & M Killen.1998. *Piaget, evolution, & development.* Psychology Press; Kuijt, Ian. 2000. *Life in Neolithic farming communities: social organization, identity, and differentiation.* Springer.

9 The stylized Cycladic Woman/Goddess figurines, such as the Pregnant Lady, dates to 4,400 BP. Other figures of identical style from Sardinia date from 5,500 BP. This stylized art gradually developed from statuettes depicting steatopygous women, having fat or prominent buttocks.

10 They are presented in extended poses of strict symmetry, with arms folded just under gently protruding breasts, as if they were clutching their abdomens.

11 Snakes were symbols of life, protection, the underlying Earth, and Goddesses. With the transition to male-centered society, they were trampled under the foot of male deities and connected to evil. This demonization of snakes was part of the reduction of the Goddess, and female power. Snakes were also a threat to males' increasing invasion of native habitats.

12 In Stone Age religions, animals and nature took part in the creation of the universe, and the difference between them is fluid. Animals become humans and vice-versa. The Goddess takes animal shape to achieve their special abilities, or animals take over part of the human soul. Animals and nature are spirited and animals can have a variety of roles, each of them defined by a specific ritual or social context.

13 Animalism is characterized by practices such as placating and begging for forgiveness of the animal killed, performing oracles with animal bones, animal dances, and fertility rites. Animals were thought to be human-like, in possession of a spirit, or equipped with magical powers. Animals are regarded as guardian spirits and "alter egos," of human forms and deities who change between human and animal forms and unifies them. Spirits exist in nature, in the forest and savannas, and in animals.

14 Individual and theological totemism are particularly close to animalism, while group or clan totemism serve a social function. Totemism occurs primarily among agrarian peoples.

15 In the popular "The Robbers and the Farm Animals" tale from Switzerland, a miller's servant had grown old and wanted to leave. The miller said: "You are free to leave if you wish, but you will receive no wages." The servant went the say goodbye to the farm animals. The horse, ox, rooster, dog, cat and goose all were sorry to see the servant go and decided to follow him. This story is a commentary on the common status of exploited animal and human workers.

16 Inuit and Chinese tales mention beautiful, seductive women who turn out to be foxes in disguise. In one Inuit story a woman enters the home of a hunter while he is out. She cooks for him and stays for some time, but eventually she puts on her fox skin and disappears.

17 JJ Tehrani. 2013. "The Phylogeny of Little Red Riding Hood." *PLoS ONE* 8(11): e78871.

18 The Goddess of the mountain has supremacy over both predator and prey. She communicates with them, shares their world and takes their shape when needed.

19 In Mesopotamia the alter ego of the healing goddesses, Gula, was the dog. In iconography, the goddesses and dogs go together, and the dog alone can represent them. In the Goddess's city Isin, archaeologists found bronze plaques scratched with images of dogs, a statue of a kneeling figure embracing a dog, and a number of small clay dogs, one of which was inscribed with a prayer to the Goddess.

20 Jan Knappert. 1992. *Pacific Mythology.* Aquarian/Thorsons

21 Áine is an Irish Goddess of summer, wealth, and sovereignty. She is connected with midsummer and the sun, and is sometimes represented by a red mare. As the Goddess of love and fertility, she had command over crops and animals and is also linked with agriculture.

22 Arnapkapfaaluk or big bad woman, was the sea Goddess of the Inuit people. She had control of the animals of the seas, and inspired fear in hunters.

23 HJ Rose. 1959. *A Handbook of Greek Mythology.* NY

24 The oldest aspect of the Cretan Goddess was as Mother of Mountains, who appears on Minoan seals with the demonic features of a Gorgon, accompanied by the double-axes of power and gripping divine snakes. Britomartis remained on the coins of Cretan cities, as herself or as Diktynna, the Goddess of Mount Dikte, Zeus' birthplace. As Diktynna, winged and depicted with a human face, she stood on her ancient mountain, and grasped an animal in each hand, in the guise of Potnia Theron, the Mistress of Animals. On the early Minoan seals, she suckles griffons, breeds of hunting dogs. Her temples were said to be guarded by vicious dogs stronger than bears.

25 Potnia Theron ("The Mistress of the Animals") is a term first used by Homer and is often used to

describe female divinities associated with animals. Many figures show a central female form grasping two animals, one to each side. The oldest depiction has been discovered in Çatalhöyük.

26 Epona was a protector of horses, donkeys, and mules. Epona is the only Celtic divinity worshiped in Rome itself. She was particularly a Goddess of fertility, as shown by her attributes of a patera, cornucopia, ears of grain and the presence of foals in some sculptures. Her worship was popular in the Roman Empire between the first and third centuries AD.

27 Nannó Marinatos. 2000. *The Goddess & the Warrior. The naked goddess & Mistress of Animals in early Greek religion.* London: Routledge

28 In ancient Roman religion, Feronia was a goddess linked to wildlife, fertility, health, and abundance. She was honored among plebeians and freedmen but her shrines were located in nature, far from human settlements. Her festival, the Feroniae, was November 13. Her sacred grove was a place where everybody was allowed to come for worship and trade, attracting people from different nations and providing everybody with a neutral territory in which the peace must not be perturbed. She received the first fruits of the harvest because she 'permits' men to domesticate the wild forces of vegetation.

29 Flidais was a Celtic Goddess. As Lady of the Forest, she protects fauna and flora. In myths she is connected to both unrestrained and domestic animals. In particular deer and cattle are her sacred animals, both of whom she milks. She called all the unrestrained animals "her cattle."

30 Medeina is one of the main deities in Lithuanian mythology, and is similar to Latvian Meža Māte. She is a ruler of forests, trees, and animals. Her sacred animal is a hare. She is depicted as a young woman and a she-wolf with an escort of wolves. Medeina is a Goddess with both divine and demonic traits. Her duty is not to help the hunters, but to protect the forest. Medeina later was replaced by Žemyna, Goddess of Earth, representing the agricultural interest of peasants (Vaitkevičius, V. 2003. "New outlook for Žvėrūna-Medeina." *Lietuvos archeologija* 24.)

31 In early Egyptian mythology, Mafdet was a Goddess who protected against snakes and scorpions and was often represented as either feline or mongoose (Wilkinson, RH. 2003. *The Complete Gods & Goddesses of Ancient Egypt.* Thames & Hudson.).

32 Rumina was a Goddess who protected breastfeeding mothers, and nursing infants in ancient Rome. Her domain extended to protecting animal mothers, not just human ones. Rumina's temple was near the fig tree at the foot of the Palatine Hill where Romulus and Remus were raised by a she-wolf. Milk, rather than the typical wine, was offered as a sacrifice at this temple (Hammond, N & Scullard, H eds. 1970. *The Oxford Classical Dictionary.* OUP.).

33 In South Asia, Aranyani is a Goddess of the forests and the animals that dwell within them.

34 Kamadhenu is a divine bovine-Goddess described as the mother of all cows.

35 Mansa Devi, is a folk Goddess of snakes, worshiped chiefly for the prevention and cure of snakebite and also for fertility and prosperity. Manasa is the sister of Vasuki, king of snakes.

36 Varahi is one of the Matrikas, a group of seven or eight mother Goddesses in South Asia. With the head of a sow, Varahi is the shakti or feminine energy of Varaha, the boar Avatar of the god Vishnu. The Buddhist Goddesses Vajravarahi and Marichi have their origins in Varahi.

37 Sarama helps the god-king Indra to recover divine cows stolen by demons. Sarama is described to have found the milk of the cattle, which nourished humanity. This is interpreted as Sarama teaching man to milk cows and use the butter created from it for fire-sacrifices.

38 Y Naito et al. 2016. "Evidence for herbivorous cave bears (Ursus spelaeus) in Goyet Cave, Belgium." *Journal of Quaternary Science,* 31:6 598-606

39 Why did the brown bear survive while the giant bear did not? It could have been climate change, different dietary preferences, hibernation strategies, geographical ranges, and habitat preferences? As modern humans moved into the caves of Europe, giant bears had fewer safe places to hibernate. So an acute housing shortage may have been the final blow for giant bears.

40 Andarta is a bear Goddess of southern Gaul. Rksavaktra is a bear-faced Dakini, a type of tantric deity most prominently found within hinduism and Tibetan buddhism. She is often depicted with a yellow or green body and the head of an Asiaic Black Bear.

41 Ina Wunn. 2000. "Beginning of Religion." *Numen* 47 (4).

42 Depending on snowfall, temperature, and food supply, bears get ready for winter hibernation in late November by eating berries, which are rich in carbohydrates. Grizzly, black, and polar bears can sleep from five to seven months, and generally do not eat, drink, defecate, or urinate during hibernation. Cubs are born about two months into hibernation but are not able to walk or feed on their own until they are about six months old.

43 The Big Dipper and the constellation as a whole have mythological significance in numerous world cultures, usually as a symbol of the north.

44 Polaris appears to remain in the same location, while all the other stars rotate around it, as if it is the center of the universe.

45 In Greek, Arktos is the word for bear, hence the name Arctic, which means bearish and describes the far northern parts of the Earth where the Great Bear constellation dominates the heavens.

46 In her travels throughout the night sky, Ursa Major constantly changes from quadrupedal to bipedal positions, seeming to run along on all fours nearest the horizon and then rising to its hind feet to begin the ascent back into the sky.

47 A Gurevich. 2013. "Forgotten Wisdom of the Chauvet Cave." *Popular Archaeology,* Mar 1

48 In Greek and Roman mythology, a harpy was a female monster in the form of a bird with a human face. Harpies steal food from their victims while they are eating and carry away evildoers. Their name means "snatchers." and they may have originally been wind spirits.

49 Sirin is a mythological creature of Russia, with head and chest of a woman and body of a bird (usually an owl). Men who heard them would forget everything, follow them, and ultimately die.

50 In Hebrew and Buddhist texts, Sirins, Alkonosts and Gamayuns turned into archangels in 'paradise.'

51 Snakes were seen as entities of strength, rebirth, and mortality. Over a vast area of South Asia, there are carved representations of cobras or nagas or stones as substitutes. Food and flowers are offered and lights are burned before the shrines.

52 Eisler 1995. ibid. Eisler suggests that prehistoric peoples viewed the Earth and Cosmos as part of sexual interplay. The seasonal rebirth of plant and animal life every Spring, and the rebirth of the sun on the Winter Solstice each year, were generated through some kind of sexual union.

53 The most powerful and sacred place of all is the vulva of the Goddess, which is depicted by Irish Sheela na gig figures. One would touch the vulva of a Sheela in order to obtain fertility, the ability to have a child.

54 Vulva images are also found in megalithic sites in Malta; on crouching stone figures from Lepenski Vir in Serbia, from around 8,800 BP; on Woman display carvings from western China around 5,000 BP; and Lajj Gauris from south Asia.

55 Dexter and Mair 2010. ibid

56 Images show Goddess Baubo sometimes as a full-bodied old Woman lifting her skirt, and sometimes only as a vulva.

57 In the Sacred Song of Inanna, 4,300 BP, it states, "moor my slender boat of heaven, my new moon crescent cunt beauty."

58 Lajja Gauri fertility aspect is emphasized by symbolic representation of the genitals, Yoni or the Womb, as blooming Lotus flower denoting blooming youth in some cases and in others through a simple yet detailed depiction of an exposed vulva. Lajja Gauri is often in a squatting position (uttanpada) with legs open, as in during childbirth. In some cases, the Lajja Gauri's right foot is placed on a platform to facilitate full opening of her vagina. A blossoming lotus is sometimes used to replace her head and neck, an icon often used in Tantra.

59 Despite their ancient history and continuing worship across South Asia and elsewhere, Lajja Gauris are entirely absent in patriarchal vedic texts and caste-based hinduism.

60 These female figures protect the villagers' health and crops and ward off evil spirits. According to another legend, Dilukai was the sister of a troublesome man who eventually departed. The images of his sister were erected to prevent his return, as it was forbidden for a brother to see his sister's genitalia.

61 Alexis Okeowo. 2011. "The Ivory Coast Effect." *The New Yorker.* 22 March.

62 Sokari Ekine. 2002. "The Curse of Nakedness: Women in Nigeria Threaten to Bare it All to Better Their Communities." *International Museum of Women.*

15: Goddess Being

1   Judith Shaw. 2016. "The Reindeer Goddess." *Feminism and Religion.* Online. Dec 18.

2   The principal lunar phases are new moon, first quarter, full moon, and third or last quarter.

3   The Maya assume the moon is female and the phases are conceived as stages of a woman's life. The Maya moon Goddess is associated with sexuality and procreation, fertility and growth, not only of human beings, but also of vegetation and crops. The moon Goddess is also a deity of disease and water, be it wells, rainfall, or the rainy season.

4   Penelope Shuttle & P Redgrove. 2005. *The Wise Wound: Menstruation & Every woman.* Marion Boyars Pub

5   The Ishango bone in the Congo, dated to 8,500 BP, has engraved marks that match lunar phases. A notched tool from an Avdeevo site in Russia show evidence of the conscious recording of the lunar cycle. The notches add up to 29, the number of days in a lunar month. And a limestone object found in an Upper Paleolithic site in Hungry is shaped like a half-moon with notched edges. (Rudgley, R. 2000. *The Lost Civilizations of the Stone Age.* Simon & Schuster.)

6   Female reproductive synchronicity leads to greater numbers of ovulating females who must be guarded simultaneously, which makes it harder for a dominant male to monopolize a harem to himself. By attending to any one fertile female, the male unavoidably leaves others to mate with his rivals. This outcome distributes paternity more widely across the total male population, reducing paternity skew.

7   Alton 2010. ibid. In Ashanti, the day of the new moon is called 'the day of blood.' The Yoruba do not work the fields on this day. And in some parts of Europe, it is believed that the moon regularly menstruates during the 'blood moon' time.

8   A Marshack. 1972. *The Roots of Civilization.* McGraw-Hill

9   Under patriarchy, the number 13 have been twisted to carry negative connotations. The fear of the number 13 has been given a scientific name, "triskaidekaphobia."

10 In Mesopotamian theology, there is a Goddess triad of Inanna, Ishtar, and Astarte; and, that of Qetesh, Astarte, and Anat.

11 In Egypt, there are the Lion-headed Goddesses, Hathor, Bast and Sekhmet. And a Goddess triad of Hathor for Birth, Nephthys for Death, and Isis for Rebirth, is common.

12 In ancient Arabian religion, there was a triad of al-Lat, Al-Uzza, and Manat.

13 In South Asian mythology, there are three Mother Goddess - Parvati, Durga, and Kali.

14 In ancient Roman religion and myth, the Parcae were the female personifications of destiny, often called the Fates in English. The Parcae were Nona, Decima and Morta.

15 In Greek mythology, the Erinyes also known as Furies, were female underworld deities of vengeance. They were sometimes referred to as 'infernal Goddesses.' They are called Furies in hell, Harpies on Earth, and Dirae in heaven.

16 Grace is one of three or more Goddesses of charm, beauty, nature, human creativity, and fertility, together known as the Charities or Graces. The usual list, from youngest to oldest is Aglaea for Splendor, Euphrosyne for Mirth, and Thalia for Good Cheer.

17 The Horae or Hours, were the Greek Goddesses of the seasons and the natural portions of time.

They were Thallo, Auxo and Carpo, who were Goddesses of nature. Horae could also be Eunomia, Diké, and Eirene, who were law-and-order Goddesses.

18 The Matres and Matronae were female deities venerated in North-West Europe from the 1st to the 5th century AD. Simek, R. 2007. *Dictionary of Northern Mythology*. D.S. Brewer.

19 The Moirai of Greek mythology were Clotho the spinner, Lachesis the allotter, and Atropos the unturnable. Hecate, a three-headed goddess of Thracian origin, guarded crossroads.

20 The Norns, the Fates of Norse mythology were Urðr of the past, Verðandi of the present, and Skuld of the future. The three Norse Mother Goddesses were Freyja, Frigg and Skaði.

21 In Celtic mythology, there are Elaine the Virgin, Margawse the Mother, and Morgan the Crone.

22 In ancient Rome, Nona spun the thread of life from a stick onto her spindle. She determined a person's lifespan on the day on which the name was chosen, which occurred on the ninth day from birth for a male and the eighth day for a female. Decima measured the thread of life with her rod, and Morta cut the thread of life and chose the manner of aperson's death.

23 The Sudice are the "Fates" of Slavic mythology - spirits that meted out fortune, destiny, judgment and in some cases, fatality, when a child was born. One story is of three old women spinners who approach cradles of every newborn child, and foretell their fate.

24 Jane Ellen Harrison.1903. *Prolegomena to the Study of Greek Religion*. Cambridge UP.

25 R Graves. 1948. *The White Goddess: a Historical Grammar of Poetic Myth*. Faber & Faber.

26 GG Jung & K Kerényi. 1949. *Essays on a Science of Mythology*. Pantheon Books.

27 Whitmont argued that mother imagery underpins many mythologies, and precedes the image of the paternal father in religious systems. EC Whitmont. 1969. *The Symbolic Quest*. Princeton UP.

28 E Neumann. 1955. *The Great Mother: an Analysis of the Archetype*. Pantheon.

29 K Kerenyi. 1952. *Athene: Virgin and Mother in Greek Religion,* translated from German by Murray Stein in 1978. Spring Publications, Zurich.

30 Gimbutas was literate in 13 languages, and an expert on the European Bronze Age.

31 Marija Gimbutas. 1989. *The Language of the Goddess*. Harper Collins.

32 Gimbutas suggested that the Great Goddess may have roots in two groups: totemic animal-Goddesses or hybrid woman-animal, and the procreative sacred female, perhaps the Original Clan Mother. The prehistoric personification of the powers and cycles of nature and cosmos as Goddess, often sculpted with her attendants, may well "reflect the role of an honored elder, the great clan mother, who was assisted by a council of women."

33 The sacred animal of the Pregnant Goddess is an unrestrained sow, and pigs are shown on lots of masks. The Earth Mother is regarded as being pregnant in the spring, and thus has to be protected and respected. There is a saying that "to strike the Earth is the same as striking your own mother."

34 Marija Gimbutas. 2001. *The Living Goddesses*. University of California Press.

35 Life-giver images were deer, bear, water-fowl and serpent. Death-wielder and Re-generator images were vulture, owl, bird of prey, fish, frog, and snake. According to Gimbutas, moths, butterflies, or bees, or alternatively, a symbols such as a frog, hedgehog, or bulls head, were representations of the uterus or fetus, and were also symbols of 'regeneration.'

36 Baba Yaga is a many-faceted figure who can be interpreted as a Cloud, Moon, Death, Winter, Snake, Bird, Pelican or Earth Goddess, totemic gynocentric ancestress, female initiator, phallic mother, or archetypal image. (Johns, Andreas. 2004. *Baba Yaga: The Ambiguous Mother and Witch of the Russian Folktale*. Peter Lang).

37 Eastern Europe was not a peaceful feminist utopia, and gynocentric theory is not romanticizing the past. Neolithic people obviously had conflicts and arguments in daily life, nonetheless, they delighted in nature and art. Moreover, they shunned war, since there was an absence of weapons and organized warfare. They built cozy settlements rather than forts.

38 EPR. 2001. "Gimbutas, Marija, & the Goddess." *Ency of Psychology & Religion*. 310423: 9329

39 Gimbutas 1991. ibid

40 Esther Jacobson. 1993. *The Deer Goddess of Ancient Siberia: A Study in the Ecology of Belief*. EJ Brill.

41 The term hierophany means 'the sacred bringing to light' or revealing of the sacred. Pre-historic female-centered art and myths may signify a manifestation of the sacred, and describe breakthroughs of the 'supernatural' into the World, that is, hierophanies.

42 In the oldest traditions, the Tree was the source of unborn souls, which would give birth to the new primal woman, Life (Lif) in the new universe after the present cycle came to an end.

43 And in southwest Asia, Hellenistic realism reshaped her as an individual human-like Goddess.

44 Lindström writes that the Moura "came to the area in the beginning of time and shaped it - its hills and valley and rivers, dolmens and menhir and red paintings on the rocks, and gave birth to children, who possibly became the ancestors of the community telling the legend. What was there before this? A feminine deity who was also the landscape itself, from whom the living things and to whom they returned in a cycle of life? Possibly."

45 Mouras may possess treasures and exist in the form of goats, bulls, or snakes but are transformed of their own accord. They may test people morally, and if people are worthy they may receive a reward. Mouras are harsh with cruel people. "Breaking a promise to a moura can also lead to death." The megalith-constructing women of the legends are supernatural, simultaneously young and old, and have everlasting life. They taught people many Neolithic skills, from herbal medicine and agriculture, to the manufacturing of iron.

46 Henna Lindstrom. 2014. "Casas das Mouras Encantadas - A Study of dolmens in Portuguese archaeology and folklore." Masters' Thesis in Archaeology, Univ. of Helsinki.

47 Palingenesis is a concept of rebirth or re-creation, used in various contexts in philosophy, theology, politics, and biology. Its meaning stems from Greek palin, meaning again, and genesis, meaning birth. In theology, the word can be used to refer to reincarnation.

48 The complex was cut into the hillside. Monolithic pillars similar to those at Göbekli Tepe were built into its dry stone walls, and its interior contained two free-standing pillars 10 feet (3 m) tall.

49 They were fired at temperatures between 500-600°C, which suggests the development of ceramic firing technology before the advent of pottery proper.

50 The two-story temple was oriented nearly east-west and made of wood and clay, surrounded by a galleried courtyard. Five rooms were on the first floor and raised family altars made of clay were on the ground floor. (J Chapman, et al. 2014. "Architectural differentiation on a Trypillia mega-site." *Journal of Neolithic Archaeology.* 16

51 The site started as a cemetery of cremation burials marked by a circle of bluestones. The UK site contains dozens of stone circles and ceremonial pits that stretch for five miles. One circle is a massive megalithic monument 12 times the size of Stonehenge, made up of more than 50 giant stones buried along a 1,082-foot-long c-shaped enclosure.

52 G Dvorsky. 2014. "Archaeologists Have Made An Incredible Discovery At Stonehenge." *Io9,* 9/10

53 The Cahokia mounds were built in the 7th to 15th centuries in Illinois by agriculturalists. The site covered 6 square miles (16 km2) and included about 120 human-made earthen mounds in a wide range of sizes, shapes, and functions. Cahokia's population at its peak in the 13th century was an estimated 40,000, more than any city in the US until the late 18th century. (G Milner. 2004. The Moundbuilders: Ancient Peoples of Eastern North America. Thames & Hudson Ltd.)

54 Unlike the megaliths built by agricultural societies, such as Stonehenge and the Egyptian pyramids, Poverty Point was built by prehistoric gatherers. In this sense, it is similar to the Göbekli Tepe complex in Turkey, that was built by gatherers around 12,000 BP. (J Gibson. 2000. *The Ancient Mounds of Poverty Point: Place of Rings.* UP of Florida.)

55 The six earthworks cover 910 acres, or 1.42 square miles (3.68 km2), and the settlement area extended for three miles (5 km) along the river terrace. The earthworks were five feet high and their construction required moving an amount of Earth over 750,000 cubic meters.

56 T Kidder et al. 2008. "Poverty Point and the Archaeology of Singularity," *Society for American Archaeology Archaeological Record,* 8 (5): 9-12 Nov

57 In Egypt the goddess Wadjet (eye of the moon) was depicted as a snake-headed woman. The oracle of Wadjet may have been the source of the oracular tradition which spread from Egypt to Greece. Wadjet was similar to the Minoan snake goddess, an underworld deity and one of the aspects of the Great Mother. (W Burkert. 1985. *Greek Religion.* Harvard UP)

58 There were lesser known temples throughout the Mediterranean. The Sibylline Oracles are a collection of oracular utterances by Sibyls, prophetesses who uttered divine revelations in spiritual states.

59 Most of the ruins that survive today date from the most intense interval of activity at the site in the 26th century BP. The Omphalos, an egg-shaped stone was situated in the innermost sanctuary of the temple. It marked the 'navel' (Omphalos) or center of the Earth.

60 The countries around the Greek world, such as Lydia, Caria, and Egypt, respected Pythia and came to Delphi for advice. The Pythian Games became the precursor of the Modern Olympics.

61 Priestesses in the sacred grove interpreted the rustling of the oak or beech leaves to determine the correct actions to be taken. Oracular sounds also came from bronze objects hanging from oak branches, and sounded with the wind, similar to a wind chime.

62 The dove symbolism was later adopted by emerging christian cults.

63 Heraclitus, fragment 92.

64 R Gottheil & S Krauss. 2011. "Sibyl." *Jewish Encyclopedia.* online

65 Mama Zogbé. 2012. *The Sibyls: the First Prophetess' of Mami (Wata):The Theft of African Prophecy by the Catholic Church.* Lulu.

66 Vivian Hindrew. 2007. *The Sibyls: The First Prophetess of Mami (Wata).* MWHS

67 The Agrippine Sibyl portrait by Abraham Janssens of the Netherlands (c. 1575) is of a black woman with a whip and scroll. Agrippine refers to Julia Agrippina, a Roman Empress who was a great-granddaughter of Emperor Augustus and mother of Emperor Nero.

68 There are various names for the Cumaean Sibyl - the Herophile of Pausanias and Lactantius, the Aeneid's Deiphobe, daughter of Glaucus, Amaltheia, Demophile, and Taraxandra.

69 Staff. 2017. "Cave of the Sibyl-Antro della Sibilla." *Atlas Obscura,* online

70 The oldest collection of written Sibylline Books appears to have been made by the Sibyl who was born near Marpessus, and whose tomb was later marked by the temple of Apollo built upon the archaic site. She appears on the coins of Gergis, c. 2,400 to 2,350 BP.

71 The main deity in vodun is a divine Creator, called Mawu or Mahu, a female being who in one tradition bore seven children and gave each rule over a realm of nature - animals, earth, and sea.

16: Gynocentric Power

1 Knight 2008. ibid

2 Not all first nations are gynocentric, especially after colonization. Some were governed by hereditary Chiefs who were counseled by a quorum of male and female elders, and others were regulated by councils where women held equal seats. Still others were governed by separate councils of male or female leadership depending on the decision that needed to be made. Interestingly, war councils were almost universally made up of women.

3 For example, a grandmother, her two daughters, and their children. When the grandmother dies, this matriarchy becomes two new ones. Often, female-centered groups belong to larger kin groups defined by a specified maximum number of generations back to a common female ancestor.

4 Matrilocal residence, or matrilocality, refers to a system in which a couple resides with or near the female's parents. The female offspring of a mother remain living in or near the mother's house, forming large clan-families, consisting of three or four generations living in the same place.

5 Matrilineality is a system in which a person's descent is traced through their mother and her maternal ancestors. It involves the inheritance of property and/or titles, and results in a higher status for females.

6 F Marlowe. 2004. "Marital residence among foragers." *Current Anthro.* 452 (45): 276-84.

7 As J Krishnamurti asks, "does authority create order? Or does it merely create a blind following which has no meaning at all except that it leads to destruction, to misery? To deny all this is not immoral; on the contrary to deny all division and resistance is the highest morality. To negate everything that man has invented, to negate all his values, ethics and gods, is to be in a state of mind in which there is no duality, therefore no resistance or conflict between opposites."

8 There are no private property and territorial claims in contemporary matrilineal and matrilocal clans. Individuals only have usage rights on the soil they till, or on pastures for animals to graze. Parcels of land are worked on communally. The oldest women of the clan, the matriarchs, have control over the most valuable goods and resources. Female elders are responsible for the sustenance and the protection of all group members. The matriarchs either work the land themselves or organize the work on the land. Crops from the fields are given to them, and the milk of the flocks as well. The big clan houses belong to them, or the tents in case of nomadic tribes.

9 Heide Göttner-Abendroth. 1988. *Das Matriarchat I.* Geschichte seiner Erforschung Kohlhammer: Stuttgart

10 In North America, European men who partnered with Indigenous females were surprised to discover that the women did not consider them to be related to their children. They were dismayed that mothers, not fathers, had control over children and property (Perdue, Theda. 1998. Cherokee Women: Gender and Culture Change, 1700-1835. U of Nebraska Press.).

11 Children are raised by mothers' extended matrilineal clan. A father does not have a valuable role in the upbringing of his children. Men do have a role in their sisters' children, or nieces and nephews.

12 In Africa, matrilocal unions were the norm from north to south, east to west. This suggests that modern humans were gynocentric from the start of the species in Africa, and remained female-centered when they migrated out of continent. Matrilocality remained the norm even with later human migration and occupation of the Americas.

13 Matrilocal unions were the custom of most nations in the Americas, including the Inuit, Hopi, Iroquois, Lenape, Choctaw, Navajo, Tlingit, and many others. The Osages, Omahas, Kiowas, Mandans, Sauk, Foxes, Yokut, Patwin, Kwakiutl, and other nations were all matrilocal. When an Osage eldest daughter made a union, she became the mistress of the house, and her parents became subordinate to her. Among the Pawnees, a man took up residence with his wife's kin and could be expelled at any time, for any reason.

14 Matrilocal unions were also practiced in Central and South America. Among the Inca of Peru, Maya of Yucatan, Tainos of the Caribbean, Amerindians of the Guianas, and Tupi of Brazil, men joined females' parental home.

15 Alice Nash. 2001. "'None of the Women Were Abused': Indigenous Contexts for the Treatment of Women Captives in the Northeast," in *Sex Without Consent,* ed. by MD Smith. NYU Press, 10-26.

16 Across the World, mating customs were female-centered. For example, if a man wanted a union with a female, he told her so and later visited her home. If the pistillate human gave him a basin of water to wash and something to eat, this communicated that she was willing.

17 When a Dene female of Alaska decided to form a union, she erected a hut next to her mother's. Aht females of Vancouver owned all property rights and children. Men's guest privileges to work on and used their partners' land could be dissolved at any time. Among the Algonquin in Canada, the woman never left her home, of which she was regarded as mistress and heiress. Children belonged to their mother and acknowledged her only. Their father was almost like a stranger to them.

18 For example, among the San of South Africa, a man needed the consent of one of the older women of a group to become a partner of one or more of the females in the clan. If a man did not work to their satisfaction, the women dissolved their association with him, and he had to leave immediately (Hilary Alton, ed. 2011. Matriarchy Really Did Exist: Selected extracts from Robert Briffault's *The Mothers.* A Radical Anthropology Group Publication.).

19 Endogamy, also called inter-marriage, is a custom enjoining one to marry within one's own group. Partnering with someone from an outside group is exogamy. There are enclaves of societies with exogamous, gynocentric patterns in Asia, Africa, the Americas, and Oceania.

20 Among the Bechuana, there is a proverb: "Happy is she who have borne a daughter. A boy is the son of his mother-in-law." Among the Banyai of Zambesi, men had to perform certain services for their mother-in-law, such as keeping her well supplied with firewood. When he came into here presence, he was obliged to sit with his knees in a bent position, as putting his feet towards her would be taken as a great offense.

21 Not all first nations were matrilineal, especially after colonization. Some followed patrilineal lines of heritage, and others allow for clan alliances to be made by the individual or their elders based on the needs of the community.

22 Johnston 2003. ibid

23 The Senecas lived together as 12 to 20 families in 'long-houses.' Each house was headed by a matron who allocated living space and controlled the distribution of food. Seneca women usually took partners from other clans. If a man did not do his fair share in providing resources to the house, he was evicted and had to return to his own clan.

24 The Sioux were matrilocal and men moved to the clan of their female partner.

25 A Cree man resided with his partner's parents, who treated him like a stranger until his first child.

26 Seminole men resided with their partner's kin. After some time, a couple could set up a household of their own anywhere, except among the man's kin.

27 Pueblo Indians were matrilocal. Related females lived together in the same clan, as did their children.

28 Pat Barcaly. 2011. The evolution of charitable behavior and the power of reputation. In SC Roberts,

ed. *Applied Evolutionary Psychology*. Oxford University Press.

29   Even though Iroquois men wielded power as chiefs, women had the ability to ensure gender balance in governance. Their law states: "If a disobedient chief persists in his disobedience... the (War) Chiefs shall then take away the title of the erring chief by order of the women in whom the title is vested... The women will then select another of their sons as a candidate and the chiefs shall elect him."

30   Johnston 2003. ibid

31   The concept of 'others' toward whom concern should be directed can vary among cultures and religions. Altruism is not the same as feelings of loyalty, which is predicated on social relationships. Altruism does not consider relationships and is the opposite of selfishness.

32   N Bird-David. 1990. "The Giving Environment." *Current Anthropology*, 31 (2); 189-96.

33   Annette Weiner writes about inalienable possessions. Weiner argues they act "as a stabilizing force against change because its presence authenticates cosmological origins, kinship, and political histories." She shows that the gift-giving traditions place women at the heart of the political process (AB Weiner. 1992. *Inalienable Possessions: The Paradox of Keeping-While Giving*. UC Press)

34   Heide Göttner-Abendroth. 1995. *The Goddess and her Heroes*. Original 1980. Anthony Pub Co.

35   A gynocentric economy is not based on accumulation, as is patriarchy. Their economic actions are geared towards a leveling of differences in living standards, which achieves an economy of balance and mutual support system, but without being a billing institution. Economy of balance is a synonym of the gift economy and liberates the most honorable human feelings such as unreserved giving, true devotion, benevolence, and friendship.

36   The status quo of the male-dominated system based on exchange attempts to defend itself by discrediting and concealing the gift model. To discredit gift-giving, patriarchy has found it necessary to create scarcity which makes giving self-sacrificial. It uses the same processes to redistribute wealth to the possession of a few.

37   Genevieve Vaughan. 1997. *For-giving: A Feminist Criticism of Exchange*. Plain View Press.

38   Shaw 2016. ibid

39   Hrdy 2011. ibid

40   In support of Marvin Harris's critique, anthropologists like Clifford Geertz and others have suggested that the cornerstone of functionalist anthropology, the theory of kinship system, is not a universal social structure. Both variants of kinship theory, 'descent theory' and the 'alliance model,' have assumed universal patriarchal family structures, and have acted as blinders on anthropology, as well as archaeology. (Geertz, C. 2002. "The Visit: Review of A Society Without Fathers or Husbands." *Annual Review of Anthropology* 3:1-19).

41   NJ Allen et al, eds. 2008. *Early Human Kinship*. Oxford UP.

42   Kramer 2010. ibid. The life-history traits of lengthy childhood, high fertility, and simultaneous, multiple, dependent offspring meant that with only support from the father, a single female's productive and reproductive roles were overly arduous.

43   Knight points out that the basis of primate social organization is predicated on the distribution of food resources and how females array themselves around these. Males then array themselves around females.

44   Knight 1995. ibid

45   ET Wood et al. 2005. "Contrasting patterns of Y chromosome and mtDNA variation in Africa." *Euro J of Human Genetics* 13:867-76.; Schlebusch, CM. 2010. Genetic variation in Khoisan-speaking populations from southern Africa. PhD thesis, Univ of the Witwatersrand.; Verdu, P. et al. 2013. "Sociocultural behaviour, sex-biased admixture & effective population sizes in Central African Pygmies & non-Pygmies." Paper at Confer. on Hunting & Gathering Societies, Liverpool, Jun 25-28.

46   MT Seielstad et al. 1994. "Construction of human Y-chromosomal haplotypes using a new polymorphic A to G transition." *Human Molecular Genetics* No3, pp 2159-61.

47   KW Alt et al. 2013. "Earliest Evidence for Social Endogamy in the 9,000-Year-Old-Population of Basta, Jordan." *PLoS ONE* 8(6).

48   After reviewing much of the 'evidence' for patrilocality by the earlier anthropologists, Helen Alvarez concluded they are based on inadequate data. Alvarez found the few ethnographies in which camp data are available support the view that individuals use a variety of kin and other links to decide where to live. And, the only discernible statistical bias was in favor of mother-daughter links. (Alvarez, Helen P. 2000. "Residence groups among hunter-gatherers: a view of the claims and evidence for patrilocal bands." In *Kinship and Behavior in Primates*. B Chapais & Carol Berman, eds, pp. 420-442. NY: Oxford.)

49   A cross-cultural study of foragers concluded that the greater the dependence on gathering, the less likely these cultures observed patrilocal residence. (Marlowe 2004).; Another study found women and men in contemporary gatherer-hunter tribes tend to have equal influence on where their group lives and who they live with. (Dyble et al 2015.)

50   N Peterson. 1976. *Tribes & Boundaries in Aboriginal Australia*. Inst of Aboriginal Studies; MV Flinn. 1989. "Household Composition & Female Reproductive Strategies." In A Rasa, et al, eds., *Sexual & Reproductive Strategies*. Chapman & Hall; BS Hewlett. 1991. "Husband-Wife Reciprocity & the Father-Infant Relationship Among Aka Pygmies." In *Father-Child Relations*. A de Gruyter; ME Lamb, ed. 1999. *Parenting & Child Development in "Nontraditional" Families*. NJ: Erlbaum; PK Ivey. 2000. "Cooperative Reproduction in Ituri Forest Hunter-Gatherers?" *Current Anthro*, 41(5), 856-66.; A Gottlieb. 2004. *The Afterlife is Where We Come From*. U of Chicago Press.; R Lee & l DeVore. 1972. "Problems in the study of hunters & gatherers." In *Man the Hunter*. Chicago: Aldine

51   J Woodburn. 1972. "Stability and flexibility in Hadza residential groupings." In Lee & DeVore, eds, *Man the Hunter*. Chicago: Aldine.

52   However, gynocentrism cannot be inferred solely from current matrilineal practices of descent.

53 Peggy Reeves Sanday. 1981. *Female Power and Male Dominance.* Cambridge UP.

54 Peggy Reeves Sanday. 2002. *Women at the Center: Life in Modern Matriarchy.* Cornell UP.

55 There is also the Karen of Burma, Bontoc of Philippines, Kerinci of Indonesia, Marshallese of Oceania, Siraya of Taiwan, Vanatinai of PNG, and some groups in eastern Sri Lanka. Matrilocal and matrilineal cultures also include lowland groups in South America, many first nations in North America, the Na, Lahu and some more groups in China, and others.

56 In 2005, Heide Göttner-Abendroth organized the Second World Congress on Matriarchal Studies, at Texas State University at San Marcos. A number of women who live or were raised in matrilineal, matrilocal, and gynocentric groups were invited to speak. Women from Polynesia, Micronesia, Mexico, Panama, Saharan Africa, West and South Africa, Northeast India, Southwest India, Sumatra, Indonesia, and China traveled to Texas. The women spoke about past and existing female-centered customs and practices in their cultures.

57 Gimbutas 1991. ibid

58 The inherited male leadership roles of the Akan people are passed down matrilineally, through a man's mothers and sisters, and their children. Often, a man is expected to not only support his own family, but those of his female relatives. (Marleen de Witte. 2001. *Long Live the Dead!: changing funeral celebrations in Asante, Ghana.* Het Spinhuis.)

59 The women's customary law refers to a system of symbols and a set of life-cycle ceremonial practices placing senior women at the social, emotional, aesthetic, political, and economic center of daily life, along with their brothers.

60 Sanday 2002. ibid

61 Khasi. 1903. *Journal of the Asiatic Society of Bengal*, Volume 71, Part 3. Asiatic Society of Bengal

62 The Khasi are no longer gynocentric. Decisions by a woman must be endorsed by her maternal uncle, and Khasi women have little political power. The former rulers of the language group left their throne to the son of their youngest sister. All the chief government ministers are men and few women even sit on village councils. (Bouissou, J. 2011. "Where women of India rule the roost and men demand gender equality." *The Guardian.* Jan 18).

63 Garos are a matrilineal society but are no longer gynocentric. While property of Garo's is owned by the women, the men govern the society and domestic affairs and manage the property.

64 Males raise livestock such as yak, water buffalo, sheep, goats, and poultry. Men deal with the slaughter of livestock, in which women never participate. (Hua, Cai. 2001. *A Society without Fathers or Husbands: The Na of China.* Asti Hustvedt, trans. New York: Zone Books).

65 Mosuo culture has "walking marriages" or "visiting relations," in which partners do not live in the same household. Children of such relationships are raised by their mothers and the mothers' families. Walking marriage is still the primary institution of family, sex and reproduction, and marriage is secondary. Women also make business decisions. However, the Mosuo have been influenced by other patriarchal cultures, and the political power tends to be in the hands of males.

66 Chuan-Kang Shih. 2001. "Genesis of Marriage among the Moso and Empire-Building in Late Imperial China." In *The Journal of Asian Studies* 60, no.2 (May):381-412.

67 For the Bribri, the cacao tree is sacred. It used to be a woman, and Sibu (God) turned into a tree. Cacao branches are never used as firewood and only used in special occasions, ceremonies, and in certain rites of passage such as when young girls have their first menstruation. Men's roles are defined by their clan, and often are exclusive for men. Examples of these roles are the "awa" or shaman, and the "oko", the only person allowed to touch the remains of the dead, sing funeral songs, and prepare the food eaten at funerals. Only certain clans are allowed to become awapa. Since the clan comes from the mother's side of the family, an awa cannot teach his own sons, but rather the sons of his female relatives. (A Skinner. 1920. *Notes on the Bribri of Costa Rica.* Heye Foundation & Museum of American Indian).

68 Women own the land upon which the couple works and are the "true garden authorities" and "originators of action." They have keen knowledge of the natural rhythm of the garden and dictate what is planted, where, and when. Men are acknowledged mostly as "facilitators" and are valued in the gardens only for their strength in clearing the land. Women's central role in producing food as well as a matrilineal inheritance structure are factors that contribute to the high status of women among the Nagovisi. (D Mitchell. 1976. *Land and Agriculture in Nagovisi, Papua New Guinea.* Institute of Applied Social and Economic Research)

69 S Beckerman & P Valentine, eds. 2002. *Cultures of Multiple Fathers.* University Press of Florida.

70 Na brothers and sisters live together their entire lives, sharing household duties and raising the women's children. Because the Na, like all cultures, prohibit incest, they practice a system of sometimes furtive, sometimes conspicuous, night time encounters at the woman's home. The woman's partners, and she frequently has more than one, bear no economic responsibility for her or her children. 'Fathers,' unless they resemble their children, remain unidentifiable. (Hua, Cai. 2001. *A Society Without Fathers Or Husbands: The Na of China.* Zone Books).

71 Du 2013. ibid

72 Kim Anderson et al. 2013. "Carriers of Water." *Journal of Cleaner Production* 60 (1): 11-17.

73 With the arrival of the Dutch and Muslims, Minangkabau traditions was gradually influenced by both western and conservative Islamic thought. The culture is mostly patriarchal since religious and political affairs are the responsibility of men. However, some women still play important roles in these areas.

17: Theorizing Prehistory

1 Johann Bachofen. 1861. *Myth, Religion & Mother-right.* Reprint 1973. Princeton University Press.

2 Lewis Morgan. 1877. *Ancient Society.* London: MacMillan.

3 Engels 1972. ibid

4 Rosa Luxembourg. 1975. "Introduction to Economics." In *Collected Works.* Institute of Marxism-

Leninism of the Central Committee of the SED. Vol. 5. Berlin: GDR. 580-612.

5   Lumsden & Wilson 1981. ibid

6   Marvin Harris. 1969. *The Rise of Anthropological Theory*. London: Routledge.

7   F Boas. 1897. *The Social Organization & Secret Societies of Kwakiutl Indians*. US Nat'l Museum

8   B Malinowski. 1956. *Marriage: Past and Present. A debate between Robert Briffault and Bronislaw Malinowski*. M Montagu, ed. Boston: Porter Sargent. Original 1931.

9   C Lévi-Strauss. 1969. *The Elementary Structures of Kinship*. London: Eyre & Spottiswoode.

10 In the place of historical analysis, anthropologists began using functionalism, examining how a cultural practice benefited the individual and group as a whole. All forms of similitude are rejected in a cultural relativist framework that permits only the existence of unique groups. The functionalist paradigm ignores wider, comparative structures and assumes the masculinist view of culture, conflict, and male domination that prevailed before Bachofen and Morgan.

11 T Deacon. 1997. *The Symbolic Species: Co-evolution of language & the human brain*. Penguin.

12 R Boyd & Joan Silk. 1997. *How Humans Evolved*. NY: Norton.

13 Gimbutas expressly avoided using the term "matriarchy," and used gynocentric instead.

14 Neolithic fortifications were sometimes massive. The walls of Jericho were ten feet thick and thirteen or more feet high. A twenty-eight foot tower that was thirty-three feet in diameter with a central stairway and an entrance at the bottom was attached to the wall. Although the entire wall remains unexcavated, it probably extended about 765 yards and enclosed an area of approximately ten acres.

15 Carol Christ. 2013. "Patriarchy as a System of Male Dominance Created at the Intersection of the Control of Women, Private Property, and War, Part 2." *Feminism and Religion*, Feb 23.

16 Charlene Spretnak. 2011. "Anatomy of a Backlash." *Journal of Archeomythology*. 7:Special Issue

17 The dismissal occurred through a repetition of disparaging comments and articles in which the initiators cite each other. Critics used mainly secondary sources, and none have conducted the decades of direct multidisciplinary research characteristic of Gimbutas's analysis.

18 B Fagan. 1992. "A Sexist View of Prehistory" *Archaeology*, 45/2. 14-18; (March-April).

19 The Woman figures are viewed as political objects revolving around issues of male power, devoid of any metaphysical or cosmological significance for Neolithic females, or males.

20 I Hodder, cited in C Renfrew & P Bahn. 2000. *Archaeology*. 3rd ed. Thames & Hudson.

21 SM Nelson. 1993. "Diversity of the Upper Paleolithic "Venus" Figurines & Archaeological Mythology," in *Gender in Cross-Cultural Perspective*. C Brettel & C Sargent, eds. Prentice Hall.

22 Margaret Conkey & Ruth Tringham. 1994. "Archaeology and the Goddess," in *Feminisms in the Academy*. Domna C Stanton & Abigail J Stewart, eds. Univ of Michigan; Lynn Meskell. 1995. "Goddesses, Gimbutas and 'New Age' Archaeology", *Antiquity* 69:74; Lauren Talalay. 1999. "(Review of) The Living Goddesses." *Bryn Mawr Classical Review* 10-05; Roberta Gilchrist. 1999. *Gender and Archaeology*. Routledge; Ruth Whitehouse. 2006. "Gender Archaeology in Europe," in Sarah M Nelson, ed., *Handbook of Gender in Archaeology*. Rowman Altamira.

23 Gimbutas was the project director of five major excavations of Neolithic sites in southeastern Europe. Most of her site reports, written in several languages, are untranslated. Therefore, many of her feminist detractors have not even read her fieldwork, which should be required as part of the scientific discipline.

24 Sarah M Nelson. 2004. *Gender Archaeology: Analyzing Power and Prestige*. AltaMira Press.

25 Cynthia Eller. 2001. *The Myth of Matriarchal Prehistory: Why an Invented Past Won't Give Women a Future*. Beacon Press.; Chapman, J. 1998. "A Biographical Sketch of Marija Gimbutas" in M García & M Sørensen, eds., *Excavating Women*. Routledge. pp.299-301

26 Talalay, for example, argues that Gimbutas's analysis only "isolate women outside of history... If women's reproductive capabilities are the source of their power, then women remain, to some extent, locked within an unchanging domestic sphere."

27 K Young & P Nathanson. 2011. *Sanctifying Misandry: Goddess Ideology & Fall of Man*. McGill UP

28 Weiner 1992.; Lepowsky, Maria 1993. *Fruit of the Motherland: Gender in an Egalitarian Society*. Columbia UP.; Du, Shanshan. 2013. *Chopsticks Only Work in Pairs: Gender Unity and Gender Equality Among the Lahu of Southwestern China*. Columbia UP.; Namu, Yang Erche & Mathieu, Christine. 2004. *Leaving Mother Lake: A Girlhood at the Edge of the World*. Back Bay Books.; Mies, M & Bennholdt-Thomsen, Veronika. 2000. *The Subsistence Perspective*. Zed Books.

29 J Corcoran. 1959. "Celtic Mythology." *New Larousse Encyclopedia of Mythology*. Prometheus.

30 JP Mallory. 1989. *In Search of the Indo-Europeans*. Thames & Hudson.; V Dergachev. 2002. "Two Studies in Defence of the Migration Concept," in *Ancient Interactions*. Katie Boyle et al eds., 93-112. Cambridge: McDonald Institute.; B Comrie. 2002. "Farming Dispersal in Europe and the Spread of the Indo-European Language Family," in *Examining the Farming Language Dispersal Hypothesis*. P Bellwood & C Renfrew, eds. Cambridge UP; Joan Marler. 2005. "The Beginnings of Patriarchy in Europe," in *The Rule of Mars*. C Biaggi, ed. Conn: Knowledge, Ideas, and Trends.

31 L Durdin-Robertson. 1982. *God the Mother: The Creatress and Giver of Life*. Eire: Cesara Pub.

32 Joan Marler. 2005b. "The Myth of Universal Patriarchy" in *Pre-historic Archaeology and Anthropological Theory Education*. L. Nikolova, et al eds., 6-7. Int'l Institute of Anthropology.

33 R Hutton. 1997. "The Neolithic Great Goddess." *Antiquity*, March.

34 ML West. 2007. *Indo-European Poetry and Myth*. Oxford University Press.

35 S Hansen. 2001. "Neolithic Sculpture: Some Remarks on an Old Problem," in *The Archaeology of Cult and Religion*. P Biehl and F Bertemes, eds., 37-52. Budapest: Archaeolingua.

36 Goddesses were superseded by bulls who were featured as gods after men's domestication of animals. (Cauvin, J. 2000. *The Birth of the Gods & the Origins of Agriculture*. Cambridge UP).

37 G Luck. 1985. *Arcana Mundi: Magic & the Occult in the Greek & Roman Worlds*. Johns Hopkins U

38 AK Coomaraswamy. 1983. "Indian Art." *Studies in Comparative Religion*, Vol. 15, No. 3 & 4
39 J Mellaart. 1975. *The Neolithic of the Near East.* Scribner.
40 Laurette Sejourne. 1978. *Burning Water: Thought & Religion in Ancient Mexico.* Thames & Hudson.

18: Taming Nature

1   Ferguson. 2003. ibid
2   KV Flannery & J Marcus. 2003. "The origin of war." *Proc. Natl. Acad. Sci.* USA 100, 11801-11805.
3   RC Kelly. 2005. "The evolution of lethal inter-group violence". *PNAS.* 102: 24-29. Oct
4   M Allentoft et al. 2015. "Population genomics of Bronze Age Eurasia." *Nature* 522:167-72, Jun 11
5   Wilma Dunaway. 1997. "Rethinking Cherokee Acculturation; Agrarian Capitalism & Women's Resistance to Cult of Domesticity, 1800-1838." *Am Indian Culture & Res Journal*, 21:1 156-64.
6   This eastern branch of the Yamnaya, or Afanasievo, persisted in central Asia and, perhaps, Mongolia and China, until as recently as 2000 BP. The Yamnaya were replaced by fierce Iron Age warriors in chariots called the Sintashta, or Andronovo culture, and other immigrants from eastern Asia who replaced these 'Caucasians' in central Asia (Gibbons, Ann. 2015. "Nomadic herders left a strong genetic mark on Europeans and Asians." American Association for the Advancement of Science, *Science Mag.* June 10.).
7   The Yamnaya were one of the first culture to make regular use of ox-drawn wheeled carts. Wagons/carts and sacrificed animals like cattle, horse, and sheep, were present in their graves, a trait typical of later European cultures. Their metal tools, axes, and daggers were mostly made of copper, with some bronze. Hunting, fishing and sporadic agriculture were practiced near rivers.
8   K Kristiansen et al. 2017. "Re-theorising mobility and the formation of culture and language among the Corded Ware Culture in Europe." *Antiquity*, 91:356 334-47 April
9   W Haak et al. 2015. "Massive migration from the steppe was a source for Indo-European languages in Europe." *Nature.* Online 2nd March.
10 The herders interbred with local farmers and created the Corded Ware culture of central Europe, named for the twisted cord imprint on its pottery. Yamnaya ancestry persisted in northern and central Europeans until at least around 3,000 BP, and is ubiquitous in present-day Europeans.
11 W Haak & A Cooper. 2015. "European invasion." *The Conversation.* March 22.
12 Countless chiefdoms and states have gone to war not for mere territory or nubile women, but to increase the numbers of commoners who can become enslaved or producers of tribute and taxes.
13 Monika Karmin, et al. 2015. "A recent bottleneck of Y chromosome diversity coincides with a global change in culture." *Genome Research.* March 13.
14 The Y bottleneck questions the psychological notion that sexual and social habits are strongly genetically programmed. The bottleneck shows that humans experience periods of dramatic social modification, and the cultural experiences, which in turn, change our genes.
15 The Y-bottleneck challenges the popular notion that farming and settlement cushioned people against 'survival of the fittest.' Whatever occurred as a consequence of domestication 8,000 years ago, has marked humans into the present.
16 A similar situation could have resulted in the extinction of Neanderthals.
17 However, after thousands of years, the numbers of men reproducing, compared to females, started to rise again. This occurred as more men became successful at domesticating plants and animals.
18 Declining intelligence could be one of the long-term effects of the Y-bottleneck and it may have started with farming. Studies show that simple reaction time has slowed since 1889, a decline of 1.16 IQ points per decade or 13.35 IQ points since Victorian times. Performance dropped most dramatically in teenagers in the upper half of the intelligence scale. Brighter teens in 2008 were on average six IQ points less intelligent than their counterparts 28 years earlier.
19 As a outcome of socialized gene expression and other factors, the Y-bottleneck may have produced biological and behavioral changes in men such as cyborg consciousness. The domestication of women may likewise have influenced females, but these are difficult issues to research.
20 When we celebrate male ceremony, ritual, and processions, we are celebrating men's historical theft of female labor and food innovations, and the evolution of misogyny.
21 Rudgley 2000 ibid
22 There were several cities that existed around the same time as Çatalhöyük. Tell Aswad in Syria was a large settlement from 11,300 to 9,500 BP. Byblos, in Lebanon was occupied between 10,800 and 9,000 BP. Tell Arpachiyah in Mesopotamia was heavily involved in the manufacture of pottery 8,100 to 5,800 BP.
23 In Catal Huyuk, there were no massive outside walls, but the houses were all interconnected, sharing contiguous inner walls. Entry into the rooms was through holes in the roofs reached by ladder. As a result the line of the outside walls of the rooms around the settlement formed a kind of fortification. When attackers approached, the inhabitants could simply scamper up their ladders, retrieve them, and if an invader broke through a wall, he simply found himself in a single room. Many other Neolithic settlements in the Near East were protected by fortifications of one kind or another.
24 Pottery and obsidian tools were major industries, and nearby obsidian was a source of trade and wealth for Catalhoyuk. Peas were grown, and almonds, pistachios, and fruit were harvested from trees in the surrounding hills. Sheep and cattle were domesticated. Anatolian obsidian was traded thousands of miles throughout the Mediterranean. Their obsidian went as far south as Jericho, in Palestine, which at its prime was half the size of Çatalhöyük. Obsidian tools were traded for items such as Mediterranean sea shells and flint from Syria.
25 Without a head, the Catalhoyuk clay figure's height is 16.5 cm. Woman/Goddess figurines were also found within bins used for storage of cereals, such as wheat and barley. The figures were probably used as a means of ensuring the harvest and protecting the food supply.

26 Ian Hodder. 2005. "New finds & new interpretations at Çatalhöyük." *Institute of Archaeology.*

27 Painted on the walls of some of the Catalhoyuk houses are wild and violent scenes. Humans are represented without heads as if they had been decapitated. Vultures or other birds of prey appear huge next to them. The narrative scenes are of dangerous interactions between people and animals. In one painting, a huge, horned unrestrained animal, probably a deer, is surrounded by small humans who are jumping or running. One of them is pulling on something sticking out of the deer's mouth, perhaps its tongue. In the scene, there is great reference to men and maleness. For example, some of the human figures are bearded and the deer has an erect penis. This could be a depiction of a dangerous masculine game or ritual of baiting and taunting an unrestrained animal as part of domesticating practice. In other paintings, men hunt or tease boars or bulls.

28 Some of the earliest cities began around 10,000 BP, when Mureybet in Syria had 500 people. By 9,000 BP, Beidha and Basta in Jordan and Catalhoyuk in Turkey each had a population of 1,000, while Jerico in Palestine had 2,000 people. By 8,000 BP Catalhoyuk had about 3,000 people. Around 7,000 BP, Tell Brak in Syria had 4,000 humans. By 6,000 BP, Tell Brak and Uruk in Iraq had around 5,000 people. Then, there was a rapid expansion and by 5,500 BP, Abydos in Egypt had 20,000 people, Uruk in Iraq had 14,000, and Susa in Iran, and Tell Brak in Syria each had 8,000. Also, Dobrovody, Maydanets and Talianki in Ukraine had 8,000 each. (Morris, I. 2010. *Why the West Rules—For Now.* Farrar, Straus and Giroux.)

29 Early builders and artists labored to construct huge temples and government buildings. Organized religion played an important role in the growth of cities, and the people who controlled rituals and the sacred sites eventually became priests.

30 Two large temple complexes in the 1,000-acre city at Uruk mark the first independent Sumerian city-state. One was dedicated to Inanna, the Goddess of love and war, while the other complex belonged to the sky god Anu. The temple platform of Anu, built up in stages over the centuries, ultimately rose to a height of about 40 feet.

31 Around 4,300 BP, Mari in Syria had a population of 50,000, while Umma in Iraq had 40,000, and Girsu in Iraq had 80,000. Also, Mohenjo-daro in Pakistan had 40,000 residents. By 4,250 BP, Akkad in Iraq and Memphis in Egypt had 35,000 people. (Modelski, G. 2003. *World Cities: 3000 to 2000.* FAROS 2000.)

32 The Pyramid of Djoser was built around 4,650 BP during the third dynasty. The Pyramid of Khufu at Giza (4,550 BP) is the most colossal and among the largest structures ever built.

33 Prehistoric gynocentric edifices were created to mimic and represent the land and nature, which remained personified subjects. The principal aim were group activities to strengthen the gynocentric community as a whole. The centers were used for gift-giving, group ritual, trade, and communication. The architecture was part of gynecological long-term land management that included fire-farming of the surrounding plains, planting of crops, water channels, and dams for irrigation. The structures were used as community cemeteries, boundary markers of territory, a reminder of past events, and to symbolize a female ancestor, Goddess, or deity.

34 For example, a traditional jewish menorah has seven lines forming an inverted triangle.

35 The Stele of Naram-Sin was found at Susa, Iran around 4,254 BP. Carved in limestone, the 6-foot-statue memorializes one of Naram-Sin's military victories over the Lullubi people of the Zagros Mountains. Watched over by three solar deities, he wears a horned helmet-crown that was worn only by gods. The hieratically scaled king stands proudly above his soldiers and fallen foes, boldly silhouetted against the sky next to the smooth surface of a mountain. Even the shape of the stone slab is used as an active part of the composition. Its tapering top perfectly accommodates the carved mountain within it, and Naram-Sin is posed to reflect the profile of both.

19: Taming the 'Beast'

1 KN Chaudhuri. 1990. *Asia Before Europe.* Cambridge UP.

2 VG Childe. 1951. *Man Makes Himself.* NY: American Library.

3 Loss of scalp hair can occur due to androgenic alopecia, an autoimmune disease.

4 The Y-chromosome is a relic of the X-chromosome. Most or all of the genes it bears, including the genes that determine sex and control sperm, are remnants of genes on the X-chromosome that have other functions altogether. In humans, all genes on the X chromosome are twice as active to account for the lack of genes on the Y. Females accommodate this by inactivating one entire X-chromosome so as not to produce too much protein.

5 The XX pair in females can recombine. However, for the Y, the only way to get rid of a bad mutation is to inactivate or delete the entire gene. Over millions of years, inactive genes are lost, and the Y shrinks. The Y has lost 90 percent of the genes it once shared with the X. It is tiny in size and only contains 27 unique genes, versus thousands on other chromosomes. The loss of one or more copies of genes has been linked to male infertility.

6 Jennifer Graves. 2009. "The Decline and Fall of the Y Chromosome, and the Future of Men." Talk at Royal College of Surgeons (RCSI) in Ireland.

7 The cells in females undergo X-inactivation in which one of the two X chromosomes is inactivated. However, around 25 percent of the genes on the inactivated X chromosome remain expressed, which provides females with added protection against defective genes coded by the X-chromosome. As a result, X-linked disorders are less common in females.

8 Jennifer Graves. 2000. "Human Y Chromosome, Sex Determination, and Spermatogenesis - A Feminist View." *Biology of Reproduction.* 63, 667-676

9 D Bachtrog et al. 2011. "Are all sex chromosomes created equal?" *Trends in Genetics,* 27:9. Sep

10 Freya Petersen. 2013. "Male producing Y chromosome likely to disappear, says geneticist Jenny Graves at ANU." *Global Post.* April 3.

11 Before the New Stone Age, there may have been earlier manipulation of herd structure to promote a secure and predictable yield of animal products. (Vigne J-D, Peters J, Helmer D., eds. 2005. *The First Steps of Animal Domestication.* Oxford: Oxbow Books).

12 The most docile animals were caught and bred in captivity, starting the irreversible evolution of domesticates. Men's taming involves restricted movement, torture, and abuse to end resistance and attempts to escape. Punishment and negative reinforcement are the training methods used. For example, dog trainers follow the Koehler method that embraces the use of dominance displays and strong corrections, delivered through shock collars and various mechanical devices.

13 Nomadic groups integrated herds to form pastoral cultures which focused on the care of domesticates for subsistence. Semi-nomadism combined animal husbandry with cultivation, and many pastoral communities included sedentary agriculturalists.

14 Domesticated animals have been selected by culturally idiosyncratic criteria, often contradicting their needs of survival in nature. Over time, the collective behavior, life cycle, and physiology of ruminants used as livestock have changed radically, and many domesticates are no longer suited to life in nature.

15 Men learned that wool is worth harvesting repeatedly over several seasons. For fiber animals, fully grown individuals have the best pulling capacity, and the investment made in training them would be wasted if they were killed for meat after only a short life.

16 Dogs and horses were regimented to extend individual male aggression, attack other humans, and to capture and guard prisoners. These two species were particularly exploited to help emerging male power in settlements broaden their base into surrounding areas, and eventually to the establishment of male-dominated, city-states and empires.

17 Gayle Rubin writes, "there are gender-stratified societies which are not necessarily patriarchy... But the power of males in these groups is not founded on their roles as fathers or patriarchy, but on their collective adult maleness, embodied in secret cults, men's houses, warfare, exchange networks, ritual knowledge, and various initiation procedures." She continues, "Patriarchy is a specific form of male dominance, and the use of the term ought to be confined to the Old Testament-type pastoral nomads from whom the term comes, or groups like them. Abraham was a Patriarch - one old man whose absolute power over wives, children, herds, and dependents was an aspect of the institution of fatherhood, as defined in the social group in which he lived." (G Rubin. 1975. "The Traffic in Women", in R Reiter, ed., *Toward an Anthropology of Women*, Monthly Review)

18 Ruth Mace & Clare Holden. 1999. "Evolutionary ecology & cross-cultural comparison." In *Comparative Primate Socioecology*, ed. by P Lee. Cambridge UP. 387-405.

19 D Aberle. 1961. "Matrilineal descent in cross-cultural perspective." In *Matrilineal Kinship*. UC Pr.

20 Other domesticates include the Alpaca, tamed ~7,000 BP from Vicuna; Guinea pig cultivated ~7,000 BP; Camel broken ~6,000 BP; Donkey manipulated ~6,000 BP from the African Wild Ass; and Buffalo tamed ~8,000 BP from the Arni. The llama was manipulated ~5,500 BP from the Guanaco; reindeer broken ~5,000 BP; Yak tamed ~4,500 BP; deer harnessed in 1st century AD; rabbit cultivated ~400 AD; bison tamed in late 19th century; and Gayal converted from the Gaur.

21 H Xianga et al. 2014. "Early Holocene chicken domestication in northern China." *PNAS* 111:49 12

22 In Mesopotamia, cattle was the only source of animal labor, so herding was oriented towards agriculture. This strategy, favoring elder, male animals is the opposite of modern carcass and dairy production strategies. The consumption of flesh was limited to elder and ill animals.

23 R Kolinsk. 2003. "Productivity of the Mesopotamian Agriculture & Animal Husbandry in the Late 3rd and 2nd Millennium BC." In F Stepniowski (ed.) *The Orient and the Aegean*, Warsaw, 87-101.

24 The consumption of non-human milk was only possible with domesticates and we became the only species that consumes the milk of another animal. Dairy consumption is a very recent dietary phenomena, as are all dairy products - from butter, cream, and ghee, to cheese and yogurt.

25 The inter-provincial importation of animals to Jerusalem to meet high demands for sacrifice by pilgrims, is the first evidence for large scale economic specialization in the city. Domesticates were also being marketed for use in surrounding areas outside of Jerusalem.

26 G Hartman et al. 2013. "The pilgrimage economy of Early Roman Jerusalem (1st century BCE - 70 CE) reconstructed from the 15N and 13C values of goat and sheep remains." *Journal of Archaeological Science* 40. 4369-4376.

27 Skeletons of 10 donkeys were found nestled in three mud graves dating to 5,000 BP, at a burial complex of one of the first pharaohs at Abydos, Egypt. (Megan Gannon. 2013. "Bronze-Age Donkey Sacrifice Found in Israel." *Live Science*, March 10).

28 Ancient Egyptian inscriptions from around 3,800 BP show that hundreds of pack donkeys were used in large-scale expeditions to mining sites in the eastern desert and southern Sinai.

29 Animal-based materials were used in elite dress as they became bodily encultured. By the Bronze Age, clothing reached a high level of sophistication, as did gender roles and social identities.

30 Elizabeth R Ellison. 1978. "A Study of Diet in Mesopotamia (c. 3000 - 600 BC) & Associated Agricultural Techniques & Methods of Food Preparation." Ph D Thesis, Arts, U. London. May.

31 The image of a fighting rooster was found on a 26th century BP seal near Jerusalem. Roosters are also pictured on other seals as a symbol of ferocity, such as on the one engraved on a late-27th-century BP seal inscribed "Jehoahaz, son of the king." (Taran, M. 1975. "Early Records of the Domestic Fowl in Ancient Judea." IBIS, *The Intl J of Avian Science* 117 (1): 109-110).

32 RD Crawford. 1990. *Poultry Breeding and Genetics*. Elsevier Health Sciences.

33 EB. 2008. Cockfighting. *Encyclopædia Britannica*.

34 R Hernandez. 1995. "A Blood Sport Gets in the Blood." *NYT* (NYC Metro) 04-11; Janette Keys. "Cock Fights / Peleas de Gallos." *Colonial Zone*, Dominican Republic

35 Plants supply over 80 percent of the total calories consumed in the world and domesticates supply one-third of the protein. Animal carcass, dairy and fish are about equal sources of animal protein, with each supplying about a third of the world's supply of total protein. (Breeds of Livestock 2014. Online. Accessed 12/6).

36 TJ Hackmann & JN Spain. 2010. "Ruminant ecology & evolution." *J of Dairy Sci*, 93:1320-34 Apr

37 During the Stone Age, men had limited access to resources and only with the permission of women. The sixth domestication gave men control over a valuable economic resource that was independent of women and gynocentric organization. Female-centered clans were plant-based and had little interest in enslaving herbivores.

38 The hunting of stags, boars, bulls and lions was an exclusive prerogative of Bronze-Age elites. But hunting was more than an elite activity or heroic test of skills and manhood. Aristotle considered the hunting of animals a training ground for young men preparing for war. The hunt served a religious purpose in transmitting power to the hunter/rulers, and restarting the life cycle. A fierce animal's blood and flesh were used in sacrifice, and the tusks of boars were mounted on helmets.

39 Before raising and breeding livestock, fertility was a mystery and men did not fully know the role males played. Clouded in mystery, reproduction was viewed as more within the realm of females, who were highly regarded as a result. When men started breeding nonhuman animals for different traits, they became knowledgeable of males' role in reproduction which in turn gave rise to male notions of supremacy. Prehistoric cultures that lacked domesticates remained gynocentric.

40 In early Mesopotamia cuneiform, references are made to male animals siring young, for instance the term 'bull' for breeding. A text from Ugarit from the second millennium refers to geldings, the practice of castration so that breeding could more easily be controlled.

41 The Assyrians typically placed massive lamassu statues prominently, at the entrances of cities and palaces. To protect houses, the lamassu were engraved on clay tablets, which were then buried under the door's threshold.

42 SJ De Laet. 1994. *History of humanity. Vol. 1, Prehistory & beginnings of civilization.* UNESCO

43 Wendy Christensen. 2014. "The NFL, the Military, and the Problem with Masculine Institutions." *Pacific Standard Mag*, Sept. 22.

44 The US Army's Mission is "To fight and win our Nation's wars by providing prompt, sustained land dominance across the full range of military operations and spectrum of conflict in support of combatant commanders."

45 Tracy Xavia Karner. 1998. "Engendering Violent Men: Oral Histories of Military Masculinity." In LH Bowker, ed. *Masculinities and Violence.* SAGE Publications.

46 DOD. 2012. "Annual Report on Sexual Assault in the Military." *US Dept of Defense.*

47 BT Locke. 2013. "The Military-Masculinity Complex: Hegemonic Masculinity and the United States Armed Forces, 1940-1963." Masters Thesis, University of Nebraska-Lincoln

48 AG Altinay. 2005. *The Myth of the Military-Nation.* Palgrave Macmillan

49 P Schouten & H Dunham. 2012. "Cynthia Enloe on Militarization, Feminism, and the International Politics of Banana Boats." *Theory Talks*, No 48, May 22.

50 Melissa T Brown. 2002. "'Be the best': Military Recruiting & the Cultural Construction of Soldiering in Great Britain." *GSC Quarterly* No 5, Summer

51 Lesley Gill. 1997. "Creating Citizens, Making Men: The Military and Masculinity in Bolivia." *Cultural Anthropology,* 12:527-50 Nov

52 Under abrahamic monotheism, all female figures and images of Goddesses or sacred animals are considered idolatrous. Corresponding with the demotion of Earth Goddesses, human female status and power were similarly reduced.

53 Ehrenreich 1998. ibid

54 A bull was tied to an iron stake so that it could move within a radius of about 30 feet. The object of the sport was for dogs to immobilize the bull. In 1835, the Cruelty to Animals Act was passed in Parliament that outlawed "Blood Sport" in Great Britain.

55 Jenkins, R and Mollett, K. 1997. *The Story of the Real Bulldog.* Neptune, NJ: TFH Publications.

56 In this blood sport, one or more bulls are fought in a bullring. In many parts of the western US, various rodeo events like calf roping and bull riding were influenced by Spanish bullfighting.

57 The Running of the Bulls is a practice that involves running in front of a small group of bulls that have been let loose on a course of a sectioned-off subset of a town's streets. Youngsters would jump among them to show off their bravado. In some other places, the six bulls in the event are those that are victimized in the afternoon bullfight.

58 Gore Vidal. 1992. "(The Great Unmentionable) Monotheism and its Discontents," *The Lowell Lecture,* Harvard University, Apr 20

20: Warhorse & Hypermasculinity

1   L Cavalli-Sforza. 2004. "The Spread of Agriculture in Nomadic Pastoralism." In DR Harris, ed., *The Origin & Spread of Agriculture & Pastoralism in Eurasia.* Routledge.

2   The horseshoe arch of arabic sacred architecture developed from the same tradition.

3   A Outram et al. 2009. "The earliest horse harnessing and milking." *Science* 323 (5919): 1332-5.

4   L Bartosiewicz. 2011. "Ex oriente equus... A brief history of horses between the early Bronze Age and the Middle Ages." *Studia Archaeologica MFME* - Studarch XII.

5   JW Evans. 1992. *Horse Breeding and Management.* Amsterdam: Elsevier Health Sciences.

6   RP Lindner. 1981. "Nomadism, Horses, and Huns." *Past & Present* 92: 5 Aug

7   Kuz'mina. 2007. ibid

8   K Kristiansen & TB Larsson, TB. 2005. *The Rise of Bronze Age Society.* Cambridge UP.

9   Some Scythian-Sarmatian cultures may have given rise to Greek stories of Amazons. Graves of armed females have been found in southern Ukraine and Russia. About 20 percent of Scythian-Sarmatian "warrior graves" on the lower Don and lower Volga contained females dressed for battle as if they were men, a style that may have inspired the Greek tales about the Amazons.

10 Bartosiewicz 2011. ibid

11 In the 17th century BP, the Great Wall of China was built to fend off western cavalry.

12 European horses were heavier than their desert counterparts. These larger breeds were used for tilling fields and pulling carts. They were hardy animals who could withstand the cold, damp climate of northern Europe.

13 Kristiansen and Larsson. 2005. ibid

14 Miriam Dexter. 1990. "The hippomorphic goddess & her offspring." *J of Indo-European Studies.*

15 The world's largest equestrian sculpture, when completed, will be the Crazy Horse Memorial, in South Dakota, USA at a planned 641 feet (195 m) wide and 563 feet (172 m) high, even though only the upper torso and head of the rider and front half of the horse will be depicted. Also the carvings on Stone Mountain in Georgia, USA, is the largest bas-relief in the world.

16 Quixote is a dreamer and buffoon, an aging gentleman who sets out from his village to perform acts of chivalry for a girl named Dulcinea. Quixote fights windmills that he imagines are giants.

17 Besides bulls, other domesticates were used as part of patriarchal symbolism, especially chickens. In the sixth century, Pope Gregory I declared the cock the emblem of christianity and another Papal enactment in the ninth century by Pope Nicholas I ordered the figure of the cock to be placed on every church steeple. In many Central European folk tales, the devil is believed to flee at the first crowing of a cock. In traditional Jewish practice, a kosher animal is swung around the head and then slaughtered on the afternoon before Yom Kippur, the Day of Atonement, in a ritual called kapparos.

18 In many ways, cows served as a substitute and replaced the role of human females. In the ancient Near Eastern texts, the Mother is called Wild Cow, and she is the mother of both gods and humans. The Egyptian great god Re was born by a Cow.

19 Burkert, Walter. 1985. *Greek Religion.* Wiley-Blackwell

20 Trimijopulos. 2011. ibid

21 Ceremonial burials of bulls indicate that ritual sacrifice was part of worship. A bull might have represented a king who became a deity after death. Each animal was buried in a separate tomb with a chapel built above it. The name of the mother-cow and the place of birth are recorded. The sarcophagi are of immense size and the burial must have entailed enormous expense.

22 Apis was protector of the dead and linked to the pharaoh. The bull symbolized the king's courage, strength, virility, and fighting spirit. A 'strong bull of his mother Hathor' was a common title for gods and pharaohs.

23 Most Bronze Age cultures did not actually worship individual animals. Instead, attributes admired or feared in the animal kingdom were thought to be directly linked with the divine.

24 Sacred animals were sacrificed, mummified, and formally presented to a temple as a sign of devotion by pilgrims. Or, devotees could pay to have an animal dedicated in their name. Priests later buried the sacrificed animals in a large cemetery.

25 F Dunand & C Zivie-Coche. 2005. *Gods and Men in Egypt.* D Lorton, transl. Cornell UP.

26 A separate practice developed in the 26th Dynasty, when people began mummifying any member of a particular animal species as an offering to the god whom the species represented. To dry out a body, the ancient Egyptians rubbed salt into the corpse. Substances such as oils, beeswax, and pine tree resins, which repel water and microbes, were then applied. (Owen, J. 2004. "Egyptian Animals Were Mummified Same Way as Humans." *National Geographic News.* September 15).

27 Many animals were killed deliberately - huge numbers of cats found in temple cemeteries had their necks broken while still relatively young. Some animal cemeteries contain millions of sacrificed mummies of one particular species.

28 The Valkyries in Norse mythology are female divine shieldmaidens, who serve Odin.

29 There were also multiple generations of Aesinoe and Berenice Queens.

21: Codifying ♂ Property

1 As pastoral farmers, nomadic herders, and traders men remained mobile and were able to maintain their knowledge of local flora and fauna.

2 Patriliny requires men to let go of married sisters and monitor the fidelity of their wives. As a result, brothers had a decreasing influence in their sisters' lives. Patriarchs choose their sons' wives, and their daughters' husbands, resulting in less choice for females.

3 Dyble et al 2015. ibid

4 The origins of war may be due to men's capturing of females and turning them into slaves to work in the textile trade. Extremely large caches of castrated sheep bones have been found in various regions of Turkey. Since the wool from castrated sheep is better, this evidence indicate that enslaved females were making cloth for the commercial trade.

5 Lerner 1986. ibid

6 When matrilocality was replaced with patrilocal unions and inheritance, this meant men were more stable. They started to develop xenophobic views about other men and establish in-group identity based on policing female sexuality. Patriarchal residential arrangements led to the development of ethnicities and increasing intra-group conflict.

7 The name comes from the Latin word cuneus for 'wedge' owing to the wedge-shaped style of writing. In cuneiform, a carefully cut writing implement known as a stylus is pressed into soft clay to produce wedge-like impressions that represent word-signs (pictographs) and, later, phonograms or 'word-concepts.' All of the great Mesopotamian civilizations used cuneiform until it was abandoned for the alphabetic script around 2,100 BP.

8 The Code of Ur-Nammu is the oldest known law code surviving today. It is from Mesopotamia and is written on tablets, in the Sumerian language around 4,100 to 4,050 BP. Only 40 of the 57 laws have been reconstructed.

9 Along with Ancient Egypt and the Indus Valley.

10 Hammurabi was the sixth king of the First Babylonian Dynasty, reigning from 3,790 BP to 3,750 BP. He was preceded by his father, Sin-Muballit, who abdicated due to failing health.

11 A shekel was 200 to 450 ka of corn. A shekel was 20 gerah, and 60 shekels was one mina.

12 From earliest Sumerian times, a mina was a unit of weight. At first, talents and shekels had not yet been introduced. By the time of Ur-Nammu, the mina had a value of 1/60 talents as well as 60 shekels. The value of the mina is calculated at 1.25 pounds or 0.571 kilograms per mina.

13 The male part of the dualism, Mary Daly writes, "implies hyper-rationality (in reality, frequently reducible to pseudo-rationality), "objectivity," aggressivity, the possession of dominating and manipulative attitudes toward persons and the environment, and the tendency to construct boundaries between the self (and those identified with the self) and the 'Other.'" She continues, "The caricature of human being which is represented by this stereotype depends for its existence upon the opposite caricature - the eternal feminine. This implies hyper-emotionalism, passivity, self-abnegation, etc."

14 The relative exception was Sparta, where women could own property, be educated, were free to exercise outdoors, and dress in revealing clothes. This prompted Aristotle to partly blame the downfall of Sparta on the freedom its women enjoyed.

15 Men defined themselves as superior by conceptually separating themselves from, and lording over, what was previously sacred. Their victims include women, sexuality, the natural world, nonhuman animals, and the body. As elite men identified themselves with a supposedly separate and abstract mind, God became transcendent, male, immaterial, asexual, and static, separate from and even antagonistic toward things on the Earth.

16 Monica Sjoo & Barbara Mor. 1987. *The Great Cosmic Mother: Rediscovering the Religion of the Earth.* Harper One.

17 DT Burgy, 2007. "Reading Europe's Paleolithic Writing." *Comp Civ. Review.* 56; Spring. 108-16

18 Gimbutas 1991. ibid

19 Joan Marler. 2008. "The Danube Script: Neo-Eneolithic Writing in Southeastern Europe." Exhibition catalogue, Brukenthal Nat. Museum, Sibiu, Romania. Sebastopol: *Institute of Archaeomythology.*

20 Shlain, L. 1999. *The Alphabet Versus the Goddess: The Conflict Between Word and Image.* Penguin Books. Shlain argues, "writing subliminally fosters a patriarchal outlook. Writing of any kind, but especially its alphabetic form, diminishes feminine values and with them, women's power in the culture." He defines the feminine outlook as a "holistic, simultaneous, synthetic, and concrete view of the world" in contrast to the masculine that is a "linear, sequential, reductionist" one characterized by abstract thinking.

21 Each monotheistic religion features an image-less Father deity whose authority shines through 'His' revealed Word, sanctified in its written form. Conceiving of a deity who has no concrete image prepares the way for the kind of abstract thinking that inevitably leads to law codes, dualistic philosophy, and objective science, the signature triad of Western culture.

22 Copies of Enheduanna's work, many dating to hundreds of years after her death, were made and kept alongside Royal inscriptions which indicates that they were of high value, perhaps equal to the inscriptions of Kings.

23 The Hurrian hymn pre-dates several other surviving early works of music, e.g., the Seikilos epitaph and the Delphic Hymns, by a millennium.

24 T Bhikkhu. 2015. *Poems of the Elders.* CA: Metta Forest Monastery

25 The Pythagoreans were notable as a sect for including women in their ranks.

26 Quoted in K Diab. 2017. "The Egyptian roots of feminism." *Al Jazeera* Feb 2.

27 Female doctors were highly regarded in Egypt. This included Peseshet, who was known as the "overseer of doctors", and Merit Ptah, who is the first woman ever recorded to have practiced medicine, some five millennia ago.

22: Sky Magic - Subduing the Earth/Goddess

1   Göttner-Abendroth 1987. ibid

2   Caputi 2004. ibid

3   For instance, the once honored canine companions of the Goddess were degraded into 'bitches.' And the former might of female leadership is sexualized and caricatured into a dominatrix, who serves as a controlled fetish despite appearances of power.

4   Gloria Anzaldúa,. 1987. *Borderlands/La Frontera.* Aunt Lute Books.

5   Helen Diner. 1973. *Mothers and Amazons.* Doubleday

6   Kim Power. 1995. *Augustine's Writings on Women.* Darton Longman Todd.

7   Cauvin 2000. ibid

8   The head of Medusa was molded into an evil-averting device known as the Gorgoneion.

9   Jane E Harrison. 1991/1908. *Prolegomena: To The Study Of Greek Religion.* Princeton UP

10 W Burkert. 1985. *Greek Religion.* Harvard UP.

11 Her common name as a vegetation goddess is Kore and in Arcadia she was worshiped under the title Despoina, "the mistress," a very old chthonic divinity. Plutarch identifies her with spring, and Cicero calls her the seed of the fruits of the fields.

12 The myth of a goddess being abducted and taken to the Underworld is probably Pre-Greek in origin. The Greek story of the abduction of Persephone may be derived from an ancient Sumerian story in which Ereshkigal, the ancient Sumerian goddess of the Underworld, is abducted by Kur, the primeval dragon of Sumerian mythology, and forced to become ruler of the Underworld against her own will.

13 Persephone as a vegetation goddess and her mother Demeter were the central figures of the Eleusinian mysteries that predated the Olympian pantheon. In Classical Greek art, Persephone is invariably portrayed robed, often carrying a sheaf of grain.

14 Such as Despoina, "the mistress of the house" in Arcadia; Hagne, "pure", originally a goddess of the springs in Messenia; Melindia or "honey" the consort of Hades, in Hermione; Melivia; Melitodes;

Aristi cthonia, "the best chthonic"; and Praxidike, etc.

15 In the Eleusinian mysteries her return is the symbol of immortality and hence she was frequently represented on sarcophagi.

16 The Goddesses were weakened to lusting after mortals. For example, Aphrodite and Persephone contended for the love of Adonis, a mortal man, and were both spurned. Clytie, a nymph, vied with Leucothoe, a mortal princess, for the love of Helios, the god who rode the sun chariot. Leucothoe was condemned to death and buried alive in the desert, while Helios abandoned Clytie forever.

17 Dionysus is called "twice-born", or "the child of the double door."

18 She was often portrayed as the daimona of the strife of war, haunting the battlefield and delighting in human bloodshed. Eris threw a golden apple among the Goddesses inscribed with "To the fairest." Three laid claim to it - Hera, Aphrodite, and Athena - and their rivalry brought the events leading up to the disastrous Trojan war.

19 This Europa and Zeus myth may have its origin in a sacred union between the Phoenician deities Astar and Astarte, in bovine form. Astarte was the Moon Goddess.

20 In Greek mythology, Chaos was the first Immortal, and she was followed by Gaia, who became the foundation of all Immortal (sky-based) and mortal (Earth-based) generations that followed. Gaia's first creation was Ouranos who was not only Gaia's son, but her first consort. Three monstrous boys were conceived as a result of their first union. Gaia next twelve children were named the Titans, and they all resided in the sky.

21 Linda Hogan. 1996. *Dwellings: A Spiritual History of the Living World*. Touchstone Books

22 Elizabeth Gould Davis. 1971. *The First Sex*. NY: Putnam.

23 Gould Davis stated that many tales in the Old Testament were actually rewritings of older stories, with Goddesses changed to male actors, or a Goddess raped or overthrown, and her powers usurped by the new father deity. This, she suggested, was part of a concerted effort to wipe out all evidence of female authority.

24 In the ancient civilizations of Crete and Mycenae, Gould Davis suggested that the monarchy was matrilineal, and that most of the tribal chiefs were women rather than men. She also claimed that even Greek women possessed rights that were presently denied by the Catholic, Orthodox, and conservative Protestant churches, such as the rights to abortion and divorce.

25 Gould Davis argued that menstrual blood was originally sacred rather than polluting or "unclean." Interestingly, she suggests that only when people began to eat animal carcass did men become bigger than women, because of selection of weak women by men.

26 Significantly, the characteristic attributes of the devil, the color red, protruding tongue, and serpentine nature, are originally associated with female divinity, including the Greek Medusa, the South Asian Kali, the Aztec Coatlicue, the Yoruban First Ancestor, and others, as well as nature gods such as the Greek Pan.

27 When christianity became the state religion of the Roman Empire in 313 AD, it led to radical changes. The writings of Paul in the New Testament were used by the Church to justify violence against women, leading to a level of barbarity unheard of in previous ages.

28 Tertullian wrote of females around 200 AD, "You are the devil's gateway... How easily you destroyed man, the image of God. Because of the death which you brought upon us, even the Son of God had to die." And in typical cyborg projection of their own depravity, Sprenger and Kramer wrote in 1486, "All witchcraft comes from carnal lust, which is in women insatiable."

29 Gould Davis showed that the beliefs used to subordinate women are myths, and in reality, women are stronger, and physically, mentally, and morally more than equal to men.

30 Gould Davis reasoned that patriarchal civilization is destroying itself, and that only the values of the "matriarchates" can save humanity, because a society based on the mechanistic, Cartesian duality of dominant and violent males leads inevitably to a focus on technology and gadgetry rather than on loving human relationships.

31 Merlin Stone. 1976. *When God Was a Woman*. Barnes and Noble. Stone spent a decade on research and gathered material from libraries, museums, universities, and excavation sites in the US, Europe and the Near East.

32 To do this, men attempted to destroy any visible symbol of the sacred feminine, including artwork, sculpture, weaving, and literature. Men wanted the Sacred Masculine to become the dominant power, to rule over women, and to co-opt Goddess energies.

33 Myrine was known also as Marian, Ay-Mari, Mariamne, and Marienna.

34 Merlin Stone's other major work, *Ancient Mirrors of Womanhood*, collects stories, myths, and prayers involving Goddess-figures from a wide variety of world religions, ancient and otherwise. She authored numerous short stories and essays, including "3,000 Years of Racism."

35 Sarah Palmer. 2016. "Recovering Female Authors of the Bible." *Studia Antiqua* 15:1 13-26.

36 C Kroeger. 1988. "The Neglected History of Women in the Early Church." *Christian History,* 17

37 C Tuckett. 2007. *The Gospel of Mary.* Oxford UP.

38 Kate Cooper. 2013. *Band of Angels: The Forgotten World of Early Christian Women.* Overlook Pr.

39 A Mar. 2016. "The Rebel Virgins and Desert Mothers Who Have Been Written Out of Christianity's Early History." *Atlas Obscura,* Jan 21

40 According to Roman law, early Christians were compelled to sacrifice to Roman gods or face imprisonment and execution. The persecution failed to check the rise of the church. By 324, Constantine was the sole ruler of the empire, and christianity had become his favored religion.

41 Around Easter 1,710 BP, Roman ruler, Urbanus, ordered the virgin Theodosia from Tyre thrown to the sea for conversing with Christians attending trial and refusing sacrifice. On another day, Urbanus sent three virgins to brothels, and imprisoned a number of others.

42 Several early christian leaders abstained from flesh out of desire for simplicity and self denial. One example was Saint Clement of Alexandria, who died around 1,800 BP. In his second treatise, the Instructor or Tutor, Clement argues against flesh-eating, and adds, "For is there not, within a

temperate simplicity a wholesome variety of eatables - vegetables, roots, olives, herbs, milk, cheese, fruits, all kinds of dry food?"

43 Jeanne Roberts. 1994. *The Shakespearean Wild: Geography, Genus, & Gender.* U Nebraska Pr.

44 Emily Oster. 2004. "Witchcraft, Weather and Economic Growth in Renaissance Europe." *Journal of Economic Perspectives*, 18:1 Winter 215-28

45 During the Witch-Hunting period, the speed and volume of female executions were astonishing. For instance, in one German town, as many as 400 people were killed in a single day. The witch trials and femicides were ubiquitous, conducted by male ecclesiastical and secular courts, and by male Catholics and Protestants.

46 The accused included older, single women or crones, unmarried females who became pregnant, and married women who had 'too many' or 'too few' children. Also, females who made rape accusations, women who gathered in groups, or those who owned cats were incriminated.

47 "Stockholm Syndrome" refers to positive reactions of four bank employees to their captor in 1973.

48 Dee Graham. 1994. *Loving to Survive: Sexual Terror, Men's Violence & Women's Lives.* NYU Pr.

1 J Derrida. 2008. *The Animal That Therefore I Am.* Ed. M Mallet. Trans. D Wills. Fordham UP.

2 René Descartes (1596 to 1650) is the "father" of "analytical geometry" and "natural philosophy" and "rationalism" and is best known for: "Cogito ergo sum" ("I think, therefore I am").

3 Immanuel Kant (1724 to 1804) was a German philosopher and a central figure in modern philosophy. Kant argued that the human mind creates the structure of human experience.

4 Martin Heidegger (1889 to 1976) was a German philosopher widely acknowledged to be one of the most original and important philosophers of the 20th century.

5 Emmanuel Levinas (1906 to 1995) was a French philosopher known for his work related to Jewish philosophy, existentialism, ethics, and ontology.

6 Jacques Lacan (1901 to 1981) was a French psychoanalyst who influenced many leading French intellectuals in the 1960s and the 1970s. His ideas had a significant impact on post-structuralism, critical theory, linguistics, 20th-century French philosophy, film theory and clinical psychoanalysis.

7 In popular conception, nonhuman animals eat without pleasure, cry without pain, and grow without knowing it. They desire nothing, fear nothing, and know nothing.

8 René Descartes. 2011. "Animals are Machines." *J of Cosmology*, Vol. 14. Reprint

9 Around 2,535 BP, Pythagoras traveled to Egypt and was initiated in temple rites. He remained for 10 years, and like Egyptian priests, Pythagoras was a strict vegetarian who dressed in linen clothes and sandals made of papyrus. As devotees of Isis, priests did not wear clothing or shoes made from animal skins.

10 Anthropomorphism is the attribution of human traits and emotions to non-human entities.

11 B Plant. 2011. "Welcoming dogs: Levinas & 'the animal' question." *Phil & Soc Crit.*, 37:1 49-71

12 M Calarco. 2008. *Zoographies: The Question of the Animal from Heidegger to Derrida.* Columbia

13 Margo DeMello. 2012. *Animals & Society: An Introduction to Human-Animal Studies.* Columbia

14 KJ Shapiro. 1998. *Animal Models of Human Psychology.* Hogrefe & Huber Pub.

15 C Choi. 2009. "10 Animals That Use Tools." *Live Science*, Dec 14

16 The list of nonhuman animals that use tools or objects is long, and includes the great apes, crows, elephants, dolphins, sea otters, octopuses, parrots, vultures, gulls, owls, herons, and others. For example, orangutans in the wild have developed and passed along a way to make improvised whistles from bundles of leaves, which they use to help ward off predators.

17 Leila Haghighat. 2013. "Baboons Can Learn to Recognize Words." *Nature News.* Apr 15.

18 Lexigrams are symbols corresponding to objects or ideas. A lexigram represents a word but is not necessarily indicative of the object to which it refers.

19 P Wedderburn. 2015. "Animals grieve just as people do." *The Telegraph*, Jan 10

20 Wells, Deborah. 2009. "The Effects of Animals on Human Health and Well-Being." *Journal of Social Issues*, Vol 65: No. 3, Sept. pp. 523-543(21).

21 DeMello 2012. ibid

22 Greta Gaard, ed. 1993. *Ecofeminism: Women, Animals, Nature.* Temple UP.

23 C Peterson. 2013. *Bestial Traces: Race, Sexuality, Animality.* Fordham UP.

24 Linda Kalof. 2007. *Looking at Animals in Human History.* Reaktion Books.

25 David A. Nibert. 2013. *Animal Oppression & Human Violence.* Columbia UP.

26 Tony Weis. 2013. *The Ecological Hoofprint.* Zed Books.

27 Seenarine 2016. ibid

28 Martha Rosenberg & R Wilbur. 2015. "Animal cruelty is a reliable predictor of criminality - which is why the FBI is taking it more seriously." *Raw Story.* May 13.

29 Shukin, Nicole. 2009. *Animal Capital: Rendering Life in Biopolitical Times.* U of Minnesota Press.

30 There are few studies on whether animals benefit at all from being made use of as service animals, circus animals, zoo animals, and so on.

31 In 2006, about 69 million US households had pets, with around 74 million dogs, 91 million cats, and 17 million birds. As part of their over-consumption, US owners spent over $38 billion on companion animals. For the rest of the world, the numbers are slightly less than US totals.

32 These cultural spectacles, founded on the mechanization of nonhuman animals, are designed to affirm the human-ness of the audience. At the same time, they clearly demonstrate the superiority of cyborg trainers, handlers, and owners who can harness the power of the tamed animals.

33 FAO. 2013. "Tackling climate change through livestock." Rome: *UN Food and Agricultural Organization;* B Chellaney. 2015. "A Healthy, Climate-Friendly Diet." *Project Syndicate.* June 23.

34 Carol Adams. 2010. *The Sexual Politics of Meat.* 20th Anniversary Edition. Bloomsbury Academic.

35 Horses and other animals are used to convey reliable communication and transportation, which perpetuates the fiction of painless transmission. These images disavow the economic, physical and representational violence upon which the animal-based technology depends.

36 MJ Lawrence et al. 2015. "The effects of modern war and military activities on biodiversity and the environment." *Environmental Reviews*, 23(4): 443-460

37 More than 1,000 military sites in the US are filled with toxins, topping the Superfund list of contaminated sites. And, across the World, US wars have contaminated the soil and water of vast regions under occupation with depleted uranium, benzene, trichloroethylene, and Perchlorate.

38 Lisa Savage. 2015. "Elephant In The Room: Pentagon's Massive Carbon Footprint." *CounterPunch*, July 23.

39 In 2015, the US will have a declared military and defense budget of $601 billion, which is more than the next 7 highest spending countries combined (China, Saudia Arabia, Russia, UK, India, France, Japan), and about 54% of the discretionary budget.

40 Sara Flounders. 2014. "The Pentagon, The Climate Elephant." *Int'l Action Center & Global Research*, Sep 17

41 The complete US military exemption from greenhouse gas emissions calculations includes more than 1,000 bases in more than 130 countries around the world, its 6,000 facilities in the US, its aircraft carriers and jet aircraft. Also excluded are its weapons testing and all multilateral operations such as the NATO, AFRICOM, and US/UN-sanctioned "peacekeeping."

42 Patricia Hynes. 2011. "The Military Assault on Global Climate." *Truthout*, Sept 08

43 The US Air Force (USAF) is the single largest consumer of jet fuel in the world. The F-4 Phantom Fighter burns more than 1,600 gallons of jet fuel per hour and peaks at 14,400 gallons per hour at supersonic speeds. The B-52 Stratocruiser, with eight jet engines, guzzles 55 gallons per minute; ten minutes of flight uses as much fuel as the average driver does in one year of driving. A quarter of the world's jet fuel feeds the USAF fleet of flying killing machines; in 2006, they consumed as much fuel as US planes did during the Second World War (1941-1945) - 2.6 billion gallons.

44 US President Wilson declared the second Sunday in May Mother's Day, but did not include Howe's antiwar message.

24: 'Civilizing' Females

1 Chris Hedges. 2017. "James Baldwin and the Meaning of Whiteness." *Truthdig*, Feb 19

2 The persistence of males' cyborg-like terrorism is due to the use of violence in maintaining domination over females for a broad range of personal and political purposes. A husband can just as easily beat his wife if she is a high school dropout or a college graduate. Or, an entire territory can be claimed if fighters rape the local women, or take them as sex slaves

3 Cyborg's domination of females occurs across all boundaries - ethnicity, race, class, religious, location, language, educational level, diet, etc. Thus far, men's false privilege and aggression are still not a real priority for most male-centered governments.

4 Eva Wiseman. 2015. "Why femicide won't end until we have a truly equal society." *Guardian*. 2/22.

5 S Sengupta. 2015. "UN Reveals 'Alarmingly High' Levels of Violence Against Women." *NYT* Mar 9

6 R Gill. 2006. *Gender and the Media*. Cambridge: Polity Press.

7 S Faludi. 1991. *Backlash: The Undeclared War Against Women*. London, Chatto and Windus.

8 Amelia Ayrelan Iuvino. 2017. The Failure of "Choice Feminism." *Jacobin Magazine*, March 15.

9 The Equal Rights Amendment that equity feminism struggled for, failed, so sexual equality, with the exception of when it pertains to the right to vote, is not protected by the US Constitution.

10 bell hooks's *Black Looks: Race and Representation* (1995), which examines white supremacist culture from a feminist perspective, was initially characterized as hate literature.

11 SJ Olshansky. 2012. "Differences In Life Expectancy Due To Race And Educational Differences Are Widening, And Many May Not Catch Up." *Health Affairs*, 31, no.8: 1803-1813.

12 Carolyn Johnston. 2003. *Cherokee Women in Crisis*. University of Alabama Press.

13 The typical prehistoric woman may have enjoyed greater freedom than the average citizen of modern democratic states. The rule of cyborgs over human egg-producers is particularly damning, as it precludes any other way of organizing society. And it keeps females in perpetual oppression since their perceived nature-based bodies will never be treated as full equals to men coupled with the strength of domesticates. The association of girls and women to animals, and the destruction of feminized nature, are direct effects of men's 'progress' in colonizing nonhuman animals.

14 Female authors who are published have usually been numbed into silence about the taboo subject of patriarchal atrocities against women and nature. And when female-authored books, particularly feminist books, have been successful in their time, they have been erased from history. Female intellect and feminist scholarship has been wiped out, over and over.

15 Silvia Federici. 2004. *Caliban & the Witch*. Autonomedia.

16 Silvia Federici. 2008. "Witch-Hunting, Globalization, & Feminist Solidarity in Africa Today." *The Commoner*.

17 Under patriarchal societies, females are viewed as property belonging to men. According to an adage, "A woman is the child of her father, her husband, and her son."

18 ILO. 2014. "Global Employment Trends 2014" *Int'l Labour Organization*.

19 AAUW. 2014. "By the Numbers: A Look at the Gender Pay Gap." *AAUW.org*. Sep 18.

20 Ariane Hegewisch et al. 2014. "The Gender Wage Gap: 2013." *Inst for Women's Policy Research*.

21 Actionaid. 2015. "Close the Gap! The cost of inequality in women's work." UK: *Actionaid*.

22 Tracey Lien. 2015. "Women are leaving the tech industry in droves." *LA Times*. February 22.

23 E Newcomer. 2015. "Sheryl Sandberg on Ellen Pao." *Seattle Times*. April 26.

24 Hill, Catherine. 2011. "Enabling Rural Women's Economic Empowerment." Ghana: *UN Women*.

25 Sex differences in access to land and credit affects the relative ability of female and male farmers and entrepreneurs to invest, operate to scale, and benefit from new economic opportunities.

26 FAO. 2011. "The State of Food & Agriculture 2011: Women & Agriculture, Closing the Gender Gap for Development." *Food & Agriculture Org* of UN.

27 Magdalena Carmona. 2013. "Extreme poverty and human rights." *UN Special Rapporteur on Extreme Poverty and Human Rights.*

28 WB. 2012. "World Development Report: Gender Equality & Development Outline." *World Bank.*

29 WHO. 2014. "Update: Progress on Sanitation and Drinking Water." *WHO & UN Children's Fund.*

30 Debbie Budlender. 2008. "The statistical evidence on care and non-care work across six countries." *UNRISD Gender and Development Programme*, No 4 Dec

31 UN Women. 2015. "Facts and Figures: Economic Empowerment." *UN Women.*

32 E Gakidou. et al., 2010, "Increased Educational Attainment and its Effect on Child Mortality in 175 Countries between 1970 and 2009: A Systematic Analysis." *The Lancet*, 376(9745), p. 969.

33 E Neumeyer & T Plumper. 2007. "The Gendered Nature of Natural Disasters." *Annals of the Association of American Geographers*, 97(3): 551.

34 Sarah Bradshaw & M Fordham. 2013. "Women, Girls & Disasters. *UK Dept for Int'l Dev.* Aug.

35 Staff. 2017. "Power and Potential." *Rights and Resources Initiative.* May 24

36 Among Australian Aborigines, the digging-stick and wooden bowls were associated with women. Annette Hamilton argues that women continued to use older traditions in technology, not because they were conservative, but because men started to monopolize Neolithic and Bronze-Age innovations for themselves. For example, females were forbidden to use lithic resources such as flint and chert, which were seen as a male prerogative. Females were not permitted to touch males' hunting spear and spear thrower, or even enter the forests where that kind of wood grew.

37 FAO. 2014. "State of Food and Agriculture." *Food & Agri Org of the UN.*

38 Rudolf, Gloria. 1999. *Panama's Poor.* Univ Press of Florida. These include works by Hoffer (1974), Brown (1975), Draper (1975), Martin & Voorhies (1975), Buenaventura-Posso & Brown (1980), Erinne & Leacock (1980), Lealock (1981), Dahlberg (1981), and Gailey (1987).

39 Including Bossen (1984), Buechler (1986), Deere and Leon de Leal (1979, 1981), Lealock and Safa (1986), Mies (1986, 1988), Nash and Safa (1986), and Safa (1981).

40 F Engels. 1972. *The Origin of the Family, Private Property & the State.* (1884). Pathfinder Press.

41 June C Nash, & Helen I Safa. 1980. *Sex & Class in Latin America.* Bergin & Garvey.

42 There is a positive correlation between female education and birth rates. In developed and developing countries alike, with increasing levels of female educational attainment, part of females' reproductive burden has improved with declining birth rates.

43 All but 32 countries have adopted laws that guarantee sexual equality. Women in legislatures has doubled in 20 years, to 22 percent. Currently, 25 women CEOs lead Fortune 500 companies, compared to just one in 1998, so they now account for five percent from near zero.

44 Mary Daly. 1973. *Beyond God the Father: Toward a Philosophy of Women's Liberation.* Beacon.

45 In development and aid policy, "men and boys" and "women and girls" are divided into neat categories that bypass any real concern with power, inequality, or difference at the household and community levels. "Women and girls" are clustered into a homogeneous category as the deserving 'objects' of empowerment, with little reference to intersecting inequalities, dismantling male privilege, or the reality of some women's interests in preserving patriarchy.

46 Amid all the talk about engaging men and boys in empowering women, there is little focus on ameliorating the harms and hazards presented by those living precarious lives in the wake of neoliberalism's structural violence. There is almost complete silence about the work that is needed to challenge and change the vested power held by those able to take full advantage of the "patriarchal dividend" - and their role in sustaining structural inequities.

47 Nimmi Gowrinathan. 2015. "'I Don't Know Why We Come': Inside the UN's Commission on the Status of Women." *Vice News.* March 20.

48 A universal basic income is a form of social security in which all citizens or residents of a country regularly receive an unconditional sum of money from the government in addition to any income received from elsewhere. Similar proposals date to Thomas Paine's Agrarian Justice of 1795, that was paired with asset-based egalitarianism

49 The Alaska Permanent Fund, Macao, and Iran are examples of partial basic income.

50 UN Women. 2015. "Progress of the World's Women 2015-2016." *UN Women.*

25: Terrorizing Females

1 Beijing20. 2015. "Gender equality: Where are we?" *UN Women.* Feb

2 Quoted in Daly. 1978. ibid

3 J Cleland et al. 2012. "Contraception and health." *Lancet.* 380 (9837): 149-56. Jul 14

4 S Ahmed et al 2012. "Maternal deaths averted by contraceptive use." *Lancet.* 380 (9837): 111-125

5 D Canning et al. 2012. "The economic consequences of reproductive health and family planning." *Lancet.* 380 (9837): 165-177.

6 D Van Braeckel et al. 2012. "Slowing population growth for wellbeing and development." *Lancet.* 380 (9837): 84-85.

7 Katha Pollitt. 2017. "Can a Feminist Be Pro-Life?" *The Nation,* Mar 10

8 The knives/penis of boys and men are rarely big enough to slice a female in two, thus fulfilling males' dark fantasies of domination. Using a condom makes men's penis smaller and less sharp, in the sense that they feel less of harm they aim to cause. Penis inadequacy is an underlying cause of pedophilia and violence against females.

9 An Oklahoma lawmaker described women as "hosts" while defending his bill that would require

women seeking abortions to gain written permission from the father of the child.

10   Starting in 1911, Margaret Sanger became a pioneer in the struggle for a woman's right to birth control in an era "when it was illegal to discuss the topic." Sanger was arrested many times for her publications and her New York City clinic.

11   Shelby McNabb. 2016. "National Clinic Violence Survey." *Feminist Majority Foundation.*

12   CRR. 2013. "The World's Abortion Laws Map 2013 Update." *Center for Reproductive Rights.*

13   WHO. 2011. "Unsafe abortion." *World Health Organization.*

14   Staff. 2015. "First woman in US sentenced for killing a fetus." *NBC*, Mar 31.

15   Women are angry at Patel for throwing the miscarriage parts of her own body into the trash. But there is a world of difference between a nonviable fetus and a baby. Besides, a miscarriage can be extremely traumatic, and females cannot always be expected to act 'rationally.'

16   B Waterfield. 2013. "Irish abortion law key factor in death of Savita Halappanavar, official report finds." *Telegraph.* June 13.

17   Nina Strochlic. 2015. "Raped 10-Year-Old Denied Abortion." *Daily Beast* 5/1

18   Amnesty International declared that the physical and psychological impact of forcing the child to continue with an unwanted pregnancy is tantamount to torture. Yet, the male Health Minister insists, "There is no indication that the health of the (girl) is at risk... therefore we are not, from any point of view, in favor of the termination of the pregnancy."

19   Fraidy Reiss. 2017. "Why does the US still let 12-year-old girls get married?" *Wash Post*, Feb 11

20   UNICEF. 2014. "Ending Child Marriage: Progress & Prospects. NY: *UNICEF.*

21   WHO. 2014. "Maternal mortality." *WHO* Fact sheet N°348. May.

22   UNICEF. 2014. "Female Genital Mutilation/Cutting: What might the future hold." NY: UNICEF.

23   ILO. 2012, "ILO Global Estimate of Forced Labour." Geneva: *International Labor Organization.*

24   US State Dept. 2005. "Trafficking in Persons Report. Washington: *USSD.*

25   Caitlin Roper. 2017. "Sexual Harassment Is Not A Compliment." *Huff Post,* May 21

26   Holly Kearl. 2014. "Unsafe and Harassed in Public Spaces." Virginia: *Stop Street Harassment.*

27   Lamiat Sabin. 2015. "Every woman in Paris polled in survey has experienced sexual harassment on trains." *Independent.* April 17.

28   Jagori & UN Women. 2010. "Safe Cities Free of Violence Against Women & Girls Initiative."

29   AAUW. 2001. "Hostile Hallways." *American Association of University Women.*

30   Courtney Kube. 2015. "Reports of Sexual Assault in Military Increase Again." *NBC News.* May 1st.

31   Patricia Jaden & Nancy Thoennes. 1998. "Stalking in America." *US DOJ,* NCJ 169592.

32   Harassment is part of the domesticating mindset that considers females as property. Stalking also occurs in the context of rape culture. The problem is not that women are inappropriately dressed for the office, school, malls, etc. It is that in male-dominated society, men and boys have unearned prerogative and are given a free pass for 'not being able to 'control themselves.'

33   Fisher, Bonnie et al. 2000. "The Sexual Victimization of College Women." *US DOJ.*, NCJ 182369.

34   GAO. 1998. "Domestic Violence," US Gen. Accounting Office, *GAO*/HEHS-99-12

35   Kim C. Lim et al. 2004. "Impact of Domestic Violence Offenders on Occupational Safety & Health." *Maine Dept of Labor & Family Crisis Services.*

36   Donna Chung. 2013. "Understanding the Statistics about Male Violence Against Women." Australia: White Ribbon, Research Series - Paper No. 5.

37   Sarah Avery-Leaf & Michele Cascardi. 2002. "Dating Violence Education," in Pa Schewe ed., *Preventing Violence in Relationships.* American Psychological Association (APA)

38   UNICEF. 2014. "Hidden in Plain Sight: A Statistical Analysis of Violence against Children."

39   JS Silverman et al. 2001. "Dating Violence Against Adolescent Girls & Associated Substance Use, Unhealthy Weight Control, Sexual Risk Behavior, Pregnancy, & Suicidality." *J. Am. Med. Ass'n* 286: 572-9

40   Vangie Foshee et al. 1996. "The Safe Date Project." *Am. J. of Preventive Med.* 12: 39.

41   Cathy Schoen et al. 1997. "The Commonwealth Fund Survey of the Health of Adolescent Girls.

42   Tjaden & Thoennes. 1998. ibid

43   WHO. 2013. "Global & regional estimates of violence against women." *World Health Organization.*

44   Bureau of Justice Statistics. 2000. "Intimate Partner Violence." DC: *US DOJ.*

45   APA. 1996. "American Psychological Assoc. Presidential Task Force on Violence the Family."

46   J Burns. 2015. "The link between animal abuse and domestic violence." *CBS News.* May 14.

47   S Stevens. 2013. "The Link Between Domestic Violence & Animal Abuse." *Feminist Wire.* 10/23

48   DOJ. 2001. "Special Report Intimate Partner Violence & Age of Victim 1993-9." *DOJ Statistics* Oct

49   MR Durose et al. 2005. "Family Violence Statistics." *US Dept of Justice*, Bureau of Justice Statistics.

50   Sengupta 2015. ibid

51   Fearon, J & Hoeffler, Anke. 2014. "Benefits and Costs of the Conflict and Violence Targets for the Post-2015 Development Agenda Post-2015 Consensus." Copenhagen Consensus Center.

52   J Messerschmidt. 1995. "From Patriarchy to Gender," in *International Feminist Perspectives in Criminology*, eds. N Rafter & F Heidensohn. Open University Press.

53   DOJ. 2006. "Extent, Nature, & Consequences of Rape Victimization: Findings From the National Violence Against Women Survey." *US Dept of Justice.* Jan.

54   CDC. 2012. "Sexual Violence: Facts at a Glance." US Centers for Disease Control.

55   K Kim. 2013. "Which country has the highest reported incidents of rape?" *Global Post.* March 18.

56   BBC. 2015. "Delhi rapist says victim shouldn't have fought back." March 2.

57 M Rahman & Tara Conlan. 2015. "Delhi rape documentary-maker appeals to Narendra Modi over broadcast ban." *The Guardian*. March 4.
58 Seenarine. 2004. ibid.
59 Makarand Purohit. 2015. "Water Untouched." *India Water Portal*. Feb 19.
60 P Dabhi. 2015. "Rape of Dalit women registers 500% increase since 2001." *Indian Express*. Mar 8
61 P Srivastava. 2015. "Dalit girl, 17, fighting for life after she was set on fire by four men 'for getting an education'" *Daily Mail India*. March 5.
62 Gokul Vannan. 2015. "Dalit Girl Found Hanging in Textile Mill." *Kractivist*, Feb 27.
63 PTI. 2015. "Teenage Dalit girl raped, body found hanging from tree." *Financial Express*. Feb 19.
64 Jill Radford & Diana EH Russell. 1992. *Femicide: The Politics of Woman Killing*. NY: Twayne.
65 UNODC. 2013. "Global Study on Homicide." *UN Office on Drugs and Crime*.
66 J McFarlane et al. 1999. "Stalking & Intimate Partner Femicide." *Homicide Studies* 3:4 300-16
67 Betty Reardon. 1996. *Sexism and the War System*. Syracuse UP
68 M Bishara. 2014. "On men and war." *Al Jazeera*, July 31.
69 Mordechai Kedar claims that if Israel threatens to dispatch agents to rape a Palestinian militant's mother or sister as retribution for his crimes, it would serve as an effective deterrent. Other Jews on social media have portrayed Gaza as an erotic woman to be violated.
70 J Goldstein. 2003. *War & Gender: How Gender Shapes the War System & Vice Versa*. Cambridge
71 In 2005 the US government amended the Manual for Courts-Martial to specifically enumerate "patronizing a prostitute" as a violation of Article 134 of the Uniform Code of Military Justice. While this provision has been in place for eight years, as of 2012 there have only been 31 cases brought for "patronizing a prostitute" or "pandering" and only 19 individuals have been convicted.
72 S Cunningham. 2000. "What we Teach about When We Teach about Violence," *HFG Review* 1:4-9.

26: Taming Females

1   A McRobbie. 2007. "Top girls?" *Cultural Studies* 21(4): 718- 737.
2   A Harris. 2004. *Future Girl: Young Women in the 21st century*. Routledge.
3   Maggie Andrews. 2012. *Domesticating the Airwaves*. Bloomsbury Academic.
4   Augie Fleras. 2011. *The Media Gaze: Representations of Diversities in Canada*. UBC Press.
5   Saba Hamedy. 2015. "'Fifty Shades of Grey' sets record at box office." *LATimes*. Feb 15.
6   Couples and females flocked to theaters. An estimated 68% of moviegoers were female, and 58% were older than 25. One theater sold a Valentine's Loveseat Package that included two tickets and a bottle of wine, blanket and dessert to share.
7   The book trilogy topped best-seller lists, selling over 100 million copies, and has been translated into 52 languages. It set a record in the UK as the fastest-selling paperback of all time.
8   NBC. 2015. "'Fifty Shades' author 'stunned' at success of erotic trilogy." *NBC News*. April 17.
9   J Hall. 2013. "Swedish man accused of killing girlfriend in Fifty Shades of Grey-style sado-masochistic sex game." UK: *Independent*. Jan 28.
10 Tara Culp-Ressler. 2015. "College Student Accused Of Brutal Rape, Uses 'Fifty Shades Of Grey' As His Defense." *Think Progress*. Feb 24.
11 The popularity of the film may indicate how frustrated and resigned females are, and it may serve as a reflection of women's permissive attitude toward cyborg desire. Daily, females are tamed and colonized to serve male desire, and the film represents an extension of that role.
12 Females are sexually repressed and may feel guilty if they become the aggressor in bed since insecure male cyborgs feel emasculated if women do. All forms of aggression must remain the sole prerogative of cyborgs, or their illusion of transcendence collapses. Plus, there is lack of education and cultural encouragement for females to own their own bodies and orgasms.
13 Domination fantasies may be a result of sexual repression and a way around guilt and shame, but not any desire to be raped. Females may have fantasies in which they are forced into sex against their will, and for some, these may be a frequent or favorite fantasy experience.
14 Rape is not taken seriously enough. The majority of cases are not reported and even when the crime is reported most rapists are not arrested or prosecuted. Only about 3% will ever go to jail. Some females have self-mutilated because they have felt betrayed by their own bodies in these horrendous situations.
15 Daly 1973. ibid
16 Rebecca Herzig. 2015. *Plucked: A History of Hair Removal (Biopolitics)*. NYU Press.
17 Sheila Jeffreys. 2005. *Beauty & Misogyny: Harmful Cultural Practices in the West*. Taylor Francis.
18 100,000 to 200,000 animals suffer and die just for cosmetics every year around the world. These are rabbits, guinea pigs, hamsters, rats and mice. They have chemicals forced down their throats and dripped into their eyes and onto their shaved skin.
19 Sydney Lupkin. 2015. "Women Put an Average of 168 Chemicals on Their Bodies Each Day, Consumer Group Says." *ABC News*. April 27.
20 Chemicals include diazolidinyl urea, lead acetate, methylene glycol formaldehyde, propyl paraben, and quaternium-15.
21 Elian Fink, et al. 2015. "Mental Health Difficulties in Early Adolescence." *Journal of Adolescent Mental Health*, 56:5 502-7. May.
22 Daly 1973. ibid
23 Andrea Dworkin. 1989. *Letters from a War Zone*. Dutton Books.
24 Tim. 2013. "The Stats on Internet Pornography." *Daily Info Graphic*. Jan 4th.
25 Catherine A Mackinnon. 1989. *Toward a Feminist Theory of the State*. Harvard UP

26 Quoted in Covenant Eyes. 2015. "Pornography Statistics: Annual Report 2015."
27 Allison Pearson. 2015. "Pornography has changed the landscape of adolescence beyond all recognition." *The Telegraph*. April 22.
28 C Marston & R Lewis. 2014. "Anal heterosex among young people and implications for health promotion: a qualitative study in the UK." *BMJ* Jul 18. 4
29 Stoltenberg 1998. ibid
30 Marti Kheel. 2009. In conversation with the author.
31 Eisler 1995. ibid
32 Caputi 2004. ibid

27: Theorizing 'Female'

1 As part of an artificially constructed, imaginary boundary, male human animals claim there are no longer animals since the temporary civilizations they have built have risen far above nature.
2 Interview with Marti Kheel by author, April 18, 2010.
3 Rosemary Ruether. 1983. *Sexism & God-Talk: Toward a Feminist Theology*. Beacon.
4 In advertising imagery, for example, both the landscape and the female body are regularly shown as conquered, rendered into property that can be taken, owned, and mapped. And as indicative of their mutual, exploited status, female sexuality is often used to market animal products, such as cow, pig and chicken flesh.
5 During the Stone Age, female reproductive roles were viewed as vital, and they formed the basis for collective female power. But male ascendancy in the New Stone Age meant that these female powers were now envied, feared, and hated by falsely entitled men. Animals' and nature's mysterious creative forces are likewise viewed with resentment, anxiety, and dislike.
6 Even though the patriarchy utilizes biological difference in gender constructions, this should not lead to an automatic denial of science and severing of all connections to nature. This position merely mirrors cyborg transcendence over the Earth and human exceptionalism. Apart from gendered constructions, there are real sex differences, and human females are unique in many important ways. Ironically, in rejecting biological difference, 'anti-essentialist' feminism accepts the traditional patriarchal division between nature and culture.
7 D Soh. 2017. "Are gender feminists & transgender activists undermining science?" *LATimes*, 2/10
8 M Bramble et al. 2016. "Sex-Specific Effects of Testosterone on the Sexually Dimorphic Transcriptome & Epigenome of Embryonic Neural Stem/Progenitor Cells." *Scientific Rep*. 6, 10/15
9 A Chekrouda et al. 2016. "Patterns in the human brain mosaic discriminate males from females." *PNAS* 113:14 Apr 5
10 Devita Singh. 2012. *A Follow-up Study of Boys with Gender Identity Disorder*. PhD Thesis, University of Toronto, Dept of Human Development and Applied Psychology.
11 In their commingling of nature and culture, gender theorists strenuously reject any biological binary. But at the same time, activists steadfastly uphold the gender dualism of 'femininity' and 'hyper-masculinity.' Trans theory does not de-construct and eliminate the patriarchal binary. Instead, it reifies transition from masculinity or femininity.
12 A born-female is biologically different from a born-male. As such, there are some universal qualities to being a female, in addition to the lived experiences of being in a subjugated group. Males do not menstruate or give birth, which are essentially female processes.
13 Trans theory was developed by European men like Foucault and Derrida whose conception of gender resistance is profoundly Eurocentric.
14 Greta R Bauer et al. 2012. "High heterogeneity of HIV-related sexual risk among transgender people in Ontario, Canada." *BMC Public Health*. 12:292
15 Queer men can perform as females, and have done so in countless cultures for thousands of years. However trans identities are far more the exception rather than the norm among humans.
16 Sarah Ditum. 2017. "It's revealing that there is so little public debate over what makes you a "real man." *New Statesman*, Mar 29.
17 Identities are often ascribed at birth according to male, class-based, racial and religious hierarchies, which generally limits an individual's performance.
18 Defining transfemmes as 'real women' does little to deconstruct the underlying forces of sexual hierarchy, systemic misogyny, and toxic masculinity.
19 Trans theory's reduction of the complex, multiple identities of individuals into one based solely on gender performance is not viewed as essentialist. Rather trans essentialism is characterized as both necessary and the final step for personal and social liberation.
20 In response to critics, ecofeminist theory has become limited, compartmentalized, reduced from a macro to a micro level, and renamed queer ecologies, global feminist environmental justice, and gender and the environment. The patriarchal dualisms are excluded from the new paradigms.
21 Trans-exclusionary radical feminist
22 The trans position on mandatory inclusion into female spaces is entirely dismissive of debate and of the legitimate fears egg-producing humans have of men, and this is an extremist position.
23 Men who used physical sex differences to construct a gender-based hierarchy with males on top, not radical feminists. And while ecofeminists recognize sex differences, they do not subscribe to sexist gender roles and male superiority. What is oppressive is not biology, and lack of fluidity, but hierarchical dualism based on gendered-biology. Radical feminists seeks to abolish gender, not increase the fluidity and transition between an oppressive and hierarchical gender binary.
24 As part of trans movement's insidious victim-blaming and abnegation of social responsibility, victimized females are blamed for their abuse due to lack of fluidity. This framing conveniently ignores the thousands of years of patriarchal oppression of females who reject femininity, and the hundred of millions who are beaten, burned, and murdered as infants, children, and adults.

25 Joan Marler. 2003. "The Body of Woman as Sacred Metaphor," in *Il Mito e il Culto della Grande Dea*. Bologna: Associazione Armonie.

26 The Babe. 2017. "Exalting the Transfeminine." *babeinbotland.com* Mar 4

27 The white liberal concern over the plight of black transfemmes conveniently ignores underlying problems of systemic racism, profiling, poverty, homelessness, and incarceration.

28 This debate is an intellectual conflict where much is at stake including a scientific understanding of females' roles in culture, mothering, reproductive health, and physiology. Also, females' significance in mating, alliances, aggression, and female intrasexual competition.

29 However, most of human thoughts, emotions, and feelings originate in the brain. And studies in biology do not reduce female agency, which is always subjective, situational, contingent, and existing in variations.

30 Maryanne Fisher et al eds. 2013. *Evolution's Empress*. Oxford UP.

31 This study rejects cyborg hierarchical separation of nature and culture. The two areas are inter-related and act upon each other in an ongoing evolutionary process. Domestication have had an organic impact on nonhuman animals, and on human animals as well. The development of male cyborg consciousness has both cultural and genetic origins and implications. Epigenetics suggests human behavior may not only be influenced by DNA sequences in genes but also by molecular processes that alter expression of genes in response to environmental changes.

32 A 1991 study found that 1 in 426 newborns, or 2.34 per 1,000, did not have strictly XX or XY chromosomes. Klinefelter's syndrome (XXY) was found in 1 per 576 boys, XYY in 1 per 851 boys, triple-X in 1 per 947 girls and Turner's syndrome (X0) in 1 per 1893 girls. Other sex chromosome aberrations were found in 1 per 11,637 children. The inter-sex ratio was similar to the most frequent autosomal abnormality, Down's syndrome, with 1 per 592 children. (J Nielsen and M Wohlert. 1991. Chromosome abnormalities found among 34,910 newborn children: results from a 13-year incidence study in Arhus, Denmark. *Human Genetics*, 87(1) May 81-3)

33 Having a "black" identity essentializes individuals with multiple, fluid identities, into just one based on skin color. A race-based strategic essentialism may be viewed as a temporary and necessary step towards liberation from racial oppression. Instead of insisting on mandatory inclusion, non-black allies can work to deconstruct "whiteness" and ending white supremacy.

34 Due to the predisposition of males to violence, female separatist spaces are relevant, like people of color space, and those of other oppressed groups. Expressing a desire for separate, female-only space should not automatically be castigated as transphobic.

35 Female-submissivity is dehumanizing, not liberating. Submissiveness limits the lives of the vast majority of born-females on the planet, and a few class-privileged men performing like women does nothing to change underprivileged women's daily misery. Neither does a few class-privileged women transitioning and performing as men.

36 Men's appropriation of female culture is glorified and structurally enshrined. And this theft is then used to silence all women's voices. Trans appropriation of feminism is egregious since trans rights tend to take precedence over females' reproductive rights and other vital issues.

37 Josephine Donovan. 2006. "Feminism & the Treatment of Animals." *Signs*, 31:2 (Winter) 305-329.

38 While conversations about Indigenous women and ecology are not exclusive to first nations, and there is other non-native aspects and relevance to feminism, these concerns are important. Self-determination and the return of stolen Indigenous lands are essential to the reclamation of females' health and environmental knowledge.

39 Native spiritual connection to nature is founded on their cultural heritage, not western notions of environmentalism and conservation.

40 Elizabeth Hoover et al. 2012. "Indigenous Peoples of North America: Environmental Exposures and Reproductive Justice." *Environmental Health Perspectives* 120 (12): 1645-49.

41 Winona LaDuke. 1999. *All Our Relations: Native Struggles for Land and Life*. South End Press.

42 Lindsay Nixon. 2015. "Eco-Feminist Appropriations of Indigenous Feminisms & Environmental Violence." *Feminist Wire*, April 30.

43 Audra Simpson. 2014. *Mohawk Interruptus*. Durham: Duke University Press.

44 Historical analysis of female-centered cultures across the Globe can help to avoid the bias of mainstream, white feminist analysis. This study explores aspects of Indigenous and minority females' relationship to the Earth through diet, myth, custom, governance, theology, and so on.

45 Andrea Smith. 2010. *Conquest: Sexual Violence & American Indian Genocide*. South End Press.

46 Aileen Moreton-Robinson. 2002. *Talkin' Up to the White Woman*. University of Queensland Press.

47 Karen Baker-Fletcher,. 1998. *Sisters of Dust, Sisters of Spirit*. Augsburg Fortress Pub.

48 Shamara Shantu Riley. 1993. "Ecology is a Sistah's Issue Too - The Politics of Emergent Afrocentric Ecowomanism." in Carol Adams, ed., *Ecofeminism and the Sacred*. Continuum Int'l.

49 In 2,131 BP, Cleopatra II of Egypt led a rebellion against Ptolemy VIII and drove him and Cleopatra III out of Egypt. In 1,975 BP, Fulvia, wife of Mark Antony, organized an uprising against Augustus. In 2,003 BP, Mother Lü led a peasant rebellion against Wang Mang of the Western Han Dynasty in China. And in 1,977 BP, the Trưng Sisters successfully rebelled against the Chinese Han-Dynasty, and are regarded as national heroines of Vietnam.

50 Close to 1,950 BP, Boudica, a Celtic female ruler in Britain, led a massive uprising against the occupying Roman forces. Around this time, Veleda of the Germanic Bructeri tribe had a great deal of influence in the Batavian rebellion. She was acknowledged as a strategic leader, a priestess, a prophet, and as a living deity. Close to 1,750 BP, Zenobia, the Syrian queen of the Palmyrene empire, took control of Roman Egypt, Arabia, and parts of Asia Minor.

51 In 1763, Gabriela Silang led a revolution against the Spanish to establish an independent Ilocos. In 1778, Baltazara Chuiza led a rebellion against the Spanish in Ecuador. In 1780, Huillac Nusca of the Kolla tribe rebelled against the Spanish in Chile. In 1781, Manuela Beltrán, a Neogranadine (now Colombia) peasant led a revolt against the Spanish Government and sparks the Revolt of the

Comuneros. In 1781, Gregoria Apaza, an Aymara woman, led an uprising against the Spanish in Bolivia. In 1782, Bartolina Sisa, an Aymara woman led an indigenous uprising in Bolivia. She was captured and executed. On October 25, 1785, Toypurina, a Tongva medicine woman rebelled against the Spanish, leading an attack against Mission San Gabriel Arcángel. In 1803, Lorenza Avemanay led a revolt against Spanish occupation in Ecuador. In 1819 Antonia Santos, a Neogranadine peasant, organized, and led the rebel guerrillas in the Province of Socorro against the invading Spanish troops during the Reconquista of the New Granada.

52 In 1896, Nehanda Nyakasikana rebelled against the colonization of Zimbabwe.

53 In 1857-1858, Rani Lakshmibai of Jhansi was one of the leaders of the Indian rebellion of 1857. Begum Hazrat Mahal also led a band of her supporters against the British in the revolt.

54 The Paris Commune was a radical socialist government that ruled Paris from 18 March to 28 May 1871. Debates over the policies and outcome of the Commune had significant influence on the ideas of Karl Marx, who described it as an example of the "dictatorship of the proletariat."

55 The most well-known female figure of the Paris Commune is the heroic Louise Michel, an anarchist and follower of Bakunin. She volunteered to assassinate the French leader at Versailles.

56 Elisabeth Dmitrieff was the leading force behind the Women's Union. Twenty years old, the Russian Dmitrieff was sent to Paris by Marx shortly before the Commune arose. She became a main advocate for women and a socialist perspective.

57 Nathalie Le Mel was an active member of the First International and a former militant strike leader in the bookbinders union. She worked alongside Dmitrieff.

58 Nadezhda Krupskaya was Vladimir Lenin's wife, but Nadezhda was a Bolshevik revolutionary and politician in her own right. She served as the Deputy Minister of Education from 1929 to 1939.

59 Rosa Luxemburg was a Marxist who co-founded the Spartacus League. She considered the Spartacist uprising of January 1919 a blunder, but supported it as events unfolded.

60 Petra Herrera was one of the most famous soldaderas of the Mexican Revolution (1910-1920). She disguised herself as a man, calling herself Pedro, until she was acknowledged as a great soldier. After leading a successful siege, Petra successfully formed a troop of all-female soldiers.

61 Constance Markievicz was an Anglo-Irish Countess, revolutionary nationalist, and suffragette. She participated in countless Irish independence causes and played a key role in the Easter Rising of 1916 where she wounded a British sniper. Constance served as the Minister for Labor of the Irish Republic for three years, making her one of the first women in the world to hold a cabinet position.

62 Nwanyeruwa was an Igbo woman in Nigeria who started the Women's War, often referred to as the first major challenge to British authority in West Africa during the colonial period. In 1929, after she was asked about her property by a census collector, Nwanyeruwa began to protest about paying taxes with other women. In two months, over 25,000 women came together to protest and the British dropped their tax plans. The peaceful Women's War triumphed.

63 Lakshmi Sahgal was a revolutionary of the Indian independence movement, an officer of the Indian National Army, and later, the Minister of Women's Affairs in the Azad Hind government. In the 40s, she commanded the Rani of Jhansi Regiment, an all-women regiment that aimed to overthrow British Raj in colonial India. The regiment was one of the very few all-female combat regiments of WWII on any side.

64 Sophie Scholl was a founder of The White Rose, a non-violent anti-Nazi resistance group that spread its beliefs via graffiti and flyers. Sophie and other members were arrested in 1942. She was convicted of high treason and was executed by guillotine along with her brother Hans.

65 Blanca Canales was a Puerto Rican Nationalist who helped organize the Daughters of Freedom, the women's branch of the Puerto Rican Nationalist Party. She was one of the few women in history to have led a revolt against the USA, known as the Jayuya Uprising.

66 Celia Sanchez played an important role in the Cuban revolution. She joined the struggle against the Batista government following the coup in 1952. She was one of the first women to assemble a combat squad and became one of the main decision-makers during the revolution. She was also the founder of the 26th of July Movement, the organization that ultimately overthrew Batista.

67 The revolutionary movements of marxism, leninism, trotskyism, and maoism are all framed around egotistical heads of all-male governments, each with their own dedicated personality cult. If they had been all-female governments people would harp endlessly on that little detail. All-male "revolutionary" socialist governments are accepted as "normal," and at the same time marxism is presented as always being at the forefront of anti-sexism.

68 Max Dashu comments, "It was Marx himself who turned a live-in servant into his concubine right in his wife's face, the same wife who struggled to manage a household with all the children he engendered without enough income."

69 Max Dashu comments, "Communism and "revolutionary humanism" ignored the horrific levels of violence against women, institutionalized the double and triple shift for women, and suppressed women activists in their ranks. All men at the top, and women kicked around by alcoholics at the bottom, at all levels for that matter."

70 Mary Daly. 1978. *Gyn/Ecology: The Metaethics of Radical Feminism.* Bacon Press.

71 Females are ostracized and harassed if they refuse to participate in the endless cycle of male processions. And, women are demoted and fired if they fail to conform to male-based norms within the phallic professions.

72 Robert Briffault. 1931. *The Mothers: The Matriarchal Theory Of Social Origins.* 2004 Reprint by Kessinger

73 The Goddess was no hidden sky magic removed from the Earth. She was present in every aspect of existence, including animals. Stone Age people lived literally as well as metaphorically within the Great Earth Goddess and were a part of her as the Earth Goddess was life itself.

74 Patricia Monaghan. 2014. *Encyclopedia of Goddesses & Heroines.* New World Library.

75 Kate Rigby. 2005. "Topographies of the Sacred." *Religion & Literature*, 37, No. 3. pp. 137-9.

76   P Allen 1986 in Caputi 2004. ibid

28: Radical Ecofeminism

1   Marti Kheel. 2007. *Nature Ethics: An Ecofeminist Perspective*. Rowman & Littlefield.
2   Under patriarchal societies, females are likewise regarded as 'stock,' reproductive vessels for future generations of cyborgs.
3   Gender dualisms are reinforced by the image of "man the hunter." Hunting is also "a symbolic display of class superiority, proclaimed through enacting the roles of conqueror and provider." For example, in the final days leading up to the 2004 presidential election, Senator John Kerry made a campaign pitch that required no words. Clad in hunting attire, with blood dripping from his hands, a double-barreled shotgun in tow, he was photographed along with his companions, emerging from an Ohio cornfield brandishing three dead geese.
4   T Roosevelt. 1893. *The Wilderness Hunter*. New York: Putnam.
5   A Naess. 1973. "The Shallow & the Deep, Long Range, Ecology Movement," *Inquiry*, 16, 95-100.
6   Holmes Rolston III. 1988. *Environmental Ethics*. Temple UP
7   Holmes Rolston III. 1995. "Duties to Endangered Species." *Ency of Environ Bio*, vol. 1 517-28
8   Marti Kheel. 1979. "Can & Ought we to Follow Nature?" *Environ. Ethics*, 1:1 28. citing Rolston III.
9   An amalgam of Naess, Buddhism, Freud's tripartite personality theory, and Maslow's need hierarchy, Fox's post-ethical vision posited an "expanded Self."
10 W Fox. 1990. *Toward Transpersonal Ecology*. Boston: Shambhala.
11 Val Plumwood. 1993. *Feminism & the Mastery of Nature*. Routledge.
12 Ariel Salleh. 1984. "Deeper than Deep Ecology," *Enviro Ethics*, 6:4 335-41; Marti Kheel. 1985. "The Liberation of Nature," *Environmental Ethics*, 7:2 135-49; Val Plumwood. 1991. "Nature, Self and Gender," *Hypatia*, 6:1 3-27; Karen Warren. 1999. "Ecofeminist Philosophy & Deep Ecology," in Nina Witosek & Andrew Brennan (eds.), *Philosophical Dialogues*. Rowman & Littlefield.
13 Males commonly use "bitch" to refer to females, the word for a female dog, or an animal. Could male aggression be overcompensation for male guilt, womb envy, and feelings of inferiority? A pang of guilt from knowing that technological ability is really womb power that cyborgs stole?
14 Haraway 2007. ibid. Feminists need not scorn all things technological in favor of the 'organic." Also, they should not reject outright the notion that a respectful and balanced interconnection between nonhuman animals and nature is a feminist issue.
15 Karen Warren. 1997. *Ecofeminism: Women, Culture, Nature*. Indiana UP.
16 Other ecofeminists are Joan Dunayer, pattrice jones, Lee Hall, Lisa Kemmerer, Lori Gruen, Breeze Harper, Lauren Ornelas, Ivone Gebara, Vandana Shiva, Susan Griffin, Alice Walker, Starhawk, Sallie McFague, Luisah Teish, Sun Ai Lee-Park, Paula Gunn Allen, Monica Sjöö, Anne Primavesi, Carol Christ and others
17 Rosemary Ruether. 1975. *New Woman/New Earth*. Seabury.
18 Dorothy Dinnerstein. 1990. "Survival on Earth: The Meaning of Feminism." *Peace Review: A Journal of Social Justice*, Volume 2, Issue 4. 7-10.
19 Ruth Harrison. 1964. *Animal Machines*. Foreword by Rachel Carson. V. Stuart.
20 The book revealed farm practices such as castration, tail-docking, beak-trimming, de-horning, adding antibiotics to feed, battery cages for laying hens and veal calf crates to the general public, who were overall ignorant of such routines.
21 Gilman writes, "Let us begin, inoffensively, with sheep. The sheep is a beast with which we are all familiar, being much used in religious imagery; the common stock of painters; a staple article of diet; one of our main sources of clothing; and an everyday symbol of bashfulness and stupidity."
22 Gilman writes, "we have had almost universally what is here called an androcentric culture. The history, such as it was, was made and written by men. The mental, the mechanical, the social development was almost wholly theirs. We have lived and suffered and died in a man-made world. We have taken it for granted, since the dawn of civilization, that 'mankind' meant men-kind, and that the world was theirs."
23 Gilman divorced her first husband and sent their daughter to live with him and his second wife. This drew far-flung public attention and criticism. She and her daughter moved to California in 1888 and Gilman became a single-parent.
24 Her characters were drawn in accord with the ideas Gilman presented in her nonfiction work *The Home: Its Work and Influence* (1903) and her serialized article "The Dress of Women" (1915).
25 There are few records of ancient Goddess customs, so Wicca and other Goddess practices are generally based on male interpretations and patriarchal rituals.
26 Gaard 1993. ibid
27 Antonia Darder. 2014. *Freire and Education*. Routledge. And Talk given at the OC Anarchist Book Fair, El Centro, Santa Ana, California. May 14, 2015.

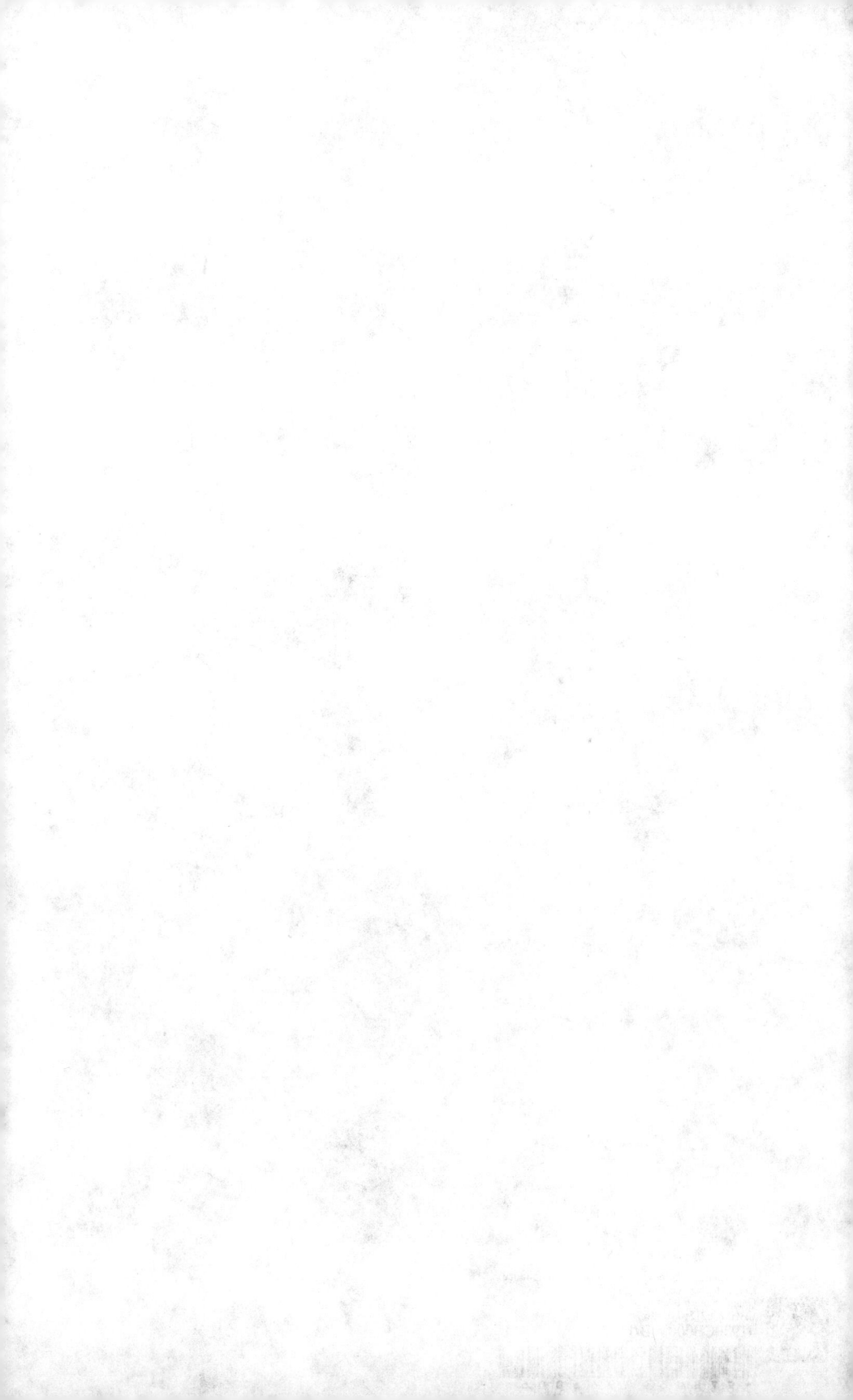

www.ingramcontent.com/pod-product-compliance
Lightning Source LLC
Chambersburg PA
CBHW062156270326
41930CB00009B/1548